THE PROSE WORKS OF
PERCY BYSSHE SHELLEY

The statement is in itself quite foreign to the merits of the Proposal in itself, & I should have suppressed it, until called upon to subscribe such a Requisition as I have suggested, if the question which it is natural to ask as to what are the sentiments of the person who originates 13 the scheme could have

subject tion of Reform. It appears to me that Annual Parliaments ought to be adopted as an immediate measure, as one which strongly tends to preserve the liberty and happiness of the nation; it would enable men to cultivate those energies on which the performance of the political duties belonging to the citizen of a free state, as the rightful guardian of its prosperity, essentially depends; it would familiarize men with liberty, by disciplining them to an habitual acquaintance with its forms. Political institution is undoubtedly susceptible of such improvements as no rational person can consider possible, in the present degraded condition to which the vital imperfections in the existing system of government has reduced the vast multitude of men. The securest method of arriving at such beneficial innovations, is to proceed gradually and with caution; or in the place of that order and freedom, which the friends of Reform assert to be violated now, anarchy and despotism will follow. Annual Parliaments have my entire assent. I will not state those general rea-

received in any other manner a more simple & direct reply

of

of

so long as

shall subject

of

THE PROSE WORKS OF
PERCY BYSSHE SHELLEY

VOLUME I

EDITED BY

E. B. MURRAY

CLARENDON PRESS · OXFORD

1993

Oxford University Press, Walton Street, Oxford OX2 6DP

Oxford New York Toronto
Delhi Bombay Calcutta Madras Karachi
Kuala Lumpur Singapore Hong Kong Tokyo
Nairobi Dar es Salaam Cape Town
Melbourne Auckland Madrid

and associated companies in
Berlin Ibadan

Oxford is a trade mark of Oxford University Press

Published in the United States
by Oxford University Press Inc., New York

British Library Cataloguing in Publication Data
Data available

Library of Congress Cataloging in Publication Data
Shelley, Percy Bysshe, 1792-1822.
The prose works of Percy Bysshe Shelley / edited by E. B. Murray.
Includes bibliographical references and index.
I. Murray, E. B. (Eugene Bernard).
PR5405.M87   1992
821'.7–dc20   91-37978
ISBN 0-19-812748-0

Set by Joshua Associates Limited, Oxford
Printed in Great Britain
on acid-free paper by
Biddles Ltd.,
Guildford and King's Lynn

Preface

SPECIFIC acknowledgement of help received during the preparation of this volume of Shelley's prose from those whose names appear below should be prefaced by a general acknowledgement of assistance which was either anonymous to begin with or has become so through time: the support of librarians, chance-met colleagues whose words lingered on but whose names have not, correspondents whose letters might have been misplaced, and the voluminous host of writers on Shelley and romanticism whose contributions to the editor's knowledge of both his subject and his procedures are subliminally present *passim* in text, apparatus, and commentary.

The following list is therefore partial but exemplary. A justified temptation to discriminate kinds, qualities, and quantities of help received is certainly recurrent to my mind as I write this. But to attempt to do that here would be both futile and invidious. Abundant and grateful thanks in widest commonality spread are therefore tendered alphabetically to the following: Stéphane Abbt, Carlene Adamson, Martha Ambrose, Anna Lou Ashby, Betty T. Bennett, Jo Ann Boydston, Malcolm S. Brown, Philip A. H. Brown, Timothy Burnett, Herbert Cahoon, John Collins, Nora Crook, Susan D. Csaky, Stuart Curran, P. M. S. Dawson, Susan Marting DeFosset, Ellen S. Dunlap, Mark R. Farrell, Max Griffin, Mihai H. Handrea, Paul T. Heffron, Kurt W. Hettler, Sally Laura Hyman, Elizabeth James, Nicholas A. Joukovsky, Thomas V. Lange, Richard M. Ludwig, Robert A. McCown, Ann Morton, Frank Paluka, Robert E. Parks, Mary A. Quinn, Charles E. Robinson, Neville Rogers, Stephen Ryan, Diana Scott-Kilvert, Anthony W. Shipps, William St Clair, Stuart M. Sperry, Peter J. Stanlis, Emily W. Sunstein, Lola L. Szladits, John B. Thomas III, James E. Tierney, Tatsuo Tokoo, J. M. S. Tompkins, D. G. Vaisey, Emily C. Walhout, Carl R. Woodring, Robert Yampolsky.

I am particularly happy to record a special debt to my co-editor, Timothy Webb, without whose willingness many years ago to join me in this edition it might never have got under way; and to Jack Stillinger, whose cordial willingness during the past few years to read and check both typescript and primary sources was equalled only by the acuteness of eye and judgement which he brought to that task. Along with the rest of the Shelley scholars of my generation, I have been recurrently indebted to Donald H. Reiman for his support, both practical and moral, during the many years this edition has been in preparation. Words of gratitude are also particularly due to Dr Bruce Barker-Benfield of the Department of Western Manuscripts at the Bodleian Library, who has saved me from many an error of form and substance.

Warm thanks are extended to the staffs of the Bodleian, British, Huntington, University of Missouri-St Louis, and Washington University (St Louis) Libraries, who not only provided me with manuscripts and monographs but also saved me time and contributed in intangible ways to the process of completing this volume.

Special thanks belong as well to the members of the Arts and Reference Division of the Clarendon Press, past and present, for their patience, encouragement, and editorial advice: these include John Bell, Dan Davin, Jon Stallworthy, Kim Scott Walwyn, and Frances Whistler.

Without expedient grants received at crucial times from the American Council of Learned Societies, from the National Endowment for the Humanities, and from the University of Missouri-St Louis, this volume would very probably still be in the making rather than in print.

The edition would not have been possible without leave to use the manuscripts and first editions in their possession kindly granted by the Bodleian Library, Harvard University (Houghton) Library, the Huntington Library, the University of Iowa Library, the Library of Congress, the Pforzheimer Foundation, and the Pierpont Morgan Library, all of whose permissions are therefore duly and gratefully acknowledged.

The last and best words of thanks are appropriately rendered to my wife Pierrette, in partial recompense for the many years during which she has aided and abetted my efforts, not only by typing (before the advent of the word processor) and proof-reading the whole several times over but also by pointing out errors and inconsistencies which would otherwise have been many more than those doubtless remaining and for which I am myself entirely responsible.

E. B. M.
June, 1992

Contents

LIST OF ILLUSTRATIONS   xi

CHRONOLOGY   xiii

ABBREVIATIONS AND SIGNS   xvii

INTRODUCTION   xxiii

The Necessity of Atheism (1811)   I

An Address, to the Irish People (1812)   7

Proposals for an Association of Philanthropists (1812)   39

Declaration of Rights (1812)   56

A Letter to Lord Ellenborough (1812)   61

A Vindication of Natural Diet (1813)   75

A Refutation of Deism (1814)   93

The Assassins: A Fragment of a Romance (1814–15)   124

On 'Memoirs of Prince Alexy Haimatoff' (1814)   140

On the Vegetable System of Diet (1814–15)   147

Journal at Geneva (1816)   156

The Elysian Fields (1815 or 1816)   162

On Learning Languages (1816)   164

A Faustian Note (1816)   165

Declaration in Chancery (1817)   166

A Proposal for Putting Reform to the Vote throughout the Kingdom (1817)   169

Preface to 'Frankenstein; or, The Modern Prometheus' (1817)   177

History of a Six Weeks' Tour (1817)   179

Letters Written in Geneva (1817)   206

An Address to the People on the Death of the Princess Charlotte
   (1817)   229

Fragment on Reform (I) (1817)   240

Fragment of 'A Refutation of Deism' (1817)   241

On Christianity (1817)   246

On the Doctrines of Christ (1817)   272

On Marriage (1817)   274

On 'Godwin's Mandeville' (1817)   276

On the Game Laws (1817)   280

On 'Frankenstein; or, The Modern Prometheus' (1818)   282

On 'Rhododaphne or The Thessalian Spell' (1818)   285

APPENDICES

   I. Newspaper Accounts of Shelley in Ireland and Wales
      (1812)   291
  II. *The Elysian Fields: An Addition?*   303
 III. The *Examiner* Account of Shelley in Chancery   310
  IV. Leigh Hunt's 'Rider' Notes on Bod. ⟨pr.⟩ Shelley e. 3   313
   V. List of Prospective Recipients of *A Proposal for Putting
      Reform to the Vote*   316

EDITORIAL COMMENTARY   319
COLLATIONS   499
   End-Line Hyphens   534
TEXTUAL NOTES   537
BIBLIOGRAPHY   567
INDEX   579

List of Illustrations

Corrected Page Proof from *A Proposal for Putting Reform to
the Vote* (1817)   *frontispiece*

REPRODUCED TITLE-PAGES

1. *The Necessity of Atheism* (1811)   1
2. *An Address, to the Irish People* (1812)   7
3. *Proposals for an Association of Philanthropists* (1812)   39
4. *A Letter to Lord Ellenborough* (1812)   61
5. *A Vindication of Natural Diet* (1813)   75
6. *A Refutation of Deism* (1814)   93
7. *A Proposal for Putting Reform to the Vote* (1817)   169
8. *A History of a Six Weeks' Tour* (1817)   179
9. *An Address to the People on the Death of the Princess
   Charlotte* (1817; ?1843 printing)   229

MAP

The Elopement Trip of Shelley and Mary, 1814   182–3

The frontispiece and Illustration 4 are reproduced by permission of the
Bodleian Library; Illustration 1 is reproduced by permission of the
Robert H. Taylor Collection, Princeton University Library; all other
title-pages are reproduced by permission of the Huntington Library.

The map (by Liam Dunne) is reprinted from *Shelley and his Circle*,
Vol. III, with permission of the Carl and Lily Pforzheimer Foundation,
Inc.

Chronology

The *Times* listing contains not only events and works of general historical and literary importance but also those of specific importance to Shelley and to his prose writings.

	Life and Works	Times
1792	Percy Bysshe Shelley born 4 Aug. at Field Place, near Horsham, Sussex, to Timothy Shelley, MP, and Elizabeth Pilford Shelley.	*Rights of Man*, pt. II (Thomas Paine), and *Vindication of the Rights of Woman* (Mary Wollstonecraft) published; Parliament passes Libel Act; Friends of the People Society founded.
1793		*Political Justice* (William Godwin) published; war between Britain and France (to 1802; renewed 1803); Reign of Terror; Marat murdered by Charlotte Corday.
1794		*The Age of Reason*, pt. I (Thomas Paine), *The Adventures of Caleb Williams* (William Godwin), *Songs of Innocence and of Experience* (William Blake), and *The Mysteries of Udolpho* (Ann Radcliffe) published; *Wat Tyler* (Southey) written.
1795		Keats born; *Esquisse ... des progrès de l'esprit humain* (Condorcet) published; Poor Law enacted.
1798		*Lyrical Ballads* (Wordsworth and Coleridge) and *An Essay on the Principle of Population* (Thomas Malthus) published; Wolf Tone's Irish rebellion put down; income tax introduced.
1799		Political associations prohibited in England; Napoleon made First Consul.
1800		Act of Union between England and Ireland; Robert Owen starts social reforms at New Lanark.

	Life and Works	Times
1801		*Thalaba the Destroyer* (Southey) published.
1802–4	Attends Syon House Academy.	*Minstrelsy of the Scottish Border* (Scott) published; *Edinburgh Review* founded (1802); Robert Emmet executed (1803); Napoleon becomes emperor (1804).
1804–10	Attends Eton.	*Lay of the Last Minstrel* (Scott) and *Madoc* (Southey) published; Battle of Trafalgar (1805); *Hours of Idleness* (Byron), *Poems in Two Volumes* (Wordsworth), and *Phenomenology of the Mind* (Hegel) published; England prohibits slave trade (1807); *Marmion* (Scott) and *Faust*, pt. 1 (Goethe), published; Leigh and John Hunt found the *Examiner* (1808); *English Bards and Scotch Reviewers* (Byron), *Elective Affinities* (Goethe), and *The High Price of Bullion* (David Ricardo) published; *Quarterly Review* founded (1809).
1810	*Zastrozzi* and *Original Poetry by Victor and Cazire* (Shelley and his sister Elizabeth) published; enters University College, Oxford; meets Thomas Jefferson Hogg; *Posthumous Fragments of Margaret Nicholson* published; *St Irvyne* (dated 1811) published in Dec.	*Lady of the Lake* (Scott) published.
1811	Meets Harriet Westbrook; financially aids Peter Finnerty, imprisoned Irish journalist; *Necessity of Atheism* published; expelled (with Hogg) from Oxford; correspondence with Elizabeth Hitchener begins; marries Harriet Westbrook; meets Robert Southey at Keswick.	*On National Education* (George Ensor), *The Missionary* (Sidney Owenson, Lady Morgan), *Sense and Sensibility* (Austen), and *Dichtung und Wahrheit* (Goethe) published; George III declared insane; Regency initiated; Hampden Clubs founded; Luddites destroy knitting-machines.
1812	Initiates correspondence with William Godwin; *An Address, to the Irish People* and *Proposals for an*	*Childe Harold*, i–ii (Byron), and *Elements of Chemical Philosophy* (Davy) published; Regent assumes

Life and Works	*Times*
Association of Philanthropists published in Dublin; speaks before the friends of Catholic Emancipation; *Declaration of Rights* printed in Dublin and later distributed in Lynmouth, Devon; *A Letter to Lord Ellenborough* printed; Shelleys move to Tremadoc, Wales (with E. Hitchener and Harriet's sister Eliza); supports Tremadoc Embankment project; to London, meets William (and probably Mary) Godwin; back to Tremadoc (without Hitchener).	full powers but frustrates Irish Catholic hopes for the alleviation of political disabilities; Prime Minister Perceval assassinated; Daniel Isaac Eaton imprisoned for publishing *The Age of Reason*, pt. III; Napoleon invades Russia; United States declares war on Britain.

	Life and Works	*Times*
1813	Mysterious assault on S at Tanyrallt (the Shelleys' Tremadoc cottage); to Ireland, thence to London; *A Vindication of Natural Diet* published; *Queen Mab* issued; Ianthe Shelley born.	*Memoirs of Prince Alexy Haimatoff* (Thomas Jefferson Hogg), *Pride and Prejudice* (Austen), and *A New View of Society* (Owen) published.
1814	*A Refutation of Deism* printed; elopes to the Continent with Mary Wollstonecraft Godwin accompanied by Jane (later Claire) Clairmont, Mary's stepsister; drafts most of *The Assassins* (finished in London, 1815); Charles Shelley born to Harriet; On '*Memoirs of Prince Alexy Haimatoff* ' printed in the *Critical Review*.	*The Corsair* (Byron), *The Excursion* (Wordsworth), and *Mansfield Park* (Austen) published; Napoleon exiled to Elba; Louis XVIII restores Bourbon monarchy; Pius VII restores Inquisition.
1815	*On the Vegetable System of Diet* probably drafted; moves to Bishopsgate.	*An Inquiry into the Nature and Progress of Rent* (Malthus), *The Influence of a Low Price of Corn on the Profits of Stock* (Ricardo), and *Progress of Metaphysical, Ethical and Political Philosophy* (Dugald Stewart) published; Napoleon's 'Hundred Days'; Waterloo; economic depression in England; Corn Law passed; massacre of the French Protestants at Nîmes.

Life and Works	*Times*
1816	William Shelley born to Mary; *Alastor* published; with Lord Byron in Switzerland; writes 'Hymn to Intellectual Beauty' and 'Mont Blanc'; drafts *Journal at Geneva*; back to England; *The Elysian Fields* drafted either in the autumn of this year or in the autumn of 1815. *On Learning Languages* and *A Faustian Note* probably drafted; Harriet Shelley commits suicide; marries Mary in London.	*Christabel*, 'Kubla Khan' (Coleridge), *The Siege of Corinth*, *Childe Harold*, III (Byron), and *The Story of Rimini* (Hunt) published; *Blackwoods Magazine* founded; income tax ended; Spa-Fields unemployment and food riot.
1817	Allegra, Claire's daughter by Byron, born; *Declaration in Chancery* drafted; loses custody of Ianthe and Charles Shelley; moves to Marlow; publishes *A Proposal for Putting Reform to the Vote*; writes *Preface to 'Frankenstein'*; publishes *History of a Six Weeks' Tour* and *Letters Written in Geneva*; writes and probably prints *An Address to the People on the Death of the Princess Charlotte*; probably drafts *Fragment on Reform* (*I*); drafts *Fragment of 'A Refutation of Deism'*, *On Christianity*, (probably) *On the Doctrines of Christ*, and *On Marriage*; *On 'Godwin's Mandeville'* printed in the *Examiner*; *On the Game Laws* probably drafted; *Laon and Cythna* published (withdrawn and reissued as *The Revolt of Islam*, Jan. 1818).	*Manfred* (Byron), *Biographia Literaria* (Coleridge), *Mandeville* (Godwin), *Paper against Gold* (William Cobbett), and *Principles of Political Economy and Taxation* (Ricardo) published; Regent's carriage stoned; suspension of Habeas Corpus; death of the Princess Charlotte; riots in Derbyshire and subsequent execution of rioters.
1818	*On 'Frankenstein'* probably drafted; 'Ozymandias' published; *On 'Rhododaphne'* transcribed; leaves for Italy.	*Frankenstein* (Mary Shelley) and *Rhododaphne* (T. L. Peacock) published.

Abbreviations and Signs

Following is a list of commonly used abbreviations of book-titles:

Baker, *Major Poetry*	Carlos Baker, *Shelley's Major Poetry: The Fabric of a Vision* (Princeton, 1948)
Barnard, *Shelley's Religion*	Ellsworth Barnard, *Shelley's Religion* (New York, 1964; repr. of the 1937 edn.)
Blunden, *Shelley*	Edmund Blunden, *Shelley: A Life Story* (New York, 1947)
Cameron, *Golden Years*	Kenneth Neill Cameron, *Shelley: The Golden Years* (Cambridge, Mass., 1974)
Cameron, *Young Shelley*	Kenneth Neill Cameron, *The Young Shelley: Genesis of a Radical* (New York, 1962)
CC	*The Journals of Claire Clairmont*, ed. Marion Kingston Stocking (Cambridge, Mass., 1968)
Clark, *Shelley's Prose*	*Shelley's Prose; Or, The Trumpet of a Prophecy*, ed. David Lee Clark (Albuquerque, N.Mex., 1954)
Dawson, *e. 4*	*Bodleian MS. Shelley e. 4*, ed. P. M. S. Dawson (The Bodleian Shelley Manuscripts, 3; New York, 1987); appears in textual annotations as '*e. 4(D)*'
Dawson, *Unacknowledged Legislator*	P. M. S. Dawson, *The Unacknowledged Legislator: Shelley and Politics* (Oxford, 1980)
DNB	*Dictionary of National Biography*
Dowden, *Life*	Edward Dowden, *The Life of Percy Bysshe Shelley*, 2 vols. (London, 1886)
Dunbar, *Bibliography*	Clement Dunbar, *A Bibliography of Shelley Studies: 1823-1950* (New York, 1976)
F	*The Works of Percy Bysshe Shelley in Verse and Prose*, ed. Harry Buxton Forman, 8 vols. (London, 1880)
Forman, *The Shelley Library*	H. Buxton Forman, *The Shelley Library: An Essay in Bibliography* ... (The Shelley Society Publications; London, 1886)

Grabo, *Magic Plant*

Carl Grabo, *The Magic Plant: The Growth of Shelley's Thought* (Chapel Hill, 1936)

Guinn, *Political Thought*

J. P. Guinn, *Shelley's Political Thought* (The Hague, 1969)

Hansard

T. C. Hansard (ed.), *Parliamentary History of England from the Earliest Period to the Year 1803* (London, 1803); continued as *Parliamentary Debates*

Hoagwood, *Scepticism*

Terence Allan Hoagwood, *Scepticism & Ideology: Shelley's Political Prose and its Philosophical Context from Bacon to Marx* (Iowa City, 1988)

Hogg, *Life*

Thomas Jefferson Hogg, in *The Life of Percy Bysshe Shelley, As Comprised in The Life of Shelley by T. J. Hogg, The Recollections of Shelley & Byron by Edward J. Trelawny, Memoirs of Shelley by Thomas Love Peacock*, with an Introduction by Humbert Wolfe, 2 vols. (London, 1933)

Hogle, *Shelley's Process*

Jerrold E. Hogle, *Shelley's Process: Radical Transference and the Development of his Major Works* (New York and Oxford, 1988)

Howell, *State Trials*

A Complete Collection of State Trials ... from the Earliest Period to the ... Present Time, ed. T. B. and Thomas Jones Howell, 31 vols. (London, 1816)

Hughes, *Nascent Mind*

A. M. D. Hughes, *The Nascent Mind of Shelley* (Oxford, 1947)

Ingpen, *Shelley in England*

Roger Ingpen, *Shelley in England: New Facts and Letters from the Shelley-Whitton Papers* (London, 1917)

J

The Complete Works of Percy Bysshe Shelley, ed. Roger Ingpen and Walter E. Peck, 10 vols. (New York, 1965; repr. of the 1926–30 'Julian' edn.)

K

Shelley's Prose in the Bodleian Manuscripts, ed. A. H. Koszul (London, 1910)

King-Hele, *Thought and Work* Desmond King-Hele, *Shelley: His Thought and Work* (Cranbury, NJ, 1971)

MacCarthy, *Early Life* — Denis Florence MacCarthy, *Shelley's Early Life from Original Sources: With Curious Incidents, Letters, and Writings, Now First Published or Collected* (London, 1872)

MacDonald, *Radicalism* — Daniel J. MacDonald, *The Radicalism of Shelley and its Sources* (New York, 1969)

McNiece, *Revolutionary Idea* — Gerald McNiece, *Shelley and the Revolutionary Idea* (Cambridge, Mass., 1969)

Medwin, *Life* — Thomas Medwin, *The Life of Percy Bysshe Shelley*, ed. H. B. Forman (London, 1913)

Notopoulos, *Platonism* — James A. Notopoulos, *The Platonism of Shelley: A Study of Platonism and the Poetic Mind* (Durham, NC, 1949)

OED — *Oxford English Dictionary*

Paine, *Writings* — *Writings of Thomas Paine*, ed. Moncure Daniel Conway, 4 vols. (New York, 1967)

Paley, *Evidences* — William Paley, *A View of the Evidences of Christianity in Three Parts* (1794; London, 1813)

Peacock, *Memoirs* — Thomas Love Peacock, *Memoirs of Shelley* (see 'Hogg, *Life*')

Peck, *Life and Work* — Walter E. Peck, *Shelley: His Life and Work*, 2 vols. (London, 1927)

PJ — William Godwin, *Enquiry Concerning Political Justice and its Influence on Morals and Happiness*, ed. F. E. L. Priestley, 3 vols. (Toronto, 1946)

Pulos, *Deep Truth* — C. E. Pulos, *The Deep Truth: A Study of Shelley's Scepticism* (Lincoln, Nebr., 1954)

Robinson, *Shelley and Byron* — Charles E. Robinson, *Shelley and Byron: The Serpent and Eagle Wreathed in Flight* (Baltimore, 1976)

Rossetti, *Memoir* — William M. Rossetti, *Memoir of Percy Bysshe Shelley* (London, 1870)

Salt, *Principles* — Henry S. Salt, *Shelley's Principles: Has Time Refuted or Confirmed them?* (London, 1892)

SC — *Shelley and his Circle, 1773-1822*, 8 vols., ed. K. N. Cameron (vols. i–iv) and Donald H. Reiman (vols. v–viii) (Cambridge, Mass., 1961–86)

Scrivener, *Radical Shelley*	Michael Henry Scrivener, *Radical Shelley* (Princeton, 1982)
Mary Shelley, *Journals*	*The Journals of Mary Shelley 1814-1844*, ed. Paula Feldman and Diana Scott-Kilvert, 2 vols. (Oxford, 1987)
Mary Shelley, *Letters*	*The Letters of Mary Wollstonecraft Shelley*, ed. Betty T. Bennett, 3 vols. (Baltimore, 1980–7)
Shelley, *Letters*	*The Letters of Percy Bysshe Shelley*, ed. Frederick L. Jones, 2 vols. (Oxford, 1964)
Shelley Memorials	*Shelley Memorials: From Authentic Sources. To Which is Added an Essay on Christianity*, ed. [Jane,] Lady Shelley (London, 1859)
Shelley Revalued	Kelvin Everest (ed.), *Shelley Revalued: Essays from the Gregynog Conference* (Leicester, 1983)
SP	Thomas Medwin, *The Shelley Papers: Memoir of Percy Bysshe Shelley* (London, 1833)
Stockdale's *Budget*	John James Stockdale, *Stockdale's Budget* (London, 1827)
Thompson, *Working Class*	E. P. Thompson, *The Making of the English Working Class* (London, 1963)
TT	'Bodleian Shelley MSS. Re-examined: A Re-edited Text of Some of Shelley's Prose Works in the Bodleian MSS. (II)' (*On Christianity*), ed. Tatsuo Tokoo, *Humanities: Bulletin of the Faculty of Letters, Kyoto Prefectural University*, 35 (Nov. 1983)
VP	*Verse and Prose from the Manuscripts of Percy Bysshe Shelley*, ed. John C. E. Shelley-Rolls and Roger Ingpen (London, 1934)
Wasserman, *Critical Reading*	Earl R. Wasserman, *Shelley: A Critical Reading* (Baltimore and London, 1971)
Webb, *Voice not Understood*	Timothy Webb, *Shelley: A Voice not Understood* (Manchester, 1977)
White, *Shelley*	Newman Ivey White, *Shelley*, 2 vols. (New York, 1940)
White, *Unextinguished Hearth*	Newman Ivey White, *The Unextinguished Hearth: Shelley and his Contemporary Critics* (Durham, NC, 1938)

Following is a list of commonly used abbreviations of periodical titles:

ELH	*English Literary History*
JEGP	*Journal of English and Germanic Philology*
K-SJ	*Keats-Shelley Journal*
K-SMB	*Keats-Shelley Memorial Bulletin*
MLN	*Modern Language Notes*
MLR	*Modern Language Review*
N&Q	*Notes and Queries*
PBSA	*The Papers of the Bibliographical Society of America*
PMLA	*Publications of the Modern Language Association*
SAQ	*The South Atlantic Quarterly*
SiR	*Studies in Romanticism*

Following is a list of commonly used signs:

C	Collation
EC	Editorial Commentary
fol.	folio
MS	manuscript
MSe	end of line in manuscript
om.	omitted word, phrase, etc.
T	the text of this edition
TN	Textual Notes
WM	watermark
?word	doubtful reading
[word etc.]	cancelled word etc.; internal brackets ([[ ]]) indicate a cancellation within a cancellation. (Cancelled words used in T also appear in square brackets)
[ ]	cancelled illegible word (the enclosed space approximates the length of the word)
⟨ ⟩	illegible word (the enclosed space approximates the length of the word)
⟨word(s)⟩	editorial conjecture or *comment*
|	marks a line-division (as on a title-page) or word-division (e.g. 'super|natural')

/word(s)/	MS insertions
~	used in c to indicate that a word in a variant is identical to a word in the lemma
∧	indicates absence of punctuation

Commonly used place-names are abbreviated as follows: BL = British Library (*BLC* = *British Library Catalogue*); Bod. = Bodleian (Library); NYPL = New York Public Library (Pf. = Pforzheimer Collection); PRO = Public Records Office (London)

Introduction

Scope of the Present Edition

This edition contains all of Shelley's prose writings except the early Gothic novels and the notes to *Queen Mab* and to *Hellas*. Significant among several items appearing here for the first time in any collected edition of Shelley's prose works are the *Declaration in Chancery*, *On Zionism*, *On the Improvvisatore Sgricci*, *A Definition of Atheism*, the *Cry of War to the Greeks*, and the fragment *On Contraception*. While *An Answer to Leslie's 'A Short and Easy Method with the Deists'* has been previously published in disparate parts in collected editions, its reintegrated form, like most of the above works, has appeared only in periodical publication. On the other hand, it has seemed expedient to print the *Letters Written in Geneva* under that title, rather than continue to subsume them under the general head of the *History of a Six Weeks' Tour*. The *Letter on Richard Carlisle* has been previously published only among the poet's letters, as has the fragment *On Learning Languages*; the short draft here entitled *A Faustian Note* associated with the latter is previously unpublished.[1]

The novels were omitted because they are available in several sufficiently well-edited texts.[2] The *Hellas* notes were omitted because of their integral relation to the poem they gloss. The two most substantial and relatively original pieces in the *Queen Mab* Notes were printed with slight variations as *The Necessity of Atheism* and *A Vindication of Natural Diet*. Significant variants between these works and the Notes of which they form the basis have been collated and/or otherwise noted here, as have anticipations or echoes of Notes incorporated into other works (e.g. *A Letter to Lord*

[1] The continuing publications of Shelley's notebooks by Garland Publishing, Inc. in their 'Bodleian Shelley Manuscripts' and 'The Manuscripts of the Younger Romantics' series will contain extraneous prose jottings and notes such as those on Humphry Davy's *Elements of Agricultural Chemistry* and on the Bible.

[2] *Zastrozzi: A Romance* (1810) and *St. Irvyne: Or, The Rosicrucian. A Romance* (1811) were reprinted with minor emendations of obvious misspellings by H. B. Forman (F, vol. v) and in the Julian edition (J, vol. v). Subsequent editions containing both works include those of Frederick S. Frank (New York, 1977) and Stephen Behrendt (Oxford, 1986). There are no extant manuscripts or authoritative later editions of either novel.

Ellenborough and *A Refutation of Deism*). Otherwise, this edition follows the precedent of previous major editions of Shelley's prose in omitting the remaining Notes, which are largely composed of more or less generous quotations and paraphrases from the works of other authors and contain relatively little of Shelley's original thinking or writing.[3]

Volume I contains all of the original prose works written before the Shelleys left England in the spring of 1818, except for the novels noted above and the prefaces to *Alastor* and *Laon and Cythna* (*The Revolt of Islam*), which have been generically grouped with the prefaces and advertisements written after their arrival in Italy. The drafts of the *Speculations on Morals and Metaphysics*, probably begun in England in 1815, were continued in Italy and provisionally integrated in early 1821, and are therefore placed chronologically according to the latter date.

Both the substance and the state of several of Shelley's letters (particularly those on religion, philosophy, and sculpture) could reasonably lead one to conclude that portions of them belong to the author's prose canon as much as the roughly drafted materials which make up much of this edition. However, except for the two noted above, only those letters related to the *History of a Six Weeks' Tour* are included in the text proper. Together with the concluding section of this Introduction, both the *Related Materials* paragraphs and the continuous commentary *passim* indicate the need for the reader to supplement the prose printed here with selected portions of the letters.

Holograph manuscripts or transcripts corrected by Shelley have been used as basic texts when available, with substantive variations and significant deletions in unique or multiple manuscripts recorded along with selected variants from important editions. With the exception of *An Address to the People on the Death of the Princess Charlotte*, the *Remarks on Sculptures in the Florentine Gallery*, *On the Revival of Literature*, *A System of Government by Juries*, and portions of *Speculations on Morals and Metaphysics*, the texts of all the original prose based on printed sources derive from first editions published during Shelley's lifetime and theoretically subject to his supervision. In some instances Shelley seems to have taken little or

---

[3] See Neville Rogers's notes on *Queen Mab* in the first volume of his OET edition of *The Complete Works of Percy Bysshe Shelley* (Oxford, 1972), 390–9, for a further account of the Notes not included here.

no advantage of any opportunity to revise such publications—he probably never saw proofs for the reviews of the *Memoirs of Prince Alexy Haimatoff* and *Mandeville*, while the Irish pamphlets, along with the *Declaration of Rights*, were apparently rushed into print and publication as soon as they came from his pen. *A Proposal for Putting Reform to the Vote* is extant in holograph, in corrected proof, and in the 1817 first edition, all of which have claims to ultimate authority that must to some extent be resolved eclectically in order to best establish inferable authorial intention. A portion of *A Refutation of Deism*, complete only in printed form, exists in a fair-copy holograph transcript whose ambiguous relation to the printed text is discussed in place. *A Refutation of Deism* is the only prose work included here which was reprinted in Shelley's lifetime under circumstances which might have allowed him to supervise and emend the text; except for compositorial error and inconsequential accidental variants, however, it is clear that the 1814 first edition served as the sole basis for the 1815 reprint in the *Theological Inquirer*. The *History of a Six Weeks' Tour* is printed from the 1817 text, though readings from Mary Shelley's 1840 text are occasionally preferred.

While the textual notes and commentary expand in detail on the facts and implications of the above summary, the following list of copy-texts used in this volume gives an overview of their relative authority. Unless otherwise noted all manuscripts are in Shelley's hand.

WORK	COPY-TEXT
The Necessity of Atheism	Original 1811 printing (Princeton Library copy)
An Address, to the Irish People	Original 1812 printing (Huntington Library copy)
Proposals for an Association of Philanthropists	Original 1812 printing (Huntington Library copy)
Declaration of Rights	Original 1812 printing (Huntington Library copy)
A Letter to Lord Ellenborough	Original 1812 printing (Bodleian ⟨pr.⟩ Shelley e. 1 (1))
A Vindication of Natural Diet	Original 1813 printing (Huntington Library copy)
A Refutation of Deism	Original 1814 printing (Huntington Library copy)

WORK	COPY-TEXT
The Assassins	Bodleian MS Shelley adds. c. 5, fols. 38^r–46^v (in both Mary and Percy Shelley's hands)
On 'Memoirs of Prince Alexy Haimatoff'	1814 *Critical Review* printing
On the Vegetable System of Diet	Bodleian MS Shelley adds. c. 4, fols. 267^r–272^v
Journal at Geneva	Bodleian Dep. d. 311 (2)
The Elysian Fields	MS (Berg Collection, NYPL)
On Learning Languages	Bodleian MS Shelley adds. c. 4, fol. 292^r
A Faustian Note	Bodleian MS Shelley adds. c. 4, fol. 292^v
Declaration in Chancery	Bodleian MS Shelley adds. c. 5, fols. 96^r–97^v (Mary Shelley draft transcript)
A Proposal for Putting Reform to the Vote	MS Lowell 36 (Houghton Library); Bodleian ⟨pr.⟩ Shelley e. 3; 1817 printing (Huntington Library copy)
Preface to 'Frankenstein; or, The Modern Prometheus'	Original 1818 printing
History of a Six Weeks' Tour	Original 1817 printing (Huntington Library copy)
Letters Written in Geneva	Original 1817 printing (Huntington Library copy)
An Address to the People on the Death of the Princess Charlotte	? 1843 printing (said to be reproduced from a lost 1817 original; Huntington Library copy)
Fragment on Reform (I)	Bodleian MS Shelley adds. c. 4, fols. 282^r–283^r
Fragment of 'A Refutation of Deism'	Bodleian MS Shelley e. 4, fols. 1^r–3^r, 4^r–5^r
On Christianity	Bodleian MS Shelley e. 4, fols. 7^r–33^v; Bodleian MS Shelley adds. c. 4, fols. 276^r–279^v
On the Doctrines of Christ	MS (Pierpont Morgan Library)
On Marriage	Bodleian MS Shelley e. 4, fols. 39^r–40^v
On 'Godwin's Mandeville'	1817 *Examiner* printing
On the Game Laws	MS (Library of Congress)
On 'Frankenstein; or, The Modern Prometheus'	MS (incomplete) (Library of Congress); 1832 *Athenaeum* printing (from a Thomas Medwin transcription which supplements the MS)
On 'Rhododaphne or The Thessalian Spell'	Mary Shelley transcript (Brewer Leigh Hunt Collection, University of Iowa Library)

Since there was no collected edition of Shelley's prose during his lifetime, the above copy-texts represent his final intentions in so far as these can be inferred from the available evidence. The fact that the printed works were often hastily got up and that the holographs are at times clearly rough drafts justifies and confirms a need, likewise warranted by the sense and syntax of a given item, for selective editorial emendation in a critical edition.

Four of the appendices to this volume include materials related to *An Address, to the Irish People*,[4] *Declaration in Chancery*, and *A Proposal for Putting Reform to the Vote*; Appendix II contains a previously unpublished work in Mary Shelley's hand which bears a close relation to *The Elysian Fields*.

Previous Printings of Shelley's Prose

While Mary Shelley projected an edition of her husband's prose as early as 1823,[5] Shelley's cousin and biographer, Thomas Medwin, was the first to print any significant amount of it, apparently from transcriptions he had made when living with the Shelleys in Italy in the autumn and early winter of 1820-1. The *Arch of Titus*, *The Coliseum*, *On Life* (part), *On a Future State* (part),[6] *On 'Frankenstein; or, The Modern Prometheus'*, *On the Revival of Literature*, and several of the descriptions in the *Remarks on Sculptures* appeared under his auspices in the 1832-3 *Athenaeum* (later reprinted in his *Shelley Papers* of 1833 and again in his *Life of Percy Bysshe Shelley*, 1847). He also first printed three additional descriptions either in or associated with the *Remarks on Sculptures*: the 'Laocoön' in his *New Anti-Jacobin* (1833), the 'Bacchus and Ampelus' in his *Angler in Wales* (1834), and the 'View from the Boboli Gardens' in the 1847 *Life*, which also reprinted the two previous descriptions. However, the first substantial attempt at collecting and editing Shelley's prose writings was Mary Shelley's *Essays, Letters from Abroad, Translations and Fragments* ('1840', actually published in 1839), which contained

---

[4] A newspaper account of a speech by Shelley first printed in J has been appended to this supplement.

[5] After she had collected and transcribed many of the MSS, she was advised that any further publication of her deceased husband's work would lead Timothy Shelley, the poet's father, to cut off the allowance he was providing her.

[6] Entitled 'Death' by Medwin, who also printed a portion of *A Discourse on the Manners of the Antient Greeks* as 'Love'. *On Love* was itself first printed in *The Keepsake* for 1829. In her 1840 edition Mary Shelley printed all of the fragments partially printed by Medwin.

all of Shelley's major prose writings with the exceptions of *On the Vegetable System of Diet*, *On Christianity*, *On the Devil, and Devils*, *A Philosophical View of Reform*, and those prose writings solely by Shelley printed during his lifetime. In 1859 Jane, Lady Shelley, printed *On Christianity* in her *Shelley Memorials*, which also included much of the previously printed *A Letter to Lord Ellenborough*. The 1862 *Relics of Shelley* edited by Richard Garnett contained the first printing of *Una Favola*, along with a few remaining prose pieces gleaned from the notebooks in Sir Percy and Lady Shelley's possession: the jotting on Love in Plato, the comment on Shakespeare's Sonnet 111, a fragment on reform (to be printed as *Fragment on Reform (II)*), a draft of the opening paragraph of *A Defence of Poetry* followed by two related fragments, and the three fragments *On Beauty* traditionally included in the canon.[7] In 1872 Denis Florence MacCarthy, in *Shelley's Early Life*, reprinted all of the political tracts Shelley had published during his lifetime, along with the 1843 printing of *An Address to the People on the Death of the Princess Charlotte*, which may have first appeared in November 1817 in a limited edition no copies of which are known to be extant.

The first truly authoritative and comprehensive collection of Shelley's prose was Harry Buxton Forman's four-volume 1880 edition of *The Prose Works of Percy Bysshe Shelley* (reprinted the same year in Forman's eight-volume *The Works of Percy Bysshe Shelley in Verse and Prose*). Except for *A Philosophical View of Reform* and *On the Vegetable System of Diet*, subsequent editors of the prose corpus have added little of consequence in either text or apparatus to the Forman edition, whose fidelity to available holographs and listings of variants, cancellations, and emendations made it one of the few nineteenth-century editions which anticipated in its essentials later twentieth-century theories of copy-text and editorial policy. But Forman's limited access to the notebooks which contained the bulk of Shelley's unique manuscripts prevented him from applying his principles and extending his apparatus through most of the holograph material that would have profited from them. Richard Herne Shepherd's *The Prose Works of Percy Bysshe Shelley* (1888) does not include any detailed statement of principles to justify a practice

---

[7] One of these, in Mary Shelley's hand, gives no certain indication of being Shelley's and will therefore be placed in an appendix. The University of Texas Library contains Garnett's transcripts of a few other prose jottings (including the so-called *On Polytheism* fragment) which he did not include in his 1862 volume.

which, for better and worse, represents the most formidable attempt at rectifying the accidentals of the text up to that time and before the time of the Clark edition noted below. In 1910 A. H. Koszul's *Shelley's Prose in the Bodleian Manuscripts* provided generally accurate transcripts of several prose drafts from notebooks left to the Bodleian Library by Lady Shelley in 1893, the most significant of which are *On Christianity*, drafts of *A Defence of Poetry*, and a large portion of the *Speculations on Morals and Metaphysics*.[8] In 1920 T. W. Rolleston published the first complete text of *A Philosophical View of Reform*, previously printed in large part by Edward Dowden in the *Fortnightly Review* (1886) and reprinted in his *Transcripts and Studies* (1888). This work has been twice edited since the notebook containing it was sold to Carl H. Pforzheimer in 1921: Walter E. Peck edited it for the Julian edition (1930; a limited issue of this version appeared separately in the same year); and Donald H. Reiman provided an annotated transcript with historical collation in volume vi of *Shelley and his Circle* (1973). With the exception of *A Philosophical View of Reform*, the prose in the Julian edition (1926–30) was edited by Roger Ingpen, who evidently had access to nearly all of the then available manuscripts. While containing some new material (including *On the Vegetable System of Diet* and a much-expanded list of emendations and cancellations), the Julian text does not offer in general any improvement over Forman and Koszul and in some specifics is less trustworthy than they. The edition of Shelley's prose most in use during the past thirty-five years has been David Lee Clark's one-volume *Shelley's Prose* (1954). This edition, though it makes some claim to manuscript authority, is, so far as it goes, essentially a reprint (including errors) of the Julian text, the editing typically limited to the accidentals, which were changed to accord with mid-twentieth-century American practice. This text has no scholarly authority of its own, though its footnoted sources and analogues are relatively expansive and sometimes helpful.

In general, it may be fairly said that the text of Shelley's original prose, comprehensively considered, has become less reliable as a basis for serious scholarly study since the publication of Forman's volumes. The major exceptions to this generalization are *A Defence of Poetry*, which has received particularly close attention from a succession of editors not only because it is Shelley's most important

---

[8] Koszul's volume also included the first publications of *On Marriage* and the *Fragment of A Refutation of Deism*, as well as a rough-draft translation of a portion of Plato's *Ion*.

prose work but also because it exists in several manuscripts, whose varying claims to authority may be adduced from the evidence and inferences offered in this edition and from the exhaustive collations in Fanny Delisle's two-volume *Study of Shelley's 'A Defence of Poetry': A Textual and Critical Evaluation* (1974); and *A Philosophical View of Reform*, which, as noted above, has received a series of editorial treatments, presently culminating in the collated transcription printed in volume vi of *Shelley and his Circle*. Lesser works—e.g. *On Love, On Life*—have been occasionally printed in anthologies by editors who have used the manuscripts directly rather than relying on the various flawed versions in the major editions of the prose works noted above.[9] *On Love* has also received a thorough historical collation in volume vi of *Shelley and his Circle*. More recently Tatsuo Tokoo has provided transcriptions and/or edited texts from the Bodleian holographs of the *Speculations on Morals and Metaphysics, On Christianity, On the Devil, and Devils*, and *A Discourse on the Manners of the Antient Greeks*. As noted, 'The Bodleian Shelley Manuscripts' and 'Manuscripts of the Younger Romantics' have provided or will provide facsimiles and annotated transcriptions of much of Shelley's manuscript prose. As also indicated earlier, certain works have received their first printing or definitive editorial treatment in less accessible form—*On Zionism* has been previously published only in a Japanese journal of 1923; the integration of *An Answer to Leslie's 'A Short and Easy Method with the Deists'* was provided by Claude Brew in the *Keats–Shelley Memorial Bulletin* (1977); *On the Improvvissatore Sgricci* was first printed in the same journal by P. M. S. Dawson (1981).

---

[9] Only A. S. B. Glover, *Selected Poetry, Prose and Letters* (London, 1951), has provided a substantial number of prose works in a form which has some claim to scholarly attention, though his use of available manuscripts seems to have been sporadic at best. Ernest Rhys's *Essays and Letters by Percy Bysshe Shelley* (London, 1886) contains a relatively large amount of Shelley's apolitical prose (supplemented by most of the political writings in an appendix), but there is no evidence that Rhys consulted manuscript materials when preparing his edition. John Shawcross's *Shelley's Literary and Philosophical Criticism* (London, 1909) is based on previous editions. It may be noted here that generous selections from the prose have also been translated into several languages, including French (*Œuvres en prose*, trans. A. Savine, Paris, 1903), Italian (*Le prose di Percy Bysshe Shelley*, trans. F. M. Martini, Rome, 1911), and Russian.

The Dating of Shelley's Prose

The dating of Shelley's prose has been a continuing and controversial problem selectively and variously resolved (or left un-
resolved) by editors and scholars from H. B. Forman through D. L.
Clark to P. M. S. Dawson.[10] Accordingly, the editorial commentary
on each work generally begins with an often lengthy discussion of
the evidence for ascertaining its date. This evidence is miscellaneous
in kind and sometimes problematical even where it may seem most
concrete. For example, the fact that the holograph of *The Elysian
Fields* is written on the reverse of the start of a letter by Shelley
which treats of house-hunting in England is not as helpful as it
seems, since Shelley was looking for a house in England in the late
summer of 1815 and in late 1816. Peripheral and internal evidence of
various kinds—newspaper concern with Princess Charlotte (the
presumed addressee of this Lucianic monologue), Shelley's
renewed interest in political matters, his readings of relevant texts,
the possible relation between this work and one in Mary Shelley's
hand—must therefore prevail in the uncertain task of assigning the
work a chronological position in the canon. The extent to which
inferences about one piece may, in default of better evidence, have
to be used to date another is illustrated by the chronological placing
of *On Learning Languages*, which is based on the debatable assumption that the Princess Charlotte was the most likely discernible
subject for such a piece, largely because of arguments adduced in
arriving at a date for *The Elysian Fields*; the associated *A Faustian
Note* has nothing in its content to indicate a better dating than can
be provided by its holograph appearance on the verso of the leaf of
On Learning Languages. The cautionary point to be derived from
this evidentiary chain is that the chronology of Shelley's manuscripts is at times tentative even when all available and possibly
relevant facts have been presented and argued. While the editor is
sometimes obliged to accept a provisional date as if it were definitive, his larger purpose has been to provide the interested reader
with all the information he needs to question as well as concur in the
chronology offered here.

---

[10] See the chronological orderings and relevant notes in F, J, and Clark, *Shelley's Prose*.
Better attempts at dating some or all of the prose appear in James A. Notopoulos's 'The
Dating of Shelley's Prose', *PMLA* 58 (1943), 477–98, and in Dawson, *Unacknowledged Legis-
lator*, 282–4.

Since many of the works in this volume were published in Shelley's lifetime, one can generally be sure of the year in which they reached the form of printer's copy, though one must keep in mind that booksellers often anticipated the title-page date—an 1817 imprint, for example, may appear in a work actually issued in December 1816. The dates of actual composition of the printed texts may be ascertained from various sources. The evidence of letters makes it clear that the Irish pamphlets were written in late 1811– early 1812, and, after some revisions, had both been printed by early March of 1812. The title-page indicates that *A Refutation of Deism* was published in 1814, though one is obliged to rely on Thomas Jefferson Hogg's memory long after the event to accept late 1813– early 1814 as the period in which the piece was composed. Mary's entries in her *Journals* establish the period during which she was preparing *A History of a Six Weeks' Tour* and the related letters to Peacock for their publication in 1817—but Shelley's share in the composition of the volume, so far as it can be certainly established, extends as far back as 1814. As its *Journals* placing demonstrates, the *Journal at Geneva*, which editorial orderings have traditionally placed after the *History* and the Peacock letters, was certainly drafted over a year before their recasting and publication.

Direct evidence from letters or the *Journals* likewise confirms the dates for *The Necessity of Atheism*, *A Letter to Lord Ellenborough*, and most of the reviews, while the topical matters treated in the *Declaration in Chancery*, *A Proposal for Putting Reform to the Vote*, and *An Address to the People on the Death of the Princess Charlotte*, abetted by letters or journal entries, sufficiently define the period of their composition. But the *Fragment on Reform (I)* has only its apparent subject-matter and generic tone to justify the editorial presumption that it belongs after the *Princess Charlotte* address.

While anything that exists in manuscript form may be taken to post-date Shelley's elopement with Mary in 1814—no original prose manuscripts survive from before that time—whether what we have represents a first or later draft of a given work is sometimes open to question. The first of such manuscripts (largely in Mary's hand) contains *The Assassins*, whose Continental dates of composition are set down in journal entries for August–September 1814 but whose fragmentary conclusion appears on English paper dated 1815. Perhaps the most problematical dating of a work in this volume concerns the holograph copy-text of *On the Vegetable*

System of Diet. The fact that it is extant at all indicates that it was composed after Shelley eloped with Mary—who was by no means consistent in her journal reportage of Shelley's literary projects. But since it so closely parallels the vegetarian interest and content of *A Vindication of Natural Diet* (1813) one wonders why the author returned to the subject so late, and also whether the draft was not itself based on earlier notes. Other references in letters and the *Journals* may be adduced to argue for a later rather than earlier date for the work, but the reader will rightly conclude that it could fall anywhere within a certain period, even if an editor is obliged to fix its position in the canon.

The notebook containing a very carefully written recension of *A Refutation of Deism* likewise contains a fairly well written fragment *On Marriage*, along with the lengthy fragment *On Christianity*, which at least starts out sufficiently well written to have derived from an earlier draft, or from notes, or perhaps from a clear memory of the lost *Biblical Extracts*, which Shelley apparently compiled in Ireland and England several years before the only dates one can, on the basis of other evidence (e.g. the notebook drafts of works known to have been composed no earlier than 1817), assign to *On Christianity*.

The Library of Congress notebook containing *On the Game Laws*, as well as most of Shelley's review of *Frankenstein*, also contains miscellaneous drafts in the hands of Mary Shelley and Claire Clairmont. The review can presumably be dated with some precision, though even here one must accept the fact that Shelley could have written it up while engaged in correcting his wife's draft of the novel several months before its publication. (Fortunately, a *Journals* entry specifies the date of Shelley's preface to his wife's novel.) As for the *Game Laws*, the only concrete evidence one has for a *terminus post quem* is a reference therein to the discontinuance of the income tax, which occurred in March 1816. Since *On the Game Laws* and the *Frankenstein* review are written on alternate pages it is plausible enough to assume that they were composed at about the same time. But Shelley's habit of using notebooks over several months (or even years) means that the inference is in fact far from secure.

Before watermarks were taken seriously by editors, internal evidence was often relied on to assign early dates to works which, at least in their extant forms, physical evidence places later. A case in point is the fragment *On Love*, whose sentiments are very close to those one may find in the 1815 *Alastor* Preface—or even in Shelley's earlier letters. But it appears in an Italian notebook and is therefore to be dated after March 1818. Internal evidence is once again worthless for dating, and, along with the comparably ambiguous fragments *On Life* and *On a Future State*, the fragment *On Love* will therefore appear in Volume II. Shelley's *magnum opus* was probably meant to result from the disparate leaves now making up the text of the *Speculations on Morals and Metaphysics*. Some of it appears on English paper dated 1815 and earlier, the remainder in an Italian notebook containing works written in 1821.

It will thus be evident that I have ordered the table of contents according to a chronology which my own arguments will (and should) on occasion call into question. The often quite plausible but now disproven chronologies of Shelley's prose put forth by previous editors and scholars are the best warning to an editor not to assume that he has pronounced the last (or even next to last) word on the dating of much of the manuscript portion of the prose canon. The editor's obligation is simply to make sure that his readers have the evidence to agree with or dissent from his own judgement in these ambiguous cases. An exhaustive attempt has been made in this edition to fulfil that obligation.

Editorial Procedures

The major textual problem an editor faces as he works his way towards a legitimate and consistent renderings of Shelley's 'final' intention is not so much deciding on a substantive reading in the holograph blurs and scratchings too often filling up and overflowing the interstices between the poet's compacted lines of furious scrawl—a decision which, however informed, is generally *ad hoc* and to that extent unprincipled—as it is deciding on the matter of accidentals, particularly but not exclusively the punctuation. Shelley's pointing, while generally justifiable in terms of one or other of the formal grammars of the late eighteenth century, was both rhetorical and impressionistic. At best this means that he pointed his sentences with special attention to pauses which would provide to his inner ear an emphasis and a syntactical definition much like those a practised speaker would provide for his audience. At worst this means that there is no pattern of consistency from text to text or, within a given text, from context to context, or in the same phrasing as it may appear in different authoritative manuscripts or printings—or even in different lines of the same holograph. At times question marks are not used in interrogative constructions because Shelley regarded the questions as rhetorical (he sometimes seems to have considered them declarative or appropriately begged); elsewhere semicolons replace the question mark, particularly in extended clausal constructions which are finally concluded with a single question mark.

As noted earlier, the *Proposal for Putting Reform to the Vote* exists in holograph, in a corrected proof, and in its printed state of 1817. In the holograph Shelley will provide one pointing in a given sentence, the printer will follow that in proof, but in correcting the proof Shelley will change it; alternatively, the printer may change the pointing from that which the holograph exhibits, and Shelley will allow the change to stand. Shelley will first write 'the Chairman of the Meeting', delete it to write 'the chairman of the Meeting', and later in the work return to 'Chairman of the Meeting'. Tempting though it may be to establish a consistency in such cases, the holographs and pamphlets demonstrate that rhetorical impressionism at best and indifference more typically defined the practice of author, house corrector, and/or printer. The question finally is whether an editor should attempt to implement what he perceives to be an underlying consistency in Shelley's use of points and capitals; or whether he should allow the natural pauses and rhetorical emphases, with their sometimes apparent inconsistencies or syntactical aberrations, to stand as Shelley's intention in such subordinate matters, except in so far as an adherence to them would interfere with the poet's pre-eminent intention—which was to be understood.

The latter alternative is preferred in this edition and the policy, while specifically justified as needed in the commentaries on given works, may be briefly defended here. With a few exceptions—notably *A Refutation of Deism* and the *History of a Six Weeks' Tour*—the prose published in Shelley's lifetime was all occasional and precipitated into print with little chance for the author to correct proofs. Dropped or misplaced words in both *The Necessity of Atheism* and *An Address, to the Irish People* illustrate the cursory attention Shelley must have paid to his proofs, if in fact he received any. The printers' copies of these and comparable writings, if extant, would doubtless in many instances be preferable to the printed texts, at least in accidentals and probably at times even in substantives. In the absence of such material, the editor is as a rule obliged to follow badly printed texts simply because he has nothing better to work with, an externally imposed ignorance which is internally compounded by his knowledge of Shelley's rhetorical impressionism. Even though a particular point, or even a substantive, is suspect, the editor is seldom justified in changing it because of his certainty that Shelley in a given instance 'must' have written something in a particular way, only to have it wrongly set by the printer. The corrected *Address, to the Irish People* does supply the place of a corrected proof, though the fact that several printer's errors still remain suggests that it was not scrupulously corrected. Evidence that Shelley did not attend as closely as he might have to the extant proof of *A Proposal for Putting Reform to the Vote* and that he had nothing to do with the emended capitalization and pointing of the work as finally printed supports a decision to prefer the holograph printer's copy to these later variants in many instances, and in a few substantive instances to argue the case for a species of transmissional corruption. Since changes in pointing between the very rough draft of *A Defence of Poetry* and the fair copy based on it are relatively few (less than twenty per cent) when weighed with syntactical reshufflings and substantive alterations, we may infer that Shelley tended to abide by his original punctuation when he was making fair copy from rough draft. In so far as the evidence of these two drafts may be generalized from (and in lieu of any certain evidence to the contrary), an editor seems warranted in accepting the accidentals of the unique and usually roughly drafted holographs which make up the great majority of Shelley's later prose writings as fairly accurate guides to his syntactical and rhetorical intentions. In this view, sporadic differences between the accidentals of the *Proposal* holograph and those in the corrected proof may be seen not as qualifying this inference because of the *ad hoc* impressionism they imply but rather as supporting an alternative inference that Shelley did not consult the holograph when correcting his proof.

It is to be hoped, at any rate, that the reader will discovery very few, if any, bothersome or unjustified aberrations[11] from the rela-

---

[11] For the most extreme instance of a necessary aberration, reserved for Volume II, see E. B. Murray, 'Shelley's *Notes on Sculptures*: The Provenance and Authority of the Text', K–SJ 32 (1983), 150–71.

tively liberal conception of copy-text which has evolved through the latter half of the twentieth century and whose flexible criteria of editorial practice are typically and perhaps inevitably adhered to in an edition as much dependent on unique copy-texts as this one is. In practice, substantive changes are rare and accidental changes modest. Because of the inconsistency of Regency house style and Shelley's rhetorical impressionism, some pointing changes from printed copy-texts are made in the interest of comprehension. However, any persistent effort at achieving clarity according to a late twentieth-century grammatical formalism would not only defeat Shelley's rhetorical intent but also prevent the reader from appreciating it, as it is hoped he will, particularly if he takes the time to read a given passage aloud and observe the emphases created by pauses which deviate from his formal expectations. In sum, for both rhetorical and substantive reasons, an attempt has been made to avoid arbitrating ambiguous contexts by imposing on them a pointing that tends to close the door on alternative readings.

Spelling variants in printed originals (e.g. 'alledge'/'allege', 'connexion'/'connection', 'judgment'/'judgement', 'enquiry'/'inquiry', 'supercede'/'supersede', 'falshood'/'falsehood') have not been normalized, partly because Shelley himself used both spellings of many such words and partly because Regency printing-house policy did not arbitrate consistency in transitional spellings, even within close contexts: the last three of the above pairings appear in both spellings in the printed text of the *Letter to Lord Ellenborough*. Normalization in such instances would risk obscuring what for some will seem a significant orthographic phenomenon. Similarly, Shelley's holograph 'shew' is retained but the 'show' of printed texts is allowed to stand as well. Holograph proper nouns which have a possible contemporary authority (e.g. 'Zerxes') or were of uncertain spelling (e.g. 'Kanstashka') are allowed to stand as Shelley wrote them unless to do so would impede the reader's understanding of what or whom they referred to. All such changes are recorded in the collation at the end of the volume.

Shelley usually spelt 'their' as 'thier' and often reversed the same letters in other words (e.g. 'recieve', 'concieve'). These misspellings have been silently corrected, partly because in some instances it is not certain whether he had reversed the letters or not (his dots tended to wander and he at times closed his 'e's and opened his 'i's) but largely because the practice does not seem to require consistent notice, except when a manuscript or other source (e.g. letters) in which the misspelling occurs is collated or quoted. Shelley sometimes seems to have spelt 'government' as either 'governnent' or 'govermnent', but uncertainty over the exact reading in a given instance would have made any attempt at recording it arbitrary guesswork. Editorial corrections of other characteristic misspellings (e.g. 'posess', 'accomodate') have been noted. Place-names obviously misspelt have been corrected; when they are recurrent, the first correction is noted and it is stated that from that point on this misspelling is silently corrected.

Since Shelley's upper- and lower-case letters are sometimes distinguished only by relative size, not always either normative or conspicuous, preferences which cannot be confirmed by context must be regarded at times as unqualified editorial decisions. His tendency in rough drafts to shape terminal '-se' and '-re' or '-r' and '-n' in very much the same way likewise leads to relatively arbitrary editorial preferences in equivocal contexts. It is sometimes difficult to distinguish 's', 'z', and 'c' in a given word: 'sacrifice', 'sacrifize', and 'sacrifise' are possible variant spellings of the same word, sometimes within the same context.

Manuscript abbreviations (e.g. 'wd.', 'Xt', and 'J. C.') are expanded and the alterations are recorded. Ampersands are given as 'and' in the text, except when they appear in the form '&c', and have not been recorded. Shelley's holograph use of the 'x' as a superscript key for a footnote has been replaced by a superscript numeral. When such footnote-numbers do not correspond to a cue in the manuscript they appear in angle brackets.

Shelley's tendency in writing to divide his words between (or sometimes within) syllables makes it difficult to be sure in a given instance which of two common alternative forms (e.g. 'can not' or 'cannot', 'for ever' or 'forever') he meant to write when they are separated in the manuscript. In all such cases the copy-text, whether holograph or printed, has been reproduced. Occasionally, less common words appear two or more times in the same context with both the characteristic space Shelley left between syllables he meant to be joined and the more generous space he left between separate words (e.g. 'pig herd' and 'pig   herd' in *On the Devil, and Devils*). In lieu of extrinsic evidence to the contrary (e.g. dictionary or contemporary usage), the space has been preserved in all instances.

Characteristic solecisms (by modern standards), such as the use of a singular verb with a plural subject (Shelley often considered plural subjects as units), are occasionally remarked on in the commentary as a Shelleyan practice but there has been no attempt at noting all such instances. However, when such solecisms seem unintended or interfere with the sense, they have been changed and the changes recorded. A few complementary exceptions are made to the general practice of preserving the punctuation of manuscript copy-texts except where retaining or failing to add a point would interfere with the sense: (1) triadic (or longer) series constructions (e.g. 'liberty, equality, fraternity'), often unpointed in Shelley's holographs, are provided with their customary commas, except before an 'and' preceding the last term of the construction (the changes are recorded); (2) words, phrases, and clauses above or below a given line of text and meant to be inserted in it are pointed when it is clear or probable that Shelley has neglected a usual or expedient pointing practice (all insertions are noted and set off by slashes in the collation); (3) missing but needed points at the end of a manuscript line are provided, with an indication (appearing as 'MSe') in the collation that the supplied comma (or whatever) is one Shelley himself might well have written had the word it follows been written in the middle rather than at the end of the line: Shelley frequently allowed the end of the line to stand for a needed syntactical point.[12]

As previous editors have noted,[13] the author tended to use the dash as an all-purpose point in contexts where he did not care to impede the flow of his thought and pen by any precise attempt at indicating syntactical relations. When the dash seems appropriate or when it is unclear what formal point would appropriately define Shelley's intentions, it has been allowed to stand unmodified. On other occasions, the Regency practice (followed by Shelley *passim*) of preceding a dash with a formal point in contexts where a greater degree of separation or emphasis was required than a comma, colon, or period alone would have provided has been followed here. In effect, the holograph dash has been groomed into a reasonable facsimile of syntactical precision rather than completely replaced by the point with which it has been conflated: thus, if the dash seems

[12] Cf. *On Learning Languages*, l. 15, which in the MS reads 'mere divisions the arbitrary points', where a comma after 'divisions' would most probably have been supplied by Shelley if the word had not appeared at the end of the line.

[13] e.g. Thomas Hutchinson in the 1905 Preface to his Oxford Standard Authors edition of the *Poetical Works*.

to represent a mark of anticipation, a holograph 'word—' becomes 'word:—' instead of 'word:'. All such changes have been recorded. Contemporary practice seems to confirm Shelley's two-dot holograph point, which has therefore been retained unless other holograph evidence (e.g. cancellation of the word(s) originally following the dots) supports an editorial change. Italic printing has been silently converted to roman where this is logically required. Double inverted commas were typically used by Shelley and Regency printers to enclose quoted matter, a practice which has been preserved here.[14]

Unless otherwise noted, Greek words are printed as they appear in the copy-text; Shelley did not use accents or breathings. Obsolete ligatures have been resolved into their constituent letters. When lacking or incorrect, French diacritical marks have been supplied or emended.

While obvious holograph changes in ink and nib-thicknesses are recorded when they may have some significance (e.g. for inferring different times of composition), clearly the writer may simply have stopped to sharpen his quill and stir his inkpot; extrinsic evidence (e.g. journal entries, letters, allusions) is required before the phenomenon can be regarded as significant.[15] Recurrent features of Shelley's holographs are the lines drawn under cancellations to indicate retention and the lines drawn under uncancelled words to indicate reconsideration. At times an editor can only hazard a guess, sometimes informed, as to whether a given underline was drawn before or after the cancel-line it might have either precipitated (if before) or retracted (if after); at other times it is unclear whether a line under an uncancelled word or phrase indicates reconsideration, and therefore should not be reproduced, or emphasis, and therefore should be reproduced (as italic). Shelley frequently failed to delete a word for which he provided a replacement. This may be an oversight but it may also be the case that he simply had not made up his mind. Typically, editorial preference is given to the insertion, as the author's latest choice.

[14] Like other marks and spellings, the quotation mark was in a state of flux whose definition in a given instance depended on the compositor. In *A Letter to Lord Ellenborough* both double and single inverted commas were used; *On 'Memoirs of Prince Alexy Haimatoff'* is the only printed work in which single inverted commas were used throughout. Since the variant usages are not distracting, they have been preserved for their potential historical interest for some readers.

[15] Cf. e.g. the textual notes on *The Assassins*, ll. 187, 310, *On the Vegetable System of Diet*, l. 122, *A Proposal for Putting Reform to the Vote*, l. 153.

Substantive editorial additions and corrections within the text itself have been kept to a necessary and consistent minimum. For example, where Shelley's manuscript note refers to 'Easton', the editorial recension appears as '⟨James⟩ Easton⟨, *Human Longevity*⟩', with additional bibliographical information reserved for the textual notes and/or editorial commentary; all references to books of the Bible have been extended to their full forms (e.g. '*Matt⟨hew⟩*' for '*Matt.*') where they are abbreviated in the original. Words or letters supplied in the text by the editor are also placed in angle brackets, while necessary words or letters retrieved from manuscript cancellations appear in square brackets. Whenever they can be discriminated, different uses of brackets in quoted and collated materials have been converted to the editorial conventions of the present text. While asterisks have been supplied to indicate vertical gaps in the copy-text manuscripts, horizontal gaps between words in a given line are always and sentence fragments concluding paragraphs are sometimes represented as they appear in the manuscript—i.e. without asterisks to indicate a gap. Where necessary, the Textual Notes will provide further information about these and other syntactical breaks in the copy-texts.

Titles have been normalized in the headmatter to each item, as in the table of contents. The parenthetical dates in the running heads are definitive (either for composition or for the publication of the copy-text); dates in angle brackets are conjectured. The reproduced title-pages of course provide fuller and/or more exact titles of the printed copy-texts. While editorial titles are noted as such in the endmatter, angle brackets have not been used in the text. In general these titles are those supplied by previous editors. Standardized rules appear under the titles regardless of how or whether they appeared in the copy-text.[16] The text below a given heading is placed full left regardless of its copy-text indentation.

The historical collation of significant editions, while generous, is not exhaustive, and is typically limited to substantive variants. The fact that a given point in the lemma is not found in the collation does not necessarily imply that it is not in the text collated.

A very few exceptions to the editorial practices defined above will be noted and justified in place. Nearly all of these occur when more than a single authoritative text of a given work, or part of a

---

[16] The evidence of Shelley's more finished manuscripts—e.g. *A Proposal for Putting Reform to the Vote, The Assassins, On the Game Laws*—indicates a preference for the rule.

work, is extant (*A Proposal for Putting Reform to the Vote, A Defence of Poetry*), or when unique circumstances prescribe a variation— *Remarks on Sculptures* (see n. 11) is the exemplary case in point.

Shelley's Social and Political Context: 1811-1817[17]

Social unrest and attempts at political reform characterized the period during which Shelley published the reactions that appear in this volume to several of their major and a few of their minor manifestations. For Shelley, as for other English reformers, the 1800 Act of Union between Ireland and England, along with the continuing political disabilities which denied Irish Catholics a place in the English Parliament, were symptomatic of an unjust political system in need of reform in order to eliminate rotten boroughs and extend the suffrage, and thereby create a true rather than 'virtual' representation in the House of Commons. In the Irish pamphlets of 1812, largely written in England, Shelley addressed himself to a 'crisis' which was for him both English and Irish, as further evidenced by his contemporary *Declaration of Rights*, printed in Ireland but disseminated in England. His *Proposal for Putting Reform to the Vote throughout the Kingdom* (1817) stressed the need for unified political action intimated in *An Address, to the Irish People* and promulgated in *Proposals for an Association of Philanthropists*. The second 1817 pamphlet, *An Address to the People on the Death of the Princess Charlotte*, dramatically portrayed the glaring inequities of the social hierarchy and the related economic distress which throughout the period 1812–17 inspired the upheavals which, in the radical shibboleth of the day, made 'Reform or Revolution' inevitable.

In 1811, the year of *The Necessity of Atheism*, George III was declared insane and his son, 'this overgrown bantling' of monarchy (Shelley to E. Hitchener, 20 June), the companion of gamblers and demireps, who at the age of fifty had done little to illustrate his capacity to rule even over himself (Leigh Hunt, *Examiner*, 22 March 1812), was declared Regent of Great Britain and Ireland. Despite conservative fears and liberal hopes concerning the Prince's liberal tendencies, by early 1812, when he was to assume full powers of monarchy, there were only the sanguine editorials of an otherwise

---

[17] Introductory remarks on Shelley's religious and metaphysical thought will appear in Volume II.

desperate reformist press to keep alive the expectation that the new
Regent would invoke the spirit of the late Whig leader Charles Fox
and replace a Tory with a Whig ministry. In Ireland such a change
might conceivably have fulfilled the promise of Catholic emancipation which William Pitt had made when the Act of Union was
agreed upon; in England peace, retrenchment, and reform were
among the hoped-for consequences of a liberal succession. But the
Regent continued the Tory ministry in power, the fact belied the
expectation, and the seeds of social upheaval, already springing up
in much of the country, were duly fertilized for further growth.

The most obvious immediate source of social unrest was the
economic distress initially occasioned among the lower classes by a
succession of bad harvests and among all classes by the continuing
French war, compounded in 1812 by the American war. Bread was
dear at home and trade abroad was practically non-existent. In the
north of England and in the Midlands the labourers' frustration
with unemployment, low wages, and high prices boiled over into
localized violence. Since technological innovation in the production of wool and cotton fabrics was often perceived as the cause of
their problems, the labourers expressed and defined their frustration by destroying the power-looms (or frames), and were so
known as frame-breakers, or Luddites, in memory of one Edward
Ludd, reputed to have been the first to vent his frustration at a loom
by breaking it. Predictably, the government's solution to an
economic problem was not social reform but legal repression. Lord
Castlereagh warned that 'all the army of the Empire could not
afford protection to the King's faithful subjects' against the
depredations of the Luddites, unless stronger laws were enacted.[18]
The Framebreaking Act of 1812 made this crime against property
punishable by death. Lord Byron's maiden speech in the House of
Lords portrayed a prospective courtroom scene whose principal
actors were a framebreaker 'meagre with famine, sullen with
despair, careless of life ... twelve butchers for a jury, and a Jeffreys
for a judge' (27 February 1812).[19] The implicit contrast between the
desperate poor and the oppressive rich had its real-life analogues. In
the north of England an old woman was hanged for stealing some
potatoes, while in London the Prince Regent spent a reported

---

[18] Quoted in Frank Ongley Darvall, *Popular Disturbances and Public Order in Regency
England* (London, 1934), 128.

[19] Quoted in White, *Shelley*, i. 272.

£120,000 on a Carlton house fête. The same Lord Eldon whose 'dear old Master',[20] George III, had seen to it that the Chancellor's pockets were lined with thousands of pounds in annual increments, upheld the principle of law by condemning a man to death for a theft of five shillings. Like Blake's Urizen, he reportedly wept, a characteristic expression of conscience which Shelley reduced to crocodile tears when he portrayed Eldon in *The Mask of Anarchy*.

Just before embarking for Ireland in 1812, Shelley had emphasized in a letter to Elizabeth Hitchener his reaction to the social and political inequities that inspired his admitted 'passion for reforming the world' when commenting on the insurrections and oppressions in the Midlands at the forefront of his mind as he wrote in *An Address, to the Irish People* of a comparably induced 'crisis' in Ireland:

I have been led into reasonings which make me *hate* more & more the existing establishment of every kind. I gasp when I think of plate & balls & tables & kings.—I have beheld scenes of misery.—The manufacture[r]s ⟨*i.e. factory workers*⟩ are reduced to starvation. My friend, the military are gone to Nottingham—Curses light on them for their motives if they destroy *one* of its famine-wasted inhabitants.—But if I were a friend to the destroyed myself about to perish, I fancy that I could bless them for saving my friend the bitter mockery of a trial. (26 December 1811)

In 1817, along with the liberal press, Shelley in his *Address to the People on the Death of the Princess Charlotte* again took up the theme of social inequality by contrasting the national mourning following the death in childbirth of the heiress presumptive to the English throne with the hanging and beheading—after a 'bitter mockery of a trial' for treason—of three leaders of a Derbyshire uprising, instigated as much by government *agents provocateurs* as by economic distress.

The 'double aristocracy' which, following William Cobbett, Shelley deplored both in the address on Princess Charlotte and later in *A Philosophical View of Reform* was already apparent to him in 1811, when he wrote to Hitchener (10 August) of the *nouveau riche* 'commercial *monopolist*' (whose closest analogues in his later published writings were the 'stockjobbers' or 'fundholders') and of the 'haughty aristocrat' (the scion of 'hereditary accumulation'),

---

[20] Lord Eldon to the Revd Dr Swine (endorsed 24 Apr. 1812), in Horace Twiss's *The Public and Private Life of Lord Chancellor Eldon*, 3 vols. (John Murray: London, 1844), iii. 196. Eldon was prominent in defending the framebreaking bill against Byron's attack on it (Twiss, iii. 190).

both of whom represent 'flagrant encroachments on liberty', neither of whom 'can be used as an antidote for the poison of the other'.

Shelley's reference to antidote and poison implies an awareness of the generally opposed interests of the traditional aristocrat, pre-eminently the agricultural landowner, and the city-based industrial-ist, who may be taken to index the new upper class at its best, in so far as they were not at the same time among the 'petty piddling slaves who have gained a right to the title of public creditors, either by gambling in the funds, or by subserviency to government, or some other villainous trade' (*An Address to the People on the Death of the Princess Charlotte*).

While many landowners were Whigs, as a class they were Tory in orientation. The industrialists, among whom may be included middle-class entrepreneurs and employers, were in a greater majority aligned with the Whigs. Both classes and parties used and feared the labouring class, who themselves had no party or rep-resentation. Enclosure laws instigated by the landowners had dis-possessed the small farmers and cottagers, who became tenants of the land they had once tilled as their own or else left for the larger towns and cities, where they helped provide cheap labour in times of relative plenty and swelled the ranks of the unemployed in times of dearth.

The political and social relations among these three classes may be illustrated by a brief (and somewhat oversimplified) account of the causes and consequences of the 1815 Corn Law. During the war bad harvests and negligible trade caused the price of bread—an accepted indicator of economic fluctuation—to rise. The agricul-tural landowner profited, while the industrialist was required to pay his workers more so that they could eke out at least a subsistence living. After the war, with good harvests and free trade, the price of grain plummeted (even during the war an abundant harvest had meant cheap grain). The landowner therefore lost, and the industri-alist, who could lower his wages accordingly, won. In either case there was no alteration in the plight of the labourer, whose wages remained at subsistence level regardless of whether landowner or industrialist profited by the grain-market fluctuations. The in-dustrialist affected social concern for his workers by expressing out-rage at the high price of grain; the landowner retaliated by pointing out that low grain prices caused the industrialist to lower wages.

Cheap imported grain after the war therefore led to the Corn Law of 1815, which set a price of 80s. for eight bushels of grain. When the price of grain went below that amount, the ports were closed so that imported grain could not undersell the consequent domestic monopoly. While theoretically the law was a benefit to the landowner, because of its inefficient operation—the authorities were slow to ban or allow imports in accordance with the changing prices of grain—it was less than satisfactory even to him. More importantly, labourers put out of work by the industrialists because of the erratic operation of the Corn Law were placed on the dole, which, by the terms of the Poor Law (another poorly functioning expedient), was subsidized by the landowners. With the labouring class effectively converted into a human shuttlecock, battered from bad to worse and back again, it became clear that legal measures designed for the amelioration of the wealthy were not working for the majority of the population. Again, the indicated remedy was reform and the implicit alternative was revolution.

Throughout the period 1811–17 reform remained a matter of speculation and debate among moderate radicals (Whiggish in so far as they had a party affiliation or tendency), who differed in matters of both principle and expediency. In principle, all of the radical and even the majority of the moderate reformers favoured annually elected parliaments, universal (manhood) suffrage, and, in fewer instances, a secret ballot. The moderates were so defined because, as a matter of expediency, they would accept triennial parliaments, restricted suffrage, and the open ballot. Radical reformers, such as Henry 'Orator' Hunt and William Hone, were suspected of revolutionary intentions by Tories and conservative Whigs and, because of their increasing tendency to alienate an otherwise sympathetic middle class, were viewed by moderate reformers as a liability to the cause of parliamentary reform. Shelley, whose goals were radical, was, as he stated or implied more than once, willing to accept what he could get and is therefore to be ranked among the moderate reformers, the radical implications of *Queen Mab* and its Notes to the contrary notwithstanding.

Because the economically motivated violence of 1811–12 was local in origin and lacked the kind of leadership Shelley called for in his *Proposals for an Association of Philanthropists*, neither its revolutionary potential nor its reformist implications stood in any likelihood of being realized. A combination of harsh repression and a good harvest in 1813 brought it to an end. A framework for more organized reformist activities was formed with the Hampden Clubs of 1811–12—named after John Hampden, the seventeenth-century parliamentary leader who refused to pay the king's taxes and otherwise abetted the imminent civil war. But these initiatives came to very little until 1816, when a combination of economic depression and high wages caused them to flourish overnight throughout the land. The undirected and localized violence of 1812 recurred in 1816 for essentially the same reasons, but with a city-based organization and a political orientation which argued the need for lasting reform as the only means to economic relief. Through much of the year petitions for reform emanated from every corner of the kingdom and found their way to the tables of Parliament, which had been 'groaning' since the 1790s with the weight of their archetypes and analogues. Moderate radicals and liberal Whigs felt their time had come.

A series of events towards the end of 1816 and at the beginning of 1817 again helped frustrate reformist expectations. London riots following two Spa-Fields meetings at which 'Orator' Hunt was the main attraction, along with turbulence in the provinces, were associated with the reformist movement in general by the ministerial press. Fears of revolutionary change swayed the middle class away from the reformist cause. In early 1817 the Prince Regent's carriage was stoned as he was on his way to the opening of Parliament. Habeas Corpus was suspended, a more severe Seditious Meetings Act was passed, and at about the time Shelley, in his holograph of *A Proposal for Putting Reform to the Vote*, called for a meeting of interested reformers to consider his propositions, whatever immediate hopes for parliamentary reform the social distress of 1816 had inspired were fast fading into the margins of non-entity.

While latter-day historians have the hindsight to know better and appear wiser, for many concerned observers of the contemporary scene in 1811–17 the alternatives of Reform or Revolution were converted into a cause–effect relationship which implied that the only possibility of achieving the first was through an implementation of the second:

Southey thinks that a revolution is *inevitable*; this is one of his reasons for supporting things as they are.—But let *us* not belie our principles.—They may feed & riot & may sin to the last moment.—The groans of the wretched may pass unheeded till the latest moment of this infamous revelry, till the storm burst upon them and the oppressed take furious vengeance on the oppressors. (Shelley to E. Hitchener, 26 December 1811)

Shelley's own sense of the inevitability of revolution was always qualified by his hopes, seldom sanguine, of a reform such as that which he outlined in 1817 and detailed in his *Philosophical View of Reform* of 1819. After broadening the intended scope of his Irish pamphlets to include his 'desire to establish on a lasting basis the happiness of human-kind', he added: 'Popular insurrections and revolutions I look upon with discountenance; if *such things must be* I will take the side of the people, but my reasonings shall endeavor to ward it from the hearts of the Rulers of the Earth, deeply as I detest them' (to E. Hitchener, 7 January 1812). Just before leaving for Ireland, he wrote to the same correspondent (?16 January 1812) that in his view the unrest in that country was only 'part of a great crisis of opinion' that he had already noted in England, where he found 'a people advanced in intellectual improvement, willfully rushing to a Revolution', an inference he drew specifically from the egregious ostentations of the rich but implicitly generalized to include the economic depression of the poor in a social hierarchy where the greedy few fed on the starving many.

Political and social equality was in fact the far goal of reform which motivated all but the most conservative among reformers. In 1817, after his *Proposal* had necessarily failed in a political atmosphere compounded of diffidence and repression, Shelley composed his longest poem, *Laon and Cythna*, a *beau ideal* of the French Revolution, where, among other variations on his historical theme, he allegorically reshuffled the Revolutionary shibboleths to indicate that for a lasting restructuring of the social and political environment equality must precede both fraternity and liberty.[21] His earliest reformist arguments, based in Rousseau but deriving as well from accounts of contemporary social and political inequalities that were the editorial staple of the liberal press, implied a comparable set of priorities: 'No one has yet been found resolute enough in dogmatizing to deny that Nature made man equal, that society has destroyed this equality is a truth not more incontrovertible' (to

---

[21] See E. B. Murray, "Elective Affinity" in *The Revolt of Islam'*, *JEGP* 67 (Oct. 1968), 581–2; Constantin François, comte de Volney, was the first to employ this criticism of the framers of the French Revolution: 'In the Declaration of Rights, there is an inversion of ideas in the first article, liberty being placed before equality, from which it springs' (*Volney's Ruins; or Meditations on the Revolution of Empires*, Dublin, 1811, 104).

E. Hitchener, ⟨25 July 1811⟩). In another letter to Hitchener, after defining his general subject as '*politics*' and his specific proposals as those of 'a moral legislator', he proceeds to an argument relating fundamental equality with the political and social inequalities currently typifying English government and society:

Equality is natural, at least many evils totally inconsistent with a state which symbolises with Nature prevail in *every* system of inequality. I will assume this point, therefore even altho it be your opinion or *my* opinion that equality is unattainable except by a parcel of peas or beans, still political virtue is to be estimated in proportion as it approximates to this ideal point of perfection *however* unattainable.—But what can be worse than the present aristocratical system? here are in England ten millions only 500,000 of whom live in a state of ease; the rest earn their livelihood with toil & care.—If therefore these 500,000 aristocrats who possess resources of various degrees of immensity were to permit these resources to be resolved into their original stock; that is, entirely to destroy it, if each earned his own living, which I do not see is at all incompatible with the *height* of intellectual refinement, then I affirm that each would be happy & contented, that crime & the temptation to crime wd. scarcely exist.... is it not worth while, that ... the remaining 9,500,000 victims to its infringement [should] make some exertions in favor of a system evidently founded on the first principles of natural justice.... and for the sake of his earth-formed schemes has the politician a right to infringe upon that which itself constitutes all right and wrong? (26 July 1811)

Shelley's *On Christianity* (1817) is largely concerned with emphasizing on one hand the benevolence of Christ's God and on the other the equality which for Shelley's Christ was the basis of justice. In 1811, with the Establishment Church in England as much in his mind as the connection between the Act of Union and the Catholic disabilities in Ireland, he was explicit about the relationship he perceived between religious persecution and political oppression which made a mockery of both liberty and equality:

Religion ... is so intimately connected with politics, & augments in so vivid a degree the evils resulting from the system before us, that I will make a few remarks on it. ... the persecutions against the Xtians, under the Greek empire their energetic retaliations, & burning each other, the excommunications bandied between the popes of Rome & the patriarchs of Constantinople, their influence upon politics—War, Assassination, the Sicilian Vespers—the Massacre of St. Bartholomew, Ld. G. Gordon's mob, & the state of Religious things at present can amply substantiate my assertions—And Liberty! Poor liberty, even the religionists who cry so much for thee, use thy name but as a mask, that they also may seize the torch, & shew their gratitude by burning their deliverer.... It is this empire of terror which is established by Religion, Monarchy is it's prototype, Aristocracy may be regarded as symbolising ... its very essence. They are mixed—one can now scarce be distinguished from the other, & equality in politics like perfection in morality appears now far removed from even the visionary anticipations of what is called the wildest theorist. (To E. Hitchener, ⟨25 July 1811⟩)

Besides *On Christianity*, *On the Game Laws* and *On Marriage* (both 1817) were responses to inveterate social and political inequities. The Game Law of 1816 was devised not only to keep the pheasant for the aristocrat but also to keep the peasant in his place by making poaching subject to seven years' transportation. The hardships the marriage laws imposed on the young as well as on the poor had been a favourite subject of parliamentary debate for decades; Shelley's personal interest in the matter was also echoed in the letter columns of the *Examiner*.[22]

Shelley's lost novel *Hubert Cauvin* seems to have been a mirror image in prose of *Laon and Cythna*, to judge from his description of it as 'a tale illustrative of the causes of the failure of the French Revolution to benefit human-kind' (to E. Hitchener, 7 January 1812). It seems further that he not only illustrated his criticisms of the character of a secular and spiritual hierarchy that brought about a revolution in France but also indicated how political morality and religious freedom might forestall in England and Ireland what had proved inevitable in France: 'You will see in my "Hubert Cauvin" ... *expediency insincerity, mystery* ... occasions of violence and blood in the French revolution; indeed their fatal effects are to be traced in every one instance of human life where vice and misery enter into the features of the portraiture' (ibid.).

As at least one historian of the social unrest of the period has noted, what was needed to precipitate a revolution in England in 1812 was precisely what Shelley was prepared to offer in his *Proposals for an Association of Philanthropists*: leadership and organ-

---

[22] See EC on *On Marriage*, pp. 479–80. For an account of the marriage laws as the subject of controversy in and out of Parliament see E. B. Murray, 'Thel, *Thelyphthora*, and the Daughters of Albion', *SiR* 20 (Fall 1981), 275–86.

ization.[23] Ireland was, after all, only a first step towards reforming the world; England was next. While the Godwinian side of Shelley's nature was content with gradualism, it is fairly clear that what Shelley had in mind when he returned to Sussex from Ireland was nothing less than what would have been construed as revolutionary activities carried on by associations—perhaps disguised as the 'Friendly Societies' still allowable under law—which would have had as their goal an organized reformation in opinion among the people at large leading to a complete reform of government—or else. When a customs official at Holyhead intercepted a box containing copies of the Irish pamphlets and the *Declaration of Rights* (the posting of which in Sussex led to the arrest of Shelley's manservant) and described them as 'Inflammatory Irish Papers', he exemplified the government's fears of the kind of uprising which some saw as warranted by the times and which Shelley might have fomented—whether he himself realized it or not—had he had power equal to his desire. In commenting on the notorious Ratcliffe Highway murders he illustrated the disparity between his official Godwinian pacifism and the unofficial firstlings of his heart: 'If the murderer of Marrs family containing 6 persons deserves a gibbet, how much more does a Prince whose conduct destroy⟨s⟩ millions deserve it?' (to E. Hitchener, ⟨? 16 April 1812⟩). The conditions for revolution were certainly there in 1812, and perhaps again in 1816. In early 1812, when William Godwin wrote in a letter to Shelley that his Irish activities were preparing a 'scene of blood' he provided a specific illustration of the middle-class fear of revolution which always qualified their general sympathies with active reform.

It may seem comfortably clear from a later historical perspective that by April 1818, when the Shelleys left for Italy, the English had successfully weathered the social reverberations of a pre-revolutionary storm akin to that which had provided France with the deluge Louis XV (or his mistress) had predicted for it. But when Shelley in 1819 drafted his longest and most thoughtful programme for *A Philosophical View of Reform*, the rigours of government

---

[23] See Darvall, *Popular Disturbances and Public Order*, 311, 314; cf. also pp. 304–6. The four-year gap in Shelley's overt interest in social and political affairs which commentators have noted is perhaps best explained by the fact that the major disorders of the period occurred in 1811–12 and 1816–17, 'years of unusual distress, of high prices, of stagnation of trade, of unemployment and low earnings' (ibid. 199).

sanctions expressed in the massacre at 'Peterloo' and further enhanced and codified in the notorious 'Six Acts' made it clear to him that the peaceful reform he had envisaged until 1817 was no longer possible.

THE

NECESSITY

OF

ATHEISM.

===

Quod clarâ et perspicuâ demonstratione careat
pro vero habere mens omnino nequit humana.

Bacon de Augment. Scient.

===

WORTHING:

PRINTED BY C. & W. PHILLIPS,

SOLD IN LONDON AND OXFORD.

1. Title-page of *The Necessity of Atheism* (1811)
Princeton University Library

Advertisement.

As a love of truth is the only motive which actuates the Author of this little tract, he earnestly entreats that those of his readers who may discover any deficiency in his reasoning, or may be in possession of proofs which his mind could never obtain, would offer them, together with their objections to the Public, as briefly, as methodically, as plainly as he has taken the liberty of doing. Thro' deficiency of proof.

AN ATHEIST.

THE NECESSITY
OF ATHEISM.

A close examination of the validity of the proofs adduced to support any proposition, has ever been allowed to be the only sure way of attaining truth, upon the advantages of which it is unnecessary to descant; our knowledge of the existence of a Deity is a subject of such importance that it cannot be too minutely investigated; in con- 5 sequence of this conviction, we proceed briefly and impartially to examine the proofs which have been adduced. It is necessary first to consider the nature of Belief.

When a proposition is offered to the mind, it perceives the agreement or disagreement of the ideas of which it is composed. A 10 perception of their agreement is termed belief; many obstacles frequently prevent this perception from being immediate; these the mind attempts to remove in order that the perception may be distinct. The mind is active in the investigation, in order to perfect the state of perception which is passive; the investigation being 15 confused with the perception has induced many falsely to imagine that the mind is active in belief, that belief is an act of volition, in consequence of which it may be regulated by the mind; pursuing, continuing this mistake they have attached a degree of criminality to disbelief of which in its nature it is incapable; it is equally so of merit. 20

The strength of belief like that of every other passion is in proportion to the degrees of excitement.

The degrees of excitement are three.

The senses are the sources of all knowledge to the mind, consequently their evidence claims the strongest assent. 25

The decision of the mind founded upon our own experience derived from these sources, claims the next degree.

The experience of others which addresses itself to the former one, occupies the lowest degree.—

Consequently no testimony can be admitted which is contrary 30 to reason; reason is founded on the evidence of our senses.

Every proof may be referred to one of these three divisions; we are naturally led to consider what arguments we receive from each of them to convince us of the existence of a Deity.

35   1st. The evidence of the senses.—If the Deity should appear to us, if he should convince our senses of his existence; this revelation would necessarily command belief;—Those to whom the Deity has thus appeared, have the strongest possible conviction of his existence.

40   Reason claims the 2nd. place—it is urged that man knows that whatever is, must either have had a beginning or existed from all eternity; he also knows that whatever is not eternal must have had a cause.—Where this is applied to the existence of the universe, it is necessary to prove that it was created; until that is clearly

45   demonstrated, we may reasonably suppose that it has endured from all eternity.—In a case where two propositions are diametrically opposite, the mind believes that which is less incomprehensible; it is easier to suppose that the Universe has existed from all eternity, than to conceive a being capable of creating it. If the mind sinks beneath

50   the weight of one, is it an alleviation to increase the intolerability of the burden?—The other argument which is founded upon a man's knowledge of his own existence, stands thus.—A man knows not only he now is, but that there was a time when he did not exist; consequently there must have been a cause.—But what does this

55   prove? We can only infer from effects causes exactly adequate to those effects;—But there certainly is a generative power which is effected by particular instruments; we cannot prove that it is inherent in these instruments, nor is the contrary hypothesis capable of demonstration; we admit that the generative power is

60   incomprehensible, but to suppose that the same effect is produced by an eternal, omniscient, Almighty Being, leaves the cause in the ⟨same⟩ obscurity, but renders it more incomprehensible.

The 3rd. and last degree of assent is claimed by Testimony—it is required that it should not be contrary to reason.—The testimony

65   that the Deity convinces the senses of men of his existence can only be admitted by us, if our mind considers it less probable that these men should have been deceived, than that the Deity should have appeared to them—our reason can never admit the testimony of men, who not only declare that they were eye-witnesses of miracles

70   but that the Deity was irrational, for he commanded that he should be believed, he proposed the highest rewards for faith, eternal

punishments for disbelief—we can only command voluntary actions, belief is not an act of volition, the mind is even passive. From this it is evident that we have not sufficient testimony, or rather that testimony is insufficient to prove the being of a God; we have before 75 shewn that it cannot be deduced from reason,—they who have been convinced by the evidence of the senses, they only can believe it.

From this it is evident that having no proofs from any of the three sources of conviction: the mind *cannot* believe the existence of a God. It is also evident that as belief is a passion of the mind, no 80 degree of criminality can be attached to disbelief; they only are reprehensible who willingly neglect to remove the false medium thro' which their mind views the subject.

It is almost unnecessary to observe, that the general knowledge of the deficiency of such proof, cannot be prejudicial to society: Truth 85 has always been found to promote the best interests of mankind.— Every reflecting mind must allow that there is no proof of the existence of a Deity. Q. E. D.

AN ADDRESS,

TO THE

IRISH PEOPLE,

By PERCY BYSSHE SHELLEY.

ADVERTISEMENT.

The lowest possible price is set on this publication, because it is the intention of the Author to awaken in the minds of the Irish poor, a knowledge of their real state, summarily pointing out the evils of that state, and suggesting rational means of remedy.—Catholic Emancipation, and a Repeal of the Union Act, (the latter, the most successful engine that England ever wielded over the misery of fallen Ireland,) being treated of in the following address, as grievances which unanimity and resolution may remove, and associations conducted with peaceable firmness, being earnestly recommended, as means for embodying that unanimity and firmness, which must finally be successful.

Dublin:
1812.

Price—5d.

2. Title-page of *An Address, to the Irish People* (1812)
Huntington Library (RB 22404)

Advertisement.

The lowest possible price is set on this publication, because it is the intention of the Author to awaken in the minds of the Irish poor, a knowledge of their real state, summarily pointing out the evils of that state, and suggesting rational means of remedy.—Catholic Emancipation, and a Repeal of the Union Act, (the latter, the most successful engine that England ever wielded over the misery of fallen Ireland,) being treated of in the following address, as grievances which unanimity and resolution may remove, and associations conducted with peaceable firmness, being earnestly recommended, as means for embodying that unanimity and firmness, which must finally be successful.

AN ADDRESS,
to the
IRISH PEOPLE.

FELLOW MEN,

I am not an Irishman, yet I can feel for you. I hope there are none among you who will read this address with prejudice or levity, because it is made by an Englishman; indeed, I believe there are not. The Irish are a brave nation. They have a heart of liberty in their breasts, but they are much mistaken if they fancy that a stranger cannot have as warm a one. Those are my brothers and my countrymen, who are unfortunate. I should like to know what there is in a man being an Englishman, a Spaniard, or a Frenchman, that makes him worse or better than he really is. He was born in one town, you in another, but that is no reason why he should not feel for you, desire your benefit, or be willing to give you some advice, which may make you more capable of knowing your own interest, or acting so as to secure it.—There are many Englishmen who cry down the Irish, and think it answers their ends to revile all that belongs to Ireland; but it is not because these men are Englishmen that they maintain such opinions, but because they wish to get money, and titles, and power. They would act in this manner to whatever country they might belong, until mankind is much altered for the better, which reform, I hope, will one day be effected.—I address you then, as my brothers and my fellow-men, for I should wish to see the Irishman who, if England was persecuted as Ireland is, who, if France was persecuted as Ireland is, who, if any set of men that helped to do a public service were prevented from enjoying its benefits as Irishmen are—I should like to see the man, I say, who would see these misfortunes, and not attempt to succour the sufferers when he could, just that I might tell him that he was no Irishman, but some bastard mongrel bred up in a court, or some coward fool who was a democrat to all above him, and an aristocrat

30 to all below him. I think there are few true Irishmen who would not
be ashamed of such a character, still fewer who possess it. I know
that there are some, not among you my friends, but among your
enemies, who seeing the title of this piece, will take it up with a sort
of hope that it may recommend violent measures, and thereby
35 disgrace the cause of freedom, that the warmth of an heart desirous
that liberty should be possessed equally by all, will vent itself in
abuse on the enemies of liberty, bad men who deserve the contempt
of the good, and ought not to excite their indignation to the harm of
their cause. But these men will be disappointed—I know the warm
40 feelings of an Irishman sometimes carries him beyond the point of
prudence. I do not desire to root out, but to moderate this honorable
warmth. This will disappoint the pioneers of oppression and they
will be sorry, that through this address nothing will occur which can
be twisted into any other meaning but what is calculated to fill you
45 with that moderation which they have not, and make you give them
that toleration which they refuse to grant to you.—You profess the
Roman Catholic religion which your fathers professed before you.
Whether it is the best religion or not, I will not here inquire: all
religions are good which make men good; and the way that a person
50 ought to prove that his method of worshipping God is best, is for
himself to be better than all other men. But we will consider what
your religion was in old times and what it is now: you may say it is
not a fair way for me to proceed as a Protestant, but I am not a
Protestant, nor am I a Catholic, and therefore not being a follower of
55 either of these religions, I am better able to judge between them. A
Protestant is my brother, and a Catholic is my brother. I am happy
when I can do either of them a service, and no pleasure is so great to
me as that, which I should feel, if my advice could make men of any
professions of faith, wiser, better and happier.
60   The Roman Catholics once persecuted the Protestants, the
Protestants now persecute the Roman Catholics—should we think
that one is as bad as the other? No, you are not answerable for the
faults of your fathers any more than the Protestants are good for the
goodness of their fathers. I must judge of people as I see them; the
65 Irish Catholics are badly used. I will not endeavour to hide from
them their wretchedness; they would think that I mocked at them if
I should make the attempt. The Irish Catholics now demand for
themselves, and profer to others, unlimited toleration, and the
sensible part among them, which I am willing to think constitutes a

very large portion of their body, know that the gates of Heaven are 70
open to people of every religion, provided they are good. But the
Protestants, although they may think so in their hearts, which
certainly, if they think at all they must, seem to act as if they thought
that God was better pleased with them than with you; they trust the
reins of earthly government only to the hands of their own sect; in 75
spite of this, I never found one of them impudent enough to say, that
a Roman Catholic, or a Quaker, or a Jew, or a Mahometan, if he was a
virtuous man, and did all the good in his power, would go to Heaven
a bit the slower for not subscribing to the thirty-nine articles—and if
he should say so, how ridiculous in a foppish courtier not six feet 80
high, to direct the spirit of universal harmony, in what manner to
conduct the affairs of the universe!

The Protestants say that there was a time when the Roman
Catholics burnt and murdered people of different sentiments, and
that their religious tenets are now as they were then. This is all very 85
true. You certainly worship God in the same way that you did when
those barbarities took place, but is that any reason that you should
now be barbarous. There is as much reason to suppose it, as to
suppose that because a man's great-grandfather, who was a Jew, had
been hung for sheep-stealing, that I, by believing the same religion as 90
he did, must certainly commit the same crime. Let us then see what
the Roman Catholic religion has been.—No one knows much of the
early times of the Christian religion, until about three hundred years
after its beginning, two great churches called the Roman and the
Greek churches, divided the opinions of men. They fought for a very 95
long time, a great many words were wasted, and a great deal of blood
shed. This as you may suppose did no good. Each party however,
thought they were doing God a service, and that he would reward
them. If they had looked an inch before their noses they might have
found, that fighting and killing men, and cursing them and hating 100
them, was the very worst way for getting into favor with a Being who
is allowed by all to be best pleased with deeds of love and charity. At
last, however, these two Religions entirely separated, and the Popes
reigned like Kings and Bishops at Rome, in Italy. The inquisition was
set up, and in the course of one year thirty thousand people were 105
burnt in Italy and Spain, for entertaining different opinions from
those of the Pope and the Priests. There was an instance of shocking
barbarity which the Roman Catholic Clergy committed in France
by order of the Pope. The bigotted Monks of that country, in cold

110 blood, in one night massacred 80,000 Protestants; this was done under the authority of the Pope, and there was only one Roman Catholic Bishop who had virtue enough to refuse to help. The vices of Monks and Nuns in their Convents were in those times shameful, people thought that they might commit any sin, however
115 monstrous, if they had money enough to prevail upon the Priests to absolve them; in truth, at that time the Priests shamefully imposed upon the people, they got all the power into their own hands, they persuaded them that a man could not be entrusted with the care of his own soul, and by cunningly obtaining possession of their secrets,
120 they became more powerful than Kings, Princes, Dukes, Lords, or Ministers: this power made them bad men; for although rational people are very good in their natural state, there are now, and ever have been very few whose good dispositions despotic power does not destroy. I have now given a fair description of what your religion
125 was; and Irishmen my brothers! will you make your friend appear a liar, when he takes upon himself to say for you, that you are not now what the professors of the same faith were in times of yore. Do I speak false when I say that the inquisition is the object of your hatred? Am I a liar if I assert that an Irishman prizes liberty dearly,
130 that he will preserve that right, and if he be wrong, does not dream that money given to a Priest, or the talking of another man erring like himself, can in the least influence the judgement of the eternal God?—I am not a liar if I affirm in your name, that you believe a Protestant equally with yourself to be worthy of the Kingdom of
135 Heaven, if he be equally virtuous; that you will treat men as brethren wherever you may find them; and that difference of opinion in religious matters, shall not, does not in the least on your part, obstruct the most perfect harmony on every other subject.—Ah! no, Irishmen, I am not a liar. I seek your confidence, not that I may
140 betray it, but that I may teach you to be happy, and wise, and good. If you will not repose any trust in me I shall lament, but I will do every thing in my power that is honorable, fair, and open, to gain it. Some teach you that others are heretics, that you alone are right; some teach that rectitude consists in religious opinions, without which no
145 morality is good, some will tell you that you ought to divulge your secrets to one particular set of men; beware my friends how you trust those who speak in this way. They will, I doubt not, attempt to rescue you from your present miserable state, but they will prepare a worse. It will be out of the frying-pan into the fire. Your present

oppressors it is true, will then oppress you no longer, but you will 150
feel the lash of a master a thousand times more blood-thirsty and
cruel. Evil designing men will spring up who will prevent your
thinking as you please, will burn you if you do not think as they do.
There are always bad men who take advantage of hard times. The
Monks and the Priests of old were very bad men; take care no such 155
abuse your confidence again. You are not blind to your present
situation, you are villainously treated, you are badly used. That this
slavery shall cease, I will venture to prophesy. Your enemies dare not
to persecute you longer, the spirit of Ireland is bent, but it is not
broken, and that they very well know. But I wish your views to 160
embrace a wider scene, I wish you to think for your children and
your children's children; to take great care (for it all rests with you)
that whilst one tyranny is destroyed another more fierce and terrible
does not spring up. Take care then of smooth-faced impostors, who
talk indeed of freedom, but who will cheat you into slavery. Can 165
there be worse slavery than the depending for the safety of your soul
on the will of another man? Is one man more favored than another by
God. No, certainly, they are all favored according to the good they
do, and not according to the rank and profession they hold. God
values a poor man as much as a Priest, and has given him a soul as 170
much to himself; the worship that a kind Being must love, is that of a
simple affectionate heart, that shews its piety in good works, and
not in ceremonies, or confessions, or burials, or processions, or
wonders. Take care then, that you are not led away. Doubt every
thing that leads you not to charity, and think of the word "heretic" as 175
a word which some selfish knave invented for the ruin and misery of
the world, to answer his own paltry and narrow ambition. Do not
inquire if a man be a heretic, if he be a Quaker, or a Jew, or a Heathen;
but if he be a virtuous man, if he loves liberty and truth, if he wish the
happiness and peace of human kind. If a man be ever so much a 180
believer and love not these things, he is a heartless hypocrite, a rascal,
and a knave. Despise and hate him, as ye despise a tyrant and a villain.
Oh! Ireland, thou emerald of the ocean, whose sons are generous and
brave, whose daughters are honorable, and frank, and fair; thou art
the isle on whose green shores I have desired to see the standard of 185
liberty erected, a flag of fire, a beacon at which the world shall light
the torch of Freedom!

We will now examine the Protestant Religion. Its origin is called
the Reformation. It was undertaken by some bigotted men, who

190 showed how little they understood the spirit of Reform, by burning each other. You will observe that these men burnt each other, indeed they universally betrayed a taste for destroying, and vied with the chiefs of the Roman Catholic Religion, in not only hating their enemies, but those men, who least of all were their enemies, or any 195 body's enemies. Now, do the Protestants, or do they not hold the same tenets as they did when Calvin burnt Servetus; they swear that they do. We can have no better proof. Then with what face can the Protestants object to Catholic Emancipation, on the plea that Catholics once were barbarous; when their own establishment is 200 liable to the very same objections, on the very same grounds? I think this is a specimen of bare-faced intoleration, which I had hoped would not have disgraced this age; this age, which is called the age of reason, of thought diffused, of virtue acknowledged, and its principles fixed.—Oh! that it may be so.—I have mentioned the 205 Catholic and Protestant Religions more to shew that any objection to the toleration of the one forcibly applies to the non-permission of the other, or rather to shew that there is no reason why both might not be tolerated, why every Religion, every form of thinking might not be tolerated.—But why do I speak of *toleration*? This word seems 210 to mean that there is some merit in the person who tolerates; he has this merit if it be one, of refraining to do an evil act, but he will share the merit with every other peaceable person who pursues his own business, and does not hinder another of his rights. It is not a merit to tolerate, but it is a crime to be intolerant: it is not a merit on me that I 215 sat quietly at home without murdering any one, but it is a crime if I do so. Besides no act of a National representation can make any thing wrong, which was not wrong before; it cannot change virtue and truth, and for a very plain reason; because they are unchangeable. An act passed in the British Parliament to take away 220 the rights of Catholics to act in that assembly, does not really take them away. It prevents them from doing it by force. This is in such cases, the last and only efficacious way. But force is not the test of truth; they will never have recourse to violence who acknowledge no other rule of behaviour but virtue and justice.

225   The folly of persecuting men for their religion will appear if we examine it. Why do we persecute them? to make them believe as we do. Can any thing be more barbarous or foolish.—For although we may make them say they believe as we do, they will not in their hearts do any such thing, indeed they cannot; this devilish method

can only make them false hypocrites. For what is belief? We cannot   230
believe just what we like, but only what we think to be true; for you
cannot alter a man's opinion by beating or burning, but by
persuading him that what you think is right, and this can only be
done by fair words and reason. It is ridiculous to call a man a heretic,
because he thinks differently from you; he might as well call you one.   235
In the same sense, the word orthodox is used: it signifies "to think
rightly" and what can be more vain and presumptuous in any man or
any set of men, to put themselves so out of the ordinary course of
things as to say—"What we think is right, no other people
throughout the world have opinions any thing like equal to ours."   240
Any thing short of unlimited toleration, and complete charity with
all men, on which you will recollect that Jesus Christ principally
insisted, is wrong, and for this reason—what makes a man to be a
good man? not his religion, or else there could be no good men in any
religion but one, when yet we find that all ages, countries, and   245
opinions have produced them. Virtue and wisdom always so far as
they went produced liberty or happiness long before any of the
religions now in the world were ever heard of. The only use of a
religion that ever I could see, is, to make men wiser or better; so far as
it does this, it is a good one. Now if people are good, and yet have   250
sentiments differing from you, then all the purposes are answered,
which any reasonable man could want, and whether he thinks like
you or not, is of too little consequence to employ means which must
be disgusting and hateful to candid minds, nay they cannot approve
of such means. For as I have before said, you cannot believe or   255
disbelieve what you like—perhaps some of you may doubt this, but
just try—I will take a common and familiar instance. Suppose you
have a friend of whom you wish to think well, he commits a crime,
which proves to you that he is a bad man. It is very painful to you to
think ill of him, and you would still think well of him if you could.   260
But mark the word, you *cannot* think well of him, not even to secure
your own peace of mind can you do so. You try, but your attempts
are vain. This shews how little power a man has over his belief, or
rather, that he cannot believe what he does not think true. And what
shall we think now? What fools and tyrants must not those men be,   265
who set up a particular religion, say that this religion alone is right,
and that every one who disbelieves it, ought to be deprived of certain
rights which are really his, and which would be allowed him if he
believed. Certainly, if you cannot help disbelief, it is not any fault in

270 you.—To take away a man's rights and privileges, to call him a heretic or to think worse of him, when at the same time you cannot help owning that he has committed no fault, is the grossest tyranny and intoleration. From what has been said, I think we may be justified in concluding, that people of all religions ought to have an

275 equal share in the state, that the words heretic and orthodox were invented by a vain villain, and have done a great deal of harm in the world, and that no person is answerable for his belief whose actions are virtuous and moral, that the religion is best whose members are the best men, and that no person can help either his belief or

280 disbelief.—Be in charity with all men. It does not therefore, signify what your Religion *was*, or what the Protestant Religion *was*, we must consider them as we find them. What are they *now*? Yours is not intolerant; indeed my friends I have ventured to pledge myself for you that it is not. You merely desire to go to Heaven, in your own

285 way, nor will you interrupt fellow travellers, although the road which you take, may not be that which they take. Believe me, that goodness of heart and purity of life are things of more value in the eye of the Spirit of Goodness, than idle earthly ceremonies, and things which have any thing but charity for their object. And is it for

290 the first or the last of these things that you or the Protestants contend. It is for the last. Prejudiced people indeed, are they who grudge to the happiness and comfort of your souls, things which can do harm to no one. They are not compelled to share in these rites. Irishmen; knowledge is more extended than in the early period of

295 your religion, people have learned to think, and the more thought there is in the world, the more happiness and liberty will there be:— men begin now to think less of idle ceremonies, and more of realities. From a long night have they risen, and they can perceive its darkness. I know no men of thought and learning who do not consider the

300 Catholic idea of purgatory, much nearer the truth than the Protestant one of eternal damnation. Can you think that the Mahometans and the Indians, who have done good deeds in this life, will not be rewarded in the next. The Protestants believe that they will be eternally damned—at least they swear that they do.—I think

305 they appear in a better light as perjurers, than believers in a falsehood so hateful and uncharitable as this.—I propose unlimited toleration, or rather the destruction, both of toleration and intoleration. The act permits certain people to worship God after such a manner, which, in fact, if not done, would as far as in it lay prevent God

from hearing their address. Can we conceive any thing more 310
presumptuous, and at the same time more ridiculous, than a set of
men granting a license to God to receive the prayers of certain of his
creatures. Oh Irishmen! I am interested in your cause; and it is not
because you are Irishmen or Roman Catholics, that I feel with you
and feel for you; but because you are men and sufferers. Were Ireland 315
at this moment, peopled with Brahmins, this very same address
would have been suggested by the same state of mind. You have
suffered not merely for your religion, but ⟨from⟩ some other causes
which I am equally desirous of remedying. The Union of England
with Ireland has withdrawn the Protestant aristocracy, and gentry 320
from their native country, and with these their friends and connections. Their resources are taken from this country, although they
are dissipated in another; the very poor people are most infamously
oppressed by the weight of burden which the superior ranks lay
upon their shoulders. I am no less desirous of the reform of these 325
evils (with many others) than for the Catholic Emancipation.

Perhaps you all agree with me on both these subjects; we now
come to the method of doing these things. I agree with the Quakers
so far as they disclaim violence, and trust their cause wholly and
solely to its own truth.—If you are convinced of the truth of your 330
cause, trust wholly to its truth; if you are not convinced, give it up. In
no case employ violence, the way to liberty and happiness is never to
transgress the rules of virtue and justice. Liberty and happiness are
founded upon virtue and justice, if you destroy the one, you destroy
the other. However ill others may act, this will be no excuse for you if 335
you follow their example; it ought rather to warn you from pursuing
so bad a method. Depend upon it, Irishmen, your cause shall not be
neglected. I will fondly hope, that the schemes for your happiness
and liberty, as well as those for the happiness and liberty of the
world, will not be wholly fruitless. One secure method of defeating 340
them is violence on the side of the injured party. If you can descend
to use the same weapons as your enemy, you put yourself on a level
with him on this score, you must be convinced that he is on these
grounds your superior. But appeal to the sacred principles of virtue
and justice, then how is he awed into nothing? how does truth shew 345
him in his real colours, and place the cause of toleration and reform
in the clearest light. I extend my view not only to you as Irishmen,
but to all of every persuasion, of every country. Be calm, mild,
deliberate, patient; recollect that you can in no measure more

350 effectually forward the cause of reform than by employing your
leisure time in reasoning, or the cultivation of your minds. Think
and talk, and discuss. The only subjects you ought to propose, are
those of happiness and liberty. Be free and be happy, but first be wise
and good. For you are not all wise or good. You are a great and a
355 brave nation, but you cannot yet be all wise or good. You may be at
some time, and then Ireland will be an earthly Paradise. You know
what is meant by a mob, it is an assembly of people who without
foresight or thought, collect themselves to disapprove of by force
any measure which they dislike. An assembly like this can never do
360 any thing but harm, tumultuous proceedings must retard the period
when thought and coolness will produce freedom and happiness,
and that to the very people who make the mob, but if a number of
human beings, after thinking of their own interests, meet together
for any conversation on them, and employ resistance of the mind,
365 not resistance of the body, these people are going the right way to
work. But let no fiery passions carry them beyond this point, let
them consider that in some sense, the whole welfare of their
countrymen depends on their prudence, and that it becomes them to
guard the welfare of others as their own. Associations for purposes
370 of violence, are entitled to the strongest disapprobation of the real
reformist. Always suspect that some knavish rascal is at the bottom
of things of this kind, waiting to profit by the confusion. All secret
associations are also bad. Are you men of deep designs, whose deeds
love darkness better than light; dare you not say what you think
375 before any man, can you not meet in the open face of day in
conscious innocence? Oh, Irishmen ye can. Hidden arms, secret
meetings and designs, violently to separate England from Ireland,
are all very bad. I do not mean to say the very end of them is bad, the
object you have in view may be just enough, whilst the way you go
380 about it is wrong, may be calculated to produce an opposite effect.
Never do evil that good may come, always think of others as well as
yourself, and cautiously look how your conduct may do good or
evil, when you yourself shall be mouldering in the grave. Be fair,
open, and you will be terrible to your enemies. A friend cannot
385 defend you, much as he may feel for your sufferings, if you have
recourse to methods of which virtue and justice disapprove. No
cause is in itself so dear to liberty as yours. Much depends on you, far
may your efforts spread, either hope or despair; do not then cover in
darkness wrongs at which the face of day, and the tyrants who bask

in its warmth ought to blush. Wherever has violence succeeded. The 390
French Revolution, although undertaken with the best intentions,
ended ill for the people, because violence was employed; the cause
which they vindicated was that of truth, but they gave it the
appearance of a lie, by using methods which will suit the purposes of
liars as well as their own. Speak boldly and daringly what you think; 395
an Irishman was never accused of cowardice, do not let it be thought
possible that he is a coward. Let him say what he thinks, a lie is the
basest and meanest employment of men, leave lies and secrets to
courtiers and lordlings; be open, sincere, and single hearted. Let it be
seen that the Irish votaries of Freedom dare to speak what they 400
think, let them resist oppression, not by force of arms, but by power
of mind, and reliance on truth and justice. Will any be arraigned for
libel—will imprisonment or death be the consequences of this mode
of proceeding: probably not—but if it were so? Is danger frightful
to an Irishman who speaks for his own liberty, and the liberty of 405
his wife and children:—No, he will steadily persevere, and sooner
shall pensioners cease to vote with their benefactors, than an
Irishman swerve from the path of duty. But steadily persevere in the
system above laid down, its benefits will speedily be manifested.
Persecution may destroy some, but cannot destroy all, or nearly 410
all; let it do its will, ye have appealed to truth and justice—shew
the goodness of your religion by persisting in a reliance on these
things, which must be the rules even of the Almighty's conduct.
But before this can be done with any effect, habits of SOBRIETY,
REGULARITY, and THOUGHT, must be entered into, and 415
firmly resolved upon.

My warm-hearted friends, who meet together to talk of the
distresses of your countrymen, until social chat induces you to drink
rather freely; as ye have felt passionately, so reason coolly. Nothing
hasty can be lasting; lay up the money with which you usually 420
purchase drunkenness and ill-health, to relieve the pains of your
fellow-sufferers. Let your children lisp of Freedom in the cradle—let
your death-bed be the school for fresh exertions—let every street of
the city, and field of the country, be connected with thoughts, which
liberty has made holy. Be warm in your cause, yet rational, and 425
charitable, and tolerant—never let the oppressor grind you into
justifying his conduct by imitating his meanness.

Many circumstances, I will own, may excuse what is called
rebellion, but no circumstances can ever make it good for your

430 cause, and however honourable to your feelings, it will reflect no credit on your judgments. It will bind you more closely to the block of the oppressor, and your children's children, whilst they talk of your exploits, will feel that you have done them injury, instead of benefit.

435 A crisis is now arriving, which shall decide your fate. The king of Great Britain has arrived at the evening of his days. He has objected to your emancipation; he has been inimical to you; but he will in a certain time be no more. The present Prince of Wales will then be king. It is said that he has promised to restore you to freedom: your

440 real and natural right will, in that case, be no longer kept from you. I hope he has pledged himself to this act of justice, because there will then exist some obligation to bind him to do right. Kings are but too apt to think little as they should do: they think every thing in the world is made for them; when the truth is, that it is only the vices of

445 men that make such people necessary, and they have no other right of being kings, but in virtue of the good they do. The benefit of the governed is the origin and meaning of government. The Prince of Wales has had every opportunity of knowing how he ought to act about Ireland and liberty. That great and good man, Charles Fox,

450 who was your friend, and the friend of freedom, was the friend of the Prince of Wales. He never flattered or disguised his sentiments, but spoke them *openly* on every occasion, and the Prince was the better for his instructive conversation. He saw the truth, and he believed it. Now I know not what to say; his staff is gone, and he leans upon a

455 broken reed; his present advisers are not like Charles Fox, they do not plan for liberty and safety, not for the happiness but for the glory of their country; and what, Irishmen, is the glory of a country divided from their happiness? it is a false light hung out by the enemies of freedom to lure the unthinking into their net. Men like

460 these surround the Prince, and whether or no he has really promised to emancipate you, whether or no he will consider the promise of a Prince of Wales binding to a King of England, is yet a matter of doubt. We cannot at least be quite certain of it: on this you cannot certainly rely. But there are men who, wherever they find a tendency

465 to freedom, go there to increase, support, and regulate that tendency. These men who join to a rational disdain of danger, a practice of speaking the truth, and defending the cause of the oppressed against the oppressor; these men see what is right and will pursue it. On such as these you may safely rely: they love you as they

love their brothers; they feel for the unfortunate, and never ask 470
whether a man is an Englishman or an Irishman, a catholic, a heretic,
a christian, or a heathen, before their hearts and their purses are
opened to feel with their misfortunes and relieve their necessities:
such are the men who will stand by you for ever. Depend then, not
upon the promises of Princes, but upon those of virtuous and 475
disinterested men: depend not upon force of arms or violence, but
upon the force of the truth of the right which you have to share
equally with others, the benefits and the evils of Government.

The crisis to which I allude as the period of your emancipation, is
not the death of the present king, or any circumstance that has to do 480
with kings, but something that is much more likely to do you good: it
is the increase of virtue and wisdom which will lead people to find
out that force and oppression is wrong and false: and this opinion,
when it once gains ground, will prevent government from severity.
It will restore those rights which government has taken away. Have 485
nothing to do with force or violence, and things will safely and surely
make their way to the right point. The Ministers have now in
Parliament a very great majority, and the Ministers are against you.
They maintain the falsehood that, were you in power you would
prosecute and burn, on the plea that you once did so. They maintain 490
many other things of the same nature.—They command the majority
of the House of Commons, or rather the part of that assembly, who
receive pensions from Government, or whose relatives receive
them. These men of course, are against you, because their employers
are. But the sense of the country is not against you, the people of 495
England are not against you—they feel warmly for you—in some
respects they feel with you. The sense of the English and of their
Governors is opposite—there must be an end of this; the goodness of
a Government consists in the happiness of the Governed, if the
Governed are wretched and dissatisfied, the Government has failed 500
in its end. It wants altering and mending. It will be mended, and a
reform of English Government will produce good to the Irish—
good to all human kind, excepting those whose happiness consists in
others' sorrows, and it will be a fit punishment for these to be
deprived of their devilish joy. This I consider as an event which is 505
approaching, and which will make the beginning of our hopes for
that period which may spread wisdom and virtue so wide, as to leave
no hole in which folly or villainy may hide themselves. I wish you, O
Irishmen, to be as careful and thoughtful of your interests as are your

510 real friends. Do not drink, do not play, do not spend any idle time, do
not take every thing that other people say for granted—there are
numbers who will tell you lies to make their own fortunes, you
cannot more certainly do good to your own cause, than by defeating
the intentions of these men. Think, read and talk; let your own
515 condition and that of your wives and children, fill your minds;
disclaim all manner of alliance with violence, meet together if ye will,
but do not meet in a mob. If you think and read and talk with a real
wish of benefiting the cause of truth and liberty, it will soon be seen
how true a service you are rendering, and how sincere you are in
520 your professions; but mobs and violence must be discarded. The
certain degree of civil and religious liberty which the usage of the
English Constitution allows, is such as the worst of men are entitled
to, although you have it not; but that liberty which we may one day
hope for, wisdom and virtue can alone give you a right to enjoy. This
525 wisdom and this virtue I recommend on every account that you
should *instantly begin* to practice. Lose not a day, not an hour, not a
moment.—Temperance, sobriety, charity and independence will
give you virtue; and reading, talking, thinking and searching, will
give you wisdom; when you have those things you may defy the
530 tyrant. It is not going often to chapel, crossing yourselves, or
confessing, that will make you virtuous; many a rascal has attended
regularly at Mass, and many a good man has never gone at all. It is not
paying Priests, or believing in what they say that makes a good man,
but it is doing good actions, or benefiting other people; this is the
535 true way to be good, and the prayers, and confessions, and masses of
him who does not these things, are good for nothing at all. Do your
work regularly and quickly, when you have done, think, read and
talk; do not spend your money in idleness and drinking, which so far
from doing good to your cause, will do it harm. If you have any thing
540 to spare from your wife and children, let it do some good to other
people, and put them in a way of getting wisdom and virtue, as the
pleasure that will come from these good acts, will be much better
than the head-ache that comes from a drinking bout. And never
quarrel between each other, be all of one mind as nearly as you can;
545 do these things, and I will promise you liberty and happiness. But if,
on the contrary of these things, you neglect to improve yourselves,
continue to use the word heretic, and demand from others the
toleration which you are unwilling to give; your friends and the
friends of liberty will have reason to lament the death-blow of their

hopes. I expect better things from you; it is for yourselves that I fear   550
and hope. Many Englishmen are prejudiced against you, they sit by
their own fire-sides and certain rumours artfully spread, are ever on
the wing against you. But these people who think ill of you and of
your nation, are often the very men who, if they had better
information, would feel for you most keenly; wherefore are these   555
reports spread, how do they begin? They originate from the warmth
of the Irish character, which the friends of the Irish nation have
hitherto encouraged rather than repressed; this leads them in those
moments when their wrongs appear so clearly, to commit acts
which justly excite displeasure. They begin therefore, from   560
yourselves, although falsehood and tyranny artfully magnify and
multiply the causes of offence.—Give no offence.

I will for the present dismiss the subject of the Catholic
Emancipation; a little reflection will convince you that my remarks
are just. Be true to yourselves, and your enemies shall not triumph. I   565
fear nothing, if charity and sobriety mark your proceedings. Every
thing is to be dreaded, you yourselves will be unworthy of even a
restoration to your rights, if you disgrace the cause, which I hope is
that of truth and liberty, by violence, if you refuse to others the
toleration which you claim for yourselves.—But this you will not do.   570
I rely upon it Irishmen, that the warmth of your characters will be
shewn as much in union with Englishmen and what are called
heretics, who feel for you, and love you as in avenging your wrongs,
or forwarding their annihilation.—It is the heart that glows and not
the cheek. The firmness, sobriety, and consistence of your outward   575
behaviour will not at all shew any hardness of heart, but will prove
that you are determined in your cause, and are going the right way to
work.—I will repeat that virtue and wisdom are necessary to true
happiness and liberty.—The Catholic Emancipation I consider, is
certain. I do not see that any thing but violence and intolerance   580
among yourselves can leave an excuse to your enemies for
continuing your slavery. The other wrongs under which you labor,
will probably also soon be done away. You will be rendered equal to
the people of England in their rights and privileges, and will be in all
respects, so far as concerns the state, as happy. And now Irishmen   585
another, and a more wide prospect opens to my view. I cannot avoid,
little as it may appear to have any thing to do with your present
situation, to talk to you on the subject. It intimately concerns the
well-being of your children, and your children's children, and will

590 perhaps, more than any thing prove to you the advantage and necessity of being thoughtful, sober, and regular; of avoiding foolish and idle talk, and thinking of yourselves, as of men who are able to be much wiser and happier than you now are; for habits like these, will not only conduce to the successful putting aside your present and
595 immediate grievances, but will contain a seed, which in future times will spring up into the tree of liberty, and bear the fruit of happiness.

There is no doubt but the world is going wrong, or rather that it is very capable of being much improved. What I mean by this improvement is, the inducement of a more equal and general dif-
600 fusion of happiness and liberty.—Many people are very rich and many are very poor. Which do you think are happiest?—I can tell you that neither are happy, so far as their station is concerned. Nature never intended that there should be such a thing as a poor man or a rich one. Being put in an unnatural situation, they can
605 neither of them be happy, so far as their situation is concerned. The poor man is born to obey the rich man, though they both come into the world equally helpless, and equally naked. But the poor man does the rich no service by obeying him—the rich man does the poor no good by commanding him. It would be much better if they could
610 be prevailed upon to live equally like brothers—they would ultimately both be happier. But this can be done neither to-day nor to-morrow, much as such a change is to be desired, it is quite impossible. Violence and folly in this, as in the other case, would only put off the period of its event. Mildness, sobriety, and reason,
615 are the effectual methods of forwarding the ends of liberty and happiness.

Although we may see many things put in train, during our life-time, we cannot hope to see the work of virtue and reason finished now; we can only lay the foundation for our posterity. Government
620 is an evil, it is only the thoughtlessness and vices of men that make it a necessary evil. When all men are good and wise, Government will of itself decay, so long as men continue foolish and vicious, so long will Government, even such a Government as that of England, continue necessary in order to prevent the crimes of bad men. Society is
625 produced by the wants, Government by the wickedness, and a state of just and happy equality by the improvement and reason of man. It is in vain to hope for any liberty and happiness, without reason and virtue—for where there is no virtue there will be crime, and where there is crime there must be Government. Before the restraints of

Government are lessened, it is fit that we should lessen the necessity 630
for them. Before Government is done away with, we must reform
ourselves. It is this work which I would earnestly recommend to
you, O Irishmen, REFORM YOURSELVES—and I do not
recommend it to you particularly because I think that you most need
it, but because I think that your hearts are warm and your feelings 635
high, and you will perceive the necessity of doing it more than those
of a colder and more distant nature.

I look with an eye of hope and pleasure on the present state
of things, gloomy and incapable of improvement as they may appear
to others. It delights me to see that men begin to think and to act 640
for the good of others. Extensively as folly and selfishness has
predominated in this age, it gives me hope and pleasure, at least, to
see that many know what is right. Ignorance and vice commonly go
together: he that would do good must be wise—a man cannot be
truly wise who is not truly virtuous. Prudence and wisdom are very 645
different things. The prudent man is he, who carefully consults for
his own good: the wise man is he, who carefully consults for the good
of others.

I look upon the Catholic Emancipation, and the restoration of
the liberties and happiness of Ireland, so far as they are compatible 650
with the English Constitution, as great and important events. I hope
to see them soon. But if all ended here, it would give me little
pleasure—I should still see thousands miserable and wicked, things
would still be wrong. I regard then, the accomplishment of these
things as the road to a greater reform—that reform after which 655
virtue and wisdom shall have conquered pain and vice. When
no Government will be wanted, but that of your neighbour's
opinion.—I look to these things with hope and pleasure, because I
consider that they will certainly happen, and because men will not
then be wicked and miserable. But I do not consider that they will or 660
can immediately happen; their arrival will be gradual, and it all
depends upon yourselves how soon or how late these great changes
will happen. If all of you, to-morrow were virtuous and wise,
Government which to-day is a safe-guard, would then become a
tyranny. But I cannot expect a rapid change. Many are obstinate and 665
determined in their vice, whose selfishness makes them think only
of their own good, when in fact, the best way even to bring that
about, is to make others happy. I do not wish to see things changed
now, because it cannot be done without violence, and we may assure

670 ourselves that none of us are fit for any change however good, if we condescend to employ force in a cause which we think right. Force makes the side that employs it directly wrong, and as much as we may pity we cannot approve the headstrong and intolerant zeal of its adherents.

675 Can you conceive, O Irishmen! a happy state of society—conceive men of every way of thinking li ing together like brothers. The descendant of the greatest Prince would there, be entitled to no more respect than the son of a peasant. There would be no pomp and no parade, but that which the rich now keep to themselves, would 680 then be distributed among the people. None would be in magnificence, but the superfluities then taken from the rich would be sufficient when spread abroad, to make every one comfortable.— No lover would then be false to his mistress, no mistress would desert her lover. No friend would play false, no rents, no debts, no 685 taxes, no frauds of any kind would disturb the general happiness: good as they would be, wise as they would be, they would be daily getting better and wiser. No beggars would exist, nor any of those wretched women, who are now reduced to a state of the most horrible misery and vice, by men whose wealth makes them 690 villainous and hardened. No thieves or murderers, because poverty would never drive men to take away comforts from another, when he had enough for himself. Vice and misery, pomp and poverty, power and obedience, would then be banished altogether.—It is for such a state as this, Irishmen, that I exhort you to prepare.—"A 695 Camel shall as soon pass through the eye of a needle, as a rich man enter the Kingdom of Heaven." This is not to be understood literally. Jesus Christ appears to me only to have meant that riches, have generally the effect of hardening and vitiating the heart; so has poverty. I think those people then are very silly, and cannot see one 700 inch beyond their noses, who say that human nature is depraved; when at the same time wealth and poverty, those two great sources of crime, fall to the lot of a great majority of people; and when they see that people in moderate circumstances are always most wise and good.—People say that poverty is no evil—they have never felt it, or 705 they would not think so. That wealth is necessary to encourage the arts—but are not the arts very inferior things to virtue and happiness—the man would be very dead to all generous feelings who would rather see pretty pictures and statues, than a million free and happy men.

It will be said, that my design is to make you dissatisfied with your 710
present condition, and that I wish to raise a Rebellion. But how
stupid and sottish must those men be, who think that violence and
uneasiness of mind have any thing to do with forwarding the views
of peace, harmony and happiness. They should know that nothing
was so well-fitted to produce slavery, tyranny, and vice, as the 715
violence which is attributed to the friends of liberty, and which the
real friends of liberty are the only persons who disdain.—As to your
being dissatisfied with your present condition, any thing that I may
say is certainly not likely to increase that dissatisfaction. I have
advanced nothing concerning your situation, but its real case, but 720
what may proved to be true. I defy any one to point out a falsehood
that I have uttered in the course of this address. It is impossible but
the blindest among you must see that every thing is not right. This
sight has often pressed some of the poorest among you to take
something from the rich man's store by violence, to relieve his own 725
necessities. I cannot justify, but I can pity him. I cannot pity the fruits
of the rich man's intemperance, I suppose some are to be found who
will justify him. This sight has often brought home to a day-labourer
the truth which I wish to impress upon you, that all is not right. But I
do not merely wish to convince you that ⟨y⟩our present state is bad, 730
but that its alteration for the better, depends on your own exertions
and resolutions.

But he has never found out the method of mending it, who does
not first mend his own conduct, and then prevail upon others to
refrain from any vicious habits which they may have contracted— 735
much less does the poor man suppose that wisdom as well as virtue is
necessary, and that the employing his little time in reading and
thinking, is really doing all that he has in his power to do towards the
state, when pain and vice shall perish altogether.

I wish to impress upon your minds, that without virtue or 740
wisdom, there can be no liberty or happiness; and that temperance,
sobriety, charity, and independence of soul, will give you virtue—as
thinking, enquiring, reading, and talking, will give you wisdom.
Without the first, the last is of little use, and without the last, the first
is a dreadful curse to yourselves and others.
745
I have told you what I think upon this subject, because I wish to
produce in your minds an awe and caution necessary, before the
happy state of which I have spoken can be introduced. This cautious
awe, is very different from the prudential fear, which leads you to

750 consider yourself as the first object, as on the contrary it is full of that warm and ardent love for others that burns in your hearts, O Irishmen! and from which I have fondly hoped to light a flame that may illumine and invigorate the world!

I have said that the rich command, and the poor obey, and that 755 money is only a kind of sign, which shews, that according to government the rich man has a right to command the poor man, or rather that the poor man being urged by having no money to get bread, is forced to work for the rich man, which amounts to the same thing. I have said that I think all this very wrong, and that I wish the 760 whole business was altered. I have also said that we can expect little amendment in our own time, and that we must be contented to lay the foundation of liberty and happiness, by virtue and wisdom.— This then, shall be my work: let this be yours, Irishmen. Never shall that glory fail, which I am anxious that you should deserve. The 765 glory of teaching to a world the first lessons of virtue and wisdom.

Let poor men still continue to work. I do not wish to hide from them a knowledge of their relative condition in society, I esteem it next ⟨to⟩ impossible to do so. Let the work of the labourer, of the artificer—let the work of every one, however employed, still be 770 exerted in its accustomed way. The public communication of this truth, ought in no manner, to impede the established usages of society; however, it is fitted in the end to do them away. For this reason it ought not to impede them, because if it did, a violent and unaccustomed and sudden sensation would take place in all ranks of 775 men, which would bring on violence, and destroy the possibility of the event of that, which in its own nature must be gradual, however rapid, and rational, however warm. It is founded on the reform of private men, and without individual amendment it is vain and foolish to expect the amendment of a state or government. I would 780 advise them therefore, whose feelings this address may have succeeded in affecting, (and surely those feelings which charitable and temperate remarks excite, can never be violent and intolerant,) if they be, as I hope, those whom poverty has compelled to class themselves in the lower orders of society, that they will as usual 785 attend to their business and the discharge of those public or private duties, which custom has ordained. Nothing can be more rash and thoughtless, than to shew in ourselves singular instances of any particular doctrine, before the general mass of the people are so convinced by the reasons of the doctrine, that it will be no longer

singular. That reasons as well as feelings, may help the establishment 790
of happiness and liberty, on the basis of wisdom and virtue, ⟨is⟩ our
aim and intention.—Let us not be led into any means which are
unworthy of this end, nor, as so much depends upon yourselves, let
us cease carefully to watch over our conduct, that when we talk of
reform it be not objected to us, that reform ought to begin at home. 795
In the interval, that public or private duties and necessary labors
allow, husband your time so, that you may do to others and
yourselves the most real good. To improve your own minds is to join
these two views: conversation and reading are the principal and chief
methods of awakening the mind to knowledge and goodness. 800
Reading or thought, will principally bestow the former of these—the
benevolent exercise of the powers of the mind in communicating
useful knowledge, will bestow an habit, of the latter, both united,
will contribute so far as lays in your individual power to that great
reform, which will be perfect and finished, the moment every one is 805
virtuous and wise. Every folly refuted, every bad habit conquered,
every good one confirmed, is so much gained in this great and
excellent cause.

To begin to reform the Government, is immediately necessary,
however good or bad individuals may be; it is the more necessary if 810
they are eminently the latter, in some degree to palliate or do away
the cause; as political institution has even the greatest influence on
the human character, and is that alone which differences the Turk
from the Irishman.

I write now not only with a view for Catholic Emancipation, but 815
for universal emancipation; and ⟨to⟩ this emancipation complete
and unconditional, that shall comprehend every individual of
whatever nation or principles, that shall fold in its embrace all that
think and all that feel, the Catholic cause is subordinate, and its
success preparatory to this great cause, which adheres to no sect but 820
society, to no cause but that of universal happiness, to no party but
the people. I desire Catholic Emancipation, but I desire not to stop
here, and I hope there are few who having perused the preceding
arguments will not concur with me in desiring a complete, a lasting
and a happy amendment. That all steps however good and salutary 825
which may be taken, all reforms consistent with the English
constitution that may be effectuated, can only be subordinate and
preparatory to the great and lasting one which shall bring about the
peace, the harmony, and the happiness of Ireland, England, Europe,

830 the World. I offer merely an outline of that picture which your own hopes may gift with the colors of reality.

Government will not allow a peaceable and reasonable discussion of its principles by any association of men, who assemble for that express purpose. But have not human beings a right to assemble to
835 talk upon what subject they please; can any thing be more evident than that as government is only of use as it conduces to the happiness of the governed; those who are governed have a right to talk on the efficacy of the safe guard employed for their benefit. Can any topic be more interesting or useful, than on⟨e⟩ discussing how far the
840 means of government, is or could be made in a higher degree effectual to producing the end. Although I deprecate violence, and the cause which depends for its influence on force, yet I can by no means think that assembling together merely to talk of how things go on, I can by no means think that societies formed for talking on
845 any subject however government may dislike them, come in any way under the head of force or violence. I think that associations conducted in the spirit of sobriety, regularity, and thought, are one of the best and most efficient of those means which I would recommend for the production of happiness, liberty, and virtue.

850 Are you slaves, or are you men? if slaves, then crouch to the rod, and lick the feet of your oppressors, glory in your shame, it will become you if brutes to act according to your nature. But you are men; a real man is free, so far as circumstances will permit him. Then firmly, yet quietly resist. When one cheek is struck, turn the other to
855 the insulting coward. You will be truly brave; you will resist and conquer. The discussion of any subject, is a right that you have brought into the world with your heart and tongue. Resign your heart's-blood, before you part with this inestimable privilege of man. For it is fit that the governed should enquire into the
860 proceedings of Government, which is of no use the moment it is conducted on any other principle but that of safety. You have much to think of.—Is war necessary to your happiness and safety. The interests of the poor gain nothing from the wealth or extension of a nation's boundaries, they gain nothing from glory, a word that has
865 often served as a cloak to the ambition or avarice of Statesmen. The barren victories of Spain, gained in behalf of a bigotted and tyrannical Government, are nothing to them. The conquests in India, by which England has gained glory indeed, but a glory which is not more honourable than that of Buonaparte, are nothing to

them. The poor purchase this glory and this wealth, at the expence of 870
their blood, and labor, and happiness, and virtue. They die in battle
for this infernal cause. Their labor supplies money and food for
carrying it into effect, their happiness is destroyed by the oppression
they undergo, their virtue is rooted out by the depravity and vice
that prevails throughout the army, and which under the present 875
system, is perfectly unavoidable. Who does not know that the
quartering of a regiment on any town, will soon destroy the
innocence and happiness of its inhabitants. The advocates for the
happiness and liberty of the great mass of the people, who pay for
war with their lives and labor, ought never to cease writing and 880
speaking until nations see as they must feel, the folly of fighting and
killing each other in uniform, for nothing at all. Ye have much to
think of. The state of your representation in the House, which is
called the collective representation of the country demands your
attention.
                                                                     885
   It is horrible that the lower classes must waste their lives and
liberty to furnish means for their oppressors to oppress them yet
more terribly. It is horrible that the poor must give in taxes what
would save them and their families from hunger and cold; it is still
more horrible that they should do this to furnish further means of 890
their own abjectness and misery; but what words can express the
enormity of the abuse that prevents them from choosing representatives with authority to enquire into the manner in which their
lives and labor, their happiness and innocence is expended, and what
advantages result from their expenditure which may counterbalance 895
so horrible and monstrous an evil. There is an outcry raised against
amendment; it is called innovation and condemned by many
unthinking people who have a good fire and plenty to eat and drink;
hard hearted or thoughtless beings, how many are famishing whilst
you deliberate, how many perish to contribute to your pleasures. I 900
hope that there are none such as these native Irishmen, indeed I
scarcely believe that there are.
   Let the object of your associations (for I conceal not my approval
of assemblies conducted with regularity, *peaceableness* and thought
for any purpose,) be the amendment of these abuses, it will have for 905
its object universal Emancipation, liberty, happiness, and virtue.
There is yet another subject, "the Liberty of the Press." The liberty of
the press consists in a right to publish any opinion on any subject
which the writer may entertain. The Attorney General in 1793 on the

910 trial of Mr. Perry, said, "I never will dispute the right of any man fully to discuss topics respecting government, and honestly to point out what he may consider a proper remedy of grievances."—"The Liberty of the Press, is placed as a centinel to alarm us when any attempt is made on our liberties."—It is this sentinel, O Irishmen 915 whom I now awaken! I create to myself a freedom which exists not. There is no liberty of the press, for the subjects of British government.

It is really ridiculous to hear people yet boasting of this inestimable blessing, when they daily see it successfully muzzled 920 and outraged by the lawyers of the crown, and by virtue of what are called ex-officio informations. Blackstone says, that "if a person publishes what is improper, mischievous, or illegal, he must take the consequences of his own temerity;" and Lord Chief Baron Comyns defines libel as "a contumely, or reproach, published to the 925 defamation of the Government, of a magistrate, or of a private person."—Now, I beseech you to consider the words, mischievous, improper, illegal, contumely, reproach, or defamation. May they not make that mischievous, or improper, which they please? Is not law with them, as clay in the potter's hand? Do not the words, 930 contumely, reproach, or defamation, express all degrees and forces of disapprobation? It is impossible to express yourself displeased at certain proceedings of Government, or the individuals who conduct it, without uttering a reproach. We cannot honestly point out a proper remedy of grievances with safety, because the very mention 935 of these grievances will be reproachful to the personages who countenance them; and therefore will come under a definition of libel. For the persons who thus directly or indirectly undergo reproach, will say for their own sakes, that the exposure of their corruption is mischievous and improper; therefore, the utterer of 940 the reproach is a fit subject for three years imprisonment. Is there any thing like the Liberty of the Press, in restrictions so positive, yet pliant, as these. The little freedom which we enjoy in this most important point, comes from the clemency of our rulers, or their fear, lest public opinion alarmed at the discovery of its enslaved 945 state, should violently assert a right to extension and diffusion. Yet public opinion may not always be so formidable, rulers may not always be so merciful or so timid: at any rate evils, and great evils do result from the present system of intellectual slavery, and you have enough to think of, if this grievance alone remained in the

constitution of society. I will give but one instance of the present 950
state of our Press.

A countryman of yours is now confined in an English gaol. His
health, his fortune, his spirits, suffer from close confinement. The air
which comes through the bars of a prison-grate, does not invigorate
the frame nor cheer the spirits. But Mr. Finnerty, much as he has lost, 955
yet retains the fair name of truth and honor. He was imprisoned for
persisting in the truth. His judge told him on his trial, that truth and
falsehood were indifferent to the law, and that if he owned the
publication any consideration, whether the facts that it related were
well or ill-founded, was totally irrelevant. Such is the libel law. Such 960
the Liberty of the Press—there is enough to think of. The right of
withholding your individual assent to war, the right of choosing
delegates to represent you in the assembly of the nation, and that of
freely opposing intellectual power, to any measures of Government
of which you may disapprove, are, in addition to the indifference 965
with which the legislative and the executive power ought to rule
their conduct towards professors of every religion, enough to
think of.

I earnestly desire peace and harmony:—peace, that whatever
wrongs you may have suffered, benevolence and a spirit of 970
forgiveness should mark your conduct towards those who have
persecuted you. Harmony, that among yourselves may be no
divisions, that Protestants and Catholics unite in a common interest,
and that whatever be the belief and principles of your countryman
and fellow-sufferer, you desire to benefit his cause, at the same time 975
that you vindicate your own; be strong and unbiassed by selfishness
or prejudice—for Catholics, your religion has not been spotless,
crimes in past ages have sullied it with a stain, which let it be your
glory to remove. Nor Protestants, hath your religion always been
characterized by the mildness of benevolence, which Jesus Christ 980
recommended. Had it any thing to do with the present subject I
could account for the spirit of intolerance, which marked both
religions; I will, however, only adduce the fact, and earnestly exhort
you to root out from your own minds every thing which may lead to
uncharitableness, and to reflect that yourselves, as well as your 985
brethren, may be deceived. Nothing on earth is infallible. The Priests
that pretend to it, are wicked and mischievous impostors; but it is an
imposture which every one, more or less, assumes, who encourages
prejudice in his breast against those who differ from him in opinion,

990 or who sets up his own religion as the only right and true one, when
no one is so blind as ⟨not⟩ to see that every religion is right and true,
which makes men beneficent and sincere. I therefore, earnestly
exhort both Protestants and Catholics to act in brotherhood and
harmony, never forgetting, because the Catholics alone are
995 heinously deprived of religious rights, that the Protestants and a
certain rank of people, of every persuasion, share with them all else
that is terrible, galling and intolerable in the mass of political
grievance.

In no case employ violence or falsehood. I cannot too often or too
1000 vividly endeavour to impress upon your minds, that these methods
will produce nothing but wretchedness and slavery—that they will
at the same time rivet the fetters, with which ignorance and
oppression bind you to abjectness, and deliver you over to a
tyranny, which shall render you incapable of renewed efforts.
1005 Violence will immediately render your cause a bad one. If you
believe in a Providential God, you must also believe that he is a good
one; and it is not likely, a merciful God would befriend a bad cause.
Insincerity is no less hurtful than violence: those who are in the
habits of either, would do well to reform themselves. A lying bravo
1010 will never promote the good of his country—he cannot be a good
man. The courageous and sincere may, at the same time, successfully
oppose corruption, by uniting their voice with that of others, or
individually raise up intellectual opposition to counteract the
abuses of Government and society. In order to benefit yourselves
1015 and your country to any extent, habits of sobriety, regularity,
and thought, are previously so necessary, that without these
preliminaries, all that you have done falls to the ground. You have
built on sand. Secure a good foundation, and you may erect a fabric
to stand for ever—the glory and the envy of the world!
1020 I have purposely avoided any lengthened discussion on those
grievances to which your hearts are from custom, and the immediate
interest of the circumstances, probably most alive at present. I have
not however wholly neglected them. Most of all have I insisted on
their instant palliation and ultimate removal; nor have I omitted a
1025 consideration of the means which I deem most effectual for the
accomplishment of this great end. How far you will consider the
former worthy of your adoption, so far shall I deem the latter
probable and interesting to the lovers of human kind. And I have
opened to your view a new scene—does not your heart bound at the

bare possibility of your posterity possessing that liberty and happiness of which during our lives powerful exertions and habitual abstinence may give us a foretaste. Oh! if your hearts do not vibrate at such as this; then ye are dead and cold—ye are not men.

I now come to the application of my principles, the conclusion of my address; and O Irishmen, whatever conduct ye may feel yourselves bound to pursue, the path which duty points to, lies before me clear and unobscured. Dangers may lurk around it, but they are not the dangers which lie beneath the footsteps of the hypocrite or temporizer.

For I have not presented to you the picture of happiness on which my fancy doats as an uncertain meteor to mislead honorable enthusiasm, or blindfold the judgment which makes virtue useful. I have not proposed crude schemes, which I should be incompetent to mature, or desired to excite in you any virulence against the abuses of political institution; where I have had occasion to point them out I have recommended moderation whilst yet I have earnestly insisted upon energy and perseverance; I have spoken of peace, yet declared that resistance is laudable; but the intellectual resistance which I recommend, I deem essential to the introduction of the millennium of virtue, whose period every one can, so far as he is concerned, forward by his own proper power. I have not attempted to shew, that the Catholic claims or the claims of the people, to a full representation in Parliament, are any of those claims to real rights, which I have insisted upon as introductory to the ultimate claim of *all*, to universal happiness, freedom, and equality; I have not attempted, I say, to shew that these can be granted consistently with the spirit of the English Constitution: this is a point which I do not feel myself inclined to discuss, and which I consider foreign to my object. But I have shewn that these claims have for their basis, truth and justice, which are immutable, and which in the ruin of Governments shall rise like a Phœnix from their ashes.[1]

Is any one inclined to dispute the possibility of a happy change in society? Do they say that the nature of man is corrupt, and that he was made for misery and wickedness? Be it so. Certain as are opposite conclusions, I will concede the truth of his, for a moment.—

[1] Note. The excellence of the Constitution of Great Britain, appears to me, to be its indefiniteness and versatility, whereby it may be unresistingly accommodated to the progression of wisdom and virtue. Such accommodation I desire: but I wish for the cause before the effect.

What are the means which I take for melioration? Violence, corruption, rapine, crime? Do I do evil, that good may come? I have recommended peace, philanthropy, wisdom.—So far as my arguments influence, they will influence to these—and if there is any one *now* inclined to say, that "private vices are public benefits," and that peace, philanthropy, and wisdom, will, if once they gain ground, ruin the human race; he may revel in his happy dreams; though were *I* this man, I should envy Satan's Hell. The wisdom and charity of which I speak, are the *only* means which I will countenance, for the redress of your grievances, and the grievances of the world. So far as they operate, I am willing to stand responsible for their *evil* effects. I expect to be accused of a desire for renewing in Ireland the scenes of revolutionary horror, which marked the struggles of France twenty years ago. But it is the renewal of that unfortunate æra, which I strongly deprecate, and which the tendency of this address is calculated to obviate. For can burthens be borne for ever, and the slave crouch and cringe the while. Is misery and vice so consonant to man's nature, that he will hug it to his heart?—but when the wretched one in bondage, beholds the emancipator near, will he not endure his misery awhile with hope and patience, then, spring to his preserver's arms, and start into a man.

It is my intention to observe the effect on your minds, O Irishmen! which this address dictated by the fervency of my love and hope will produce. I have come to this country to spare no pains where expenditure may purchase your real benefit. The present is a crisis, which of all others, is the most valuable for fixing the fluctuation of public feeling; as far as my poor efforts may have succeeded in fixing it to virtue, Irishmen, so far shall I esteem myself happy. I intend this address as introductory to another. The organization of a society, whose institution shall serve as a bond to its members, for the purposes of virtue, happiness, liberty, and wisdom, by the means of intellectual opposition to grievances, would probably be useful. For the formation of such a society, I avow myself anxious.

Adieu, my friends! May every Sun that shines on your green Island see the annihilation of an abuse, and the birth of an Embryon of melioration! Your own hearts—may they become the shrines of purity and freedom, and never may smoke to the Mammon of unrighteousness, ascend from the unpolluted altar of their devotion!

No. 7, Lower Sackville-street, Feb. 22.

Postscript.

I have now been a week in Dublin, during which time I have ₁₁₀₅ endeavoured to make myself more accurately acquainted with the state of the public mind, on those great topics of grievances which induced me to select Ireland as a theatre, the widest and fairest, for the operations of the determined friend of religious and political freedom.

1110

The result of my observations has determined me to propose, an association for the purposes of restoring Ireland to the prosperity which she possessed before the Union Act; and the religious freedom, which the involuntariness of faith, ought to have taught all monopolists of Heaven, long, long ago, that every one had a right to ₁₁₁₅ possess.

For the purpose of obtaining the Emancipation of the Catholics, from the penal laws that aggrieve them, and a Repeal of the Legislative Union act: and grounding upon the remission of the church-craft and oppression, which caused these grievances; *a plan* ₁₁₂₀ *of amendment and regeneration in the moral and political state of society, on a comprehensive and systematic philanthropy, which shall be sure, though slow in its projects; and as it is without the rapidity and danger of revolution, so will it be devoid of the time servingness of temporizing reform*—which in its deliberative capacity, having ₁₁₂₅ investigated the state of the government of England, shall oppose those parts of it, by intellectual force, which will not bear the touchstone of reason.

For information respecting the principles which I possess, and the nature and spirit of the association which I propose, I refer the ₁₁₃₀ reader to a small pamphlet, which I shall publish on the subject, in the course of a few days.

I have published the above address (written in England) in the cheapest possible form, and have taken pains that the remarks which it contains, should be intelligible to the most uneducated minds. ₁₁₃₅ Men are not slaves and brutes, because they are poor: it has been the policy of the thoughtless, or wicked of the higher ranks, (as a proof of the decay, of which policy, I am happy to see the rapid success of a comparatively enlightened system of education,) to conceal from the poor the truths which I have endeavoured to teach them. In doing so, I have but translated my thoughts into another language; and as language is only useful as it communicates ideas, I shall think my style so far good, as it is successful as a means to bring about the end which I desire, on any occasion, to accomplish.

A Limerick Paper, which I suppose, professes to support certain *loyal* and *John Bullish* principles of freedom—has, in an essay for advocating the Liberty of the Press, the following clause: "For lawless license of discussion never did we advocate, nor do we now."—What is lawless license of discussion? Is it not as indefinite as the words, *contumely*, *reproach*, *defamation*, that allow at present, such latitude to the outrages that are committed on the free expression of individual sentiment. Can they not see that what is rational will stand by its reason, and what is true stand by its truth, as all that is foolish will fall by its folly, and all that is false be controverted by its own falsehood.—Liberty gains nothing by the reform of politicians of this stamp, any more than it gains from a change of Ministers in London. What at present, is contumely and defamation, would at the period of this Limerick amendment, be "lawless license of discussion"; and such would be the mighty advantage, which this doughty champion of liberty proposes to effect.

I conclude, with the words of Lafayette—a name endeared, by its peerless bearer, to every lover of the human race. "For a nation to love Liberty it is sufficient that she knows it, to be free it is sufficient that she wills it."

PROPOSALS

FOR AN

ASSOCIATION

OF THOSE

PHILANTHROPISTS,

WHO CONVINCED OF THE INADEQUACY OF THE
MORAL AND POLITICAL STATE OF IRELAND TO
PRODUCE BENEFITS WHICH ARE NEVERTHELESS
ATTAINABLE ARE WILLING TO UNITE TO AC-
COMPLISH ITS REGENERATION.

BY

PERCY BYSSHE SHELLEY.

Dublin:

PRINTED BY I. ETON, WINETAVERN-STREET,

1812.

3. Title-page of *Proposals for an Association of Philanthropists* (1812)
Huntington Library (RB 23000; '1812' written in)

PROPOSALS
for
AN ASSOCIATION, &c.

I propose an association which shall have for its immediate objects,
Catholic Emancipation, and the Repeal of the Act of Union between Great
Britain and Ireland; and grounding on the removal of these grievances, an
annihilation or palliation, of whatever moral or political evil, it may be
within the compass of human power to assuage or eradicate. 5

===

Man cannot make occasions, but he may seize those that offer. None
are more interesting to Philanthropy, than those which excite the
benevolent passions, that generalize and expand private into public
feelings, and make the hearts of individuals vibrate not merely for
themselves, their families, and their friends, but for posterity, *for a* 10
people; till their country becomes the world, and their family the
sensitive creation.

A recollection of the absent, and a taking into consideration the
interests of those unconnected with ourselves, is a principal source
of that feeling which generates occasions, wherein a love for 15
human kind may become eminently useful and active. Public
topics of fear and hope, such as sympathize with general grievance,
or hold out hopes of general amendment, are those on ⟨which⟩ the
Philanthropist would dilate with the warmest feeling. Because these
are accustomed to place individuals at a distance from self; for in 20
proportion as he is absorbed in public feeling, so will a consideration
of his proper benefit be generalized. In proportion as he feels with, or
for, a nation or a world, so will man consider himself less as that
centre, to which we are but too prone to believe that every line of
human concern does, or ought to converge. 25

I should not here make the trite remark, that selfish motive
biasses, brutalizes, and degrades the human mind, did it not thence

follow, that to seize those occasions wherein the opposite spirit predominates, is a duty which Philanthropy imperiously exacts of her votaries; that occasions like these are the proper ones for leading mankind to their own interest; by awakening in their minds a love for the interest of their fellows. A plant that grows in every soil, though too often it is choaked by tares before its lovely blossoms are expanded. Virtue produces pleasure, it is as the cause to the effect; I feel pleasure in doing good to my friend, because I love him. I do not love him for the sake of that pleasure.

I regard the present state of the public mind in Ireland, to be one of those occasions, which the ardent votary of the religion of Philanthropy dare not leave unseized. I perceive that the public interest is excited, I perceive that individual interest has, in a certain degree, quitted individual concern to generalize itself with universal feeling. Be the Catholic Emancipation a thing of great or of small misfortune[1], be it a means of adding happiness to four millions of people, or a reform which will only give honor to a few of the higher ranks, yet a benevolent and distinterested feeling has gone abroad, and I am willing that it should never subside. I desire that means should be taken with energy and expedition, in this important, yet fleeting crisis, to feed the unpolluted flame, at which nations and ages may light the torch of Liberty and Virtue!

It is my opinion that the claims of the Catholic inhabitants of Ireland, if gained to-morrow, would in a very small degree, aggrandize their liberty and happiness. The disqualifications principally affect the higher orders of the Catholic persuasion, these would principally be benefited by their removal. Power and wealth do not benefit, but injure the cause of virtue and freedom. I am happy however, at the near approach of this emancipation, because I am inimical to all disqualifications for opinion. It gives me pleasure to see the approach of this enfranchisement, not for the good which it will bring with it, but because it is a sign of benefits approaching, a prophet of good about to come; and therefore, do I sympathize with the inhabitants of Ireland, in this great cause; a cause, which, though in its own accomplishment, will add not one comfort to the cottager, will snatch not one from the dark dungeon, will root not out one vice, alleviate not one pang, yet it is the fore-ground of a picture, in the dimness of whose distance, I behold the lion lay down with the lamb, and the infant play with the basilisk.—For it supposes the

[1] ⟨importance *cj*⟩

extermination of the eyeless monster bigotry, whose throne has
tottered for two hundred years. I hear the teeth of the palsied
beldame Superstition chatter, and I see her descending to the grave!
Reason points to the open gates of the Temple of Religious 70
Freedom, Philanthropy kneels at the altar of the common God!
There, wealth and poverty, rank and abjectness, are names known
but as memorials of past time: meteors which play over the
loathsome pool of vice and misery, to warn the wanderer where
dangers lie. Does a God rule this illimitable universe? Are you 75
thankful for his beneficence—do you adore his wisdom—do you
hang upon his altar the garland of your devotion? Curse not your
brother, though he hath enwreathed with his flowers of a different
hue; the purest religion is that of Charity, its loveliness begins to
proselyte the hearts of men. The tree is to be judged of by its fruit. I 80
regard the admission of the Catholic claims, and the Repeal of the
Union Act, as blossoms of that fruit, which the Summer Sun of
improved intellect and progressive virtue are destined to mature.

I will not pass unreflected on the Legislative Union of Great
Britain and Ireland, nor will I speak of it as a grievance so tolerable or 85
unimportant in its own nature as that of Catholic disqualification. The latter affects few, the former affects thousands. The one
disqualifies the rich from power, the other impoverishes the
peasant, adds beggary to the city, famine to the country, multiplies
abjectness, whilst misery and crime play into each other's hands, 90
under its withering auspices. I esteem then, the annihilation of this
second grievance to be something more than a mere sign of coming
good. I esteem it to be in itself a substantial benefit. The aristocracy
of Ireland (for much as I may disapprove other distinctions than
those of virtue and talent, I consider it useless, hasty, and violent, not 95
for the present to acquiesce in their continuance.) The aristocracy of
Ireland suck the veins of its inhabitants and consume the blood in
England. I mean not to deny the unhappy truth, that there is much
misery and vice in the world. I mean to say that Ireland shares largely
of both.—England has made her poor; and the poverty of a rich 100
nation will make its people very desperate and wicked.

I look forward then, to the redress of both these grievances, or
rather, I perceive the state of the public mind, that precedes them
as the crisis of beneficial innovation. The latter I consider to be
the cause of the former, as I hope it will be the cause of more 105
comprehensively beneficial amendments. It forms that occasion

which should energetically and quickly be occupied. The voice of the whole human race; their crimes, their miseries, and their ignorance, invoke us to the task. For the miseries of the Irish poor, exacerbated by the Union of their country with England, are not peculiar to themselves. England, the whole civilized world, with few exceptions, is either sunk in disproportioned abjectness, or raised to unnatural elevation. The Repeal of the Union Act will place Ireland on a level, so far as concerns the well-being of its poor, with her sister nation. Benevolent feeling has gone out in this country in favor of the happiness of its inhabitants—may this feeling be corroborated, methodized, and continued! May it never fail!—But it will not be kept alive by each citizen sitting quietly by his own fire-side, and saying that things are going on well, because the rain does not beat on *him*, because *he* has books and leisure to read them, because *he* has money and is at liberty to accumulate luxuries to *himself*. Generous feeling dictates no such sayings. When the heart recurs to the thousands who have no liberty and no leisure, it must be rendered callous by long contemplation of wretchedness, if after such recurrence it can beat with contented evenness.—Why do I talk thus. Is there any one who doubts that the present state of politics and morals is wrong? They say—shew us a safe method of improvement. There is no safer than the corroboration and propagation of generous and Philanthropic feeling, than the keeping continually alive a love for the human race, than the putting in train causes which shall have for their consequences virtue and freedom, and because I think that individuals acting singly, with whatever energy can never ⟨e⟩ffect so much as a society; I propose that all those, whose views coincide with those that I have avowed, who perceive the state of the public mind in Ireland, who think the present a fit opportunity for attempting to fix its fluctuations at Philanthropy; who love all mankind, and are willing actively to engage in its cause, or passively to endure the persecutions of those who are inimical to its success; I propose to these to form an association for the purposes, first, of debating on the propriety of whatever measures may be agitated, and secondly, for carrying, by united or individual exertion, such measures into effect when determined on. That it should be an association for discussing[1] knowledge and virtue throughout the poorer classes of society in Ireland, for co-operating with any enlightened system of education;

[1] ⟨diffusing *cj*⟩

for discussing topics calculated to throw light on any methods of alleviation of moral and political evil, and as far as lays in its power, actively interesting itself in whatever occasion may arise for benefiting mankind.

When I mention Ireland, I do not mean to confine the influence of the association to this, or to any other country, but for the time being. Moreover, I would recommend, that this association should attempt to form others, and to actuate them with a similar spirit, and I am thus indeterminate in my description of the association which I propose; because I conceive that an assembly of men meeting, to do all the good that opportunity will permit them to do, must be in its nature, as indefinite and varying as the instances of human vice and misery that precede, occasion, and call for its institution.

As political institution and its attendant evils constitute the majority of those grievances, which Philanthropists desire to remedy, it is probable that existing Governments will frequently become the topic of their discussion, the results of which may little coincide with the opinions which those who profit by the supineness of human belief, desire to impress upon the world. It is probable that this freedom may excite the odium of certain well-meaning people, who pin their faith upon their grandmother's apron string. The minority in number are the majority in intellect and power. The former govern the latter, though it is by the sufferance of the latter that this originally delegated power is exercised. This power is become hereditary, and hath ceased to be necessarily united with intellect.

It is certain, therefore, that any questioning of established principles would excite the abhorrence and opposition of those who derived power and honour (such as it is) from their continuance.

As the association which I recommend would question those principles (however they may be hedged in with antiquity and precedent) which appeared ill adapted for the benefit of human kind; it would probably excite the odium of those in power. It would be obnoxious to the government, though nothing would be farther from the views of associated philanthropists than attempting to subvert establishments forcibly, or even hastily. Aristocracy would oppose it, whether oppositionists or ministerialists, (for philanthropy is of no party,) because its ultimate views look to a subversion of all factitious distinctions, although from its immediate intentions I fear that aristocracy can have nothing to dread. The

priesthood would oppose it, because a union of church and state;
contrary to the principles and practice of Jesus, contrary to that
equality which he fruitlessly endeavoured to teach mankind, is of all
institutions that from the rust of antiquity are called venerable, the
190 least qualified to stand free and cool reasoning, because it least
conduces to the happiness of human kind: yet did either the
minister, the peer, or the bishop, know their true interest, instead of
that virulent opposition which some among them have made to
freedom and philanthropy, they would rejoice and co-operate with
195 the diffusion and corroboration of those principles that would
remove a load of paltry equivocation, paltrier grandeur, and of wigs
that crush into emptiness the brains below them, from their
shoulders; and by permitting them to reassume the degraded and
vilified title of man would preclude the necessity of mystery and
200 deception, would bestow on them a title more ennobling, and a
dignity which though it would be without the gravity of an ape,
would possess the ease and consistency of a man.

For the reasons above alleged, falsely, prejudicedly, and narrowly
will those very persons whose ultimate benefit is included in the
205 general good whose promotion is the essence of a philanthropic
association, will they persecute those who have the best intentions
towards them, malevolence towards none.

I do not, therefore, conceal that those who make the favour of
government the sunshine of their moral day, confide in the political
210 creed makers of the hour, are willing to think things that are rusty
and decayed venerable, and are unenquiringly satisfied with evils as
these are, because they find them established and unquestioned as
they do sunlight and air when they come into existence; that they
had better not even think of philanthropy. I conceal not from them
215 that the discountenance which government will shew to such an
association as I am desirous to establish will come under their
comprehensive definition of danger: that virtue and any assembly
instituted under its auspices demands a voluntariness on the part
of its devoted individuals to sacrifice personal to public benefit;
220 and that it is possible that a party of beings associated for the
purposes of disseminating virtuous principles, may, considering
the ascendency which long custom has conferred on opposite
motives to action, meet with inconveniencies that may amount to
personal danger. These considerations are, however, to the mind of
225 the philanthropist as is a drop to an ocean; they serve by their

possible existence as tests whereby to discover the really virtuous man from him who calls himself a patriot for dishonourable and selfish purposes. I propose then to such as think with me, a Philanthropic Association, in spite of the danger that may attend the attempt. I do not this beneath the shroud of mystery and darkness. I propose not an Association of Secrecy. Let it open as the beam of day. Let it rival the sunbeam in its stainless purity, as in the extensiveness of its effulgence.

I disclaim all connection with insincerity and concealment. The latter implies the former, as much as the former stands in need of the latter. It is a very latitudinarian system of morality that permits its professor to employ bad means for any end whatever. Weapons which vice *can* use are unfit for the hands of virtue. Concealment implies falsehood; it is bad, and can therefore never be serviceable to the cause of philanthropy.

I propose, therefore, that the association shall be established and conducted in the open face of day, with the utmost possible publicity. It is only vice that hides itself in holes and corners whose effrontery shrinks from scrutiny, whose cowardice lets I *dare not* wait upon I would, like the poor cat in the adage. But the eye of virtue, eagle-like, darts through the undazzling beam of eternal truth, and from the undiminished fountain of its purity gathers wherewith to vivify and illuminate a universe.

I have hitherto abstained from inquiring whether the association which I recommend be or be not consistent with the English constitution. And here it is fit, briefly to consider what a constitution is.

Government can have no rights, it is a delegation for the purpose of securing them to others. Man becomes a subject of government, not that he may be in a worse but that he may be in a better state than that of unorganized society. The strength of government is the happiness of the governed. All government existing for the happiness of others is just only so far as it exists by their consent, and useful only so far as it operates to their well-being. Constitution is to government what government is to law. Constitution may, in this view of the subject, be defined to be, not merely something constituted for the benefit of any nation or class of people, but something constituted by themselves for their own benefit. The nations of England and Ireland have no constitution, because at no one time did the individuals that compose them constitute a system

for the general benefit: if a system determined on by a very few, at a great length of time; if magna charta, the bill of rights, and other usages for whose influence the improved state of human knowledge is rather to be looked to, than any system which courtiers pretend to
270 exist and perhaps believe to exist; a system whose spring of agency they represent as something secret, undiscoverable and awful as the law of nature. If these make a constitution then England has one. But if (as I have endeavoured to shew they do not) a constitution is something else, then the speeches of kings or commissioners, the
275 writings of courtiers, and the journals of parliament, which teem with its glory, are full of political cant; exhibit the skeleton of national freedom, and are fruitless attempts to hide evils in whose favor they cannot prove an alibi. As therefore, in the true sense of the expression, the spot of earth on which we live is destitute of
280 constituted Government, it is impossible to offend against its principles, or to be with justice accused of wishing to subvert what has no real existence. If a man was accused of setting fire to a house, which house never existed, and from the nature of things could not have existed, it is impossible that a jury in their senses would find
285 him guilty of arson. The English constitution then, could not be offended by the principles of virtue and freedom. In fact, the manner in which the Government of England has varied since its earliest establishment, proves that its present form is the result of a progressive accommodation to existing principles. It has been a
290 continual struggle for liberty on the part of the people, and an uninterrupted attempt at tightening the reins of oppression and encouraging ignorance and imposture by the oligarchy to whom the first William parcelled out the property of the aborigines at the conquest of England by the Normans. I hear much of its being a tree
295 so long growing which to cut down is as bad as cutting down an oak where there are no more. But the best way, on topics similar to these, is, to tell the plain truth, without the confusion and ornament of metaphor. I call expressions similar to these political cant, which like the songs of Rule Britannia and God save the king, are but
300 abstracts of the caterpillar creed of courtiers, cut down to the taste and comprehension of a mob; the one to disguise to an alehouse politician the evils of that devilish practice of war, and the other to inspire among clubs of all descriptions a certain feeling which some call loyalty and others servility. A philanthropic association has
305 nothing to fear from the English constitution, but it may expect

danger from its government. So far however from thinking this an argument against its institution, establishment and augmentation, I am inclined to rest much of the weight of the cause which my duties call upon me to support, on the very fact that government forcibly interferes when the opposition that is made to its proceedings is 310 professedly and undeniably nothing but intellectual. A good cause may be shewn to be good, violence instantly renders bad what might before have been good. "Weapons that falsehood can use are unfit for the hands of truth."—Truth can reason and falsehood cannot.

A political or religious system may burn and imprison those who 315 investigate its principles; but it is an invariable proof of their falsehood and hollowness. Here then is another reason for the necessity of a Philanthropic Association, and I call upon any fair and rational opponent to controvert the argument which it contains; for there is no one who even calls himself a philanthropist that thinks 320 personal danger or dishonour terrible in any other light than as it affects his usefulness.

Man has a heart to feel, a brain to think, and a tongue to utter. The laws of his moral as of his physical nature are immutable, as is every thing of nature; nor can the ephemeral institutions of human society 325 take away those rights, annihilate or strengthen the duties that have for their basis the imperishable relations of his constitution.

Though the parliament of England were to pass a thousand bills to inflict upon those who determined to utter their thoughts, a thousand penalties, it could not render that criminal which was in its 330 nature innocent before the passing of such bill.

Man has a right to feel, to think, and to speak, nor can any acts of legislature destroy that right. He will feel, he must think, and he *ought* to give utterance to those thoughts and feelings with the readiest sincerity and the strictest candour. A man must have a right 335 to do a thing before he can have a duty; this right must permit before his duty can enjoin him to any act. Any law is bad which attempts to make it criminal to do what the plain dictates within the breast of every man tells him that he ought to do.

The English government permits a fanatic to assemble any num- 340 ber of persons to teach them the most extravagant and immoral systems of faith; but a few men meeting to consider its own principles are marked with its hatred, and pursued by its jealousy.

The religionist who agonizes the death-bed of the cottager, and by picturing the hell, which hearts black and narrow as his own alone 345 could have invented, and which exists but in their cores, spreads the uncharitable doctrines which devote *heretics* to eternal torments, and represents heaven to be what earth is, a monopoly in the hands of certain favoured ones whose merit consists in slavishness, whose success is the reward of sycophancy. Thus much is permitted, but a public inquiry that involves any doubt of their rectitude into the principles of government is not permitted. When Jupiter and a countryman were one day walking out, conversing familiarly on the affairs of earth, the countryman listened to Jupiter's assertions on the subject for some time in acquiescence, at length happening to hint a doubt, Jupiter threatened him with his thunder; ah, ha, says the countryman, now Jupiter I know that you are wrong: you are always wrong when you appeal to your thunder. The essence of virtue is disinterestedness. Disinterestedness is the quality which preserves the character of virtue distinct from that of either innocence or vice. This, it will be said, is mere assertion. It is so: but it is an assertion, whose truth, I believe, the hearts of philanthropists are disinclined to deny. Those who have been convinced by their grandam of the doctrine of an original hereditary sin, or by the apostles of a degrading philosophy of the necessary and universal selfishness of man cannot be philanthropists. Now as an action, or a motive to action, is only virtuous so far as it is disinterested, or partakes (I adopt this mode of expression to suit the taste of some) of the nature of generalized self-love, then reward or punishment, attached even by omnipotence to any action, can in no wise make it either good or bad.

It is no crime to act in contradiction to an English judge or an English legislator, but it is a crime to transgress the dictates of a monitor, which feels the spring of every motive, whose throne is the human sensorium, whose empire the human conduct. Conscience is a Government before which, all others sink into nothingness; it surpasses, and where it can act supercedes, all other, as nature surpasses art, as God surpasses man.

In the preceding pages, during the course of an investigation of the possible objections which might be urged by Philanthropy, to an association such as I recommend, as I have rather sought to bring forward than conceal my principles, it will appear that they have their origin from the discoveries in the sciences of politics and morals, which preceded and occasioned the Revolutions of America and France. It is with openness that I confess, nay with pride I assert, that they are so. The names of Paine and Lafayette will outlive the poetic aristocracy of an expatriated Jesuit,[1] as the executive of a bigotted policy will die before the disgust at the sycophancy of their eulogists can subside.

It will be said, perhaps, that much as principles, such as these, may appear marked on the outside with peace, liberty, and virtue, that their ultimate tendency is to a Revolution, which like that of France, will end in bloodshed, vice, and slavery. I must offer, therefore, my thoughts on that event, which so suddenly and so lamentably extinguished the overstrained hopes of liberty which it excited. I do not deny that the Revolution of France was occasioned by the literary labors of the Encyclopedists. When we see two events together, in certain cases, we speak of one as the cause, the other the effect. We have no other idea of cause and effect, but that which arises from necessary connection; it is therefore, still doubtful, whether D'Alembert, Boulanger, Condorcet, and other celebrated characters, were the causes of the overthrow of the antient monarchy of France. Thus much is certain, that they contributed greatly to the extension and diffusion of knowledge, and that knowledge is incompatible with slavery. The French nation was bowed to the dust by ages of unintermitted despotism. They were plundered and insulted by a succession of oligarchies, each more blood-thirsty and unrelenting than the foregoing. In a state like this, her soldiers learned to fight for Freedom on the plains of America, whilst at this very conjuncture, a ray of science burst through the clouds of bigotry that obscured the moral day of Europe. The French were in the lowest state of human degradation, and when the truth, unaccustomed to their ears, that they were men and equals was promulgated, they were the first to vent their indignation on the monopolizers of earth, because they were most glaringly defrauded of the immunities of nature.

Since the French were furthest removed by the sophistications of political institution from the genuine condition of human beings, they must have been most unfit for that happy state of equal law, which proceeds from consummated civilization, and which demands habits of the strictest virtue before its introduction.

The murders during the period of the French Revolution, and the despotism which has since been established, prove that the doctrines of Philanthropy and Freedom, were but shallowly understood. Nor

[1] See *Mémoires du Jacobinisme*, par l'Abbé Barruel.

425 was it until after that period, that their principles became clearly to be explained, and unanswerably to be established.

Voltaire was the flatterer of Kings, though in his heart he despised them:—so far has he been instrumental in the present slavery of his country. Rousseau gave licence by his writings, to 430 passions that only incapacitate and contract the human heart:—so far hath he prepared the necks of his fellow-beings for that yoke of galling and dishonorable servitude, which at this moment, it bears. Helvetius and Condorcet established principles, but if they drew conclusions, their conclusions were unsystematical, and 435 devoid of the luminousness and energy of method:—they were little understood in the Revolution. But this age of ours is not stationary. Philosophers have not developed the great principles of the human mind, that conclusions from them should be unprofitable and impracticable. We are in a state of continually 440 progressive improvement. One truth that had been discovered can never die, but will prevent the revivification of its apportioned opposite falsehood. By promoting truth and discouraging its opposite, the means of Philanthropy are principally to be forwarded.—Godwin wrote during the Revolution of France, and 445 certainly his writings were totally devoid of influence, with regard to its purposes. Oh! that they had not!—In the Revolution of France, were engaged men, whose names are inerasible from the records of Liberty. Their genius penetrated with a glance the gloom and glare which Church-craft and State-craft had spread 450 before the imposture and villainy of their establishments. They saw the world—were they men? Yes! They felt for it! They risked their lives and happiness for its benefit!—Had there been more of these men France would not now be a beacon to warn us of the hazard and horror of Revolutions, but a pattern of society, rapidly 455 advancing to a state of perfection, and holding out an example for the gradual and peaceful regeneration of the world. I consider it to be one of the effects of a Philanthropic Association, to assist in the production of such men as these, in an extensive developement of those germs of excellence, whose favorite soil is the cultured 460 garden of the human mind.

Many well-meaning persons may think that the attainment of the good, which I propose, as the ultimatum of Philanthropic exertion, is visionary and inconsistent with human nature: they would tell me not to make people happy, for fear of overstocking the world, and to

permit those who found dishes placed before them on the table of ₄₆₅
partial nature, to enjoy their superfluities in quietness, though
millions of wretches crowded around but to pick a morsel,[1] which
morsel was still refused to the prayers of agonizing famine.

I cannot help thinking this an evil, nor help endeavouring, by the
safest means that I can devise, to palliate at present, and in fine to ₄₇₀
eradicate this evil; war, vice, and misery are undeniably bad, they
embrace all that we can conceive of temporal and eternal evil. Are we
to be told that these are remedyless, because the earth would, in case
of their remedy, be overstocked? That the rich are still to glut, that
the ambitious are still to plan, that the fools whom these knaves ₄₇₅
mould, are still to murder their brethren and call it glory, and that
the poor are to pay with their blood, their labor, their happiness, and
their innocence, for the crimes and mistakes which the hereditary
monopolists of earth commit? Rare sophism! How will the heartless
rich hug thee to their bosoms, and lull their conscience into slum- ₄₈₀
ber with the opiate of thy reconciling dogmas! But when the
Philosopher and Philanthropist contemplates the universe, when he
perceives existing evils that admit of amendment, and hears tell of
other evils, which, in the course of sixty centuries, may again
derange the system of happiness, which the amendment is calculated ₄₈₅
to produce, does he submit to prolong a positive evil, because if that
were eradicated, after a millennium of 6000 years (for such space of
time would it take to people the earth) another evil would take place.

To how contemptible a degradation of grossest credulity will not
prejudice lower the human mind!—We see in Winter that the foliage ₄₉₀
of the trees is gone, that they present to the view nothing but leafless
branches—we see that the loveliness of the flower decays, though
the root continues in the earth. What opinion should we form of that
man, who, when he walked in the freshness of the spring, beheld the
fields enamelled with flowers, and the foliage bursting from the ₄₉₅
buds, should find fault with all this beautiful order, and murmur his
contemptible discontents because winter must come, and the
landscape be robbed of its beauty for a while again? Yet this man is
Mr. Malthus. Do we not see that the laws of nature perpetually act by
disorganization and reproduction, each alternately becoming cause ₅₀₀
and effect. The ⟨analogies⟩ that we can draw from physical to moral
topics are of all others the most striking.

Does any one yet question the possibility of inducing radical

[1] See ⟨Thomas R.⟩ Malthus⟨, An Essay⟩ on ⟨the Principle of⟩ Population.

reform of moral and political evil. Does he object from that
impossibility to the Association which I propose, which I frankly
confess to be one of the means whose instrumentality I would
employ to attain this reform. Let them look to the methods which I
use. Let them put my object out of their view and propose their own,
how would they accomplish it? By diffusing virtue and knowledge,
by promoting human happiness. Palsied be the hand, for ever dumb
be the tongue that would by one expression convey sentiments
differing from these: I will use no bad means for any end whatever,
know then ye philanthropists, to whatever profession of faith, or
whatever determination of principles, chance, reason, or education,
may have conducted you, that the endeavours of the truly virtuous
necessarily converge to one point, though it be hidden from them
what point that is: they all labour for one end, and that controversies
concerning the nature of that end, serve only to weaken the strength
which for the interest of virtue should be consolidated.

The diffusion of true and virtuous principles (for in the first
principles of morality *none* disagree) will produce the best of
possible terminations.

I invite to an Association of Philanthropy those of whatever
ultimate expectations, who will employ the same means that I
employ; let their designs differ as much as they may from mine, I
shall rejoice at their co-operation; because if the ultimatum of my
hopes be founded on the unity of truth, I shall then have auxiliaries in
its cause, and if it be false I shall rejoice that means are not neglected
for forwarding that which is true.

The accumulation of evil which Ireland has for the last twenty
years sustained, and considering the unremittingness of its pressure
I may say patiently sustained; the melancholy prospect which the
unforeseen conduct of the Regent of England holds out of its
continuance, demands of every Irishman, whose pulses have not
ceased to throb with the life-blood of his heart, that he should
individually consult, and unitedly determine on some measures for
the liberty of his countrymen. That those measures should be pacific
though resolute, that their movers should be calmly brave, and
temperately unbending, though the whole heart and soul should go
with the attempt, is the opinion which my principles command me
to give.

And I am induced to call an Association, such as this occasion
demands, an Association of philanthropy, because good men ought

never to circumscribe their usefulness by any name which denotes their exclusive devotion to the accomplishment of its signification. ₅₄₅

When I began the preceding remarks I conceived that on the removal of the restrictions from the Regent a ministry less inimical than the present to the interests of liberty would have been appointed. I am deceived and the disappointment of the hopes of freedom on this subject afford an additional argument towards the ₅₅₀ necessity of an Association.

I conclude these remarks which I have indited principally with a view of unveiling my principles, with a proposal for an Association for the purposes of catholic emancipation, a repeal of the union act, and grounding upon the attainment of these objects a reform of ₅₅₅ whatever moral or political evil it may be within the compass of human power to remedy.

Such as are favourably inclined towards the institution would highly gratify the proposer, if they would personally communicate with him on this important subject, by which means the plan might ₅₆₀ be matured, errors in the proposer's original system be detected, and a meeting for the purpose convened with that resolute expedition which the nature of the present crisis demands.

No. 7, Lower Sackville Street.

DECLARATION OF RIGHTS.

Government has no rights; it is a delegation from several individuals for the purpose of securing their own. It is therefore just, only so far as it exists by their consent, useful only so far as it operates to their well-being.

2

IF these individuals think that the form of government which they, or their forefathers constituted is ill adapted to produce their happiness, they have a right to change it.

3

Government is devised for the security of rights. The rights of man are liberty, and an equal participation of the commonage of nature.

4

As the benefit of the governed, is, or ought to be the origin of government, no men can have any authority that does not expressly emanate from their will.

5

Though all governments are not so bad as that of Turkey, yet none are so good as they might be; the majority of every country have a right to perfect their government, the minority should not disturb them, they ought to secede, and form their own system in their own way.

6

All have a right to an equal share in the benefits, and burdens of Government. Any disabilities for opinion, imply by their existence, barefaced tyranny on the side of government, ignorant slavishness on the side of the governed.

7

The rights of man in the present state of society, are only to be

secured by some degree of coercion to be exercised on their violator.
The sufferer has a right that the degree of coercion employed be as
slight as possible.   25

8

It may be considered as a plain proof of the hollowness of any
proposition, if power be used to enforce instead of reason to
persuade its admission. Government is never supported by fraud
until it cannot be supported by reason.

9

No man has a right to disturb the public peace, by personally   30
resisting the execution of a law however bad. He ought to acquiesce,
using at the same time the utmost powers of his reason, to promote
its repeal.

10

A man must have a right to act in a certain manner before it can be his
duty. He may, before he ought.   35

11

A man has a right to think as his reason directs, it is a duty he owes to
himself to think with freedom, that he may act from conviction.

12

A man has a right to unrestricted liberty of discussion, falsehood is a
scorpion that will sting itself to death.

13

A man has not only a right to express his thoughts, but it is his duty   40
to do so.

14

No law has a right to discourage the practice of truth. A man ought to
speak the truth on every occasion, a duty can never be criminal, what
is not criminal cannot be injurious.

15

Law cannot make what is in its nature virtuous or innocent, to be   45
criminal, any more than it can make what is criminal to be innocent.
Government cannot make a law, it can only pronounce that which

was law before its organization, viz. the moral result of the imperishable relations of things.

16

The present generation cannot bind their posterity. The few cannot promise for the many.

17

No man has a right to do an evil thing that good may come.

18

Expediency is inadmissible in morals. Politics are only sound when conducted on principles of morality. They are in fact the morals of nations.

19

Man has no right to kill his brother, it is no excuse that he does so in uniform. He only adds the infamy of servitude to the crime of murder.

20

Man, whatever be his country, has the same rights in one place as another, the rights of universal citizenship.

21

The government of a country ought to be perfectly indifferent to every opinion. Religious differences, the bloodiest and most rancorous of all, spring from partiality.

22

A delegation of individuals for the purpose of securing their rights, can have no undelegated power of restraining the expression of their opinion.

23

Belief is involuntary; nothing involuntary is meritorious or reprehensible. A man ought not to be considered worse or better for his belief.

24

A Christian, a Deist, a Turk, and a Jew, have equal rights: they are men and brethren.

25

If a person's religious ideas correspond not with your own, love him nevertheless. How different would yours have been, had the chance of birth placed you in Tartary or India.

26

Those who believe that Heaven is, what earth has been, a monopoly in the hands of a favored few, would do well to reconsider their opinion: if they find that it came from their priest or their grandmother, they could not do better than reject it.

27

No man has a right to be respected for any other possessions, but those of virtue and talents. Titles are tinsel, power a corruptor, glory a bubble, and excessive wealth, a libel on its possessor.

28

No man has a right to monopolize more than he can enjoy; what the rich give to the poor, whilst millions are starving, is not a perfect favour, but an imperfect right.

29

Every man has a right to a certain degree of leisure and liberty, because it is his duty to attain a certain degree of knowledge. He may before he ought.

30

Sobriety of body and mind is necessary to those who would be free, because, without sobriety a high sense of philanthropy cannot actuate the heart, nor cool and determined courage, execute its dictates.

31

The only use of government is to repress the vices of man. If man were to day sinless, to-morrow he would have a right to demand that government and all its evils should cease.

Man! thou whose rights are here declared, be no longer forgetful of the loftiness of thy destination. Think of thy rights; of those possessions which will give thee virtue and wisdom, by which thou mayest arrive at happiness and freedom. They are declared to thee by one who knows thy dignity, for every hour does his heart swell with 100 honorable pride in the contemplation of what thou mayest attain, by one who is not forgetful of thy degeneracy, for every moment brings home to him the bitter conviction of what thou art.

Awake!—arise!—or be for ever fallen.

A LETTER

TO

LORD ELLENBOROUGH,

Occasioned by the Sentence which he passed on

MR D. I. EATON,

As Publisher of

The THIRD PART of PAINE's AGE OF REASON.

Deorum offensa, Diis curæ.

——It is contrary to the mild spirit of the Christian Religion, for no sanction can be found under that dispensation which will warrant a Government to impose disabilities and penalties upon any man, on account of his religious opinions. [*Hear, Hear.*]

Marquis Wellesley's Speech., Globe, July 2.

4. Title-page of *A Letter to Lord Ellenborough* (1812)
Bodleian Library (shelfmark Bod. ⟨pr.⟩ Shelley e. i(i))

Advertisement.

I have waited impatiently for these last four months, in the hopes, that some pen, fitter for the important task, would have spared me the perilous pleasure of becoming the champion of an innocent man.—This may serve as an excuse for delay, to those who think that I have let pass the aptest opportunity—but it is not to be supposed that in four short months the public indignation, raised by Mr. Eaton's unmerited suffering, can have subsided.

LETTER.

My Lord,

As the station to which you have been called by your country is important, so much the more awful is your responsibility, so much the more does it become you to watch lest you inadvertently punish the virtuous and reward the vicious.

You preside over a court which is instituted for the suppression of crime, and to whose authority the people submit on no other conditions than that its decrees should be conformable to justice.

If it should be demonstrated that a judge had condemned an innocent man, the bare existence of laws in conformity to which the accused is punished, would but little extenuate his offence. The inquisitor when he burns an obstinate heretic may set up a similar plea, yet few are sufficiently blinded by intolerance to acknowledge its validity. It will less avail such a judge to assert the policy of punishing one who has committed no crime. Policy and morality ought to be deemed synonimous in a court of justice, and he whose conduct has been regulated by the latter principle, is not justly amenable to any penal law for a supposed violation of the former. It is true, my Lord, laws exist which suffice to screen you from the animadversion of any constituted power, in consequence of the unmerited sentence which you have passed upon Mr. Eaton; but there are no laws which screen you from the reproof of a nation's disgust, none which ward off the just judgment of posterity, if that posterity will deign to recollect you.

By what right do you punish Mr. Eaton? What but antiquated precedents gathered from times of priestly and tyrannical domination, can be adduced in palliation of an outrage so insulting to humanity and justice? Whom has he injured? What crime has he committed? Wherefore may he not walk abroad like other men and follow his accustomed pursuits? What end is proposed in confining this man, charged with the commission of no dishonorable action? Wherefore did his aggressor avail himself of popular prejudice, and

return no answer but one of common place contempt, to a defence of plain and simple sincerity? Lastly, when the prejudices of the jury, as
35 Christians, were strongly and unfairly inflamed[1] against this injured man as a Deist, wherefore did not you, my Lord, check such unconstitutional pleading, and desire the jury to pronounce the accused innocent or criminal[2] without reference to the particular faith which he professed?
40 In the name of justice what answer is there to these questions? The answer which Heathen Athens made to Socrates, is the same with which Christian England must attempt to silence the advocates of this injured man—"He has questioned established opinions." —Alas! the crime of enquiry is one which religion never has
45 forgiven. Implicit faith and fearless enquiry have in all ages been irreconcileable enemies. Unrestrained philosophy has in every age opposed itself to the reveries of credulity and fanaticism.—The truths of astronomy demonstrated by Newton have superseded astrology; since the modern discoveries in chemistry the philo-
50 sopher's stone has no longer been deemed attainable. Miracles of every kind have become rare, in proportion to the hidden principles which those who study nature have developed. That which is false will ultimately be controverted by its own falsehood. That which is true needs but publicity to be acknowledged. It is ever
55 a proof that the falsehood of a proposition is felt by those who use power and coercion, not reasoning and persuasion, to procure its admission.—Falsehood skulks in holes and corners, "it lets I dare not wait upon I would, like the poor cat in the adage,"[3] except when it has power, and then, as it was a coward, it is a tyrant; but the eagle-
60 eye of truth darts thro' the undazzling sunbeam of the immutable and just, gathering thence wherewith to vivify and illuminate a universe!
Wherefore, I repeat, is Mr. Eaton punished?—Because he is a Deist?—and what are you my Lord?—A Christian. Ha then! the
65 mask is fallen off; you persecute him because his faith differs from your's. You copy the persecutors of christianity in your actions, and are an additional proof that your religion is as bloody, barbarous, and intolerant as theirs.—If some deistical Bigot in power (supposing such a character for the sake of illustration) should in

---

[1] See the Attorney General's Speech.
[2] By Mr. Fox's bill (1791) Juries are, in cases of libel, judges both of the law and the fact.
[3] Shakespeare⟨, *Macbeth*, i. vii. 43–4⟩.

dark and barbarous ages have enacted a statute, making the 70
profession of christianity criminal, if you my Lord were a christian
bookseller and Mr. Eaton a judge, those arguments which you
consider adequate to justify yourself for the sentence which you
have passed, must likewise suffice in this suppositionary case to
justify Mr. Eaton, in sentencing you to Newgate and the pillory for 75
being a christian. Whence is any right derived but that which power
confers for persecution? Do you think to convert Mr. Eaton to your
religion by embittering his existence? You might force him by
torture to profess your tenets, but he could not believe them, except
you should make them credible, which perhaps exceeds your power. 80
Do you think to please the God you worship by this exhibition of
your zeal? If so, the Demon to whom savage nations offer human
hecatombs is less barbarous than the Deity of civilized society.

You consider man as an accountable being—but he can only be
accountable for those actions which are influenced by his will.   85

Belief and disbelief are utterly distinct from and unconnected
with volition. They are the apprehension of the agreement or
disagreement of the ideas which compose any proposition. Belief is
an involuntary operation of the mind, and, like other passions, its
intensity is precisely proportionate to the degrees of excitement.— 90
Volition is essential to merit or demerit. How then can merit or
demerit be attached to what is distinct from that faculty of the mind
whose presence is essential to their being? I am aware that religion is
founded on the voluntariness of belief, as it makes it a subject of
reward and punishment; but before we extinguish the steady ray of 95
reason and common sense, it is fit that we should discover, which we
cannot do without their assistance, whether or no there be any other
which may suffice to guide us thro' the labyrinth of life.

If the law 'de heretico comburendo' has not been formally
repealed, I conceive that from the promise held out by your 100
Lordship's zeal, we need not despair of beholding the flames of
persecution rekindled in Smithfield. Even now the lash that drove
Descartes and Voltaire from their native country, the chains which
bound Galileo, the flames which burned Vanini, again resound:—
And where? in a nation that presumptuously calls itself the 105
sanctuary of freedom. Under a government which, whilst it infringes
the very right of thought and speech, boasts of permitting the liberty
of the press; in a civilized and enlightened country, a man is pilloried
and imprisoned because he is a Deist, and no one raises his voice in

110 the indignation of outraged humanity. Does the Christian God, whom his followers eulogize as the Deity of humility and peace; he, the regenerator of the world, the meek reformer, authorize one man to rise against another, and because lictors are at his beck, to chain and torture him as an Infidel?

115 When the Apostles went abroad to convert the nations, were they enjoined to stab and poison all who disbelieved the divinity of Christ's mission; assuredly they would have been no more justifiable in this case, than he is at present who puts into execution the law which inflicts pillory and imprisonment on the Deist.

120 Has not Mr. Eaton an equal right to call your Lordship an Infidel, as you have to imprison him for promulgating a different doctrine from that which you profess?—What do I say!—Has he not even a stronger plea?—The word *Infidel* can only mean any thing when applied to a person who professes that which he disbelieves. The test 125 of truth is an undivided reliance on its inclusive powers;—the test of conscious falsehood is the variety of the forms under which it presents itself, and its tendency towards employing whatever coercive means may be within its command, in order to procure the admission of what is unsusceptible of support from reason or 130 persuasion. A dispassionate observer would feel himself more powerfully interested in favor of a man, who depending on the truth of his opinions, simply stated his reasons for entertaining them, than in that of his aggressor, who daringly avowing his unwillingness to answer them by argument, proceeded to repress the activity, 135 and break the spirit of their promulgator, by that torture and imprisonment whose infliction he could command.

I hesitate not to affirm that the opinions which Mr. Eaton sustained, when undergoing that mockery of a trial at which your Lordship presided, appear to me more true and good than those of 140 his accuser;—but were they false as the visions of a Calvinist, it still would be the duty of those who love liberty and virtue, to raise their voice indignantly against a reviving system of persecution, against the coercively repressing any opinion which, if false, needs but the opposition of truth; which if true, in spite of force, must ultimately 145 prevail.

Mr. Eaton asserted that the scriptures were, from beginning to end, a fable and imposture,[1] that the Apostles were liars and deceivers. He denied the miracles, resurrection, and ascension of

[1] See the Attorney General's Speech.

Jesus Christ.—He did so, and the Attorney General denied the propositions which he asserted, and asserted those which he denied. 150 What singular conclusion is deducible from this fact? None, but that the Attorney General and Mr. Eaton sustained two opposite opinions. The Attorney General puts some obsolete and tyrannical laws in force against Mr. Eaton, because he publishes a book tending to prove that certain supernatural events, which are supposed to 155 have taken place eighteen centuries ago, in a remote corner of the world, did actually not take place. But how are the truth or falsehood of the facts in dispute relevant to the merit or demerit attachable to the advocates of the two opinions? No man is accountable for his belief, because no man is capable of directing it. Mr. Eaton is 160 therefore totally blameless. What are we to think of the justice of a sentence, which punishes an individual against whom it is not even attempted to attach the slightest stain of criminality?

It is asserted that Mr. Eaton's opinions are calculated to subvert morality—How? What moral truth is spoken of with irreverence or 165 ridicule in the book which he published? Morality, or the duty of a man and a citizen, is founded on the relations which arise from the association of human beings, and which vary with the circumstances produced by the different states of this association.—This duty in similar situations must be precisely the same in all ages and 170 nations.—The opinion contrary to this has arisen from a supposition that the will of God is the source or criterion of morality: It is plain that the utmost exertion of Omnipotence could not cause that to be virtuous which actually is vicious. An all-powerful Demon might indubitably annex punishments to virtue and rewards to 175 vice, but could not by these means effect the slightest change in their abstract and immutable natures.—Omnipotence could vary by a providential interposition the relations of human society;—in this latter case, what before was virtuous would become vicious, according to the necessary and natural result of the alteration; but 180 the abstract natures of the opposite principles would have sustained not the slightest change; for instance, the punishment with which society restrains the robber, the assassin, and the ravisher is just, laudable, and requisite. We admire and respect the institutions which curb those who would defeat the ends for which society was 185 established;—but, should a precisely similar coercion be exercised against one who merely expressed his disbelief of a system admitted by those entrusted with the executive power, using at the same time

no methods of promulgation but those afforded by reason, certainly
190 this coercion would be eminently inhuman and immoral; and the
supposition that any revelation from an unknown power, avails to
palliate a persecution so senseless, unprovoked, and indefensible, is
at once to destroy the barrier which reason places between vice and
virtue, and leave to unprincipled fanaticism a plea, whereby it may
195 excuse every act of frenzy, which its own wild passions, not the
inspirations of the Deity, have engendered.

Moral qualities are such, as only a human being can possess. To
attribute them to the Spirit of the Universe, or to suppose that it is
capable of altering them, is to degrade God into man, and to annex to
200 this incomprehensible being, qualities incompatible with any *possible* definition of his nature.—It may here be objected—ought
not the Creator to possess the perfections of the creature? No. To
attribute to God the moral qualities of man, is to suppose him
susceptible of passions which, arising out of corporeal organization,
205 it is plain that a pure spirit cannot possess. A bear is not perfect
except he is rough, a tyger is not perfect if he be not voracious, an
elephant is not perfect if otherwise than docile. How *deep* an
argument must that not be which proves that the Deity is as rough as
a bear, as voracious as a tyger, and as docile as an elephant! But even
210 suppose with the vulgar, that God is a venerable old man, seated on a
throne of clouds, his breast the theatre of various passions,
analogous to those of humanity, his will changeable and uncertain as
that of an earthly king,—still goodness and justice are qualities
seldom nominally denied him, and it will be admitted that he
215 disapproves of any action incompatible with these qualities. Persecution for opinion is unjust. With what consistency, then, can
the worshippers of a Deity whose benevolence they boast, embitter
the existence of their fellow being, because his ideas of that Deity are
different from those which they entertain.—Alas! there is no
220 consistency in those persecutors who worship a benevolent Deity;
those who worship a Demon would alone act consonantly to these
principles, by imprisoning and torturing in his name.

Persecution is the only name applicable to punishment inflicted
on an individual in consequence of his opinions.—What end is
225 persecution designed to answer? Can it convince him whom it
injures? Can it prove to the people the falsehood of his opinions? It
may make him a hypocrite and them cowards, but bad means can
promote no good end. The unprejudiced mind looks with suspicion
on a doctrine that needs the sustaining hand of power.

Socrates was poisoned because he dared to combat the degrading superstitions in which his countrymen were educated. Not long after his death, Athens recognized the injustice of his sentence; his accuser Melitus was condemned, and Socrates became a demigod.

Jesus Christ was crucified because he attempted to supercede the ritual of Moses with regulations more moral and humane—his very judge made public acknowledgment of his innocence, but a bigotted and ignorant mob demanded the deed of horror.—Barrabbas the murderer and traitor was released. The meek reformer Jesus was immolated to the sanguinary Deity of the Jews. Time rolled on, time changed the situations, and with them, the opinions of men.

The vulgar, ever in extremes, became persuaded that the crucifixion of Jesus was a supernatural event, and testimonies of miracles, so frequent in unenlightened ages, were not wanting to prove that he was something divine. This belief rolling thro' the lapse of ages, acquired force and extent, until the divinity of Jesus became a dogma, which to dispute was death, which to doubt was infamy.

Christianity is now the established religion; he who attempts to disprove it must behold murderers and traitors take precedence of him in public opinion, tho', if his genius be equal to his courage, and assisted by a peculiar coalition of circumstances, future ages may exalt him to a divinity, and persecute others in his name, as he was persecuted in the name of his predecessor, in the homage of the world.

The same means that have supported every other popular belief have supported Christianity. War, imprisonment, murder, and falsehood; deeds of unexampled and incomparable atrocity have made it what it is. We derive from our ancestors a belief thus fostered and supported.—We quarrel, persecute, and hate for its maintenance.—Does not analogy favour the opinion, that as like other systems it has arisen and augmented, so like them it will decay and perish; that as violence and falshood, not reasoning and persuasion, have procured its admission among mankind; so, when enthusiasm has subsided, and time, that infallible controverter of false opinions, has involved its pretended evidences in the darkness of antiquity, it will become obsolete, and that men will then laugh as heartily at grace, faith, redemption, and original sin, as they now do at the metamorphoses of Jupiter, the miracles of Romish Saints, the efficacy of witchcraft, and the appearance of departed spirits?

Had the christian religion commenced and continued by the mere

270 force of reasoning and persuasion, by its self-evident excellence and fitness, the preceding analogy would be inadmissible. We should never speculate upon the future obsoleteness of a system perfectly conformable to nature and reason. It would endure as long as they endured, it would be a truth as indisputable as the light of the sun, the

275 criminality of murder, and other facts, physical and moral, which, depending on our organization, and relative situations, must remain acknowledged so long as man is man.—It is an incontrovertible fact, the consideration of which ought to repress the hasty conclusions of credulity, or moderate its obstinacy in maintaining them, that had

280 the Jews not been a barbarous and fanatical race of men, had even the resolution of Pontius Pilate been equal to his candour, the christian religion never could have prevailed, it could not even have existed. Man! the very existence of whose most cherished opinions depends from a thread so feeble, arises out of a source so equivocal, learn at

285 least humility; own at least that it is possible for thyself also to have been seduced by education and circumstance into the admission of tenets destitute of rational proof, and the truth of which has not yet been satisfactorily demonstrated. Acknowledge at least that the falshood of thy brother's opinions is no sufficient reason for his

290 meriting thy hatred.—What! because a fellow being disputes the reasonableness of thy faith, wilt thou punish him with torture and imprisonment? If persecution for religious opinions were admitted by the moralist, how wide a door would not be opened by which convulsionists of every kind might make inroads on the peace of

295 society! How many deeds of barbarism and blood would not receive a sanction!—But I will demand, if that man is not rather entitled to the respect than the discountenance of society, who, by disputing a received doctrine, either proves its falshood and inutility, thereby aiming at the abolition of what is false and useless, or give⟨s⟩ to

300 its adherents an opportunity of establishing its excellence and truth.—Surely this can be no crime. Surely the individual who devotes his time to fearless and unrestricted inquiry into the grand questions arising out of our moral nature, ought rather to receive the patronage, than encounter the vengeance, of an enlightened

305 legislature. I would have you to know, my Lord, that fetters of iron cannot bind or subdue the soul of virtue. From the damps and solitude of its dungeon it ascends free and undaunted, whither thine, from the pompous seat of judgment, dare not soar. I do not warn you to beware lest your profession as a Christian, should make you

forget that you are a man;—but I warn you against festinating that period, which, under the present coercive system, is too rapidly maturing, when the seats of justice shall be the seats of venality and slavishness, and the cells of Newgate become the abodes of all that is honorable and true.

I mean not to compare Mr. Eaton with Socrates or Jesus; he is a man of blameless and respectable character, he is a citizen unimpeached with crime; if, therefore, his rights as a citizen and a man have been infringed, they have been infringed by illegal and immoral violence. But I will assert that should a second Jesus arise among men; should such a one as Socrates again enlighten the earth, lengthened imprisonment and infamous punishment (according to the regimen of persecution revived by your Lordship) would effect, what hemlock and the cross have heretofore effected, and the stain on the national character, like that on Athens and Judea, would remain indelible, but by the destruction of the history in which it is recorded. When the Christian Religion shall have faded from the earth, when its memory like that of Polytheism now shall remain, but remain only as the subject of ridicule and wonder, indignant posterity would attach immortal infamy to such an outrage; like the murder of Socrates, it would secure the execration of every age.

The horrible and wide wasting enormities which gleam like comets thro' the darkness of gothic and superstitious ages, are regarded by the moralist as no more than the necessary effects of known causes: but when an enlightened age and nation signalizes itself by a deed, becoming none but barbarians and fanatics, Philosophy itself is even induced to doubt whether human nature will ever emerge from the pettishness and imbecility of its childhood. The system of persecution at whose new birth, you, my Lord, are one of the presiding midwives, is not more impotent and wicked than inconsistent. The press is loaded with what are called (ironically I should conceive) *proofs* of the Christian Religion: these books are replete with invective and calumny against Infidels, they presuppose that he who rejects Christianity must be utterly divested of reason and feeling. They advance the most unsupported assertions and take as first principles the most revolting dogmas. The inferences drawn from these assumed premises are imposingly logical and correct; but if a foundation is weak, no architect is needed to foretell the instability of the superstructure.—If the truth of Christianity is not disputable, for what purpose are these books

350 written? If they are sufficient to prove it, what further need of controversy? *If God has spoken, why is not the universe convinced?* If the Christian Religion needs deeper learning, more painful investigation, to establish its genuineness, wherefore attempt to accomplish that by force, which the human mind can alone effect

355 with satisfaction to itself? If, lastly, its truth *cannot* be demonstrated, wherefore impotently attempt to snatch from God the government of his creation, and impiously assert that the Spirit of Benevolence has left that knowledge most essential to the well being of man, the only one which, since its promulgation, has been the subject of

360 unceasing cavil, the cause of irreconcileable hatred?—Either the Christian Religion is true, or it is not. If true, it comes from God, and its authenticity can admit of doubt and dispute no further than its Omnipotent Author is willing to allow;—if true, it admits of rational proof, and is capable of being placed equally beyond controversy, as

365 the principles which have been established concerning matter and mind, by Locke and Newton; and in proportion to the usefulness of the fact in dispute, so must it be supposed that a benevolent being is anxious to procure the diffusion of its knowledge on the earth.—If false, surely no enlightened legislature would punish the reasoner,

370 who opposes a system so much the more fatal and pernicious as it is extensively admitted; so much the more productive of absurd and ruinous consequences, as it is entwined by education, with the prejudices and affections of the human heart, in the shape of a popular belief.

375   Let us suppose that some half-witted philosopher should assert that the earth was the centre of the universe, or that ideas could enter the human mind independently of sensation or reflection. This man would assert what is demonstrably incorrect;—he would promulgate a false opinion. Yet would he therefore deserve pillory

380 and imprisonment? By no means; probably few would discharge more correctly the duties of a citizen and a man. I admit that the case above stated is not precisely in point. The thinking part of the community has not received as indisputable the truth of Christianity as they have that of the Newtonian system. A very large

385 portion of society, and that powerfully and extensively connected, derives its sole emolument from the belief of Christianity, as a popular faith.

To torture and imprison the asserter of a dogma, however ridiculous and false, is highly barbarous and impolitic:—How then, does not the cruelty of persecution become aggravated when it is ₃₉₀ dictated against the opposer of an opinion *yet under dispute*, and which men of unrivalled acquirements, penetrating genius, and stainless virtue, have spent, and at last sacrificed, their lives in combating.

The time is rapidly approaching—I hope, that you, my Lord, ₃₉₅ may live to behold its arrival—when the Mahometan, the Jew, the Christian, the Deist, and the Atheist, will live together in one community, equally sharing the benefits which arise from its association, and united in the bonds of charity and brotherly love.—My Lord, you have condemned an innocent man—no crime ₄₀₀ was imputed to him—and you sentenced him to torture and imprisonment. I have not addressed this letter to you with the hopes of convincing you that you have acted wrong. The most unprincipled and barbarous of men are not unprepared with sophisms, to prove that they would have acted in no other manner, ₄₀₅ and to shew that vice is virtue. But I raise my solitary voice, to express my disapprobation, so far as it goes, of the cruel and unjust sentence you passed upon Mr. Eaton; to assert, so far as I am capable of influencing, those rights of humanity, which you have wantonly and unlawfully infringed.   ₄₁₀

My Lord,
Yours, &c.

A

VINDICATION

OF

NATURAL DIET.

——◈◦✦◦◈——

BEING ONE IN A SERIES OF NOTES TO QUEEN MAB.
A PHILOSOPHICAL POEM.

Ιαπέλιονιδη, παντων περι μηδεα ειδωσ,
Χαιρεισ μεν πυρ κλεψασ, και εμασ φρενασ ηπεροπευσασ;
Σοισ' αυτω μεγα πημα και ανδρασιν εσσομενοισι.
Τοισ δ'εγω αυλι πυροσ δωσω κακον, ω κεν απαγτεσ
Τερπωνται κατα θυμον, εον κακον αμφαγαπωντεσ.

HΣΙΩΔ. Op. et Dies. I. 54.

══════════════

London:
PRINTED FOR J. CALLOW, MEDICAL BOOKSELLER, CROWN
COURT, PRINCES STREET, SOHO,
By SMITH and DAVY, Queen Street, Seven Dials.
1813.

Price One Shilling and Sixpence.

5. Title-page of *A Vindication of Natural Diet* (1813)
Huntington Library (RB 22262)

A VINDICATION
Of
NATURAL DIET.

I hold that the depravity of the physical and moral nature of man originated in his unnatural habits of life. The origin of man, like that of the universe of which he is a part, is enveloped in impenetrable mystery. His generations either had a beginning, or they had not. The weight of evidence in favour of each of these suppositions seems tolerably equal; and it is perfectly unimportant to the present argument which is assumed. The language spoken however by the mythology of nearly all religions seems to prove, that at some distant period man forsook the path of nature, and sacrificed the purity and happiness of his being to unnatural appetites. The date of this event, seems to have also been that of some great change in the climates of the earth, with which it has an obvious correspondence. The allegory of Adam and Eve eating of the tree of evil, and entailing upon their posterity the wrath of God, and the loss of everlasting life, admits of no other explanation, than the disease and crime that have flowed from unnatural diet. Milton was so well aware of this, that he makes Raphael thus exhibit to Adam the consequence of his disobedience.

    ————————— Immediately a place,
Before his eyes appeared: sad, noisome, dark:
A lazar-house it seem'd; wherein were laid
Numbers of all diseased: all maladies
Of ghastly spasm, or racking torture, qualms
Of heart-sick agony, all feverous kinds,
Convulsions, epilepsies, fierce catarrhs,
Intestine stone and ulcer, cholic pangs,
Dæmoniac frenzy, moping melancholy,
And moon-struck madness, pining atrophy,
Marasmus, and wide-wasting pestilence,
Dropsies, and asthmas, and joint-racking rheums.

And how many thousand more might not be added to this frightful catalogue!

The story of Prometheus, is one likewise which, although universally admitted to be allegorical, has never been satisfactorily
35 explained. Prometheus stole fire from heaven, and was chained for this crime to mount Caucasus, where a vulture continually devoured his liver, that grew to meet its hunger.—Hesiod says, that before the time of Prometheus, mankind were exempt from suffering; that they enjoyed a vigorous youth, and that death, when at length it came,
40 approached like sleep, and gently closed their eyes.—Again, so general was this opinion, that Horace, a poet of the Augustan age, writes—

> Audax omnia perpeti,
> Gens humana ruit per vetitum nefas,
45 > Audax Iapeti genus,
> Ignem fraude mala gentibus intulit,
> Post ignem ætheriâ domo,
> Subductum, macies et nova febrium,
> Terris incubuit cohors
50 > Semotique prius tarda necessitas,
> Lethi corripuit gradum.—

How plain a language is spoken by all this.—Prometheus, (who represents the human race) effected some great change in the condition of his nature, and applied fire to culinary purposes; thus
55 inventing an expedient for screening from his disgust the horrors of the shambles. From this moment his vitals were devoured by the vulture of disease. It consumed his being in every shape of its loathsome and infinite variety, inducing the soul-quelling sinkings of premature and violent death. All vice arose from the ruin of
60 healthful innocence. Tyranny, superstition, commerce, and inequality, were then first known, when reason vainly attempted to guide the wanderings of exacerbated passion. I conclude this part of the subject with an extract from Mr. Newton's Defence of Vegetable Regimen, from whom I have borrowed this interpretation of the
65 fable of Prometheus.

"Making allowance for such transposition of the events of the allegory, as time might produce after the important truths were forgotten, which the portion of the antient mythology was intended to transmit, the drift of the fable seems to be this:—Man at his
70 creation was endowed with the gift of perpetual youth; that is, he

was not formed to be a sickly suffering creature as we now see him, but to enjoy health, and to sink by slow degrees into the bosom of his parent earth without disease or pain. Prometheus first taught the use of animal food (*primus bovem occidit Prometheus*[1]) and of fire, with which to render it more digestible and pleasing to the taste. Jupiter, [75] and the rest of the gods, foreseeing the consequences of the inventions, were amused or irritated at the short-sighted devices of the newly-formed creature, and left him to experience the sad effects of them. Thirst, the necessary concomitant of a flesh diet," (perhaps of all diet vitiated by culinary preparation) "ensued; water was [80] resorted to, and man forfeited the inestimable gift of health which he had received from heaven: he became diseased, the partaker of a precarious existence, and no longer descended slowly to his grave" ⟨pp. 8–9⟩.

> But just disease to luxury succeeds,   [85]
> And every death its own avenger breeds;
> The fury passions from that blood began,
> And turned on man a fiercer savage—Man.

Man, and the animals whom he has infected with his society, or depraved by his dominion, are alone diseased. The wild hog, the [90] mouflon, the bison, and the wolf, are perfectly exempt from malady, and invariably die either from external violence, or natural old age. But the domestic hog, the sheep, the cow, and the dog, are subject to an incredible variety of distempers; and, like the corrupters of their nature, have physicians who thrive upon their miseries. The [95] supereminence of man is like Satan's, a supereminence of pain; and the majority of his species, doomed to penury, disease, and crime, have reason to curse the untoward event, that by enabling him to communicate his sensations, raised him above the level of his fellow animals. But the steps that have been taken are irrevocable. The [100] whole of human science is comprised in one question:—How can the advantages of intellect and civilization, be reconciled with the liberty and pure pleasures of natural life? How can we take the benefits, and reject the evils of the system, which is now interwoven with all the fibres of our being?—I believe that abstinence from [105] animal food and spirituous liquors, would in a great measure capacitate us for the solution of this important question.

Comparative anatomy teaches us that man resembles frugivorous

---

[1] Plin⟨y,⟩ *Nat⟨uralis⟩ Hist⟨oria⟩* lib. vii. sect. 57.

animals in every thing, and carnivorous in nothing; he has neither
110 claws wherewith to seize his prey, nor distinct and pointed teeth to
tear the living fibre. A Mandarin of the first class, with nails two
inches long, would probably find them alone inefficient to hold even
a hare. After every subterfuge of gluttony, the bull must be degraded
into the ox, and the ram into the wether, by an unnatural and
115 inhuman operation, that the flaccid fibre may offer a fainter
resistance to rebellious nature. It is only by softening and disguising
dead flesh by culinary preparation, that it is rendered susceptible of
mastication or digestion; and that the sight of its bloody juices and
raw horror, does not excite intolerable loathing and disgust. Let the
120 advocate of animal food, force himself to a decisive experiment on its
fitness, and as Plutarch recommends, tear a living lamb with his
teeth, and plunging his head into its vitals, slake his thirst with the
steaming blood; when fresh from the deed of horror let him revert to
the irresistible instincts of nature that would rise in judgment against
125 it, and say, Nature formed me for such work as this. Then, and then
only, would he be consistent.

Man resembles no carnivorous animal. There is no exception,
except man be one, to the rule of herbivorous animals having
cellulated colons.

130 The orang-outang perfectly resembles man both in the order and
number of his teeth. The orang-outang is the most anthropo-
morphous of the ape tribe, all of which are strictly frugivorous.
There is no other species of animals in which this analogy exists.[1] In
many frugivorous animals, the canine teeth are more pointed and
135 distinct than those of man. The resemblance also of the human
stomach to that of the orang-outang, is greater than to that of any
other animal.

The intestines are also identical with those of herbivorous
animals, which present a larger surface for absorption, and have
140 ample and cellulated colons. The cæcum also, though short, is larger
than that of carnivorous animals; and even here the orang-outang
retains its accustomed similarity. The structure of the human frame
then is that of one fitted to a pure vegetable diet, in every essential
particular. It is true, that the reluctance to abstain from animal food,
145 in those who have been long accustomed to its stimulus, is so great in
some persons of weak minds, as to be scarcely overcome; but this is

---

[1] ⟨Georges⟩ Cuvier, *Leçons d'Anat⟨omie⟩ Comp⟨arée,⟩* tom. iii. p⟨p⟩. 169, 373, 448, 465, 480.
Rees's *Cyclopædia*, article Man.

far from bringing any argument in its favour.—A lamb, which was fed for some time on flesh by a ship's crew, refused its natural diet at the end of the voyage. There are numerous instances of horses, sheep, oxen, and even wood-pigeons, having been taught to live 150 upon flesh, until they have loathed their accustomed aliment. Young children evidently prefer pastry, oranges, apples, and other fruit, to the flesh of animals; until, by the gradual depravation of the digestive organs, the free use of vegetables has for a time produced serious inconveniences; *for a time*, I say, since there never was an instance 155 wherein a change from spirituous liquors and animal food, to vegetables and pure water, has failed ultimately to invigorate the body, by rendering its juices bland and consentaneous, and to restore to the mind that cheerfulness and elasticity, which not one in fifty possess on the present system. A love of strong liquors is also 160 with difficulty taught to infants. Almost every one remembers the wry faces, which the first glass of port produced. Unsophisticated instinct is invariably unerring; but to decide on the fitness of animal food, from the perverted appetites which its constrained adoption produces, is to make the criminal a judge in his own cause:—it is even 165 worse, it is appealing to the infatuated drunkard in a question of the salubrity of brandy.

What is the cause of morbid action in the animal system? Not the air we breathe, for our fellow denizens of nature, breathe the same uninjured; not the water we drink, (if remote from the pollutions of 170 man and his inventions[1]) for the animals drink it too; not the earth we tread upon; not the unobscured sight of glorious nature, in the wood, the field, or the expanse of sky and ocean; nothing that we are or do in common, with the undiseased inhabitants of the forest. Something then wherein we differ from them: our habit of altering 175 our food by fire, so that our appetite is no longer a just criterion for the fitness of its gratification. Except in children there remain no traces of that instinct, which determines in all other animals what aliment is natural or otherwise, and so perfectly obliterated are they in the reasoning adults of our species, that it has become necessary to 180 urge considerations drawn from comparative anatomy to prove that we are naturally frugivorous.

[1] The necessity of resorting to some means of purifying water, and the disease which arises from its adulteration in civilized countries, is sufficiently apparent.—See Dr. (William) Lambe's *Reports on Cancer*. I do not assert that the use of water is in itself unnatural, but that the unperverted palate would swallow no liquid capable of occasioning disease.

Crime is madness. Madness is disease. Whenever the cause of disease shall be discovered, the root from which all vice and misery have so long overshadowed the globe, will lay bare to the axe. All the exertions of man, from that moment, may be considered as tending to the clear profit of his species. No sane mind in a sane body resolves upon a real crime. It is a man of violent passions, blood-shot eyes, and swollen veins, that alone can grasp the knife of murder. The system of a simple diet promises no Utopian advantages. It is no mere reform of legislation, whilst the furious passions and evil propensities of the human heart, in which it had its origin, are still unassuaged. It strikes at the root of all evil, and is an experiment which may be tried with success, not alone by nations, but by small societies, families, and even individuals. In no cases has a return to vegetable diet produced the slightest injury; in most it has been attended with changes undeniably beneficial. Should ever a physician be born with the genius of Locke, I am persuaded that he might trace all bodily and mental derangements to our unnatural habits, as clearly as that philosopher has traced all knowledge to sensation. What prolific sources of disease are not those mineral and vegetable poisons that have been introduced for its extirpation! How many thousands have become murderers and robbers, bigots and domestic tyrants, dissolute and abandoned adventurers, from the use of fermented liquors; who, had they slaked their thirst only at the mountain stream, would have lived but to diffuse the happiness of their own unperverted feelings. How many groundless opinions and absurd institutions have not received a general sanction, from the sottishness and intemperance of individuals! Who will assert, that had the populace of Paris drank at the pure source of the Seine, and satisfied their hunger at the ever-furnished table of vegetable nature, that they would have lent their brutal suffrage to the proscription-list of Robespierre? Could a set of men, whose passions were not perverted by unnatural stimuli, look with coolness on an auto da fé? Is it to be believed that a being of gentle feelings, rising from his meal of roots, would take delight in sports of blood? Was Nero a man of temperate life? could you read calm health in his cheek, flushed with ungovernable propensities of hatred for the human race? Did Muley Ismael's pulse beat evenly, was his skin transparent, did his eyes beam with healthfulness, and its invariable concomitants cheerfulness and benignity? Though history has decided none of these questions, a child could not hesitate to answer in the negative. Surely the bile-suffused cheek of Buonaparte, his wrinkled brow, and yellow eye, the ceaseless inquietude of his nervous system, speak no less plainly the character of his unresting 225 ambition than his murders and his victories. It is impossible, had Buonaparte descended from a race of vegetable feeders, that he could have had either the inclination or the power to ascend the throne of the Bourbons. The desire of tyranny could scarcely be excited in the individual, the power to tyrannize would certainly not 230 be delegated by a society, neither frenzied by inebriation, nor rendered impotent and irrational by disease. Pregnant indeed with inexhaustible calamity, is the renunciation of instinct, as it concerns our physical nature; arithmetic cannot enumerate, nor reason perhaps suspect, the multitudinous sources of disease in civilized life. 235 Even common water, that apparently innoxious pabulum, when corrupted by the filth of populous cities, is a deadly and insidious destroyer.[1] Who can wonder that all the inducements held out by God himself in the Bible to virtue, should have been vainer than a nurse's tale; and that those dogmas, apparently favourable to the 240 intolerant and angry passions, should have alone been deemed essential; whilst christians are in the daily practice of all those habits, which have infected with disease and crime, not only the reprobate sons, but these favoured children of the common Father's love. Omnipotence itself could not save them from the consequences of 245 this original and universal sin.

There is no disease, bodily or mental, which adoption of vegetable diet and pure water has not infallibly mitigated, wherever the experiment has been fairly tried. Debility is gradually converted into strength, disease into healthfulness; madness in all 250 its hideous variety, from the ravings of the fettered maniac, to the unaccountable irrationalities of ill temper, that make a hell of domestic life, into a calm and considerate evenness of temper, that alone might offer a certain pledge of the future moral reformation of society. On a natural system of diet, old age would be our last 255 and our only malady; the term of our existence would be protracted; we should enjoy life, and no longer preclude others from the enjoyment of it. All sensational delights would be infinitely more exquisite and perfect. The very sense of being would then be a continued pleasure, such as we now feel it in some 260 few and favoured moments of our youth. By all that is sacred in

[1] ⟨William⟩ Lambe's *Reports on Cancer*.

our hopes for the human race, I conjure those who love happiness and truth, to give a fair trial to the vegetable system. Reasoning is surely superfluous on a subject, whose merits an experience of six 265 months would set for ever at rest. But it is only among the enlightened and benevolent, that so great a sacrifice of appetite and prejudice can be expected, even though its ultimate excellence should not admit of dispute. It is found easier, by the short-sighted victims of disease, to palliate their torments by medicine, than to 270 prevent them by regimen. The vulgar of all ranks are invariably sensual and indocile; yet I cannot but feel myself persuaded, that when the benefits of vegetable diet are mathematically proved; when it is as clear, that those who live naturally are exempt from premature death, as that nine is not one, the most sottish of mankind 275 will feel a preference towards a long and tranquil, contrasted with a short and painful life. On the average, out of sixty persons, four die in three years. In April 1814, a statement will be given, that sixty persons, all having lived more than three years on vegetables and pure water, are then *in perfect health*. More than two years have now 280 elapsed; *not one of them has died*; no such example will be found in any sixty persons taken at random. Seventeen persons of all ages (the families of Dr. Lambe and Mr. Newton) have lived for seven years on this diet, without a death and almost without the slightest illness. Surely when we consider that some of these were infants, and one a 285 martyr to asthma now nearly subdued, we may challenge any seventeen persons taken at random in this city to exhibit a parallel case. Those who may have been excited to question the rectitude of established habits of diet, by these loose remarks, should consult Mr. Newton's luminous and eloquent essay.[1] It is from that book, and 290 from the conversation of its excellent and enlightened author, that I have derived the materials which I here present to the public.

When these proofs come fairly before the world, and are clearly seen by all who understand arithmetic, it is scarcely possible that abstinence from aliments demonstrably pernicious should not 295 become universal. In proportion to the number of proselytes, so will be the weight of evidence, and when a thousand persons can be produced living on vegetables and distilled water, who have to dread no disease but old age, the world will be compelled to regard animal flesh and fermented liquors, as slow, but certain poisons. The change 300 which would be produced by simpler habits on political economy is

---

[1] ⟨John Frank Newton,⟩ *Return to Nature, or Defence of Vegetable Regimen*. Cadell, 1811.

sufficiently remarkable. The monopolizing eater of animal flesh would no longer destroy his constitution by devouring an acre at a meal, and many loaves of bread would cease to contribute to gout, madness and apoplexy, in the shape of a pint of porter, or a dram of gin, when appeasing the long-protracted famine of the hard-working peasant's hungry babes. The quantity of nutritious vegetable matter, consumed in fattening the carcase of an ox, would afford ten times the sustenance, undepraving indeed, and incapable of generating disease, if gathered immediately from the bosom of the earth. The most fertile districts of the habitable globe are now actually cultivated by men for animals, at a delay and waste of aliment absolutely incapable of calculation. It is only the wealthy that can, to any great degree, even now, indulge the unnatural craving for dead flesh, and they pay for the greater licence of the privilege by subjection to supernumerary diseases. Again, the spirit of the nation that should take lead in this great reform, would insensibly become agricultural; commerce, with all its vice, selfishness and corruption, would gradually decline; more natural habits would produce gentler manners, and the excessive complication of political relations would be so far simplified, that every individual might feel and understand why he loved his country, and took a personal interest in its welfare. How would England, for example, depend on the caprices of foreign rulers, if she contained within herself all the necessaries, and despised whatever they possessed of the luxuries of life? How could they starve her into compliance with their views? Of what consequence would it be, that they refused to take her woollen manufactures, when large and fertile tracts of the island ceased to be allotted to the waste of pasturage? On a natural system of diet, we should require no spices from India; no wines from Portugal, Spain, France, or Madeira; none of those multitudinous articles of luxury, for which every corner of the globe is rifled, and which are the causes of so much individual rivalship, such calamitous and sanguinary national disputes. In the history of modern times, the avarice of commercial monopoly, no less than the ambition of weak and wicked chiefs, seems to have fomented the universal discord, to have added stubbornness to the mistakes of cabinets, and indocility to the infatuation of the people. Let it ever be remembered, that it is the direct influence of commerce to make the interval between the richest and the poorest man wider and more unconquerable. Let it be remembered, that it is a foe to

every thing of real worth and excellence in the human character. The odious and disgusting aristocracy of wealth, is built upon the ruins of all that is good in chivalry or republicanism; and luxury is the forerunner of a barbarism scarce capable of cure. Is it impossible to
345 realize a state of society, where all the energies of man shall be directed to the production of his solid happiness? Certainly if this advantage (the object of all political speculation) be in any degree attainable, it is attainable only by a community, which holds out no factitious incentives to the avarice and ambition of the few, and
350 which is internally organized for the liberty, security and comfort of the many. None must be entrusted with power (and money is the completest species of power) who do not stand pledged to use it exclusively for the general benefit. But the use of animal flesh and fermented liquors, directly militates with this equality of the rights
355 of man. The peasant cannot gratify these fashionable cravings without leaving his family to starve. Without disease and war, those sweeping curtailers of population, pasturage would include a waste too great to be afforded. The labour requisite to support a family is far lighter[1] than is usually supposed. The peasantry work, not only
360 for themselves, but for the aristocracy, the army and the manu-facturers.

The advantage of a reform in diet, is obviously greater than that of any other. It strikes at the root of the evil. To remedy the abuses of legislation, before we annihilate the propensities by which they are
365 produced, is to suppose, that by taking away the effect, the cause will cease to operate. But the efficacy of this system depends entirely on the proselytism of individuals, and grounds its merits as a benefit to the community, upon the total change of the dietetic habits in its members. It proceeds securely from a number of particular cases, to
370 one that is universal, and has this advantage over the contrary mode, that one error does not invalidate all that has gone before.

Let not too much however be expected from this system. The healthiest among us is not exempt from hereditary disease. The most symmetrical, athletic, and long-lived, is a being inexpressibly in-
375 ferior to what he would have been, had not the unnatural habits of

---

[1] It has come under the author's experience, that some of the workmen on an embankment in North Wales, who, in consequence of the inability of the proprietor to pay them, seldom received their wages, have supported large families by cultivating small spots of sterile ground by moonlight. In the notes to Pratt's Poem, "Bread, or the Poor," is an account of an industrious labourer, who, by working in a small garden, before and after his day's task, attained to an enviable state of independence.

his ancestors accumulated for him a certain portion of malady and deformity. In the most perfect specimen of civilized man, something is still found wanting, by the physiological critic. Can a return to nature, then, instantaneously eradicate predispositions that have been slowly taking root in the silence of innumerable ages?— Indubitably not. All that I contend for is, that from the moment of the relinquishing all unnatural habits, no new disease is generated; and that the predisposition to hereditary maladies, gradually perishes, for want of its accustomed supply. In cases of consumption, cancer, gout, asthma and scrofula, such is the invariable tendency of a diet of vegetables and pure water.

Those who may be induced by these remarks to give the vegetable system a fair trial, should, in the first place, date the commencement of their practice from the moment of their conviction. All depends upon breaking through a pernicious habit, resolutely and at once. Dr. Trotter[1] asserts, that no drunkard was ever reformed by gradually relinquishing his dram. Animal flesh in its effects on the human stomach is analogous to a dram. It is similar in the kind, though differing in the degree, of its operation. The proselyte to a pure diet, must be warned to expect a temporary diminution of muscular strength. The subtraction of a powerful stimulus will suffice to account for this event. But it is only temporary, and is succeeded by an equable capability for exertion, far surpassing his former various and fluctuating strength. Above all, he will acquire an easiness of breathing, by which the same exertion is performed, with a remarkable exemption from that painful and difficult panting now felt by almost every one, after hastily climbing an ordinary mountain. He will be equally capable of bodily exertion, or mental application, after as before his simple meal. He will feel none of the narcotic effects of ordinary diet. Irritability, the direct consequence of exhausting stimuli, would yield to the power of natural and tranquil impulses. He will no longer pine under the lethargy of ennui, that unconquerable weariness of life, more dreaded than death itself. He will escape the epidemic madness, that broods over its own injurious notions of the Deity, and "realizes the hell that priests and beldams feign." Every man forms as it were his god from his own character; to the divinity of one of simple habits, no offering would be more acceptable than the happiness of his creatures. He would be incapable of hating or persecuting others for the love of

[1] See ⟨Thomas⟩ Trotter⟨, A View of⟩ the Nervous Temperament.

415 God. He will find, moreover, a system of simple diet to be a system of perfect epicurism. He will no longer be incessantly occupied in blunting and destroying those organs, from which he expects his gratification. The pleasures of taste to be derived from a dinner of potatoes, beans, peas, turnips, lettice, with a dessert of apples,
420 gooseberries, strawberries, currants, raspberries, and in winter, oranges, apples and pears, is far greater than is supposed. Those who wait until they can eat this plain fare, with the sauce of appetite, will scarcely join with the hypocritical sensualist at a lord mayor's feast, who declaims against the pleasures of the table. Solomon kept a
425 thousand concubines, and owned in despair that all was vanity. The man whose happiness is constituted by the society of one amiable woman, would find some difficulty in sympathizing with the disappointment of this venerable debauchee.

I address myself not only to the young enthusiast: the ardent
430 devotee of truth and virtue; the pure and passionate moralist, yet unvitiated by the contagion of the world. He will embrace a pure system, from its abstract truth, its beauty, its simplicity, and its promise of wide-extended benefit; unless custom has turned poison into food, he will hate the brutal pleasures of the chace by instinct; it
435 will be a contemplation full of horror and disappointment to his mind, that beings capable of the gentlest and most admirable sympathies, should take delight in the death-pangs and last convulsions of dying animals. The elderly man, whose youth has been poisoned by intemperance, or who has lived with apparent
440 moderation, and is afflicted with a variety of painful maladies, would find his account in a beneficial change produced without the risk of poisonous medicines. The mother, to whom the perpetual restlessness of disease, and unaccountable deaths incident to her children, are the causes of incurable unhappiness, would on this diet
445 experience the satisfaction of beholding their perpetual healths and natural playfulness.[1] The most valuable lives are daily destroyed by

---

[1] See Mr. Newton's Book. His children are the most beautiful and healthy creatures it is possible to conceive; the girls are perfect models for a sculptor; their dispositions are also the most gentle and conciliating; the judicious treatment, which they experience in other points, may be a correlative cause of this. In the first five years of their life, of 18000 children that are born, 7500 die of various diseases; and how many more of those that survive are not rendered miserable by maladies not immediately mortal? The quality and quantity of a woman's milk, are materially injured by the use of dead flesh. In an island near Iceland, where no vegetables are to be got, the children invariably die of tetanus, before they are three weeks old, and the population is supplied from the mainland.—Sir G⟨eorge⟩ Mackenzie's ⟨Travels in the Island⟩ of Iceland, ⟨p. 413⟩. See also ⟨Rousseau's⟩ Emile, i, p⟨p⟩. 53, 54, 56.

diseases, that it is dangerous to palliate and impossible to cure by medicine. How much longer will man continue to pimp for the gluttony of death, his most insidious, implacable, and eternal foe?

The proselyte to a simple and natural diet who desires health,   450
must from the moment of his conversion attend to these rules—

NEVER TAKE ANY SUBSTANCE INTO THE STOMACH THAT ONCE HAD LIFE.

DRINK NO LIQUID BUT WATER RESTORED TO ITS ORIGINAL PURITY BY DISTILLATION.
                                                                    455

APPENDIX.

Persons on vegetable diet have been remarkable for longevity. The first Christians practised abstinence from animal flesh, on a principle of self-mortification.

1	Old Parr	152
2	Mary Patten	136
3	A shepherd in Hungary	126
4	Patrick O'Neale	113
5	Joseph Elkins	103
6	Elizabeth de Val	101
7	Aurungzebe	100[1]
	St. Anthony	105
	James the Hermit	104
	Arsenius	120
	St. Epiphanius	115
	Simeon	112
	Rombald	120

Mr. Newton's mode of reasoning on longevity is ingenious and conclusive.

"Old Parr, healthy as the wild animals, attained to the age of 152 years.

"All men might be as healthy as the wild animals.

"Therefore all men might attain to the age of 152 years."[2]

The conclusion is sufficiently modest. Old Parr cannot be supposed to have escaped the inheritance of disease, amassed by the

---

[1] 1 Cheyne's *Essay on Health*, p. 62.

2 *Gentleman's Magazine*, vii. 449.

3 *Morning Post*, Jan. 28, 1800.

4 *Emile*, i. 44.

5 He died at Coombe in Northumberland.

6 *Scot's Magazine*, xxxiv. 696.

7 Aurungzebe, from the time of his Usurpation adhered strictly to the Vegetable System.

[2] *Return to Nature* ⟨p. 64 n., *slightly modified*⟩.

unnatural habits of his ancestors. The term of human life may be ₄₈₀
expected to be infinitely greater, taking into the consideration all the
circumstances that must have contributed to abridge even that of
Parr.

It may be here remarked, that the author and his wife have lived
on vegetables for eight months. The improvements of health and ₄₈₅
temper here stated is the result of his own experience.

A

REFUTATION

OF

DEISM:

IN

A DIALOGUE.

ΣΥΝΕΤΟΙΣΙΝ.

London:

PRINTED BY SCHULZE AND DEAN,

13, POLAND STREET.

1814.

6. Title-page of *A Refutation of Deism* (1814)
Huntington Library (RB 22752)

Preface.

The object of the following Dialogue is to prove that the system of Deism is untenable. It is attempted to shew that there is no alternative between Atheism and Christianity; that the evidences of the Being of a God are to be deduced from no other principles than those of Divine Revelation.

The Author endeavours to shew how much the cause of natural and revealed Religion has suffered from the mode of defence adopted by Theosophistical Christians. How far he will accomplish what he proposed to himself, in the composition of this Dialogue, the world will finally determine.

The mode of printing this little work may appear too expensive, either for its merits or its length. However inimical this practice confessedly is, to the general diffusion of knowledge, yet it was adopted in this instance with a view of excluding the multitude from the abuse of a mode of reasoning, liable to misconstruction on account of its novelty.

EUSEBES AND THEOSOPHUS.

O Theosophus, I have long regretted and observed the strange infatuation which has blinded your understanding. It is not without acute uneasiness that I have beheld the progress of your audacious scepticism trample on the most venerable institutions of our forefathers, until it has rejected the salvation which the only be-gotten Son of God deigned to proffer in person to a guilty and unbelieving world. To this excess then has the pride of the human understanding at length arrived? To measure itself with Omni-science! To scan the intentions of Inscrutability!

You can have reflected but superficially on this awful and important subject. The love of paradox, an affectation of singularity, or the pride of reason has seduced you to the barren and gloomy paths of infidelity. Surely you have hardened yourself against the truth with a spirit of coldness and cavil.

Have you been wholly inattentive to the accumulated evidence which the Deity has been pleased to attach to the revelation of his will? The antient books in which the advent of the Messiah was predicted, the miracles by which its truth has been so conspicuously confirmed, the martyrs who have undergone every variety of tor-ment in attestation of its veracity? You seem to require mathe-matical demonstration in a case which admits of no more than strong moral probability. Surely the merit of that faith which we are required to repose in our Redeemer would be thus entirely done away. Where is the difficulty of according credit to that which is perfectly plain and evident? How is he entitled to a recompense who believes what he cannot disbelieve?

When there is satisfactory evidence that the witnesses of the Christian miracles passed their lives in labours, dangers and sufferings, and consented severally to be racked, burned and strangled, in testimony of the truth of their account, will it be asserted that they were actuated by a disinterested desire of

deceiving others? That they were hypocrites for no end but to teach the purest doctrine that ever enlightened the world, and martyrs
50 without any prospect of emolument or fame? The sophist who gravely advances an opinion thus absurd, certainly sins with gratuitous and indefensible pertinacity.

The history of Christianity is itself the most indisputable proof of those miracles by which its origin was sanctioned to the world. It is
55 itself one great miracle. A few humble men established it in the face of an opposing universe. In less than fifty years an astonishing multitude was converted, as Suetonius[1], Pliny[2], Tacitus[3] and Lucian attest; and shortly afterwards thousands who had boldly overturned the altars, slain the priest and burned the temples of Paganism, were
60 loud in demanding the recompense of martyrdom from the hands of the infuriated Heathens. Not until three centuries after the coming of the Messiah did his holy religion incorporate itself with the institutions of the Roman Empire, and derive support from the visible arm of fleshly strength. Thus long without any assistance but
65 that of its Omnipotent author, Christianity prevailed in defiance of incredible persecutions, and drew fresh vigour from circumstances the most desperate and unpromising. By what process of sophistry can a rational being persuade himself to reject a religion, the original propagation of which is an event wholly unparalleled in the sphere
70 of human experience?

The morality of the Christian religion is as original and sublime, as its miracles and mysteries are unlike all other portents. A patient acquiescence in injuries and violence; a passive submission to the will of sovereigns; a disregard of those ties by which the feelings of

---

[1] Judæi, impulsore Chresto, turbantes, facile comprimuntur.—Suet⟨onius⟩ in ⟨Claudio⟩. Affecti suppliciis Christiani, genus hominum superstitionis novæ et maleficæ.—Id⟨em⟩ in Neron⟨e⟩.

[2] Multi omnis ætatis utriusque sexûs etiam; neque enim civitates tantum, sed vicos etiam et agros superstitionis istius contagio pervagata est.—Plin⟨y⟩ Epist⟨ulae⟩.

[3] Ergo abolendo rumori Nero subdidit reos et quæsitissimis pœnis adfecit, quos, suo flagitio invisos, vulgus "Christianos" appellabat. Auctor nominis ejus Christus, Tiberio imperitante, per procuratorem Pontium Pilatum supplicio adfectus erat. Repressaque in præsens exitiabilis superstitio rursus erumpebat, non modo per Judæam, originem ejus mali, sed per urbem etiam, quò cuncta, undique atrocia aut pudenda, confluunt concelebranturque. Igitur primo correpti, qui fatebantur; deinde indicio eorum multitudo ingens haud perinde in crimine incendii, quam odio humani generis convicti sunt, et pereuntibus addita ludibria, ut, ferarum tergis contecti, laniatu canum interirent, aut crucibus affixi, aut flammandi, atque ubi defecisset dies, in usum nocturni luminis urerentur. Hortos suos ei spectaculo Nero obtulerat, et Circense ludibrium edebat, habitu aurigæ permixtus plebi, vel curriculo insistens. Unde quanquam adversus sontes, et novissima exempla meritos, miseratio oriebatur, tanquam non utilitate publicâ, sed in saevitiam unius absumerentur. Tacitus Annal⟨es⟩, L⟨ib⟩. XV, Sect. XLV.

humanity have ever been bound to this unimportant world; 75
humility and faith, are doctrines neither similar nor comparable
to those of any other system.[1] Friendship, patriotism and magnanimity; the heart that is quick in sensibility, the hand that is
inflexible in execution; genius, learning and courage, are qualities
which have engaged the admiration of mankind, but which we are 80
taught by Christianity to consider as splendid and delusive vices.

I know not why a Theist should feel himself more inclined to
distrust the historians of Jesus Christ, than those of Alexander the
Great. What do the tidings of redemption contain which render
them peculiarly obnoxious to discredit? It will not be disputed that a 85
revelation of the Divine will is a benefit to mankind[2]. It will not be
asserted that even under the Christian revelation, we have too clear a
solution of the vast enigma of the Universe, too satisfactory a
justification of the attributes of God. When we call to mind the
profound ignorance in which, with the exception of the Jews, the 90
philosophers of antiquity were plunged; when we recollect that men
eminent for dazzling talents and fallacious virtues, Epicurus,
Democritus, Pliny, Lucretius, Euripides,[3] and innumerable others,

[1] See the *Internal Evidence of Christianity*; see also ⟨William⟩ Paley's ⟨*A View of the*⟩ *Evidences* ⟨*of Christianity*⟩, Vol. II, p. 27.

[2] Paley's *Evidences*, Vol. I, p. 3.

[3] Imperfectæ verò in homine naturæ præcipua solatia ne Deum quidem posse omnia. Namque nec sibi potest mortem cons⟨c⟩iscere, si velit, quod homini dedit optimum in tantis vitæ pœnis; nec mortales æternitate donare, aut revocare defunctos; nec facere ut qui vixit non vixerit, qui honores gessit non gesserit, nullumque habere in præteritum jus præterquam oblivionis, atque ut facetis quoque argumentis societas hæc cum Deo copuletur ut bis dena viginti non sint, et multa similiter efficere non posse. Per quæ, declaratur haud dubiè, naturæ potentiam id quoque esse, quod Deum vocamus.

> Plin⟨y⟩ *Nat*⟨*uralis*⟩ *His*⟨*toria*⟩ *Cap. de Deo.*

Hunc igitur terrorem animi, tenebrasque necesse est
Non radii solis, neque lucida tela diei
Discuti⟨a⟩nt, sed naturæ species ratioque.
Principium hinc cuius nobis exordia sumet,
NULLAM REM NIHILO GIGNI DIVINITUS UNQUAM.

> Luc⟨retius⟩ *de Rer*⟨*um*⟩ *Nat*⟨*ura,*⟩ *Lib. I.*

Φησιν τις, ειναι δητ' εν ουρανω Θεους;
Ουκ εισιν, ουκ εισ'. ει τις ανθρωπων λεγει,
Μη τω παλαιω μωρος ων χρησθω λογω·
Εκεψασθε δ' αυτα, μη 'πι τοις εμοις λογοις
Γνωμην εχοντες. Φημ' εγω, τυραννιδα
Κτεινειν τε πολλους, κτηματων τ' αποστερειν,
Ορκους τε παραβαινοντας εκπορθειν πολεις.
Και ταυτα δρωντες μαλλον εισ' ευδαιμονες
Των ευσεβουντων ήσυχῃ καθ' ήμεραν.

dared publicly to avow their faith in Atheism with impunity,
95 and that the Theists, Anaxagoras, Pythagoras and Plato, vainly
endeavoured by that human reason, which is truly incommensurate
to so vast a purpose, to establish among philosophers the belief in
one Almighty God, the creator and preserver of the world; when we
recollect that the multitude were grossly and ridiculously idol-
100 atrous, and that the magistrates, if not Atheists, regarded the
being of a God in the light of an abstruse and uninteresting
speculation;[1] when we add to these considerations a remembrance
of the wars and the oppressions, which about the time of the advent
of the Messiah, desolated the human race, is it not more credible that
105 the Deity actually interposed to check the rapid progress of human
deterioration, than that he permitted a specious and pestilent
imposture to seduce mankind into the labyrinth of a deadlier
superstition? Surely the Deity has not created man immortal, and
left him for ever in ignorance of his glorious destination. If the
110 Christian Religion is false, I see not upon what foundation our belief
in a moral governor of the universe, or our hopes of immortality can
rest.

Thus then the plain reason of the case, and the suffrage of the
civilized world conspire with the more indisputable suggestions of
115 faith, to render impregnable that system which has been so vainly
and so wantonly assailed. Suppose, however, it were admitted that
the conclusions of human reason and the lessons of worldly virtue
should be found, in the detail, incongruous with Divine Revelation;
by the dictates of which would it become us to abide? Not by that
120 which errs whenever it is employed, but by that which is incapable of
error: not by the ephemeral systems of vain philosophy, but by the
word of God, which shall endure for ever.

Reflect, O Theosophus, that if the religion you reject be true, you
are justly excluded from the benefits which result from a belief in its
125 efficiency to salvation. Be not regardless, therefore, I entreat you, of
the curses so emphatically heaped upon infidels by the inspired

Πολεις τε μικρας οιδα τιμουσας Θεους,
Αι μειζονων κλυουσι δυσσεβεστερων
Λογχης αριθμῳ πλειονος κρατουμεναι.
Οιμαι δ' αν υμας, ει τις αργος ων Θεοις
Ευχοιτο, και μη χειρι συλλεγοι Βιον * * *

Euripides Be⟨l⟩lerophon. Frag. XXV.

[1] See Cicero de Natura Deorum.

organs of the will of God: the fire which is never quenched, the worm
that never dies. I dare not think that the God in whom I trust for
salvation would terrify his creatures with menaces of punishment,
which he does not intend to inflict. The ingratitude of incredulity is, 130
perhaps, the only sin to which the Almighty cannot extend his
mercy without compromising his justice. How can the human heart
endure, without despair, the mere conception of so tremendous an
alternative? Return, I entreat you, to that tower of strength which
securely overlooks the chaos of the conflicting opinions of men. 135
Return to that God who is your creator and preserver, by whom
alone you are defended from the ceaseless wiles of your eternal
enemy. Are human institutions so faultless that the principle upon
which they are founded may strive with the voice of God? Know
that faith is superior to reason, in as much as the creature is surpassed 140
by the Creator; and that whensoever they are incompatible, the
suggestions of the latter, not those of the former, are to be
questioned.

Permit me to exhibit in their genuine deformity the errors which
are seducing you to destruction. State to me, with candour the train 145
of sophisms by which the evil spirit has deluded your understanding.
Confess the secret motives of your disbelief; suffer me to administer
a remedy to your intellectual disease. I fear not the contagion of such
revolting sentiments: I fear only lest patience should desert me
before you have finished the detail of your presumptuous credulity. 150

THEOSOPHUS.

I am not only prepared to confess, but to vindicate my sentiments. I
cannot refrain, however, from premising, that in this controversy I
labour under a disadvantage from which you are exempt. You
believe that incredulity is immoral, and regard him as an object of
suspicion and distrust whose creed is incongruous with your own. 155
But truth is the perception of the agreement or disagreement of
ideas. I can no more conceive that a man who perceives the
disagreement of any ideas, should be persuaded of their agreement,
than that he should overcome a physical impossibility. The
reasonableness or the folly of the articles of our creed is therefore no 160
legitimate object of merit or demerit; our opinions depend not on
the will, but on the understanding.

If I am in error (and the wisest of us may not presume to deem

himself secure from all illusion) that error is the consequence of the
165 prejudices by which I am prevented, of the ignorance by which I am
incapacitated from forming a correct estimation of the subject.
Remove those prejudices, dispel that ignorance, make truth apparent, and fear not the obstacles that remain to be encountered. But
do not repeat to me those terrible and frequent curses, by whose
170 intolerance and cruelty I have so often been disgusted in the perusal
of your sacred books. Do not tell me that the All-Merciful will
punish me for the conclusions of that reason by which he has
thought fit to distinguish me from the beasts that perish. Above all,
refrain from urging considerations drawn from reason, to degrade
175 that which you are thereby compelled to acknowledge as the
ultimate arbiter of the dispute. Answer my objections as I engage to
answer your assertions, point by point, word by word.

You believe that the only and ever-present God begot a Son
whom he sent to reform the world, and to propitiate its sins; you
180 believe that a book, called the Bible, contains a true account of this
event, together with an infinity of miracles and prophecies which
preceded it from the creation of the world. Your opinion that
these circumstances really happened appears to me, from some
considerations which I will proceed to state, destitute of rational
185 foundation.

To expose all the inconsistency, immorality and false pretensions
which I perceive in the Bible, demands a minuteness of criticism at
least as voluminous as itself. I shall confine myself, therefore, to the
confronting of your tenets with those primitive and general
190 principles which are the basis of all moral reasoning.

In creating the Universe, God certainly proposed to himself the
happiness of his creatures. It is just, therefore, to conclude that he
left no means unemployed, which did not involve an impossibility to
accomplish this design. In fixing a residence for this image of his own
195 Majesty, he was doubtless careful that every occasion of detriment,
every opportunity of evil should be removed. He was aware of the
extent of his powers, he foresaw the consequences of his conduct,
and doubtless modelled his being consentaneously with the world of
which he was to be the inhabitant, and the circumstances which
200 were destined to surround him.

The account given by the Bible has but a faint concordance with
the surmises of reason concerning this event.

According to this book, God created Satan, who instigated by the impulses of his nature contended with the Omnipotent for the throne of Heaven. After a contest, for the empire, in which God was victorious, Satan was thrust into a pit of burning sulphur. On man's creation God placed within his reach a tree whose fruit he forbade him to taste, on pain of death; permitting Satan at the same time, to employ all his artifice to persuade this innocent and wondering creature to transgress the fatal prohibition.

The first man yielded to this temptation; and to satisfy Divine Justice the whole of his posterity must have been eternally burned in hell, if God had not sent his only Son on Earth, to save those few whose salvation had been foreseen and determined before the creation of the world.

God is here represented as creating man with certain passions and powers, surrounding him with certain circumstances, and then condemning him to everlasting torments because he acted as omniscience had foreseen, and was such as omnipotence had made him. For to assert that the Creator is the author of all good, and the creature the author of all evil, is to assert that one man makes a straight line and a crooked one, and that another makes the incongruity.[1]

Barbarous and uncivilized nations have uniformly adored, under various names, a God of which themselves were the model; revengeful, blood-thirsty, groveling and capricious. The idol of a savage is a demon that delights in carnage. The steam of slaughter, the dissonance of groans, the flames of a desolated land, are the offerings which he deems acceptable, and his innumerable votaries throughout the world have made it a point of duty to worship him to his taste.[2] The Phenicians, the Druids and the Mexicans have immolated hundreds at the shrines of their divinity, and the high and holy name of God has been in all ages the watch word of the most unsparing massacres, the sanction of the most atrocious perfidies.

But I appeal to your candour, O Eusebes, if there exist a record of such groveling absurdities and enormities so atrocious, a picture of the Deity so characteristic of a demon as that which the sacred writings of the Jews contain. I demand of you, whether as a conscientious Theist you can reconcile the conduct which is attributed to the God of the Jews with your conceptions of the purity and benevolence of the divine nature.

[1] Hobbes.
[2] See preface to ⟨Baron d'Holbach's⟩ *Le Bon Sens.*

The loathsome and minute obscenities to which the inspired writers perpetually descend, the filthy observances which God is described as personally instituting,[1] the total disregard of truth and
245 contempt of the first principles of morality, manifested on the most public occasions by the chosen favourites of Heaven, might corrupt, were they not so flagitious as to disgust.

When the chief of this obscure and brutal horde of assassins asserts that the God of the Universe was enclosed in a box of shittim
250 wood[2] "two feet long and three feet wide[3]," and brought home in a new cart, I smile at the impertinence of so shallow an imposture. But it is blasphemy of a more hideous and unexampled nature to maintain that the Almighty God expressly commanded Moses to invade an unoffending nation, and on account of the difference of
255 their worship utterly to destroy every human being it contained, to murder every infant and unarmed man in cold blood, to massacre the captives, to rip up the matrons, and to retain the maidens alone for concubinage and violation.[4] At the very time that philosophers

[1] See *Hosea*, Chap. I. Chap. IX. *Ezekiel*, Chap. IV. Chap. XVI. Chap. XXIII. Heynë, speaking of the opinions entertained of the Jews by antient poets and philosophers says: *Meminit quidem superstitionis Judaicæ Horatius, verum ut eam risu exploderet.* Heyn⟨e,⟩ *ad Virg⟨ilim⟩ Poll⟨ionem⟩ in Arg⟨umento; Tom.* I, *Pars* I, 73.⟩

[2] *Sam⟨uel,⟩* Chap. V, v. 8.

[3] Wordsworth's ('The Thorn', l. 33,) *Lyrical Ballads* ⟨1798⟩.

[4] When Moses stood in the gate of the court and said—Who is of the Lord's side? Let him come unto me. And all the sons of Levi gathered themselves together unto him. *Thus saith the Lord God of Israel*, put every man his sword by his side, and go in and out from gate to gate throughout the camp, and *slay every man his brother, and every man his companion, and every man his neighbour*. And the children of Levi did according to the word of Moses, and there fell of the people on that day twenty three thousand men. *Exodus*, Chap. XXXII, v⟨v⟩. 26⟨-8⟩.

And they warred against the Midianites as the Lord commanded Moses, and they slew all the males; and the children of Israel took all the women of Midian captives, and their little ones, and took up the spoil of all their cattle, and all their flocks, and all their goods. And they burned all their huts wherein they dwelt and all their goodly castles with fire. And Moses and Eleazer the priest, and all the princes of the congregation came forth to meet them without the camp. And Moses was ⟨wroth⟩ with the officers of the post, with the captains over hundreds and the captains over thousands that came from the battle. And Moses said unto them—*Have ye saved all the women alive?*—Behold these caused the children of Israel through the counsel of Balaam to commit trespass against the Lord in the matter of Peor, and there was a plague among the congregation of the Lord. *Now therefore kill every male among the little ones, and kill every woman that hath known man by lying with him. And all the women-children that have not known a man by lying with him*, KEEP ALIVE FOR YOURSELVES. *Numbers*, Chap. XXXI ⟨,vv. 7-18⟩.

And we utterly destroyed them, as we did unto Sihon King of Heshbon utterly destroying the men, women and children of every city. *Deut⟨eronomy,⟩* Chap. III, v. 6.

And they utterly destroyed all that was in the city both man and woman, young and old, and ox and sheep and ass with the edge of the sword. *Joshua⟨,* Chap. VI, v. 21⟩.

So Joshua fought against Debir, and utterly destroyed all the souls that were therein, he left

of the most enterprising benevolence were founding in Greece those
institutions which have rendered it the wonder and luminary of the 260
world, am I required to believe that the weak and wicked king of an
obscure and barbarous nation, a murderer, a traitor and a tyrant was
the man after God's own heart? A wretch, at the thought of whose
unparalleled enormities the sternest soul must sicken in dismay! An
unnatural monster who sawed his fellow beings in sunder, harrowed 265
them to fragments under harrows of iron, chopped them to pieces
with axes and burned them in brick-kilns, because they bowed
before a different, and less bloody idol than his own. It is surely no
perverse conclusion of an infatuated understanding that the God of
the Jews is not the benevolent author of this beautiful world. 270

The conduct of the Deity in the promulgation of the Gospel,
appears not to the eye of reason more compatible with His immutability and omnipotence than the history of his actions under
the law accords with his benevolence.

You assert that the human race merited eternal reprobation 275
because their common father had transgressed the divine command, and that the crucifixion of the Son of God was the only
sacrifice of sufficient efficacy to satisfy eternal justice. But it is no
less inconsistent with justice and subversive of morality that
millions should be responsible for a crime which they had no share 280
in committing; than that, if they had really committed it, the
crucifixion of an innocent being could absolve them from moral
turpitude. *Ferretne ulla civitas latorem istiusmodi legis, ut condem-
naretur filius, aut nepos, si pater aut avus deliquisset?* Certainly this is a
mode of legislation peculiar to a state of savageness and anarchy; 285
this is the irrefragable logic of tyranny and imposture.

The supposition that God has ⟨n⟩ever supernaturally revealed his
will to man at any other period than the original creation of the
human race, necessarily involves a compromise of his benevolence.
It assumes that he withheld from mankind a benefit which it was in 290
his power to confer. That he suffered his creatures to remain in
ignorance of truths essential to their happiness and salvation. That
during the lapse of innumerable ages every individual of the human

none remaining, but utterly destroyed all that breathed, as the *Lord God of Israel commanded.
Joshua*, Chap. X ⟨vv. 38–40 *conflated*⟩.

And David gathered all the people together and went to Rabbah and took it, and he brought
forth the people therein, and *put them under saws and under harrows of iron, and made them pass
through the brick-kiln. This did he also unto all the children of Ammon.* II *Sam*⟨*uel*⟩, Chap. XII,
v⟨v⟩. 29, ⟨31⟩.

race had perished without redemption from an universal stain which
the Deity at length descended in person to erase. That the good and
wise of all ages, involved in one common fate with the ignorant and
wicked, have been tainted by involuntary and inevitable error which
torments infinite in duration may not avail to expiate.

In vain will you assure me with amiable inconsistency that the
mercy of God will be extended to the virtuous, and that the vicious
will alone be punished. The foundation of the Christian Religion
is manifestly compromised by a concession of this nature. A
subterfuge thus palpable plainly annihilates the necessity of the
incarnation of God for the redemption of the human race, and
represents the descent of the Messiah as a gratuitous display of
Deity, solely adapted to perplex, to terrify and to embroil mankind.

It is sufficiently evident that an omniscient being never conceived
the design of reforming the world by Christianity. Omniscience
would surely have foreseen the inefficacy of that system, which
experience demonstrates not only to have been utterly impotent in
restraining, but to have been most active in exhaling the malevolent
propensities of men. During the period which elapsed between the
removal of the seat of empire to Constantinople in 328, and
its capture by the Turks in 1453, what salutary influence did
Christianity exercise upon that world which it was intended to
enlighten? Never before was Europe the theatre of such ceaseless
and sanguinary wars; never were the people so brutalized by
ignorance and debased by slavery.

I will admit that one prediction of Jesus Christ has been
indisputably fulfilled. *I come not to bring peace upon earth, but a sword.*
Christianity indeed has equalled Judaism in the atrocities, and
exceeded it in the extent of its desolation. Eleven millions of men,
women and children have been killed in battle, butchered in their
sleep, burned to death at public festivals of sacrifice, poisoned,
tortured, assassinated and pillaged in the spirit of the Religion of
Peace, and for the glory of the most merciful God.

In vain will you tell me that these terrible effects flow not from
Christianity, but from the abuse of it. No such excuse will avail to
palliate the enormities of a religion pretended to be divine. A limited
intelligence is only so far responsible for the effects of its agency
as it foresaw, or might have foreseen them; but Omniscience is
manifestly chargeable with all the consequences of its conduct.
Christianity itself declares that the worth of the tree is to be

determined by the quality of its fruit. The extermination of infidels; the mutual persecutions of hostile sects; the midnight massacres and slow burning of thousands because their creed contained either more or less than the orthodox standard, of which Christianity has been the immediate occasion; and the invariable opposition which philosophy has ever encountered from the spirit of revealed religion, plainly show that a very slight portion of sagacity was sufficient to have estimated at its true value the advantages of that belief to which some Theists are unaccountably attached.

You lay great stress upon the originality of the Christian system of morals. If this claim be just, either your religion must be false, or the Deity has willed that opposite modes of conduct should be pursued by mankind at different times, under the same circumstances; which is absurd.

The doctrine of acquiescing in the most insolent despotism; of praying for and loving our enemies; of faith and humility, appears to fix the perfection of the human character in that abjectness and credulity which priests and tyrants of all ages have found sufficiently convenient for their purposes. It is evident that a whole nation of Christians (could such an anomaly maintain itself a day) would become, like cattle, the property of the first occupier. It is evident that ten highwaymen would suffice to subjugate the world if it were composed of slaves who dared not to resist oppression.

The apathy to love and friendship, recommended by your creed, would, if attainable, not be less pernicious. This enthusiasm of anti-social misanthropy if it were an actual rule of conduct, and not the speculation of a few interested persons, would speedily annihilate the human race. A total abstinence from sexual intercourse is not perhaps enjoined, but is strenuously recommended,[1] and was actually practised to a frightful extent by the primitive Christians.[2]

The penalties inflicted by that monster Constantine, the first Christian Emperor, on the pleasures of unlicenced love are so iniquitously severe, that no modern legislator could have affixed them to the most atrocious crimes.[3] This cold-blooded and

---

[1] Now concerning the things whereof ye wrote to me. It is good for a man not to touch a woman.

I say, therefore, to the unmarried and widows, it is good for them if they abide even as I; but if they cannot contain, let them marry; it is better to marry than burn. I *Corinthians*, Chap. VII⟨, 1, 8–9⟩.

[2] See ⟨Edward⟩ Gibbon's *Decline and Fall*, Vol. II, p. 210.

[3] See Gibbon's *Decline and Fall*, Vol. II, p. 269.

hypocritical ruffian cut his son's throat, strangled his wife, murdered his father-in-law and his brother-in-law, and maintained at
370 his court a set of blood-thirsty and bigoted Christian Priests, one of
whom was sufficient to excite the one half of the world to massacre
the other.

I am willing to admit that some few axioms of morality, which
Christianity has borrowed from the philosophers of Greece and
375 India, dictate, in an unconnected state, rules of conduct worthy of
regard; but the purest and most elevated lessons of morality must
remain nugatory, the most probable inducements to virtue must fail
of their effect, so long as the slightest weight is attached to that
dogma which is the vital essence of revealed religion.

380 Belief is set up as the criterion of merit or demerit; a man is to be
judged not by the purity of his intentions but by the orthodoxy of his
creed; an assent to certain propositions, is to outweigh in the balance
of Christianity the most generous and elevated virtue.

But the intensity of belief, like that of every other passion, is
385 precisely proportionate to the degrees of excitement. A graduated
scale, on which should be marked the capabilities of propositions to
approach to the test of the senses, would be a just measure of the
belief which ought to be attached to them: and but for the influence
of prejudice or ignorance this invariably *is* the measure of belief.
390 That is believed which is apprehended to be true, nor can the mind
by any exertion avoid attaching credit to an opinion attended with
overwhelming evidence. Belief is not an act of volition, nor can it be
regulated by the mind: it is manifestly incapable therefore of either
merit or criminality. The system which assumes a false criterion of
395 moral virtue, must be as pernicious as it is absurd. Above all, it
cannot be divine, as it is impossible that the Creator of the human
mind should be ignorant of its primary powers.

The degree of evidence afforded by miracles and prophecies in
favour of the Christian Religion is lastly to be considered.

400 Evidence of a more imposing and irresistible nature is required in
proportion to the remoteness of any event from the sphere of
our experience. Every case of miracles is a contest of opposite
improbabilities, whether it is more contrary to experience that a
miracle should be true, or that the story on which it is supported
405 should be false: whether the immutable laws of this harmonious
world should have undergone violation, or that some obscure
Greeks and Jews should have conspired to fabricate a tale of wonder.

The actual appearance of a departed spirit would be a circumstance truly unusual and portentous; but the accumulated testimony of twelve old women that a spirit had appeared is neither 410 unprecedented nor miraculous.

It seems less credible that the God whose immensity is uncircumscribed by space, should have committed adultery with a carpenter's wife, than that some bold knaves or insane dupes had deceived the credulous multitude.[1] We have perpetual and mournful 415 experience of the latter: the former is yet under dispute. History affords us innumerable examples of the possibility of the one: Philosophy has in all ages protested against the probability of the other.

Every superstition can produce its dupes, its miracles and its 420 mysteries; each is prepared to justify its peculiar tenets by an equal assemblage of portents, prophecies and martyrdoms.

Prophecies, however circumstantial, are liable to the same objection as direct miracles: it is more agreeable to experience that the historical evidence of the prediction really having preceded the 425 event pretended to be foretold should be false, or that a lucky conjuncture of events should have justified the conjecture of the prophet, than that God should communicate to a man the discernment of future events.[2] I defy you to produce more than one instance of prophecy in the Bible, wherein the inspired writer speaks 430 so as to be understood, wherein his prediction has not been so unintelligible and obscure as to have been itself the subject of controversy among Christians.

That one prediction which I except is certainly most explicit and circumstantial. It is the only one of this nature which the 435 Bible contains. Jesus himself here predicts his own arrival in the clouds to consummate a period of supernatural desolation, before the generation which he addressed should pass away.[3] Eighteen

---

[1] See Paley's *Evidences*, Vol. I, Chap. I.

[2] See the Controversy of Bishop Watson and Thomas Paine.—Paine's Criticism on the XIXth Chapter of *Isaiah*.

[3] Immediately after the tribulation of these days, shall the sun be darkened and the moon shall not give her light, and the stars shall fall from Heaven, and the powers of the heavens shall be shaken; and then shall appear the sign of the son of man in Heaven: and then shall all the tribes of the Earth mourn, and they shall see the son of man coming in the clouds of Heaven with power and great Glory: and he shall send his Angel with a great sound of a trumpet, and they shall gather together his elect from the four winds, from one end of Heaven to the other. *Verily I say unto you: This generation shall not pass until all these things be fulfilled. Matthew*, Chap. XXIV⟨, vv. 29–31, 34).

hundred years have past, and no such event is pretended to have
440 happened. This single plain prophecy, thus conspicuously false, may
serve as a criterion of those which are more vague and indirect, and
which apply in an hundred senses to an hundred things.

Either the pretended predictions in the Bible were meant to be
understood, or they were not. If they were, why is there any dispute
445 concerning them: if they were not, wherefore were they written at
all? But the God of Christianity spoke to mankind in parables, that
seeing they might not see, and hearing they might not understand.

The Gospels contain internal evidence that they were not written
by eye-witnesses of the event which they pretend to record. The
450 Gospel of St. Matthew was plainly not written until some time after
the taking of Jerusalem, that is, at least forty years after the execution
of Jesus Christ: for he makes Jesus say *that upon you may come all the
righteous blood shed upon the earth, from the blood of righteous Abel unto
the blood of Zacharias son of Barachias whom ye slew between the altar
455 and the temple.*[1] Now Zacharias son of Barachias was assassinated
between the altar and the temple by a faction of zealots, during the
siege of Jerusalem.[2]

You assert that the design of the instances of supernatural
interposition which the Gospel records was to convince mankind
460 that Jesus Christ was truly the expected Redeemer. But it is as
impossible that any human sophistry should frustrate the manifestation of Omnipotence, as that Omniscience should fail to
select the most efficient means of accomplishing its design. Eighteen
centuries have passed and the tenth part of the human race have a
465 blind and mechanical belief in that Redeemer, without a complete
reliance on the merits of whom, their lot is fixed in everlasting
misery: surely if the Christian system be thus dreadfully important
its Omnipotent author would have rendered it incapable of those
abuses from which it has never been exempt, and to which it is
470 subject in common with all human institutions, he would not have
left it a matter of ceaseless cavil or complete indifference to the
immense majority of mankind. Surely some more conspicuous
evidences of its authenticity would have been afforded than driving
out devils, drowning pigs, curing blind men, animating a dead body,
475 and turning water into wine. Some theatre worthier of the
transcendant event, than Judea, would have been chosen, some

---

[1] See *Matthew*, Chap. XXIII, v. 35.
[2] Josephus⟨, *The Jewish War*⟩.

historians more adapted by their accomplishments and their genius to record the incarnation of the immutable God. The humane society restores drowned persons; every empiric can cure every disease; drowning pigs is no very difficult matter, and driving out devils was far from being either an original or an unusual occupation in Judea. Do not recite these stale absurdities as proofs of the Divine origin of Christianity.

If the Almighty has spoken, would not the Universe have been convinced? If he had judged the knowledge of his will to have been more important than any other science to mankind, would he not have rendered it more evident and more clear?

Now, O Eusebes, have I enumerated the general grounds of my disbelief of the Christian Religion.—I could have collated its Sacred Writings with the Brahminical record of the early ages of the world, and identified its institutions with the antient worship of the Sun. I might have entered into an elaborate comparison of the innumerable discordances which exist between the inspired historians of the same event. Enough however has been said to vindicate me from the charge of groundless and infatuated scepticism. I trust therefore to your candour for the consideration, and to your logic for the refutation, of my arguments.

EUSEBES.

I will not dissemble, O Theosophus, the difficulty of solving your general objections to Christianity, on the grounds of human reason. I did not assist at the councils of the Almighty when he determined to extend his mercy to mankind, nor can I venture to affirm that it exceeded the limits of his power to have afforded a more conspicuous or universal manifestation of his will.

But this is a difficulty which attends Christianity in common with the belief in the being and attributes of God. This whole scheme of things might have been, according to our partial conceptions, infinitely more admirable and perfect. Poisons, earthquakes, disease, war, famine and venomous serpents; slavery and persecution are the consequences of certain causes, which according to human judgment might well have been dispensed with in arranging the economy of the globe.

Is this the reasoning which the Theist will choose to employ? Will he impose limitations on that Deity whom he professes to regard

with so profound a veneration? Will he place his God between the
horns of a logical dilemma which shall restrict the fulness either of
his power or his bounty?

Certainly he will prefer to resign his objections to Christianity,
than pursue the reasoning upon which they are founded, to the
dreadful conclusions of cold and dreary Atheism.

I confess, that Christianity appears not unattended with difficulty
to the understanding which approaches it with a determination to
judge its mysteries by reason. I will ever confess that the discourse,
which you have just delivered, ought to unsettle any candid mind
engaged in a similar attempt. The children of this world are wiser in
their generation than the children of light.

But, if I succeed in convincing you that reason conducts to
conclusions destructive of morality, happiness, and the hope of
futurity, and inconsistent with the very existence of human society, I
trust that you will no longer confide in a director so dangerous and
faithless.

I require you to declare, O Theosophus, whether you would
embrace Christianity or Atheism, if no other systems of belief shall
be found to stand the touchstone of enquiry.

THEOSOPHUS.

I do not hesitate to prefer the Christian system, or indeed any system
of religion, however rude and gross, to Atheism.—Here we truly
sympathise; nor do I blame, however I may feel inclined to pity, the
man who in his zeal to escape this gloomy faith, should plunge into
the most abject superstition.

The Atheist is a monster among men. Inducements, which are
Omnipotent over the conduct of others, are impotent for him. His
private judgment is his criterion of right and wrong. He dreads no
judge but his own conscience, he fears no hell but the loss of his self
esteem. He is not to be restrained by punishments, for death is
divested of its terror, and whatever enters into his heart, to conceive,
that will he not scruple to execute. *Iste non timet omnia providentem
et cogitantem, et animadvertentem, et omnia ad se pertinere putantem,
curiosum et plenum negotii Deum.*

This dark and terrible doctrine was surely the abortion of some
blind speculator's brain: some strange and hideous perversion of
intellect, some portentous distortion of reason. There can surely be

no metaphysician sufficiently bigotted to his own system to look upon this harmonious world, and dispute the necessity of intelligence; to contemplate the design and deny the designer; to enjoy the spectacle of this beautiful Universe and not feel himself instinctively persuaded to gratitude and adoration. What arguments of the slightest plausibility can be adduced to support a doctrine rejected alike by the instinct of the savage and the reason of the sage?   555

I readily engage, with you, to reject reason as a faithless guide, if you can demonstrate that it conducts to Atheism. So little however do I mistrust the dictates of reason, concerning a supreme Being, that I promise, in the event of your success, to subscribe the wildest and most monstrous creed which you can devise. I will call credulity, faith; reason, impiety; the dictates of the understanding shall be the temptations of the Devil, and the wildest dreams of the imagination, the infallible inspirations of Grace.   560   565

EUSEBES.

Let me request you then to state, concisely, the grounds of your belief in the being of a God. In my reply I shall endeavour to controvert your reasoning, and shall hold myself acquitted by my zeal for the Christian religion, of the blasphemies which I must utter in the progress of my discourse.   570

THEOSOPHUS.

I will readily state the grounds of my belief in the being of a God. You can only have remained ignorant of the obvious proofs of this important truth, from a superstitious reliance upon the evidence afforded by a revealed religion. The reasoning lies within an extremely narrow compass: *quicquid enim nos vel meliores vel beatiores facturum est, aut in aperto, aut in proximo posuit natura.*   575

From every design we justly infer a designer. If we examine the structure of a watch, we shall readily confess the existence of a watch-maker. No work of man could possibly have existed from all eternity. From the contemplation of any product of human art, we conclude that there was an artificer who arranged its several parts. In like manner, from the marks of design and contrivance exhibited in the Universe, we are necessitated to infer a designer, a contriver. If   580

585 the parts of the Universe have been designed, contrived and adapted, the existence of a God is manifest.

But design is sufficiently apparent. The wonderful adaptation of substances which act to those which are acted upon; of the eye to light, and of light to the eye; of the ear to sound, and of sound to the ear; of every object of sensation to the sense which it impresses prove 590 that neither blind chance, nor undistinguishing necessity has brought them into being. The adaptation of certain animals to certain climates, the relations borne to each other by animals and vegetables, and by different tribes of animals; the relation, lastly, between man and the circumstances of his external situation are so 595 many demonstrations of Deity.

All is order, design and harmony, so far as we can descry the tendency of things, and every new enlargement of our views, every new display of the material world, affords a new illustration of the power, the wisdom and the benevolence of God.

600 The existence of God has never been the topic of popular dispute. There is a tendency to devotion, a thirst for reliance on supernatural aid inherent in the human mind. Scarcely any people, however barbarous, have been discovered, who do not acknowledge with reverence and awe the supernatural causes of the natural effects 605 which they experience. They worship, it is true, the vilest and most inanimate substances, but they firmly confide in the holiness and power of these symbols, and thus own their connexion with what they can neither see nor perceive.

If there is motion in the Universe, there is a God.[1] The power of 610 beginning motion is no less an attribute of mind than sensation or thought. Wherever motion exists it is evident that mind has operated. The phenomena of the Universe indicate the agency of powers which cannot belong to inert matter.

Every thing which begins to exist must have a cause: every 615 combination, conspiring to an end, implies intelligence.

EUSEBES.

Design must be proved before a designer can be inferred. The matter in controversy is the existence of design in the Universe, and it is not permitted to assume the contested premises and thence infer the matter in dispute. Insidiously to employ the words contrivance,

¹ See Dugald Stewart's *Outlines of Moral Philosophy* and Paley's *Natural Theology*.

design and adaptation before these circumstances are made appar- 620
ent in the Universe, thence justly infering a contriver, is a popular
sophism against which it behoves us to be watchful.

To assert that motion is an attribute of mind, that matter is inert,
that every combination is the result of intelligence is also an
assumption of the matter in dispute.   625

Why do we admit design in any machine of human contrivance?
Simply, because innumerable instances of machines having been
contrived by human art are present to our mind, because we are
acquainted with persons who could construct such machines; but if,
having no previous knowledge of any artificial contrivance, we had 630
accidentally found a watch upon the ground, we should have been
justified in concluding that it was a thing of Nature, that it was a
combination of matter with whose cause we were unacquainted, and
that any attempt to account for the origin of its existence would be
equally presumptuous and unsatisfactory.   635

The analogy which you attempt to establish between the
contrivances of human art, and the various existences of the
Universe, is inadmissible. We attribute these effects to human
intelligence, because we know before hand that human intelligence
is capable of producing them. Take away this knowledge, and the 640
grounds of our reasoning will be destroyed. Our entire ignorance,
therefore, of the Divine Nature leaves this analogy defective in its
most essential point of comparison.

What consideration remains to be urged in support of the
creation of the Universe by a supreme Being? Its admirable fitness 645
for the production of certain effects, that wonderful consent of
all its parts, that universal harmony by whose changeless laws
innumerable systems of worlds perform their stated revolutions,
and the blood is driven through the veins of the minutest animalcule
that sports in the corruption of an insect's lymph: on this account 650
did the Universe require an intelligent Creator, because it exists
producing invariable effects, and inasmuch as it is admirably
organised for the production of these effects, so the more did it
require a creative intelligence.

Thus have we arrived at the substance of your assertion. "That 655
whatever exists, producing certain effects, stands in need of a
Creator, and the more conspicuous is its fitness for the production
of these effects, the more certain will be our conclusion that it would
not have existed from eternity, but must have derived its origin from
an intelligent creator."

660

In what respect then do these arguments apply to the Universe, and not apply to God? From the fitness of the Universe to its end you infer the necessity of an intelligent Creator. But if the fitness of the Universe, to produce certain effects, be thus conspicuous and
665 evident, how much more exquisite fitness to his end must exist in the Author of this Universe? If we find great difficulty from its admirable arrangement, in conceiving that the Universe has existed from all eternity, and to resolve this difficulty suppose a Creator, how much more clearly must we perceive the necessity of this very
670 Creator's creation whose perfections comprehend an arrangement far more accurate and just.

The belief of an infinity of creative and created Gods, each more eminently requiring an intelligent author of his being than the foregoing, is a direct consequence of the premises which you have
675 stated. The assumption that the Universe is a design, leads to a conclusion that there are ⟨an⟩ infinity of creative and created Gods, which is absurd. It is impossible indeed to prescribe limits to learned error, when Philosophy relinquishes experience and feeling for speculation.

680 Until it is clearly proved that the Universe was created, we may reasonably suppose that it has endured from all eternity. In a case where two propositions are diametrically opposite, the mind believes that which is less incomprehensible: it is easier to suppose that the Universe has existed, from all eternity, than to conceive an
685 eternal being capable of creating it. If the mind sinks beneath the weight of one, is it an alleviation to encrease the intolerability of the burthen?

A man knows, not only that he now is, but that there was a time when he did not exist; consequently there must have been a cause.
690 But we can only infer, from effects, causes exactly adequate to those effects. There certainly is a generative power which is effected by particular instruments; we cannot prove that it is inherent in these instruments, nor is the contrary hypothesis capable of demonstration. We admit that the generative power is
695 incomprehensible, but to suppose that the same effects are produced by an eternal Omnipotent and Omniscient Being, leaves the cause in the same obscurity, but renders it more incomprehensible.

We can only infer from effects causes exactly adequate to those effects.—An infinite number of effects demand an infinite number of
700 causes, nor is the philosopher justified in supposing a greater

connection or unity in the latter, than is perceptible in the former. The same energy cannot be at once the cause of the serpent and the sheep; of the blight by which the harvest is destroyed, and the sunshine by which it is matured; of the ferocious propensities by which man becomes a victim to himself, and of the accurate judgment by which his institutions are improved. The spirit of our accurate and exact philosophy is outraged by conclusions which contradict each other so glaringly.

The greatest, equally with the smallest motions of the Universe, are subjected to the rigid necessity of inevitable laws. These laws are the unknown causes of the known effects perceivable in the Universe. Their effects are the boundaries of our knowledge, their names the expressions of our ignorance. To suppose some existence beyond, or above them, is to invent a second and superfluous hypothesis to account for what has already been accounted for by the laws of motion and the properties of matter. I admit that the nature of these laws is incomprehensible, but the hypothesis of a Deity adds a gratuitous difficulty, which so far from alleviating those which it is adduced to explain, requires new hypotheses for the elucidation of its own inherent contradictions.

The laws of attraction and repulsion, desire and aversion, suffice to account for every phenomenon of the moral and physical world. A precise knowledge of the properties of any object, is alone requisite to determine its manner of action. Let the mathematician be acquainted with the weight and volume of a cannon ball, together with the degree of velocity and inclination with which it is impelled, and he will accurately delineate the course it must describe, and determine the force with which it will strike an object at a given distance. Let the influencing motive, present to the mind of any person be given, and the knowledge of his consequent conduct will result. Let the bulk and velocity of a comet be discovered, and the astronomer, by the accurate estimation of the equal and contrary actions of the centripetal and centrifugal forces, will justly predict the period of its return.

The anomalous motions of the heavenly bodies, their unequal velocities and frequent aberrations, are corrected by that gravitation by which they are caused. The illustrious Laplace, has shewn, that the approach of the Moon to the Earth and the Earth to the Sun, is only a secular equation of a very long period, which has its maximum and minimum. The system of the Universe then is upheld solely by

physical powers. The necessity of matter is the ruler of the world. It is vain philosophy which supposes more causes than are exactly adequate to explain the phenomena of things. *Hypotheses non fingo: quicquid enim ex phænomenis non deducitur, hypothesis vocanda est; et*
745 *hypotheses vel metaphysicæ, vel physicæ, vel qualitatum occultarum, seu mechanicæ, in philosophiâ locum non habent.*

You assert that the construction of the animal machine, the fitness of certain animals to certain situations, the connexion between the organs of perception and that which is perceived; the relation
750 between every thing which exists, and that which tends to preserve it in its existence, imply design. It is manifest that if the eye could not see, nor the stomach digest, the human frame could not preserve its present mode of existence. It is equally certain, however, that the elements of its composition, if they did not exist in one form, must
755 exist in another; and that the combinations which they would form, must so long as they endured, derive support for their peculiar mode of being from their fitness to the circumstances of their situation.

It by no means follows, that because a being exists, performing certain functions, he was fitted by another being to the performance
760 of these functions. So rash a conclusion would conduct, as I have before shewn, to an absurdity; and it becomes infinitely more unwarrantable from the consideration that the known laws of matter and motion, suffice to unravel, even in the present imperfect state of moral and physical science, the majority of those difficulties
765 which the hypothesis of a Deity was invented to explain.

Doubtless no disposition of inert matter, or matter deprived of qualities, could ever have composed an animal, a tree, or even a stone. But matter deprived of qualities, is an abstraction, concerning which it is impossible to form an idea. Matter, such as we behold it, is
770 not inert. It is infinitely active and subtile. Light, electricity and magnetism are fluids not surpassed by thought itself in tenuity and activity: like thought they are sometimes the cause and sometimes the effect of motion; and, distinct as they are from every other class of substances, with which we are acquainted, seem to possess equal
775 claims with thought to the unmeaning distinction of immateriality.

The laws of motion and the properties of matter suffice to account for every phenomenon, or combination of phenomena exhibited in the Universe. That certain animals exist in certain climates, results from the consentaneity of their frames to the circumstances of their
780 situation: let these circumstances be altered to a sufficient degree,

and the elements of their composition, must exist in some new combination no less resulting than the former from those inevitable laws by which the Universe is governed.

It is the necessary consequence of the organization of man, that his stomach should digest his food: it inevitably results also from his gluttonous and unnatural appetite for the flesh of animals that his frame be diseased and his vigour impaired; but in neither of these cases is adaptation of means to end to be perceived. Unnatural diet, and the habits consequent upon its use are the means, and every complication of frightful disease is the end, but to assert that these means were adapted to this end by the Creator of the world, or that human caprice can avail to traverse the precautions of Omnipotence, is absurd. These are the consequences of the properties of organized matter; and it is a strange perversion of the understanding to argue that a certain sheep was created to be butchered and devoured by a certain individual of the human species, when the conf⟨o⟩rmation of the latter, as is manifest to the most superficial student of comparative anatomy, classes him with those animals who feed on fruits and vegetables.[1]

The means by which the existence of an animal is sustained, requires a designer in no greater degree than the existence itself of the animal. If it exists, there must be means to support its existence. In a world where *omne mutatur nihil interit*, no organized being can exist without a continual separation of that substance which is incessantly exhausted, nor can this separation take place otherwise, than by the invariable laws which result from the relations of matter.

[1] See ⟨Georges⟩ Cuvier *Leçons d'Anat⟨omie⟩ Comp⟨arée⟩*, tom. iii⟨,⟩ p⟨p⟩. 169, 373, 448, 465, 480.—Rees's *Cyclopædia*, Art⟨icle⟩ Man.

Ουκ αιδεισθε τους ημερους καρπους αιματι και φονῳ μιγνυοντες; αλλα δρακοντας αγριους καλειτε, και παρδαλεις και λεοντας, αθτοι δε μιαιφονειτε εις ωμοτητα καταλιποντες εκεινοις ουδεν. Εκεινοις μεν ὁ φονος τροφη, ὑμιν δε οψον εστιν.

Ὁτι γαρ ουκ εστιν ανθρωπῳ κατα φυσιν το σαρκοφαγειν, πρωτον μεν απο των σωματων δηλουται της κατασκευης. Ουδενι γαρ εοικε το ανθρωπου σωμα των ⟨επι⟩ σαρκοφαγιᾳ γεγονοτων. ου γρυποτης χειλους, ουκ οξυτης ονυχος, ου τραχυτης οδοντων προσεστιν, ου κοιλιας ευτονια και πνευματος θερμοτης τρεψαι και κατεργασασθαι το βαρυ και κρεωδες. Αλλ᾽ αυτοθεν ἡ φυσις τῃ λειοτητι των οδοντων, και τῃ σμικροτητι του σ⟨το⟩ματος, και τῃ μαλακοτητι της γλωσσης, και τῃ προς πεψιν αμβλυτητι του πνευματος, εξομνυται την σαρκοφαγιαν· Ει δε λεγεις πεφυκεναι σεαυτον επι τοιαυτην εδωδην, ὁ βουλει φαγειν, πρωτον αυτος αποκτεινον, αλλ᾽ αυτος δια σεαυτου, μη χρησαμενος κοπιδι, μηδε τυμπανῳ τινι, μηδε πελεκει· αλλα ὡς λυκοι και αρκτοι και λεοντες αυτοι ὡς εσθιουσι φονευουσιν, ανελε δηγματι βουν, η σ⟨το⟩ματι συν, η αρνα η λαγωον διαρρηξον, και φαγε προσπεσων ετι ζωντος, ὡς εκεινα.

Πλουτ⟨αρχου⟩ περι Σαρκοφαγ⟨ιας⟩ Λογ⟨ος⟩ ⟨α⟩.

We are incapacitated only by our ignorance from referring every phenomenon, however unusual, minute or complex, to the laws of motion and the properties of matter; and it is an egregious offence 810 against the first principles of reason, to suppose an immaterial creator of the world, *in quo omnia moventur sed sine mutuâ passione*; which is equally a superfluous hypothesis in the mechanical philosophy of Newton, and an useless excrescence on the inductive logic of Bacon.

815   What then is this harmony, this order which you maintain to have required for its establishment, what it needs not for its maintenance, the agency of a supernatural intelligence? Inasmuch as the order visible in the Universe requires one cause, so does the disorder whose operation is not less clearly apparent, demand another. 820 Order and disorder are no more than modifications of our own perceptions of the relations which subsist between ourselves and external objects, and if we are justified in inferring the operation of a benevolent power from the advantages attendant on the former, the evils of the latter bear equal testimony to the activity of a 825 malignant principle, no less pertinacious in inducing evil out of good than the other is unremitting in procuring good from evil.

If we permit our imagination to traverse the obscure regions of possibility, we may doubtless imagine, according to the complexion of our minds, that disorder may have a relative tendency to 830 unmingled good, or order be relatively replete with exquisite and subtile evil. To neither of these conclusions, which are equally presumptuous and unfounded, will it become the philosopher to assent. Order and disorder are expressions denoting our perceptions of what is injurious or beneficial to ourselves, or to the 835 beings in whose welfare we are compelled to sympathize by the similarity of their conformation to our own.[1]

A beautiful antelope panting under the fangs of a tiger, a defenceless ox, groaning beneath the butcher's axe, is a spectacle which instantly awakens compassion in a virtuous and unvitiated 840 breast. Many there are, however, sufficiently hardened to the rebukes of justice and the precepts of humanity, as to regard the deliberate butchery of thousands of their species, as a theme of exultation and a source of honour, and to consider any failure in these remorseless enterprises as a defect in the system of things. The

[1] See ⟨William⟩ Godwin's *Political Justice*, Vol. I, p. 449.

criteria of order and disorder are as various as those beings from 845 whose opinions and feelings they result.

Populous cities are destroyed by earthquakes, and desolated by pestilence. Ambition is every where devoting its millions to incalculable calamity. Superstition, in a thousand shapes, is employed in brutalizing and degrading the human species, and 850 fitting it to endure without a murmur the oppression of its innumerable tyrants. All this is abstractedly neither good nor evil because good and evil are words employed to designate that peculiar state of our own perceptions, resulting from the encounter of any object calculated to produce pleasure or pain. Exclude the idea of 855 relation, and the words good and evil are deprived of import.

Earthquakes are injurious to the cities which they destroy, beneficial to those whose commerce was injured by their prosperity, and indifferent to others which are too remote to be affected by their influence. Famine is good to the corn-merchant, evil to the poor, and 860 indifferent to those whose fortunes can at all times command a superfluity. Ambition is evil to the restless bosom it inhabits, to the innumerable victims who are dragged by its ruthless thirst for infamy, to expire in every variety of anguish, to the inhabitants of the country it depopulates, and to the human race whose improvement 865 it retards; it is indifferent with regard to the system of the Universe, and is good only to the vultures and the jackalls that track the conqueror's career, and to the worms who feast in security on the desolation of his progress. It is manifest that we cannot reason with respect to the universal system from that which only exists in 870 relation to our own perceptions.

You allege some considerations in favor of a Deity from the universality of a belief in his existence.

The superstitions of the savage, and the religion of civilized Europe appear to you to conspire to prove a first cause. I maintain 875 that it is from the evidence of revelation alone that this belief derives the slightest countenance.

That credulity should be gross in proportion to the ignorance of the mind which it enslaves, is in strict consistency with the principles of human nature. The idiot, the child and the savage, agree 880 in attributing their own passions and propensities[1] to the inanimate substances by which they are either benefited or injured. The former become Gods and the latter Demons; hence prayers and sacrifices,

[1] See ⟨Robert⟩ Southey's *History of Brazil*, p. 255.

by the means of which the rude Theologian imagines that he may
885 confirm the benevolence of the one, or mitigate the malignity of the
other. He has averted the wrath of a powerful enemy by supplications and submission; he has secured the assistance of his
neighbour by offerings; he has felt his own anger subside before the
entreaties of a vanquished foe, and has cherished gratitude for the
890 kindness of another. Therefore does he believe that the elements will
listen to his vows. He is capable of love and hatred towards his fellow
beings, and is variously impelled by those principles to benefit or
injure them. The source of his error is sufficiently obvious. When the
winds, the waves and the atmosphere, act in such a manner as to
895 thwart or forward his designs, he attributes to them the same
propensities of whose existence within himself he is conscious when
he is instigated by benefits to kindness, or by injuries to revenge. The
bigot of the woods can form no conception of beings possessed of
properties differing from his own: it requires, indeed, a mind
900 considerably tinctured with science, and enlarged by cultivation to
contemplate itself, not as the centre and model of the Universe, but
as one of the infinitely various multitude of beings of which it is
actually composed.

There is no attribute of God which is not either borrowed from
905 the passions and powers of the human mind, or which is not a
negation. Omniscience, Omnipotence, Omnipresence, Infinity,
Immutability, Incomprehensibility, and Immateriality, are all
words which designate properties and powers peculiar to organized
beings, with the addition of negations, by which the idea of
910 limitation is excluded.[1]

That the frequency of a belief in God (for it is not Universal)
should be any argument in its favour, none to whom the innumerable mistakes of men are familiar, will assert. It is among
men of genius and science that Atheism alone is found, but among
915 these alone is cherished an hostility to those errors, with which the
illiterate and vulgar are infected.

How small is the proportion of those who really believe in God, to
the thousands who are prevented by their occupations from ever
bestowing a serious thought upon the subject, and the millions who
920 worship butterflies, bones, feathers, monkeys, calabashes and
serpents. The word God, like other abstractions, signifies the

---

[1] See (Baron d'Holbach's) Le Système de la Nature: this book is one of the most eloquent
vindications of Atheism.

agreement of certain propositions, rather than the presence of any idea. If we found our belief in the existence of God on the universal consent of mankind, we are duped by the most palpable of sophisms. The word God cannot mean at the same time an ape, a snake, a bone, a calabash, a Trinity and a Unity: Nor can that belief be accounted universal against which men of powerful intellect and spotless virtue have in every age protested. *Non pudet igitur physicum, id est speculatorem venatoremque naturæ, ex animis consuetudine imbutis petere testimonium veritatis?*

Hume has shewn, to the satisfaction of all philosophers, that the only idea which we can form of causation is ⟨derivable⟩ from the constant conjunction of objects, and the consequent inference of one from the other. We denominate that phenomenon the cause of another which we observe with the fewest exceptions to precede its occurrence. Hence it would be inadmissible to deduce the being of a God from the existence of the Universe; even if this mode of reasoning did not conduct to the monstrous conclusion of an infinity of creative and created Gods, each more eminently requiring a Creator than its predecessor.

If Power[1] be an attribute of existing substance, substance could not have derived its origin from power. One thing cannot be at the same time the cause and the effect of another.—The word power expresses the capability of any thing to be or act. The human mind never hesitates to annex the idea of power to any object of its experience. To deny that power is the attribute of being, is to deny that being can be. If power be an attribute of substance, the hypothesis of a God is a superfluous and unwarrantable assumption.

Intelligence is that attribute of the Deity, which you hold to be most apparent in the Universe. Intelligence is only known to us as a mode of animal being. We cannot conceive intelligence distinct from sensation and perception, which are attributes to organized bodies. To assert that God is intelligent, is to assert that he has ideas; and Locke has proved that ideas result from sensation. Sensation can exist only in an organized body, and organized body is necessarily limited both in extent and operation. The God of the rational Theosophist is a vast and wise animal.

You have laid it down as a maxim that the power of beginning motion is an attribute of mind as much as thought and sensation.

[1] For a very profound disquisition on this subject, see Sir William Drummond's *Academical Questions*, Chap. I, p. 1.

960   Mind cannot create, it can only perceive. Mind is the recipient of impressions made on the organs of sense, and without the action of external objects we should not only be deprived of all knowledge of the existence of mind, but totally incapable of the knowledge of any thing. It is evident therefore that mind deserves to be considered as
965   the effect, rather than the cause of motion. The ideas which suggest themselves too are prompted by the circumstances of our situation, these are the elements of thought, and from the various combinations of these our feelings, opinions and volitions, inevitably result.

That which is infinite necessarily includes that which is finite. The
970   distinction therefore between the Universe, and that by which the Universe is upheld, is manifestly erroneous. To devise the word God, that you may express a certain portion of the universal system, can answer no good purpose in philosophy: In the language of reason, the words God and Universe are synonimous. *Omnia*
975   *enim per Dei potentiam facta sunt: imo, quia naturæ potentia nulla est nisi ipsa Dei potentia, certum est nos eatenus Dei potentiam non intelligere quatenus causas naturales ignoramus; adeoque stultè ad eandem Dei potentiam recurritur, quando rei alicujus, causam naturalem, hoc est, ipsam Dei potentiam ignoramus.* [1]

980   Thus, from the principles of that reason to which you so rashly appealed as the ultimate arbiter of our dispute, have I shewn that the popular arguments in favour of the being of a God are totally destitute of colour. I have shewn the absurdity of attributing intelligence to the cause of those effects which we perceive in the
985   Universe, and the fallacy which lurks in the argument from design. I have shewn that order is no more than a peculiar manner of contemplating the operation of necessary agents, that mind is the effect, not the cause of motion, that power is the attribute, not the origin of Being. I have proved that we can have no evidence of the
990   existence of a God from the principles of reason.

You will have observed, from the zeal with which I have urged arguments so revolting to my genuine sentiments, and conducted to a conclusion in direct contradiction to that faith which every good man must eternally preserve, how little I am inclined to sympathise
995   with those of my religion who have pretended to prove the existence of God by the unassisted light of reason. I confess that the necessity of a revelation has been compromised by treacherous friends to

---

[1] Spinosa, *Tract⟨atus⟩ Theologico-Pol⟨iticus,⟩* Chap. I, p. 14.

Christianity, who have maintained that the sublime mysteries of the being of a God and the immortality of the soul are discoverable from other sources than itself.

I have proved, that on the principles of that philosophy to which Epicurus, Lord Bacon, Newton, Locke and Hume were addicted, the existence of God is a chimera.

The Christian Religion then, alone, affords indisputable assurance that the world was created by the power, and is preserved by the Providence of an Almighty God, who, in justice has appointed a future life for the punishment of the vicious and the remuneration of the virtuous.

Now, O Theosophus, I call upon you to decide between Atheism and Christianity; to declare whether you will pursue your principles to the destruction of the bonds of civilized society, or wear the easy yoke of that Religion which proclaims "peace upon earth, good-will to all men."

THEOSOPHUS.

I am not prepared at present, I confess, to reply clearly to your unexpected arguments. I assure you that no considerations, however specious, should seduce me to deny the existence of my Creator.

I am willing to promise that if, after mature deliberation, the arguments which you have advanced in favour of Atheism should appear incontrovertible, I will endeavour to adopt so much of the Christian scheme as is consistent with my persuasion of the goodness, unity and majesty of God.

THE ASSASSINS
A FRAGMENT OF A ROMANCE

Chapter First

Jerusalem, goaded on to resistance by the incessant usurpations and insolence of Rome, leagued together its discordant factions to rebel against the common enemy and tyrant. Inferior to their foe in all but the unconquerable hope of liberty they surrounded their city with
5 fortifications of uncommon strength and placed in array before the temple a band rendered desperate by patriotism and religion. Even the women preferred to die rather than survive the ruin of their country. When the Roman army approached the walls of the sacred city, its preparations, its discipline and its numbers evinced the
10 conviction of its leader that he had no common barbarians to subdue. At the approach of the Roman army the strangers withdrew from the city.

Among the multitudes which from every nation of the East had assembled at Jerusalem was a little congregation of Christians. They
15 were remarkable neither for their numbers nor their importance. They contained among them neither philosophers nor poets. Acknowledging no laws but those of God they modelled their conduct towards their fellow men by the conclusions of their individual judgement on the practical application of these laws. And
20 it was apparent from the simplicity and severity of their manners that this contempt for human institutions had produced among them a character superior in singleness and sincere self apprehension to the slavery of pagan customs and the gross delusions of antiquated superstition. Many of their opinions considerably
25 resembled those of the sect afterwards known by the name of Gnostics. They esteemed the human understanding to be the paramount rule of human conduct, they maintained that the obscurest religious truth required for its complete elucidation no more than the strenuous application of the energies of mind. It
30 appeared impossible to them that any doctrine could be subversive

of social happiness which is not capable of being confuted by arguments derived from the nature of existing things. With the devoutest submission to the law of Christ they united an intrepid spirit of enquiry as to the correctest mode of acting in particular instances of conduct that occur among men. Assuming the doctrines of the Messiah concerning benevolence and justice for the regulation of their actions they could not be persuaded to acknowledge that there was apparent in the divine code any prescribed rule whereby for its own sake one action rather than another, as fulfilling the will of their great master, should be preferred.

The contempt with which the magistracy and priesthood regarded this obscure community of speculators had hitherto protected them from persecution. But they had arrived at that precise degree of eminence and prosperity which is peculiarly obnoxious to the hostility of the rich and powerful. The moment of their departure from Jerusalem was the crisis of their future destiny. Had they continued to seek a precarious refuge in a city of the Roman empire this persecution would not have delayed to impress a new character on their opinions and their conduct. Narrow views and the illiberality of sectarian patriotism would not have failed speedily to obliterate the magnificence and beauty of their wild and wonderful condition.

Attached from principle to peace, despising and hating the pleasures and the customs of the ⟨de⟩generate mass of mankind, this unostentatious community of good and happy men fled to the solitudes of Lebanon. To Arabians and enthusiasts the solemnity and grandeur of these desolate recesses possessed peculiar attractions. It well accorded with the justice of their conceptions on the relative duties of man towards his fellow in society that they should labour in unconstrained equality to dispossess the wolf and the tiger of their empire and establish on its ruins the dominion of intelligence and virtue. No longer would the worshippers of the God of nature be indebted to a hundred hands for the accommodation of their simple wants. No longer would the poison of a diseased civilization embrue their very nutriment with pestilence. They would no longer owe their very existence to the vices, the fears and the follies of mankind. Love, friendship and philanthropy would now be the characteristic disposers of their industry. It is for his mistress or his friend that the labourer consecrates his toil. Others are mindful but he is forgetful of himself. "God feeds the hungry ravens, and clothes the lillies of the fields, and yet Solomon in all his glory is not like to one of these."

Rome was now the shadow of her former self. The light of her grandeur and loveliness had passed away. The latest and the noblest of her poets and historians had foretold in agony her approaching slavery and degradation. The ruins of the human mind, more awful and portentous than the desolation of the most solemn temples, threw a shade of gloom upon her golden palaces which the brutal vulgar could not see but which the mighty felt with inward trepidation and despair. The ruins of Jerusalem lay defenceless and uninhabited upon the burning sands. None visited, but in the depth of solemn awe, this accursed and solitary spot. Tradition says that there was seen to linger among the scorched and shattered fragments of the temple one being, whom he that saw dared not to call man, with clasped hands, immoveable eyes and a visage horribly serene. Not on the will of the capricious multitude nor the constant fluctuations of the many and the weak depends the change of empires and religions. These are the mere insensible elements from which a subtler intelligence moulds its enduring statuary. They that direct the changes of this mortal scene breathe the decrees of their dominion from a throne of darkness and of tempest. The power of man is great.

After many days of wandering the Assassins pitched their tents in the valley of Bethzatanai. For ages had this fertile valley lain concealed from the adventurous search of man among mountains of everlasting snow. The men of elder days had inhabited this spot. Piles of monumental marble and fragments of columns that in their integrity almost seemed the work of some intelligence more sportive and fantastic than the gross conceptions of mortality lay in heaps beside the lake and were visible beneath its transparent waves. The flowering orange tree, the balsam and innumerable odoriferous shrubs grew wild in the desolated portals. The fountain tanks had overflowed and amid the luxuriant vegetation of their margin the yellow snake held its unmolested dwelling. Hither came the tiger and the bear to contend for those once domestic animals who had forgotten the secure servitude of their ancestors. No sound, when the famished beast of prey had retreated in despair from the awful desolation of this place at whose completion he had assisted, but the shrill cry of the stork and the flapping of his heavy wings from the capital of the solitary column and the scream of the hungry vulture baffled of its only victim. The lore of ancient wisdom was sculptured in mystic characters on the rocks. The human spirit and the human hand had been busy here to accomplish its profoundest miracles. It was a temple dedicated to the God of knowledge and of truth. The palaces of the Califs and the Cæsars might easily surpass these ruins in magnitude and sumptuousness. But they were the design of tyrants and the work of slaves. Piercing genius and consummate prudence had planned and executed Bethzatanai. There was deep and important meaning in every lineament of its fantastic sculpture. The unintelligible legend once so beautiful and perfect, so full of poetry and history, spoke, even in destruction, volumes of mysterious import, and obscure significance.

But in the season of its utmost prosperity and magnificence art might not aspire to vie with nature in the valley of Bethzatanai. All that was wonderful and lovely was collected in this deep seclusion. The fluctuating elements seemed to have been rendered ever-lastingly permanent in forms of wonder and delight. The moun-tains of Lebanon had been divided to their base to form this happy valley; on every side their icy summits darted their white pin-nacles into the clear blue sky, imaging in their grotesque outline minarets and ruined domes and columns worn with time. Far below the silver clouds rolled their bright volumes in many beautiful shapes and fed the eternal springs that spanning the dark chasms like a thousand radiant rainbows leaped into the quiet vale, then lingering in many a dark glade among the groves of cypress and of palm lost themselves in the lake. The immensity of those precipitous mountains with their starry pyramids of snow excluded the sun, which overtopped not even in its meridian their overhanging rocks. But a more heavenly and serener light was reflected from their icy mirrors, which piercing through the many tinted clouds produced lights and colours of inexhaustible variety. The herbage was per-petually verdant and clothed the darkest recesses of the caverns and the woods.

Nature undisturbed had become an enchantress in these solitudes. She had collected here all that was wonderful and divine from the armory of her omnipotence. The very winds breathed health and renovation and the joyousness of youthful courage. Fountains of chrystalline water played perpetually among the aromatic flowers and mingled a freshness with their odour. The pine boughs became instruments of exquisite contrivance among which every varying breeze waked music of new and more delightful melody. Meteoric shapes more effulgent than the moonlight hung on the wandering clouds and mixed in discordant dance around the spiral fountains. Blue vapours assumed strange lineaments under the rocks and among the ruins, lingering like ghosts with slow and solemn step. Through a dark chasm to the east, in the long perspective of a portal glittering with the unnumbered riches of the subterranean world, shone the broad moon, pouring in one yellow and unbroken stream her horizontal beams. Nearer the icy region autumn and spring held an alternate reign. The sear leaves fell and choked the sluggish brooks. The chilling fogs hung diamonds on every spray and in the dark cold evening the howling winds made melancholy music in the trees. Far above shone the bright throne of winter, clear, cold and dazzling. Sometimes there was seen the snow flakes to fall before the sinking orb of the beamless sun like a shower of fiery sulphur. The cataracts arrested in their course seemed with their transparent columns to support the dark browed rocks. Sometimes the icy whirlwind scooped the powdery snow aloft to mingle with the hissing meteors and scatter spangles through the rare and rayless atmosphere.

Such strange scenes of chaotic confusion and harrowing sublimity surrounding and shutting in the vale added to the delights of its secure and voluptuous tranquillity. No spectator could have refused to believe that some spirit of great intelligence and power had hallowed these wild and beautiful solitudes to a deep and solemn mystery.

The immediate effect of such a scene suddenly presented to the contemplation of mortal eyes is seldom the subject of authentic record. The coldest slave of custom cannot fail to recollect some few moments in which the breath of spring or the crowding clouds of sunset with the pale moon shining through their fleecy skirts, or the song of some lonely bird perched on the only tree of an unfrequented heath, has awakened the touch of nature. And they were Arabians who entered the valley of Bethzatanai, men who idolized nature and the God of nature, to whom love and lofty thoughts and the apprehensions of an uncorrupted spirit were sustenance and life. Thus securely excluded from an abhorred world, all thought of its judgement was cancelled by the rapidity of their fervid imaginations. They ceased to acknowledge or deigned not to advert to the distinctions with which the majority of base and vulgar

minds controul the longings and struggles of the soul towards its
place of rest. A new and sacred fire was kindled in their hearts and
sparkled in their eyes. Every gesture, every feature, the minutest
action was modelled to beneficence and beauty by the holy
inspiration that had descended on their searching spirits. The 195
epidemic transport communicated itself through every heart with
the rapidity of a blast from heaven. They were already disembodied
spirits, they were already the inhabitants of Paradise. To live, to
breathe, to move was itself a sensation of immeasurable transport.
Every new contemplation of the condition of his nature brought to 200
the happy enthusiast an added measure of delight, impelled to every
organ where mind is united with external things a keener and more
exquisite perception of all that they contain of lovely and divine. To
love, to be beloved suddenly became an insatiable famine of his
nature which the wide circle of the universe comprehending beings 205
of such inexhaustible variety and stupendous magnitude of
excellence appeared too narrow and confined to satiate.

Alas! that these visitings of the spirit of life should fluctuate
and pass away. That the moments when the human mind is
commensurate with all that it can conceive of excellent and power- 210
ful should not endure with its existence and survive its most
momentous change. But the beauty of a vernal sunset with its
overhanging curtains of empurpled cloud is rapidly dissolved to
return at some unexpected period and spread an alleviating
melancholy over the dark vigils of despair. 215

It is true the enthusiasm of overwhelming transport which had
inspired every breast among the Assassins is no more. The necessity
of daily occupation and the ordinariness of that human life, the
burthen of which it is the destiny of every human being to bear, had
smothered, not extinguished, that divine and eternal fire. Not the 220
less indelible and permanent were the impressions communicated to
all; not the more unalterably were the features of their social
character modelled and determined by its influence.

Chapter Second

Rome had fallen. Her senate house had become a polluted den of
thieves and liars. Her solemn temples, the arena of Theological 225
disputants who made fire and sword the missionaries of their
inconceivable beliefs. The city of the monster Constantine, sym-
bolizing in the consequences of its foundation the wickedness

and weakness of his successors, feebly imaged with declining power
230 the substantial eminence of the Roman name. Pilgrims of a new and
mightier faith crowded to visit the lonely ruins of Jerusalem and
weep and pray before the sepulchre of the eternal God. The earth
was filled with discord, tumult and ruin. The spirit of disinterested
virtue had armed one half of the civilized world against the other.
235 Monstrous and detestable creeds poisoned and blighted the
domestic charities. There was no appeal to natural love or ancient
faith from pride, superstition and revenge.

Four centuries had passed thus terribly characterized by the most
calamitous revolutions. The Assassins mean while undisturbed by
240 the surrounding tumult possessed and cultivated their fertile valley.
The gradual operation of their peculiar condition had matured and
perfected the singularity and excellence of their character. That
cause which had ceased to act as an immediate and overpowering
excitement became the unperceived law of their lives and sustenance
245 of their natures. Their religious tenets had also undergone a change
corresponding with the exalted condition of their moral being. The
gratitude which they owed to the benignant spirit by which their
limited intelligences had not only been created but redeemed was
less frequently adverted to, became less the topic of comment or
250 contemplation. Not therefore did it cease to be their presiding
guardian, the guide of their inmost thoughts, the tribunal of appeal
for the minutest particulars of their conduct. They learned to
identify this mysterious benefactor with the delight that is bred
among the solitary rocks and has its dwelling alike in the changing
255 colours of the clouds and the inmost recesses of the caverns. Their
future also no longer existed but ⟨in the⟩ blissful tranquillity of the
present. Time was measured and created by the vices and the
miseries of men between whom and the happy nation of the
Assassins there was no analogy or comparison. Already had their
260 eternal peace commenced. The darkness had passed away from the
open gates of death.

The practical results produced by their faith and condition upon
their external conduct were singular and memorable. Excluded from
the great and various community of mankind these solitudes
265 became to them a sacred hermitage in which all formed, as it were,
one being divided against itself by no contending will or factious passions. Every impulse conspired to one end and tended to a single
object. Each devoted his powers to the happiness of the other. Their

republic was the scene of the perpetual contentions of benevolence; not the heartless and assumed kindness of commercial man but the genuine virtue that has a legible superscription in every feature of the countenance and every motion of the frame. The perverseness and calamities of those who dwelt beyond the mountains that encircled their undisturbed possession were unknown and unimagined. Little embarrassed by the complexities of civilized society they knew not to conceive of any happiness that can be satiated without participation or that thirsts not to reproduce and perpetually generate itself. The path of virtue and felicity was plain and unimpeded. They clearly acknowledged in every case that conduct to be entitled to preference which would obviously produce the greatest pleasure. They could not conceive an instance in which it would be their duty to hesitate in causing at whatever expence the greatest and most unmixed delight.

Hence arose a peculiarity which only failed to germinate in uncommon and momentous consequences because the Assassins had retired from the intercourse of mankind over whom other motives and principles of conduct than justice and benevolence prevail. It would be a difficult matter for men of such a sincere and simple faith to estimate the final results of their intentions among the corrupt and slavish multitude. They would be perplexed also in their choice of the means whereby their intentions might be fulfilled. To produce immediate pain or disorder for the sake of future benefit is consonant indeed with the purest religion and philosophy; but never fails to excite invincible repugnance in the feelings of the many. Against their predilections and distastes an Assassin accidentally the inhabitant of a civilized community would wage unremitting hostility from principle. He would find himself compelled to adopt means which they would abhor for the sake of an object which they could not conceive that he should propose to himself. Secure and self enshrined in the magnificence and pre-eminence of his conceptions, spotless as the light of Heaven, he would be the victim among men of calumny and persecution. Incapable of distinguishing his motives they would rank him among the vilest and most atrocious criminals. Great beyond all comparison with them they would despise him in the presumption of their ignorance. Because his spirit burned with an unquenchable passion for their welfare they would lead him like his illustrious master amidst scoffs and mockery and insult to the remuneration of an ignominious death.

310　Who hesitates to destroy a venemous serpent that has crept near his sleeping friend but the man who selfishly dreads lest the malignant reptile should turn its fury on himself. And if the poisoner has assumed a human shape, if the bane be distinguished only from the viper's venom by the excess and extent of its devastation, will the
315　saviour and avenger here retract and pause entrenched behind the superstition of the indefeasible divinity of man? Is the human form then the mere badge of a prerogative for unlicenced wickedness and mischief? Can the power derived from the weakness of the oppressed or the ignorance of the deceived confer the right in
320　security to tyrannize and defraud?

The subject of regular governments and the disciple of established superstition dares not to ask this question. For the sake of the eventual benefit, he endures what he esteems a transitory evil: and the moral degradation of man disquiets not his patience. But the
325　religion of an Assassin imposes other virtues than endurance, when his fellow men groan under tyranny, or have become so bestial and abject that they cannot feel their chains.—An Assassin believes that man is eminently man, and only then enjoys the prerogatives of his priviledged condition when his affections and his judgement pay
330　tribute to the God of [Nature]. The perverse and vile and vicious— what were they? Shapes of some unholy vision moulded by the Spirit of Evil, which the sword of the merciful destroyer should sweep from this beautiful world. Dreamy nothings, phantasms of misery and mischief that hold their deathlike state on glittering thrones and
335　in the loathsome dens of poverty. No Assassin would submissively temporize with vice, and in cold charity became a pandar to falshood and desolation. His path thro' the wilderness of civilized society would be marked with the blood of the oppressor and the ruiner. The wretch whom nations tremblingly adore would expiate in his
340　throttling grasp a thousand licensed and venerable crimes. How many holy liars, and parasites in solemn guise, would his saviour arm drag from their luxurious couches, and plunge in the cold charnel, that the green and many legged monsters of the slimy grave might eat off at their leisure the lineaments of rooted malignity and
345　detested cunning. [The respectable man, the smooth, smiling, polished villain, whom all the city honours, whose very trade is lies and murder, who buys his daily bread with the blood and tears of men, would feed the ravens with his limbs. The Assassin would cater nobly for the eyeless worms of Earth and the carrion fowls of
350　Heaven.—

Yet pure religion and human love had imbued the manners of those solitary people with inexpressible gentleness and benignity. Courage and active virtue and the indignation against vice which becomes a hurrying and irresistible passion slept like the imprisoned earthquake, or the lightning-shafts that hang ⟨id⟩ly in the golden clouds of evening. They were innocent, but they were capable of more than innocence; for the great principles of their faith were perpetually acknowledged and adverted [to]. Nor had they forgotten in this uninterrupted quiet the author of their felicity.] 355

Four centuries had thus worn away without producing an event. Men had died and natural tears had been shed upon their graves in sorrow that improves the heart. Those who had been united by love had gone to death together, leaving to their friends the bequest of a most sacred grief and of a sadness that is allied to pleasure.—Babes that hung upon their mothers' breasts had become men. Men had died ... and many a wild, luxuriant weed that overtopped the habitations of the vale had twined its roots round their disregarded bones. Their tranquil state was like a summer sea whose gentle undulations disturb not the reflected stars, and break not the long still line of the rainbow hues of sunrise. 360

365

370

⟨Chapter⟩ Third

Where all is thus calm the slightest circumstance is recorded and remembered. Before the sixth century had expired one incident occurred remarkable and strange. A young man named Albedir, wandering in the woods, was startled by the screaming of a bird of prey, and looking up, saw blood fall drop by drop from among the intertwined boughs [of a lofty cedar]. Having climbed the tree, he beheld a terrible and dismaying spectacle. A naked human body was impaled on a broken branch. It was maimed and mangled horribly .. every limb bent and bruised into frightful distortion, exhibiting a breathing image of the most sickening mockery of life. A monstrous snake that had scented its prey from among the mountains fed eagerly, whilst innumerable worms disputed for the putrid morsel even at his pestilential jaws .. Above hovered a hungry vulture, who dared not tho' mad with raging famine pick from their sockets eyes endowed so excellently with majesty and empire: he waited for a secure but ignobler victim, till the gluttonous serpent should be sated with his meal .... In the hair of the head was matted a mass of 375

380

385

bloody snow that melted slowly in the warmer atmosphere ... A pointed rock had torn away the flesh from the right side ... His
390 naked heart was beating violently against his naked ribs, whilst the action of the tortured muscles of his back was grinding slowly the bark from the branch on which he hung, which intermixed with foam and gore fell to the ground. From amid this mass of desolated humanity two eyes black and inexpressibly brilliant shone with an
395 unearthly lustre. Beneath the bloodstained eyebrows their steady rays manifested the serenity of an immortal power, the collected energy of a deathless mind spell-secured from dissolution. They calmly appeared to observe and measure all around. Self possession had not deserted the shattered mass of life. A bitter smile of mingled
400 abhorrence and scorn distorted his wounded lips.

The youth approached the branch on which the breathing corpse was hung. As he approached, the serpent reluctantly unwreathed his glittering coils, and crept towards his dank and loathsome cave. The vulture, impatient of his meal, pecked the eyes from the unsated
405 reptile and fled with his writhing prey to the mountains that reechoed with his hoarse screams of triumph. The cedar branches creaked with their agitating weight, faintly, as the dismal wind arose. All else was deadly silent.

At length a voice issued from the mangled man. It rattled in hoarse
410 murmurs from his throat and lungs. His words were the conclusion of some strange and mysterious soliloquy. They were broken and without apparent connection completing wide intervals of inexpressible conceptions.

"The great Tyrant is baffled even in success ... Joy! Joy to his
415 tortured foe! Triumph to the worm whom he tramples under his feet! ... Ha! his suicidal hand might dare as well abolish this mighty frame of things.—Delight and exultation sit before the closed gates of death. I fear not to dwell beneath their black and ghastly shadow. There thy power may not avail. Thou createst.. 'tis mine to ruin and
420 destroy ... design ... execute ... I was thy slave .. I am thine equal and thy foe.—Thousands tremble before thy throne who at my voice shall dare to pluck the golden crown from thine unholy head, the golden crown whose gnawing rust has ?already mingled with thy ?cankered brain."—He ceased. The silence of noon swallowed up his
425 words. Albedir clung tighter to the tree; he dared not for dismay remove his eyes. He remained mute in the perturbation of deep and creeping horror.

"Albedir!" said the same voice, "Albedir! in the name of God approach. He that suffered me to fall, watches thee: the gentle and the merciful spirits of sweet human love delight not in agony and horror. For pity's sake approach .. in the name of thy good God approach, Albedir!" The tones were mild and clear as the responses of æolian music. ⟨They⟩ floated to Albedir's ear like the warm breath of June that lingers in the lawny groves subduing all to softness. Tears of tender affection started to his eyes. It was as the voice of a beloved friend. The partner of ⟨his⟩ childhood, the brother of his soul seemed to call for aid, and pathetically to remonstrate with delay. He resisted not the magic impulse but advanced towards the spot and tenderly attempted to remove the wounded man. He cautiously descended the tree with his wretched burthen, and deposited it on the ground.

A period of strange silence intervened. Awe and cold horror were slowly succeeding to the softer sensations of tumultuous pity when again he heard the silver modulations of the same enchanting voice. "Weep not for me Albedir! What wretch so utterly lost but might inhale peace and renovation from this Paradise! I am wounded and in pain: but having found a refuge in this seclusion, a friend in you, I am worthier of envy than compassion. Bear me to your cottage secretly. I would not disturb your gentle partner by my appearance. She must love me more dearly than a brother. I must be the playmate of your children; already I regard them with all a father's love. My arrival must not be regarded as a thing of mystery and wonder. What indeed, but that men are prone to error and exaggeration, is less inexplicable than that a stranger wandering on Lebanon fell from the rocks into the vale. Albedir", he continued—and his deepening voice assumed awful solemnity—"in return for the affection with which I cherish thee and thine thou owest this submission." Albedir implicitly submitted. Not even a thought had the power to refuse its deference. He reassumed his burthen, and proceeded towards the cottage. He watched until Khaled should be absent, and conveyed [the] stranger into an apartment appropriated for the reception of those who occasionally visited their habitation. He desired that the door should be securely fastened, and that he might not be visited until the morning of the following day.

Albedir waited with impatience the return of Khaled. The unaccustomed weight of even so transitory a secret hung on his ingenuous and unpractised nature like a blighting, clinging curse.

The stranger's accents had lulled him to a trance of wild and delightful imagination. Hopes so visionary and aerial that they had assumed no denomination had spread themselves over his intellectual frame, and phantoms as they were, had modelled his being to their shape. Still his mind was not exempt from the visitings of disquietude and perturbation. It was a troubled stream of thought over whose fluctuating waves unsearchable fate seemed to preside, guiding its unforeseen alternations with an inexorable hand.— Albedir paced earnestly the garden of his cottage, revolving every circumstance attendant on the incident of the day. He reimaged with intense thought the minutest recollections of the scene. In vain . . . he was the slave of suggestions not to be controlled. Astonishment, horror and awe, tumultuous sympathy and a mysterious elevation of soul hurried away all activity of judgement, overwhelmed with stunning force every attempt at deliberation or inquiry.

His reveries were interrupted at length by the return of Khaled. She entered the cottage, that scene of undisturbed repose, in the confidence, [the tranquil confidence that change might as soon overwhelm the eternal world] as disturb this inviolable sanctuary. She started to behold Albedir. Without preface or remark he recounted with eager haste the occurrences of the day. Khaled's tranquil spirit could hardly keep pace with the breathless rapidity of his narration. She was bewildered with staggering wonder even to hear his confused tones and behold his agitated countenance.

Chapter Fourth

On the following morning Albedir arose at sunrise and visited the stranger. He found him already risen and employed in adorning the lattice of his chamber with flowers from the garden. There was something in his attitude and occupation singularly expressive of his entire familiarity with the scene; Albedir's habitation seemed to have been his accustomed home. He addressed his host in a tone of gay and affectionate welcome such as never fails to communicate by sympathy the feelings from which it flows.

"My friend", said he, "the balm of the dew of our vale is sweet—or is this garden the favoured spot where the winds conspire to scatter the best odours they can find? Come lend me your arm awhile; I feel very weak". He motioned to walk forth but as if unable to proceed rested on the seat beside the door. For a few moments they were

silent, if the interchange of cheerful and happy looks is to be called   505
silence. At last he observed a spade that rested against the wall. "You
have only one spade, brother", said he; "you have only one, I
suppose, of any of the instruments of tillage. Your garden ground,
too, occupies a certain space which it will be necessary to enlarge;
this must be quickly remedied; I cannot earn my supper of tonight   510
nor of tomorrow but thenceforward I do not mean to eat the bread
of idleness. I know that you would willingly perform the additional
labour which my nourishment would require: I know also that you
would feel a degree of pleasure in the fatigue arising from this
employment but I shall contest with you such pleasures as these, and   515
such pleasures as these alone". His eyes were somewhat wan, and the
tone of his voice languid as he spoke.

As they were thus engaged Khaled came towards them: the
stranger beckoned to her to sit beside him, and taking her hands
within his own, looked attentively on her mild countenance. Khaled   520
enquired if he had been refreshed by sleep. He replied by a laugh of
careless and inoffensive glee; and placing one of her hands within
Albedir's [said] "If this be sleep here in this odorous vale, where these
sweet smiles encompass us, and the voices of those who love are
heard—if these be the visions of sleep, sister, those who lie down in   525
misery shall arise lighter than the butterflies.—I came from amid the
tumult of a world how different from this! I am unexpectedly among
you, in the midst of a scene such as my imagination never dared to
promise—I must remain here, I must not depart".—Khaled,
recovering from the admiration and astonishment caused by the   530
stranger's words and manner, assured him of the happiness which
she should feel in such an addition to her society. Albedir too, who
had been more deeply impressed than Khaled by the event of his
arrival, earnestly reassured him of the ardour of the affection with
which he had inspired them.—The stranger smiled gently to hear the   535
unaccustomed fervour of sincerity which animated their address
and was rising to retire, when Khaled said—"You have not yet seen
our children, Maimuna and Abdallah. They are by the water side
playing with their favourite snake. We have only to cross yonder
little wood, and wind down a path cut in the rock that overhangs the   540
lake, and we shall find them beside a recess which the shore makes
there, and which a chasm as it were among the rocks and woods
encloses.—Do you think you could walk there"?—"To see your
children, Khaled? I think I could with the assistance of Albedir's arm

545 and yours".—So they went thro' the wood of antient cypress intermingled with [odoriferous shrubs] the brightness of whose many tinted blooms gleamed like stars thro' its romantic glens. They crossed the green meadow, and entered among the broken chasms, beautiful as they were in their investiture of odoriferous shrubs.

550 They came at last, after pursuing a path which wound thro' the intricacies of a little wilderness, to the borders of the lake. They stood on the rock which overhung it, from which there ⟨was⟩ a prospect of all the miracles of nature and of art which encircle⟨d⟩ and adorn⟨ed⟩ its shores.—The stranger gazed upon it, with a

555 countenance unchanged by any emotion, but as it were thoughtfully and contemplatively.—As she gazed Khaled ardently pressed his hand and said in a low yet eager voice, "*Look, look,* Lo there—lo there!"—he turned towards her but her eyes were not on him. She looked below, her lips were parted by the feelings which possessed

560 her soul—her breath came and went regularly but inaudibly.—She leaned over the precipice, and her dark hair hanging beside her face, gave relief to its fine lineaments, animated by such love as exceeds utterance. The stranger followed her eyes, and saw that her children were in the glen below; then raising his eyes, exchanged with her

565 affectionate looks of congratulation and delight. The boy was apparently eight years old—the girl about two years younger. The beauty of their form and countenance was something so divine and strange, as overwhelmed the senses of the beholder like a delightful dream with insupportable ravishment. They were arrayed in a loose

570 robe of linen thro' which the exquisite proportions of their form appeared. Unconscious that they were observed they did not relinquish the occupation in which they were engaged. They had constructed a little boat of the bark of trees, and had given it sails of interwoven feathers and launched it on the water. They sate beside a

575 white flat stone, on which a small snake lay coiled, and when their work was finished they arose and called to the snake in melodious tones, so that it understood their language. For it unwreathed its shining circles and crept to the boat, into which no sooner had it entered than the girl loosened the band which held it to the shore,

580 and it sailed away. Then they ran round and round the little creek, clapping their hands, and melodiously pouring out wild sounds which the snake seemed to answer by the restless glancing of his neck. At last a breath of wind came from the shore, and the boat changed its course and was about to leave the creek, which the snake

perceived and leaped into the water, and came to the little children's   585
feet. The girl sang to it, and it leaped into her bosom, and she crossed
her fair hands over it, as if to cherish it there. Then the boy answered
with a song, and it glided from her hands, and crept towards him.
While they were thus employed, Maimuna looked up, and seeing her
parents on the cliff, ran to meet them up the steep path that wound   590
around it, and Abdallah, leaving his snake, followed joyfully.

ON 'MEMOIRS OF PRINCE
ALEXY HAIMATOFF'

Is the suffrage of mankind the legitimate criterion of intellectual
energy? Are complaints of the aspirants to literary fame, to be
considered as the honourable disappointment of neglected genius,
or the sickly impatience of a dreamer miserably self deceived? The
5 most illustrious ornaments of the annals of the human race, have
been stigmatised by the contempt and abhorrence of entire
communities of man; but this injustice arose out of some temporary
superstition, some partial interest, some national doctrine: a
glorious redemption awaited their remembrance. There is indeed,
10 nothing so remarkable in the contempt of the ignorant for the
enlightened: the vulgar pride of folly, delights to triumph upon
mind. This is an intelligible process: the infamy or ingloriousness
that can be thus explained, detracts nothing from the beauty of
virtue or the sublimity of genius. But what does utter obscurity ex-
15 press? If the public do not advert even in censure to a performance,
has that performance already received its condemnation?

The result of this controversy is important to the ingenuous critic.
His labours are indeed, miserably worthless, if their objects may
invariably be attained before their application. He should know
20 the limits of his prerogative. He should not be ignorant, whether
it is his duty to promulgate the decisions of others, or to cultivate
his taste and judgment that he may be enabled to render a reason for
his own.

Circumstances the least connected with intellectual nature have
25 contributed, for a certain period, to retain in obscurity, the most
memorable specimens of human genius. The author refrains perhaps
from introducing his production to the world with all the pomp of
empirical bibliopolism. A sudden tide in the affairs of men may make
the neglect or contradiction of some insignificant doctrine, a badge
30 of obscurity and discredit: those even who are exempt from the
action of these absurd predilections, are necessarily in an indirect

manner affected by their influence. It is perhaps the product of an imagination daring and undisciplined: the majority of readers ignorant and disdaining toleration refuse to pardon a neglect of common rules; their canons of criticism are carelessly infringed, it is less religious than a charity sermon, less methodical and cold than a French tragedy, where all the unities are preserved: no excellencies, where prudish cant and dull regularity are absent, can preserve it from the contempt and abhorrence of the multitude. It is evidently not difficult to imagine an instance in which the most elevated genius shall be recompensed with neglect. Mediocrity alone seems unvaryingly to escape rebuke and obloquy, it accommodates its attempts to the spirit of the age, which has produced it, and adopts with mimic effrontery the cant of the day and hour for which alone it lives.

We think that 'the Memoirs of Prince Alexy Haimatoff,' deserves to be regarded as an example of the fact, by the frequency of which, criticism is vindicated from the imputation of futility and impertinence. We do not hesitate to consider this fiction, as the product of a bold and original mind. We hardly remember eve⟨r⟩ to have seen surpassed the subtle delicacy of imagination, by which the manifest distinctions of character and form, are seized and pictured in colours, that almost make nature more beautiful than herself. The vulgar observe no resemblances or discrepancies, but such as are gross and glaring. The science of mind to which history, poetry, biography serve as the materials, consists in the discernment of shades and distinctions where the unenlightened discover nothing but a shapeless and unmeaning mass. The faculty for this discernment distinguishes genius from dulness. There are passages in the production before us, which afford instances of just and rapid intuition belonging only to intelligences, that possess this faculty in no ordinary degree. As a composition the book is far from faultless. Its abruptness and angularities do not appear to have received the slightest polish or correction. The author has written with fervor but has disdained to revise at leisure. These errors are the errors of youth and genius and the fervid impatience of sensibilities impetuously disburthening their fulness. The author is proudly negligent of connecting the incidents of his tale. It appears more like the recorded day dream of a poet, not unvisited by the sublimest and most lovely visions, than the tissue of a romance skilfully interwoven for the purpose of maintaining the interest of the reader, and conducting his sympathies by dramatic gradations to the

denouement. It is, what it professes to be, a memoir, not a novel.
Yet its claims to the former appellation are established, only by the
impatience and inexperience of the author, who, possessing in an
75 eminent degree, the higher qualifications of a novelist—we had
almost said a poet—has neglected the number by which that
success would probably have been secured, which, in this instance,
merit⟨s⟩, of a far nobler stamp, have unfortunately failed to acquire.
Prince Alexy is by no means an unnatural, although no common
80 character. We think we can discern his counterpart in Alfieri's
delineation of himself. The same propensities, the same ardent
devotion to his purposes, the same chivalric and unproductive
attachment to unbounded liberty, characterizes both. We are
inclined to doubt whether the author has not attributed to his
85 hero, the doctrines of universal philanthropy in a spirit of
profound and almost unsearchable irony: at least he appears
biassed by no peculiar principles, and it were perhaps an insoluble
inquiry whether any, and if any, what moral truth he designed to
illustrate by his tale. Bruhle, the tutor of Alexy, is a character
90 delineated with consummate skill; the power of intelligence and
virtue over external deficiencies, is forcibly exemplified. The
calmness, patience and magnanimity of this singular man, are truly
rare and admirable: his disinterestedness, his equanimity, his
irresistible gentleness form a finished and delightful portrait. But
95 we cannot regard his commendation to his pupil to indulge in
promiscuous concubinage without horror and detestation. The
author appears to deem the loveless intercourse of brutal appetite,
a venial offense against delicacy and virtue! he asserts that a
transient connection with a cultivated female, may contribute to
100 form the heart without essentially vitiating the sensibilities. It is
our duty to protest against so pernicious and disgusting an
opinion. No man can rise pure from the poisonous embraces of a
prostitute, or sinless from the desolated hopes of a confiding heart.
Whatever may be the claims of chastity, whatever the advantages
105 of simple and pure affections, these ties, these benefits are of equal
obligation to either sex. Domestic relations depend for their
integrity upon a complete reciprocity of duties. But the author
himself has in the adventure of the sultana, Debesh-Sheptuti,
afforded a most impressive and tremendous allegory of the cold
110 blooded and malignant selfishness of sensuality.
    We are incapacitated by the unconnected and vague narrative

from forming an analysis of the incidents; they would consist indeed, simply of a catalogue of events, which, divested of the aërial tinge of genius might appear trivial and common. We shall content ourselves, therefore, with selecting some passages calculated to exemplify the peculiar powers of the author. The following description of the simple and interesting Rosalie is in the highest style of delineation: 'Her hair was unusually black, she truly had raven locks, the same glossiness, the same varying shade, the same mixture of purple and sable for which the plumage of the raven is remarkable, were found in the long elastic tresses depending from her head and covering her shoulders. Her complexion was dark and clear: the colours which composed the brown that dyed her smooth skin, were so well mixed, that not one blot, not one varied tinge injured its brightness, and when the blush of animation or of modesty flushed her cheek, the tint was so rare, that could a painter have dipped his pencil in it, that single shade would have rendered him immortal. The bone above her eye was sharp, and beautifully curved; much as I have admired the wonderful properties of curves, I am convinced that their most stupendous properties collected, would fall far short of that magic line. The eyebrow was pencilled with extreme nicety; in the centre it consisted of the deepest shade of black, at the edges it was hardly perceptible, and no man could have been hardy enough to have attempted to define the precise spot at which it ceased: in short the velvet drapery of the eyebrow was only to be rivalled by the purple of the long black eyelashes that terminated the ample curtain. Rosalie's eyes were large and full; they appeared at a distance uniformly dark, but upon close inspection the innumerable strokes of various hues of infinite fineness and endless variety drawn in concentric circles behind the pellucid chrystal, filled the mind with wonder and admiration, and could only be the work of infinite power directed by infinite wisdom.'

Alexy's union with Aür-Ahebeh the Circassian slave is marked by circumstances of deep pathos, and the sweetest tenderness of sentiment. The description of his misery and madness at her death, deserves to be remarked as affording evidence of an imagination vast, profound and full of energy.

'Alexy, who gained the friendship, perhaps the love of the native Rosalie: the handsome Haimatoff, the philosophic Haimatoff, the haughty Haimatoff, Haimatoff the gay, the witty, the accomplished, the bold hunter, the friend of liberty, the chivalric lover of all that is

feminine, the hero, the enthusiast: see him now, that is he, mark him! he appears in the shades of evening, he stalk⟨s⟩ as a spectre, he has just risen from the damps of the charnel house; see, the dews still
155 hang on his forehead. He will vanish at cock-crowing, he never heard the song of the lark, nor the busy hum of men; the sun's rays never warmed him, the pale moonbeam alone shews his unearthly figure, which is fanned by the wing of the owl, which scarce obstructs the slow flight of the droning beatle, or of the drowsy bat. Mark him! he
160 stops, his lean arms are crossed on his bosom; he is bowed to the earth, his sunken eye gazes from its deep cavity on vacuity, as the toad skulking in the corner of a sepulchre, peeps with malignity through the circum⟨am⟩bient gloom. His cheek is hollow; the glowing tints of his complexion, which once resembled the
165 autumnal sunbeam on the autumnal beech, are gone, the cadaverous yellow, the livid hue have usurped their place, the sable honours of his head have perished, they once waved in the wind like the jetty pinions of the raven, the skull is only covered by the shrivelled skin, which the rook views wistfully, and calls to her young ones. His
170 gaunt bones start from his wrinkled garments, his voice is deep, hollow, sepulchral; it is the voice which wakes the dead, he has long held converse with the departed. He attempts to walk he knows not whither, his legs totter under him, he falls, the boys hoot him, the dogs bark at him, he hears them not, he sees them not.—Rest, there,
175 Alexy, it beseemeth thee, thy bed is the grave, thy bride is the worm, yet once thou stoodest erect, thy cheek was flushed with joyful ardour, thy eye blazing told what thy head conceived, what thy heart felt, thy limbs were vigour and activity, thy bosom expanded with pride, ambition, and desire, every nerve thrilled to feel, every muscle
180 swelled to execute.

'Haimatoff, the blight has tainted thee, thou ample roomy web of life, whereon were traced the gaudy characters, the gay embroidery of pleasure, how has the moth battened on thee; Haimatoff, how has the devouring flame scorched the plains, once yellow with the
185 harvest! the simoon, the parching breath of the desert, has swept over the laughing plains, the carpet of verdure rolled away at its approach, and has bared a⟨r⟩id desolation. Thou stricken deer, thy leather coat, thy dappled hide hangs loose upon thee, it was a deadly arrow, how has it wasted thee, thou scathed oak, how has the red
190 lightning drank thy sap: Haimatoff, Haimatoff, eat thy soul with vexation. Let the immeasurable ocean roll between thee and pride: you must not dwell together.' p. 129.

The episode of Viola is affecting, natural and beautiful. We do not ever remember to have seen the unforgiving fastidiousness of family honor more awfully illustrated. After the death of her lover, Viola 195 still expects that he will esteem, still cherishes the delusion that he is not lost to her for ever.

'She used frequently to go to the window to look for him, or walk in the Park to meet him, but without the least impatience, at his delay. She learnt a new tune, or a new song to amuse him, she stood 200 behind the door to startle him as he entered, or disguised herself to surprise him.'

The character of Mary, deserves, we think, to be considered as the only complete failure in the book. Every other female whom the author has attempted to describe is designated by an individuality 205 peculiarly marked and true. They constitute finished portraits of whatever is eminently simple, graceful, gentle, or disgustingly atrocious and vile. Mary alone is the miserable parasite of fashion, the tame slave of drivelling and drunken folly, the cold hearted coquette, the lying and meretricious prude. The means employed to 210 gain this worthless prize corresponds exactly with its worthlessness. Sir Fulke Hildebrand is a strenuous tory; Alexy, on his arrival in England professes himself inclined to the principles of the whig party; finding that the Baronet had sworn that his daughter should never marry a whig, he sacrifices his principles and with incon- 215 ceivable effrontery thus palliates his apostacy and falsehood.

'The prejudices of the Baronet, were strong in proportion as they were irrational. I resolved rather to humour than to thwart them. I contrived to be invited to dine in company with him; I always proposed the health of the minister, I introduced politics and 220 defended the tory party in long speeches, I attended clubs and public dinners of that interest. I do not know whether this conduct was justifiable; it may certainly be excused when the circumstances of my case are duly considered. I would tear myself in pieces, if I suspected that I could be guilty of the slightest falsehood or 225 prevarication; (see Lord Chesterfield's letters for the courtier-like distinction between simulation and dissimulation,) but there was nothing of that sort here. I was of no party, consequently, I could not be accused of deserting any one. I did not defend the injustice of any body of men, I did not detract from the merits of any virtuous 230 character. I praised what was laudable in the tory party, and blamed what was reprehensible in the whigs: I was silent with regard to whatever was culpable in the former or praiseworthy in the latter.

The stratagem was innocent which injured no one, and which
235 promoted the happiness of two individuals, especially of the most
amiable woman the world ever knew.'

An instance of more deplorable perversity of the human
understanding we do not recollect ever to have witnessed. It almost
persuades us to believe that scepticism or indifference concerning
240 certain sacred truths may occasionally produce a subtlety of
sophism, by which the conscience of the criminal may be bribed to
overlook his crime.

Towards the conclusion of this strange and powerful performance it must be confessed that *aliquando bonus dormitat Homerus*.
245 The adventure of the Eleutheri, although the sketch of a profounder
project, is introduced and concluded with unintelligible abruptness.
Bruhle dies, purposely as it should seem that his pupil may renounce
the romantic sublimity of his nature, and that his inauspicious
union and prostituted character, might be exempt from the censure
250 of violated friendship. Numerous indications of profound and
vigorous thought are scattered over even the most negligently
compacted portions of the narrative. It is an unweeded garden where
nightshade is interwoven with sweet jessamine, and the most
delicate spices of the East, peep over struggling stalks of rank and
255 poisonous hemlock.

In the delineation of the more evanescent feelings and uncommon
instances of strong and delicate passion we conceive the author to
have exhibited new and unparalleled powers. He has noticed some
peculiarities of female character, with a delicacy and truth singularly
260 exquisite. We think that the interesting subject of sexual relations
requires for its successful development the application of a mind
thus organised and endowed. Yet even here how great the deficiencies; this mind must be pure from the fashionable superstitions of gallantry, must be exempt from the sordid feelings which
265 with blind idolatry worship the image and blaspheme the deity,
reverence the type, and degrade the reality of which it is an emblem.

We do not hesitate to assert that the author of this volume is a man
of ability. His great though indisciplinable energies and fervid
rapidity of conception embodies scenes and situations, and passions
270 affording inexhaustible food for wonder and delight. The interest is
deep and irresistible. A moral enchanter seems to have conjured up
the shapes of all that is beautiful and strange to suspend the faculties
in fascination and astonishment.

ON THE VEGETABLE SYSTEM OF DIET

The wisest of the moral philosophers have justly remarked that man is the willing victim of innumerable errors, the habitual slave of a thousand perverse propensities. The madness of ambition and the abject idiotism of slavery, the impudence of imposture and the ignorance of credulity have furnished inexhaustible themes for the indignant reprobation of enlightened virtue. Moralists have contented themselves, however, with tracing these evils to the defective institutions of human society. They have shewn that the narrow and malignant passions which have turned man against man, as a beast of blood, the unenlightened brutality of the multitude and the profligate selfishness of courts are cherished by errors which have been rendered venerable by antiquity and consecrated by custom. This however is a loose and superficial estimate of the case. These pernicious institutions derive their origin from human error. This therefore is the legitimate object of scientific disquisition. This is the cause, as well as the consequence, of what we seek to remedy. The source of the errors of mankind is to be found not only in the external circumstances of his situation, but in those peculiarities of internal organization which modify their operation.

It is surprising that philosophers have never been induced to ascribe much of the violent and unreasonable conduct of human beings to diseased organization. They admit the influence of body on mind, they admit that the flames of a fever will calcine the brazen vase of our knowledge, that old age will extinguish the enthusiasm of virtue and of science; and that the faculties of the mind are so connected with the body that they sympathise minutely in its infancy and perfection, in its decrepitude and decay.—Does then a slighter degree of bodily derangement fail to limit in some degree the energies of intellect and to excite some slighter perversities of passion? Is idiotism and frenzy to be traced to one cause, ill temper and stupidity the result of another? A certain degree of violent and injudicious conduct has been invariably ascribed to organic derangement: whilst the cause of those slighter specimens of folly and malignity which constitute the mass of human misery, have 35 never been the subject ⟨of⟩ philosophical investigation. Moral instruction has been thought a sufficient antidote to a malady which is the inevitable result of physical derangement. The speculative truths of moral science, when perceived, never fail perhaps to acquire an empire over the conduct: the difficulty consists in 40 impressing them durably on the conviction of men, and this can only be effected by previously securing an understanding, unvitiated by bodily disease. With arguments shall philosophy assail superstition, so long as terrifying phantasms crowd round the couch of its pale and prostrate victim: refuting with the indisputable evidence of 45 sense, the metaphysical scepticism of reason? whilst portentous dreams and reveries of indescribable horror testify [that]

How shall we inspire the miserable man with kindness and humanity whose social feelings are jaundiced by a torturer that lurks within his vitals, (*esse omnia providentem et cogitantem et* 50 *animadvertentem et omnia ad se pertinere putantem curiosum et plenum negotii deum*) and forces him to contemplate every cheerful sight and sound as a bitter mockery of his own intolerable anguish?[1] How will you inspire that imbecile being with a persuasion of the import- ance of active virtue and the faithful discharge of the numerous 55 duties of social life who is by the physical imperfections of his nature constituted the canting nurse of his own morbid sensibilities? The attempt is more common, but is scarcely less absurd than to reason with a lunatic, or to require from a dying man the exertion of that mental power, and enlightened subtlety of research for which when 60 in health he had been conspicuous.

---

[1] A poet dear to every lover of Nature, has illustrated this fact with his exquisite and original pencil:

—Ladurlad hears their distant voices
And with their joy no more his heart rejoices;
And how their old companion now may fare
Little they know, and less they care;
The torment he is doomed to bear
Was but to them the wonder of a day
A burthen of sad thoughts soon put away.
They knew not that the wretched man was near
And yet it seemed to his distempered ear
As if they wronged him with their merriment.
Resentfully he turned away his eyes.

⟨Robert Southey,⟩ *Curse of Kehama*: IX. ⟨ll. 71–81⟩

The use of ardent spirits and irritating food deranges the mental faculties in a greater or less degree as is evident to daily experience. Not only is inebriety temporarily subversive of the understanding, and gluttony productive of immediate grossness of perception (The Benevolent, the Selfish, ?the ?slave of the Passions, the Malignant 65 and the ?Mixed) but habits of indigestion are peculiarly favorable to stupidity, and the consequences of a fit of drunkenness are inimical to intellectual exertion. It is impossible to dispute a fact of which every fireside circle affords more than one melancholy example, but it belongs to philosophy alone to trace the remoter effects of 70 mistakes consecrated by habit, to mark their influence on individual character, to estimate the sum of a thousand unregarded events as affecting the welfare of society, and to trace to the influence of unnatural habits of life hatred, murder and rapine, wars, massacres and revolutions.

75

A popular objection which never fails to be opposed to every reasoning of this nature is, that it is incorrect to ascribe such mighty effects to causes so comparatively trivial. Such nevertheless are the laws of the world which we inhabit. A spark well kindled will consume the most sumptuous palace. Some slight derangement in 80 the association of a Monarch's ideas may involve his subjects in a long and sanguinary war. The dream of a frantic woman has lighted the piles of persecution in every corner of the civilized globe.—Man is an whole the complicated parts of which are so interwoven with each other, that the most remote and subtile springs of his machine 85 are connected with those which are more gross and obvious, and reciprocally act and react upon each other. The vital principle by some inexplicable process influences, and is influenced [by], the nerves and muscles of the body.—The flesh is wasted by an excess of grief and passion: Thought is suspended by the languor of a lethargy, 90 and deranged by the excitement of a fever. The conclusion therefore to which we have arrived and which is neither contradicted by the experience of daily life, nor the more subtile speculations of profound philosophy, ⟨is⟩ that much of the violent and unreasonable conduct of human beings is to be ascribed to diseased organiza- 95 tion.

The establishment of this axiom is of considerable moment to the subject of the present investigation. It attaches a degree of importance to the issue of the enquiry which would scarcely seem to belong to a mere question of dietetics. Much of that spirit in which 100

human beings persecute and destroy each other arises from the morbid disquietude of their physical constitutions. It is not easy to conceive an object more worthy of the philanthropist and the philosopher, than to investigate the nature and to oppose the
105 influence of a principle thus eminently hostile to the peace and welfare of mankind.—

It will readily be admitted that Disease is not a natural state of the human frame; that there are certain habits which have a tendency to preserve health, and others on the practise of which organic
110 derangement inevitably ensues.—It will not be disputed that there is a peculiar mode of life which would effectually secure the human race from the invasions of malady. The assertion therefore that disease is the consequence of unnatural habits of life is liable to no conceivable objection. To every species of animal, excepting man,
115 and those miserable creatures whom he has subjected to his contaminating dominion, there is an average period of existence which few exceed, and which few fail to attain. But no hour of the life of man is exempt from the dreaded invasion of a mortal malady. Some isolated instances of longevity stand upon record as proofs of
120 the natural term of human life.[1] But death ordinarily seizes alike upon old age and childhood, vigour and debility: Not the innocence of infancy, ⟨the⟩ strength of manhood, the bloom of dawning youth, nay, not the strictest individual temperance can guard against the secret wiles of this insidious destroyer.

125 Human beings possesst of the most admirable and glorious propensities are suddenly cut off in their full career of usefulness. Beings to whom nations have turned anxiously as to their expected saviours, whom families have regarded as their only comfort and support, who have dispensed concord, happiness and hope through-
130 out the sphere of their exertions, are abruptly swept away by that mysterious principle which visits the sins of the fathers on the children. Hospitals are filled with a thousand screaming victims; the palaces of luxury and the hovels of indigence resound alike with the bitter wailings of disease, idiotism and madness grin and rave
135 amongst us—and all these complicated calamities result from those unnatural habits of life to which the human race has addicted itself during innumerable ages of mistake and misery.

By an unnatural habit is to be understood such an habit as is manifestly inconsistent with the conformation of any animal; and

[1] ⟨James⟩ Easton⟨, *Human Longevity*.⟩

this inconsistency is to be esteemed a sufficient evidence of its 140
pernicious consequences. It is probable that no anatomist will be
inclined to deny that if a lion were fed on grass, or a cow on flesh the
health of these animals would be materially injured. In fact the
experiment has been tried, and has uniformly been attended with the
consequences here alledged.—The wild boar is healthy and active, 145
and one of the most formidable of the beasts of the forests. In his
natural state he is frugivorous: domestication has rendered him
omnivorous, has rendered him in consequence miserable, languid
and filthy, inflicted on him an immense variety of diseases. The argali
or wild sheep is an animal of remarkable sagacity, and strength, and 150
attains the age of fourteen years: the domestic sheep is weak and
timorous, and would be devoured by innumerable diseases long
before the natural term of its existence, if the butcher's knife ⟨did⟩
not anticipate its miserable end. Many similar facts might be
adduced if the fact that disease is the result of unnatural habits of life 155
required any additional confirmation.

The object of the present enquiry is to prove that one of those
unnatural habits which produce disease is the use of animal food. It is
confessed [that] the substances which we take into the stomach,
constitute one of the principal sources of malady. The remotest 160
parts of the body sympathise [with] the stomach; groundless terrors,
vertigo and delirium are frequently consequent upon a disease of the
digestive organs; tremours and spasmodic affections remote both in
their nature[1] and position from disorders of the stomach are yet in
many cases to be traced to its derangement; and those whose 165
digestive powers are strongly and regularly exerted are particularly
exempt from illness. If, therefore, the cause of the disorders of the
digestive organs be discovered, disease may be successfully assailed
in its source by a system of diet, the reverse of that by which it is
produced.[2]
170

That man is naturally a frugivorous animal numerous considerations conspire to demonstrate. The most obvious of these has
not failed to suggest itself to the antient advocates of simple diet. The
manifest natural disqualification of the human frame for rapine and
destruction, his want of those instruments of offence with which the 175
carnivorous animals are furnished, sufficiently evinces how ill he is
adapted to provide himself with the flesh of animals without the

---

[1] See ⟨John⟩ Abernethy⟨, 'Essay on the Constitutional Origin of Local Disease'.⟩
[2] It is not here asserted that mental and bodily derangement &c; see *Queen Mab*, p. 223.

artifices which result from the experience of many centuries. It demanded surely no great profundity of anatomical research to perceive that man has neither the fangs of a lion nor the claws of a tiger, that his instincts are inimical to bloodshed, and that the food which is not to be eaten without the most intolerable loathing until it is altered by the action of fire and disguised by the addition of condiments, is not that food for which he is adapted by his physical construction. The bull must be degraded into the ox, the ram into the wether by an unnatural and inhuman operation that the flaccid fibre may offer less resistance to [a nature]   Sows big with young are indeed no longer stamped upon until they die, and sucking pigs roasted alive; but lobsters are slowly boiled [to death] and express by their inarticulate cries the dreadful agony they endure. Chickens are mutilated and imprisoned until they fatten, calves are bled to death that their flesh may appear white: and a certain horrible process of torture furnishes brawn for the gluttonous repasts with which Christians celebrate the anniversary of their Saviour's birth.—What beast of prey compels its victim to undergo such protracted, such severe and such degrading torments? The single consideration that man cannot swallow a piece of raw flesh would be sufficient to prove that the natural diet of the human species did not consist in the carcases of butchered animals.

Custom has been found to reconcile the animal system to habits the most unnatural and pernicious. Narcotic poisons have been gradually swallowed until they have ceased to [produce] their accustomed effect, although they have never failed eventually to produce disease and death. Every being with which we are acquainted invariably attempts to accommodate itself to the circumstances of its situation; it nevertheless exhausts in the effort much of its vital energy. A willow will attain to its perfection by the bank of a river, because this situation is analogous to its nature; place it ⟨in⟩ that soil which is congenial to the fir tree: it will live indeed if it survive the shock of transplantation but will become a diseased and stunted shrub. Horses, sheep, oxen and even wood pidgeons have been taught to live upon flesh until they have loathed their natural aliment.[1] No argument therefore can be adduced in favour of any system of diet from the mere fact of its being generally used, so long as disease and meagreness and misery are observed among [its] unfailing concomitants.

[1] ⟨Joseph⟩ Ritson, ⟨*An Essay on Abstinence from Animal Food, as a Moral Duty*⟩.

Here then lies exposed one of the most important sources of the wretchedness of man. If these reasoni⟨n⟩g⟨s⟩ have any force mankind is in the daily practise of an unnatural habit, the consequences of which cannot fail to be eminently pernicious. It is a duty which every individual owes to himself, to posterity, to those who are influenced by his example, and to those who depend in any manner on his health and existence for any portion of their happiness, resolutely to break this unnatural practise thus pregnant with inexhaustible and measureless calamity. Those who are persuaded of the point which it is the object of this enquiry to establish, are bound by the most sacred obligations of morality to adopt in practise what he admits in theory. He is bound to disregard the seductive titillations of a perverted appetite, to despise that false and hollow hearted conviviality which is founded on intemperance, and to content himself with those purer and more constant elations of nature which invariably accompany a virtuous mind and an unvitiated body.

Before [?the] human race shall be capable of any considerable advance towards that happiness which is the ultimate object of all human exertion, habits demonstrably unnatural must be unsparingly discarded. Let not however the expectations which may reasonably be indulged from the dereliction of a destructive custom be exaggerated. Disease is hereditary. The mass which is now existing in the world has been produced by a mistake of unfathomable antiquity. With what rapidity the adoption of vegetable food might diminish this accumulation it is impossible to predict. We are authorized only to assert that it would in some degree be diminished by the use of aliment to which man is adapted by his construction in every essential particular.

Meanwhile facts are not wanting which may serve to shew that the vegetable system of diet is innocent and even salutary; and may reconcile it to the selfishness of some by the promise of immediate advantages.—Specimens of longevity have been far more common among vegetable eaters in proportion to their numbers, than among those who use animal food.[1] The philosophers of antient Greece,[2]

[1] Old Parr 152. Mary Patten 136. A shepherd in Hungary 126. Patric O Neale 113. Joseph Elkins 103. Elizabeth de Val 101. Aurungzebe 100. Rombald 120. Arsenius 120. Epiphanius 115. Simeon 112. St. Anthony 105. James the Hermit 104. See Essay.—Many other instances are to be found in Easton's catalogue of longevity; in which however the habits of life of the individuals are incorrectly omitted. These examples are procured from another source.

[2] Zeno used απυρω τρ⟨o⟩φη. Notes to ⟨Euripides'⟩ *Hippolytus* 953⟨.⟩

and the hermits of primitive Christianity, adopted a rigid system of diet from which the flesh of animals was almost entirely excluded; they afford numerous examples of longevity.—Constitutional
255 diseases which have resisted every other method, have yielded to vegetable diet.[1] Whoever fairly makes the experiment of the change here recommended will speedily perceive the benefit of his abstinence. He will find himself equally capable of bodily or intellectual exertion after, as before his simple meal. His spirits will
260 be more equally constant and less subject ⟨to⟩ those invincible depressions by which the lightest heart is so frequently invaded ... Such are the recommendations of the vegetable system, and such are the argument⟨s⟩ upon which it is founded.... So far as just philosophy and natural sentiments shall prevail among mankind, so
265 far, I am persuaded, the practise of destroying and devouring animals will be contemplated in the light of an unnatural and pernicious outrage.

The mere destruction of any sentient being, abstractedly considered, is perhaps an event of exceedingly minute importance. It is
270 of little moment to the welfare of animated beings that a Volcano burst out in Kanstashka and destroyed some villages and some heads of cattle.—It is because, a malevolent and ferocious disposition is generated by the commission of murder that this crime is so tremendous and detestable. Who that is accustomed to the sight of
275 wounds and anguish will scruple to inflict them, when he shall deem it expedient? With what measure of evil is anger, vengeance and malignity contented? How interminable is the series of calamity which that man who first slew his brother, unthinkingly produced?—It is evident that those who are necessitated by their
280 profession to trifle with the sacredness of life, and think lightly of the agonies of living beings, are unfit for the benevolence and justice which is required for the performance of the offices of civilized society. They are by necessity brutal, coarse, turbulent and sanguinary. Their habits form even a more admirable apprenticeship
285 to the more wide wasting wickedness of war, in which men are hired to mangle and murder their fellow beings by ⟨the⟩ thousands. How can he be expected to preserve a vivid sensibility to the benevolent sympathies of our nature, who is familiar with carnage, agony and groans? The very sight of animals in the fields who are destined to the

[1] See ⟨John Frank Newton⟩, *Return to Nature* and Dr. ⟨William⟩ Lambe⟨, *Cure of*⟩ *Constitutional Diseases*.

axe must encourage obduracy if it fails to awaken compassion. The 290
butchering of harmless animals cannot fail to produce much of that
spirit of insane and hideous exultation in which news of a victory is
related, altho' purchased by the massacre of an hundred thousand
men. If the use of animal food, be in consequence thus subversive to
the peace of human society; how unwarrantable is the injustice and 295
barbarity which is exercised toward these miserable victims. They
are called into existence by human artifice, that their bodies may be
then mutilated, their social feelings outraged, that they may drag out
a short and miserable existence of slavery and disease. It were much
better that a sentient being should never have existed, than that it 300
should have existed only to endure unmitigated misery.[1]

[1] The attachment of animals to their young is very strong. The monstrous and unfeeling
sophism that beasts are pure machines and do not reason scarcely requires a confutation.

JOURNAL AT GENEVA

Geneva, Sunday, 18th August, 1816.

See Apollo's Sexton,[1] who tells us many mysteries of his trade. We talk of Ghosts.—Neither Lord B⟨yron⟩ or M.G.L. seem to believe in them, and they both agree in the very face of reason, that none could believe in Ghosts without also believing in God.—I do not think that all the persons who profess to discredit these visitations, really discredit them or, if they do in the daylight, are not admonished by the approach of loneliness and midnight to think more respectfully of the world of Shadows.

Lewis recited a poem which he had composed at the request of the Princess of Wales. The Princess of Wales, he premised, was not only a believer in ghosts, but in magic and witchcraft, and asserted that prophecies made in her youth had been accomplished since.—The tale was of a Lady of her court in Germany.—

This lady, Mina, had been exceedingly attached to her husband, and they had made a vow that the one who died first should return after death and visit the other as a Ghost.—She was sitting one day alone in her chamber when she heard an unusual sound of footsteps on the stairs.—The door opened, and her husband's spectre gashed with a deep wound across the forehead, and in military habiliments, entered.—She appeared startled at the apparition, and the ghost told her, that when he should visit her in future, she would hear a passing bell toll, and these words distinctly uttered close to her ear, "Mina, I am here".—On enquiry it was found that her husband had fallen in battle on the very day that she was visited by the vision.—The intercourse between the Ghost and the woman continued for some time, until the latter had laid aside all terror, and indulged herself in

[1] Mr. ⟨Matthew⟩ G. Lewis—so named in *English Bards and Scotch Reviewers*. When Lewis first saw Lord Byron, he asked him earnestly,—"Why did you call me Apollo's Sexton?" The noble Poet found it difficult to reply to this categorical species of reproof. The above stories have, some of them, appeared in print; but, as a ghost story depends entirely on the mode in which it is told, I think the reader will be pleased to read these, written by S, fresh from their relation by Lewis ⟨Mary Shelley's *1840* note⟩.

the affection which she had felt for him whilst living.—One evening she went to a ball, and permitted her thoughts to be alienated by the attentions of a Florentine gentleman, more witty, more graceful and more gentle, as it appeared to her, than any person she had ever seen. As he was conducting her thro' the dance a death bell tolled: Mina, lost in the fascination of the Florentine's attentions, disregarded or did not hear the sound.—A second peal, louder and more deep, startled the whole company; when Mina heard the ghost's accustomed whisper, and raising her eyes saw in an opposite mirror the reflexion of the ghost, standing over her.—She is said to have died of terror.

He told us four other stories—all grim.

1

A young man who had taken orders had just been presented with a living on the death of the incumbent. It was in the Catholic part of Germany.—He arrived at the parsonage on a Saturday night; it was summer, and waking about 3 o'clock in the morning, and it being already broad day he saw a venerable looking man, but with an aspect exceedingly melancholy, sitting at a desk in the window reading, and two beautiful boys standing near him, whom he regarded with looks expressive of the profoundest grief. Presently he rose from his seat, the boys followed him, and they were no more to be seen. The young man, much troubled, arose, hesitating whether he should regard what he had seen as a dream or as a waking phantasy. To divert his dejection he walked towards the church which the sexton was already preparing for the morning service. The first sight that struck him was a portrait, the exact resemblance of the man whom he had seen sitting in his chamber.—It was the custom in this district to place the portrait of each minister after his death in the church.—

He made the minutest enquiries respecting his predecessor, and learned that he was universally beloved as a man of unexampled integrity and benevolence, but that he was the prey of a secret and perpetual sorrow. His grief was supposed to have arisen from an attachment to a young lady with whom his situation did not permit him to unite himself—others however asserted that a connection did subsist between them, and that even she occasionally brought to his house, two beautiful boys, the offspring of their connection.—Nothing further occurred until the cold weather came, and the new

65 minister desired a fire to be lighted in the stove of the room where he slept.—A hideous stench arose from the stove as soon as it was lighted, and on examining it, the bones of two male children were found within.—

2

Lord Lyttleton and a number of his friends were joined during the
70 chase by a stranger.—He was excellently mounted and displayed such courage, or rather so much desperate rashness that no other person in the hunt could follow him. The gentlemen, when the chase was concluded, invited the stranger to dine with them. His conversation was something of a wonderful kind. He astonished, he
75 interested, he commanded the attention of the most inert.—As night came on, the company being weary began to retire one by one; much later than the usual hour. The most intellectual among them were retained the latest by his fascination. As he perceived that they began to depart he redoubled his efforts to retain them. At last when few
80 remained, he entreated them to stay with him, but all pleaded the fatigue of a hard day's chase, and all at last retired. They had been in bed about an hour when they were awakened by the most horrible screams, which issued from the stranger's room. Every one rushed towards it.—The door was locked. After a moment's deliberation
85 they burst it open, and found the stranger stretched on the ground— writhing with agony and weltering in blood.—On their entrance he arose, and collecting himself, apparently with a strong effort, intreated them to leave him—not to disturb him—that he would give every possible explanation in the morning.—They complied—in the
90 morning his chamber was found vacant and he was seen no more.

3

Miles Andrews, the friend of Lord Lyttleton, was sitting one night alone when Lord Lyttleton came in, and informed ⟨him⟩ that he was dead, and that this was his ghost which he saw before him.— Andrews pettishly told him not to play any ridiculous tricks upon
95 him, for he was not in a temper to bear them.—The ghost then departed. In the morning Andrews asked his servant at what hour Lord Lyttleton had arrived? The servant said he did not know that he had arrived but that he would enquire. On enquiry it was found that Lord Lyttleton had not arrived, nor had the door been opened
100 to any one during the whole night.—Andrews sent to Lord

Lyttleton's and discovered that he had died precisely at the hour of the apparition.—

4

A gentleman on a visit to a friend who lived on the skirts of an extensive forest in the East of Germany lost his way. He wandered for some hours among the trees when he saw a light at a distance. On approaching it he was surprised to observe that it proceeded from the interior of a ruined monastery. Before he knocked at the gate he thought it prudent to look thro' the window.—He saw a multitude of cats assembled round a small grave, four of whom were at that moment letting down a coffin with a crown upon it. The gentleman, startled at this unusual sight, and imagining that he had arrived among the retreat of fiends or witches, mounted his horse and rode away with the utmost precipitation. He arrived at his friend's house at a late hour, who sate up waiting for him. On his arrival, his friend questioned him as to the cause of the traces of trouble visible in his face. He began to recount his adventure, after much difficulty, knowing that it was scarcely possible that his friend should give faith to his relation. No sooner had he mentioned the coffin with a crown upon it, than his friend's cat who seemed to have been lying asleep before the fire, leaped up, saying "Then I am the King of the cats", and scrambled up the chimney and was seen no more.

——————

Thursday ⟨August⟩ 29[*]

We depart from Geneva at nine in the morning.—The Swiss are very slow drivers and besides which we have Jura to mount; we, therefore go a very few posts today. The scenery is very beaut⟨iful⟩ and we see many magnificent views.—We pass *La Vattaz* and *Les Rousses* which when we passed in the spring were in snow. We sleep at Morrez.

Friday 30

We leave Morrez and arrive in the evening at Dole, after a various day.

Saturday 31

From Dole we go to Rouvray where we sleep. We pass thro' Dijon and after Dijon take a different route to that which we followed on

⟨* Mary Shelley wrote this entry.⟩

the two other occasions.—The scenery has some beauty and singularity on the line of the mountains which surround the Val de Suzon. Low yet precipitous hills, covered with vines or woods, and with streams, meadows and poplars at the bottom.

Sunday September 1

135 Leave Rouvray, pass Auxerre where we dine, a pretty town, and arrive at 2 o'clock at Villene⟨u⟩ve le Guiard.—

Monday 2

From Villeneuve le Guiard we arrive at Fontainbleau.—The scenery around this palace is wild and even savage. The soil is full of rocks, apparently granite, which on every side break thro' the ground. The
140 hills are low but precipitous and rough. The vallies, equally wild, are shaded by forests. In the midst of this wilderness stands the Palace and town of Fontainbleau. We visited the palace.—Some of the apartments equal in magnificence any thing that I could conceive. The roofs are fretted with Gold, and the canopies of velvet.—From
145 Fontainbleau we passed to Versailles in the route towards Rouen.— We arrived at Versailles at 9.

Tuesday 3

We saw the Palace and gardens of Versailles and le Grand et Petit Trianon. They surpass those of Fontainbleau.—The gardens are full of statues of the most exquisite workmanship—vases, fountains, and
150 colonnades.—In all that essentially belongs to a garden they are extraordinarily deficient. The orangery is a stupid piece of expense. There was one orange tree, not apparently so old, sown in 1442. We saw only the gardens and the theatre at the Petit Trianon. The gardens are in the English taste, and extremely pretty. The Grand
155 Trianon was open. It is a summer palace, light, yet magnificent.—We were unable to devote the time it deserved to the gallery of paintings here. There was a portrait of Mad⟨ame⟩ Lavallière, the repentant mistress of Louis 14th. She was melancholy but exceedingly beautiful, and was represented as holding a skull, and sitting before a
160 crucifix—pale, and with downcast eyes.

We then went to the great Palace.—The apartments are un-furnished, but even with this disadvantage are more magnificent than those of Fontainbleau. They are lined with marble of various colours, whose pedestals and capitals are gilt, and the ceiling is richly

gilt with compartments of exquisite painting. The arrangement of these precious materials has in it, it is true, something effeminate and royal. Could a Grecian architect have commanded all the labour and money which was expended on Versailles, he would have produced a fabric which the whole world has never equalled.—We saw the Hall of Hercules, the balcony where the King and Queen exhibited themselves to the Parisian mob. The people who shewed us the palace obstinately refused to say anything about the Revolution: we could not even find out in which Chambre the rioters of the 10th of August found the King.—We saw the Salon d'Opéra, where are now preserved the portraits of the Kings. There was the race of the house of Orléans with the exception of Egalité, all extremely handsome. There was Mad⟨ame⟩ de Maintenon and beside her a beautiful little girl, the daughter of Lavallière. The pictures had been hidden during the Revolution.—We saw the Library of Louis 16th. The Librarian had held some place in the antient court near Marie Antoinette. He returned with the Bourbons, and was waiting for some better situation.—He shewed us a book which he had preserved during the Revolution. It was a book of paintings representing a tournament at the Court of Louis 14.—and it seemed that the present desolation of France, the fury of the injured people, and all the horrors to which they abandoned themselves stung by their long sufferings, flowed naturally enough from expenditures so immense as must have been demanded by the magnificence of this tournament. The vacant rooms of this palace imaged well the hollow shew of monarchy.—
—   After seeing these things we departed towards Hâvre and slept at Auxonne.

Wednesday 4

We passed thro' Rouen, and saw the Cathedral, an immense specimen of the most costly and magnificent gothic. The interior of the Church disappoints.—We saw the burial place of Richard Cœur de Lion and his brother.—The altar of the Church is a fine piece of marble. Sleep at Yvetot.

Thursday 5

We arrive at Hâvre, and wait for the Packet.—wind contrary.

THE ELYSIAN FIELDS

I am not forgetful in this dreary scene of the country which whilst I lived in the upper air, it was my whole aim to illustrate and render happy. Indeed, altho' immortal, we are not exempted from the enjoyments and the sufferings of mortality. We sympathise in all the proceedings of mankind, and we experience joy or grief in all intelligence from them according to our various opinions and views. Nor do we resign those opinions, even those which the grave has utterly refuted. Frederic of Prussia has lately arrived amongst us, and persists in maintaining that "death is an eternal sleep" to the great discomfiture of Philip 2ᵈ of Spain, who on the furies refusing to apply the torture, expects the roof of Tartarus to fall upon his head, and laments that at least in his particular instance the doctrine should be false.—Religion is more frequently the subject of discussion among the departed dead, than any other topic, for we know as little which mode of faith is true as you do. Every one maintains the doctrine he maintained on Earth, and accommodates the appearances which surround us to his peculiar tenets.—

I am one of those who esteeming political science capable of certain conclusions, have ever preferred it to these airy speculations, which when they assume an empire over the passions of mankind render them so mischievous and unextinguishable, that they subsist even among the dead. The art of employing the power entrusted to you for the benefit of those who entrust it, is something more definite, and subject as all its details must ever be to innumerable limitations and exceptions arising out of the change in the habits, ⟨and⟩ opinions of mankind, is the noblest and the greatest, and the most universal of all. It is not as a queen, but as a human being that this science must be learned; the same discipline which contributes to domestic happiness and individual distinction secures true welfare and genuine glory to a nation.—

You will start, I do not doubt, to hear the language of philosophy. You will have been informed that those who approach sovereigns

with warnings that they have duties to perform, that they are
elevated above the rest of mankind simply to prevent their tearing
one another to pieces, and for the purpose of putting into effect all 35
practical equality and justice, are insidious traitors who devise their
ruin. But if the character which I bore on earth should not reassure
you, it would be well to recollect the circumstances under which you
will ascend the throne of England, and what is the spirit of the times.
There are better examples to emulate than those who have only 40
refrained from depraving or tyrannizing over their subjects, because
they remembered the fates of Pisistratus and Tarquin. If generosity
and virtue should have dominion over your actions, my lessons can
hardly be needed; but the discipline of a narrow education may have
extinguished all thirst of genuine excellence, all desire of becoming 45
illustrious for the sake of the illustriousness of the actions which I
would incite you to perform. Should you be thus—and no pains have
been spared to make you so—make your account with holding your
crown on this condition: of deserving it alone. And that this may be
evident, I will expose to you the state in which the nation will be 50
found at your accession, for the very dead know more than the
counsellors by whom you will be surrounded.

The English nation does not, as has been imagined, inherit
freedom from its ancestors. Public opinion rather than positive
institution maintains it in whatever portion it may now possess; 55
which is in truth the acquirement of their own incessant struggles.

As yet the gradations [by] which this freedom has advanced have
been contested step by step.

ON LEARNING LANGUAGES

it is probable that they will be earnest to employ the sacred talismans of language. To acquire these you are now necessitated to sacrifize many hours of the time when instead of being conversant with particles and verbs your nature incites you to contemplation and enquiry concerning the objects which they conceal. You desire to enjoy the beauties of eloquence and poetry, to sympathise in thei⟨r⟩ original language with the institutors and the martyrs of antient freedom. The generous and inspiriting examples of philosophy and virtue you desire intimately to know and feel, not as mere facts detailing names and dates and motions of the human body, but clothed in the very language of the actors—that language dictated by and expressive of the passions or principles which governed their conduct. Facts are not what we want to know in poetry, in history, in the lives of individual men, in satire or in panegyric. They are the mere divisions, the arbitrary points on which we hang and to which we refer those delicate and evanescent hues of mind ⟨with⟩ which language delights and instructs us in precise proportion as it expresses. What is a translation of Homer into English? A person who is ignorant of Greek need only look at Paradise Lost or the tragedy of Lear translated into French to obtain an analogical conception of its worthless and miserable inadequacy. Tacitus or Livius or Herodotus are equally undelightful and uninstructive in translation. You require to know and to be intimate with those persons who have acted a distinguished part to benefit, to enlighten, or even to pervert and injure human kind. Before you can do this four years are yet to be consumed in the discipline of the antient languages, and those of modern Europe which you only imperfectly know and which conceal from your intimacy such names as Ariosto, Tasso, Petrarch and Macchiavelli, or Goethe, Schiller, Wieland &ᶜ. The French language you, like every other respectable female, already know, and if the great name of Rousseau did not redeem it from   it would have been perhaps as well had you remained entirely ignorant of it.

A FAUSTIAN NOTE

It has been conceded to some men to pass the boundaries of the knowledge of the age in which they live.—Circumstances distinct from their own wisdom frequently conspire to invest them with this prerogative. Let none suppose that the preeminence which it confers is useful to the possessor! If his fellow men neither worship him as a God, fear ⟨him⟩ as a demon or persecute him as an enemy—yet the power itself if disproportioned to the skill which should wield it might contain a germ of inexhaustible misfortune. 5

DECLARATION IN CHANCERY⟨*⟩

I understand the opinions which I hold on religious matters to be
abandoned as a ground of depriving me of the guardianship of my
children; the allegations from which this unfitness is argued to
proceed, are reduced to a simple statement of my holding doctrines
inimical to the institution of marriage as established in this country,
and my having [differed] ⟨*contravened*⟩ in practise, as well as
speculation, [from] that institution. If I have attacked Religion, it is
agreed that I am punishable; but not by the loss of my children—
if I have imagined a system of social life inconsistent with the
constitution of England, I am punishable; but not by the loss of my
children.

I understand that it is argued that I am to be [rendered] ⟨*declared*⟩
incapable of the most sacred of human duties, and the most
inestimable of human rights, because I have reasoned against the
institution of marriage in its present state, because I have in my own
person violated that institution and because I have justified that
violation by my reasoning. If [indeed its] ⟨*the*⟩ consequence ⟨*of this
charge*⟩ be so dreadful as to justify the interference of a Court of
[Chancery] ⟨*law*⟩ with my paternal rights, I shall leave it to my
adversaries to establish against me.

[This] ⟨*The*⟩ argument ⟨*of my adversaries then*⟩, as it presents itself
to the Lord Chancellor's mind, reduces itself, I imagine, to this plain
consideration—not whether I shall teach my children religious
infidelity—not whether I shall teach them political heterodoxy, but
whether I shall educate them in immodest and loose sentiments of
sexual connexion. I feel that on this particular point I ought to be
heard in explanation.

The institutions and opinions of all ages and countries have
admitted in various degrees the principle of divorce. They have
admitted that the sexual connexion once having taken place may be

⟨(*)⟩ The copy-text for this work is in Mary Shelley's hand. Square brackets enclose material
from her transcription deleted from the manuscript by William Godwin; Godwin's
emendations are italicized within angle brackets.⟩

dissolved by some causes, which according to their respective maxims, are to be considered destructive of the design of its institution. Adultery, incompatibility of temper, difference of religion, madness, have all been established ⟨by different codes⟩ as conditions under which the parties to this union might be free to amend their choice. [Milton] ⟨Selden, perhaps the most learned man and the greatest lawyer this country has produced,⟩ and other illustrious writers have already vindicated these doctrines with impunity. My reasonings, I solemnly affirm, amount ⟨to⟩ as much and no more than I here state. I [have a right I believe to] consider the institution of marriage as it exists precisely in the laws and opinions of this country, a mischievous and tyrannical institution, [and to] ⟨or shall⟩ express publickly the reasonings on which that persuasion is founded. If I am judged to be an improper guardian for my children on this account; no men ⟨of a liberal and enquiring spirit⟩ will remain in the community, [of a liberal and inquiring spirit] ⟨who if they are not more free from human feelings, or more fortunate in their developement and growth, than most men can sincerely state their own to be, must not⟩ [who] for some protest against the opinions of the multitude, equivalent to my tenets, [must not] live in the daily terror [that] ⟨lest⟩ a court of justice [may] ⟨should⟩ be converted into an instrument of private vengeance, ⟨and its edicts be⟩ directed ⟨under some remote allegement of public good⟩ against the most deep and sacred interests of ⟨their⟩ heart⟨s⟩.

I am aware [not only that] ⟨of the nature of⟩ the institution of marriage [exists] in this country [but] ⟨and⟩ that the opinions exist which give its vitality to that institution. So far as my own practise has been concerned I have done my utmost, in my peculiar situation, to accommodate myself to the feelings of the community as is expressed in these opinions and laws. It was matter of the deepest grief to me, to instance my particular case, that, at the commencement of my union with the present Mrs. Shelley, I was legally married to a woman of whom delicacy forbids me to say more than that we were disunited by incurable dissentions [and rendered incapable by that marriage] of exhibiting to the world according to those formalities which the world requires, that my motives of preference towards [her] ⟨my present wife⟩ arose from no light or frivolous attachment[, but such as in their sense of the word, as well as in mine, I wish to express by the word "wife".] And that these feelings were sincere, and that I gave [a due] weight to public opinion, there can be no better proof; than that immediately on the death of my late wife, I married the lady whose ⟨*previous*⟩ connexion with me, [alledged to be the consequence not of the common affections of human nature, but] of my peculiar tenets, [is now to be made the ground of depriving me of my children].

75

[My opinions with respect to] my notions of the education of my children with respect

𝔄 𝔓roposal

FOR PUTTING

REFORM TO THE VOTE

THROUGHOUT THE KINGDOM.

BY THE HERMIT OF MARLOW.

LONDON:

PRINTED FOR C. AND J. OLLIER,
3, WELBECK STREET, CAVENDISH SQUARE;
By C. H. Reynell, 21, Piccadilly.

1817.

7. Title-page of *A Proposal for Putting Reform to the Vote* (1817)
Huntington Library (RB 22406)

A PROPOSAL, &c.

A great question is now agitating this nation, which no man or no party of men is competent to decide; indeed there are no materials of evidence which can afford a foresight of the result. Yet on its issue depends whether we are to be slaves or freemen.

It is needless to recapitulate all that has been said about *reform*. Every one is agreed that the House of Commons is not a representation of the people. The only theoretical question that remains, is whether the people ought to legislate for themselves, or be governed by laws and impoverished by taxes originating in the edicts of an assembly which represents somewhat less than a thousandth part of the intire community. I think they ought not to be so taxed and governed. An hospital for lunatics is the only theatre where we can conceive so mournful a comedy to be exhibited as this mighty nation now exhibits: a single person bullying and swindling a thousand of his comrades out of all they possessed in the world, and then trampling and spitting upon them, tho' he were the most contemptible and degraded of mankind, and they had strength in their arms and courage in their hearts. Such a parable realised in political society is a spectacle worthy of the utmost indignation and abhorrence.—

The prerogatives of Parliament constitute a sovereignty which is exercised in contempt of the people, and it is in strict consistency with the laws of human nature, that it should have been exercised for the people's misery and ruin. Those whom they despise, men instinctively seek to render slavish and wretched, that their scorn may be secure. It is the object of the Reformers to restore the people to a sovereignty thus held in their contempt. It is my object, or I would be silent now.

Servitude is sometimes voluntary. Perhaps the people choose to be enslaved, perhaps it is their will to be degraded and ignorant and famished. Perhaps Custom is their only God, and they its fanatic worshippers will shiver in frost and waste in famine rather than deny

that Idol. Perhaps the majority of this nation decree that they will
not be represented in Parliament, that they will not to deprive of
35 power those who have reduced them to the miserable condition in
which they now exist. It is *their* will—it is their own concern. If such
be their decision, the champions of the rights, and the mourners over
the errors and calamities of man, must retire to their homes in
silence, until accumulated sufferings shall have produced the effect
40 of reason:—

The question now at issue, is whether the majority of the adult
individuals of the United Kingdom of Great Britain and Ireland,
desire or no a complete representation in the Legislative Assembly.—

45 I have no doubt that such is their will, and I believe this is the
opinion of most persons conversant with the state of public feeling.
But the fact ought to be formally ascertained before we proceed. If
the majority of the adult population should solemnly state their
desire to be, that the representatives whom they might appoint
50 should constitute the Commons House of Parliament there is
an end of the dispute. Parliament would then be required, not
petitioned to prepare some effectual plan for carrying the general
will into effect; and if Parliament should then refuse—the consequences of the contest that might ensue, would rest on its
55 presumption and temerity alone. Parliament would then have
rebelled against the people.

If the majority of the adult population shall, when seriously called
upon for their opinion, determine on grounds however erroneous,
that the experiment of innovation by reform in Parliament is an evil
60 of greater magnitude than the consequences of misgovernment to
which Parliament has afforded a constitutional sanction . . . then it
becomes us to be silent.—and we should be guilty of the great crime
which I have conditionally imputed to the House of Commons, if
after unequivocal evidence that it was the national will to acquiesce
65 in the existing system we should, by partial assembles of the
multitude, or by any party acts, excite the minority to disturb this
decision.

The first step towards reform is to ascertain this point. For which
purpose I think the following plan would be effectual:—

70 That a meeting should be appointed to be held at the *Crown and
Anchor Tavern* on the   of   , to take into
consideration the most effectual measures for ascertaining whether

or no, a Reform in Parliament is the will of the majority of the individuals of the British Nation.—

That the most eloquent and the most virtuous and the most venerable among the Friends of Liberty should employ their authority and intellect to persuade men to lay aside all animosity and even discussion respecting the topics on which they are disunited, and by the love they bear to their suffering country conjure them to contribute all their energies to set this great question at rest.— whether the Nation desires a reform in Parliament or no?

That the friends of Reform residing in any part of the country, be earnestly intreated to lend perhaps their last and decisive effort to set their hopes and fears at rest.—that those who can, should go to London, and those who cannot but who yet feel that the aid of their talents might be beneficial should address a letter to the chairman of the meeting explaining their sentiments—let these letters be read aloud, let all things be transacted in the face of day. Let Resolutions of an import similar to those that follow, be proposed.

1. That those who think that it is the duty of the People of this Nation to exact such a reform in the Commons House of Parliament as should make that House a complete representation of their will, and that the People have a right to perform this duty, assemble here for the purpose of collecting evidence as to how far it is the will of the majority of the People to acquit themselves of this duty and to exercise this right.

2. That the population of Great Britain and Ireland be divided into three hundred distinct portions, each to contain an equal number of inhabitants, and three hundred persons be commissioned each personally to visit every individual within the district named in his commission, and to inquire whether or no that individual is willing to sign the declaration contained in the third resolution, requesting him to annex to his signature any explanation or exposure of his sentiments which he might choose to place on record. That the following declaration be proposed for signature.

3. That "the House of Commons does not represent the will of the People of the British Nation; we the undersigned therefore declare and publish, and our signatures annexed shall be evidence of our firm and solemn conviction that the liberty, the happiness, and the majesty of the great nation to which it is our boast to belong, have been brought into danger and suffered to decay thro' the corrupt and inadequate manner in which members are chosen to sit

in the Commons' House of Parliament.—We hereby express, before God and our Country, a deliberate and unbiassed persuasion, that it 115 is our duty if we shall be found in the minority in this great question incessantly to petition; if among the majority to require and exact that that House should originate such measures of Reform, as would render its members the actual representatives of the nation."

4. That this meeting shall be held day after day, until it determines 120 on the whole detail of the plan for collecting evidence as to the will of the Nation on the subject of a reform in Parliament.

5. That this meeting disclaims any design, however remote, of lending ⟨its⟩ sanction to the revolutionary and disorganizing schemes which have been most falsely imputed to the Friends of 125 Reform, and declares that its object is purely constitutional.

6. That a subscription be set on foot to defray the expenses of this plan.

In the foregoing proposal of Resolutions to be submitted to a National Meeting of the Friends of Reform, I have purposely 130 avoided detail. If it shall prove that I have in any degree afforded a hint to men who have earned and established their popularity by personal sacrifizes and intellectual eminence such as I have not the presumption to rival, let it belong to them to pursue and develope all suggestions relating to the great cause of Liberty which has been 135 nurtured (I am scarcely conscious of a metaphor) with their very sweat and blood and tears: Some have tended it in dungeons, others have cherished it in famine, all have been constant to it amidst persecution and calumny, and in the face of the sanctions of Power. —So accomplish what ye have begun.—

140 I shall mention therefore only one point relating to the practical part of my proposal. Considerable expenses, according to my present conception, would be necessarily incurred: funds should be created by subscription to meet these demands. I have an income of a thousand a year on which I support my wife and children in decent 145 comfort and from which I satisfy certain large claims of general justice.—Should any plan resembling that which I have proposed, be determined on by you, I will give £100, being a tenth part of one year's income, towards its object. And I will not deem so proudly of myself as to believe that I shall stand alone in this respect when any 150 rational and consistent scheme for the public benefit shall have received the sanction of those great and good men, who have devoted themselves for its preservation.

A certain degree of coalition among the sincere friends of Reform in whatever shape, is indispensable to the success of this proposal. The friends of Universal or of limited Suffrage, of Annual or Triennial Parliaments, ought to settle these subjects on which they disagree, when it is known whether the Nation wills that measure on which they are all agreed. It is trivial to discuss what species of Reform shall have place, when it yet remains a question whether there will be any Reform or no.—

Meanwhile, nothing remains for me but to state explicitly my sentiments on this subject of Reform.—The statement is indeed quite foreign to the merits of the Proposal in itself, and I should have suppressed it, until called upon to subscribe such a Requisition as I have suggested, if the question which it is natural to ask as to what are the sentiments of the person who originates the scheme could have received in any other manner a more simple and direct reply. It appears to me that Annual Parliaments ought to be adopted as an immediate measure, as one which strongly tends to preserve the liberty and happiness of the nation. It would enable men to cultivate those energies on which the performance of the political duties belonging to the citizen of a free state as the rightful guardian of its prosperity, essentially depends. It would familiarise men with liberty by disciplining them to an habitual acquaintance with its forms. Political institution is undoubtedly susceptible of such improvements as no rational person can consider possible so long as the present degraded condition to which the vital imperfections in the existing system of government has reduced the vast multitude of men shall subsist. The securest method of arriving at such beneficial innovations is to proceed gradually and with caution, or in the place of that order and freedom which the friends of reform assert to be violated now, anarchy and despotism will follow. Annual Parliaments have my intire assent.—I will not state those general reasonings in their favour which Mr. Cobbett and other writers have already made familiar to the public mind.—

With respect to Universal Suffrage, I confess I consider its adoption in the present unprepared state of public knowledge and feeling, a measure fraught with peril. I think that none but those who register their names as paying a certain small sum in *direct taxes* ought, at present, to send members to Parliament. The consequences of the *immediate* extension of the elective franchise to *every* male adult would be to place power in the hands of men who have been rendered brutal and torpid and ferocious by ages of slavery. It is to suppose that the qualities belonging to a demagogue are such as are sufficient to endow a legislator. I allow Major Cartwright's arguments to be unanswerable; abstractedly it is the right of every human being to have a share in the government. But Mr. Paine's arguments are also unanswerable; a pure republic may be shewn, by inferences the most obvious and irresistible, to be that system of social order the fittest to produce the happiness and promote the genuine eminence of man. Yet, nothing can less consist with reason, or afford smaller hopes of any beneficial issue than the plan which should abolish the regal and the aristocratical branches of our constitution, before the public mind, thro' many gradations of improvement, shall have arrived at the maturity which can disregard these symbols of its childhood.

PREFACE TO 'FRANKENSTEIN; OR, THE MODERN PROMETHEUS'

The event on which this fiction is founded has been supposed, by Dr. Darwin, and some of the physiological writers of Germany, as not of impossible occurrence. I shall not be supposed as according the remotest degree of serious faith to such an imagination; yet, in assuming it as the basis of a work of fancy, I have not considered myself as merely weaving a series of supernatural terrors. The event on which the interest of the story depends is exempt from the disadvantages of a mere tale of spectres or enchantment. It was recommended by the novelty of the situations which it developes; and, however impossible as a physical fact, affords a point of view to the imagination for the delineating of human passions more comprehensive and commanding than any which the ordinary relations of existing events can yield.

I have thus endeavoured to preserve the truth of the elementary principles of human nature, while I have not scrupled to innovate upon their combinations. The *Iliad*, the tragic poetry of Greece,—Shakespeare, in the *Tempest* and *Midsummer Night's Dream*,—and most especially Milton, in *Paradise Lost*, conform to this rule; and the most humble novelist, who seeks to confer or receive amusement from his labours, may, without presumption, apply to prose fiction a licence, or rather a rule, from the adoption of which so many exquisite combinations of human feeling have resulted in the highest specimens of poetry.

The circumstance on which my story rests was suggested in casual conversation. It was commenced, partly as a source of amusement, and partly as an expedient for exercising any untried resources of mind. Other motives were mingled with these, as the work proceeded. I am by no means indifferent to the manner in which whatever moral tendencies exist in the sentiments or characters it contains shall affect the reader; yet my chief concern in this respect has been limited to the avoiding the enervating effects of the novels of the present day, and to the exhibition of the amiableness of domestic affection, and the excellence of universal virtue. The opinions which naturally spring from the character and situation of the hero are by no means to be conceived as existing always in my own conviction; nor is any inference justly to be drawn from the following pages as prejudicing any philosophical doctrine of whatever kind.

It is a subject also of additional interest to the author, that this story was begun in the majestic region where the scene is principally laid, and in society which cannot cease to be regretted. I passed the summer of 1816 in the environs of Geneva. The season was cold and rainy, and in the evenings we crowded around a blazing wood fire, and occasionally amused ourselves with some German stories of ghosts, which happened to fall into our hands. These tales excited in us a playful desire of imitation. Two other friends (a tale from the pen of one of whom would be far more acceptable to the public than any thing I can ever hope to produce) and myself agreed to write each a story, founded on some supernatural occurrence.

The weather, however, suddenly became serene; and my two friends left me on a journey among the Alps, and lost, in the magnificent scenes which they present, all memory of their ghostly visions. The following tale is the only one which has been completed.

HISTORY

OF

A SIX WEEKS' TOUR

THROUGH

A PART OF FRANCE,
SWITZERLAND, GERMANY, AND HOLLAND:

WITH LETTERS

DESCRIPTIVE OF

A SAIL ROUND THE LAKE OF GENEVA, AND OF
THE GLACIERS OF CHAMOUNI.

LONDON:

PUBLISHED BY T. HOOKHAM, JUN.
OLD BOND STREET;

AND C. AND J. OLLIER,
WELBECK STREET.

1817.

8. Title-page of *A History of a Six Weeks' Tour* (1817)
Huntington Library (RB 23003)

Preface.

Nothing can be more unpresuming than this little volume. It contains the account of some desultory visits by a party of young people to scenes which are now so familiar to our countrymen, that few facts relating to them can be expected to have escaped the many more experienced and exact observers, who have sent their journals to the press. In fact, they have done little else than arrange the few materials which an imperfect journal, and two or three letters to their friends in England afforded. They regret, since their little History is to be offered to the public, that these materials were not more copious and complete. This is a just topic of censure to those who are less inclined to be amused than to condemn. Those whose youth has been past as their's (with what success it imports not) in pursuing, like the swallow, the inconstant summer of delight and beauty which invests this visible world, will perhaps find some entertainment in following the author, with her husband and sister, on foot, through part of France and Switzerland, and in sailing with her down the castled Rhine, through scenes beautiful in themselves, but which, since she visited them, a great Poet has clothed with the freshness of a diviner nature. They will be interested to hear of one who has visited Meillerie, and Clarens, and Chillon, and Vevai—classic ground, peopled with tender and glorious imaginations of the present and the past.

They have perhaps never talked with one who has beheld in the enthusiasm of youth the glaciers, and the lakes, and the forests, and the fountains of the mighty Alps. Such will perhaps forgive the imperfections of their narrative for the sympathy which the adventures and feelings which it recounts, and a curiosity respecting scenes already rendered interesting and illustrious, may excite.

The Poem, entitled "Mont Blanc," is written by the author of the two letters from Chamouni and Vevai. It was composed under the immediate impression of the deep and powerful feelings excited by the objects which it attempts to describe; and as an undisciplined

overflowing of the soul, rests its claim to approbation on an attempt
to imitate the untameable wildness and inaccessible solemnity from
which those feelings sprang.   35

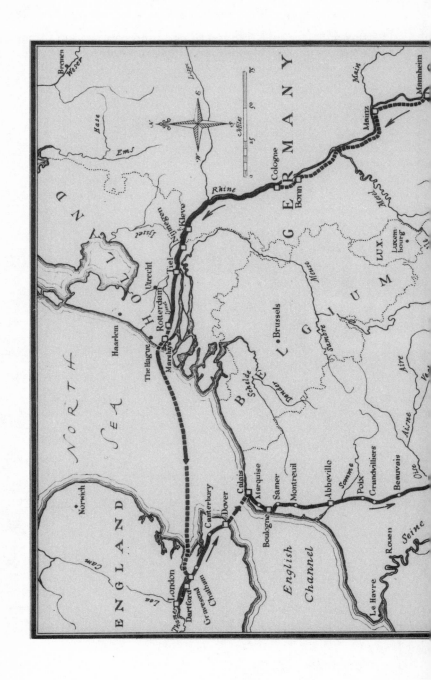

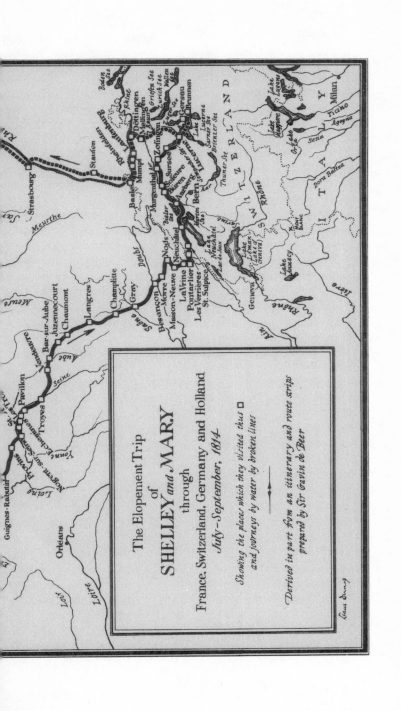

The Elopement Trip
of
SHELLEY and MARY
through
France, Switzerland, Germany and Holland
July–September, 1814

Showing the places which they visited thus □
and journeys by water by broken lines

Derived in part from an itinerary and route strips
prepared by Sir Gavin de Beer

HISTORY OF A SIX WEEKS' TOUR

It is now nearly three years since this Journey took place, and the journal I then kept was not very copious; but I have so often talked over the incidents that befel us, and attempted to describe the scenery through which we passed, that I think few occurrences of any interest will be omitted.

We left London July 28th, 1814, on a hotter day than has been known in this climate for many years. I am not a good traveller, and this heat agreed very ill with me, till, on arriving at Dover, I was refreshed by a sea-bath. As we very much wished to cross the channel with all possible speed, we would not wait for the packet of the following day (it being then about four in the afternoon) but hiring a small boat, resolved to make the passage the same evening, the seamen promising us a voyage of two hours.

The evening was most beautiful; there was but little wind, and the sails flapped in the flagging breeze: the moon rose, and night came on, and with the night a slow, heavy swell, and a fresh breeze, which soon produced a sea so violent as to toss the boat very much. I was dreadfully seasick, and as is usually my custom when thus affected, I slept during the greater part of the night, awaking only from time to time to ask where we were, and to receive the dismal answer each time—"Not quite half way."

The wind was violent and contrary; if we could not reach Calais, the sailors proposed making for Boulogne. They promised only two hours' sail from shore, yet hour after hour passed, and we were still far distant, when the moon sunk in the red and stormy horizon, and the fast-flashing lightning became pale in the breaking day.

We were proceeding slowly against the wind, when suddenly a thunder squall struck the sail, and the waves rushed into the boat: even the sailors acknowledged that our situation was perilous; but they succeeded in reefing the sail;—the wind was now changed, and we drove before the gale directly to Calais. As we entered the harbour I awoke from a comfortless sleep, and saw the sun rise broad, red, and cloudless over the pier.

FRANCE.

Exhausted with sickness and fatigue, I walked over the sands with
70 my companions to the hotel. I heard for the first time the confused
buzz of voices speaking a different language from that to which I had
been accustomed; and saw a costume very unlike that worn on the
opposite side of the channel; the women with high caps and short
jackets; the men with earrings; ladies walking about with high
75 bonnets or *coiffures* lodged on the top of the head, the hair dragged
up underneath, without any stray curls to decorate the temples or
cheeks. There is, however, something very pleasing in the manners
and appearance of the people of Calais, that prepossesses you in
their favour. A national reflection might occur, that when Edward
80 III. took Calais, he turned out the old inhabitants, and peopled it
almost entirely with our own countrymen; but unfortunately the
manners are not English.

We remained during that day and the greater part of the next at
Calais: we had been obliged to leave our boxes the night before at the
85 English custom-house, and it was arranged that they should go by
the packet of the following day, which, detained by contrary wind,
did not arrive until night. S*** and I walked among the fortifications
on the outside of the town; they consisted of fields where the hay
was making. The aspect of the country was rural and pleasant.
90 On the 30th of July, about three in the afternoon, we left Calais, in
a cabriolet drawn by three horses. To persons who had never before
seen any thing but a spruce English chaise and post-boy, there was
something irresistibly ludicrous in our equipage. A cabriolet is
shaped somewhat like a post-chaise, except that it has only two
95 wheels, and consequently there are no doors at the sides; the front is
let down to admit the passengers. The three horses were placed
abreast, the tallest in the middle, who was rendered more formidable
by the addition of an unintelligible article of harness, resembling a
pair of wooden wings fastened to his shoulders; the harnesses were
100 of rope; and the postillion, a queer, upright little fellow with a long
pigtail, *craquéed* his whip, and clattered on, while an old forlorn
shepherd with a cocked hat gazed on us as we passed.

The roads are excellent, but the heat was intense, and I suffered
greatly from it. We slept at Boulogne the first night, where there was

an ugly but remarkably good-tempered femme de chambre. This 105
made us for the first time remark the difference which exists
between this class of persons in France and in England. In the latter
country they are prudish, and if they become in the least degree
familiar they are impudent. The lower orders in France have the
easiness and politeness of the most well-bred English; they treat you 110
unaffectedly as their equal, and consequently there is no scope for
insolence.

We had ordered horses to be ready during the night, but we were
too fatigued to make use of them. The man insisted on being paid for
the whole post. *Ah! Madame*, said the femme-de-chambre, *pensez-y;* 115
ç'est pour dédommager les pauvres chevaux d'avoir perdues leur douce
sommeil. A joke from an English chamber-maid would have been
quite another thing.

The first appearance that struck our English eyes was the want of
enclosures; but the fields were flourishing with a plentiful harvest. 120
We observed no vines on this side Paris.

The weather still continued very hot, and travelling produced a
very bad effect upon my health; my companions were induced by
this circumstance to hasten the journey as much as possible; and
accordingly we did not rest the following night, and the next day, 125
about two, arrived in Paris.

In this city there are no hotels where you can reside as long or as
short a time as you please, and we were obliged to engage apartments
at an hotel for a week. They were dear, and not very pleasant. As
usual in France, the principal apartment was a bedchamber; there 130
was another closet with a bed, and an ante-chamber, which we used
as a sitting-room.

The heat of the weather was excessive, so that we were unable to
walk except in the afternoon. On the first evening we walked to the
gardens of the Thuilleries; they are formal and uninteresting, in the 135
French fashion, the trees cut into shapes, and without any grass. I
think the Boulevards infinitely more pleasant. This street nearly
surrounds Paris, and is eight miles in extent; it is very wide, and
planted on either side with trees. At one end is a superb cascade
which refreshes the senses by its continual splashing: near this stands 140
the gate of St. Denis, a beautiful piece of sculpture. I do not know
how it may at present be disfigured by the Gothic barbarism of the
conquerors of France, who were not contented with retaking the
spoils of Napoleon, but with impotent malice, destroyed the

145 monuments of their own defeat. When I saw this gate, it was in its
splendour, and made you imagine that the days of Roman greatness
were transported to Paris.

After remaining a week in Paris, we received a small remittance
that set us free from a kind of imprisonment there which we found
150 very irksome. But how should we proceed? After talking over and
rejecting many plans, we fixed on one eccentric enough, but which,
from its romance, was very pleasing to us. In England we could not
have put it in execution without sustaining continual insult and
impertinence: the French are far more tolerant of the vagaries of
155 their neighbours. We resolved to walk through France; but as I was
too weak for any considerable distance, and my sister could not be
supposed to be able to walk as far as S*** each day, we determined to
purchase an ass, to carry our portmanteau and one of us by turns.

Early, therefore, on Monday, August 8th, S*** and C*** went to
160 the ass market, and purchased an ass, and the rest of the day, until
four in the afternoon, was spent in preparations for our departure;
during which, Madame l'hôtesse paid us a visit, and attempted to
dissuade us from our design. She represented to us that a large army
had been recently disbanded, that the soldiers and officers wandered
165 idle about the country, and that *les Dames seroient certainement
enlevées.* But we were proof against her arguments, and packing up a
few necessaries, leaving the rest to go by the diligence, we departed
in a fiacre from the door of the hotel, our little ass following.

We dismissed the coach at the barrier. It was dusk, and the ass
170 seemed totally unable to bear one of us, appearing to sink under the
portmanteau, although it was small and light. We were, however,
merry enough, and thought the leagues short. We arrived at
Charenton about ten.

Charenton is prettily situated in a valley, through which the Seine
175 flows, winding among banks variegated with trees. On looking at
this scene, C*** exclaimed, "Oh! this is beautiful enough; let us live
here." This was her exclamation on every new scene, and as each
surpassed the one before, she cried, "I am glad we did not stay at
Charenton, but let us live here."

180 Finding our ass useless, we sold it before we proceeded on our
journey, and bought a mule, for ten Napoleons. About nine o'clock
we departed. We were clad in black silk. I rode on the mule, which
carried also our portmanteau; S*** and C*** followed, bringing a
small basket of provisions. At about one we arrived at Gros Bois,

where, under the shade of trees, we ate our bread and fruit, and drank 185
our wine, thinking of Don Quixote and Sancho.

The country through which we passed was highly cultivated, but
uninteresting; the horizon scarcely ever extended beyond the
circumference of a few fields, bright and waving with the golden
harvest. We met several travellers; but our mode, although novel, did 190
not appear to excite any curiosity or remark. This night we slept at
Guignes, in the same room and beds in which Napoleon and some of
his Generals had rested during the late war. The little old woman of
the place was highly gratified in having this little story to tell, and
spoke in warm praise of the Empress Josephine and Marie Louise, 195
who had at different times passed on that road.

As we continued our route, Provins was the first place that struck
us with interest. It was our stage of rest for the night; we approached
it at sunset. After having gained the summit of a hill, the prospect of
the town opened upon us as it lay in the valley below; a rocky hill 200
rose abruptly on one side, on the top of which stood a ruined citadel
with extensive walls and towers; lower down, but beyond, was the
cathedral, and the whole formed a scene for painting. After having
travelled for two days through a country perfectly without interest,
it was a delicious relief for the eye to dwell again on some 205
irregularities and beauty of country. Our fare at Provins was coarse,
and our beds uncomfortable, but the remembrance of this prospect
made us contented and happy.

We now approached scenes that reminded us of what we had
nearly forgotten, that France had lately been the country in which 210
great and extraordinary events had taken place. Nogent, a town we
entered about noon the following day, had been entirely desolated
by the Cossacs. Nothing could be more entire than the ruin which
these barbarians had spread as they advanced; perhaps they
remembered Moscow and the destruction of the Russian villages; 215
but we were now in France, and the distress of the inhabitants,
whose houses had been burned, their cattle killed, and all their
wealth destroyed, has given a sting to my detestation of war, which
none can feel who have not travelled through a country pillaged and
wasted by this plague, which, in his pride, man inflicts upon his 220
fellow.

We quitted the great route soon after we had left Nogent, to strike
across the country to Troyes. About six in the evening we arrived at
St. Aubin, a lovely village embosomed in trees; but on a nearer view

225 we found the cottages roofless, the rafters black, and the walls
     dilapidated;—a few inhabitants remained. We asked for milk—they
     had none to give; all their cows had been taken by the Cossacs. We
     had still some leagues to travel that night, but we found that they
     were not post leagues, but the measurement of the inhabitants, and
230 nearly double the distance. The road lay over a desert plain, and as
     night advanced we were often in danger of losing the track of wheels,
     which was our only guide. Night closed in, and we suddenly lost all
     trace of the road; but a few trees, indistinctly seen, seemed to
     indicate the position of a village. About ten we arrived at Trois
235 Maisons, where, after a supper on milk and sour bread, we retired to
     rest on wretched beds: but sleep is seldom denied, except to the
     indolent, and after the day's fatigue, although my bed was nothing
     more than a sheet spread upon straw, I slept soundly until the
     morning was considerably advanced.
240   S*** had hurt his ancle so considerably the preceding evening,
     that he was obliged, during the whole of the following day's journey,
     to ride on our mule. Nothing could be more barren and wretched
     than the track through which we now passed; the ground was chalky
     and uncovered even by grass, and where there had been any attempts
245 made towards cultivation, the straggling ears of corn discovered
     more plainly the barren nature of the soil. Thousands of insects,
     which were of the same white colour as the road, infested our path;
     the sky was cloudless, and the sun darted its rays upon us, reflected
     back by the earth, until I nearly fainted under the heat. A village
250 appeared at a distance, cheering us with a prospect of rest. It gave us
     new strength to proceed; but it was a wretched place, and afforded us
     but little relief. It had been once large and populous, but now the
     houses were roofless, and the ruins that lay scattered about, the
     gardens covered with the white dust of the torn cottages, the black
255 burnt beams, and squalid looks of the inhabitants, presented in every
     direction the melancholy aspect of devastation. One house, a
     cabaret, alone remained; we were here offered plenty of milk,
     stinking bacon, sour bread, and a few vegetables, which we were to
     dress for ourselves.
260   As we prepared our dinner in a place, so filthy that the sight of it
     alone was sufficient to destroy our appetite, the people of the village
     collected around us, squalid with dirt, their countenances ex-
     pressing every thing that is disgusting and brutal. They seemed
     indeed entirely detached from the rest of the world, and ignorant of

all that was passing in it. There is much less communication between 265
the various towns of France than in England. The use of passports
may easily account for this: these people did not know that
Napoleon was deposed, and when we asked why they did not
rebuild their cottages, they replied, that they were afraid that the
Cossacs would destroy them again upon their return. Echemine (the 270
name of this village) is in every respect the most disgusting place I
ever met with.

Two leagues beyond, on the same road, we came to the village of
Pavillon, so unlike Echemine, that we might have fancied ourselves
in another quarter of the globe; here every thing denoted cleanliness 275
and hospitality; many of the cottages were destroyed, but the
inhabitants were employed in repairing them. What could occasion
so great a difference?

Still our road lay over this track of uncultivated country, and our
eyes were fatigued by observing nothing but a white expanse of 280
ground, where no bramble or stunted shrub adorned its barrenness.
Towards evening we reached a small plantation of vines, it appeared
like one of those islands of verdure that are met with in the midst of
the sands of Lybia, but the grapes were not yet ripe. S*** was totally
incapable of walking, and C*** and I were very tired before we 285
arrived at Troyes.

We rested here for the night, and devoted the following day to a
consideration of the manner in which we should proceed. S***'s
sprain rendered our pedestrianism impossible. We accordingly sold
our mule, and bought an open *voiture* that went on four wheels, for 290
five Napoleons, and hired a man with a mule for eight more, to
convey us to Neufchâtel in six days.

The suburbs of Troyes were destroyed, and the town itself dirty
and uninviting. I remained at the inn writing, while S*** and C***
arranged this bargain and visited the cathedral of the town; and the 295
next morning we departed in our *voiture* for Neufchâtel. A curious
instance of French vanity occurred on leaving this town. Our
voiturier pointed to the plain around, and mentioned, that it had
been the scene of a battle between the Russians and the French. "In
which the Russians gained the victory?"—"Ah no, Madame," replied 300
the man, "the French are never beaten." "But how was it then," we
asked, "that the Russians had entered Troyes soon after?"—"Oh,
after having been defeated, they took a circuitous route, and thus
entered the town."

305 Vandeuvres is a pleasant town, at which we rested during the hours of noon. We walked in the grounds of a nobleman, laid out in the English taste, and terminated in a pretty wood; it was a scene that reminded us of our native country. As we left Vandeuvres the aspect of the country suddenly changed; abrupt hills, covered with
310 vineyards, intermixed with trees, enclosed a narrow valley, the channel of the Aube. The view was interspersed by green meadows, groves of poplar and white willow, and spires of village churches, which the Cossacs had yet spared. Many villages, ruined by the war, occupied the most romantic spots.

315 In the evening we arrived at Bar-sur-Aube, a beautiful town, placed at the opening of the vale where the hills terminate abruptly. We climbed the highest of these, but scarce had we reached the top, when a mist descended upon every thing, and the rain began to fall: we were wet through before we could reach our inn. It was evening,
320 and the laden clouds made the darkness almost as deep as that of midnight; but in the west an unusually brilliant and fiery redness occupied an opening in the vapours, and added to the interest of our little expedition: the cottage lights were reflected in the tranquil river, and the dark hills behind, dimly seen, resembled vast and
325 frowning mountains.

As we quitted Bar-sur-Aube, we at the same time bade a short farewel to hills. Passing through the towns of Chaumont, Langres (which was situated on a hill, and surrounded by ancient fortifications), Champlitte, and Gray, we travelled for nearly three
330 days through plains, where the country gently undulated, and relieved the eye from a perpetual flat, without exciting any peculiar interest. Gentle rivers, their banks ornamented by a few trees, stole through these plains, and a thousand beautiful summer insects skimmed over the streams. The third day was a day of rain, and the
335 first that had taken place during our journey. We were soon wet through, and were glad to stop at a little inn to dry ourselves. The reception we received here was very unprepossessing, the people still kept their seats round the fire, and seemed very unwilling to make way for the dripping guests. In the afternoon, however, the
340 weather became fine, and at about six in the evening we entered Besançon.

Hills had appeared in the distance during the whole day, and we had advanced gradually towards them, but were unprepared for the scene that broke upon us as we passed the gate of this city. On quitting the walls, the road wound underneath a high precipice; on the other side the hills rose more gradually, and the green valley that intervened between them was watered by a pleasant river; before us arose an amphitheatre of hills covered with vines, but irregular and rocky. The last gate of the town was cut through the precipitous rock that arose on one side, and in that place jutted into the road.

This approach to mountain scenery filled us with delight; it was otherwise with our *voiturier:* he came from the plains of Troyes, and these hills so utterly scared him, that he in some degree lost his reason. After winding through the valley, we began to ascend the mountains which were its boundary: we left our *voiture*, and walked on, delighted with every new view that broke upon us.

When we had ascended the hills for about a mile and a half, we found our *voiturier* at the door of a wretched inn, having taken the mule from the *voiture*, and obstinately determined to remain for the night at this miserable village of Mort. We could only submit, for he was deaf to all we could urge, and to our remonstrances only replied, *Je ne puis plus.*

Our beds were too uncomfortable to allow a thought of sleeping in them: we could only procure one room, and our hostess gave us to understand that our *voiturier* was to occupy the same apartment. It was of little consequence, as we had previously resolved not to enter the beds. The evening was fine, and after the rain the air was perfumed by many delicious scents. We climbed to a rocky seat on the hill that overlooked the village, where we remained until sunset. The night was passed by the kitchen fire in a wretched manner, striving to catch a few moments of sleep, which were denied to us. At three in the morning we pursued our journey.

Our road led to the summit of the hills that environ Besançon. From the top of one of these we saw the whole expanse of the valley filled with a white undulating mist, which was pierced like islands by the piny mountains. The sun had just risen, and a ray of red light lay upon the waves of this fluctuating vapour. To the west, opposite the sun, it seemed driven by the light against the rocks in immense masses of foaming cloud, until it became lost in the distance, mixing its tints with the fleecy sky.

Our *voiturier* insisted on remaining two hours at the village of Noé, although we were unable to procure any dinner, and wished to go on to the next stage. I have already said, that the hills scared his senses, and he had become disobliging, sullen, and stupid. While he

385 waited we walked to the neighbouring wood: it was a fine forest, carpeted beautifully with moss, and in various places overhung by rocks, in whose crevices young pines had taken root, and spread their branches for shade to those below; the noon heat was intense, and we were glad to shelter ourselves from it in the shady retreats of 390 this lovely forest.

On our return to the village we found, to our extreme surprise, that the *voiturier* had departed nearly an hour before, leaving word that he expected to meet us on the road. S***'s sprain rendered him incapable of much exertion; but there was no remedy, and we 395 proceeded on foot to Maison Neuve, an *auberge*, four miles and a half distant.

At Maison Neuve the man had left word that he should proceed to Pontarlier, the frontier town of France, six leagues distant, and that if we did not arrive that night, he should the next morning leave the 400 *voiture* at an inn, and return with the mule to Troyes. We were astonished at the impudence of this message, but the boy of the inn comforted us by saying, that by going on a horse by a cross road, where the *voiture* could not venture, he could easily overtake and intercept the *voiturier*, and accordingly we dispatched him, walking 405 slowly after. We waited at the next inn for dinner, and in about two hours the boy returned. The man promised to wait for us at an *auberge* two leagues further on. S***'s ancle had become very painful, but we could procure no conveyance, and as the sun was nearly setting, we were obliged to hasten on. The evening was most 410 beautiful, and the scenery lovely enough to beguile us of our fatigue: the horned moon hung in the light of sunset, that threw a glow of unusual depth of redness over the piny mountains and the dark deep vallies they enclosed; at intervals in the woods were beautiful lawns interspersed with picturesque clumps of trees, and dark pines 415 overshadowed our road.

In about two hours we arrived at the promised termination of our journey, but the *voiturier* was not there: after the boy had left him, he again pursued his journey towards Pontarlier. We were enabled, however, to procure here a rude kind of cart, and in this manner 420 arrived late at Pontarlier, where we found our conductor, who blundered out many falsehoods for excuses; and thus ended the adventures of that day.

SWITZERLAND.

On passing the French barrier, a surprising difference may be observed between the opposite nations that inhabit either side. The Swiss cottages are much cleaner and neater, and the inhabitants ₄₂₅ exhibit the same contrast. The Swiss women wear a great deal of white linen, and their whole dress is always perfectly clean. This superior cleanliness is chiefly produced by the difference of religion: travellers in Germany remark the same contrast between the protestant and catholic towns, although they be but a few leagues ₄₃₀ separate.

The scenery of this day's journey was divine, exhibiting piny mountains, barren rocks, and spots of verdure surpassing imagination. After descending for nearly a league between lofty rocks, covered with pines, and interspersed with green glades, where the ₄₃₅ grass is short, and soft, and beautifully verdant, we arrived at the village of St. Sulpice.

The mule had latterly become very lame, and the man so disobliging, that we determined to engage a horse for the remainder of the way. Our *voiturier* had anticipated us, without in the least ₄₄₀ intimating his intention to us: he had determined to leave us at this village, and taken measures to that effect. The man we now engaged was a Swiss, a cottager of the better class, who was proud of his mountains and his country. Pointing to the glades that were interspersed among the woods, he informed us that they were very ₄₄₅ beautiful, and were excellent pasture; that the cows thrived there, and consequently produced excellent milk, from which the best cheese and butter in the world were made.

The mountains after St. Sulpice became loftier and more beautiful. We passed through a narrow valley between two ranges of ₄₅₀ mountains, clothed with forests, at the bottom of which flowed a river, from whose narrow bed on either side the boundaries of the vale arose precipitously. The road lay about half way up the mountain, which formed one of the sides, and we saw the overhanging rocks above us and below, enormous pines, and the ₄₅₅ river, not to be perceived but from its reflection of the light of heaven, far beneath. The mountains of this beautiful ravine are so little asunder, that in time of war with France an iron chain is thrown

across it. Two leagues from Neufchâtel we saw the Alps: range after
460 range of black mountains are seen extending one before the other,
and far behind all, towering above every feature of the scene, the
snowy Alps. They were an hundred miles distant, but reach so high
in the heavens, that they look like those accumulated clouds of
dazzling white that arrange themselves on the horizon during
465 summer. Their immensity staggers the imagination, and so far surpasses all conception, that it requires an effort of the understanding to believe that they indeed form a part of the earth.

From this point we descended to Neufchâtel, which is situated in
a narrow plain, between the mountains and its immense lake, and
470 presents no additional aspect of peculiar interest.

We remained the following day at this town, occupied in a
consideration of the step it would now be advisable for us to
take. The money we had brought with us from Paris was nearly
exhausted, but we obtained about £38. in silver upon discount from
475 one of the bankers of the city, and with this we resolved to journey
towards the lake of Uri, and seek in that romantic and interesting
country some cottage where we might dwell in peace and solitude.
Such were our dreams, which we should probably have realized, had
it not been for the deficiency of that indispensible article money,
480 which obliged us to return to England.

A Swiss, whom S*** met at the post-office, kindly interested
himself in our affairs, and assisted us to hire a *voiture* to convey us
to Lucerne, the principal town of the lake of that name, which is
connected with the lake of Uri. This man was imbued with the
485 spirit of true politeness, and endeavoured to perform real services,
and seemed to regard the mere ceremonies of the affair as things of
very little value. The journey to Lucerne occupied rather more
than two days. The country was flat and dull, and, excepting that
we now and then caught a glimpse of the divine Alps, there was
490 nothing in it to interest us. Lucerne promised better things, and as
soon as we arrived (August 23d) we hired a boat, with which we
proposed to coast the lake until we should meet with some suitable
habitation, or perhaps, even going to Altorf, cross Mont St.
Gothard, and seek in the warm climate of the country to the south
495 of the Alps an air more salubrious, and a temperature better fitted
for the precarious state of S***'s health, than the bleak region to
the north. The lake of Lucerne is encompassed on all sides by high
mountains that rise abruptly from the water;—sometimes their

bare fronts descend perpendicularly and cast a black shade upon the waves;—sometimes they are covered with thick wood, whose dark foliage is interspersed by the brown bare crags on which the trees have taken root. In every part where a glade shews itself in the forest it appears cultivated, and cottages peep from among the woods. The most luxuriant islands, rocky and covered with moss, and bending trees, are sprinkled over the lake. Most of these are decorated by the figure of a saint in wretched waxwork.

The direction of this lake extends at first from east to west, then turning a right angle, it lies from north to south; this latter part is distinguished in name from the other, and is called the lake of Uri. The former part is also nearly divided midway, where the jutting land almost meets, and its craggy sides cast a deep shadow on the little strait through which you pass. The summits of several of the mountains that enclose the lake to the south are covered by eternal glaciers; of one of these, opposite Brunen, they tell the story of a priest and his mistress, who, flying from persecution, inhabited a cottage at the foot of the snows. One winter night an avalanche overwhelmed them, but their plaintive voices are still heard in stormy nights, calling for succour from the peasants.

Brunen is situated on the northern side of the angle which the lake makes, forming the extremity of the lake of Lucerne. Here we rested for the night, and dismissed our boatmen. Nothing could be more magnificent than the view from this spot. The high mountains encompassed us, darkening the waters; at a distance on the shores of Uri we could perceive the chapel of Tell, and this was the village where he matured the conspiracy which was to overthrow the tyrant of his country; and indeed this lovely lake, these sublime mountains, and wild forests, seemed a fit cradle for a mind aspiring to high adventure and heroic deeds. Yet we saw no glimpse of his spirit in his present countrymen. The Swiss appeared to us then, and experience has confirmed our opinion, a people slow of comprehension and of action; but habit has made them unfit for slavery, and they would, I have little doubt, make a brave defence against any invader of their freedom.

Such were our reflections, and we remained until late in the evening on the shores of the lake conversing, enjoying the rising breeze, and contemplating with feelings of exquisite delight the divine objects that surrounded us.

The following day was spent in a consideration of our

circumstances, and in contemplation of the scene around us. A
540 furious *vent d'Italie* (south wind) tore up the lake, making immense
waves, and carrying the water in a whirlwind high in the air, when it
fell like heavy rain into the lake. The waves broke with a tremendous
noise on the rocky shores. This conflict continued during the whole
day, but it became calmer towards the evening. S*** and I walked on
545 the banks, and sitting on a rude pier, S*** read aloud the account of
the Siege of Jerusalem from Tacitus.

In the mean time we endeavoured to find an habitation, but could
only procure two unfurnished rooms in an ugly big house, called the
Chateau. These we hired at a guinea a month, had beds moved into
550 them, and the next day took possession. But it was a wretched place,
with no comfort or convenience. It was with difficulty that we could
get any food prepared: as it was cold and rainy, we ordered a fire—
they lighted an immense stove which occupied a corner of the room;
it was long before it heated, and when hot, the warmth was so
555 unwholesome, that we were obliged to throw open our windows to
prevent a kind of suffocation; added to this, there was but one
person in Brunen who could speak French, a barbarous kind of
German being the language of this part of Switzerland. It was with
difficulty, therefore, that we could get our most ordinary wants
560 supplied.

These immediate inconveniences led us to a more serious
consideration of our situation. The £28. which we possessed, was all
the money that we could count upon with any certainty, until the
following December. S***'s presence in London was absolutely
565 necessary for the procuring any further supply. What were we to do?
we should soon be reduced to absolute want. Thus, after balancing
the various topics that offered themselves for discussion, we
resolved to return to England.

Having formed this resolution, we had not a moment for delay:
570 our little store was sensibly decreasing, and £28. could hardly appear
sufficient for so long a journey. It had cost us sixty to cross France
from Paris to Neufchâtel; but we now resolved on a more
economical mode of travelling. Water conveyances are always the
cheapest, and fortunately we were so situated, that by taking
575 advantage of the rivers of the Reuss and Rhine, we could reach
England without travelling a league on land. This was our plan; we
should travel eight hundred miles, and was this possible for so small
a sum? but there was no other alternative, and indeed S*** only
knew how very little we had to depend upon.

We departed the next morning for the town of Lucerne. It rained 580
violently during the first part of our voyage, but towards its
conclusion the sky became clear, and the sun-beams dried and
cheered us. We saw again, and for the last time, the rocky shores of
this beautiful lake, its verdant isles, and snow-capt mountains.

We landed at Lucerne, and remained in that town the following 585
night, and the next morning (August 28th) departed in the *diligence
par-eau* for Loffenburgh, a town on the Rhine, where the falls of that
river prevented the same vessel from proceeding any further. Our
companions in this voyage were of the meanest class, smoked
prodigiously, and were exceedingly disgusting. After having landed 590
for refreshment in the middle of the day, we found, on our return to
the boat, that our former seats were occupied; we took others, when
the original possessors angrily, and almost with violence, insisted
upon our leaving them. Their brutal rudeness to us, who did not
understand their language, provoked S*** to knock one of the 595
foremost down: he did not return the blow, but continued his
vociferations until the boatmen interfered, and provided us with
other seats.

The Reuss is exceedingly rapid, and we descended several falls,
one of more than eight feet. There is something very delicious in the 600
sensation, when at one moment you are at the top of a fall of water,
and before the second has expired you are at the bottom, still rushing
on with the impulse which the descent has given. The waters of the
Rhône are blue, those of the Reuss are of a deep green. I should think
that there must be something in the beds of these rivers, and that the 605
accidents of the banks and sky cannot alone cause this difference.

Sleeping at Dettingen, we arrived the next morning at
Loffenburgh, where we engaged a small canoe to convey us to
Mumph. I give these boats this Indian appellation, as they were of
the rudest construction—long, narrow, and flat-bottomed: they 610
consisted merely of straight pieces of deal board, unpainted, and
nailed together with so little care, that the water constantly poured
in at the crevices, and the boat perpetually required emptying. The
river was rapid, and sped swiftly, breaking as it passed on
innumerable rocks just covered by the water: it was a sight of some 615
dread to see our frail boat winding among the eddies of the rocks,
which it was death to touch, and when the slightest inclination on
one side would instantly have overset it.

We could not procure a boat at Mumph, and we thought

620 ourselves lucky in meeting with a return *cabriolet* to Rheinfelden; but our good fortune was of short duration: about a league from Mumph the *cabriolet* broke down, and we were obliged to proceed on foot. Fortunately we were overtaken by some Swiss soldiers, who were discharged and returning home, who carried our box for us as 625 far as Rheinfelden, when we were directed to proceed a league farther to a village, where boats were commonly hired. Here, although not without some difficulty, we procured a boat for Basle, and proceeded down a swift river, while evening came on, and the air was bleak and comfortless. Our voyage was, however, short, and we 630 arrived at the place of our destination by six in the evening.

GERMANY.

Before we slept, S*** had made a bargain for a boat to carry us to Mayence, and the next morning, bidding adieu to Switzerland, we embarked in a boat laden with merchandize, but where we had no fellow-passengers to disturb our tranquillity by their vulgarity and 635 rudeness. The wind was violently against us, but the stream, aided by a slight exertion from the rowers, carried us on; the sun shone pleasantly, S*** read aloud to us Mary Wollstonecraft's Letters from Norway, and we passed our time delightfully.

The evening was such as to find few parallels in beauty; as it 640 approached, the banks which had hitherto been flat and uninteresting, became exceedingly beautiful. Suddenly the river grew narrow, and the boat dashed with inconceivable rapidity round the base of a rocky hill covered with pines; a ruined tower, with its desolated windows, stood on the summit of another hill that jutted 645 into the river; beyond, the sunset was illuminating the distant mountains and clouds, casting the reflection of its rich and purple hues on the agitated river. The brilliance and contrasts of the colours on the circling whirlpools of the stream, was an appearance entirely new and most beautiful; the shades grew darker as the sun descended 650 below the horizon, and after we had landed, as we walked to our inn round a beautiful bay, the full moon arose with divine splendour, casting its silver light on the before-purpled waves.

The following morning we pursued our journey in a slight canoe, in which every motion was accompanied with danger; but the 655 stream had lost much of its rapidity, and was no longer impeded by rocks, the banks were low, and covered with willows. We passed Strasburgh, and the next morning it was proposed to us that we should proceed in the *diligence par-eau*, as the navigation would become dangerous for our small boat.

There were only four passengers besides ourselves, three of these 660 were students of the Strasburgh university: Schwitz, a rather handsome, good tempered young man; Hoff, a kind of shapeless animal, with a heavy, ugly, German face; and Schneider, who was nearly an ideot, and on whom his companions were always playing a thousand tricks: the remaining passengers were a woman, and an 665 infant.

The country was uninteresting, but we enjoyed fine weather, and slept in the boat in the open air without any inconvenience. We saw on the shores few objects that called forth our attention, if I except the town of Manheim, which was strikingly neat and clean. It was 670 situated at about a mile from the river, and the road to it was planted on each side with beautiful acacias. The last part of this voyage was performed close under land, as the wind was so violently against us, that even with all the force of a rapid current in our favour, we were hardly permitted to proceed. We were told (and not without reason) 675 that we ought to congratulate ourselves on having exchanged our canoe for this boat, as the river was now of considerable width, and tossed by the wind into large waves. The same morning a boat, containing fifteen persons, in attempting to cross the water, had upset in the middle of the river, and every one in it perished. We saw 680 the boat turned over, floating down the stream. This was a melancholy sight, yet ludicrously commented on by the *batelier;* almost the whole stock of whose French consisted in the word *seulement.* When we asked him what had happened, he answered, laying particular emphasis on this favourite dissyllable, *Ç'est seule-* 685 *ment un bateau, qui étoit seulement renversée, et tous les peuples sont seulement noyés.*

Mayence is one of the best fortified towns in Germany. The river, which is broad and rapid, guards it to the east, and the hills for three leagues around exhibit signs of fortifications. The town itself is old, 690 the streets narrow, and the houses high: the cathedral and towers of the town still bear marks of the bombardment which took place in the revolutionary war.

We took our place in the *diligence par-eau* for Cologne, and the next morning (September 4th) departed. This conveyance appeared 695 much more like a mercantile English affair than any we had before seen; it was shaped like a steam-boat, with a cabin and a high deck. Most of our companions chose to remain in the cabin; this was fortunate for us, since nothing could be more horribly disgusting 700 than the lower order of smoking, drinking Germans who travelled with us; they swaggered and talked, and what was hideous to English eyes, kissed one another: there were, however, two or three merchants of a better class, who appeared well-informed and polite.

The part of the Rhine down which we now glided, is that so 705 beautifully described by Lord Byron in his third canto of *Childe Harold*. We read these verses with delight, as they conjured before us these lovely scenes with the truth and vividness of painting, and with the exquisite addition of glowing language and a warm imagination. We were carried down by a dangerously rapid current, and saw 710 on either side of us hills covered with vines and trees, craggy cliffs crowned by desolate towers, and wooded islands, where picturesque ruins peeped from behind the foliage, and cast the shadows of their forms on the troubled waters, which distorted without deforming them. We heard the songs of the vintagers, and if 715 surrounded by disgusting Germans, the sight was not so replete with enjoyment as I now fancy it to have been; yet memory, taking all the dark shades from the picture, presents this part of the Rhine to my remembrance as the loveliest paradise on earth.

We had sufficient leisure for the enjoyment of these scenes, for the 720 boatmen, neither rowing nor steering, suffered us to be carried down by the stream, and the boat turned round and round as it descended.

While I speak with disgust of the Germans who travelled with us, I should in justice to these borderers record, that at one of the inns 725 here we saw the only pretty woman we met with in the course of our travels. She is what I should conceive to be a truly German beauty; grey eyes, slightly tinged with brown, and expressive of uncommon sweetness and frankness. She had lately recovered from a fever, and this added to the interest of her countenance, by adorning it with an 730 appearance of extreme delicacy.

On the following day we left the hills of the Rhine, and found that, for the remainder of our journey, we should move sluggishly through the flats of Holland: the river also winds extremely, so that, after calculating our resources, we resolved to finish our journey in a 735 land diligence. Our water conveyance remained that night at Bonn, and that we might lose no time, we proceeded post the same night to Cologne, where we arrived late; for the rate of travelling in Germany seldom exceeds a mile and a half an hour.

Cologne appeared an immense town, as we drove through street after street to arrive at our inn. Before we slept, we secured places in 740 the diligence, which was to depart next morning for Clêves.

Nothing in the world can be more wretched than travelling in this German diligence: the coach is clumsy and comfortless, and we proceeded so slowly, stopping so often, that it appeared as if we should never arrive at our journey's end. We were allowed two hours 745 for dinner, and two more were wasted in the evening while the coach was being changed. We were then requested, as the diligence had a greater demand for places than it could supply, to proceed in a *cabriolet* which was provided for us. We readily consented, as we hoped to travel faster than in the heavy diligence; but this was not 750 permitted, and we jogged on all night behind this cumbrous machine. In the morning when we stopped, we for a moment indulged a hope that we had arrived at Clêves, which was at the distance of five leagues from our last night's stage; but we had only advanced three leagues in seven or eight hours, and had yet eight 755 miles to perform. However, we first rested about three hours at this stage, where we could not obtain breakfast or any convenience, and at about eight o'clock we again departed, and with slow, although far from easy travelling, faint with hunger and fatigue, we arrived by noon at Clêves.

760

HOLLAND.

Tired by the slow pace of the diligence, we resolved to post the remainder of the way. We had now, however, left Germany, and travelled at about the same rate as an English post-chaise. The country was entirely flat, and the roads so sandy, that the horses proceeded with difficulty. The only ornaments of this country are 765 the turf fortifications that surround the towns. At Nimeguen we passed the flying bridge, mentioned in the letters of Lady Mary Montague. We had intended to travel all night, but at T⟨h⟩iel where we arrived at about ten o'clock, we were assured that no post-boy was to be found who would proceed at so late an hour, on account of 770 the robbers who infested the roads. This was an obvious imposition;

but as we could procure neither horses nor driver, we were obliged to sleep here.

During the whole of the following day the road lay between 775 canals, which intersect this country in every direction. The roads were excellent, but the Dutch have contrived as many inconveniences as possible. In our journey of the day before, we had passed by a windmill, which was so situated with regard to the road, that it was only by keeping close to the opposite side, and passing 780 quickly, that we could avoid the sweep of its sails.

The roads between the canals were only wide enough to admit of one carriage, so that when we encountered another we were obliged sometimes to back for half a mile, until we should come to one of the drawbridges which led to the fields, on which one of the *cabriolets* 785 was rolled, while the other passed. But they have another practice, which is still more annoying: the flax when cut is put to soak under the mud of the canals, and then placed to dry against the trees which are planted on either side of the road; the stench that it exhales, when the beams of the sun draw out the moisture, is scarcely endurable. 790 We saw many enormous frogs and toads in the canals; and the only sight which refreshed the eye by its beauty was the delicious verdure of the fields, where the grass was as rich and green as that of England, an appearance not common on the continent.

Rotterdam is remarkably clean: the Dutch even wash the outside 795 brickwork of their houses. We remained here one day, and met with a man in a very unfortunate condition: he had been born in Holland, and had spent so much of his life between England, France, and Germany, that he had acquired a slight knowledge of the language of each country, and spoke all very imperfectly. He said that he 800 understood English best, but he was nearly unable to express himself in that.

On the evening of the 8th of September we sailed from Rotterdam, but contrary winds obliged us to remain nearly two days at Marsluys, a town about two leagues from Rotterdam. Here our 805 last guinea was expended, and we reflected with wonder that we had travelled eight hundred miles for less than thirty pounds, passing through lovely scenes, and enjoying the beauteous Rhine, and all the brilliant shews of earth and sky, perhaps more, travelling as we did, in an open boat, than if we had been shut up in a carriage, and passed 810 on the road under the hills.

The captain of our vessel was an Englishman, and had been a

king's pilot. The bar of the Rhine a little below Marsluys is so dangerous, that without a very favourable breeze none of the Dutch vessels dare attempt its passage; but although the wind was a very few points in our favour, our captain resolved to sail, and although 815 half repentant before he had accomplished his undertaking, he was glad and proud when, triumphing over the timorous Dutchmen, the bar was crossed, and the vessel safe in the open sea. It was in truth an enterprise of some peril; a heavy gale had prevailed during the night, and although it had abated since the morning, the breakers at the bar 820 were still exceedingly high. Through some delay, which had arisen from the ship having got a-ground in the harbour, we arrived half an hour after the appointed time. The breakers were tremendous, and we were informed that there was the space of only two feet between the bottom of the vessel and the sands. The waves, which broke 825 against the sides of the ship with a terrible shock, were quite perpendicular, and even sometimes overhanging in the abrupt smoothness of their sides. Shoals of enormous porpoises were sporting with the utmost composure amidst the troubled waters.

We safely past this danger, and after a navigation unexpectedly 830 short, arrived at Gravesend on the morning of the 13th of September, the third day after our departure from Marsluys.

M.

LETTERS

WRITTEN DURING A RESIDENCE OF THREE
MONTHS
IN THE ENVIRONS OF GENEVA,

In the Summer of the Year 1816.

LETTER I.

Hôtel de Sécheron, Geneva,
May 17, 1816.

We arrived at Paris on the 8th of this month, and were detained two
days for the purpose of obtaining the various signatures necessary to
our passports, the French government having become much more
circumspect since the escape of Lavalette. We had no letters of
5 introduction, or any friend in that city, and were therefore confined
to our hotel, where we were obliged to hire apartments for the week,
although when we first arrived we expected to be detained one
night only; for in Paris there are no houses where you can be
accommodated with apartments by the day.

10 The manners of the French are interesting, although less attractive, at least to Englishmen, than before the last invasion of the
Allies: the discontent and sullenness of their minds perpetually
betrays itself. Nor is it wonderful that they should regard the
subjects of a government which fills their country with hostile
15 garrisons, and sustains a detested dynasty on the throne, with an
acrimony and indignation of which that government alone is the
proper object. This feeling is honourable to the French, and
encouraging to all those of every nation in Europe who have a fellow
feeling with the oppressed, and who cherish an unconquerable hope
20 that the cause of liberty must at length prevail.

Our route after Paris, as far as Troyes, lay through the same
uninteresting tract of country which we had traversed on foot nearly
two years before, but on quitting Troyes we left the road leading to

Neufchâtel, to follow that which was to conduct us to Geneva. We entered Dijon on the third evening after our departure from Paris, 25 and passing through Dole, arrived at Poligny. This town is built at the foot of Jura, which rises abruptly from a plain of vast extent. The rocks of the mountain overhang the houses. Some difficulty in procuring horses detained us here until the evening closed in, when we proceeded, by the light of a stormy moon, to Champagnolles, a 30 little village situated in the depth of the mountains. The road was serpentine and exceedingly steep, and was overhung on one side by half distinguished precipices, whilst the other was a gulph, filled by the darkness of the driving clouds. The dashing of the invisible mountain streams announced to us that we had quitted the plains of 35 France, as we slowly ascended, amidst a violent storm of wind and rain, to Champagnolles, where we arrived at twelve o'clock, the fourth night after our departure from Paris.

The next morning we proceeded, still ascending among the ravines and vallies of the mountain. The scenery perpetually grows 40 more wonderful and sublime: pine forests of impenetrable thickness, and untrodden, nay, inaccessible expanse spread on every side. Sometimes the dark woods descending, follow the route into the vallies, the distorted trees struggling with knotted roots between the most barren clefts; sometimes the road winds high into the 45 regions of frost, and then the forests become scattered, and the branches of the trees are loaded with snow, and half of the enormous pines themselves buried in the wavy drifts. The spring, as the inhabitants informed us, was unusually late, and indeed the cold was excessive; as we ascended the mountains, the same clouds which 50 rained on us in the vallies poured forth large flakes of snow thick and fast. The sun occasionally shone through these showers, and illuminated the magnificent ravines of the mountains, whose gigantic pines were some laden with snow, some wreathed round by the lines of scattered and lingering vapour; others darting their dark 55 spires into the sunny sky, brilliantly clear and azure.

As the evening advanced, and we ascended higher, the snow, which we had beheld whitening the overhanging rocks, now encroached upon our road, and it snowed fast as we entered the village of Les Rousses, where we were threatened by the apparent 60 necessity of passing the night in a bad inn and dirty beds. For from that place there are two roads to Geneva; one by Nion, in the Swiss territory, where the mountain route is shorter, and comparatively

easy at that time of the year, when the road is for several leagues
65 covered with snow of an enormous depth; the other road lay
through Gex, and was too circuitous and dangerous to be attempted
at so late an hour in the day. Our passport, however, was for Gex,
and we were told that we could not change its destination; but all
these police laws, so severe in themselves, are to be softened by
70 bribery, and this difficulty was at length overcome. We hired four
horses, and ten men to support the carriage, and departed from Les
Rousses at six in the evening, when the sun had already far
descended, and the snow pelting against the windows of our
carriage, assisted the coming darkness to deprive us of the view of
75 the lake of Geneva and the far distant Alps.

The prospect around, however, was sufficiently sublime to
command our attention—never was scene more awfully desolate.
The trees in these regions are incredibly large, and stand in scattered
clumps over the white wilderness; the vast expanse of snow was
80 chequered only by these gigantic pines, and the poles that marked
our road: no river or rock-encircled lawn relieved the eye, by adding
the picturesque to the sublime. The natural silence of that
uninhabited desert contrasted strangely with the voices of the men
who conducted us, who, with animated tones and gestures, called to
85 one another in a *patois* composed of French and Italian, creating
disturbance, where but for them, there was none.

To what a different scene are we now arrived! To the warm
sunshine and to the humming of sun-loving insects. From the
windows of our hotel we see the lovely lake, blue as the heavens
90 which it reflects, and sparkling with golden beams. The opposite
shore is sloping, and covered with vines, which however do not so
early in the season add to the beauty of the prospect. Gentlemen's
seats are scattered over these banks, behind which rise the various
ridges of black mountains, and towering far above, in the midst of its
95 snowy Alps, the majestic Mont Blanc, highest and queen of all. Such
is the view reflected by the lake; it is a bright summer scene without
any of that sacred solitude and deep seclusion that delighted us at
Lucerne.

We have not yet found out any very agreeable walks, but you
100 know our attachment to water excursions. We have hired a boat, and
every evening at about six o'clock we sail on the lake, which is
delightful, whether we glide over a glassy surface or are speeded
along by a strong wind. The waves of this lake never afflict me with

that sickness that deprives me of all enjoyment in a sea voyage; on the contrary, the tossing of our boat raises my spirits and inspires me with unusual hilarity. Twilight here is of short duration, but we at present enjoy the benefit of an increasing moon, and seldom return until ten o'clock, when, as we approach the shore, we are saluted by the delightful scent of flowers and new mown grass, and the chirp of the grasshoppers, and the song of the evening birds.

We do not enter into society here, yet our time passes swiftly and delightfully. We read Latin and Italian during the heats of noon, and when the sun declines we walk in the garden of the hotel, looking at the rabbits, relieving fallen cockchaffers, and watching the motions of a myriad of lizards, who inhabit a southern wall of the garden. You know that we have just escaped from the gloom of winter and of London; and coming to this delightful spot during this divine weather, I feel as happy as a new-fledged bird, and hardly care what twig I fly to, so that I may try my new-found wings. A more experienced bird may be more difficult in its choice of a bower; but in my present temper of mind, the budding flowers, the fresh grass of spring, and the happy creatures about me that live and enjoy these pleasures, are quite enough to afford me exquisite delight, even though clouds should shut out Mont Blanc from my sight. Adieu!

M.

LETTER II.

COLIGNY—GENEVA—PLAINPALAIS.

Campagne C⟨haupuis,⟩ near Coligny,
1st June.

You will perceive from my date that we have changed our residence since my last letter. We now inhabit a little cottage on the opposite shore of the lake, and have exchanged the view of Mont Blanc and her snowy *aiguilles* for the dark frowning Jura, behind whose range we every evening see the sun sink, and darkness approaches our valley from behind the Alps, which are then tinged by that glowing rose-like hue which is observed in England to attend on the clouds of an autumnal sky when day-light is almost gone. The lake is at our feet, and a little harbour contains our boat, in which we still enjoy our evening excursions on the water. Unfortunately we do not now enjoy those brilliant skies that hailed us on our first arrival to this country. An almost perpetual rain confines us principally to the house; but when the sun bursts forth it is with a splendour and heat unknown in England. The thunder storms that visit us are grander and more terrific than I have ever seen before. We watch them as they approach from the opposite side of the lake, observing the lightning play among the clouds in various parts of the heavens, and dart in jagged figures upon the piny heights of Jura, dark with the shadow of the overhanging cloud, while perhaps the sun is shining cheerily upon us. One night we *enjoyed* a finer storm than I had ever before beheld. The lake was lit up—the pines on Jura made visible, and all the scene illuminated for an instant, when a pitchy blackness succeeded, and the thunder came in frightful bursts over our heads amid the darkness.

But while I still dwell on the country around Geneva, you will expect me to say something of the town itself: there is nothing, however, in it that can repay you for the trouble of walking over its rough stones. The houses are high, the streets narrow, many of them on the ascent, and no public building of any beauty to attract your eye, or any architecture to gratify your taste. The town is surrounded by a wall, the three gates of which are shut exactly at ten o'clock, when no bribery (as in France) can open them. To the south of the town is the promenade of the Genevese, a grassy plain planted with a few trees, and called Plainpalais. Here a small obelisk is erected to the glory of Rousseau, and here (such is the mutability of human life) the magistrates, the successors of those who exiled him from his native country, were shot by the populace during that revolution, which his writings mainly contributed to mature, and which, notwithstanding the temporary bloodshed and injustice with which it was polluted, has produced enduring benefits to mankind, which all the chicanery of statesmen, nor even the great conspiracy of kings, can entirely render vain. From respect to the memory of their predecessors, none of the present magistrates ever walk in Plainpalais. Another Sunday recreation for the citizens is an excursion to the top of Mont Salève. This hill is within a league of the town, and rises perpendicularly from the cultivated plain. It is ascended on the other side, and I should judge from its situation that your toil is rewarded by a delightful view of the course of the Rhône and Arve, and of the shores of the lake. We have not yet visited it.

There is more equality of classes here than in England. This occasions a greater freedom and refinement of manners among the lower orders than we meet with in our own country. I fancy the haughty English ladies are greatly disgusted with this consequence of republican institutions, for the Genevese servants complain very much of their *scolding*, an exercise of the tongue, I believe, perfectly 55 unknown here. The peasants of Switzerland may not however emulate the vivacity and grace of the French. They are more cleanly, but they are slow and inapt. I know a girl of twenty, who although she had lived all her life among vineyards, could not inform me during what month the vintage took place, and I discovered she was 60 utterly ignorant of the order in which the months succeed one to another. She would not have been surprised if I had talked of the burning sun and delicious fruits of December, or of the frosts of July. Yet she is by no means deficient in understanding.

The Genevese are also much inclined to puritanism. It is true that 65 from habit they dance on a Sunday, but as soon as the French government was abolished in the town, the magistrates ordered the theatre to be closed, and measures were taken to pull down the building.

We have latterly enjoyed fine weather, and nothing is more 70 pleasant than to listen to the evening song of the vine-dressers. They are all women, and most of them have harmonious although masculine voices. The theme of their ballads consists of shepherds, love, flocks, and the sons of kings who fall in love with beautiful shepherdesses. Their tunes are monotonous, but it is sweet to hear 75 them in the stillness of evening, while we are enjoying the sight of the setting sun, either from the hill behind our house or from the lake.

Such are our pleasures here, which would be greatly increased if the season had been more favourable, for they chiefly consist in such enjoyments as sunshine and gentle breezes bestow. We have not yet 80 made any excursion in the environs of the town, but we have planned several⟨; and⟩ when you shall again hear of us, we will endeavour, by the magic of words, to transport the ethereal part of you to the neighbourhood of the Alps, and mountain streams, and forests, which, while they clothe the former, darken the latter with 85 their vast shadows. Adieu!

M.

LETTER III.
To T. P. Esq.

MEILLERIE—CLARENS—CHILLON—VEVAI—LAUSANNE.

> Montalègre, near Coligni, Geneva,
> July 12th.

It is nearly a fortnight since I have returned from Vevai. This journey has been on every account delightful, but most especially, because then I first knew the divine beauty of Rousseau's imagination, as it exhibits itself in Julie. It is inconceivable what an
5 enchantment the scene itself lends to those delineations, from which its own most touching charm arises. But I will give you an abstract of our voyage, which lasted eight days, and if you have a map of Switzerland, you can follow me.

We left Montalègre at half past two on the 23d of June. The lake
10 was calm, and after three hours of rowing we arrived at Hermance, a beautiful little village, containing a ruined tower, built, the villagers say, by Julius Cæsar. There were three other towers similar to it, which the Genevese destroyed for their own fortifications in 1560. We got into the tower by a kind of window.
15 The walls are immensely solid, and the stone of which it is built so hard, that it yet retained the mark of chisels. The boatmen said, that this tower was once three times higher than it is now. There are two staircases in the thickness of the walls, one of which is entirely demolished, and the other half ruined, and only acces-
20 sible by a ladder. The town itself, now an inconsiderable village inhabited by a few fishermen, was built by a Queen of Burgundy, and reduced to its present state by the inhabitants of Berne, who burnt and ravaged every thing they could find.

Leaving Hermance, we arrived at sunset at the village of Nerni.
25 After looking at our lodgings, which were gloomy and dirty, we walked out by the side of the lake. It was beautiful to see the vast expanse of these purple and misty waters broken by the craggy islets near to its slant and "beached margin." There were many fish sporting in the lake, and multitudes were collected close to the
30 rocks to catch the flies which inhabited them.

On returning to the village, we sat on a wall beside the lake, looking at some children who were playing at a game like ninepins. The children here appeared in an extraordinary way deformed and diseased. Most of them were crooked, and with enlarged throats; but one little boy had such exquisite grace in his mien and motions, as I never before saw equalled in a child. His countenance was beautiful for the expression with which it overflowed. There was a mixture of pride and gentleness in his eyes and lips, the indications of sensibility, which his education will probably pervert to misery or seduce to crime; but there was more of gentleness than of pride, and it seemed that the pride was tamed from its original wildness by the habitual exercise of milder feelings. My companion gave him a piece of money, which he took without speaking, with a sweet smile of easy thankfulness, and then with an unembarrassed air turned to his play. All this might scarcely be; but the imagination surely could not forbear to breathe into the most inanimate forms some likeness of its own visions, on such a serene and glowing evening, in this remote and romantic village, beside the calm lake that bore us hither.

On returning to our inn, we found that the servant had arranged our rooms, and deprived them of the greater portion of their former disconsolate appearance. They reminded my companion of Greece: it was five years, he said, since he had slept in such beds. The influence of the recollections excited by this circumstance on our conversation gradually faded, and I retired to rest with no unpleasant sensations, thinking of our journey tomorrow, and of the pleasure of recounting the little adventures of it when we return.

The next morning we passed Yvoire, a scattered village with an ancient castle, whose houses are interspersed with trees, and which stands at a little distance from Nerni, on the promontory which bounds a deep bay, some miles in extent. So soon as we arrived at this promontory, the lake began to assume an aspect of wilder magnificence. The mountains of Savoy, whose summits were bright with snow, descended in broken slopes to the lake: on high, the rocks were dark with pine forests, which become deeper and more immense, until the ice and snow mingle with the points of naked rock that pierce the blue air; but below, groves of walnut, chesnut, and oak, with openings of lawny fields, attested the milder climate.

As soon as we had passed the opposite promontory, we saw the river Drance, which descends from between a chasm in the mountains, and makes a plain near the lake, intersected by its

divided streams. Thousands of *besolets*, beautiful water-birds, like
75 sea-gulls, but smaller, with purple on their backs, take their station
on the shallows, where its waters mingle with the lake. As we
approached Evian, the mountains descended more precipitously to
the lake, and masses of intermingled wood and rock overhung its
shining spire.

80   We arrived at this town about seven o'clock, after a day which
involved more rapid changes of atmosphere than I ever recollect to
have observed before. The morning was cold and wet; then an
easterly wind, and the clouds hard and high; then thunder showers,
and wind shifting to every quarter; then a warm blast from the south,
85 and summer clouds hanging over the peaks, with bright blue sky
between. About half an hour after we had arrived at Evian, a few
flashes of lightning came from a dark cloud, directly over head, and
continued after the cloud had dispersed. "Diespiter, per pura
tonantes egit equos:" a phenomenon which certainly had no
90 influence on me, corresponding with that which it produced on
Horace.

The appearance of the inhabitants of Evian is more wretched,
diseased and poor, than I ever recollect to have seen. The contrast
indeed between the subjects of the King of Sardinia and the citizens
95 of the independent republics of Switzerland, affords a powerful
illustration of the blighting mischiefs of despotism, within the space
of a few miles. They have mineral waters here, *eaux savonneuses*, they
call them. In the evening we had some difficulty about our passports,
but so soon as the syndic heard my companion's rank and name, he
100 apologized for the circumstance. The inn was good. During our
voyage, on the distant height of a hill, covered with pine-forests, we
saw a ruined castle, which reminded me of those on the Rhine.

We left Evian on the following morning, with a wind of such
violence as to permit but one sail to be carried. The waves also were
105 exceedingly high, and our boat so heavily laden, that there appeared
to be some danger. We arrived however safe at Meillerie, after
passing with great speed mighty forests which overhung the lake,
and lawns of exquisite verdure, and mountains with bare and icy
points, which rose immediately from the summit of the rocks,
110 whose bases were echoing to the waves.

We here heard that the Empress Maria Louisa had slept at
Meillerie, before the present inn was built, and when the
accommodations were those of the most wretched village, in

remembrance of St. Preux. How beautiful it is to find that the common sentiments of human nature can attach themselves to those who are the most removed from its duties and its enjoyments, when Genius pleads for their admission at the gate of Power. To own them was becoming in the Empress, and confirms the affectionate praise contained in the regret of a great and enlightened nation. A Bourbon dared not even to have remembered Rousseau. She owed this power to that democracy which her husband's dynasty outraged, and of which it was however in some sort the representative among the nations of the earth. This little incident shews at once how unfit and how impossible it is for the ancient system of opinions, or for any power built upon a conspiracy to revive them, permanently to subsist among mankind. We dined there, and had some honey, the best I have ever tasted, the very essence of the mountain flowers, and as fragrant. Probably the village derives its name from this production. Meillerie is the well known scene of St. Preux's visionary exile; but Meillerie is indeed inchanted ground, were Rousseau no magician. Groves of pine, chesnut, and walnut overshadow it; magnificent and unbounded forests to which England affords no parallel. In the midst of these woods are dells of lawny expanse, inconceivably verdant, adorned with a thousand of the rarest flowers and odourous with thyme.

The lake appeared somewhat calmer as we left Meillerie, sailing close to the banks, whose magnificence augmented with the turn of every promontory. But we congratulated ourselves too soon: the wind gradually increased in violence, until it blew tremendously; and as it came from the remotest extremity of the lake, produced waves of a frightful height, and covered the whole surface with a chaos of foam. One of our boatmen, who was a dreadfully stupid fellow, persisted in holding the sail at a time when the boat was on the point of being driven under water by the hurricane. On discovering his error, he let it entirely go, and the boat for a moment refused to obey the helm; in addition, the rudder was so broken as to render the management of it very difficult; one wave fell in, and then another. My companion, an excellent swimmer, took off his coat, I did the same, and we sat with our arms crossed, every instant expecting to be swamped. The sail was however again held, the boat obeyed the helm, and still in imminent peril from the immensity of the waves, we arrived in a few minutes at a sheltered port, in the village of St. Gingoux.

I felt in this near prospect of death a mixture of sensations, among
155 which terror entered, though but subordinately. My feelings would
have been less painful had I been alone; but I know that my
companion would have attempted to save me, and I was overcome
with humiliation, when I thought that his life might have been risked
to preserve mine. When we arrived at St. Gingoux, the inhabitants,
160 who stood on the shore, unaccustomed to see a vessel as frail as our's,
and fearing to venture at all on such a sea, exchanged looks of
wonder and congratulation with our boatmen, who, as well as
ourselves, were well pleased to set foot on shore.

St. Gingoux is even more beautiful than Meillerie; the mountains
165 are higher, and their loftiest points of elevation descend more
abruptly to the lake. On high, the aerial summits still cherish great
depths of snow in their ravines, and in the paths of their unseen
torrents. One of the highest of these is called Roche de St. Julien,
beneath whose pinnacles the forests become deeper and more
170 extensive; the chesnut gives a peculiarity to the scene, which is most
beautiful, and will make a picture in my memory, distinct from all
other mountain scenes which I have ever before visited.

As we arrived here early, we took a *voiture* to visit the mouth of
the Rhône. We went between the mountains and the lake, under
175 groves of mighty chesnut trees, beside perpetual streams, which are
nourished by the snows above, and form stalactites on the rocks,
over which they fall. We saw an immense chesnut tree, which had
been overthrown by the hurricane of the morning. The place where
the Rhône joins the lake was marked by a line of tremendous
180 breakers; the river is as rapid as when it leaves the lake, but is muddy
and dark. We went about a league farther on the road to La Valais,
and stopped at a castle called La Tour de Bouverie, which seems to be
the frontier of Switzerland and Savoy, as we were asked for our
passports, on the supposition of our proceeding to Italy.

185 On one side of the road was the immense Roche de St. Julien,
which overhung it; through the gateway of the castle we saw the
snowy mountains of La Valais, clothed in clouds, and on the other
side was the willowy plain of the Rhône, in a character of striking
contrast with the rest of the scene, bounded by the dark mountains
190 that overhang Clarens, Vevai, and the lake that rolls between. In the
midst of the plain rises a little isolated hill, on which the white spire
of a church peeps from among the tufted chesnut woods. We
returned to St. Gingoux before sun-set, and I passed the evening in
reading Julie.

As my companion rises late, I had time before breakfast, on the 195 ensuing morning, to hunt the waterfalls of the river that fall into the lake at St. Gingoux. The stream is indeed, from the declivity over which it falls, only a succession of waterfalls, which roar over the rocks with a perpetual sound, and suspend their unceasing spray on the leaves and flowers that overhang and adorn its savage banks. The 200 path that conducted along this river sometimes avoided the precipices of its shores, by leading through meadows; sometimes threaded the base of the perpendicular and caverned rocks. I gathered in these meadows a nosegay of such flowers as I never saw in England, and which I thought more beautiful for that rarity. 205

On my return, after breakfast, we sailed for Clarens, determining first to see the three mouths of the Rhône, and then the castle of Chillon; the day was fine, and the water calm. We passed from the blue waters of the lake over the stream of the Rhône, which is rapid even at a great distance from its confluence with the lake; the turbid 210 waters mixed with those of the lake, but mixed with them unwillingly. (*See Nouvelle Héloïse, Lettre 17, Part 4.*) I read Julie all day; an overflowing, as it now seems, surrounded by the scenes which it has so wonderfully peopled, of sublimest genius, and more than human sensibility. Meillerie, the Castle of Chillon, Clarens, the mountains 215 of La Valais and Savoy, present themselves to the imagination as monuments of things that were once familiar, and of beings that were once dear to it. They were created indeed by one mind, but a mind so powerfully bright as to cast a shade of falsehood on the records that are called reality. 220

We passed on to the Castle of Chillon, and visited its dungeons and towers. These prisons are excavated below the lake; the principal dungeon is supported by seven columns, whose branching capitals support the roof. Close to the very walls, the lake is 800 feet deep; iron rings are fastened to these columns, and on them were 225 engraven a multitude of names, partly those of visitors, and partly doubtless of the prisoners, of whom now no memory remains, and who thus beguiled a solitude which they have long ceased to feel. One date was as ancient as 1670. At the commencement of the Reformation, and indeed long after that period, this dungeon was 230 the receptacle of those who shook, or who denied the system of idolatry, from the effects of which mankind is even now slowly emerging.

Close to this long and lofty dungeon was a narrow cell, and

235 beyond it one larger and far more lofty and dark, supported upon two unornamented arches. Across one of these arches was a beam, now black and rotten, on which prisoners were hung in secret. I never saw a monument more terrible of that cold and inhuman tyranny, which it has been the delight of man to exercise over man. It 240 was indeed one of those many tremendous fulfilments which render the "pernicies humani generis" of the great Tacitus, so solemn and irrefragable a prophecy. The gendarme, who conducted us over this castle, told us that there was an opening to the lake, by means of a secret spring, connected with which the whole dungeon might be 245 filled with water before the prisoners could possibly escape!

We proceeded with a contrary wind to Clarens, against a heavy swell. I never felt more strongly than on landing at Clarens, that the spirit of old times had deserted its once cherished habitation. A thousand times, thought I, have Julia and St. Preux walked on this 250 terrassed road, looking towards these mountains which I now behold; nay, treading on the ground where I now tread. From the window of our lodging our landlady pointed out "le bosquet de Julie." At least the inhabitants of this village are impressed with an idea, that the persons of that romance had actual existence. In the 255 evening we walked thither. It is indeed Julia's wood. The hay was making under the trees; the trees themselves were aged, but vigorous, and interspersed with younger ones, which are destined to be their successors, and in future years, when we are dead, to afford a shade to future worshippers of nature, who love the memory of that 260 tenderness and peace of which this was the imaginary abode. We walked forward among the vineyards, whose narrow terraces overlook this affecting scene. Why did the cold maxims of the world compel me at this moment to repress the tears of melancholy transport which it would have been so sweet to indulge, im- 265 measurably, even until the darkness of night had swallowed up the objects which excited them?

I forgot to remark, what indeed my companion remarked to me, that our danger from the storm took place precisely in the spot where Julie and her lover were nearly overset, and where St. Preux 270 was tempted to plunge with her into the lake.

On the following day we went to see the castle of Clarens, a square strong house, with very few windows, surrounded by a double terrace that overlooks the valley, or rather the plain of Clarens. The road which conducted to it wound up the steep ascent through woods of walnut and chesnut. We gathered roses on the terrace, in the feeling that they might be the posterity of some planted by Julia's hand. We sent their dead and withered leaves to the absent.

We went again to "the bosquet de Julie," and found that the precise spot was now utterly obliterated, and a heap of stones marked the place where the little chapel had once stood. Whilst we were execrating the author of this brutal folly, our guide informed us that the land belonged to the convent of St. Bernard, and that this outrage had been committed by their orders. I knew before, that if avarice could harden the hearts of men, a system of prescriptive religion has an influence far more inimical to natural sensibility. I know that an isolated man is sometimes restrained by shame from outraging the venerable feelings arising out of the memory of genius, which once made nature even lovelier than itself; but associated man holds it as the very sacrament of his union to forswear all delicacy, all benevolence, all remorse, all that is true, or tender, or sublime.

We sailed from Clarens to Vevai. Vevai is a town more beautiful in its simplicity than any I have ever seen. Its market-place, a spacious square interspersed with trees, looks directly upon the mountains of Savoy and La Valais, the lake, and the valley of the Rhône. It was at Vevai that Rousseau conceived the design of Julie.

From Vevai we came to Ouchy, a village near Lausanne. The coasts of the Pays de Vaud, though full of villages and vineyards, present an aspect of tranquillity and peculiar beauty which well compensates for the solitude which I am accustomed to admire. The hills are very high and rocky, crowned and interspersed with woods. Water-falls echo from the cliffs, and shine afar. In one place we saw the traces of two rocks of immense size, which had fallen from the mountain behind. One of these lodged in a room where a young woman was sleeping, without injuring her. The vineyards were utterly destroyed in its path, and the earth torn up.

The rain detained us two days at Ouchy. We however visited Lausanne, and saw Gibbon's house. We were shewn the decayed summer-house where he finished his History, and the old acacias on the terrace, from which he saw Mont Blanc, after having written the last sentence. There is something grand and even touching in the regret which he expresses at the completion of his task. It was conceived amid the ruins of the Capitol. The sudden departure of his cherished and accustomed toil must have left him, like the death of a dear friend, sad and solitary.

315 My companion gathered some acacia leaves to preserve in remembrance of him. I refrained from doing so, fearing to outrage the greater and more sacred name of Rousseau; the contemplation of whose imperishable creations had left no vacancy in my heart for mortal things. Gibbon had a cold and unimpassioned spirit. I 320 never felt more inclination to rail at the prejudices which cling to such a thing, than now that Julie and Clarens, Lausanne and the Roman Empire, compelled me to a contrast between Rousseau and Gibbon.

When we returned, in the only interval of sunshine during the 325 day, I walked on the pier which the lake was lashing with its waves. A rainbow spanned the lake, or rather rested one extremity of its arch upon the water, and the other at the foot of the mountains of Savoy. Some white houses, I know not if they were those of Meillerie, shone through the yellow fire.

330 On Saturday the 30th of June we quitted Ouchy, and after two days of pleasant sailing arrived on Sunday evening at Montalègre.

S.

LETTER IV.
To T. P. Esq.

ST. MARTIN—SERVOZ—CHAMOUNI—MONTANVERT—
MONT BLANC.

Hôtel de Londres, Chamouni,
July 22d, 1816.

Whilst you, my friend, are engaged in securing a home for us, we are wandering in search of recollections to embellish it. I do not err in conceiving that you are interested in details of all that is majestic or beautiful in nature; but how shall I describe to you the scenes by 5 which I am now surrounded? To exhaust the epithets which express the astonishment and the admiration—the very excess of satisfied astonishment, where expectation scarcely acknowledged any boundary, is this, to impress upon your mind the images which fill mine now even till it overflow? I too have read the 10 raptures of travellers; I will be warned by their example; I will simply detail to you all that I can relate, or all that, if related, would enable you to conceive of what we have done or seen since the morning of the 20th, when we left Geneva.

We commenced our intended journey to Chamouni at half-past eight in the morning. We passed through the champain country, which extends from Mont Salève to the base of the higher Alps. The country is sufficiently fertile, covered with corn fields and orchards, and intersected by sudden acclivities with flat summits. The day was cloudless and excessively hot, the Alps were perpetually in sight, and as we advanced, the mountains, which form their outskirts, closed in around us. We passed a bridge over a stream, which discharges itself into the Arve. The Arve itself, much swollen by the rains, flows constantly to the right of the road.

As we approached Bonneville through an avenue composed of a beautiful species of drooping poplar, we observed that the corn fields on each side were covered with inundation. Bonneville is a neat little town, with no conspicuous peculiarity, except the white towers of the prison, an extensive building overlooking the town. At Bonneville the Alps commence, one of which, clothed by forests, rises almost immediately from the opposite bank of the Arve.

From Bonneville to Cluses the road conducts through a spacious and fertile plain, surrounded on all sides by mountains, covered like those of Meillerie with forests of intermingled pine and chesnut. At Cluses the road turns suddenly to the right, following the Arve along the chasm, which it seems to have hollowed for itself among the perpendicular mountains. The scene assumes here a more savage and colossal character: the valley becomes narrow, affording no more space than is sufficient for the river and the road. The pines descend to the banks, imitating with their irregular spires, the pyramidal crags which lift themselves far above the regions of forest into the deep azure of the sky, and among the white dazzling clouds. The scene, at the distance of half a mile from Cluses, differs from that of Matlock in little else than in the immensity of its proportions, and in its untameable, inaccessible solitude, inhabited only by the goats which we saw browsing on the rocks.

Near Maglans, within a league of each other, we saw two waterfalls. They were no more than mountain rivulets, but the height from which they fell, at least of *twelve* hundred feet, made them assume a character inconsistent with the smallness of their stream. The first fell from the overhanging brow of a black precipice on an enormous rock, precisely resembling some colossal Egyptian statue of a female deity. It struck the head of the visionary image, and gracefully dividing there, fell from it in folds of foam more like to

cloud than water, imitating a veil of the most exquisite woof. It then
55 united, concealing the lower part of the statue, and hiding itself in a
winding of its channel, burst into a deeper fall, and crossed our route
in its path towards the Arve.

The other waterfall was more continuous and larger. The violence
with which it fell made it look more like some shape which an
60 exhalation had assumed, than like water, for it streamed beyond the
mountain, which appeared dark behind it, as it might have appeared
behind an evanescent cloud.

The character of the scenery continued the same until we arrived
at St. Martin (called in the maps Sallanches) the mountains per-
65 petually becoming more elevated, exhibiting at every turn of the
road more craggy summits, loftier and wider extent of forests,
darker and more deep recesses.

The following morning we proceeded from St. Martin on mules to
Chamouni, accompanied by two guides. We proceeded, as we had
70 done the preceding day, along the valley of the Arve, a valley
surrounded on all sides by immense mountains, whose rugged
precipices are intermixed on high with dazzling snow. Their bases
were still covered with the eternal forests, which perpetually grew
darker and more profound as we approached the inner regions of the
75 mountains.

On arriving at a small village, at the distance of a league from St.
Martin, we dismounted from our mules, and were conducted by our
guides to view a cascade. We beheld an immense body of water fall
two hundred and fifty feet, dashing from rock to rock, and casting a
80 spray which formed a mist around it, in the midst of which hung a
multitude of sunbows, which faded or became unspeakably vivid, as
the inconstant sun shone through the clouds. When we approached
near to it, the rain of the spray reached us, and our clothes were
wetted by the quick-falling but minute particles of water. The
85 cataract fell from above into a deep craggy chasm at our feet, where,
changing its character to that of a mountain stream, it pursued its
course towards the Arve, roaring over the rocks that impeded its
progress.

As we proceeded, our route still lay through the valley, or rather,
90 as it had now become, the vast ravine, which is at once the couch and
the creation of the terrible Arve. We ascended, winding between
mountains whose immensity staggers the imagination. We crossed
the path of a torrent, which three days since had descended from the
thawing snow, and torn the road away.

We dined at Servoz, a little village, where there are lead and ₉₅
copper mines, and where we saw a cabinet of natural curiosities, like
those of Keswick and Bethgelert. We saw in this cabinet some
chamois' horns, and the horns of an exceedingly rare animal called
the bouquetin, which inhabits the desarts of snow to the south of
Mont Blanc: it is an animal of the stag kind; its horns weigh at least ₁₀₀
twenty-seven English pounds. It is inconceivable how so small an
animal could support so inordinate a weight. The horns are of a very
peculiar conformation, being broad, massy, and pointed at the ends,
and surrounded with a number of rings, which are supposed to
afford an indication of its age: there were seventeen rings on the ₁₀₅
largest of these horns.

From Servoz three leagues remain to Chamouni.—Mont Blanc
was before us—the Alps, with their innumerable glaciers on high all
around, closing in the complicated windings of the single vale—
forests inexpressibly beautiful, but majestic in their beauty— ₁₁₀
intermingled beech and pine, and oak, overshadowed our road, or
receded, whilst lawns of such verdure as I have never seen before
occupied these openings, and gradually became darker in their
recesses. Mont Blanc was before us, but it was covered with cloud; its
base, furrowed with dreadful gaps, was seen above. Pinnacles of ₁₁₅
snow intolerably bright, part of the chain connected with Mont
Blanc, shone through the clouds at intervals on high. I never knew—I
never imagined what mountains were before. The immensity of
these aerial summits excited, when they suddenly burst upon the
sight, a sentiment of extatic wonder, not unallied to madness. And ₁₂₀
remember this was all one scene, it all pressed home to our regard
and our imagination. Though it embraced a vast extent of space, the
snowy pyramids which shot into the bright blue sky seemed to
overhang our path; the ravine, clothed with gigantic pines, and black
with its depth below, so deep that the very roaring of the untameable ₁₂₅
Arve, which rolled through it, could not be heard above—all was as
much our own, as if we had been the creators of such impressions in
the minds of others as now occupied our own. Nature was the poet,
whose harmony held our spirits more breathless than that of the
divinest. ₁₃₀

As we entered the valley of Chamouni (which in fact may be
considered as a continuation of those which we have followed from
Bonneville and Cluses) clouds hung upon the mountains at the
distance perhaps of 6000 feet from the earth, but so as effectually to

135 conceal not only Mont Blanc, but the other *aiguilles*, as they call them here, attached and subordinate to it. We were travelling along the valley, when suddenly we heard a sound as of the burst of smothered thunder rolling above; yet there was something earthly in the sound, that told us it could not be thunder. Our guide hastily
140 pointed out to us a part of the mountain opposite, from whence the sound came. It was an avalanche. We saw the smoke of its path among the rocks, and continued to hear at intervals the bursting of its fall. It fell on the bed of a torrent, which it displaced, and presently we saw its tawny-coloured waters also spread themselves over the
145 ravine, which was their couch.

We did not, as we intended, visit the *Glacier des Bossons* to-day, although it descends within a few minutes' walk of the road, wishing to survey it at least when unfatigued. We saw this glacier which comes close to the fertile plain, as we passed, its surface was broken
150 into a thousand unaccountable figures: conical and pyramidical crystalizations, more than fifty feet in height, rise from its surface, and precipices of ice, of dazzling splendour, overhang the woods and meadows of the vale. This glacier winds upwards from the valley, until it joins the masses of frost from which it was produced above,
155 winding through its own ravine like a bright belt flung over the black region of pines. There is more in all these scenes than mere magnitude of proportion: there is a majesty of outline; there is an awful grace in the very colours which invest these wonderful shapes—a charm which is peculiar to them, quite distinct even from
160 the reality of their unutterable greatness.

July 24.

Yesterday morning we went to the source of the Arveiron. It is about a league from this village; the river rolls forth impetuously from an arch of ice, and spreads itself in many streams over a vast space of the valley, ravaged and laid bare by its inundations. The
165 glacier by which its waters are nourished, overhangs this cavern and the plain, and the forests of pine which surround it, with terrible precipices of solid ice. On the other side rises the immense glacier of Montanvert, fifty miles in extent, occupying a chasm among mountains of inconceivable height, and of forms so pointed and
170 abrupt, that they seem to pierce the sky. From this glacier we saw as we sat on a rock, close to one of the streams of the Arveiron, masses of ice detach themselves from on high, and rush with a loud dull

noise into the vale. The violence of their fall turned them into powder, which flowed over the rocks in imitation of waterfalls, whose ravines they usurped and filled.

In the evening I went with Ducrée, my guide, the only tolerable person I have seen in this country, to visit the glacier of Bossons. This glacier, like that of Montanvert, comes close to the vale, overhanging the green meadows and the dark woods with the dazzling whiteness of its precipices and pinnacles, which are like spires of radiant crystal, covered with a net-work of frosted silver. These glaciers flow perpetually into the valley, ravaging in their slow but irresistible progress the pastures and the forests which surround them, performing a work of desolation in ages, which a river of lava might accomplish in an hour, but far more irretrievably; for where the ice has once descended, the hardiest plant refuses to grow; if even, as in some extraordinary instances, it should recede after its progress has once commenced. The glaciers perpetually move onward, at the rate of a foot each day, with a motion that commences at the spot where, on the boundaries of perpetual congelation, they are produced by the freezing of the waters which arise from the partial melting of the eternal snows. They drag with them from the regions whence they derive their origin, all the ruins of the mountain, enormous rocks, and immense accumulations of sand and stones. These are driven onwards by the irresistible stream of solid ice; and when they arrive at a declivity of the mountain, sufficiently rapid, roll down, scattering ruin. I saw one of these rocks which had descended in the spring, (winter here is the season of silence and safety) which measured forty feet in every direction.

The verge of a glacier, like that of Bossons, presents the most vivid image of desolation that it is possible to conceive. No one dares to approach it; for the enormous pinnacles of ice which perpetually fall, are perpetually reproduced. The pines of the forest, which bound it at one extremity, are overthrown and shattered to a wide extent at its base. There is something inexpressibly dreadful in the aspect of the few branchless trunks, which, nearest to the ice rifts, still stand in the uprooted soil. The meadows perish, overwhelmed with sand and stones. Within this last year, these glaciers have advanced three hundred feet into the valley. Saussure, the naturalist, says, that they have their periods of increase and decay: the people of the country hold an opinion entirely different; but as I judge, more probable. It is agreed by all, that the snow on the summit of Mont Blanc and the neighbouring mountains perpetually augments, and that ice, in the form of glaciers, subsists without melting in the valley of Chamouni during its transient and variable summer. If the snow which produces this glacier must augment, and the heat of the valley is no obstacle to the perpetual existence of such masses of ice as have already descended into it, the consequence is obvious; the glaciers must augment and will subsist, at least until they have overflowed this vale.

I will not pursue Buffon's sublime but gloomy theory—that this globe which we inhabit will at some future period be changed into a mass of frost by the encroachments of the polar ice, and of that produced on the most elevated points of the earth. Do you, who assert the supremacy of Ahriman, imagine him throned among these desolating snows, among these palaces of death and frost, so sculptured in this their terrible magnificence by the adamantine hand of necessity, and that he casts around him, as the first essays of his final usurpation, avalanches, torrents, rocks, and thunders, and above all these deadly glaciers, at once the proof and symbols of his reign;—add to this, the degradation of the human species—who in these regions are half deformed or idiotic, and most of whom are deprived of any thing that can excite interest or admiration. This is a part of the subject more mournful and less sublime; but such as neither the poet nor the philosopher should disdain to regard.

This morning we departed, on the promise of a fine day, to visit the glacier of Montanvert. In that part where it fills a slanting valley, it is called the Sea of Ice. This valley is 950 toises, or 7600 feet above the level of the sea. We had not proceeded far before the rain began to fall, but we persisted until we had accomplished more than half of our journey, when we returned, wet through.

Chamouni, July 25th.

We have returned from visiting the glacier of Montanvert, or as it is called, the Sea of Ice, a scene in truth of dizzying wonder. The path that winds to it along the side of a mountain, now clothed with pines, now intersected with snowy hollows, is wide and steep. The cabin of Montanvert is three leagues from Chamouni, half of which distance is performed on mules, not so sure footed, but that on the first day the one which I rode fell in what the guides call a *mauvais pas*, so that I narrowly escaped being precipitated down the mountain. We passed over a hollow covered with snow, down which vast stones are accustomed to roll. One had fallen the preceding day, a little time after we had returned: our guides desired us to pass quickly, for it is said that sometimes the least sound will accelerate their descent. We arrived at Montanvert, however, safe.

On all sides precipitous mountains, the abodes of unrelenting frost, surround this vale: their sides are banked up with ice and snow, broken, heaped high, and exhibiting terrific chasms. The summits are sharp and naked pinnacles, whose overhanging steepness will not even permit snow to rest upon them. Lines of dazzling ice occupy here and there their perpendicular rifts, and shine through the driving vapours with inexpressible brilliance: they pierce the clouds like things not belonging to this earth. The vale itself is filled with a mass of undulating ice, and has an ascent sufficiently gradual even to the remotest abysses of these horrible desarts. It is only half a league (about two miles) in breadth, and seems much less. It exhibits an appearance as if frost had suddenly bound up the waves and whirlpools of a mighty torrent. We walked some distance upon its surface. The waves are elevated about 12 or 15 feet from the surface of the mass, which is intersected by long gaps of unfathomable depth, the ice of whose sides is more beautifully azure than the sky. In these regions every thing changes, and is in motion. This vast mass of ice has one general progress, which ceases neither day nor night; it breaks and bursts for ever: some undulations sink while others rise; it is never the same. The echo of rocks, or of the ice and snow which fall from their overhanging precipices, or roll from their aerial summits, scarcely ceases for one moment. One would think that Mont Blanc, like the god of the Stoics, was a vast animal, and that the frozen blood for ever circulated through his stony veins.

We dined (M***, C***, and I) on the grass, in the open air, surrounded by this scene. The air is piercing and clear. We returned down the mountain, sometimes encompassed by the driving vapours, sometimes cheered by the sunbeams, and arrived at our inn by seven o'clock.

Montalègre, July 28th.

The next morning we returned through the rain to St. Martin. The scenery had lost something of its immensity, thick clouds hanging over the highest mountains; but visitings of sunset intervened between the showers, and the blue sky shone between the accumulated clouds of snowy whiteness which brought them; the

dazzling mountains sometimes glittered through a chasm of the
290 clouds above our heads, and all the charm of its grandeur remained.
We repassed *Pont Pellisier*, a wooden bridge over the Arve, and the
ravine of the Arve. We repassed the pine forests which overhang the
defile, the château of St. Michel, a haunted ruin, built on the edge of a
precipice, and shadowed over by the eternal forest. We repassed the
295 vale of Servoz, a vale more beautiful, because more luxuriant, than
that of Chamouni. Mont Blanc forms one of the sides of this vale
also, and the other is inclosed by an irregular amphitheatre of
enormous mountains, one of which is in ruins, and fell fifty years ago
into the higher part of the valley: the smoke of its fall was seen in
300 Piedmont, and people went from Turin to investigate whether a
volcano had not burst forth among the Alps. It continued falling
many days, spreading, with the shock and thunder of its ruin,
consternation into the neighbouring vales. In the evening we arrived
at St. Martin. The next day we wound through the valley, which I
305 have described before, and arrived in the evening at our home.

We have bought some specimens of minerals and plants, and two
or three crystal seals, at Mont Blanc, to preserve the remembrance of
having approached it. There is a cabinet of *Histoire Naturelle* at
Chamouni, just as at Keswick, Matlock, and Clifton; the proprietor
310 of which is the very vilest specimen of that vile species of quack that,
together with the whole army of aubergistes and guides, and indeed
the entire mass of the population, subsist on the weakness and
credulity of travellers as leaches subsist on the sick. The most
interesting of my purchases is a large collection of all the seeds of rare
315 alpine plants, with their names written upon the outside of the
papers that contain them. These I mean to colonize in my garden in
England, and to permit you to make what choice you please from
them. They are companions which the Celandine—the classic
Celandine, need not despise; they are as wild and more daring than
320 he, and will tell him tales of things even as touching and sublime as
the gaze of a vernal poet.

Did I tell you that there are troops of wolves among these
mountains? In the winter they descend into the vallies, which the
snow occupies six months of the year, and devour every thing that
325 they can find out of doors. A wolf is more powerful than the fiercest
and strongest dog. There are no bears in these regions. We heard,
when we were at Lucerne, that they were occasionally found in the
forests which surround that lake. Adieu.

S.

"WE PITY THE PLUMAGE, BUT FORGET
THE DYING BIRD."

A N

ADDRESS TO THE PEOPLE

O N

The Death of the Princess Charlotte.

B Y

𝕮𝖍𝖊 𝕳𝖊𝖗𝖒𝖎𝖙 𝖔𝖋 𝕸𝖆𝖗𝖑𝖔𝖜.

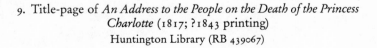

9. Title-page of *An Address to the People on the Death of the Princess Charlotte* (1817; ?1843 printing)
Huntington Library (RB 439067)

AN ADDRESS, &c.

I. The Princess Charlotte is dead. She no longer moves, nor thinks, nor feels. She is an inanimate as the clay with which she is about to mingle. It is a dreadful thing to know that she is a putrid corpse, who but a few days since was full of life and hope; a woman young, innocent, and beautiful, snatched from the bosom of domestic peace, and leaving that single vacancy which none can die and leave not.

II. Thus much the death of the Princess Charlotte has in common with the death of thousands. How many women die in childbed and leave their families of motherless children and their husbands to live on, blighted by the remembrance of that heavy loss? How many women of active and energetic virtues; mild, affectionate, and wise, whose life is as a chain of happiness and union, which once being broken, leaves those whom it bound to perish, have died, and have been deplored with bitterness, which is too deep for words? Some have perished in penury or shame, and their orphan baby has survived, a prey to the scorn and neglect of strangers. Men have watched by the bedside of their expiring wives, and have gone mad when the hideous death-rattle was heard within the throat, regardless of the rosy child sleeping in the lap of the unobservant nurse. The countenance of the physician had been read by the stare of this distracted husband, till the legible despair sunk into his heart. All this has been and is. You walk with a merry heart through the streets of this great city, and think not that such are the scenes acting all around you. You do not number in your thought the mothers who die in childbed. It is the most horrible of ruins:—In sickness, in old age, in battle, death comes as to his own home; but in the season of joy and hope, when life should succeed to life, and the assembled family expects one more, the youngest and the best beloved, that the wife, the mother—she for whom each member of the family was so dear to one another, should die!—Yet thousands of the poorest poor, whose misery is aggravated by what cannot be spoken now, suffer

this. And have they no affections? Do not their hearts beat in their bosoms, and the tears gush from their eyes? Are they not human
35 flesh and blood? Yet none weep for them—none mourn for them—none when their coffins are carried to the grave (if indeed the parish furnishes a coffin for all) turn aside and moralize upon the sadness they have left behind.

III. The Athenians did well to celebrate, with public mourning,
40 the death of those who had guided the republic with their valour and their understanding, or illustrated it with their genius. Men do well to mourn for the dead: it proves that we love something beside ourselves; and he must have a hard heart who can see his friend depart to rottenness and dust, and speed him without emotion on
45 his voyage to "that bourne whence no traveller returns." To lament for those who have benefitted the state, is a habit of piety yet more favourable to the cultivation of our best affections. When Milton died it had been well that the universal English nation had been clothed in solemn black, and that the muffled bells had tolled from
50 town to town. The French nation should have enjoined a public mourning at the deaths of Rousseau and Voltaire. We cannot truly grieve for every one who dies beyond the circle of those especially dear to us; yet in the extinction of the objects of public love and admiration, and gratitude, there is something, if we enjoy a liberal
55 mind, which has departed from within that circle. It were well done also, that men should mourn for any public calamity which has befallen their country or the world, though it be not death. This helps to maintain that connexion between one man and another, and all men considered as a whole, which is the bond of social life. There
60 should be public mourning when those events take place which make all good men mourn in their hearts,—the rule of foreign or domestic tyrants, the abuse of public faith, the wresting of old and venerable laws to the murder of the innocent, the established insecurity of all those, the flower of the nation, who cherish an
65 unconquerable enthusiasm for public good. Thus, if Horne Tooke and Hardy had been convicted of high treason, it had been good that there had been not only the sorrow and the indignation which would have filled all hearts, but the external symbols of grief. When the French Republic was extinguished, the world ought to have
70 mourned.

IV. But this appeal to the feelings of men should not be made lightly, or in any manner that tends to waste, on inadequate objects, those fertilising streams of sympathy, which a public mourning should be the occasion of pouring forth. This solemnity should be used only to express a wide and intelligible calamity, and one which is felt to be such by those who feel for their country and for mankind; its character ought to be universal, not particular.

V. The news of the death of the Princess Charlotte, and of the execution of Brandreth, Ludlam, and Turner, arrived nearly at the same time. If beauty, youth, innocence, amiable manners, and the exercise of the domestic virtues could alone justify public sorrow when they are extinguished for ever, this interesting Lady would well deserve that exhibition. She was the last and the best of her race. But there were thousands of others equally distinguished as she, for private excellencies, who have been cut off in youth and hope. The accident of her birth neither made her life more virtuous nor her death more worthy of grief. For the public she had done nothing either good or evil; her education had rendered her incapable of either in a large and comprehensive sense. She was born a Princess; and those who are destined to rule mankind are dispensed with acquiring that wisdom and that experience which is necessary even to rule themselves. She was not like Lady Jane Grey, or Queen Elizabeth, a woman of profound and various learning. She had accomplished nothing, and aspired to nothing, and could understand nothing respecting those great political questions which involve the happiness of those over whom she was destined to rule. Yet this should not be said in blame, but in compassion: let us speak no evil of the dead. Such is the misery, such the impotence of royalty.—Princes are prevented from the cradle from becoming any thing which may deserve that greatest of all rewards next to a good conscience, public admiration and regret.

VI. The execution of Brandreth, Ludlam, and Turner, is an event of quite a different character from the death of the Princess Charlotte. These men were shut up in a horrible dungeon, for many months, with the fear of a hideous death and of everlasting hell thrust before their eyes; and at last were brought to the scaffold and hung. They too had domestic affections, and were remarkable for the exercise of private virtues. Perhaps their low station permitted the growth of those affections in a degree not consistent with a more exalted rank. They had sons, and brothers, and sisters, and fathers, who loved them, it should seem, more than the Princess Charlotte could be loved by those whom the regulations of her rank had held in perpetual estrangement from her. Her husband was to her as father, mother, and brethren. Ludlam and Turner were men of mature years, and the affections were ripened and strengthened within them. What these sufferers felt shall not be said. But what must have been the long and various agony of their kindred may be inferred from Edward Turner, who, when he saw his brother dragged along upon the hurdle, shrieked horribly and fell in a fit, and was carried away like a corpse by two men. How fearful must have been their agony, sitting in solitude on that day when the tempestuous voice of horror from the crowd, told them that the head so dear to them was severed from the body! Yes—they listened to the maddening shriek which burst from the multitude: they heard the rush of ten thousand terror-stricken feet, the groans and the hootings which told them that the mangled and distorted head was then lifted into the air. The sufferers were dead. What is death? Who dares to say that which will come after the grave?[1] Brandreth was calm, and evidently believed that the consequences of our errors were limited by that tremendous barrier. Ludlam and Turner were full of fears, lest God should plunge them in everlasting fire. Mr. Pickering, the clergyman, was evidently anxious that Brandreth should not by a false confidence lose the single opportunity of reconciling himself with the Ruler of the future world. None knew what death was, or could know. Yet these men were presumptuously thrust into that unfathomable gulf, by other men, who knew as little and who reckoned not the present or the future sufferings of their victims. Nothing is more horrible than that man should for any cause shed the life of man. For all other calamities there is a remedy or a consolation. When that Power through which we live ceases to maintain the life which it has conferred, then is grief and agony, and the burthen which must be borne: such sorrow improves the heart. But when man sheds the blood of man, revenge, and hatred, and a long train of executions, and assassinations, and proscriptions, is perpetuated to remotest time.

VII. Such are the particular, and some of the general considerations depending on the death of these men. But however deplorable, if it were a mere private or customary grief, the public, as the public, should not mourn. But it is more than this. The events which led to the death of those unfortunate men are a public calamity. I will not impute blame to the jury who pronounced them

---

[1] "Your death has eyes in his head—mine is not painted so." *Cymbeline* (V. I. 184–5).

guilty of high treason, perhaps the law requires that such should be the denomination of their offence. Some restraint ought indeed to be imposed on those thoughtless men who imagine they can find in violence a remedy for violence, even if their oppressors had tempted them to this occasion of their ruin. They are instruments of evil, not so guilty as the hands that wielded them, but fit to inspire caution. But their death, by hanging and beheading, and the circumstances of which it is the characteristic and the consequence, constitute a calamity such as the English nation ought to mourn with an unassuageable grief.

VIII. Kings and their ministers have in every age been distinguished from other men by a thirst for expenditure and bloodshed. There existed in this country, until the American war, a check, sufficiently feeble and pliant indeed, to this desolating propensity. Until America proclaimed itself a republic, England was perhaps the freest and most glorious nation subsisting on the surface of the earth. It was not what is to the full desirable that a nation should be, but all that it can be, when it does not govern itself. The consequences however of that fundamental defect soon became evident. The government which the imperfect constitution of our representative assembly threw into the hands of a few aristocrats, improved the method of anticipating the taxes by loans, invented by the ministers of William III, until an enormous debt had been created. In the war against the republic of France, this policy was followed up, until now, the *mere interest* of the public debt amounts to more than twice as much as the lavish expenditure of the public treasure, for maintaining the standing army, and the royal family, and the pensioners, and the placemen. The effect of this debt is to produce such an unequal distribution of the means of living, as saps the foundation of social union and civilized life. It creates a double aristocracy, instead of one which was sufficiently burthensome before, and gives twice as many people the liberty of living in luxury and idleness, on the produce of the industrious and the poor. And it does not give them this because they are more wise and meritorious than the rest, or because their leisure is spent in schemes of public good, or in those exercises of the intellect and the imagination, whose creations ennoble or adorn a country. They are not like the old aristocracy men of pride and honour, *sans peur et sans tache*, but petty piddling slaves who have gained a right to the title of public creditors, either by gambling in the funds, or by subserviency to

government, or some other villainous trade. They are not the
"Corinthian capital of polished society," but the petty and creeping
weeds which deface the rich tracery of its sculpture. The effect of this
195 system is, that the day labourer gains no more now by working
sixteen hours a day than he gained before by working eight. I put the
thing in its simplest and most intelligible shape. The labourer, he that
tills the ground and manufactures cloth, is the man who has to
provide, out of what he would bring home to his wife and children,
200 for the luxuries and comforts of those, whose claims are represented
by an annuity of forty-four millions a year levied upon the English
nation. Before, he supported the army and the pensioners, and the
royal family, and the landholders; and this is a hard necessity to
which it was well that he should submit. Many and various are the
205 mischiefs flowing from oppression, but this is the representative of
them all; namely, that one man is forced to labour for another in a
degree not only not necessary to the support of the subsisting
distinctions among mankind, but so as by the excess of the injustice
to endanger the very foundations of all that is valuable in social
210 order, and to provoke that anarchy which is at once the enemy of
freedom, and the child and the chastiser of misrule. The nation,
tottering on the brink of two chasms, began to be weary of a
continuance of such dangers and degradations, and the miseries
which are the consequence of them; the public voice loudly
215 demanded a free representation of the people. It began to be felt that
no other constituted body of men could meet the difficulties which
impend. Nothing but the nation itself dares to touch the question as
to whether there is any remedy or no to the annual payment of forty-
four millions a year, beyond the necessary expenses of state, for ever
220 and for ever. A nobler spirit also went abroad, and the love of liberty,
and patriotism, and the self-respect attendant on those glorious
emotions, revived in the bosoms of men. The government had a
desperate game to play.

IX. In the manufacturing districts of England discontent and
225 disaffection had prevailed for many years; this was the consequence
of that system of double aristocracy produced by the causes before
mentioned. The manufacturers, the helots of our luxury, are left by
this system famished, without affections, without health, without
leisure or opportunity for such instruction as might counteract
230 those habits of turbulence and dissipation, produced by the
precariousness and insecurity of poverty. Here was a ready field for

any adventurer who should wish for whatever purpose to incite a few ignorant men to acts of illegal outrage. So soon as it was plainly seen that the demands of the people for a free representation must be conceded if some intimidation and prejudice were not conjured up, 235 a conspiracy of the most horrible atrocity was laid in train. It is impossible to know how far the higher members of the government are involved in the guilt of their infernal agents. It is impossible to know how numerous or how active they have been, or by what false hopes they are yet inflaming the untutored multitude to put their 240 necks under the axe and into the halter. But thus much is known, that so soon as the whole nation lifted up its voice for parliamentary reform, spies were sent forth. These were selected from the most worthless and infamous of mankind, and dispersed among the multitude of famished and illiterate labourers. It was their business if 245 they found no discontent to create it. It was their business to find victims, no matter whether right or wrong. It was their business to produce upon the public an impression, that if any attempt to attain national freedom, or to diminish the burthens of debt and taxation under which we groan, were successful, the starving multitude 250 would rush in, and confound all orders and distinctions, and institutions and laws, in common ruin. The inference with which they were required to arm the ministers was, that despotic power ought to be eternal. To produce this salutary impression, they betrayed some innocent and unsuspecting rustics into a crime 255 whose penalty is a hideous death. A few hungry and ignorant manufacturers seduced by the splendid promises of these remorseless blood-conspirators, collected together in what is called rebellion against the state. All was prepared, and the eighteen dragoons assembled in readiness, no doubt, conducted their 260 astonished victims to that dungeon which they left only to be mangled by the executioner's hand. The cruel instigators of their ruin retired to enjoy the great revenues which they had earned by a life of villainy. The public voice was overpowered by the timid and the selfish, who threw the weight of fear into the scale of public 265 opinion, and parliament confided anew to the executive government those extraordinary powers which may never be laid down, or which may be laid down in blood, or which the regularly constituted assembly of the nation must wrest out of their hands. Our alternatives are a despotism, a revolution, or reform. 270

X. On the 7th of November, Brandreth, Turner, and Ludlam

ascended the scaffold. We feel for Brandreth the less, because it seems he killed a man. But recollect who instigated him to the proceedings which led to murder. On the word of a dying man,

275 Brandreth tells us, that "OLIVER *brought him to this*"—that, "*but for* OLIVER, *he would not have been there.*" See, too, Ludlam and Turner, with their sons and brothers, and sisters, how they kneel together in a dreadful agony of prayer. Hell is before their eyes, and they shudder and feel sick with fear, lest some unrepented or some wilful

280 sin should seal their doom in everlasting fire. With that dreadful penalty before their eyes—with that tremendous sanction for the truth of all he spoke, Turner exclaimed loudly and distinctly, *while the executioner was putting the rope round his neck*, "THIS IS ALL OLIVER AND THE GOVERNMENT." What more he might have said

285 we know not, because the chaplain prevented any further observations. Troops of horse, with keen and glittering swords, hemmed in the multitudes collected to witness this abominable exhibition. "When the stroke of the axe was heard, there was a burst of horror from the crowd.[1] The instant the head was exhibited, there

290 was a tremendous shriek set up, and the multitude ran violently in all directions, as if under the impulse of sudden frenzy. Those who resumed their stations, groaned and hooted." It is a national calamity, that we endure men to rule over us, who sanction for whatever ends a conspiracy which is to arrive at its purpose through

295 such a frightful pouring forth of human blood and agony. But when that purpose is to trample upon our rights and liberties forever, to present to us the alternatives of anarchy and oppression, and triumph when the astonished nation accepts the latter at their hands, to maintain a vast standing army, and add, year by year, to a public

300 debt, which, already, they know, cannot be discharged; and which, when the delusion that supports it fails, will produce as much misery and confusion through all classes of society as it has continued to produce of famine and degradation to the undefended poor; to imprison and calumniate those who may offend them, at will; when

305 this, if not the purpose, is the effect of that conspiracy, how ought we not to mourn?

XI. Mourn then People of England. Clothe yourselves in solemn black. Let the bells be tolled. Think of mortality and change. Shroud yourselves in solitude and the gloom of sacred sorrow. Spare no

310 symbol of universal grief. Weep—mourn—lament. Fill the great

---

[1] These expressions are taken from the *Examiner*, Sunday, Nov. 9.

City—fill the boundless fields, with lamentation and the echo of groans. A beautiful Princess is dead:—she who should have been the Queen of her beloved nation, and whose posterity should have ruled it for ever. She loved the domestic affections, and cherished arts which adorn, and valour which defends. She was amiable and would 315 have become wise, but she was young, and in the flower of youth the despoiler came. LIBERTY is dead. Slave! I charge thee disturb not the depth and solemnity of our grief by any meaner sorrow. If One has died who was like her that should have ruled over this land, like Liberty, young, innocent, and lovely, know that the power through 320 which that one perished was God, and that it was a private grief. But *man* has murdered Liberty, and whilst the life was ebbing from its wound, there descended on the heads and on the hearts of every human thing, the sympathy of an universal blast and curse. Fetters heavier than iron weigh upon us, because they bind our souls. We 325 move about in a dungeon more pestilential than damp and narrow walls, because the earth is its floor and the heavens are its roof. Let us follow the corpse of British Liberty slowly and reverentially to its tomb: and if some glorious Phantom should appear, and make its throne of broken swords and sceptres and royal crowns trampled in 330 the dust, let us say that the Spirit of Liberty has arisen from its grave and left all that was gross and mortal there, and kneel down and worship it as our Queen.

FRAGMENT ON REFORM (I)

The hopes of the world were bound up in the claims which the people of England made to be delivered from the oppression under which the⟨y⟩ groaned, and to abolish the symbols of those impostures which surrounded their tyrants with sanctity. The claim on the part of the people was, that the institutions of government should be provided for, at certain limited periods, by the people themselves; those for whose benefit alone, it was declared, any of the regulations of social life ought to be permitted to subsist. The voice of public opinion had by no means decided as to the precise form of political institution which should supersede that already existing: but a general persuasion prevailed that the multitude was deluded and oppressed by its rulers; thousands of miserable men and women and children wandered thro' the streets famished, naked and houseless, cottages and farm houses became tenantless whilst

FRAGMENT OF
'A REFUTATION OF DEISM'

The word God signifies an intelligent Creator and
be any force in terms, or discrimination in
of Nature. Nature is the mass of events,
all things of which by means of our sen⟨ses⟩
and which is therefore the only legitim⟨ate⟩
deductions are founded upon their evidence   5
some Being above, or beyond Nature, its
and whose intelligence is the guide of its
-tinged God from Nature, that the mis⟨takes⟩
have fallen by confounding them, may
The attributes of God are usually supposed   10
Omnipresence, infinite goodness, and Immutab⟨ility⟩
of his existence are supposed to be afforded
displayed in the Universe.—It is propo⟨sed⟩
these proofs, and then to discuss the
universe, and how far the qualities usua⟨lly⟩   15
compatible with each other.

              in favour of the Existence of a Deity.
              a Deity.

                    ine the structure of a   20
                    aker. No work of Man
                    the contemplation of
                    was an artificer
                    the Universe is
                    shall be proved   25
                    signed, adapted
                    philosophical
                    inferred. The
                    erse; and it
                    thence infer a   30
                    e, design and

parent in the
a popular
ntrivance?

35 Simply, because innumerable instances of machines having been
contrived by human art are present to our mind—because we are
acquainted with persons who could construct such machines; but, if
having no knowledge of any contrivance of art we had accidentally
found a watch upon the ground, we should have been justified in
40 concluding that it was a thing of Nature, that it was a combination of
matter with whose cause we were unacquainted, and that the
attempt to account for the origin of its existence would be equally
presumptuous and unsatisfactory.

The analogy which some philosophers have attempted to
45 establish, between the contrivances of human art, and the various
existences of the Universe is inadmissable. We attribute these effects
to human intelligence, because we know before hand that human
intelligence is capable of producing them. Take away this knowledge, and the grounds of our reasoning will be destroyed. But
50 our entire ignorance of the divine Nature, leaves this analogy
defective in its most essential point of comparison.

What consideration then remains to be urged by the Deist in
support of the creation of the Universe by a Supreme Being? Its
admirable fitness for the production of certain effects; that won-
55 derful consent of all its parts; that universal harmony by whose
invariable laws innumerable systems of worlds perform their stated
revolutions, and the blood is driven thro' the veins of the minutest
animalcule that sports in the corruption of an insect's lymph: on this
account did the Universe require an intelligent Creator, because it
60 exists producing invariable effects; and inasmuch as it is admirably
organized for the production of these effects, so the more did it
require a creative intelligence.

Thus we have arrived at the Deist's true proposition "That
whatever exists producing certain effects stands in need of a Creator,
65 and the more conspicuous is its fitness for the production of these
effects, the more certain will be our conclusion, that it could not
have existed from eternity, but derives its origin from an Intelligent
Creator."

In what respects then does God differ from the Universe? From
70 the admirable fitness of the Universe to its end the Deist infers that it
must have been created. How much more wonderful is the fitness of

the Deity itself. If the fitness of the Universe to produce certain effects be so conspicuous and evident, how much more fitness to his end must exist in the Author of this universe. If we find great difficulty from its admirable arrangement in conceiving that the Universe has existed from all eternity, and to resolve this difficulty suppose a Creator; how much more clearly must we feel the necessity of this very Creator's creation whose perfections comprehend an arrangement far more accurate and just. The belief of an infinity of creative and created Gods, each more eminently requiring an Intelligent Author of their being than the foregoing is a direct consequence of these premises. It is impossible indeed to prescribe limits to learned error, when philosophy relinguishes experience for speculation.

The assumption that the Universe is a design, leads to a conclusion that there are an infinity of creative and created Gods.— which is absurd.

Until it is proved that the Universe was created, we may reasonably suppose that it has endured from all eternity. In a case where two propositions are diametrically opposite the mind believes that which is less incomprehensible: it is easier to suppose that the Universe has existed from all eternity, than to conceive an eternal Being capable of creating it. If the mind sinks beneath the weight of one, is it an alleviation to increase the intolerability of the burden?

A Man knows not only that he now is, but that there was a time when he did not exist; consequently there must have been a cause. But we can only infer from effects causes exactly adequate to those effects; but there certainly is a generative power which is effected by particular instruments; we cannot prove that it is inherent in these instruments, nor is the contrary hypothesis capable of demonstration; we admit that the generative power is incomprehensible, but to suppose that the same effects are produced by an Eternal, Omniscient and Omnipotent Being, leaves the cause in the same obscurity but renders it more incomprehensible.

Of the argument in favour of a Deity from the
universality of a belief in his existence

———

God may be defined to be, an Intelligent Creator and Preserver of
the Universe. How small is the proportion of those who believe in
this Being, to the thousands who are prevented by their occupations
from ever bestowing one thought upon the subject; to the millions
110 who worship butterflies, bones, feathers, monkeys, calabashes and
serpents. The word God, like other abstractions, signifies the
agreement of certain propositions, rather than the presence of any
idea. Certainly not the half of mankind, ever heard the reasoning on
which philosophers ground the existence of God; nor has an idea of
115 the Cause of all things yet been received into any human mind. If we
found our belief in the existence of God on the universal consent of
mankind, we are duped by the most palpable of sophisms. The word
God cannot mean at the same time a snake, an ape, a bone, a calabash,
a Trinity and a Unity. The universal belief of mankind in the divinity
120 of a calabash would afford no proof of the Trinity; nor from the
simple fact that few nations have neglected to endow real or
imaginary beings with human qualities, could we justly infer an
Intelligent and Supreme First Cause.

But, there is a tendency to devotion in the human mind. Scarcely
125 any people however barbarous have been discovered, who do not
acknowledge with reverence and awe the supernatural causes of the
natural effects which they experience. They worship it is true, the
vilest and most inanimate substances, but they believe firmly in their
holiness and power, owning thus their dependance on what they can
130 neither see nor conceive.

That credulity should be gross in proportion to the ignorance of
the mind which it enslaves, is strictly consistent with the principles
of human Nature. The idiot, the child and the savage agree in
attributing their own passions and propensities to those inanimate
135 substances by which they are either benefited or injured. The former
become Gods and the latter Demons; hence sacrifizes and prayers
by the means of which the rude theologian imagines that he may
confirm the beneficence of the one, or mitigate the malevolence of
the other. He has averted the wrath of a powerful enemy by
140 supplications and submission, he has secured the assistance of his
neighbour by offerings, he has felt his own fury subside before the

entreaties of a vanquished foe, and has cherished gratitude for the kindness of another. Therefore does he believe that the elements will listen to his vows. He is capable of love and hatred towards his fellow beings; and is variously impelled by these principles to benefit or 145 injure them.—The source then of his error is sufficiently obvious: When the winds, the waves and the atmosphere act in such a manner as to thwart or forward his designs, he attributes to them the same propensities, of whose existence in his own mind, he is conscious, when he is instigated by benefits to kindness, or by injuries to 150 revenge. The only knowledge, at which we are capable of arriving, of cause and effect is, the knowledge of their necessary connexion and the subsequent inference of one to the other. We call that event the cause of another which invariably precedes and is connected with it. Much science and experience is required to ascertain the true cause 155 of any event, or that circumstance which is found with the fewest exceptions to precede its occurrence.

ON CHRISTIANITY

The being who has influenced in the most memorable manner the opinions and the fortunes of the human species, is Jesus Christ. At this day his name is connected with the devotional feelings of two hundred millions of the race of man. The institutions of the most
5 civilised portion of the globe derive their authority from the sanction of his doctrines and to a certain extent are [imbued by ⟨their⟩ Spirit.] He is the God of our popular religion. His extraordinary Genius, the wide and rapid effect of his unexampled doctrines, his invincible gentleness and benignity, the devoted love
10 borne to him by his adherents suggested a persuasion to them that he was something divine. The supernatural events which the historians of this wonderful man subsequently asserted to have been connected with every gradation of his career established the opinion. His death is said to have been accompanied by an accumula-
15 tion of tremendous prodigies. Utter darkness fell upon the earth blotting the noonday Sun, dead bodies arising from their graves walked thro' the public streets, and an earthquake shook the astonished city, rending the rocks of the surrounding mountains. The philosopher may attribute the application of these events to the
20 death of a reformer or the events themselves to a visitation of that Universal Pan who

* * * * * *

I protest against any prejudication of the controversy (if indeed it can be considered a disputable point) as to whether Jesus Christ was something divine or no. I make an abstraction of whatever
25 miraculous or mysterious is connected with his character and his history. Enough remains to afford a theme for amplest elucidation.
The remarkable consequences which resulted from the doctrines of Jesus Christ produced a number of historians among his immediate followers who eagerly recorded the uncommon tale of his
30 genius, his virtues, his sufferings and his death. Four only of these

have been permitted to descend to posterity, and these agree in the most important particulars of the tale. It is a simple tale, natural, probable, full of heart moving truth. Every religion and every revolution can furnish with regard to some of its most important particulars a parallel series of events. A man of ardent genius, and impatient virtue perishes in stern and resolute opposition to tyranny, injustice and superstition. He refuses, he despises pardon. He exults in the torturing flames and the insolent mockery of the oppressor. It is a triumph to him beyond all triumphs that the multitude accumulate scorn and execration on his head solely because his heart has known no measure in the love it bore them, and because the zeal which dragged him to his torments is so pure and ardent that it can make their very hatred sweet.—Most dear to the human heart, and in all its shapes sweet and soothing, is the consciousness of self-sacrifize. Not for this is the history of Jesus Christ unparalleled in the annals of mankind. The honour of the human race rests not solely on the atchievements of a being concerning whom it is disputed whether he be a God or man. It is the profound wisdom and the comprehensive morality of his doctrines which essentially distinguish him from the crowd of martyrs and of patriots who have exulted to devote themselves for what they conceived would contribute to the benefit of their fellow men.—

The birth of the Christ occurred at a period which may be considered as a crisis the most stupendous and memorable in the progress of the human race. The splendour of the Roman name, the vital spirit of the Roman power had vanished. A race of despicable usurpers had assumed the dominion of the world, and power was no longer distributed but as the price of the basest artifices of slavery. Sentiments of liberty and heroism no longer lived but in the lamentations of those who had felt, but had survived their influence; even from these they were speedily effaced. Accumulations of wealth and power were inordinately great. The most abject of mankind, freedmen, eunuchs, and every species of satellite attendant on a court became invested with inexhaustible resources. The consequences of this system speedily became manifest, and they accurately corresponded to the pernicious character of their cause. Refinement in arts and letters distorted from its natural tendency to promote benevolence and truth, became subservient to lust and luxury. All communication among human beings was vitiated and polluted in its sources. The prosperity of the republic no longer excited disinterested care. The intercourse of man with man was that of tyrant with slave, the one stipulating as the price of his submission, the other as the prerogative of his superiority some personal advantage. Selfishness became a system whose gradations were so nicely ascertained that the balance never inclined to the minutest disadvantage of the estimator. And as intellectual objects betray their pursuer more readily into situations of self-sacrifize, sensual pleasures occupied the interest of mankind; hence those persons who occupied the most eminent stations in society, public opinion having lost its value, became habituated to the most monstrous and complicated perversities of appetite and sentiment. The national affections were first destroyed, the domestic affections now vanished away; man lived like a beast of prey among his fellow men, uniting more than a serpent's cunning to its deadliest malignity and venom.

Meanwhile other effects indirectly favourable to the progress of mankind sprung from the same causes. Good and evil subsist in so intimate an union that few situations of human affairs can be affirmed to contain either of these principles in an unconnected state. The dominion which Rome had usurped over the civilized world was essentially iniquitous. It was procured by a series of aggressions, and preserved by sanguinary despotism. The national religion of Rome and of the Greek republics perished when Rome lost the character and priviledges of a nation. It was incorporated with the ceremonies and institutions of a free people, and disjoined from these lost the   by which it was preserved. Without exciting any powerful enthusiasm the Polytheism of Rome was calculated to satiate the vulgar belief and tranquillize that curiosity concerning the mystery of the Universe inseparable from the human mind. The established faith began to decline from the moment of the subversion of the republic, [and] lost by regular gradations from that æra its influence on the world. Involved in its ruin was the important moral system inseparably connected with it. The splendid devotions of patriotism, the emulation of military fame, such atchievements as Scævola, the Decii and Regulus performed had fulfilled their impersonations on the scene and contributed their allotted portion to the improvement of mankind. It was time that new and more accurate maxims of social duty should replace the decaying influence of opinions which derived no sanctity but from immemorial usage, and which had survived the end and intention of their institution. The speculations of the severer philosophers on the subject of moral science, contributed to mature this revolution. The Stoics in particular earnestly assailed the popular superstitions of glory and revenge and personal prowess, asserting as the chief characteristic of wisdom and virtue, internal sanctity and inviolability of soul. The Epicureans employed other terms to express the same sentiments. The sceptics narrowly investigated the foundations of all human knowledge, and produced a systematic deliberation and independance of mind not compatible with the impetuosity of assent required by the enterprises of Roman virtue. Meanwhile some impulse was

*   *   *   *   *   *

God.

The thoughts which the word, God, suggests to the human mind are susceptible of as many variations as human minds themselves. The Stoic the Platonist and the Epicurean, the Polytheist the Dualist and the Trinitarian differ infinitely in their conceptions of its meaning. They agree only in considering it the most awful and most venerable of names, as a common term devised to express all of mystery or majesty or power which the invisible world contains. And not only has every sect distinct conceptions of the application of this name, but scarcely two individuals of the same sect, who exercise in any degree the freedom of their judgement, or yield themselves with any candour of feeling to the influencings of the visible world find perfect coincidence of opinions to exist between them. It is interes⟨ting⟩ to enquire in what acceptation Jesus Christ employed this term.

We may conceive his mind to have been predisposed on this subject to adopt the opinions of his countrymen. Every human being is indebted for a multitude of his sentiments to the religion of his early years. Jesus Christ probably studied the historians of his country with the ardour of a spirit seeking after truth. They were undoubtedly the companions of his childish years, the food and nutriment and materials of his youthful meditations. The sublime dramatic poem entitled *Job*, had familiarized his imagination with the boldest imagery afforded by the human mind and the material world. *Ecclesiastes* had diffused a seriousness and solemnity over the frame of his spirit glowing with youthful hope, and made audible to his listening heart

> The still, sad music of humanity,
> Not harsh or grating, but of ample power
> To chasten and subdue.

150

He had contemplated this name as having been prophanely perverted to the sanctioning of the most enormous and abominable crimes. We can distinctly trace in the tissue of his doctrines the persuasion that God is some universal being, differing both from man and from the mind of man.—According to Jesus Christ God is neither the Jupiter who sends rain upon the earth, nor the Venus thro' whom all living things are produced, nor the Vulcan who presides over the terrestrial element of fire, nor the Vesta that preserves the light which is inshrined in the sun and moon and stars. He is neither the Proteus or the Pan of the material world. But the word God according to the acceptation of Jesus Christ unites all the attributes which these denominations contain, and is the interfused and overruling Spirit of all the energy and wisdom included within the circle of existing things. It is important to observe that the author of the Christian system had a conception widely differing from the gross imaginations of the vulgar relatively to the ruling Power of the Universe. He every where represents this power as something mysteriously and illimitably pervading the frame of things. Nor do his doctrines practically assume any proposition which they theoretically deny. They do not represent God as a limitless and inconceivable mystery affirming at the same time his existence as a being subject to passion and capable

155

160

165

170

*　　*　　*　　*　　*　　*

Blessed are the pure in heart, for they shall see God—blessed are those who have preserved internal sanctity of soul, who are conscious of no secret deceit, who are the same in act as they are in desire, who conceal no thought, no tendencies of thought, from their own conscience, who are faithful and sincere witnesses before the tribunal of their own judgement of all that passes within their mind. Such as these shall see God. What! after death shall their awakened eyes behold the King of Heaven, shall they stand in awe before the golden throne on which he sits, and gaze upon the

175

180

venerable countenance of the paternal Monarch. Is this the reward of the virtuous and the pure? These are the idle dreams of the visionary or the pernicious representations of impostors who have fabricated from the very materials of wisdom a cloak for their own 185 dwarfish and imbecile conceptions. Jesus Christ has said no more than the most excellent philosophers have felt and expressed—that virtue is its own reward. It is true that such an expression as he has used was prompted by the energy of genius, it was the overflowing enthusiasm of a   poet, but it is not the less literally true, 190 clearly repugnant to the mistaken conceptions of the multitude.— God, it has been asserted, was contemplated by Jesus Christ as every poet and every philosopher must have contemplated that mysterious principle. He considered that venerable word to express the overruling Spirit of the collective energy of the moral and 195 material world. He affirms therefore no more than that a simple and sincere mind is an indispensable requisite of true knowledge and true happiness. He affirms that a being of pure and gentle habits will not fail in every thought, in every object of every thought, to be aware of benignant visitings from the invisible energies by which he 200 is surrounded. Whosoever is free from the contamination of luxury and licence may go forth to the fields and to the woods inhaling joyous renovation from the breath of Spring, or catching from the odours and the sounds of autumn, some diviner mood of sweetest sadness which improves the solitary heart. Whosoever is no deceiver 205 or destroyer of his fellow men, no liar, no flatterer, no murderer may walk among his species, deriving from the communion with all which they contain of beautiful or of majestic, some intercourse with the Universal God. Whoever has maintained with his own heart the strictest correspondence of confidence, who dares to 210 examine and to estimate every imagination which suggests itself to his mind, who is that which he designs to become, and only aspires to that which the divinity of his own nature shall consider and approve .. he, has already seen God.

We live and move and think, but we are not the creators of our 215 own origin and existence, we are not the arbiters of every motion of our own complicated nature, we are not the masters of our own imaginations and moods of mental being .. There is a power by which we are surrounded, like the atmosphere in which some motionless lyre is suspended, which visits with its breath our silent 220 chords, at will. Our most imperial and stupendous qualities, those

on which the majesty and power of humanity is erected are, relatively to the inferiour portion of its mechanism indeed active and imperial; but they are the passive slaves of some higher and more
225 omnipresent Power. This power is God. And those who have seen God, have, in the periods of their purer and more perfect nature, been harmonized by their own will, to so exquisite a consentaneity of powers, as to give forth divinest melody when the breath of universal being sweeps over their frame.
230   That those who are pure in heart shall see God, and that virtue is its own reward, may be considered as equivalent assertions. The former of these propositions is a metaphorical repetition of the latter. The advocates of literal interpretation have been the most efficacious enemies of those doctrines whose institutor they profess
235 to venerate. They would assert, it

*   *   *   *   *   *

Thucydides in particular affords a number of instances calculated to establish this opinion:

και οσα μεν λογω ειπον εκαστοι χαλεπον την ακριβειαν αυτην των
λεχθεντων διαμνημονευσαι ην, εμοι τε ων αυτος ηκουσα, και τοις
240 αλλοθεν ποθεν εμοι απαγγελλουσιν· ως δ' αν εδοκουν μοι εκαστοι περι
των αει παροντων τα δεοντα μαλιστα ειπειν εχομενω οτι εγγυτατα της
ξυμπασης γνωμης των αληθως λεχθεντων, ουτως ειρηται.

Tacitus says that "the Jews hold God to be something eternal and supreme, neither subject to change nor to decay. Therefore they
245 permit no statues in their cities or their temples." The universal being can only be described or defined by negatives, which deny his subjection to the laws of all inferior existences. Where indefiniteness ends idolatry and anthropomorphism begin. God is as Lucan has expressed

250   quodcunque vides quodcunque moveris
           Et cælum et virtus.

   The doctrine of what some fanatics have termed a peculiar Providence, that is of some power beyond and superiour to that which ordinar⟨il⟩y guides the operations of the Universe interfering
255 to punish the vicious and reward the virtuous, is explicitly denied by Jesus Christ. The absurd and execrable doctrine of vengeance seems

to have been contemplated in all its shapes by this great moralist with the profoundest disapprobation. Nor would he permit the most venerable of names to be perverted into a sanction for the meanest and most contemptible propensities incident to the nature of man: "Love your enemies, bless those who curse you that ye may be the sons of your heavenly Father who makes the sun to shine on the good and on the evil, and the rain to fall on the just and the unjust." How monstrous a calumny have not impostors dared to advance against the mild and gentle Author of this just sentiment, and against the whole tenor of his doctrines and his life overflowing with benevolence and forbearance and compassion! They have represented him asserting that the omnipotent God, that merciful and benignant power who scatters equally upon this beautiful earth all the elements of security and happiness, whose influencings are distributed to all whose natures admit of a participation in them, who sends to the weak and vicious creatures of his will all the benefits which they are capable of sharing, that this God has devised a scheme whereby the body shall live after its apparent dissolution and be rendered capable of indefinite torture.

He is said to have compared the agonies which the vicious shall then endure, to the excruciations of a living body bound among the flames and being consumed sinew by sinew and bone by bone. And this is to be done, not because it is supposed (and the supposition would be sufficiently detestable) that the moral nature of the sufferer would be improved by his tortures. It is done because it *is just* to be done. My neighbour or my servant or my child has done me an injury and it is just that he should suffer an injury in return. Such is the doctrine which Jesus Christ summoned his whole resources of persuasion to oppose. Love your enemy, bless those who curse you ⟨, do good to them that hate you, and pray for them which despitefully use you, and persecute you—⟩such he says is the practise of God, and such must ye imitate if ye would be the children of God; Jesus Christ would hardly have cited as an example of all that is gentle and beneficent and compassionate a being who shall deliberately scheme to inflict on a large portion of the human race tortures indescribably intense and indefinitely protracted .. who shall inflict them too without any mistake as to the true nature of pain, without any view to future good .. merely because it is just! This, and no other is justice. To consider under all the circumstances and consequences of a particular case how the greatest quantity and

the purest quality of happiness will ensue from any action is to be
just, and there is no other justice. The distinction between justice
and mercy was first imagined in the courts of tyrants. Inslaved to the
300 usurpation of their rulers mankind receives every relaxation of their
tyranny as a circumstance of grace and favour. Such was the
clemency of Julius Cæsar who having atchieved by a series of
treachery and bloodshed the ruin of the liberties of his country
receives the fame of mercy because, possessing the power to slay and
305 torture the noblest men of Rome, he restrained his sanguinary soul,
and arrogat⟨ed⟩ to himself as a merit an abstinence from actions
which if he had committed, he would only have added one other
atrocity to his enormous deeds. His assassins understood justice
better. They saw the most virtuous and civilized community of
310 mankind under the insolent dominion of one wicked man, and they
murdered him. They destroyed the usurper of the liberties of their
countrymen, not because they hated him, not because they would
revenge the wrongs which they had sustained. Brutus, it is said, was
his most familiar friend. Most of the conspirators were habituated to
315 domestic intercourse with the man whom they destroyed. It was in
affection, in inextinguishable love for all that is *venerable and dear* to
the human heart in the names of country, liberty and virtue, it was in
serious and solemn and reluctant mood that these holy patriots
murdered their *father and their friend*. They would have spared his
320 violent death if he could have deposited the rights which he had
assumed. His own selfish and narrow nature necessitated the
sacrifice they made. They required that he should change all those
habits which debauchery and bloodshed had twined around the
fibres of his inmost frame of thought, that he should participate with
325 them and with his country those priviledges which having corrupted
by assuming to himself he would no longer value. They would have
sacrificed their lives if they could have made him worthy of the
sacrifice.—Such are the feelings, which Jesus Christ asserts to belong
to the ruling Power of the world. He desireth not the death of a
330 sinner, he makes the sun to shine upon the just and upon the unjust.
    The nature of a narrow and malevolent spirit is so essentially
incompatible with happiness, as to render it inaccessible even to the
influencings of the benignant God. All that his own perverse
propensities will permit him to receive, that God abundantly pours
335 forth upon him. If there is the slightest overbalance of happiness
which can be allotted to the most atrocious offender consistently

with the nature of things, that is rigidly made his portion by the ever watchful power of good. In every case the human mind enjoys the utmost pleasure which it is capable of enjoying. God is represented by Jesus Christ as the [Power] from which or thro' which the streams 340 of all that is excellent and delightful flow: The power which models as they pass all the elements of this mixed universe to the purest and most perfect shape which it belongs to their nature to assume. Jesus Christ attributes to this power the faculty of will. How far such a doctrine in its ordinary sense may be philosophically true, or how 345 far Jesus Christ intentionally availed himself of a metaphor easily understood, is foreign to the subject to consider. Thus much is certain, that Jesus Christ represents God as the fountain of all goodness, the eternal enemy of pain and evil: the uniform and unchanging motive of the salutary operations of the material world. 350 The supposition that this cause is excited to action by some principle analogous to the human will adds weight to the persuasion that it is foreign to its benevolent nature to inflict the slightest pain. According to Jesus Christ, and according to the indisputable facts of the case, some evil Spirit has dominion in this imperfect world. But 355 there will come a time when the human mind shall be visited exclusively by the influences of the benignant power. Men shall die and their bodies shall rot under the ground, all the organs thro' which their knowledge and their feelings have flowed, or in which they have originated shall assume other forms, and become 360 ministrant to purposes the most foreign from their former tendencies. There is a time when we shall neither hear nor see, neither be heard or be seen by the multitude of beings like ourselves by whom we have been so long surrounded.—They shall go ⟨to⟩ the grave where "there is ⟨no work, nor device, nor knowledge, nor 365 wisdom".⟩ It appears that we [moul]der to a heap of senseless dust, a few worms that arise and perish like ourselves. Jesus Christ asserts that these appearances are fallacious, that a gloomy and cold imagination alone suggests the conception that thought can cease to be. 370

Another and a more extensive state of being, rather than the complete extinction of being will follow from that mysterious change which we call death. There shall be no misery, no pain, no fear. The empire of the evil Spirit extends not beyond the boundaries of the grave. The unobscured irradiations from the fountain fire of all 375 goodness shall reveal all that is mysterious and unintelligible until

the mutual communications of knowledge and of happiness throughout all thinking natures constitute a harmony of good that ever varies and never ends. This is Heaven, when pain and evil cease,
380 and when the benignant principle untram⟨mel⟩led and uncontrolled visits in the fulness of its power the universal frame of things. Human life with all its unreal ills and transitory hopes is as a dream which departs before the dawn leaving no trace of its evanescent hues. All that it contains of pure or of divine visits the passive mind in some
385 serenest mood. Most holy are the affections thro' which our fellow beings are rendered dear and venerable to the heart; the remembrance of their sweetness and the completion of the hopes which they did excite constitute when we awaken from the sleep of life the fulfilment of the prophecies of its most majestic [and]
390 beautiful visions.

We die, says Jesus Christ, and when we awaken from the languor of disease the glories and the happiness of Paradise are around us. All evil and pain have ceased for ever. . Our happiness also corresponds with and is adapted to, the nature of our being; the nature of what is
395 most excellent in our being. We see God, and we see that he is good. How delightful a picture even if it be not true! How magnificent and illustrious is the conception which this bold theory suggests to the contemplation, even if it be no more than the imagination of some sublimest and most holy poet, who impressed with the loveliness
400 and majesty of his own nature, is impatient, discontented, with the narrow limits which this imperfect life, and the dark grave have assigned forever as his melancholy portion.

It is not to be believed that Hell or punishment was the conception of this daring mind. It is not to be believed that the most
405 prominent group of the picture which it framed so heartmoving and lovely; the accomplishment of all human hope, the extinction of all mortal fear and anguish, would consist [of] millions of sensitive beings enduring in every variety of torture which omniscient vengeance could invent, immortal agony.

410   Jesus Christ opposed with earnest eloquence the panic fears and hateful superstitions which have enslaved mankind for ages. Nations had risen against nations employing the subtilest devices of mechanism and mind to waste and excruciate and overthrow. The great community of mankind had been subdivided into ten
415 thousand communities each organised for the ruin of the other. Wheel within wheel the vast machine was instinct with the restless

spirit of desolation. The most conspicuous instance of this spirit is
revenge. Pain has been inflicted, therefore pain should be inflicted in
return. Retaliation is the only remedy which can be applied to
violence, because it teaches the injurer the true nature of his own   420
conduct, and operates as a warning against its repetition. Nor must
the same measure [of] calamity be returned as was received. If a man
borrows a certain sum from me, he is bound to repay that sum. Shall
no more be required from the enemy who destroys my reputation or
ravages my fields? It is just that he should suffer ten times the loss   425
which he has inflicted that the legitimate consequences of his deed
may never be obliterated from his remembrance, and that others
may clearly discern and feel the danger of invading the peace of
human society. Such reasonings and the impetuous feelings arising
from them have armed nation against nation, family against family,   430
man against man. An Athenian soldier in the Ionian army which had
assembled for the purpose of vindicating the liberty of the Asiatic
Greeks, accidentally set fire to Sardis. The city being composed of
combustible materials was burned to the ground. The Persians
believed that this circumstance of aggression made it their duty to   435
retaliate on Athens. They assembled successive expeditions on the
most extensive scale. Every nation of the East was united to ruin the
Græcian states. Athens was burned to the ground, the whole
territory laid waste, and every living thing which it contain⟨ed⟩. The
markets, temples with their statues and columns, and the ?tracery   440
          After suffering and inflicting incalculable mischiefs
they desisted from their purpose only when they became impotent
to effect it. The desire of revenge for the aggression of Persia outlived
among the Greeks that love of liberty which had been their most
glorious distinction among the nations of mankind, and Alexander   445
became the instrument of its completion. The mischiefs attendant
on this consummation of fruitless ruin are too manifold and too
tremendous to be related. If all the thought which had been
expended on the construction of engines of agony and death, the
modes of aggression and defence, the raising of armies, and the   450
acquirement of those arts of tyranny and falshood without which
mixed multitudes deluded and goaded to mutual ruin could neither
be led nor governed, had been employed to promote the true
welfare, and extend the real empire of man, how different would
have been the present situation of human society. How different the   455
state of knowledge on physical and moral science from which the

happiness and the power of mankind essentially depend! What
nation has the example of the desolation of Attica by Mardonius and
Zerxes, or the extinction of the Persian Empire by Alexander of
460 Macedon restrained from outrage? Was not the pretext of this latter
system of spoliation derived immediately from the former? Had
revenge in this instance any other effect than to increase instead of
diminishing the mass of malice and evil already existing in the world?

The emptiness and folly of retaliation is apparent from every
465 example which can be brought forward. Not only Jesus Christ, but
the most eminent professors of every sect of philosophy have
reasoned against this futile superstition. Legislation is, in one point
of view, to be considered as an attempt to provide against the
excesses of this deplorable mistake. It professes to assign the penalty
470 of all private injuries, and denies to individuals the right of
vindicating their proper cause. This end is certainly not attained
without some accommodation to the propensities which it desires
to destroy. Still it [professes] to recognize no principle but the
production of the greatest eventual good with the least immediate
475 injury, and to regard the torture or the death of any human being as
unjust, of whatever mischief he may have been the author; so long as
the result shall not more than compensate for the immediate pain.
Such are the only justifiable principles and such is the true reason of
law.

*   *   *   *   *   *

480 Mankind, transmitting from generation to generation this
horrible legacy of accumulated vengeances, and pursuing with the
feelings of duty the misery of their fellow beings have not failed to
attribute to the universal cause a character analogous with their
own. The image of this invisible, mysterious being is more or less
485 excellent and perfect, resembles more or less its original and object
in proportion to the *perfectness* of the mind on which it is impressed.
Thus the nation which has arrived at the highest step in the scale of
moral progression will believe most purely in that God the
knowledge of whose real attributes ⟨has⟩ been considered as the
490 firmest basis of the true religion. The ?nature of the belief of each
individual also will be so far regulated by his conceptions of what is
good. Thus, the conceptions which any nation or indiv⟨id⟩uals
entertain of the God of its popular worship may be inferred from
their own actions and opinions, and from the actions and opinions

which are the subjects of their approbation among their fellow men. 495
Jesus Christ, instructed his disciples to be perfect as their father in
Heaven is perfect, declaring at the same time his belief that human
perfection required the refraining from revenge or retribution in any
of its various shapes. The perfection of the human and the divine
character is thus asserted to be the same: man by resembling God 500
fulfills most accurately the tendencies of his nature, and God
comprehends within itself all that constitutes human perfection.
Thus God is a model thro' which the excellence of man is to be
measured, whilst the *abstract* perfection of the human character is
the type of the actual *perfection* of the divine. It is not to ⟨be⟩ believed 505
that a person of such comprehensive views as Jesus Christ could
have fallen into so manifest a contradiction as to assert that men
would be tortured after death by that being whose character is held
up as a model to human kind because he is incapable of malevolence
or revenge. All the arguments which have been brought forward to 510
justify retribution, fail when retribution is destined neither to
operate as an example to other agents, nor to the offender himself.
How feeble such reasoning is to be considered has been already
shewn. But it is the character of an evil dæmon to consign the beings
whom he has endowed with sensation to improfitable anguish. The 515
peculiar circumstances attendant on the conception of God casting
sinners to burn in Hell forever, combine to render that conception
the most perfect specimen of the greatest imaginable crime. Jesus
Christ represented God as the principle of all good, the source of
all happiness, the wise and benevolent creator and preserver of all 520
living things. But the interpreters of his doctrine have confounded
the good and the evil principle. They observed the emanations of
these universal natures to be inextricably intangled in the world,
and trembling before the power of the cause of all things addressed
to it such flattery as is acceptable to the ministers of human tyranny, 525
attributing love and wisdom to those energies which they felt to be
exerted indifferently for the purposes of benefit and calamity.—
Jesus Christ expressly asserts that distinction between the good and
evil principle which it has been the practise of all theologians to
confound. How far his doctrine or their interpretation may be true, 530
it would scarcely have been worth while to enquire, if the one did not
afford an example and an incentive to the attainment of true virtue,
whilst the other holds out a sanction and apology for every species of
mean and cruel vice.

535   It cannot be precisely ascertained to what degree Jesus Christ accommodated his doctrines to the opinions of his auditors, or in what degree he really said all that he is related to have said. He has left no written record of himself, and we are compelled to judge from the imperfect and obscure information which his biographers, persons
540   certainly of very undisciplined and undiscriminating minds, have transmitted to posterity. These writers, our only guides, impute sentiments to Jesus Christ which flatly contradict each other.—They represent him as narrow, superstitious, or exquisitely vindictive and malicious.—They insert in the midst of a strain of impassioned
545   eloquence, or sagest exhortation, a sentiment only remarkable for its naked and drivelling folly. But it is not difficult to distinguish the inventions by which these historians have filled up the interstices of tradition, or corrupted the simplicity of truth, from the real character of the object of their rude amazement. They have left
550   sufficiently clear indications of the genuine character of Jesus Christ to rescue it forever from the imputations cast upon it by their ignorance and fanaticism. We discover that he is the enemy of oppression and of falshood, that he is the advocate of equal justice, that he is neither disposed to sanction bloodshed or deceit under
555   whatsoever pretences their practise may be vindicated. We discover that he was a man of meek and majestic demeanour, calm in danger, of natural and simple thoughts and habits, beloved to adoration by his adherents, unmoved and solemn and serene. It is utterly incredible that this man said that if you hated your enemy you
560   would find it to your account to return him good for evil, since by such temporary oblivion of vengeance you would heap coals of fire upon his head. Where such contradictions occur, a favourable construction is warranted by the general innocence of manners and comprehensiveness of views which he is represented to possess.—
565   The rule of criticism to be adopted in judging of the life, actions and words of a man who has acted any conspicuous part in the revolutions of the world should not be narrow. We ought to form a general image of his character and of his doctrines and refer to this whole the distinct portions of action and of speech by which they are
570   diversified. It is not here asserted that no contradictions are to be admitted to have place in the system of Jesus Christ between doctrines promulgated in different states of feeling or information, or even such as are implied in the enunciation of a scheme of thought various and obscure thro' its immensity and depth. It is not asserted

that no degree of human indignation ever hurried him beyond the 575
limits which his calmer mood had placed to disapprobation against
vice and folly. Those deviations from the history of his life are alone
to be vindicated which represent his own essential character in
contradiction with itself. Every human mind has, what Lord Bacon
calls its *idola specus*, peculiar images which reside in the inner cave of 580
thought. These constitute the essential and distinctive character of
every human being, to which every action and every word bears
intimate relation, and by which in depicturing a character the
genuineness and meaning of those words and actions are to be
determined.[1]
                                                                    585
Every fanatic or enemy of virtue is not at liberty to misrepresent
the greatest geniuses and the most heroic defenders of all that is
valuable in this mortal world. His story to gain any credit must
contain some truth, and that truth shall thus be a sufficient
indication of his prejudice and his deceit.
                                                                    590
With respect to the miracles which these biographers have
related: I have already declined to enter into any discussion on their
nature or their existence. The supposition of their falshood or their
truth would modify in no degree the hues of the picture which is
attempted to be delineated. To judge truly of the moral and 595
philosophical character of Socrates it is not necessary to determine
the question of the familiar Spirit which it is supposed that he
believed to attend him. The power of [the] human mind relatively to
intercourse with or dominion over the invisible world is doubtless
an interesting theme of discussion, but the connection of the 600
instance of Jesus Christ with the established religion of the country
in which I write renders it dangerous to subject oneself to the
imputation of introducing new gods or abolishing old ones, nor is
the duty of mutual forbearance sufficiently understood to render it
certain that the metaphysician and the moralist, even tho' he 605
carefully sacrifize a cock to Esculapius, may not receive something
analogous to the bowl of hemlock for the reward of his labours.
Much however of what his biographers have asserted is not to be
rejected merely because inferences inconsistent with the general
spirit of his system are to be deduced from its admission. Jesus Christ 610
did, what every other reformer who has produced any considerable
effect upon the world has done.—He accommodated his doctrines
to the prepossessions of those whom he addressed. He used a

[1] Bacon⟨,⟩ *Novum Organum*⟨,⟩ Aph⟨orism⟩ 53.—*De aug⟨mentis⟩ Scien⟨tiarum⟩*. Lib. V.
C⟨ap⟩. 4.

language, for this view, sufficiently familiar to our comprehensions.
615 He said—However new or strange my doctrines may appear to you, they are, in fact, only the restoration and reestablishment of the original institutions, and antient customs of your own law and religion. The constitution of your faith and policy, altho' perfect in their origin, have become corrupt and altered, and have fallen into
620 decay. I profess to restore them to their pristine authority and splendour. "Think not that I am come to destroy the law and the prophets: I am not come to destroy but to fulfill. Till Heaven and Earth pass away, one jot or one tittle shall in no wise pass from the law till all be fulfilled."—Thus like a skilful orator he secures the
625 prejudices of his auditors, and induces them by his professions of sympathy with their feelings, to enter with a willing mind into the exposition of his own.[1] The art of persuasion differs from that of reasoning; and it is of no small moment to the success even of a true cause that the judges who are to determine on its merits should be
630 free from those national and religious predilections which render the multitude both deaf and blind. Let not this practise be considered as an unworthy artifice. It were best for the cause of reason that mankind should acknowledge no authority but its own, but it is useful to a certain extent, that they should not consider those
635 institutions which they have been habituated to reverence as opposing an obstacle to its admission. All reformers have been compelled to practise this misrepresentation of their own true feelings and opinions. It is deeply to be lamented that a word should ever issue from human lips which contains the minutest alloy of
640 dissimulation or simulation, or hypocrisy or exaggeration or any thing but the precise and rigid image which is present to the mind, and which ought to dictate the expression. But the practise of entire sincerity towards other men would avail to no good end, if they were incapable of practising it towards their own minds. In fact, truth
645 cannot be communicated until it is perceived. The interests therefore of truth required that an orator should so far as possible produce in his hearers that state of mind in which alone his exhortations could fairly be contemplated and examined.

Having produced this favourable disposition of mind Jesus Christ
650 proceeds to qualify and finally to abrogate the system of the Jewish [law]. He descants upon its insufficiency as a code of moral conduct, which it professed to be,[2] and absolutely selects the law of retaliation

---

[1] See Cicero de Oratore(.)   [2] See (Matthew Chap. V,) verse(s) 21, 27, 31, 33.

as an instance of the absurdity and immorality of its institutions.[1]
The conclusion of the speech   is in a strain
of most daring and most impassioned speculation. He seems 655
emboldened by the success of his exculpation to the multitude to
declare in public the utmost singularity of his faith. He tramples
upon all received opinions, on all the cherished luxuries and
superstitions of mankind. He bids them cast aside the chains of
custom and blind faith by which they have been encompassed from 660
the very cradle of their being, and become the imitators and
ministers of the Universal God.

Equality of Mankind.

The spirit of the Lord is upon me because he hath chosen me to
preach the gospel to the poor, he hath sent me to heal the broken
hearted, to preach deliverance to the captives, and recovery of sight 665
to the blind, and to set at liberty them that are bruised. (*Luke*,
C⟨hap⟩. iv, v. 18.)

This is an enunciation of all that Plato and Diogenes have
speculated upon of the equality of mankind. They saw that the great
majority of the human species were reduced to the situation of 670
squalid ignorance, and moral imbecility, for the purpose of
purveying for the luxury of a few, and contributing to the
satisfaction of their thirst for power. Too mean spirited and too
feeble in resolve to attempt the conquest of their own evil passions,
and of the difficulties of the material world, men sought dominion 675
over their fellow men as an easy method to gain that apparent
majesty and power which the instinct of their nature requires. Plato
wrote the scheme of a republic in which laws should watch over the
equal distribution of the external instruments of unequal power:
honours, property and   . Diogenes devised a 680
nobler and more worthy system of opposition to the system of slave
and tyrant. He said, it is in the power of each individual to level the
inequality which is the topic of the complaint of mankind. Let him
be aware of his own worth and the station which he really occupies
in the scale of moral beings. Diamonds and gold, palaces and sceptres 685
derive their value from the opinion of mankind. The only sumptuary
law which can be imposed on the use and fabrication of these
instruments of mischief and deceit, these symbols of successful
injustice, is the law of opinion. Every man possesses the power in

[1] *Matt⟨hew⟩* Chap. V⟨, verse⟩ 38.

690 this respect, to legislate for himself. Let him be well aware of his own worth, and moral dignity. Let him yield in   to any wiser or worthier than he so long as he accords no veneration to the splendour of his apparel, the luxury of his food, the multitude of his flatterers and slaves. It is because, O mankind, ye value and seek the

695 empty pageantry of wealth and social power that ye are enslaved to its possessors. Circumscribe your physical wants, learn to live, so far as nourishment and shelter are concerned, like the beasts of the forest and the birds of the air; ye will need not to complain that other individuals of your species are surrounded by the diseases of luxury

700 and the vices of oppression. With all those who are truly wise, there will be an entire community, not only of thoughts and feelings, but also of external possessions. Insomuch therefore as ye love one another, ye may enjoy the community of whatsoever benefits arise from the inventions of civilised life. They are of value only for

705 purposes of mental power, they are of value only as they are capable of being shared and applied to the common advantage of philosophy and [mankind].—If there be no love among men, whatever institutions they may frame, must be subservient to the same purpose: to the continuance of inequality. If there be no love among

710 men, it is best that he who sees thro' the hollowness of their professions, should fly from their society and suffice to his own soul. In wisdom he will thus lose nothing, in peace he will gain every thing. In proportion to the love existing among men, so will be the community of property and power. Among true and real friends all

715 is common, and were ignorance and envy, and superstition banished from the world all mankind would be as friends. The only perfect and genuine republic is that which comprehends every living being. Those distinctions which have been artificially set up of nations and cities and families and religions are only general names expressing

720 the abhorrence and contempt with which men blindly consider their fellow men. I love my country, I love the city in which I was born, my parents and my wife, and the children of my care, and to this city, this woman and this nation, it is incumbent on me to do all the benefit in my power.—To what do these distinctions point, but to an

725 indirect denial of the duty which humanity imposes on you of doing every possible good, to every individual, under whatever denomination he may be comp⟨re⟩hended, to whom you have the power of doing it. You ought to love all mankind, nay, every individual of mankind; you ought not to love the individuals of your

domestic circle less, but to love those who exist beyond it, more. 730
Once make the feelings of confidence and affection universal and the
distinctions of property and power will vanish: nor are they to be
abolished, without substituting something equivalent in mischief to
them, until all mankind shall acknowledge an entire community of
rights.—But as the shades of night are dispelled by the faintest 735
glimmerings of dawn, so shall the minutest progress of the benevolent feelings disperse in some degree the gloom of tyranny and
slavery, ministers of mutual suspicion and abhorrence.

Your physical wants are few, whilst those of your mind and heart
cannot be numbered or described from their multitude and 740
complication. To secure the gratification of the former men have
made themselves the bond slaves of each other. They have cultivated
these meaner wants to so great an excess as to judge nothing valuable
or desirable but what relates to their gratification. Hence has arisen a
system of passions which loses sight of the end which they were 745
originally awakened to attain: Fame, power and gold are loved for
their own sakes, are worshipped with a blind and habitual idolatry.
The pageantry of empire, and the fame of irresistible might is
contemplated by its possessor with unmeaning complacency,
without a retrospect to the properties which first made him consider 750
them of value. It is from the cultivation of the most contemptible
properties of human nature, that the discord and torpor and
            by which the moral universe is disordered essen-
tially depend. So long as these are the ties by which human
society is connected, let it not be admired that they are fragile. 755
Before man can be free and equal and truly wise he must cast aside
the chains of habit and superstition, he must strip sensuality of its
pomp and selfishness of its excuses, and contemplate actions and
objects as they really are: He will discover the wisdom of universal
love. He will feel the meanness and the injustice of sacrifising the 760
leisure and the liberty of his fellow men to the indulgence of his
physical appetites and becoming a party to their degradation by the
consummation of his own. He will consider ευγενειας δε και δοξας
προ⟨σ⟩κοσμ⟨ν⟩ματα κακιας ειναι, μονην τε ορθην πολιτειαν
ειναι την εν κοσμω.

Such, with those differences only incidental to the age and the 765
state of society [in which] they were promulgated, appear to have
been the doctrines of Jesus Christ. It is not too much to assert that
they have been the doctrines of every just and compassionate mind

770 that ever speculated on the social nature of man. The dogma of the
equality of mankind has been advocated with various success in
different ages of the world. It was imperfectly understood, but thro'
a kind of instinct in its favour influenced considerably on the
practise of antient Greece or Rome. Attempts to establish usages
775 founded on this dogma have been made in modern Europe, in
several instances, since the revival of literature and the arts.
Rousseau has vindicated this opinion with all the eloquence of
sincere and earnest faith, and is perhaps the philosopher among the
moderns who in the structure of his feelings and understanding
780 resembles most nearly the mysterious sage of Judæa. It is impossible
to read those passionate words in which Jesus Christ upbraids the
pusillanimity and sensuality of mankind without being strongly
reminded of the more connected and systematic enthusiasm of
Rousseau. "No man" says Jesus Christ "can serve two masters

*　　*　　*　　*　　*　　*

785   Take therefore no thought for the morrow, for the morrow shall
take thought for the things of itself. Sufficient unto the day is the evil
thereof."—If we would profit by the wisdom of a sublime and
poetical mind we must beware of the vulgar error of interpreting
literally every expression which ⟨it⟩ employ⟨s⟩. Nothing can well be
790 more remote from truth than the literal and strict construction of
such expressions as Jesus Christ here delivers, or than it were best for
man that he should abandon all his acquirements in physical and
intellectual science, and depend on the spontaneous productions of
Nature for his subsistence. Nothing is more obviously false than that
795 the remedy for the inequality among men consists in their return to
the condition of savages and beasts. Philosophy will never be
understood if we approach the study of its mysteries with so narrow
and illiberal conceptions of its universality. Rousseau certainly did
not mean to persuade the immense population of his country to
800 abandon all the arts of life, destroy their habitations and their
temples and become the inhabitants of the woods. He addressed the
most enlightened of his compatriots, and endeavoured to persuade
them to set the example of a pure and simple life, by placing in the
strongest point of view his conceptions of the calamitous and
805 diseased aspect which, overshadowed as it is with the vices of
sensuality and selfishness, is exhibited by civilized society. Nor, can

it be believed that Jesus Christ endeavoured to prevail on the inhabitants of Jerusalem, neither to till their fields nor to frame a shelter against the sky, nor to provide food for the morrow. He simply exposes with the passionate rhetoric of enthusiastic love 810 towards all human beings the miseries and mischiefs of that system which makes all things subservient to the subsistence of the material frame of man. He warns them that no man can serve two masters, God and mammon: that it is impossible at once to be high minded and just, and wise, and comply with the accustomed forms of human 815 society, seek honour, wealth or empire either from the idolatry of habit, or as the direct instruments of sensual gratification. He instructs them that clothing and food and shelter are not, as they suppose, the true end of human life but only certain means to be valued in proportion to their subserviency to that end. These means 820 it is the right of every human being to possess, and that in the same degree. In this respect the fowls of the air and the lilies of the field are examples for the imitation of mankind. They are clothed and fed by the Universal God. Permit, therefore, the spirit of this benignant principle to visit your intellectual frame, or, in other words, become 825 just and pure. When you understand the degree of attention which the requisitions of your physical nature demand, you will perceive how little labour suffices for their satisfaction. Your heavenly father knoweth that you have need of these things. The universal Harmony or Reason which makes your passive frame of thought its dwelling in 830 proportion to the purity and majesty of its nature, will instruct you if ye are willing to attain that exalted condition, in what manner to possess all the objects necessary for your material subsistence. All men are invocated to become thus pure and happy. All men are called to participation in the community of nature's gifts. Ye can 835 expend thus no labour on mechanisms consecrated to luxury and pride. How abundant will not be your progress in all that truly ennobles and extends human nature! The man who has fewest bodily wants approaches nearest to the divine nature. Satisfy these wants, at the cheapest rate, and expend the remaining energies of your nature 840 in the attainment of virtue and knowledge. The mighty frame of this wonderful and lovely world is the food of your contemplation, and living beings who resemble your own nature and are bound to you by similarity of sensations are destined to the nutriment of your affections: united they are the consummation of the widest hopes 845 that your mind can contain. By rendering yourselves thus worthy, ye will be as free in your imaginations as the swift and many coloured fowls of the air, and as beautiful in your simplicity as the lilies of the field.

850 In proportion as mankind becomes wise, yes, in exact proportion to that wisdom should be the extinction of the unequal system under which they now subsist. Government is in fact the mere badge of their depravity. They are so little aware of the inestimable benefits of mutual love as to indulge without thought and almost without 855 motive in the worst excesses of selfishness and malice. Hence without graduating human society into a scale of empire and subjection, its very existence has become impossible. It is necessary that universal benevolence should supersede the regulations of precedent and prescription, before these regulations can safely be 860 abolished. Meanwhile their very subsistence depends on the [system] of injustice and violence which they have been devised to palliate. They suppose men endowed with the power of deliberating and determining for their equals; whilst these men, as frail and as ignorant as the multitude whom they rule, possess, as a practical 865 consequence of this power, the right, which they of necessity exercise to pervert, together with their own, the physical and moral and intellectual nature of all mankind. It is the object of wisdom to equalize the distinctions on which this power depends; by exhibiting in their proper worthlessness the objects, a contention 870 concerning which renders its existence a necessary evil. The evil in fact is virtually abolished wherever *justice* is practised, and it is abolished in precise proportion to the prevalence of true virtue.— The whole frame of human things is infected by the insidious poison. Hence it is that man is blind in his understanding, corrupt in his 875 moral sense and diseased in his physical functions. The wisest and most sublime of the antient Poets saw this truth, and embodied their conceptions of its value in retrospect to the earliest ages of mankind. They represented equality as the reign of Saturn, and taught that mankind had gradually degenerated from the virtue which enabled 880 them to enjoy or maintain this happy state. Their doctrine was philosophically false. Later and more correct observations have instructed us that uncivilized man is the most pernicious and miserable of beings, and that the violence and injustice which are the genuine indications of real inequality obtain in the society of these 885 beings without mixture and without palliation. Their imaginations of a happier state of human society were referred indeed to the

period, they ministered indeed to thoughts of despondency and sorrow. But they were the children of airy hope, the prophets and the parents of mysterious futurity. Man was once as a wild beast, he has become a moralist, a metaphysician, ⟨a⟩ poet and an astronomer;—Lucretius or Virgil might have referred the comparison to themselves and as a proof of ⟨the⟩ progress of the nature of man challenged a comparison with the cannibals of Scythia. Jesus Christ foresaw what these Poets retrospectively imagined.

The experience of the ages which have intervened between the present period and that in which Jesus Christ taught tends to prove his doctrine and to illustrate theirs. There is more equality, because there is more justice among mankind, and there is more justice because there is more, or more universal, knowledge. To the accomplishment of such mighty hopes were the views of Jesus Christ extended, such did he believe to be the tendency of his doctrines: the abolition of artificial distinctions among mankind so far as the love which it becomes all human beings to bear towards each other, and the knowledge of truth from which that love will never fail to be produced, avail to their destruction.—

A young man came to Jesus Christ struck by the miraculous dignity and simplicity of his character, and attracted by the words of power which he uttered. He demanded to be considered as one of the followers of his creed. [Sell all that] thou hast, replied the philosopher, give it to the poor and follow me. But the young man had large possessions and he ⟨went away sorrowing.⟩

※　※　※　※　※　※

The system of equality was attempted, after Christ's death, to be carried into effect by his followers. "They that believed had all things common: they sold their possessions and goods and parted them to all men as every man had need, and they continued daily with one accord in the temple and breaking bread from house to house did eat their meat with gladness and singleness of heart" *Acts*, Chap. 2, v. 44 &⟨c⟩. The practical application of the doctrines of strict justice to a state of society established in its contempt was such as might have been expected. After the transitory glow of enthusiasm had faded from the minds of men precedent and habit resumed their empire, broke like a universal deluge on one shrinking and solitary island.

Men to whom birth had allotted these possessions looked with
complacency on sumptuous apartments and luxurious food and
those ceremonials of delusive majesty which surround the throne of
power and the court of wealth.—Men from whom these things were
withheld by their condition began again to gaze with stupid envy on
their pernicious splendour, and by desiring the false greatness of
another's state to sacrifise the intrinsic majesty of their own. The
demagogues of the infant republic of the Christian sect attaining
thro' eloquence or artifice to influence among its members, first
violated, under the pretence of watching over its integrity, the
institutions established for the common and equal benefit of all.
These demagogues artfully silenced the voice of the moral sense
among them by engaging them to attend not so much to the
cultivation of a virtuous and happy life in this mortal scene as to the
attainment of a fortunate condition after death; not so much to the
consideration of those means by which the state of man is adorned
or improved as ⟨to⟩ an enquiry into the secrets of the connection
between God and the world, things which they well knew were not
to be explained or even to be conceived.—The system of equality
which they established, necessarily fell to the ground, because it is a
system that must result from, rather than precede the moral
improvement of human kind. It was a circumstance of no moment
that the first adherents of the system of Jesus Christ cast their
property into a common stock. The same degree of real community
of property would have subsisted without this formality, which
served only to extend a temptation of dishonesty to the treasurers of
so considerable a patrimony. Every man, in proportion to his virtue,
considers himself with respect to the great community of mankind
as the steward and guardian of their interests in the property which
he chances to possess. Every man, in proportion to his wisdom, sees
the manner in which it is his duty to employ the resources which the
consent of mankind has entrusted to his discretion. Such is the
annihilation of the unjust inequality of powers and conditions
subs⟨is⟩ting in the world, and so gradually and inevitably is the
progress of equality accommodated to the progress of wisdom and
of virtue among mankind. Meanwhile some benefit has not failed to
flow from the imperfect attempts which have been made to erect a
system of equal rights to property and power upon the basis of
arbitrary institutions. They have undoubtedly in every case from the
very instability of their foundation, failed. Still they constitute a

record of those epochs at which a true sense of justice suggested itself to the understandings of men, so that they consented to forego 965 all the cherished delights of luxury, all the habitual gratifications arising out of the possession or the expectations of power, all the superstitions which the accumulated authority of ages had made dear and venerable to them. They are so many trophies erected in the enemies' land to mark the limits of the victorious progress of truth 970 and justice.

Jesus Christ did not fail to advert to the

ON THE DOCTRINES OF CHRIST

No mistake is more to be deplored than the conception that a system of morals and religion should derive any portion of its authority either from the circumstance of its novelty or its antiquity, that it should be judged excellent, not because it is reasonable or true, but because no person has ever thought of it before, or because it has been thought of from the beginning of time. The vulgar mind delights to ⟨abstract⟩ from the most ⟨u⟩seful maxims or institutions the true reasons of their preferableness, and to accommodate to the loose inductions of their own indisciplinable minds

　　　*　　*　　*　　*　　*　　*

Thus mankind is governed by precedents for actions which were never, or are no longer, useful; deluded by the pretensions of any bold impostor

　　　*　　*　　*　　*　　*　　*

Such has been, most unfortunately, the process of the human mind relatively to the doc⟨trin⟩es of Jesus Christ. Their original promulgation was authorized by an appeal to the antiquity of the institutions of Judæa; and in vindication of a superstition professing to be founded on them, it is asserted, that nothing analogous to their tenor was ever before produced. The doctrines of Jesus Christ have scarcely the smallest resemblance to the Jewish law.—Nor have wisdom and benevolence and pity failed in whatsoever age of the world to generate such persuasions as those which are the basis of the moral system he announced.

Chap⟨ter⟩ 2

The most eminent philosophers of Greece had long been famil-
iarised to the boldest and most sublime speculations ⟨o⟩n God, on
the visible world and on the moral and the intellectual Nature of
Man. The universality and unity of God, the omnipotence of the
mind of man, the equality of human beings and the duty of internal
purity is either asserted by Pythagoras, Plato, Diogenes, Zeno, and
their followers or may be directly inferred from their assertions.
Nothing would be gained by the establishment of the originality of
Jesus Christ's doctrines but the casting a suspicion upon its
practicability. Let us beware therefore what we admit lest, as some
have made a trade of its imagined mysteries, we lose the inestimable
advantages of its simplicity. Let us beware, if we love liberty and
truth, if we loathe tyranny and imposture, if, imperfect ourselves, we
still aspire to the freedom of internal purity, and cherish the elevated
hope that Mankind may not be everlastingly condemned to the
bondage of their own passions and the passions of their fellow
beings, let us beware. An established religion turns to deathlike
apathy, the sublimest ebullitions of most exalted genius, and the
spirit stirring truths of a mind inflamed with the desire of benefiting
mankind. It is the characteristic of a cold and tame spirit to imagine
that such doctrines as Jesus Christ promulgated are destined to
follow the fortunes and share the extinction of a popular religion.
That priests

ON MARRIAGE

Before the commencement of human society, if such a state can be conceived to have existed, it is probable that men like other animals used promiscuous concubinage. Force or persuasion regulated the particular instances of this general practise. No moral affections
5 arose from the indulgence of a physical impulse, nor did the relations of parent and child endure longer than is essential for the preservation of the latter. The circumstance of pleasure being attached to the fulfilment of the sexual functions rendered that which was the object of their exercise a possession analogous in
10 value to those articles of luxury or necessity which maintain or delight the existence of a savage. The superiority of strength inherent in the male rendered him the possessor and the female the possession, in the same manner as beasts are the property of men thro' their preeminence of reason, and men are the property of each
15 other thro' the inequality of opportunity and the success of fraud.— Women therefore, in rude ages and in rude countries have been considered as the property of men, because they are the materials of usefulness or pleasure. They were valuable to them in the same manner as their flocks and herds were valuable, and it was as
20 important to their interests that they should retain undisturbed possession. The same dread of insecurity which gave birth to those laws or opinions which defend the security of property suggested also the institution of marriage: that is a contrivance to prevent others from deriving advantage from that which any individual has
25 succeeded in preoccupying. I am aware that this institution has undergone essential modifications from an infinite multitude of circumstances which it is unnecessary to enumerate: such as I describe was however the original spirit of marriage.

    If any assemblage of men agree to command or prohibit any
30 action, with reference to their society the omission or the commission of this action is to be called criminal.—If it be an action manifestly and most extensively beneficial such is nevertheless the

denomination under which, by the universal practise of language, it is to be ranged. To consider whether any particular action of any human being is really right or wrong we must estimate that action by a standard strictly universal. We must consider the degree of substantial advantage which the greatest number of the worthiest beings are intended to derive from that action. I say thus much to distinguish what is really right and wrong from that which from the equivocal application of the idea of criminality, has falsely been called right and wrong. The ideas are sufficiently distinguishable from the circumstance of one being measured by a standard common to all human beings, and the other by a standard peculiar only to a portion of mankind. A superficial observer considers the laws of his own society universal, in the same manner and with the same justice as all that to which no limits have been discovered is called infinite.

The origin of law therefore was the origin of crime, altho' the ideas of right and wrong must have subsisted from the moment that one human being could sympathise in the pains and pleasure of another.—Every law supposes the criminality of its own infraction. If it be a law which has a tendency to produce in every case the greatest good, this supposition, and even the consideration of what is lawful as what is right, is salutary and may be innocent. If it is partial and unjust the greatest evils would flow from the abolition of this distinction. Such in fact is the unhappy cause whence all the doctrinal perversions of ethical science have arisen.

ON 'GODWIN'S MANDEVILLE'

To the Editor of the *Examiner*.

Sir,—The author of *Mandeville* is one of the most illustrious examples of intellectual power in the present age. He has exhibited that variety and universality of talent which distinguishes him who is destined to inherit lasting renown from the possessors of tem-
5 porary celebrity. If his claims were to be measured solely by the comprehension and accuracy of his researches into ethical and political science, still it would be difficult to name a contemporary competitor. Let us make a deduction of all those parts of his moral system which are liable to any possible controversy, and consider
10 simply those which only to alledge is to establish, and which belong to that most important class of truths, which he that announces to mankind seems less to teach than to recall.

Political Justice is the first moral system, explicitly founded upon the doctrine of the negativeness of rights and the positiveness of
15 duties, an obscure feeling of which has been the basis of all the political liberty and private virtue in the world. But he is also the author of *Caleb Williams*, and if we had no other record of a mind but simply some fragment containing the conception of the character of Falkland, doubtless we should say,—"This is an extraordinary mind,
20 and undoubtedly was capable of the very sublimest enterprises of thought." *St. Leon* and *Fleetwood* are moulded, with somewhat inferior distinctness, in the same character of an union of delicacy and power. The *Essay on Sepulchres* has all the solemnity and depth of passion which belongs to a mind that sympathises, as one man with
25 his friend, in the interests of future ages, and in the concerns of vanished generations of mankind.

It may be said with truth, that Godwin has been treated unjustly by those of his countrymen, upon whose favour temporary distinction depends. If he had devoted his high accomplishments to
30 flatter the selfishness of the rich, or enforce those doctrines on which the powerful depend for power, they would no doubt have

rewarded him with their countenance, and he might have been more fortunate in that sunshine than Mr. Malthus or Dr. Paley. But the difference would still have been as wide as that which must for ever divide notoriety from fame. Godwin has been to the present age in 35 moral philosophy what Wordsworth is in poetry. The personal interest of the latter would probably have suffered from his pursuit of the true principles of taste in poetry, as much as all that is temporary in the fame of Godwin has suffered from his daring to announce the true foundation of morals, if servility and depend- 40 ance and superstition had not been too easily reconcileable with Wordsworth's species of dissent from the opinions of the great and the prevailing. It is singular, that the other nations of Europe should have anticipated in this respect the judgment of posterity, and that the name of Godwin, and that of his late illustrious and admirable 45 wife, should be pronounced, even by those who know but little of English literature, with reverence; and that the writings of Mary Wollstonecraft should have been translated and universally read in France and Germany, long after the bigotry of faction had stifled them in our own country.

Mandeville is Godwin's last production. The interest of this novel 50 is undoubtedly equal, in some respects superior, to that of *Caleb Williams*. Yet there is no character like Falkland, whom the author, with that sublime casuistry which is the parent of toleration and forbearance, persuades us personally to love, whilst his actions must 55 for ever remain the theme of our astonishment and abhorrence. Mandeville challenges our compassion, and no more. His errors arise from an immutable necessity of internal nature, and from much of a constitutional antipathy and suspicion, which soon sprang up into a hatred and contempt and barren misanthropy, which, as it had 60 no root in genius or in virtue, produces no fruit uncongenial with the soil wherein it grew. Those of Falkland arose from a high, though perverted conception of the majesty of human nature, from a powerful sympathy with his species, and from a temper which led him to believe that the very reputation of excellence should walk 65 among mankind, unquestioned and undefiled. So far as it was a defect to link the interest of the tale with any thing inferior to Falkland, so is Mandeville defective. But if the varieties of human character, the depth and the complexity of human motive, those sources of the union of strength and weakness, those useful 70 occasions for pleading in favour of universal kindness and toleration, are just subjects for illustration and developement in a work of fiction, Mandeville yields in interest and importance to none of the productions of the Author.

75 The language is more rich and various, and the expressions more eloquently sweet, without losing that energy and distinctness which characterises *Political Justice* and *Caleb Williams*. The moral speculations have a strength and consistency and boldness which has been less clearly aimed at in his other works of fiction. The
80 pleadings of Henrietta to Mandeville, after his recovery from madness, in favour of virtue and benevolent energy, compose, in every respect, the most perfect and beautiful piece of writing of modern times. It is the genuine doctrine of *Political Justice* presented in one perspicuous and impressive view, and clothed in such
85 enchanting melody of language, as seems, scarcely less than the writings of Plato, to realize those lines of Milton:—

> How charming is divine Philosophy!
> Not harsh and crabbed, as dull fools suppose,
> But musical as is Apollo's lute.

90 Clifford's talk, too, about wealth, has a beautiful and readily to be disentangled intermixture of truth and error. Clifford is a person, who, without those characteristics which usually constitute the sublime, is sublime from the mere excess of loveliness and innocence. Henrietta's first appearance to Mandeville at Mandeville
95 House is an occurrence resplendent with the sunrise of life; it recalls to the memory many a vision,—or perhaps but one,—which the delusive exhalations of unbaffled hope has invested with a rose-like lustre as of morning, yet, unlike morning, a light, which, once extinguished, never can return. Henrietta seems at first to be all that
100 a susceptible heart imagines in the object of its earliest passion. We scarcely can see her, she is so beautiful. There is a mist of dazzling loveliness which encircles her, and shuts out from the sight all that is mortal in her transcendant charms. But the veil is gradually withdrawn, and she "fades into the light of common day." Her
105 actions and even her sentiments do not correspond with the elevation of her speculative opinions, and the fearless purity which should be and is the accompaniment of truth and virtue. But she has a divided affection, and she is faithful there only where infidelity would have been self-sacrifice. Could the spotless Henrietta have
110 subjected her love for Clifford to the vain and insulting accidents of

wealth and reputation, and the babbling of a miserable old woman, and have proceeded unshrinkingly to her nuptial feast from the expostulations of Mandeville's impassioned and pathetic madness? It might be well in the Author to shew the foundations of human hope thus overturned, for his picture would otherwise have been   115 illumined with one gleam of light; it was his skill to enforce the moral, that "all things are vanity;" and that "the house of mourning is better than the house of feasting;" and we are indebted to those who make us feel the instability of our nature, that we may lay the knowledge which is its foundation deep, and make the affections   120 which are its cement strong. But one regrets that Henrietta, who soared far beyond her contemporaries in her opinions, who was so beautiful, that she seemed a spirit among mankind, should act and feel no otherwise than the least exalted of her sex; and still more, that the Author capable of conceiving something so admirable and   125 lovely, should have been withheld, by the tenour of the fiction which he chose, from executing it to its full extent. It almost seems in the original conception of the character of Henrietta, that something was imagined too vast and too uncommon to be realized; and the feeling weighs like disappointment on the mind.   130

But these, considered with reference to the core of the story, are extrinsical. The events of the tale flow on like the stream of fate, regular and irresistible, and growing at once darker and swifter in their progress;—there is no surprise, there is no shock; we are prepared for the worst from the very opening of the scene, though   135 we wonder whence the Author drew the shadows which render the moral darkness every instant more profound, and, at last, so appalling and complete. The interest is awfully deep and rapid. To struggle with it would be gossamere attempting to bear up against the tempest. In this respect it is more powerful than *Caleb Williams*;   140 the interest of *Caleb Williams* being as rapid but not so profound as that of *Mandeville*. It is a wind which tears up the deepest waters of the ocean of mind. The reader's mind is hurried on, as he approaches the end, with breathless and accelerated impulse. The noun *Smorfia* comes at last, and touches some nerve, which jars the inmost soul,   145 and grates as it were along the blood; and we can scarcely believe that the grin, which must accompany Mandeville to his grave, is not stamped upon our own visage.

E. K.

ON THE GAME LAWS.

It is said that the House of Commons tho' not an actual, is a virtual representation of the people.—Undoubtedly such cannot be the case.—They actually represent that which is a distortion and a shadow; ⟨they⟩ virtually represent none but the powerful and the rich.—

If a doubt is ever excited in our minds as to whether that Assembly does or does not provide for the welfare of the community as well as any Assembly more legally constituted, we need only consider the legislative provisions in force in this country for the preservation of Game to set in its clearest point of view, the despotism which is exercised by an oligarchical minority amongst us. We may doubt whether the Parliament repealed the Income Tax because it demanded a tenth of the incomes of its own members; we may doubt whether it ?loads the necessaries which the labouring poor consume with imposts, whilst the most productive as well as the most legitimate object of all taxation is spared—namely, vast accumulations of wealth—because it is the species of possession which its own members enjoy, from ignorance or ill-faith; tho' their conduct would scarcely justify such a question.—But the laws which are in force for the preservation of Game will admit of no excuse, and bring home to this assembly, a charge of corrupting the taste and morals, sacrifizing the lives, imprisoning the persons, and trampling upon the property of the inhabitants of this same country; and that with the barefaced insolence of power, without deigning even to alledge the remotest pretext of general good, in order that they may indulge themselves in a barbarous and bloody sport, from which every enlightened and amiable mind shrinks in abhorrence and disgust.

There is a distinction of ranks—the inequality of Property is established amongst us; so that one man enjoys all the productions of human art and industry without any exertion of his own, whilst another earns the right of seeing his wife and children famish before

his eyes, by providing for the superfluous luxuries of the former.
Society submits to this enormous injustice for the sake of an
overbalance of what it considers an eventual benefit. It supposes that 35
refinement of sentiment, that literature, that philosophy and the
imitative arts are kept alive by the enforcement of this condition of
things. To a certain degree this opinion is correct—Gentlemen, or
persons of wealth and leisure, are usually found to possess more
courage, generosity and gentleness, than men chained to the soil, 40
and occupied in providing for their physical necessities.—But
the system of the game-laws, so far as it ?proceeds, is a direct
contravention of this compact. It leaves to the poor the same
grinding misery as was their lot before, and deprives the community
of the contemplation of so much of that moral grace which it has a 45
right to demand in return for a sacrifise so prodigious, and alas, so
feebly compensated, as that misery.—

Persons of great property nurture animals on their estates for the
sake of destroying them. For this they banish, for this they imprison,
for this they persecute and overbear their feebler neighbours; for this 50
they lay in train the whole horrors of that devilish enginery which
the law places within the grasp of the wealthy to grind the weak to
the dust of the earth. For what?—that they may kill and torture living
beings for their sport. When an ox or a sheep is put to death that their
flesh may serve for human food the pang to the beast is sudden and 55
unforseen—the necessity of the action to the very existence of man is
supposed to be indispensible.—The justifiableness of such an action
flows directly from the right of self preservation. Yet the authors of
our common law forbid butchers to decide as jurymen on the life of a
man because ⟨they are⟩ familiar, however innocently, with the death 60
of beasts.—But how shall those men be considered who go forth not
from necessity, not for the preservation but for the insult and
outrage of the rights of their fellow-men, to the mangling of living
beings. And the case is as widely different between the mode of death
of [an] ox and a sheep and that ⟨of⟩ a pheasant or a hare or a deer, as 65
are the

ON 'FRANKENSTEIN; OR, THE MODERN PROMETHEUS'

The novel of "Frankenstein, or the Modern Prometheus," is undoubtedly, as a mere story, one of the most original and complete productions of the age. We debate with ourselves in wonder as we read it, what could have been the series of thoughts, what could have been the peculiar experiences that awakened them, which conducted in the author's mind, to the astonishing combination of motives and incidents and the startling catastrophe which compose this tale. There are perhaps some points of subordinate importance which prove that it is the Author's first attempt. But in this judgement, which requires a very nice discrimination, we may be mistaken. For it is conducted throughout with a firm and steady hand. The interest gradually accumulates, and advances towards the conclusion with the accelerated rapidity of a rock rolled down a mountain. We are held breathless with suspense and sympathy, and the heaping up of incident on incident, and the working of passion out of passion. We cry "hold, hold, enough"—but there is yet something to come, and like the victim whose history it relates we think we can bear no more, and yet more is to be borne. Pelion is heaped on Ossa, and Ossa on Olympus. We climb Alp after Alp, until the horizon is seen, blank, vacant and limitless, and the head turns giddy, and the ground seems to fail under the feet.

This Novel thus rests its claim on being a source of powerful and profound emotion. The elementary feelings of the human mind are exposed to view, and those who are accustomed to reason deeply on their origin and tendency, will perhaps be the only persons who can sympathise to the full extent in the interest of the actions which are their result. But, founded on nature as they are, there is perhaps no reader who can endure any thing beside a new love-story, who will not feel a responsive string touched in his inmost soul. The sentiments are so affectionate and so innocent, the characters of the subordinate agents in this strange drama are clothed in the light of such a mild and gentle mind.—The pictures of domestic manners are every where of the most simple and attaching character. The pathos is irresistible and deep. Nor are the crimes and malevolence of the single Being, tho' indeed withering and tremendous, the offspring of any unaccountable propensity to evil, but flow inevitably from certain causes fully adequate to their production. They are the children, as it were, of Necessity and Human Nature. In this the direct moral of the book consists; and it is perhaps the most important, and of the most universal application, of any moral that can be enforced by example. Treat a person ill, and he will become wicked. Requite affection with scorn;—let one being be selected, for whatever cause, as the refuse of his kind—divide him, a social being, from society, and you impose upon him the irresistible obligations— malevolence and selfishness. It is thus that, too often in society, those who are best qualified to be its benefactors and its ornaments, are branded by some accident with scorn, and changed, by neglect and solitude of heart, into a scourge and a curse.

The Being in "Frankenstein" is, no doubt, a tremendous creature. It was impossible that he should not have received among men that treatment which led to the consequences of his being a social nature. He was an abortion and an anomaly, and tho' his mind was such as its' first impressions formed it, affectionate and full of moral sensibility, yet the circumstances of his existence were so monstrous and uncommon, that when the consequences of them became developed in action, his original goodness was gradually turned into the fuel of an inextinguishable misanthropy and revenge. The scene between the Being and the blind de Lacey in the cottage is one of the most profound and extraordinary instances of pathos that we ever recollect. It is impossible to read this dialogue—and indeed many other situations of a somewhat similar character—without feeling the heart suspend its pulsations with wonder, and the tears stream down the cheeks! The encounter and argument between Frankenstein and the Being on the sea of ice almost approaches in effect to the expostulations of Caleb Williams with Falkland. It reminds us indeed somewhat of the style and character of that admirable writer to whom the Author has dedicated his work, and whose productions he seems to have studied. There is only one instance however in which we detect the least approach to imitation, and that is, the conduct of the incident of Frankenstein's landing and trial in Ireland.—The general character of the tale indeed resembles

nothing that ever preceded it. After the death of Elisabeth, the story, like a stream which grows at once more rapid and profound as it proceeds, assumes an irresistible solemnity, and the magnificent
75 energy and swiftness as of a tempest.

The church yard scene, in which Frankenstein visits the tombs of his family, his quitting Geneva and his journey thro' Tartary to the shores of the Frozen Ocean, resembles at once the terrible reanimation of a corpse, and the supernatural career of a spirit. The
80 scene in the cabin of Walton's ship, the more than mortal enthusiasm and grandeur of the Being's speech over the dead body of his victim, is an exhibition of intellectual and imaginative power, which we think the reader will acknowledge has seldom been surpassed.

ON '*RHODODAPHNE*
or
THE THESSALIAN SPELL'
a Poem

———

Rhododaphne is a poem of the most remarkable character, and the nature of the subject no less than the spirit in which it is written forbid us to range it under any of the classes of modern literature. It is a Greek and Pagan poem. In sentiment and scenery it is essentially antique. There is a strong *religio loci* throughout which almost compels us to believe that the author wrote from the dictation of a voice heard from some Pythian cavern in the solitudes where Delphi stood. We are transported to the banks of the Peneus, and linger under the crags of Tempe, and see the water lilies floating on the stream. We sit with Plato by Old Ilissus under the sacred Plane tree among the sweet scent of flowering sallows; and above there is the nightingale of Sophocles in the ivy of the pine, who is watching the sunset so that it may dare to sing; it is the radiant evening of a burning day, and the smooth hollow whirlpools of the river are overflowing with the aërial gold of the level sunlight. We stand in the marble temples of the Gods, and see their sculptured forms gazing and almost breathing around. We are led forth from the frequent pomp of sacrifize into the solitude of mountains and forests where Pan, "the life, the intellectual soul of grove and stream," yet lives and yet is worshipped. We visit the solitudes of Thessalian magic, and tremble with new wonder to hear statues speak and move and to see the shaggy changelings minister to their witch queen with the shape of beasts and the reason of men, and move among the animated statues who people her enchanted palaces and gardens. That wonderful overflowing of fancy, the *Syria Dea* of Lucian, and the impassioned and elegant pantomime of Apuleius, have contributed to this portion of the poem. There is here, as in the songs of ancient times, music and dancing and the luxury of voluptuous delight. The

Bacchanalians toss on high their leaf-inwoven hair, and the tumult
and fervour of the chase is depicted; we hear its clamour gathering
among the woods, and she who impels it is so graceful and so fearless
that we are charmed—and it needs no feeble spell to see nothing of
the agony and blood of that royal sport. This it is to be a scholar; this
it is to have read Homer and Sophocles and Plato.

Such is the scenery and the spirit of the tale. The story itself
presents a more modern aspect, being made up of combinations of
human passion which seem to have been developed since the pagan
system has been outworn. The poem opens in a strain of elegant but
less powerful versification than that which follows. It is descriptive
of the annual festival of Love at his temple in Thespia. Anthemion is
among the crowd of votaries; a youth from the banks of Arcadian
Ladon:

> The flower of all Arcadia's youth
> Was he: such form and face in truth
> As thoughts of gentlest maidens seek
> In their day-dreams: soft glossy hair
> Shadowed his forehead, snowy-fair,
> With many a hyacinthine cluster:
> Lips that in silence seemed to speak,
> Were his, and eyes of mild blue lustre:
> And even the paleness of his cheek,
> The passing trace of tender care,
> Still shewed how beautiful it were
> If its own natural bloom were there.   Canto I. p. 11.

He comes to offer his vows at the shrine for the recovery of his
mistress Calliroë, who is suffering under some strange, and as we are
led to infer, magical disease. As he presents his wreath of flowers at
the altar they are suddenly withered up. He looks and there is
standing near him a woman of exquisite beauty who gives him
another wreath, which he places on the altar and it does not wither.
She turns to him and bids him wear a flower which she presents,
saying, with other sweet words

> Some meet for once and part for aye,
> Like thee and me, and scarce a day
> Shall each by each remembered be:
> But take the flower I give to thee,
> And till ⟨it⟩ fades remember me.—   Canto I. p. 22.

As Anthemion passes from the temple among the sports and dances of the festival "with vacant eye"

———— the trains   70
Of youthful dancers round him float,
As the musing bard from his sylvan seat
Looks on the dance of the noontide heat,
Or on the play of the watery flowers, that quiver
In the eddies of a lowland river.   75

C⟨anto⟩ I⟨I⟩ p. 29.

He there meets an old man who tells him that the flower he wears is the profane laurel-rose which grows in Larissa's unholy gardens, that it is impious to wea⟨r⟩ it in the temple of Love, and that he, who has suffered evils which he dares not tell from Thessalian 80 enchantments, knows that the gift of this flower is a spell only to be dissolved by invoking his natal genius and casting the flower into some stream with the caution of not looking upon it after he has thrown it away. Anthemion obeys his direction but so soon as he has

*   *   *   *   *   *

———— round his neck   85
Are closely twined the silken rings
Of Rhododaphne's glittering hair,
And round him her bright arms she flings,
And cinctured thus in loveliest bands
The charmed waves in safety bear   90
The youth and the enchantress fair,
And leave them on the golden sands.

C⟨anto⟩ V. p⟨p⟩. 110⟨-11⟩.

They now find themselves on a lonely moor on which stands a solitary cottage—ruined and waste; this scene is transformed by 95 Thessalian magic to a palace surrounded by magnificent gardens. Anthemion enters the hall of the palace where, surrounded by sculptures of divine workmanship, he sees the earthly image of Uranian Love. Plato says, with profound allegory, that Love is not itself beautiful but seeks the possession of beauty; this idea seems 100 embodied in the deformed dwarf who bids, with a voice as from a trumpet, Anthemion enter. After feast and music the natural result of the situation of the lovers is related by the poet to have place.

The last Canto relates the enjoyments and occupations of the
105 lovers; and we are astonished to discover that any thing can be added
to the gardens of Armida and Alcina, and the Bower of Bliss; the
following description, among many, of a Bacchanalian dance is a
remarkable instance of fertile and elegant imagination:

> Oft, 'mid those palace gardens fair,
> The beauteous nymph (her radiant hair
110 With mingled oak and vine-leaves crowned)
> Would grasp the thyrsus ivy-bound,
> And fold, her festal vest around,
> The Bacchic nebris, leading thus
> The swift and dizzy thiasus:
115 And as she moves, in all her charms,
> With springing feet and flowing arms,
> 'Tis strange in one fair shape to see
> How many forms of grace may be.
> The youths and maids, her beauteous train,
120 Follow fast in sportive ring,
> Some the torch and mystic cane
> Some the vine-bough, brandishing;
> Some, in giddy circlets fleeting,
> The Corybantic timbrel beating:
125 Maids, with silver flasks advancing,
> Pour the wine's red-sparkling tide,
> Which youths, with heads recumbent dancing
> Catch in goblets as they glide:
> All upon the odorous air
130 Lightly toss their leafy hair,
> ⟨Ever singing, as they move,
> —"Io Bacchus! son of Jove!"—
>   Canto VII. pp. 148–50.⟩

Appendices

Newspaper Accounts of Shelley in Ireland and Wales (1812)

S's speech of 28 Feb. 1812 to the Aggregate Meeting of the Catholics of
Ireland at the Fishamble Theatre in Dublin is extant only in the summary
reportage provided by three Dublin newspapers. According to S, the
speech lasted over an hour and was generally well received, though S himself qualifies the positive appraisal of the newspaper reports by noting that
they printed only 'that which did not excite dissaprobation' (to Elizabeth
Hitchener, 14 Mar.). In the same letter he states that 'the hisses with which
they greeted me when I spoke of *religion*, tho' in terms of respect, were
mixed with applause when I avowed my mission'. On the whole, he felt
the speech had been 'misinterpreted' (ibid.). Previously (10 Mar.) he had
stated in a letter to Hitchener that 'more hate me as a freethinker, than
love me as a votary of Freedom'. Thomas Jefferson Hogg (*Life*, i. 337)
wrote that S told him in later years that the ill will shown towards Protestants at a meeting (presumably this one), the 'savage yells' which greeted his
arguments for equal rights and toleration for the Protestants, followed by
threats of personal violence, convinced S that the Irish Catholics really
desired to 'tyrannize over and oppress their Protestant brethren'. Given
S's creative paranoia, perhaps activated by a recollection of the 'hisses' and
even a few more articulate verbal assaults, Hogg's account might not be, as
sometimes supposed, a mere fabrication of his own, though neither the
newspaper reports nor the Catholic attempts to conciliate the Protestants
indicate that 'savage yells' or 'tremendous uproar' greeted anything S said.
He was in fact speaking to a Catholic resolution extending 'the grateful
thanks of this Meeting' to the 'DISTINGUISHED PROTESTANTS who have this
day honoured us with their presence' (*Dublin Weekly Messenger*, 7 Mar.
1812). Whatever S said, the most passionately eloquent speech of the meeting was probably that of the young Thomas (later Sir Thomas) Wyse,
reported at length in the same issue of the *Weekly Messenger*, which concluded with a fervent acknowledgement of the 'PROTESTANT *who stood by
us in our struggle, and bore our broken standard to the front of the battle*, whilst
we prepare the sacrifice to the spirit of UNDISTINGUISHED BROTHERHOOD
AND UNIVERSAL EMANCIPATION'. The reference to the 'Protestant' is probably generic but it is tempting to suppose that the young Wyse was bowing
in the direction of the even younger S, who in his recently published
Address, to the Irish People had himself made use of the prevalent shibboleth
of 'Universal Emancipation'. Wyse's speech in much of its rhetoric and

sentiments sounds quite Shelleyan—or perhaps suggests the extent to which S echoed contemporary reformists. The resolution to which S spoke was seconded by Wyse.

All of those at the meeting risked arrest under the 1793 Convention Act prohibiting assemblies which 'under the pretence of petitioning' sought to alter matters of Church or State. Harriet's fears that a suspension of Habeas Corpus might lead to S's imprisonment (to Hitchener, 14 Mar.) were at least partly justified by the recent arrests of Irishmen in attendance at meetings like that at the Fishamble Theatre on 28 Feb. (see Dowden, *Life*, i. 239–41). The precipitating cause for the gathering, as defined in the meeting of 27 Dec. 1811 which proposed its agenda, was 'the recent violation committed on the rights of the subject, while engaged in the very act of preparing Petitions to both Houses of Parliament' (*Examiner*, 5 Jan. 1812). The meeting was to consider an address (the word 'petition' was avoided) to the Prince Regent pointing out the inequities of the disability laws, which might threaten the Union unless the Prince, in his 'unrestricted wisdom', provided the Irish Catholics some relief from them. The address was to be presented to him after he had succeeded to the full powers of the regency. For further accounts of the Fishamble speech and reaction to it, see MacCarthy, *Early Life*, 226–61, Cameron, *Young Shelley*, 166–8.

All of the accounts printed below agree that S traced the miseries of Ireland to the Act of Union, two of them note that he therefore 'blushes' for his country, and one of them notes that he considered repeal more important than emancipation. Identical phrasing in the two longer accounts suggests verbatim reportage rather than reprinting, since each account contains material not in the other. The first account alone refers to Timothy Shelley's position as an MP, which suggests that S provided his listeners with an autobiographical sketch that went beyond his generic characterization as an English Protestant. The 'fane of liberty converted to the temple of Mammon' was the Houses of Parliament, which had been converted to the Bank of Ireland. The reference to the 'founder of our religion' and his toleration anticipates S's *On Christianity* and may index some of the content of the lost *Biblical Extracts* which S probably began while in Ireland.

These accounts, and reprints of them in other newspapers, were supplemented by general reactions both to S's speech and to his publications; two of these reactions appeared as letters to the editor, another as a biographical sketch and eulogium. The letters may be from the same correspondent (Cameron, *Young Shelley*, 387, suggests that the first might have been written by S himself—to inspire controversy), while the sketch was probably written by John Lawless, for whose then unpublished Irish history S solicited subvention (to Thomas Charles Medwin, 20 Mar. 1812), and with whom the poet thought to establish a newspaper, 'a powerful engine of melioration' (to Elizabeth Hitchener, 14 Mar.). The visionary naïvety generously assigned to S in the sketch anticipates S's paraphrase of Lawless's estimate of his millennial expectations: 'Mr. L. tho he regards my ultimate hopes as visionary, is willing to acquiesce in my *means*. He is a republican' (ibid.). As S's letters to Godwin on the subject of minority secession indicate, the 'means' were all-important, the specific ends, within a general framework of reform, were immaterial (to Godwin, 24 Feb., 8 Mar., 18 Mar.). The sketch's hypothetical characterization of S as 'an imaginary Legislator' might have stuck in his mind to resurface as a positive predication in *A Philosophical View of Reform* and *A Defence of Poetry*, wherein the poet becomes the 'unacknowledged legislator of the world'.

S apparently took no notice of the letters in the newspapers—though the reference in the first to those who prejudice the cause they mean to support anticipates his much later criticism of his own *Queen Mab* as more likely to injure than aid the cause it advocated. He was ambiguous in his response to the sketch: he stated in a letter to Godwin that he was 'rather piqued than gratified at the eulogia of a Journal' (8 Mar.) but none the less asked Hitchener to reprint it in the Sussex papers as a 'preparative' in the minds of the people he clearly meant to convert (10 Mar.). In the same letter he promises a letter 'to the Editor of the panegerizing paper', which 'some will call . . . violent'. The letter does not seem to have been printed. MacCarthy (*Early Life*, 238, 249) records two other possible references to the speech, one by a government spy, the other by Chief Baron Woulfe, who recalled that S was 'a cold, methodical, and ineffective speaker'—an evaluation at odds with the implications of the newspaper accounts and one of the letters below (see also White, *Shelley*, i. 217).

On the fifth ⟨*actually* sixth⟩ resolution being proposed, Mr. Shelley, an English gentleman (very young), the son of a Member of Parliament, rose to address the meeting. He was received with great kindness, and declared that the greatest misery this country endured was the Union Law, the Penal Code, and the state of the representation. He drew a lively picture of the misery of the country, which he attributed to the unfortunate Act of Legislative Union.

(*Freeman's Journal*, 29 Feb.)

Mr. Shelley requested a hearing. He was an Englishman, and when he reflected on *the crimes committed by his nation on Ireland*, he could not but blush for his countrymen, did he not know that arbitrary power never failed to corrupt the heart of man. (Loud applause for several minutes.)

He had come to Ireland for the sole purpose of interesting himself in her misfortunes. He was deeply impressed with a sense of the evils which Ireland endured, and he considered them to be truly ascribed to the fatal effects of the legislative union with Great Britain.

He walked through the streets, and he saw the *fane of liberty converted into a temple of Mammon*. (Loud applause.) He beheld beggary and famine in the country, and he could lay his hand on his heart and say that the cause of such sights was the union with Great Britain. (Hear, hear.) He was resolved to do his utmost to promote a Repeal of the Union. Catholic Emancipation would do a great deal towards the amelioration of the condition of the people, but he was convinced that the Repeal of the Union was of more importance. He considered that the victims whose members were vibrating on gibbets were driven to the commission of the crimes which they expiated by their lives by the effects of the Union.

(*Dublin Evening Post*, 29 Feb.)

Mr. Shelly then addressed the Chair. He hoped he should not be accounted a transgressor on the time of the meeting. He felt inadequate to the task he had undertaken, but he hoped the feelings which urged him forward would plead his pardon. He was an Englishman; when he reflected on the outrages that his countrymen had committed here for the last twenty years he confessed that he blushed for them. He had come to Ireland for the sole purpose of interesting himself in the misfortunes of this country, and impressed with a full conviction of the necessity of Catholic Emancipation, and of the baneful effects which the union with Great Britain had entailed upon Ireland. He had walked through the fields of the country and the streets of the city, and he had in both seen the miserable effects of that fatal step. He had seen that edifice which ought to have been the fane of their liberties converted to a temple of Mammon. Many of the crimes which are daily committed he could not avoid attributing to the effect of that measure, which had thrown numbers of people out of the employment they had in manufacture, and induced them to commit acts of the greatest desperation for the support of their existence.

He could not imagine that the religious opinion of a man should exclude him from the rights of society. The original founder of our religion taught no such doctrine. Equality in this respect was general in the American States, and why not here? Did a change of place change the nature of man? He would beg those in power to recollect the French Revolution: the suddenness, the violence with which it burst forth, and the causes which gave rise to it.

Both the measures of Emancipation and a Repeal of the Union should meet his decided support, but he hoped many years would not pass over his head when he would make himself conspicuous at least by his zeal for them.

(*Saunders's News-Letter*, 29 Feb.)

[To the Editor of *The Dublin Journal*]

Saturday, March 7th, 1812.

SIR,—Our public meetings now-a-days, instead of exhibiting the deliberations of men of acknowledged wisdom and experience, resemble mere debating societies, when unfledged candidates for national distinction rant out a few trite and commonplace observations with as much exultation and self-applause as if they possessed the talents or eloquence of a Saurin or a Burke. This remark is particularly applicable to almost the whole of the meetings which have been assembled within the last twelve months by the Catholics; at which young gentlemen of this description have constantly intruded themselves upon the public notice, and by the unseasonable and injudicious violence of their language, have not a little prejudiced the cause they attempted to support. Curiosity and the expected gratification of hearing a display of oratory by some of the leading members of the Catholic body led me on Friday, for the first time, to the Aggregate Meeting in Fishamble Street. Being rather late I missed the orations of Mr. ⟨Daniel O'⟩Connell and the leading orators, and only heard a dry montonous effusion from Counsellor——, and, to me, a most disgusting harangue from a stripling, with whom I am unacquainted, but who, I am sorry to say, styled himself my countryman—an Englishman. This young gentleman, after stating that he had been only a fortnight in Ireland, expatiated on the miseries which this country endured in consequence of its connexion with his own, and asserted (from the knowledge, I presume, which his peculiar sagacity enabled him to acquire in so short a period) that its cities were depopulated, its fields laid waste, and its inhabitants degraded and enslaved; and all this by its union with England. If it revolted against my principles, Mr. Editor, to hear such language from one of my own countrymen, you will readily conceive that my disgust was infinitely heightened to observe with what transport the invectives of this renegade Englishman against his native country were *hailed* by the assembly he addressed. Joy beamed in every countenance and rapture glistened in every eye at the aggravated detail: the delirium of ecstasy got the better of prudential control; the veil was for a moment withdrawn. I thought I saw the *purpose*, in spite of the *pretence*, written in legible characters in each of their faces, and though emancipation *alone* flowed from the tongue, separation and ascendancy were rooted in the heart.

As for the young gentleman alluded to, I congratulate the Catholics of Ireland on the acquisition of so *patriotic* and *enlightened* an advocate; and England, I dare say, will spare him without regret. I must, however, remark that as the love of his country is one of the strongest principles implanted in the breast of man by his Maker, and as the affections are more ardent in youth than in maturer years, that this young gentleman should at so early an age have overcome the strongest impulses of nature, seems to me a complete refutation of the hitherto supposed infallible maxim that *Nemo fuit repente turpissimus* ⟨No man ever became utterly base all at once⟩.

'AN ENGLISHMAN.'

PIERCE BYSHE SHELLY, ESQ.

The highly interesting appearance of this young Gentleman, at the late Aggregate Meeting of the Catholics of Ireland, has naturally excited a spirit of enquiry as to his objects and views, in coming forward at *such* a Meeting; and the publications which he has circulated, with such uncommon industry, through the Metropolis, has set curiosity on the wing to ascertain who he is, from whence he comes, and what his pretensions are to the confidence he solicits, and the character he assumes—To those who have read the productions we have alluded to, we need bring forward no evidence of the cultivation of his mind—the benignity of his principles—or the peculiar fascination with which he seems able to recommend them.

Of this Gentleman's family we can say but little—but we can set down what we have heard from respectable authority.—That his Father is a Member of the Imperial Parliament, and that this young Gentleman, whom we have seen, is the *immediate* heir of one of the *first* fortunes in England.—Of his principles and his manners we can say more, because, we can collect from conversation, as well as from reading, that he seems devoted to the propagation of those divine and christian feelings which purify the human heart, give shelter to the poor, and consolation to the unfortunate.—That he is the *bold* and *intrepid* advocate of those principles which are calculated to give energy to truth, and to depose from their guilty eminence the bad and vicious passions of a corrupt community;—that a universality of charity is *his* object, and a perfectibility of human society *his* end, which cannot be attained by the *conflicting* dogmas of religious sects, *each* priding itself on the extinction of the *other*, and *all* existing by the mutual misfortunes which flow from polemical warfare,—The principles of this young Gentleman embrace *all* sects, and all persuasions—His doctrines, *political* and *religious*, may be accomodated to *all*; every friend to true Christianity will be his religious friend, and every enemy to the liberties of Ireland will be his *political* enemy—The weapons he wields are those of reason, and the most *social benevolence*—He deprecates violence in the accomplishment of his views, and relies upon the mild and merciful spirit of toleration for the completion of all his designs, and the consummation of all his wishes.—To the religious bigot such a *missionary of truth* is a formidable opponent, by the political monopolist he will be considered the child of Chimera—the creature of Fancy—an imaginary Legislator, who presumes to make laws without reflecting upon *his materials*, and despises these considerations which have baffled the hopes of the most philanthropic, and the efforts of the most wise.—It is true, human nature may be too depraved for such a hand as Mr. Shelly's, to form to anything that is good, or liberal, or beneficent.—Let him but take down *one* of the rotten pillars by which society is *now* propped, and substitute the purity of his own principles, and Mr. Shelly shall have done a great and lasting service to human nature.—To this Gentleman Ireland is much indebted, for selecting *her* as the theatre of his first attempts in this holy work of human regeneration;—the Catholics of Ireland should listen to him with respect, because, they will find that an enlightened Englishman has interposed between the treason of their own countrymen and the almost conquered spirit of their country;—that Mr. Shelly has come to Ireland to demonstrate in his person, that there are hearts in his own country not rendered callous by six hundred years of injustice; and that the genius of freedom, which has communicated comfort and content to the cottage of the Englishman, has found its way to the humble roof of the Irish peasant, and promises, by its presence to dissipate the sorrows of past ages—to obliterate the remembrance of persecution—and close the long and wearisome scene of centuries of human depression.—We extract from Mr. Shelly's last production, which he calls PROPOSALS FOR AN ASSOCIATION ⟨&c; *lines 1-149 of the* Proposals *follow*⟩.

We have but one word more to add—Mr. Shelly commiserating the sufferings of our distinguished countryman, Mr. Finerty, whose exertions in the cause of political freedom he much admired, wrote a very beautiful poem, the profits of the sale of which we understand, from *undoubted*, authority, Mr. Shelly remitted to Mr. Finerty;—we have heard they amounted to nearly an hundred pounds.—This fact speaks a volume in favour of our new Friend.

(*Dublin Weekly Messenger*, 7 March 1812)

To the Editor of *The Dublin Journal*

Saturday, 21 March, 1812.

SIR,—I question the propriety of contributing to the public introduction of those literary nondescripts and political adventurers who figure occasionally on the Catholic stage. Men there are who, preferring distinction procured by infamy to inglorious obscurity, do not hesitate at the violation of any law, civil or sacred, in order to attain it: swimming at the surface by their own putrescence, these merit not our attention; silence and contempt are all we owe to the individual whose sole ambition is to become the idol of a mob, and who like Herostratus, could fire a temple the wonder of the world, merely for the sake of transmitting to posterity a name which might otherwise rot.

Through the medium of your paper, however, the attention of the public has been called to another of the Catholic performers, and a late worthy correspondent has obliged you with some deserved and judicious animadversions upon his debut. In a weekly paper, the appearance of this 'very interesting' personage is announced with as much parade as if Dogberry, Verges, and the Watch graced the scene. 'Oh, a stool and a cushion for the sexton.' 'An two men ride of a horse, one must ride behind.' 'The ewe that will not hear her lamb when it baes, will never answer a calf when he bleats.' His panegyrist has described him with the minuteness of an interested biographer; the prospects and the talents of the 'stranger' and his generosity, his amazing generosity to an incarcerated individual ⟨Mr. Peter Finnerty⟩, whose crime was not loyalty, are made the subjects of commendation; and in illustration of the excellence of this modern Apollonius, who travels but for the improvement of the human race, a specimen of his composition is printed and circulated. I do not find that he, like the Cappadocian, has laid claims to miraculous powers, but he is a poet, and his very prose is so full of poetic fire, so vivid, so redundant with words, which, like those often used by a celebrated female novelist, were probably never intended to represent any specific idea—one is tempted to think he must now and then compose under the influence of the moon. Now, sir, though I really can neither 'make occasions,' nor 'improve those that offer,' for perusing the whole of a production which is scarcely to be paralleled in the ravings of Diderot, the rhapsodies of Rousseau, or the soft sentimental stuff of the Prebend of York, I have read enough of this specimen to confirm me in the old-fashioned but honest and conscientious prejudices which it is evidently the wish of its author to eradicate. He proposes to 'exterminate the eyeless monster Bigotry,' and 'make the teeth of the palsied beldame Superstition chatter.' This, which is doubtless designed as an allegorical allusion to the Romish Church, must, if actually accomplished, be its death; and when 'the teeth of the beldame chatter,' her brats may go beg; he proposes to make us 'kneel at the altar of the common God,' and to 'hang upon that altar the garland of devotion,' figures which Deism borrows from the old Heathen mythology, which are mere poetic smoke, and resemble most the steams of a perfumer's shop, or the smock of an Eastern bride smelling of 'myrrh, aloes, and cassia.'

In a style less elevated and Heliconian this modern annihilator of moral and political evil roundly proposes an association throughout Ireland for the attainment of 'Catholic Emancipation and the repeal of the Union Act.' That the abolition of the aristocracy of the country is a feature in his picture of Utopian amelioration, though, for reasons obvious, but lightly touched, and as yet kept in the shade, is evident from the manner and connexion in which he disapproves 'of other distinctions than those of virtue and talent'—a disapproval specious indeed, worthy the head of him who expects a new Jerusalem on earth, or seeks divine perfection among created beings. But ignorant, shamefully ignorant, must they be of human nature, and of the awful events which have taken place in Europe of late years, who can be gulled by such a pretext now. It is 'Vox et præterea nihil ⟨mere words and nothing besides⟩,' the very cant of republicans. I would suspect the cause which recommends itself by such a pretext, as I would the chastity of a wanton assuming the dress of a nun—the loyalty of a friar or a presbyter armed with a pike, or the honesty of a beggar with a casquet of jewels. 'No distinctions but those of virtue and talent' was the pretext of Monsieur Egalité, of Legendre the butcher, of the bloody Roland, and of that monster in human shape Marat, who proposed, and was applauded by a banditti of ruffians calling themselves a National Convention for professing, the cutting off one hundred and fifty thousand heads as a sovereign specific for the disorders of France.

It is said in a book to whose pages the 'very interesting' Philanthropist seems not be a stranger, that 'burning lips and a wicked heart' are 'like a potsherd covered with silver;' the man I mean has himself quoted the phrase 'a tree is known by its fruits,' and if I mistake not, such expressions warrant the opinion that from certain noisy but worthless characters nothing but what is noxious can be expected. Men whose private life and known habits make them the refuse of the political, and the terror or the stain of the moral world, would make but sorry reformers of public abuse. I need not whisper 'whence I steal the waters' when I say, 'Physician, heal thyself.' It is usual to commend the Catholic body for their loyalty; that they are generally loyal is sometimes acknowledged even by those who, in their official situations, reprobate the proceedings of the Catholic Committee. That there are loyal Catholics, both lay and clerical, is, I believe, probable, but it would puzzle a conjuror to reconcile with loyalty, as it is by loyalists understood, some of the Catholic measures.... Leaving this 'interesting stranger' to amuse the admirers of the Catholic Drama by puffing at 'the meteors' of his own creation, 'which play over the loathsome pool' of his own pantomimic invention, I will ask you, sir, what has the Protestant cause, and what has that consummation of political wisdom the

British constitution, to fear from a party which has to shelter in the shade of such paltry and unmeaning bombast? The Philanthropist talks bigly of 'blossoms to be matured by the summer sun of improved intellect and progressive virtue,'—but if his root be rotten his blossoms will be dust. . . . From such corrections and such apologists, and from the machinations of all pseudo-philanthropists, may the good Lord deliver us!

I have the honour to be, Sir,

yours, &c.,

A Dissenter.

⟨Except for the *Dublin Weekly Messenger* account, all of the above are reprinted from MacCarthy, *Early Life*.⟩

*   *   *   *   *   *

In September 1812 S was in Tremadoc, Wales, where he provided both material and verbal support to the completion of an embankment or dike built to add further land to that which had already been reclaimed from the sea to base the town. The principal entrepreneur behind the project was William Alexander Madocks, after whom the town was named. The following paraphrase of a speech which S made at a meeting of the town corporation at Beaumaris in Wales on 28 Sept. 1812 is excerpted from a report of that meeting in the *North Wales Gazette* for 1 Oct., as printed in J vii. 326–30. For the best and fullest account of both the project and S's involvement in it see White, *Shelley*, i. 253–8, 267–9.

Mr. Shelley requested the indulgence of the meeting; though a stranger he knew that he carried with him a legal passport to their indulgence—the desire of benefiting their country. Mr. J. Williams, who had just sat down, would testify to them the sincerity and disinterestedness of his intentions. That man he was proud to call his friend—he was proud that Mr. Williams permitted him to place himself on an equality with him; inasmuch as one yet a novice in the great drama of life, whose integrity was untried, whose strength was unascertained, must consider himself honoured when admitted on an equal footing with one who had struggled for twelve years with incessant and unparalleled difficulties, in honesty, faithfulness, and fortitude. As to Mr. Madocks, he had never seen him—but if unshaken public spirit and patriotism, if zeal to accomplish a work of national benefit, be a claim, then was *he* the strongest. The

Embankment at Tremadoc is one of the noblest works of human power—it is an exhibition of human nature as it appears in its noblest and most natural shape—benevolence—it saves, it does not destroy. Yes! the unfruitful sea once rolled where human beings now live and earn their honest livelihood. Cast a look round these islands, through the perspective of these times—behold famine driving millions even to madness; and own how excellent, how glorious, is the work which will give no less than three thousand souls the means of competence. How can anyone look upon that work and hesitate to join me, when I here publicly pledge myself to spend the last shillings of my fortune, and devote the last breath of my life, to this great, this glorious Cause.

Sir R. Williams then rose, and returning Mr. Shelley thanks in the name of the meeting, for his honourable and liberal exertions, proposed his health.

Mr. Shelley expressed his thanks for the indulgence and liberality of the meeting, and said that he now took the opportunity of remarking what before he had through inadvertence omitted, that it was no little argument in his favour, that Lord Bulkeley and Sir R. Williams had given the Tremadoc Embankment their generous and praiseworthy support.

APPENDIX II

The Elysian Fields: An Addition?

saw the necessity of oppressing the impious people over whom he reigned.

But let us turn from the unhappy view of your exile to that of your glorious restoration. We receive the gazettes here with tolerable regularity, and I not only read there the lists of the proscribed and the imprisoned but I see their poor puling souls enter these regions. Continue, Princess, in your noble work—allow not the more merciful disposition of your royal uncle to turn you from the work of righteousness. He is weak and through his means you hold the rod of retribution, and what must that mind be who after so many injuries could not return in blood a hundred fold, and is not the life of a king worth ten thousand of his subjects. Let your motto be—better ten innocent should suffer than one guilty escape—

I must also express the satisfaction which your exalted piety gives me. And although I cannot judge of the part your highness took in the murder of the Protestants at Nismes, yet I am fully satisfied that your royal highness has always the prosperity of the holy Catholic Church near your heart. How it was dear to me the souls of three hundred heretics now wandering in Tartarus can testify for me. But your royal highness rules (for it ⟨is⟩ you that have the real power in France) over a nation the established religion of which acknowledges ... And however painful it is to me I must remind your royal highness that it was the mercy of your ancestors that allowed that demoniac wretch Voltaire to propagate his opinions. Catherine de Medicis and Charles IX, her son, shed tears of blood every minute that that incarnate devil breathed the upper air; they exclaimed that the day of St. Bartholomew was in vain—and that the family had miserably degenerated—but no blood was spilt. The Revolution began and I saw with horror the calm and intrepid conduct of the reformists.—No blood is spilt, exclaimed I, and all is lost. Marat and Robespierre revived my hopes—and when the flames of war were every where lighted up in Europe I saw that you would finally conquer and I was comforted.

And you are triumphant. But besides my sympathy in your
35 success I have another subject of happiness. You well know that
during my life my subjects hated me, and you of course know of the
detestable epithet which since then

Collation (MS)

1 saw] *fol. 92ʳ*   regularity,] ~∧ *MS*   5 read] [see] /~/ *MS*   there] [their]~ *MS*
7 Princess] [royal] ~ *MS*   the] ~ [the] *MS*   8 merciful] meciful *MS*   9 righteous-
ness] [⟨   ⟩] rhiteousness *MS* (*see Commentary*)   10 retribution,] ~∧ *MS*   11 fold,]
~∧ *MS*   and] [as]~ *MS*   14 the] [my] /~/ *MS*   which] *fol. 92 v*   15 me.] ~.
[[Your royal father and mother] although the removing of their bones did not give them any
immediate addition of happiness—yet [they feel] [they express ?their] [the ?doom of posts help
the]] *MS*(*see Commentary*)   16 Nismes,] ~∧ *MS*   17 royal] [hi] ~ *MS*
18 me] ~ [fo] [three] *MS*   21 nation] ~ [who now are generally] *MS*   22 acknowledges . . .] ~— *MS* (*see Commentary*)   24 that] *fol. 93ʳ*   25 and] ~ [her] [the] *MS*
IX, her son,] ~∧ ~ ~∧ *MS*   27 air;] ~∧ *MS*   Bartholomew] Batholomew *MS*
28 and] /~/ *MS*   the] th[eir]e *MS*   30 reformists.—] ~∧— *MS*   No] ~[t] *MS*
spilt, exclaimed I,] ~∧ ~ ~∧ *MS*   32 when] [then] ~ *MS*   34 you] ~[r] *MS*
triumphant. But] triumphant but *MS*   35 happiness. You] happiness you *MS*
36 subjects] ~ [my] *MS*   me,] ~∧ *MS*

Commentary

Date: ?Sept. 1815 or ?Nov.–Dec. 1816.
   Copy-text: Bod. MS Shelley adds c. 5, fols. 92ʳ–93ʳ.
   Description: Ink holograph by Mary Shelley consisting of one sheet folded to
form two leaves or four pages, each measuring 22.7 cm. × 18.6 cm. (9″ × 7.3″); laid
paper; WM: posthorn in crowned shield (with ?cipher); the text starts at the top of
fol. 92ʳ and is continuous through the bottom of fol. 93ʳ, where it breaks off 5.6
cm. (2″) from the right edge of the page; fol. 92ᵛ contains sketches of trees written
between and over part of the text; fol. 93ᵛ is blank. The manuscript is contained in
a paper folder, along with *Cry of War to the Greeks*, and is entitled 'Part of
Imaginary letter' on the folder cover.
   Provenance: Sir Percy Shelley and Jane, Lady Shelley; John Shelley-Rolls;
Bodleian.
   Printed: Previously unpublished.

When S wrote in a letter to Hogg (end of Aug. 1815) that he had seen 'in
the papers . . . a most spirited remonstrance of the king of France's
ministers against the enormities of ⟨the Allied occupation⟩ troops' he was
referring most directly to a letter by Joseph Fouché to Louis XVIII which
had appeared in the *Examiner* for 27 Aug. He then told Hogg that he tried
to take a dispassionate view of such political events by considering them
as 'already historical'. Both *The Elysian Fields* and this apparent addition
and counterpoint to it in Mary's hand illustrate an attempt at achieving

that historical perspective through the use of a Lucianic device, a dialogue—or, here, a monologue—of the dead.

The person addressed is almost certainly Marie-Thérèse Charlotte, Duchesse d'Angoulême, who was the only surviving child of Louis XVI and was generally accounted the most intimate source of the ultra-conservatism which characterized Louis XVIII's reign from 1814 to 1816. In Napoleon's oft-quoted *mot*, she was 'the only man in the family'. The speaker is almost certainly Mary Tudor—'Bloody Mary'—who here objects to the epithet history has assigned her (l. 37), though the persona here created for her amply demonstrates its aptness.

If the Shelleys responded immediately to the massacre at Nîmes (which was detailed in the *Examiner* for 3 Sept. 1815), their knowledge of the Princess Charlotte's liberal opinions and presumptive destiny would have been sufficient for them to hit on the idea of a composite set of essays soon after the 'murder of the Protestants' referred to in this fragment. See the headnote to *The Elysian Fields* for an argument in favour of an alternative date of composition (Nov.–Dec. 1816).

Additional reasons in favour of a later date also help explain why so promising a pair of political fantasies were abandoned so soon after they were begun. On 5 Sept. 1816 Louis XVIII dissolved the Ultra-Royalist 'Chambre Introuvable'. While the English Tories were for obvious reasons disgruntled at this sign of political moderation from the French king, the English liberals were likewise affected because such a revisionist policy seriously impeded the inevitable and speedy overthrow of the Bourbons which the reactionary measures of the king had hitherto given them every reason to anticipate. Leigh Hunt was obliged to note (*Examiner*, 8 Sept.) that the dissolution of the Chamber seemed a step in the direction of liberalism, but he then continued through several issues to nourish implicit expectations of a conservative backlash by ascribing Louis's deviant political behaviour to his constitutional weakness, intimidated by public opinion and overlaid with hypocrisy. With the formation of a Chamber largely free of Ultras in late November, the practical effects of Louis's weakness (he was seldom allowed the relatively positive attributes of shrewdness or expediency) became dramatically apparent to friend and foe alike, as they would have seemed to the speaker from Elysium who admonishes the duchess to counteract the 'merciful disposition' of the king by wielding in his place the 'rod of retribution' which had apparently proved too heavy for him. The speaker is explicit about the real power in France—it is not Louis, in all his weakness, but the Ultras as led by the duchess. Liberally—and ironic-ally—speaking then, S and/or Mary in this fragment were not merely creating a foil to Princess Charlotte and her instructor but also recreating from their current wreck liberal hopes for a continued Bourbon reaction in France that would lead to the dynasty's inevitable overthrow. However, as the conspicuous silence about France in the pages of the *Examiner* continued to indicate, there was simply not enough evidence forthcoming that the Ultras were to reassume their control over the government in spite of the reformed Chamber.

From late 1816 the Duchesse d'Angoulême's power was diminished: by 1819 she had become, for Louis, 'l'ennemie'. With many other affairs, political and domestic, to occupy them, the Shelleys could well have felt that the news from France did not provide them with enough substance to carry on with one side of their political fiction. In so far as the two fragments were considered as working together to effect a political point and counterpoint, the lagging inspiration for one of them was bound to affect a continuation of the other.

The engaging idea of so counterpointing the two Princess Charlottes in two Lucianic monologues (which could have become dialogues) has a significant precedent and perhaps a source in a genealogical parallel which the *Examiner* for 12 May 1816 pointed up after noting that Leopold was descended from Alfred and, in marrying Charlotte, thus united divergent streams from the same source: 'In this respect the elegant . . . simile of the Abbé de Lille in speaking of the marriage of the Duke and Duchess of Angoulême ⟨who were cousins⟩, whom he compares to two streams long separated and at last united, would have been remarkably happy in the present instance, as the Royal Bride can trace her descent from the same glorious fountain'. As a general rule of editorial policy Hunt used the Bourbons as a collective whipping boy from under whose cloak he could attack the House of Hanover by intimating a political kinship that might breed even in England both the repression and its bloody aftermath which the Bourbons had once motivated and were now, with the Regent's blessing, on the verge of repeating. Louis's deviation into moderate channels in late 1816 clearly took the wind out of Hunt's editorial sails.

The form and content of this holograph of Mary Shelley's are sufficiently like those of *The Elysian Fields* to warrant its inclusion in this volume under the same title, a title also justified within the text by the speaker's evident condition and locale. While it is possible that at least part of the work was transcribed from a lost original in S's hand, or perhaps taken from his dictation, the textual evidence rather suggests that, in so far as it may relate to *The Elysian Fields*, it represents Mary's contribution to a co-authored topical critique of which the two fragments were intended to be a part. If it was so intended, then an implicitly satirical anti-monarchical dimension, comparable to that recurrent in Leigh Hunt's *Examiner* from the time of the Bourbon Restoration, was meant to be added to the positive reformist instruction the speaker in *The Elysian Fields* seems on the brink of conveying to the Princess Charlotte when that fragment breaks off. The advice given by the speaker to the auditor in this fragment is precisely the opposite of (but for that reason akin to) that offered and intimated to the Princess Charlotte in *The Elysian Fields*: a monarchist from the hereafter preaches an absolute despotism which thereby provides a satirical counterpoint to the ingratiating liberalism which Charles Fox, or someone like him, is attempting to instil in the heiress presumptive to the English throne in S's dramatic monologue.

Similar measurements (the difference of a few centimetres in one measurement may be accounted for by the accidents of different provenances and variable shrinkage) and watermarks (posthorns) suggest that the same paper was used for both Elysianic fragments, but the identity of the ciphers is uncertain. Besides their generic likeness of format and their political motivations, the fragments contain substantive parallels suggesting their kinship—both refer to the 'upper air' and both speakers receive 'intelligence' ('gazettes' here) of contemporary events. The only certain sign of S's hand at work in this fragment is a group of trees sketched at the top of fol. 92ᵛ. They appear over several lines previously deleted by a laterally expanded 'X' supplementing several strikeovers *passim* (see the Collation to l. 15).

1–2. *saw ... reigned*. The reference is probably to Louis XVI, as the antithesis introducing the next paragraph suggests; fol. 92ʳ continues the thought and syntax of a lost preceding leaf.

3. *exile*. The duchess's exile began in effect with the deposition of her father in 1792 and continued until the Bourbon Restoration of 1814, to which the speaker refers.

5–6. *I not only read ... regions*. As an alternative to murdering them, the Ultras in the south of France (and the mob which followed them) proscribed and exiled the Protestants, particularly the wealthy ones. The present tense used by the speaker may support 1815 as the date of composition, but rumours and retrospective accounts of the harsh treatment accorded the Protestants continued well into 1816.

8–9. *merciful ... righteousness*. One member of the Chamber in late Oct. 1815 succinctly anticipated the speaker here by telling the Ultra majority 'ç'est à vous ⟨de⟩ garantir ce Roi qui ne s'appartient pas à lui-même', while another early in 1816 defined the deputies' duty in words close enough to these to suggest a source: 'de défendre le souverain contre sa propre clémence' (quoted in Philip Mansel, *Louis XVIII*, London, 1981, 326). The sole reference to the Angoulêmes in the Shelleys' correspondence appears in a contrast between them and Louis made by an imperialist in Lyons and partially quoted by Mary in a letter to the Hunts: 'When the Angoulême party had the lead dreadful atrocities were committed here mais ce

Monsieur qu'on apelle Louis XVIII is a better man and restrained them'
(22 Mar. 1818). Like Hunt, S disallowed any moral preference to Louis,
whom he considered to be merely the latest in a series of 'tyrants' France
had suffered under since Robespierre.

9. *righteousness*. 'rhiteousness', the manuscript spelling (see the Collation), supports Mary's claim to authorship, since her spelling tended to be
more erratic than S's. She would of course have provided the same spelling
if she had been transcribing from S's dictation. But the reasonably accurate
pointing makes this latter alternative unlikely (see the headnote to *The
Assassins* for inferences about pointing, or the lack of it, in a transcript by
Mary).

11–12. *life of a king ... subjects*. The evident contrast between this
evaluation of a king relative to his subjects and the humane attributes
desired for the 'queen' in *The Elysian Fields* corresponds with a like contrast
between the 'divine right' assumed for sovereigns here and the need to
'deserve' one's crown insisted on there.

15c. *removing... bones*. The bones of Louis XVI and Marie-Antoinette
were removed to Saint-Denis on 21 Jan. 1815. Again, the character of the
deletion (which has been sketched over by drawings of foliage by S)
suggests either original composition or false starts in dictation.

15–16. *I cannot judge ... Nismes*. 'As to the religious discord in the
South, its origin stares one in the face. The Duke and Duchess of
Angoulême, who have been there, are notorious bigots . . . an endeavour is
made to connect religion with politics in the people's minds; the weakest of
these minds run mad with the mixture' (*Examiner*, 17 Sept. 1815). Hunt,
like Napoleon (and, implicitly, the speaker here), discounts the duke as a
'poor creature', whose wife seemed to 'run away with the manly reputation
of the family . . . but how much of her spirit she owes to bigotry also,
remains to be disproved' (ibid.). The speaker in *The Elysian Fields* is once
again opposed to the speaker here, as well as to the endeavour in France,
because he admonishes his pupil not 'to connect religion with politics'
(ll. 18–24).

20. ⟨*is*⟩. The omission of the verb suggests error in transcription.

22. *acknowledges*. The failure to provide an object for the verb is
puzzling. An illegible holograph in S's hand, a change of mind in the
course of his dictation or of Mary's original thought, are plausible alternative solutions. Likely objects—e.g. 'the Pope as spiritual authority'—
might have seemed rhetorically inappropriate, given some of the liberal
(and pro-Catholic) sympathies the author might have hoped to solicit
here.

25–8. *Catherine de Medicis... vain*. Charles IX of France, influenced by
his mother, initiated the massacre of some 50,000 French Protestants
which began in Paris on St Bartholomew's Day (24 Aug.) 1572 and eventu-

ally spread through most of France. The massacre at Nîmes was immediately seen as a second St Bartholomew's day.

31–2. *Marat ... hopes.* Marat presumably instigated the September (1792) Massacre, while Robespierre was considered largely responsible for the Reign of Terror which followed the Revolution. Behind the implicit irony lies S's typical view of the inevitable effects of a violent anarchy.

APPENDIX III

The Examiner *Account of Shelley in Chancery*

The *Examiner* for 2 Feb. 1817, appearing on the very day on which Mary wrote out the *Declaration in Chancery*, expresses concern that Sir Samuel Romilly should be retained by the wrong side in the 'agitation of subjects connected with the remotest doubt of universal ⟨religious⟩ toleration' but further notes that 'we understand that this part of the business in dispute is to be abandoned'. By suggesting a week earlier the implications of the case (which was not identified by name), the *Examiner* might have provided Romilly with sufficient argument to drop its more controversial aspects:

> A cause is now privately pending before the Chancellor, which involves considerations of the greatest importance to all the most tolerant and best affections of humanity, public and private. It is of a novel description, and not only threatens to exhibit a most impolitic distinction between the Prince and the subject, but trenches already upon questions, which the progress of liberality and self-knowledge has been tacitly supposed to have swept aside, and the return of which would be bringing new and frightful obstacles in the way of the general harmony. But it remains to see, by the result, whether we shall be under the painful necessity of recurring to it.
>
> We have given a short Report of the above case from the *Morning Chronicle*; As the Reporters were not admitted, that report must have been hearsay, and is consequently brief and perhaps not perfectly accurate. It relates however to a question, to which the following quotation from the account of the persecution of the Hugonots in France is not inappropriate:—
>
> "Many Arrêts of the Council were issued, blow upon blow, to extirpate the remains of the proscribed religion. (The Protestant religion.) That which threatened to be the most fatal, was the order to tear their children from the pretended Reformés, to put them in the hands of the nearest Catholic relations,—an order against which *Nature cried with so loud a voice*, that it was not executed."— *Voltaire's History of Louis XIV.* Chapter *Du Calvinisme*.

The 'short report' is dated 24 Jan. and titled 'Westbrooke v. Shelley' in the legal section of the newspaper:

Sir S. Romilly moved for an order to prevent the defendant exercising any guardianship over his children, on the ground of his Deistical principles. It appeared the defendant had some time since written a book, called *Queen Mab*, which openly avowed the principles of Deism, and in such a case he could certainly not be considered a proper person for educating youth. The interests of society would obviously be endangered were persons of these principles permitted to instil them into their children. Interference in such a case was peremptorily called for, and he (Sir S.) had no doubt, from his Lordship's well known attention to the duties of parents, and his anxiety respecting every thing where morals were concerned, what his decision in this instance would be.

Sir A. Piggott (actually Basil Montagu), on the other hand, contended, that as his client had written this work merely for his own amusement, without the most distant idea of his children seeing it, it was extremely hard that he should be deprived of the exercise of his parental rights, as the work was a mere effusion of imagination.

His Lordship is to give judgment on a future day.

The *Examiner*'s implied threat to bring the Regent's domestic affairs into a political relation with S's case, along with the further implications of a religious controversy, doubtless aided Lord Eldon in his decision to keep the proceedings private. The *Chronicle*'s reportage could well have been a reminder to the Reformists of the potential ammunition someone accused of blasphemy and adultery could provide to conservative critics of the movement to which S was on the verge of publicly attaching himself with his *Proposal for Putting Reform to the Vote*. Several reformers (including Sir Francis Burdett) had, and were to have, their political platforms undermined by newspaper and pamphlet attacks on their personal lives. S's use of the pen-name 'Hermit' for his political pamphlets of 1817 probably indicates an awareness of the damage he might do to the cause he supported if the 'criminal part of the business' (to Claire Clairmont, 30 Jan. 1817) was carried forward, as he clearly expected it to be. Much of the draft of the *Declaration* is concerned with generalizing his case on political rather than on strictly domestic grounds. Recognizing that he might have sought such an assessment of his case, the prosecution were shrewd to abandon their argument that S's religious opinions were a ground for depriving him of his children. S notes in ll. 25–6 that sexual immorality seems the key charge against him, though he immediately avoids the specifications of that charge by translating it into a political and historical context where it receives no further notice, except perhaps as the 'light and frivolous attachment' (ll. 67–8) which he denies by implication.

The 'institution of marriage', particularly as codified by the marriage law of 1753, had been under attack in and out of Parliament for decades.

The *Examiner's* 1818 index lists several contemporary reactions against the religious sanctions required for a ceremony many thought should be secular in order to be comprehensively civil (see the EC on *On Marriage*).

A rather ambivalent sidelight on the Chancery affair is provided by the fact that the counsel for Westbrook, Sir Samuel Romilly, was just then advocating the repeal of the game laws, the subject of one of S's fragmentary polemics, while S's own counsel, Basil Montagu, was an ardent opponent of capital punishment, another subject of S's reformist writings. Lord Eldon (whose only reformist vote was for the abolition of trial by combat) was appropriately a staunch defender of the status quo on both subjects.

Appendix IV

Leigh Hunt's 'Rider' Notes on Bod. ⟨pr.⟩ Shelley e. 3

Much the most important extrinsic feature of the corrected proof of *A Proposal for Putting Reform to the Vote* (Bod. ⟨pr.⟩ Shelley e. 3) is the set of jottings on the verso of the last page, all or nearly all of which were written by Leigh Hunt as preliminary notes for the 'Rider' eventually added to his original Preface to S's *Masque of Anarchy*.[1] They were written across, upside-down, up or down the margin, some were blocked off in small rectangles, many of the words are illegible, several fade into a vagueness of line that makes it difficult to discriminate the hand even when the words are inferable.

The major jotting, which begins in the centre of the page to the right and runs up the right margin, refers to S and the pamphlet, and, except for the reference to the pamphlet, begins Hunt's Rider: 'His countrymen know how anxious he was for the advancement of the general welfare; but they are yet to be made aware how earnest he was on the subject of this particular means of it, Reform. Anonymous Pamphlet.' Apparently related to the foregoing but written up the right margin is the following, much of which is given as transcribed by Koszul (K 147), though I have not myself been able to discern some of his readings: 'Mr. Shelley could have been one of the most passionate and impatient of men, if his sense and imagination had not been equal to this physical excitability. . . . He resented nothing but the sight of selfishness and he knew how to find excuses for that. He had the most unbounded sympathy with all things of any human being I ever knew.' This passage does not appear in the published Rider. At the top left of the page appear two descriptions of *P*: 'Proof sheet', 'Trees on title-page', with a notation between them, 'Letter from college', which probably refers to S's first letter to Hunt, also referred to in the Rider. To the right of these begins what seems to be a further description of S, though not used in the Rider: 'If he waited for you any where—So ?mixed up [in his] with the habits of his thought were the /noblest hostilities/ & the sweetest images of peace.' Below this, in a rectangular box: 'Aristocrat no.—moral vulgarity only', a discrimination of S's character which the Rider fills in. Below this appear a few illegible words followed by 'Extracts fr. ?H', perhaps referring to the extracts from the proof Hunt included in the Rider, and below that 'Three days',

[1] See Percy Bysshe Shelley, *The Mask of Anarchy*, ed. Donald H. Reiman (Garland Publishing, Inc.: New York, 1985), 123 ff.

preceded by a superscript 'x'. To the right of both the latter jottings is a set of figures of the sort that recur in S's notebooks and which may be in his hand: '6000,000,000/12, 6000,000,000/ 20 ⟨divided into⟩ 5000,000,000 ⟨with a subtrahend of⟩ 250, oo ooo' (all of these figures have then been crossed over). At the bottom of the page appears a relatively long but largely indecipherable metaphysical comment which includes the following words:

> thoughtfully & forcefully were   acting   upon
> an agent & ? moral taste
> according to the   existing state of   feel-
> ings.

This does not appear to be in S's hand, nor is it in the Rider. A jotting which reads 'Pleasure of seeing my name in title-page' might have been made by Charles Ollier—the *Proposal* was among his earliest publications—but Koszul (loc. cit.) suggests it refers to the printer, Reynell, and the hand could well be Hunt's. A rectangular box surrounds a comparison which sounds Shelleyan but was probably Hunt's: 'Theocritus would have been a Greek Ariosto.' In his chapters on Theocritus in *A Jar of Honey from Hybla* (1848) Hunt compares Theocritus to Ariosto three times. S did not particularly admire Ariosto and nowhere makes such a comparison.

The overall provenance of the proof is indicated by the above but its earlier and more interesting progress is better established by the fact that a vertical line in the margins adjacent to pages 11–12 of the proof (ll. 140–52) distinguishes the passage Hunt used in the *Examiner* of 2 Mar. 1817. The inference is that he received the proof from Ollier (possibly from Reynell) immediately after it had been used to correct the 1817 text into its printed form. In the Rider Hunt describes the sheets as 'scrawled over with sketches of trees and foliage, which was a habit of his in the intervals of thinking, whenever he had pen or pencil in hand'.

The Rider also seems to account for the names 'Murray' and 'Buccleuch' written in the margin of page 12 of the proof next to the vertical line which marks the passage in which S promises a hundred pounds to defray expenses for the project he is proposing. As noted, Hunt first used the passage in the *Examiner* of 2 Mar. 1817; when he also quoted most of it in the Rider of 1832 he compared S's generosity to that of the 'manager of a Scottish theatre' who had contributed as much as a much wealthier 'Scottish Duke' towards the construction of a monument to the recently deceased Sir Walter Scott. In reviewing the proof in 1832, Hunt jotted down the names to remind himself to refer in the Rider to William Murray, the manager of the Theatre Royal in Edinburgh from 1830 to 1848, and to Walter Francis Scott, 5th Duke of Buccleuch. The fact that more of the excerpt to the right of the marginal line was used in 1817 than in 1832 would seem to indicate that the line was drawn in 1817.

Sir Percy and Lady Shelley apparently received the proof from Hunt (along with several letters by Shelley and Mary) shortly before his death in 1859; in 1893 it went to the Bodleian along with the rest of Lady Shelley's bequest.

List of Prospective Recipients of A Proposal for Putting Reform to the Vote

The following list contains the names of those to whom S asked Charles Ollier to send additional copies of the pamphlet in a letter of ?Feb. 1817; square brackets enclose Ollier's notations. Most of the names may be found in the *DNB*. Many of the less prominent were in attendance at Reformist meetings in London during February, as noted in the *Examiner*, from the pages of which S could have made up the bulk of his list; see also William H. Davenport, 'Footnote for a Political Letter of Shelley', *N&Q* (8 Apr. 1939), 236–7.

Sir Francis Burdett, M.P. [sent[
Mr. Peters of Cornwall
Mr. Brougham. M.P. [sent]
Lord Grosvenor—[sent]
Lord Holland—[sent]
Lord Grey—[sent]
Mr. Cobbett [sent]
Mr. Waithman [sent]
Mr. Curran
Mr. [Hon.] Douglas Kinnaird [32 Clarges St.—sent]
Mr. [Hon. Thos.] Brand. M.P. [61 Albany—sent]
Lord Cochrane. M.P.
Sir R. Heron. M.P.
The Lord Mayor [sent]
Mr. Montague Burgoyne
Major Cartwright. [sent]
Messrs. Taylor. Sen. & Jun. of Norwich   2 copies
Mr. Place, Charing Cross. [sent]
Mr. Walker (of Westminster)
Lord Essex. [sent]
Mr. [Captn.] Bennet M.P. [Privy Gardens, Whitehall—sent]
The Birmingham Hampden Club   5 copies.
Mr. J. Thomas, St. Albans Monmouthshire
Mr. Philipps, Whitson, d°.—
Mr. Andrew Duncan, Provost of Arbroath, Scotland

The Duke of Sussex.
Mr. Alderman Goodbehere [sent]
Mr. Jones Burdett [sent]
Mr. Hallet of Berkshire 5 copies
The London Hampden Club 10 copies [sent]
To the Editors of
    the Statesman [sent]
    the Morning Chronicle [sent]
    the Independent Whig [sent]
Mr. Montgomery (the Poet) of Sheffield
Mr. R. Owen of Lanark
Mr. Madocks. M.P.
Mr. George Ensor.
Mr. Bruce
Mr. Sturch (of Westminster) [sent]
Mr. Creevy M.P.
[Genl.] Sir R. Ferguson M.P. 1 Clarges St. [sent]

Editorial Commentary

THE NECESSITY OF ATHEISM

Date: Composed and printed 17 Dec. 1810–25 Jan. 1811; privately distributed 13 Feb.–25 Mar. 1811.

Copy-text: *1811* (Princeton University copy).

Locations: BL (Ashley); Bodleian; St John's College, Cambridge; Princeton University; University of Texas.

Description: Undated octavo pamphlet measuring 16.0 cm. × 10.4 cm. (6.3″ × 4.1″) and made up of a single gathering (⟨A⟩⁸), which consists of a half-title (verso blank; ⟨1–2⟩), title-page (verso blank; ⟨3–4⟩), Advertisement (verso blank; ⟨5–6⟩), a drop-head title and centrally numbered text (⟨7⟩–13; ⟨14⟩ blank), followed by a blank leaf conjugate with the half-title leaf; wove paper; WM: ?IM&S | 1809 (lacking in the defective Bodleian copy); no running heads; a printer's slug at the foot of p. 13 reads: 'Phillips, Printers, Worthing.' The copy-text title-page is reproduced on page 1. The bifolium which consists of the half-title and final blank leaf is not in the Bodleian and St John's College copies. The Princeton copy is wrapped in a leaf advertising the *New Family Bible* and printed at the 'Sussex Press, Lewes, July 31, 1810.' The half-title page of the Princeton copy has written below it: 'by Percy Bysshe Shelley | Univsy. Coll.'; the wrapper of the same copy has written on its blank verso: 'The Duplicate Shelley Tract *very valuable* SR | the other copy is ?locked in my sitting | Room'; the title-page of the University of Texas copy has 'Impious' written below 'Atheism'—probably by Timothy Shelley; the imprint of the Bodleian title-page is cut away.

Reprinted: F; J. (*1811* was reproduced by T. J. Wise and Percy Vaughan, Rationalist Press, Watts & Co., London, 1906.)

The printing of *The Necessity of Atheism* in Sussex indicates that S drafted it at Field Place, near Horsham, during his Christmas vacation from Oxford, 17 Dec. 1810–25 Jan. 1811; the latter part of this period is the most probable time of its composition. During the night of 13–14 Jan. S capped a flurry of correspondence with his friend and Oxford classmate Thomas Jefferson Hogg on the metaphysical basis of belief in a deity (and related topics) when he filled five sheets of paper with an argument meant to disprove Christianity by affirming the existence of God (to Hogg, 14 Jan.). A reference to an early form or analogue of *Necessity* may appear in a letter of 17 Jan. to Hogg, in which S wrote that he had made use of his friend's 'systematic cudgel for Xtianity' on his father. In any case, it seems probable that this intensified and shared interest in God and religion inspired S to put together *The Necessity of Atheism* around the middle of January.

The printer's copy must have been in the hands of the Sussex

compositor by 21 Jan., because S advised Hogg in the letter of 17 Jan. that
he intended to be in London on the 22nd, apparently while on his way to
Oxford. In his next letter to Hogg he promised to be in Oxford by the
25th. If the pamphlets did not accompany him there, they must have
arrived on or before 14 Feb., when he sent a copy to his friend Edward
Graham in London with a request that the latter advertise it in eight
'famous papers', a request which was rescinded in a letter of 17 Feb.
because 'the Atheism . . . is not yet published'. It had none the less been
circulated, as the same letter states, among 'All the Bishops', a fact which
apparently led S to cancel a proposed trip to London, lest his absence
from Oxford cause him to be suspected of being its author. In a letter of
15 Mar. Charles Kirkpatrick Sharpe, an older contemporary of S's at
Oxford, wrote that he had not seen a copy of the pamphlet but, evidently
having heard of it, knew it was written by S (*Letters from and to Charles
Kirkpatrick Sharpe, Esq.*, Edinburgh, 1888; see *Related materials* below).
While S had advertised in the *Oxford University and City Herald* of 9 Feb.
that the tract was 'speedily to be published', its distribution was
apparently limited to those copies which S sent to clerics and college
heads and to those which he placed in the shop of the Oxford booksellers
Munday and Slatter, though an unpublished letter (see below) at the
Bodleian indicates that some copies had made their way to the London
booksellers as well. According to the traditional account, the copies in
Munday and Slatter's shop remained on sale, at sixpence each, for twenty
minutes before being discovered by a local clergyman, who had them
removed and burnt. Munday and Slatter further ensured that no other
copies would remain to incriminate them by advising the printer Phillips
to destroy any he had, together with the manuscript and type, and so
avoid the risk of prosecution. In what seems to be the first public reference to *Necessity*, a writer in the *Political Register* of 1813 did ask why its
printer had not been prosecuted: see Louise Boas, '"Erasmus Perkins"
and Shelley', *MLN* (June 1955), 412. A batch of correspondence once
belonging to John Hogg, Thomas Jefferson's father, and recently (Nov.
1990) acquired by the Bodleian Library contains a letter of 8 Apr. 1811 to
Hogg senior from Robert Clarke, a family friend, who provides the
additional but second-hand information that in fact all of the Oxford
copies had been bought up by S himself and that the Bishop of London
had himself stopped their sale in his jurisdiction (MS Don. c. 180, fol. 32).

However that may be, the fact that, along with the *Declaration of
Rights*, it was adversely reviewed by the *Brighton Magazine* in May 1822
suggests that several copies besides those now extant were both disseminated and available throughout the poet's lifetime. The earliest certain
account of anyone's actually having read a copy appears in a letter by the
Reverend George S. Faber, a neighbour of the Hogg family, who about
7 Mar. 1811 had received the pamphlet from an elderly cleric named

Charles Meyton, who wrote that he had been tempted to renounce his living by the pamphlet's arguments and wondered whether Faber could answer them. Faber did that, but to no avail, since Meyton was in fact really S, as Faber, to his later distress and irritation, discovered (to John Hogg, 7 Apr. 1811; MS Don. c. 180, fol. 27). In a 23 Apr. 1811 letter (MS Don. c. 180, fols. 41-5) sent to T. J. Hogg through his father, Faber provides the first critical reaction to *Necessity* when he asserts that the 'sum and substance of the whole pamphlet is an attempt to decide *a matter of fact* by a *shew of metaphysical reasoning*.' Faber argues from the historical fact of Christ and the religion his followers founded to conclude that 'If Christianity be true, and if its founders had the power of working miracles, then there must be a God.' Whether or not S. (or for that matter Hogg) ever saw this letter, which John Hogg at least put off sending to his son (John Hogg to G. S. Faber, 6 May 1811; MS Don. c. 180, fol. 47ʳ), S's letters of this period (and his later writings on the general subject from *A Refutation of Deism* through *An Answer to Leslie's 'A Short and Easy Method with the Deists'*) indicate that Faber's trite and derivative arguments would have elicited at best another verbal brickbat from one or both of the indicated recipients, as perhaps they did.

The best evidence confirms that the pamphlet was in some way the joint composition of S and Hogg, S being responsible for its final form, its printing, and its distribution. The pronoun 'we' is recurrent in references to it in letters, most relevantly in S's of 29 Mar. to his father, in which he provides his perhaps not altogether 'candid' account of the origin of the pamphlet, its purpose, and its consequences:

> The case was this—You well know that a train of reasoning, & not any great profligacy has induced me to disbelieve the scriptures—this train myself & my friend pursued. We found to our surprise that ... the proofs of an existing Deity were as far as we had observed, defective. We therefore embodied our doubts on the subject, & arranged them methodically in the form of 'The Necessity of Atheism', thinking thereby to obtain a satisfactory, or unsatisfactory answer from men who had made Divinity the study of their lives.—How then were we treated? not as our fair, open, candid conduct might demand, no argument was publickly brought forward to disprove our reasoning, & it at once demonstrated the weakness of their cause, & their inveteracy on discovering it, when they publickly expelled myself & my friend.—

The aforementioned correspondence recently acquired by the Bodleian Library casts some new but not unambiguous light on Hogg's share in the composition of *Necessity*. Several of the letters, written to Hogg senior, characterize S as being the only begetter of the pamphlet. However, T. J. Hogg, writing to an unnamed correspondent in a letter of 11 Jan. 1811 (which might have been the 'systematic cudgel' referred to in S's letter of

17 Jan.), advances arguments much like those in the *Necessity* and adduces evidence of Biblical discrepancies and immorality much like that appearing in S's *Refutation of Deism*. While John Hogg's correspondents assured him that his son had been made the 'dupe' of an insane and depraved young man, Thomas Jefferson himself, in one of the latest letters in the batch, provides his father with a series of unpointed reasons for his unalterable friendship with S that could confirm as well his joint authorship of *Necessity*: '. . . we are of the same age the same disposition the same pursuits the same sentiments the same principles and we have read the same books we read the same books we have had similar educations we have lived in the strictest intimacy for some time we have been similarly unfortunate we are brothers in every respect except in the least important point being born of the same parents . . .' (13 Nov. 1811). Hogg ends this list of quasi-Lockian arguments, which tangentially support S's early description of him as the 'brother' of his soul (letter to E. Hitchener, 16 Oct. 1811), with a reservation that might have confirmed the inferences of those who felt he had been taken in by S, though later readers may well find it a salutary qualification of the patronizing Hogg of the *Life*: '. . . we are in short in every thing precisely similar excepting only that Shelley is much wiser and much better than myself wch disparity is an additional inducement to me not to destroy the connection indeed how can I destroy a connection with a person who will chearfully travel any distance live anywhere submit to any inconvenience that I may enjoy the pleasure of his society . . .'. In an earlier (25 Mar. 1811) letter advising his father of his expulsion, Hogg states that he felt it his duty to inform the college that he 'was as much the author ⟨of *Necessity*⟩ as the person accused'. It may finally seem that if the question of authorship cannot be altogether resolved, it can be rendered more or less academic by observing that whatever share Hogg had in the original pamphlet, its later recension as the substance of S's *Queen Mab* Note to 'There is no God,' established S's willingness to accept, and even require, complete responsibility for the piece.

Historically, the pamphlet has acquired a generic significance as one of the first overtly labelled arguments on behalf of atheism to be printed in England. However, the many writings attacking atheism from the seventeenth century onwards indicate that inquiring minds under less flagrantly honest titles ('Deism' was the most popular euphemism) had anticipated the subject and methodology of *Necessity*. S's later fame has given the piece a kind of specious authority best indicated by its numerous reprintings by advocates of agnosticism, secular humanism, and free speech, as well as of atheism.

Biographically, its significance lies in its consquences for S, whose Oxford career was cut short with his expulsion from the University on 25 Mar. for refusing to answer questions concerning his part in its composition and distribution. Along with the related and subsequent alienation from his father, the arbitrary handling of his case by the Oxford authorities confirmed him as a rebel against repressive authority both temporal and spiritual. It is clear that S was as much concerned in the culpable 'syllabus' (as S's cousin, Thomas Medwin, later and perhaps rightly defined it in his *Life*, 83) with testing the limits of free speech as he was in advocating the theoretical necessity of atheism. The general cast of his life as pariah-poet received its first lasting impression when Oxford predictably failed the test.

By 'Necessity' S probably meant philosophical inevitability as logically demonstrated in the pamphlet's argument. 'Atheism' was ostensibly used (though was not understood) in an allied philosophical/etymological sense. While S later allowed that in the popular sense of the word 'God' he regarded himself as an atheist, he never considered himself as he considered his grandfather, Sir Bysshe Shelley, 'a complete Atheist ⟨who⟩ builds all his hopes on annihilation' (to E. Hitchener, 26 Jan. 1812); neither his emotional predilections nor his maturing sceptical idealism would have inclined towards or posited nihilism as a necessary attribute of atheism. In a notebook jotting of 1819[1] he distinguished *atheos* from 'atheist' by supposing the Greek word to have been pejoratively used to reproach the impious, while the latter word was a relatively neutral term defining a logically stipulated philosophical position, a definition which is perhaps at least nominally anticipated here. In so far as S contemned orthodox Christianity he was willing and honest enough to set himself down as an *atheos* (which he did more than once), but in so far as he rationally disbelieved in a creative deity he was appropriately an atheist, as (so he implied in the 1819 jotting) were a host of classical philosophers from the pre-Socratics through the late Academics. William Nicholson's 1809 *Encyclopedia* (which S refers to in his *Queen Mab* Notes) in its entry s.v. 'Atheist' provides the following traditional applications of the term: (1) materialism; (2) denial of God; (3) acceptance of God but not of his concern with human beings; (4) a belief in gods and providence accompanied by a belief in forgiveness of sins 'for the smallest supplication' (e.g., one infers, Roman Catholicism). With some qualification, the second would best define S's use of the term. Hogg provides a supplementary qualification when he notes that at Eton, where S had been given the title of atheist, 'the word Atheist was used . . . not in a modern, but in an ancient and classical sense, meaning an Antitheist, rather than an Atheist; for an opposer and contemner of the gods, not one who denies their existence' (Hogg, *Life*, i. 92), an understanding of the term which tends to blur S's distinction of 1819 noted above.

The God S necessarily doubts or denies may be seen as the one defined

---

[1] To be printed in this edition as *A Definition of Atheism*.

by a contemporary follower of William Paley: 'an intelligent nature, to whose wisdom and power we ascribe the creation of the world, and all things in it' (*Further Evidences of the Existence of the Deity . . . Intended as an Humble Supplement to Archdeacon Paley's Natural Theology*, George Clark: London, printed for the author, 1806, p. i). While scholars and apologists have sporadically felt it necessary to point out that S is really putting a case for agnosticism, 'atheism' is in fact the more exact description of his specific concern if some such sense of the word and the strictly empirical limitations of S's argument from necessity are given their contextual due. In so far as S in 1811 might have been in agreement with William Drummond's position in *Academical Questions* (a work he singles out for critical attention in the *Queen Mab* Notes), that because God cannot be compelled, necessity, philosophically defined, was consistent only with atheism (347), the title may be construed as a religious truism. The fact that John Leland, an eighteenth-century epitomist of the earlier English Deists, wrote on *The Advantage and Necessity of the Christian Revelation* and an anonymous near contemporary of S's wrote a *Necessity of Divine Revelation* (1778) may suggest that S's title was chosen for its ironic potential as well as for its aptness to his logical argument. Conversely, the generalized scope of kindred titles (ranging from *The Necessity of Monarchy*, 1681, to the *Necessity for Universal Toleration*, 1808) suggests that whatever imperative associations the word 'Necessity' in such usages might originally have elicited in prospective readers had been neutralized into rhetorical commonplaces long before S (and his later reputation) revitalized it.

S's letters indicate that, in its practical applications, his atheism was contingent on his argumentative purpose at a given time. Early and late, the recurrent subject of his meaningful attacks on religion (or 'superstition') was orthodox Christianity, its versions of God, and its repressive bigotry, a subject initially and most feelingly taken up when he blamed Christianity for frustrating his love affair with his cousin Harriet Grove (to Hogg, 20, 23 Dec. 1810; 3 Jan. 1811). The terms and methodology of *Necessity* derive largely from Locke and Hume, its tenor is agnostic and sceptical, and the restrictively logical presentation of the 'syllabus' as a whole is implicitly at odds with S's early willingness (indicated *passim* in his letters) to feel or imagine a species of overseeing agency, benevolent if impersonal. The significant difference between this pamphlet and its revised form in the *Queen Mab* Note on 'There is no God' is S's qualifying addition in the Note that he did not mean either his negation or its supportive argument to interfere with a belief in a 'pervading spirit co-eternal with the universe'. On Bod. MS adds. e. 4, fol. 84ᵛ S pencilled in a favourite Lockian aphorism, 'Mind cannot create, it can only perceive', and followed it with an apparent reminder to himself that the sentence could ground 'an Atheist Essay'; he thereby suggested, as he later did in the fragment *On Life*, that the species of theism he denied was the one that essentially identified the creative mind of God with the merely perceptive mind of man. The prolusory character of the tract, Hogg's probable share in it, and S's later writings on the same general subject, along with relevant letters to Hogg and Elizabeth Hitchener, should be considered when estimating the ideological commitment of his first published venture into the fields of religious and, tangentially, political controversy.

The spelling and punctuation used by the printer reflect S's practice—'posession' and 'Thro'' are so spelt and dashes are characteristically abundant—while at least one printing and proofreading lapse (the omission of a word before 'obscurity', l. 62) suggests that the copy was indifferently set up and corrected, as do the battered letters occasionally found. The *Queen Mab* Note seems generally to have profited from a keener eye—'same' is supplied before 'obscurity'—though the major purpose of its revisions is to increase the Humean content and to qualify (as noted above) the character of the deity denied. Further groomings of particular sentences and passages appear in the *Declaration of Rights*, *A Letter to Lord Ellenborough*, and *A Refutation of Deism*. Both *Zastrozzi* and *St. Irvyne* contain earlier dramatizations of the atheistic reasonings adduced or implied in *Necessity*.

Related primary and secondary materials: LETTERS, to Hogg, 20 Dec. 1810, 3,[1] 6, 11, 12 Jan., 26, 28 Apr., 8, 12, 14, 17 May 1811, to Timothy Shelley, 6 Feb., ?13 Apr. 1811, to Janetta Philipps, 16, ?May 1811, to Elizabeth Hitchener, 11 June 1811 (and subsequent letters *passim*), to William Godwin, 10 Jan., 24 Feb. 1812; *Zastrozzi*; *St. Irvyne*; *A Letter to Lord Ellenborough*; *A Refutation of Deism*; *On Christianity*; SC ii. 608-9, 685-7, 721-4, 730-50 *passim*; T. J. Hogg to Mrs Timothy Shelley, SC ii. 820-9; Paine, *The Age of Reason, Writings*, iv. 23-5, 49, 79, 181, 183-4; George Ensor, *On National Government*, i. 418-28, ii. 390-2; *Letters from and to Charles Kirkpatrick Sharpe*, i. 443, 483; Bod. MS Shelley adds. c. 7, fols. 6-7 (copy of a letter of 2 Apr. 1811 on Hogg's expulsion; cf. Bod. MS Don. c. 180, fols. 19-20); [anon.], *Reply to the Anti-Matrimonial Hypothesis and Supposed Atheism of Percy Byssche ⟨sic⟩ Shelley, as Laid down in Queen Mab* (London, 1821); 'Percy Bysshe Shelley', *Stockdale's Budget*, 26 (3 Jan. 1827); Robert Montgomery, *Oxford: A Poem*, 3rd edn. (Oxford, 1833), 173-4 (the bookseller Henry Slatter's account); Charles Bradlaugh, 'Percy Bysshe Shelley', *Half-hours with the Free-thinkers*, 1/4 (15 Nov. 1856), 25-32; Hogg, *Life*, i. 163-72; Washington Frothingham, *Atheos: Or, The Tragedies of Unbelief* (New York, 1862), chapter on S; J. C. Jeaffreson, *The Real Shelley* (London, 1885), i. 5, 272-91; Dowden, *Life*, i. 114-25; Forman, *The Shelley Library*, 17-19; Percy Vaughan, *Early Shelley Pamphlets* (London, 1905), 16-21; A. Lang, 'Shelley's Oxford Martyrdom', *The Fortnightly Review*, NS 81 (Feb. 1907), 230-40; Medwin, *Life*, 82-8; Ingpen, *Shelley in England*, 186-205; Solomon Gingerich,

---

[1] See *SC* ii. 685 n. for the dating of this letter. The transcriptions of S's letters in *SC* are generally preferable to the versions found in Shelley, *Letters*.

'Shelley's Doctrine of Necessity versus Christianity', *PMLA* 33 (Sept. 1918), 444–73; J v. 299–300; Grabo, *Magic Plant*, 22–33, 38–45; F. L. Jones, 'Hogg and The Necessity of Atheism', *PMLA* 52 (June 1937), 423–6; Barnard, *Shelley's Religion*, 22–32; Edmund Blunden, 'Shelley is Expelled', and Gavin de Beer, 'The Atheist: An Incident at Chamonix', in *On Shelley*; White, *Shelley*, i. 110–18, 597–600; F. E. Ratchford, 'Shelley Meets the Texas Legislature', *Southwest Review*, 30 (Winter 1945), 161–6; Hughes, *Nascent Mind*, 63–73; Baker, *Major Poetry*, 29–38; Cameron, *Young Shelley*, 38–9, 92–5, 101–7, 358–63; Pulos, *Deep Truth*, 90–1; Clark, *Shelley's Prose*, 5–9; Bice Chiappelli, *Il pensiero religioso di Shelley con particolare riferimento alla 'Necessity of Atheism'* (Rome, 1956), 28–48; Gavin de Beer, 'An "Atheist" in the Alps', *K-SMB* 9 (1958), 1–15; George Mathewson, 'Shelley's Atheism: An Early Victorian Explanation', *K-SJ* 15 (1966), 7–9; Harold Orel, 'Another Look at *The Necessity of Atheism*', *Mosaic*, 2 (1969), 27–37; Timothy Webb, 'The Avalanche of Ages: Shelley's Defence of Atheism and *Prometheus Unbound*', *K-SMB* 35 (1984), 1–39; Hogle, *Shelley's Process*, 6–7, 28–9. Presently unpublished letters in the Bod. MS Don. c. 180 correspondence with special relevance to *Necessity* appears on fols. 7–12 (T. J. Hogg to an unnamed correspondent, 11 Jan. 1811), 13–16 (S to Felicia Browne ⟨Hemans⟩, 13 or 19 Mar. 1811), 17–18 (T. J. Hogg to John Hogg, 25 Mar. 1811), 25 (G. S. Faber to John Hogg, 30 Mar. or 6 Apr. 1811), 27–8 (G. S. Faber to John Hogg, 7 Apr. 1811), 38–9 (T. J. Hogg to G. S. Faber, 18 Apr. 1811), 41–5 (G. S. Faber to T. J. Hogg, 23 Apr. 1811), 63–4 (T. J. Hogg to John Hogg, 13 Nov. 1811). See also B. C. Barker-Benfield, 'Hogg–Shelley papers of 1810–12', *The Bodleian Library Record*, 14/1 (Oct. 1991), 14–29. (As indicated above, John Locke's *Essay Concerning Human Understanding* and David Hume's *Essays*, particularly 'Of Miracles', were the major philosophical sources of *Necessity*.)

EPIGRAPH. *Quod clarâ et perspicuâ demonstratione careat pro vero habere mens omnino nequit humana.* 'The human mind can by no means consider true that which lacks clear and manifest demonstration.' I have not located the quotation either in *De augmentis scientiarum* or in any other of Bacon's Latin works.

ADVERTISEMENT. C. J. Ridley, resident in the University in 1811, later wrote that Hogg was generally supposed responsible for the Advertisement (Dowden, *Life*, i. 123). S asked Edward Graham to 'advertise the Advertisement' in the third page of the *Globe* (?14 Feb. 1811), which may mean print it, a request S was more likely to make for his own rather than for Hogg's writing. For a compilation and assessment of the evidence concerning authorship of the pamphlet as a whole and in its parts see Cameron, *Young Shelley*, 95, 358–60, which, however, should now be considered along with relevant letters in the recently discovered correspondence (Bod. MS Don. c. 180) noted above.

1. *A close.* The *Queen Mab* Note on 'There is no God' has the following paragraph before these words: 'This negation ⟨i.e. 'There is no God'⟩ must be understood solely to affect a creative Deity. The hypothesis of a pervading Spirit coeternal with the universe, remains unshaken.' This position corresponds with that of Baron d'Holbach, from whose *Système*

de la Nature S takes the extensive passage making up the bulk of this Note.

17. *that belief . . . volition.* Among those who 'falsely' asserted that belief could be willed was Soame Jenyns, in his *View of the Internal Evidence of the Christian Religion* (London, 1776), who specifically refuted a doctrine of involuntary faith 'necessarily dependent on the degree of evidence, which is offered to our senses' (82–3). Jenyns's anonymously published volume, admired by William Paley and footnoted by S in *A Refutation of Deism*, went into at least ten editions before 1800 and could well have been one of the texts drawn on by G. S. Faber for his refutation of *Necessity* noted above. As S indicates, those who made belief a voluntary act therefore made it a moral decision.

88. *Q. E. D.* 'Quod Erat Demonstrandum' ('which was to be demonstrated'). The formulaic tag, dropped in the *Queen Mab* Note, is at least partly ironic. As the recurrent conclusion to Isaac Newton's propositions in the *Principia Mathematica*, it had become the seal of unquestioned scientific truth.

AN ADDRESS, TO THE IRISH PEOPLE

Date: Dec. 1811–Feb. 1812.

Copy-text: *1812* (Huntington Library copy; shelfmark RB 22404) corrected from the Pf. copy containing 'Holograph Ms alterations and corrections (PBS 268)'.

Locations: Include BL (2, one in Ashley); Bodleian; Pf. (2); Yale; Harvard; Berg Collection (NYPL); Princeton; Pierpont Morgan; University of Texas (2); Huntington.

Description: Octavo pamphlet measuring 22 cm. × 13.8 cm. (8.75″ × 5.5″, untrimmed) made up of an unsigned singleton and three gatherings (⟨A⟩¹ B–D⁴ (− D4, probably the ⟨A⟩¹ title-leaf)) and consisting of a title-page (verso blank; ⟨i–ii⟩), a drop-head title followed by a centrally numbered text (⟨1⟩–20), and Postscript (⟨21⟩–2); machine-wove paper; no WM, running heads, or imprint; 'FINIS.' appears below the text on p. 22. The Huntington copy has the original stitching through three stab-holes; the Bodleian copy has what seems an autograph 'P. B. Shelley' on its title-page; the BL copy has a facsimile Postscript. The copy-text title-page is reproduced on p. 7.

Reprinted: MacCarthy, *Early Life*; F; J. (T. J. Wise edited an 1890 facsimile edition for the Shelley Society, Reeves and Turner, London.)

S first refers to *An Address, to the Irish People* in a letter of 16 Jan. 1812 to Elizabeth Hitchener which contains an early version of ll. 161–77 ('. . . think . . . ambition'). On the same date he wrote in a letter to William Godwin that 'We go ⟨to Ireland⟩ principally to forward as much as we can the Catholic Emancipation', a purpose he heavily qualified in a letter of 26 Jan. to Hitchener when he stated that the *Address* 'is *secretly* intended also as a preliminary to other pamphlets to shake Catholicism at its basis, and to induce Quakerish and Socinian principle[s] of politics . . .'. Several passages in the second half of the *Address* are clearly drawn from the speeches of John Philpot Curran, an Irish liberal whom Godwin had recalled to S's attention in a letter received on 'the eve of our departure for Dublin' (to Godwin, ?26 Jan.). In the same letter he assures Godwin that nothing in the address he is then preparing can 'excite rebellion' because its sentiments will be those of 'universal philanthropy'.

The bulk of the *Address* was certainly drafted Dec. 1811-Jan. 1812 in Keswick, where S had been disagreeing with Robert Southey on the Irish question in general and Catholic Emancipation in particular. S left England on 3 Feb., arrived in Dublin on 12 Feb., revised and perhaps completed the *Address* there, and by 18 Feb. had apparently received 'the first sheet of my first address' from the printer (to Hitchener, ?18 Feb.). S himself dates the conclusion of his pamphlet proper 'Feb. 22'; the Postscript following contains a reference to a newspaper of 18 Feb. The completed 'little pamphlet' was enclosed in a letter of 24 Feb. to Godwin. On 25 Feb. (as on 29 Feb. and 3 Mar.) it was advertised in the *Dublin Evening Post*. Four hundred copies (of 1,500) had been distributed, mainly without charge, to public houses and passers-by by 27 Feb., as S then wrote to Hitchener in support of his claim to be congratulated on the 'rapid success' he was convinced he had achieved. Less than three weeks later he wrote to Godwin: 'I have withdrawn from circulation the publications wherein I erred & am preparing to quit Dublin' (18 Mar.). The Shelleys left Dublin on 4 Apr.

The decline and fall of S's hopes for initiating world reform in Ireland were more rapid than their rise had been but not by very much. He had originally intended to visit Ireland in the summer of 1812 (to Hitchener, ?10 Dec. 1811). Events both public and private probably led him to bring the date forward by several months. Foremost among the public events was the imminent accession of the Prince Regent to the full powers of the regency in February, an elevation which was now generally expected to bring with it the betrayal of the Irish hopes for Catholic Emancipation it had originally been expected to fulfil. In late 1811 and early 1812 the repressive measures taken against Irish militants who spoke for Catholic Emancipation and repeal of the Act of Union were recurrent features of the daily and weekly press, which also advised their readers in late Dec. 1811 of a meeting in Dublin on 28 Feb. of the General Committee of the Catholics of Ireland for the purpose of addressing or petitioning the Regent in protest against these infringements of their right to protest. Not only the trip but also the *Address* itself was probably precipitated by S's desire to speak at that meeting, where he could best take advantage of a crisis 'generalized by catholic disqualifications and the oppressive

influence of the Union act' but specifically occasioned by 'the conduct of
the prince which might lead to blind insurrections' (to Godwin, 24 Feb.).
He did speak at the meeting and, though his remarks on the clergy were
not well received, the Dublin newspapers gave him favourable coverage
(see Appendix I). S's private reasons for making the trip so early were the
conversations with Southey and the correspondence with Godwin,
which the poet had initiated on 3 Jan. S was probably inclined to demonstrate to the former that he did 'not feel the least disposition to be Mr. S's
proselyte' (to Godwin, 16 Jan.) and to the latter that he had a great disposition to be considered his disciple and accepted exegete.

A sufficient cause for S's leaving his Irish project a broken purpose was
surely Godwin's vehement disapproval of the poet's schemes for the
unenlightened masses, as set forth in the *Address*, and for the enlightened
philanthropists (as defined to Godwin on 24 Feb., 8 Mar.) to whom S
addressed his second Irish pamphlet (see Shelley, *Letters*, i. 260–2 n., 269–
70 n.). But the *Address* itself illustrates why it was that S achieved little
more than a patient hearing. He failed sufficiently to observe his own
axiom—'to preserve in some measure the good opinion of prejudice is
necessary to its destruction' (to Hitchener, 28 Oct. 1811)—by alienating
his Catholic audience with his implicit attacks on their religion. His error
was tactical as well as rhetorical: the grass-roots organization he needed
to effect his goals was already in place as the Catholic clergy. By too
patently attempting to 'shake Catholicism at its basis' he predictably
stumbled in his first step towards world reform. His discomfiting
insistence on repeal was likewise (if unwittingly) geared to alienate the
Catholic aristocracy, who would have found neither their political nor
their religious ends well served by the resurgence of an issue which could
only irritate a Parliament (and a Regent) they wished at that time to
conciliate.

Some of the 1,100 copies of the *Address* left undistributed after 27 Feb.
were packed into a box, along with the *Proposals for an Association of Philanthropists* and the *Declaration of Rights*, and sent to Elizabeth Hitchener;
clearly S meant to propagate in Sussex what he had agitated in Dublin.
The box was intercepted by the Customs and both its contents and their
author brought to the attention of the appropriate government officials,
though there were no overt repercussions (see the headnote to *Declaration of Rights*). In Aug. 1812, his enthusiasm rekindled by a volume of
revolutionary apologetics partially entitled *Pieces of Irish History* (by W. J.
MacNeven and T. A. Emmet), S asked the London bookseller Thomas
Hookham to publish both the *Address* and the *Proposals*, intending that
they might somehow 'find their way to Dublin' (to Hookham, 18 Aug.).
The compendium was also to include an explanatory preface and a set of
'suggestions', which were probably an expansion of the 'suggestions'
respecting his Association sent to mollify Godwin in a letter of 8 Mar.

(see the headnote to the *Proposals*). Nothing came of the proposal, which seems to contain S's last word on the *Address*, though either it or the *Proposals* must have been the 'little pamphlet . . . sent up to Government' which Harriet Shelley referred to in a letter of 12 Mar. 1813 to Hookham (Shelley, *Letters*, i. 356 n.).

Together the two pamphlets represent not only S's first public utterance on contemporary political issues and the way to resolve them but also a characteristic distinction between two audiences, popular and refined, which in poetry as well as in prose he would continue to define and individually address in later writings. As S recurrently allowed, his republicanism had an aristocratic leavening which found him very early despairing of the 'swinish multitude' (to Hitchener, 7 May 1812) and very late turning to the poet as the unacknowledged legislator whose radical idealism would gradually effect its practical changes as the multitude became increasingly able to accommodate them through the upward-spiralling trial and error of perfectible self-reform which Godwin had envisaged and which S was typically willing to believe in. While Godwin will occasionally intimate that institutional reform should precede individual reform (*PJ* i. 5), his general thrust was that lasting reform required a change in the opinions of men through collective self-reform motivated by individually enlightened understandings. S's own position was less ambiguous, as his emphatic imperative 'REFORM YOUR-SELVES' to his Irish audience demonstrates. His letters and his later activities in England make it clear that in 1812 he was still sufficiently unsure of his own best inferences (and Godwin's protestations) to continue agitating for peaceful reform through associations not very different from the reformist Hampden Clubs, which were just then getting under way. It is likewise clear that not only was he willing to use Catholic Emancipation as a stalking-horse for his generalized antipathy to all established religion but he was also interested in the Irish question as a whole only because he felt the answers given to that question could serve as a preliminary to and paradigm for the comprehensive world reform which continued to be his goal. T. W. Rolleston's comment in the Wise reprint of the *Address* (1890), that S at no time seemed to possess 'the gift of placing himself with imaginative sympathy in the attitude of other and otherwise-constituted minds' (22), seems at least recurrently applicable. Given S's own definition of the imagination (in *A Defence of Poetry*) as an outgoing of the spirit which allows us to identify with others, his passion for reforming the world might seem to have required the poetic sublimination it received in works like *Queen Mab* and *Prometheus Unbound* in order for it to be effective and acknowledged in the long run. S very early recognized that posterity was his indicated audience when he wrote to Godwin about the far goal of time he disinterestedly worked towards in his compositions (18 Mar. 1812); he later reaffirmed more directly his lack of contemporary appeal when he wrote that he was 'undec‹e›ived in the belief that ‹he had› powers deeply to interest, or substantially to improve, mankind' (to Leigh Hunt, 8 Dec. 1816).

As the Collation demonstrates, the poorly printed and negligently corrected text of 1812 contains a good many quite obvious typographical errors. While the long 's' prevalent in the *Proposals* is the rare exception in the *Address*, the argument from expediency is abetted by the title-page similarities (the open type and Gothic 'Dublin') in the two works to make it probable that the *Address* was printed by the same printer who printed the *Proposals*. (The *Declaration of Rights* was probably also printed by the same printer, though apparently not distributed until S returned to England.) The spellings 'honor', 'honourable', 'labor', 'labourer', 'judgement', and 'judgment' suggest different compositors in different parts of the *Address*.

The important advance of the present text of the *Address* over its predecessors is that it contains S's latest corrections as written into the Pforzheimer copy which S sent to his father, Timothy Shelley. The substantive character of several of these corrections (indicated in c by '*Pf*'), together with the numerous uncorrected printer's errors, is prima-facie evidence that S probably did not proofread the *Address* before it was published.

Related primary and secondary materials: LETTERS (see above); *The Speeches of the Hon. Thomas Erskine... on Subjects connected with the Liberty of the Press*, collected by James Ridgway (London, 1810), esp. the account of the trial of James Perry (also in Howell, *State Trials*, xxii. 953 ff.); John Joseph Dillon, *Considerations on the Necessity of Catholic Emancipation: or, The Propriety of Repealing the Act of Union with Ireland* (London, 1811), a coda to a series of letters by Dillon (under the pseudonym 'Hibernus-Anglus'), which appeared in the *Morning Chronicle* in the latter part of 1811; George Ensor, *On National Government*, i. 408-18, ii. 116-30, 332-5, 356-62; Hogg, *Life*, i. 316-17; MacCarthy, *Early Life*, 130-77; Dowden, *Life*, i. 228-64; T. W. Rolleston's Introduction to T. J. Wise's 1890 facsimile edition (Shelley Society Publications, Second Series, No. 6); Percy Vaughan, *Early Shelley Pamphlets* (London, 1905), 21-5; Peck, *Life and Work*, ii. 341-3 (S's indebtedness to John Philpot Curran's *Speeches*); Wilfred H. Woollen, 'Shelley and Catholic Emancipation', *The Downside Review*, 44 (Oct. 1926), 271-84; Grabo, *Magic Plant*, 64-76; Barnard, *Shelley's Religion*, 116-17; David Lee Clark, 'Shelley and *Pieces of Irish History*', *MLN* 53 (Nov. 1938), 522-5; White, *Shelley*, i. 207-21; Hughes, *Nascent Mind*, 131-6; Bennet Weaver, 'Pre-Promethean Thought in the Prose of Shelley', *Philological Quarterly*, 27 (July 1948), 193-208; Cameron, *Young Shelley*, 154-68, 382-9; Guinn, *Political Thought*, 27-36; Art Young, *Shelley and Nonviolence* (Mouton: The Hague, 1975), 35-58; E. B. Murray, 'The Trial of Mr. Perry, Lord Eldon, and Shelley's *Address to the Irish*', *SiR* 17 (Winter 1978), 35-49; P. M. S. Dawson, 'Shelley and the Irish Catholics in 1812', *K-SMB* 29 (1978), 18-31; Dawson, *Unacknowledged Legislator*, 134-65; Scrivener, *Radical Shelley*, 59-62; Hoagwood, *Scepticism*, 141-3. (William Godwin and

Thomas Paine are the political writers whose influence on the *Address* is most pervasive but for that reason less readily specified. Newspapers such as the *Examiner* and the *Morning Chronicle* provided S with topical information and sympathetic editorials.) See also the EC on *Proposals for an Association of Philanthropists* and *Declaration of Rights*.

ADVERTISEMENT. Newman White supposes that the following postscript in a letter of 1844 from H. White to Robert Peele refers to this Advertisement: 'As a matter of curiosity I send the title page of a pamphlet of which I believe no other copy exists but mine. It is curious for recommending the very course of peaceable agitation and of political science of which O'Connell boasts himself the originator. It is also curious for the fulfillment of one of its prophecies. Beware the other. Beyond this page the pamphlet is not worth reading. In matter and style it has all the marks of boyhood. The language is often vague ... and ungrammatical, like the advertisement' (White, *Shelley*, i. 631). Both the substantive account and the stylistic critique make White's supposition plausible. Daniel O'Connell (1775–1847) founded the Catholic Association (1823), which was largely responsible for the Catholic Emancipation Act of 1829. He later agitated as well for repeal of the Act of Union. O'Connell spoke at the meeting of 28 Feb. 1811, but in later years did not recall S's speech; he could have read the *Address*. But 'peaceable agitation' was hardly a novel recommendation when S made it, and O'Connell's 'political science' was shrewd enough to make positive use of the Catholic clergy, whom S tended to alienate.

79. *thirty-nine articles*. The theological creed of the Church of England which established the supremacy of the monarch over the prelacy.

110. *one night*. On St Bartholomew's day (24 Aug.) 1572 Catherine de Medici instigated a massacre of Protestants in Paris which eventually spread throughout France. The total killed during the period was estimated at about 50,000. Pope Gregory XIII had a medal struck in commemoration of the event.

111–12. *one ... help*. According to a historical account now considered apocryphal, the Bishop Jean le Hennuyer (1497–1578) was supposed to have saved the Protestants at Lisieux during the Massacre. S's information probably derived from a mid-eighteenth-century French play based on le Hennuyer's reputed heroism (translated into English in 1773). Richard Monckton Milnes in an article 'On the Apologies for the Massacre of Saint Bartholomew' (*Miscellanies of the Philobiblon Society*, London, vol. 3, 1856–7), 65 n., provides a brief account of the controversy concerning the Bishop's actions and indicates that the false account was accepted as true at least through the middle of the nineteenth century. See also the entry under le Hennuyer in the *Biographie Universelle* (Michaud).

196. *Servetus.* Michael Servetus (1511–53), Spanish physician and dissident writer on theological subjects, was condemned as a heretic largely through information provided by John Calvin.

279–80. *no person . . . disbelief.* A recurrent tenet in S's early attacks on religious orthodoxy.

435. *crisis.* The specific crisis referred to is the Prince's assumption of full regency powers and his consequent acts as they may affect the Irish. But as S makes clear elsewhere in the *Address* and in a letter to Godwin written on the same day the *Address* was printed, the predisposing crisis to individual and collective reform which he meant to take advantage of had a psychological character. He meant to 'improve' the warm sentiments of the brutalized Irish by allaying any tendency to 'blind insurrection' the 'conduct of the prince' might further precipitate, and so beguile their 'benevolent passions' into peaceful channels of constructive reform (to Godwin, 24 Feb. 1812). 'Crisis' as a political shibboleth had become a decreasingly potent call to arms after forty years of deadening repetition in reformist (and anti-reformist) circles, with titles such as *Hints to All Classes of the State of the Country in This Momentous Crisis* (Stockdale: London, 1812) and *A View of the State of the Nation at the Present Crisis* (Hatchard and Richardson: London, 1814) defining the word and its application according to the varying theses of the works they headed.

438–9. *The present . . . freedom.* As the rest of the paragraph, the *Proposals*, and his letters indicate, S had no real faith in the Prince's good intentions but he was calculating enough to remind the Irish (and the Prince) of them. As late as 28 Dec. 1811 the *Morning Chronicle* reported that the Irish still regarded the Regent as their 'proudest hope'. With, it seems, the rather forlorn hope of embarrassing him into some allegiance to his earlier liberal pretentions, the *Chronicle* continued ostensibly to believe that the Regent still held these beliefs by reminding him (and the people) of them. But when in mid-Feb. 1812 the Prince's devious invitation to certain Whig ministers to join a coalition government was predictably refused, even the *Chronicle* finally admitted in print what its editor must have known to be true for some time. Other liberal and radical publications such as the *Oxford University and City Herald* and the *Scourge* had long since given up on the Prince, in so far as they had ever attached any credence to his reformist tendencies. Here as elsewhere the *Address* illustrates S's formal rhetorical training rather than his beliefs or even his hopes.

455. *Charles Fox.* The Whig leader, who had died in 1806, was a friend of the Regent and favoured concessions to the Roman Catholics; the 'broken reed' (455) could refer specifically to Lord Chancellor Eldon, but S seems to have in mind the Tory ministry in general. Reformist meetings consistently toasted the Regent (and the heiress presumptive Princess Charlotte) with the hope that he (and she) would never lose sight of the

principles of Charles Fox, which had become somewhat idealized since his death.

474-5. *Depend . . . Princes.* Cf. 'Put not your trust in princes' (*Psalms* 146: 3).

479-80. *The crisis . . . king.* James Perry's trial in 1810 for seditious libel (cf. 910EC) resulted from his reprinting in the *Morning Chronicle* of 2 Oct. 1809 a paragraph from the *Examiner* which noted that the successor of George III could become 'nobly popular' by 'a total change of system'. By an accustomed stretch of the Attorney-General's legal imagination, this prediction was construed as 'a direct libel on the person of the king' because it suggested that his death was necessary for the country's betterment. S wished to avoid such a construction.

498-9. *the goodness . . . Governed.* Cf. *Proposals for an Association of Philanthropists*, ll. 256-7, and Paine's *Common Sense, Writings*, i. 69.

619-21. *Government . . . necessary evil.* Cf. Paine's *Common Sense, Writings*, i. 69.

624-5. *Society . . . wickedness.* Almost verbatim from Paine's *Common Sense, Writings*, i. 69.

633. *REFORM YOURSELVES.* While S felt that self-reform and political reform were symbiotic, his emphasis when addressing the lower classes (as the *Address* redundantly illustrates) was on the former. George Ensor, an Irish writer whose *On National Education* (London, 1811) S recommended to Elizabeth Hitchener as 'the production of a very clever man' (to Hitchener, 5 June 1811), wrote in *Defects of the English Laws and Tribunals* (J. Johnson & Co.: London, 1812), 288, 'Reform the state, reform yourselves, and defy the crown.' Newman White has noted (*Shelley*, i. 624-6) the possible influence of Ensor on S. In religion and politics he is representative of the radical opinion S often echoed, though, while no believer in self-interest as the mainspring of human interaction, he is less sanguine than S concerning the innate tendencies in human nature towards the disinterested reform which S typically envisaged. In spite of his suggestion that Ensor might have been S's pre-Godwinian preceptor, White sensibly notes that 'constant attacks upon priestcraft, aristocracy, patronage, monarchy, luxury, and the educational system are too common to radical literature for Shelley's indebtedness to any particular expression of them to be demonstrable . . . from general similarity' (625). While the 1812 *Defects* was probably not available to S before he printed the *Address*, certain parallels between the two works are close enough to support both of White's suggestions: there was a clear compatibility in thought and phrasing between the two writers which, if merely accidental, demonstrates a cognate influence of the radical press which they echoed in kindred terms.

668. *to make others happy.* Cf. 'Learn to make others happy' (*Queen Mab*, II. 64).

694–6. *"A Camel...Heaven."* Matt. 19: 24.

806–8. *Every folly ... cause.* Cf. '*Every prejudice conquered every error rooted out, every virtue given is so much gained in the case of reform*' (to Elizabeth Hitchener, ?10 Dec. 1811). The letter's version confirms the correction of *1812*'s 'as' to 'is'.

835–7. *can ... governed.* Cf. *Declaration of Rights*, 1–2 and EC. The sentiment was a reformist commonplace.

907. *"the Liberty of the Press."* The quotation marks here and later highlight the irony of using Lord Eldon, who (as John Scott) was the Attorney-General in 1793, in defence of free speech. There is no question that Eldon's words (910–12) are quoted out of context (see Erskine's *Speeches*, ii. 404 and *passim*) to reverse his real sentiments. A general defence of those accused of libel was that their intention had been perverted by quotation out of context: during S's lifetime there was no more persistent enemy of liberty of the press in England than Lord Eldon. Thomas Erskine, the foremost advocate of a free press in his time, defended Perry in 1793; all of the references to the trial noted here appear in the account of Erskine's speeches printed by Ridgway in 1810 (see *Related materials*).

910. *Mr. Perry.* James Perry, proprietor and editor of the *Morning Chronicle*, the foremost liberal London newspaper. His trial in 1793 was for seditious libel, a charge which was again brought against him in 1810. The earlier case was of particular relevance because it represented the first real test of Charles Fox's Libel Act of 1792, which gave the jury (rather than the judge) the right to decide on the question of libel, not simply on the facts of a given case. Eldon tried to subvert the new law but was easily foiled by the much more astute Erskine (see previous note), and Perry was found not guilty. In view of S's rather offhand allusions here, the trial and its significance must have been fairly common knowledge. According to a later appraisal, Perry was the standard-bearer and eventual hero for the many dailies and weeklies that feared the opposite verdict, which would have 'shackled the Liberty of the Press forever' (quoted from the London *World* ⟨12 Dec. 1793⟩ in Lucyle Werkmeister, *A Newspaper History of England 1792–3*, Lincoln, 1967, 454). The account of the 1793 trial might have had a further relevance to S's present act of calculated sedition, since it took the general form of an address to the English people, questioned (as S was later to question) heavy taxes, regressive wars, lack of representation, the 'army of placemen, pensioners, &c. fighting in the cause of corruption and prejudice ... a proclamation tending to cramp the liberty of the press ...', and—most pertinently—advocated the formation of 'a union founded on principles of benevolence and humanity, disclaiming all connexion with riots and disorders' (Erskine's *Speeches*, ii. 377–9).

912–14. *"The Liberty ... liberties".* Quoted from the summary remarks of Lord Kenyon, who presided at Perry's trial in 1793. The original context (in Erskine's *Speeches*, ii. 448) indicates that, like Eldon's, Kenyon's remarks are here used against the grain of his intent: 'Gentlemen, it ⟨liberty of the press⟩ is placed as the sentinel to alarm us, when any attempt is made on our liberties; and we ought to be watchful, and to take care that the sentinel is not abused and converted into a traitor. . . . It is therefore for the protection of liberty, that its licentiousness is brought to punishment.' Cf. S's remarks on the Limerick newspaper in the Postscript below.

916–19. *There is . . . blessing*. George Ensor had written, 'let no man speak of liberty of the press in England. . . . It is absurd to talk of a free press, and to prohibit politics, morals, laws, religion, public characters, or any such subject from being discussed' (*Defects of the English Laws and Tribunals*, 358, 364).

921. *ex-officio informations*. The Attorney-General was empowered to file these informations against those responsible for publishing material regarded as libellous and/or seditious. While they often resulted in a trial, they seldom led to a conviction. They were notably less effective in intimidating the press than they were in motivating its opposition to the ministry which proliferated them, though they often proved costly to the defendants even when a jury eventually found them not guilty. The Finnerty case (see 955EC) became a *cause célèbre* partly because it precipitated a Parliamentary motion for the repeal of the act providing for ex-officio informations. In effect, they allowed the government to manipulate every aspect of a trial, even to the extent of picking the jury.

Blackstone. Sir William Blackstone (1723–80), whose *Commentaries on the Laws of England* (1765–9) served as the final authority on the principles of English law. S wrote in a letter to Hitchener (7 Jan. 1812) that 'they shall not get at me' because 'I shall refer to Blackstone, he will tell me what points are criminal and what innocent in the eyes of the law'. However, the quotation he uses here—which he could have found in the lengthy excerpt from the *Commentaries* used by Eldon in his opening statement to the jury in 1793—demonstrates some exasperation with the vagueness he found in Blackstone on the liberty or licence of the press.

923. *Lord . . . Comyns*. Sir John Comyns (d. 1740). The ultimate source of S's quotation is probably the English translation of Comyns's (originally French) *A Digest of the Laws of England* (1762–7; 1792 edn.), iv. 713, though S himself might well have found it among the trial accounts in Lord Erskine's *Speeches* of 1810. George Ensor likewise criticized Comyns's definition (*Defects of the English Laws and Tribunals*, 331), noting too that 'Among the broadest pleasantries of the law is the assertion that truth is a libel' (p. 326). The *DNB* quotes both Lords Kenyon and Ellenborough (who presided at Perry's trial in 1810) in praise of Comyns's legal opinions and authority.

955. *Mr. Finnerty*. The Irish journalist Peter Finnerty was sentenced to jail in 1811 for a libel against Lord Castlereagh printed in the *Morning Chronicle*. As S suggests, the real motive for his imprisonment was political. While at Oxford, S contributed to Finnerty's maintenance in prison with the proceeds from the sale of a lost poem called *A Poetical Essay on the Existing State of Things*. See MacCarthy, *Early Life*, 77–91, for the *Examiner*'s account of the Finnerty affair, and Cameron, *Young Shelley*, 65–6, for an account of S's interest in him.

1032. *hearts ... vibrate*. Cf. S's letter of 26 Jan. to Hitchener, who would 'command the conviction of those whose hearts vibrate in unison with justice and benevolence'.

1061 n. *The excellence ... effect*. The note is not keyed to any specific word or phrase in the original. The last sentence may be glossed by S's letter of 27 Feb. to Hitchener, in which he outlines his hopes for instigating revolution in England through a proposed Philanthropic Society which he meant to initiate in Sussex: 'How is Sussex disposed? Is there much intellect there? We must have the cause before the effect.' That is, reform must begin in the appropriately conditioned and expanded minds of men. In the note, 'wisdom and virtue' are the 'cause', the 'accommodation' of the constitution is the 'effect'.

1070. *"private vices are public benefits"*. The ultimate source of the quotation is Bernard Mandeville's *The Fable of the Bees: Or, Private Vices, Public Benefits* (1714), which advanced the paradox that luxury, pride, avarice, etc. make for a prosperous society. In opposition to the thesis of man's essential goodness, as proposed by his contemporary the Earl of Shaftesbury, Mandeville argued that man was essentially selfish. For S, apologists for the economic status quo such as William Paley and Thomas Malthus were present-day exponents of the Mandevillean thesis in opposition to Godwin's concept of mankind's perfectibility.

1090. *expenditure*. '*Expenditure* is used in my Address in a moral sense' (to Godwin, 8 Mar. 1812).

1104. *Lower Sackville-street*. S's Dublin address.

1139. *enlightened ... education*. Probably the monitorial system, wherein better students were taught directly by the teachers and in turn taught the inferior students. The system was popularized by the Quaker Joseph Lancaster, who on 11 Dec. 1811 attended a meeting of the 'Friends of Religious Liberty' sponsored by the Irish Catholics. S would have been attracted to a system which was akin to his own purposes in soliciting the enlightened classes to lead the vulgar in their collective pursuit of reform. Attacks on traditional—particular classical—education in George Ensor's *On National Education* and in Godwin's *Political Justice* were negative supplements to a system of mass education calculated to disturb the social and political status quo by a democratic emphasis on the individual, whatever his ancestry.

1145. *A Limerick Paper*. The *Limerick Evening Post*. The article referred to was reprinted in the *Dublin Freeman's Journal* of 18 Feb. 1812, where S probably saw it.

1162. *Lafayette*. S probably found this oft-quoted ascription in Paine's *Rights of Man, Writings*, ii. 282.

PROPOSALS FOR AN ASSOCIATION OF PHILANTHROPISTS

Date: Feb. 1812.

Copy-text: *1812* (Huntington Library copy; shelfmark RB 23000).

Locations: BL (Ashley); Bodleian; Harvard; Huntington; Princeton.

Description: Undated octavo pamphlet measuring 22.7 cm. × 14.5 cm. (8.9″ × 5.75″, untrimmed) and made up of three gatherings (⟨A⟩1 (= D2 wrap-around) B–C⁴ ⟨D⟩² (— D2)), which consist of a title-page (verso blank; ⟨i–ii⟩), a drop-head title ('Proposals for an Association, &c.') and centrally numbered text (⟨1⟩–18); machine-wove paper; no WM or running heads; 'FINIS.' appears below the text on p. 18. The copy-text title-page is reproduced on page 39 (the '1812' under the imprint has been added in pencil). The Huntington copy has been restitched into a later cover with the *Declaration of Rights* and associated correspondence.

Reprinted: MacCarthy, *Early Life*; F; J.

The *Proposals for an Association of Philanthropists* probably predated the *Address, to the Irish People* in conception but was not published until 2 Mar. 1812, exactly one year after S first broached the subject of such an association in his first letter to Leigh Hunt. In his letter of 14 Feb. to Elizabeth Hitchener he states that the 'address will soon come out; it will be instantly followed by another, with downright proposals for instituting assoc⟨i⟩ations for bettering the condition of human kind'. On 18 Feb. he wrote in a letter to Hitchener that the *Proposals* would 'make about 30 such pages as the inclosed ⟨first sheet of the *Address*⟩'. In fact the *Proposals* contains about half as many words per page as the *Address* (though only two pages less) and is about half its length, which suggests that S had not at that date finished it and that he meant to include more material than he eventually did. The conclusion of the *Address*, dated 22 Feb., further defines the scope of the *Proposals*, while the first half of the Postscript to the *Address* is in effect a prefatory summary of it. On 24 Feb. S went to the printer's, probably to pick up the completed *Address* (which was sent to Godwin on that date) and to deliver copy for the *Proposals*, which, he wrote to Godwin, was 'in the press' (to Hitchener and to Godwin, 24 Feb.). While the *Proposals* carries the imprint of 'I. Eton, Winetavern-Street' and the *Address* does not, the poor quality of the printing and paper in both pamphlets, their shared misspelling of 'philanthropy' (as 'philanthrophy'), and the distinctive title-page printing of 'Dublin' which they both exhibit strongly suggest that they (and the *Declaration of Rights*) were printed by the same Dublin printer, in spite of the fact that the long 's' standard in the *Proposals* appears only towards the end of the *Address*.

On 27 Feb. S announced to Hitchener that his 'next book' would appear the following Monday, 2 Mar. In the *Dublin Weekly Messenger* of 7 Mar., following a short sketch of 'Pierce Byshe Shelly, Esq.', the full title and ll. 1–149 of the *Proposals* are printed (see Appendix I). In a letter of 8 Mar. to Godwin S writes that he is also sending copies of the *Messenger* of 7 Mar. and the *Proposals* itself. The same letter contains S's expansive defence against Godwin's attack (4 Mar.) on his 'Association' as defined to the philosopher in S's letter to him of 24 Feb. S struggles in the letter of 8 Mar. to align his scheme with the 'friendly discussion' Godwin approved of in *Political Justice* by including 'some suggestions respecting' the sort of association he intended. It was apparently an enlarged form of these suggestions which S sent to Thomas Hookham the following summer, when he thought to reprint his Irish pamphlets, along with a preface, in London (to Hookham, 18 Aug.). In a letter of 10 Mar. to Hitchener he notes that the 'Association proceeds slowly, and I fear will not be established'. Writing to Godwin on 18 Mar., he allows that his 'schemes of organizing the ignorant' had been 'ill-timed', though he still defends the principle of association against Godwin's reiterated attacks on it. Around the same time Harriet wrote to Hitchener that 'All thoughts of an Association are given up as impracticable' (Shelley, *Letters*, i. 280 n.).

S's sources for an association such as he proposes here may be found in his readings of the Abbé Augustin Barruel's *Memoirs, Illustrating the History of Jacobinism* (referred to in a letter of 27 Feb. 1812 to Hitchener), with its accounts of the Illuminati and kindred societies; or in the general concept and implementation of political organizations rife in Great Britain and France for at least three decades. But his own statements to Godwin, that he regarded his 'Philanthropic Association' as 'strictly compatible with the principles of "Political Justice"' (8 Mar.) and as 'undoubtedly' growing 'out of my notions of political justice, first generated by your book on that subject' (18 Mar.), define the theoretical basis S thought he was implementing in his *Proposals*. Godwin's distinct opposition to S's 'scheme' was at least as potent as the indifference and ignorance of the Irish themselves in causing him to abandon Ireland as the 'theatre' in which to realize his hopes for brotherhood and universal emancipation.

As distinguished from the *Address, to the Irish People*, the *Proposals* was addressed to 'a different class' (to Godwin, 24 Feb.) and composed in S's 'natural style tho in the same strain' (to Hitchener, 18 Feb.). At its best it is representative of his mature style and of some aspects of his later thought both political and metaphysical; in some parts both the prose and the thought are convoluted. In S's mind it was clearly the more important of the two pamphlets because it devised a *modus operandi* for reform which emphasized enlightened leadership of the masses indiscriminately addressed in the first pamphlet, who would be directed by peaceful means to deserve their rights by learning their duties. From the outset of his political activities S was a pragmatic moderate in his means, however radical his long-range goals appeared. None the less, his failure to attract the upper-class leadership to his idea of an association was at least partly due to his misunderstanding of the practical ends desired by that class and of the means by which they felt these ends could be achieved. He implicitly came to realize that some of the leaders to whom he made his proposals were part of the problem he felt his associations should solve. 'The rich', he wrote to Elizabeth Hitchener, '*grind* the poor into abjectness & then complain that they are abject' (10 Mar.). By 14 Mar. his alienation from the Catholic hierarchy was complete: 'I do not like Lord Fingal or *any* of the Catholic aristocracy' (to Hitchener; Fingal chaired the meeting of 28 Feb. at which S spoke).

S's subsequent activities in Devon (see the headnote to *Declaration of Rights*), his hopes of forming associations in Wales and Sussex (to Hitchener, 10 Mar.), and his plan to publish the Irish pamphlets in London noted above are signs that his resolution had been momentarily frustrated but not daunted by Ireland and Godwin.

The 'suggestions' with which S intended to define and further modify his *Proposals* were apparently complete when he first mentioned them to Godwin, and ready for publication when offered for that purpose to Hookham in the letter of 18 Aug. They were not published and are extant only in the selectively Godwinian extracts written into S's apologia of 8 Mar. to his ruffled mentor: 'That any number of persons who meet together for philanthropical purposes should ascertain by friendly discussion, those points of opinion wherein they differ, & those wherein they coincide: and should by subjecting them to rational analysis produce an unanimity founded on reason, and not the superficial agreement, too often exhibited at associations for mere party purposes; that the minority whose belief could not subscribe to the opinion of the majority on a division in any question of moment & interest should recede ⟨?secede⟩. Some associations might by refinement of secessions contain not more than three or four members.' S then comments that he does not think such a society as this 'incompatible with your chapter on associations'. These suggestions do in fact echo significant parts of that chapter (*PJ* i. 285 ff.), as well as the segment on majorities in the chapter on 'Resistance' (i. 247 ff.). S apparently intended to send the suggestions *in toto* to Godwin ('the proposals . . . will be followed by ⟨the⟩ "suggestions"', letter of 8 Mar.), either because he felt them to be an intrinsic qualification to that work or because he would have liked Godwin to think he felt them so. In his letter of 18 Mar. to Godwin, a mixture of general contrition and uncertain defiance, S defends his associations by reiterating his major suggestion concerning minority voices: 'the refinement of secessions would prevent a fictitious unanimity . . .'.

It seems clear from his original hopes for a society of some sort resulting from his *Proposals* that S intended to spend more time in Ireland than he did. He did not leave abruptly (as Hogg states), nor does he seem to have been unduly concerned about police action (so long as Habeas Corpus was in effect), but he certainly foreshortened a stay that (*pace* Godwin) would quite possibly have continued through later spring or early summer had he met with a positive response from those whom he solicited to form an association for Ireland's social and political betterment. If he had been successful in gaining the management of a Dublin newspaper (probably through John Lawless, in whose Irish history he apparently took an authorial as well as material part—see S's letter to Thomas Charles Medwin, 20 Mar. 1812), he would have been obliged, or at least strongly tempted, to stay on. But his own miscalculations concerning the religious opinions and secular goals of the Irish Catholics were abetted by the government's intolerance of associations of any sort so as to render his scheme, in his own understatement, 'ill-timed'. He had hoped that a confluence of public sentiments concerning repeal and emancipation, further stimulated by the Regent's imminent betrayal, would have enlarged the hearts and minds of the Irish of every class to the point of the 'crisis' his apparition in Ireland was meant to take advantage of. In basic and recurrent Shelleyan terms, the principle of self would have been momentarily replaced by the principle of disinterestedness. S's miscalculations as regards particular aspects of prejudice, political and religious, were symptomatic of a larger miscalculation concerning the contemporary state of human nature. As S's *Weekly Messenger* reporter and eulogist (probably Lawless) noted, he felt it as ready generically as he was specifically to realize a millennium and discard or at least discount those ideological symbols of a self-interested and intolerant childhood which stood in its way. (See Appendix I.)

S's long-range programme extended beyond Ireland and the Irish pamphlets. It called for select cadres crucially placed in different parts of Great Britain to function as a nucleus and pattern for non-violent but radical social change through moral and political education of the masses. Such groups would '*quietly* revolutionize the country' through a politically innocent subversion which would demonstrate the inutility of government (to Hitchener, 27 Feb. 1812). He subsequently prepared the way for continued political activity in England by asking Elizabeth Hitchener (10 Mar.) to place the 'account of me' which had appeared in the *Dublin Weekly Messenger* in a Sussex paper. He had previously asked her to have the *Address, to the Irish People* printed, apparently at Lewes in Sussex—Harriet supposed that this had in fact been done (10 Mar., her addition to S's letter). The negative result of Hitchener's efforts is summed up in an ambiguous rejection notice printed in the *Sussex Weekly Advertiser* of 6 Apr.:

> We have been favoured with the address of P.B.S., Esq., and entertain no doubt of his benevolent and humane intentions. Nevertheless, after due consideration, we are of opinion that any especial notice of the accompanying letter would have a tendency to defeat the ends he has in view, as a public exposure of the accused parties, however just, might irritate their minds and lead them to direct, with greater severity, the lash of tyranny and oppression against the object of his commiseration ⟨Peter Finnerty?⟩, who appears to be completely within their power.

S, as well as Harriet, apparently assumed that Hitchener would have no trouble placing his *Address*, since on 20 Mar. he wrote in a letter to his uncle, Thomas Charles Medwin, 'you will see by the Lewes paper, I am in the midst of overwhelming engagements'.

The last evaluation of the Irish venture appears in a letter of 16 Apr. to Hitchener, written in Wales, in which S states that he left Dublin because he 'had done all that ⟨he⟩ could do', that the beneficial effects of his efforts had been minimal, but that he was none the less not dissatisfied with his attempt. He continued throughout his life to support the justifying tenet of the *Proposals*, that the 'only true religion' was philanthropy as formulated in a 'society of peace and love' (to Hitchener, 14 Feb.), a proposition which not only backs Newman White's astute observation that S's radicalism was 'always more social and moral than political' (*Shelley*, i. 214) but also suggests the parallel inference that his plans for associations were typically more metaphysical than empirical in derivation.

Like the *Address, to the Irish People*, the *Proposals* was poorly printed, with several words misspelt, though the loose or questionable pointing probably derives as often as not from S himself and is therefore generally allowed to stand as printed. Variants appearing in the lines reprinted in the *Dublin Weekly Messenger* represent mistranscriptions or printer's changes and are not recorded here.

Related primary and secondary materials: LETTERS (see above); Arthur Swann, 'A Rare Shelley Pamphlet', *American Book Collector*, 1 (June 1932), 353-6; Grabo, *Magic Plant*, 76-81; Hughes, *Nascent Mind*, 131-3, 137-40; Cameron, *Young Shelley*, 168-73; Guinn, *Political Thought*, 36-9; Dawson, *Unacknowledged Legislator*, 138-41, 157-65; Scrivener, *Radical Shelley*, 49-52, 63-4; Hoagwood, *Scepticism*, 144-5; Hogle, *Shelley's Process*, 252-4. (See also EC on *An Address, to the Irish People* and *A Proposal for Putting Reform to the Vote*.)

6. *Man . . . offer.* Cf. Paine, *Rights of Man*, *Writings*, ii. 336: 'Man cannot . . . make circumstances for his purpose, but he always has it in his power to improve them when they occur'.

11. *their country . . . world.* Cf. ibid. 472: 'my country is the world, and my religion is to do good'.

56. *near approach.* Catholic emancipation did not arrive until 1829.

68–9. *I hear . . . grave!* This was readily interpreted as an attack on the Catholic Church (see Appendix I). However, in this context S means religious bigotry and superstition of whatever persuasion.

73. *meteors.* I.e. ignes fatui or will-o'-the-wisps.

78. *enwreathed with his.* I.e. with 'garland' implied after 'his'.

104–5. *The latter . . . former.* S's references are obscure though his general sense is not. He means that the general spirit of benevolence will effect redress of grievances through the disinterestedness then focused on the question of Catholic emancipation.

106–7. *It forms . . . occupied.* Cf. S's letter of ?26 Jan. 1812 to Godwin, in which he regards the state of Irish affairs as an 'opportunity' which he should not 'permit to pass unoccupied'.

133. ⟨*e*⟩*ffect . . . society.* That is, individuals can never bring about as much as a society can bring about. *1812*'s 'affect' would provide the rather lame and probably contradictory sense (given S's own hopes for success in Ireland and in the world) that single individuals cannot influence even a society. It would have been quite easy for the printer to mistake S's 'e' for an 'a' or to simply have nodded a bit over two words often confused.

159. *political institution.* Like Godwin (and Rousseau), S located the origin of social inequities in governmental institutions. S parted company with Godwin by believing that the spirit of benevolence he found in Ireland indicated that the people needed only the direction he meant his associations to supply for the restructuring of political institutions to begin.

168–70. *The former . . . exercised.* The confusion of this sentence is compounded by its relation to the sentence preceding it, though both are somewhat clarified when taken in context with the last sentence in the paragraph. The overall meaning may be as follows: 'Since the minority govern the majority they are in effect its intellect and power. This same governing minority originally received its power from the majority. However, the present minority, while holding the governing power through heredity, no longer possesses the intellect which justified ⟨so the implication⟩ the powers its forefathers had had delegated to them.' The first sentence seems to be elliptical at best, with the ambiguous 'majority' apparently doing double service. On the one hand, it is a minority which possesses the majority of intellect and power; on the other, it is the majority of the people as opposed to this same minority to whom they once delegated power because of its ⟨the minority's⟩ superior intellect. It is quite possible that the printer dropped a phrase or clause. S's meaning is clear both from the context of his reformist writings in general and from the oft-reiterated Lockian/Painite/Godwinian confluence of ideas which it draws on.

234. *I disclaim... concealment.* Since S meant secretly to undermine the Catholicism whose emancipation he advocated, he was in fact guilty of the deceit he disclaimed. However, perhaps unintentionally, his rhetoric elsewhere in the Irish pamphlets makes his true sentiments obvious enough, as they must have been in his Fishamble speech (see Appendix I).

244–5. *I dare not... adage.* This adaptation from Shakespeare (*Macbeth*, I. vii. 44–5) is recurrent in S. It appears also in the *Letter to Lord Ellenborough* (see ll. 57–8) and *A Defence of Poetry*.

245–8. *But the eye... universe.* The eagle was traditionally supposed to gain its nourishment from the sun, which it, alone among living creatures, could look on without blinking. The image is recurrent among romantic writers. S repeats this sentence, nearly verbatim, in the *Letter to Lord Ellenborough* (ll. 59–62).

253–4. *Government ... others.* S introduces his *Declaration of Rights* with this revolutionary commonplace and rings changes on it through many of the passages following.

259–60. *Constitution... law.* Cf. Paine, *Rights of Man*, *Writings*, ii. 310: 'A constitution ... is to a government what the laws made afterwards by that government are to a court of judicature.' Paine, like S and like other radical reformers in England, made much of the fact that the English had no formal constitution. Paine's conclusion, which S did not care to repeat, is that the English government was established by right of conquest, not by the will of the people, and continues to suffer from that original defect. S carefully modifies Paine's argument in this context (ibid., 308–12) to suit his rhetorical purposes.

278. *prove an alibi.* S's use of this legalistic phrase is vague, though his general sense seems to be that the Establishment tries to hide evils which it cannot prove are absent or do not exist. For a parallel usage, see Paine, *Writings*, iv. 162.

292–4. *the oligarchy ... Normans.* William the Conqueror (1027–87) consolidated his hold on England by dispossessing the Saxon landholders and installing in their place an aristocracy made up of those who aided him.

313–14. *"Weapons ... truth."* S does not note his source, though he comes very close to repeating his own words, ll. 237–8: 'Weapons which vice *can* use are unfit for the hands of virtue.' In contrasting S's Godwinian concept of open associations with the secret association of the eighteenth-century Illuminati, P. M. S. Dawson notes that this last statement directly opposes the inverted wisdom of the serpent as preached by the founder of Illuminism, Adam Weishaupt, who advocated employing 'the same means for a good purpose which impostors employ for evil' (*Unacknowledged Legislator*, 160; quoted from Augustin Barruel's *Memoirs, illustrating the History of Jacobinism*, iii. 115). As noted below (on l. 387), at about the time S was composing his *Proposals for an Association* he was recommending (with reservations) Barruel's book to Elizabeth Hitchener.

335–6. *A man ... duty.* Cf. On *'Godwin's Mandeville'*, 13–16: '*Political Justice* is the first moral system, explicitly founded upon the doctrine of the negativeness of rights and the positiveness of duties, an obscure feeling of which has been the basis of all the political liberty and private virtue in the world'. Godwin, however, typically allowed for the necessary pre-eminence of private judgement, which seems to be the species of individual right S argues for here. Like Godwin (and Rousseau), S recognized that man's natural rights were appropriately defined in a social and political context. His basic right was finally a disinterested right to do his duty towards his fellow men so that the general stock of happiness could be increased. Queen Mab's advice to Ianthe—'Learn to make others happy'—is the apposite revelation of Godwinian duty intuitively arrived at. S's *Declaration of Rights*, which repeats ll. 335–6 as its tenth right, is essentially a statement of man's right to perform his duties towards his fellow men for their collective benefit.

352–8. *When Jupiter ... thunder.* S repeats, with few changes, the anecdote as it appears in Thomas Erskine's *Speeches*, ii. 181. See *An Address, to the Irish People* and relevant commentary for evidence that S had read these speeches before writing his Irish polemics.

386. *Lafayette.* The Marquis de La Fayette (1757–1834) was a leading participant in both the French and American revolutions. He was distinguished from most of his revolutionary compatriots by his advocacy of religious tolerance, trial by jury, and freedom of the press.

387. *poetic ... Jesuit.* S refers to the Abbé ⟨Augustin⟩ Barruel's *Histoire du Jacobinisme* (1797) in a letter of 27 Feb. 1812 to Elizabeth Hitchener as a book 'half filled with the vilest and most unsupported falsehoods' but none the less 'worth reading' by those (like Hitchener) who know how to 'distinguish truth'. S's later references to the Encyclopedists D'Alembert, Boulanger, and Condorcet may be coloured by his critical reading of Barruel in an English translation by R. Clifford in four volumes (1797–8). See Walter E. Peck, 'Shelley and the Abbé Barruel', *PMLA* 36 (Sept. 1921), 347–53. S's remarks on the French here anticipate similar remarks in *A Philosophical View of Reform* (1819). The hybrid title in the footnote is here allowed to stand as originally printed (except for the addition of italic).

397. *Encyclopedists.* A group of French Enlightenment humanists

(several of whom S later mentions) whose *Encyclopédie* (1751-80), philosophically based in British empiricism as exemplified by Bacon and Locke and in French scepticism as comprehended in the works of Pierre Bayle, was avowedly meant to 'change the general way of thinking' (*Encyclopédie*, vol. v, s.v. 'Encyclopédie' ⟨Diderot⟩). They were advocates of reason, human perfectibility and civil liberties, explicit critics of dogmatic religion, and *de facto* critics of the monarchy under which they wrote. S remained selectively and critically appreciative of their efforts throughout his life. As his subsequent introduction of the Humean concept of cause and effect indicates, he is unwilling to do more here than to allow the probability of the Encyclopedists' causal connection with the French Revolution. Cf. Paine, *Rights of Man, Writings*, ii. 333-4.

401. *D'Alembert ... Condorcet.* Jean le Rond D'Alembert (1717-83), French mathematician and sceptic, wrote the 'Discours préliminaire' to the *Encyclopédie* (1751); Nicolas-Antoine Boulanger (1722-59), writer on various subjects, including religion, astronomy, and geology, who contributed several articles to the *Encyclopédie*; Jean-Antoine-Nicolas Caritat, Marquis de Condorcet (1743-94), French mathematician, science historian, political and social reformer, who, alone among the more significant Encyclopedists, actively engaged in the French Revolution; other 'celebrated characters' associated with the *Encyclopédie* were Rousseau, Voltaire, Diderot, Montesquieu, Quesnay, and Holbach.

427-8. *Voltaire ... them.* François-Marie Arouet de Voltaire (1694-1778), French *philosophe*, satirist, poet, sceptic, deist, was the 'flatterer' and sometime critic of several contemporary kings and queens. Cf. Paine, *Rights of Man, Writings*, ii. 334. S follows Paine in this context but tends to be harsher on the Encyclopedists, whom both agree had had a mixed effect on France and the Revolution. S's association of Voltaire with Frederic in *The Triumph of Life* (1822; ll. 235-6) suggests that he had in mind Voltaire's fulsome praise of the eighteenth-century Prussian 'demagogue' (variously apostrophized as a Horace, a Catullus, a Maecenas, an Alexander, an Augustus, and even as *Gott-Frederick*), to whom he was not only the 'sage' (ibid. l. 237) but also an inveterate gadfly. Voltaire was to S the greatest among the 'mere reasoners' (so generalized in *A Defence of Poetry*) who dominated pre-Revolutionary French thinking, though also among those whom he implicitly discounts in *On Learning Languages* (ll. 30-3). The side of Voltaire which S most admired is epitomized in the former's anti-Establishment 'Ecrasez l'infame' ('Smash the infamous'—by which he meant superstition in general but most immediately sectarian Christianity), a shibboleth which S put into his early correspondence (to T. J. Hogg, 20 Dec. 1810) and later used as an epigraph to *Queen Mab* (1813). S's statement in *An Address to the People on the Death of the Princess Charlotte* that the French 'should have enjoined a public mourning at the deaths of Rousseau and Voltaire' (ll. 50–1) is in its context a particularly apt Voltairian barb.

429–30. *Rousseau ... heart.* Jean-Jacques Rousseau (1712–78), Swiss/ French philosopher, essayist, and novelist, was for S the only name that redeemed French literature (see *On Learning Languages*, ll. 30–3). S's moral criticism seems directed at Rousseau's *Confessions*, which in 1811 he referred to as 'either a disgrace to the confessor or a string of false-hoods' (to T. J. Hogg, 14 May). While still in Dublin in 1812 S would have found his earlier appraisal implicitly confirmed in a letter of 4 Mar. from William Godwin, who cites Rousseau as an example of an individual who had sacrificed general usefulness by presenting to the world too un-varnished a tale of his heart and mind (Shelley, *Letters*, p. 261 n.). While S came to a more profound, comprehensive, and sympathetic understand-ing of Rousseau in later years (cf. *Letters Written in Geneva*, Letter III, *passim*), his early reservations reappeared in *The Triumph of Life* (1822), where Rousseau, the major speaker of the fragment, is made to reconfess himself as one whose infected heart and impure spirit had produced 'seeds of misery'—unlike, one may conjecture, those seeds of millennial potential which S had hoped to sow among mankind in his 'Ode to the West Wind'.

433. *Helvetius.* Claude-Adrien Helvetius (1715–71) was a thorough-going euthenicist who believed that social and political reform could be brought about only by universal education. In writing to Elizabeth Hitchener (?13 July 1811) S apparently quotes from Helvetius's *Treatise on Man* (trans. 1777): 'Modes of worship differ, they are therefore the work of man—morality is accordant *universal* and uniform, therefore it is the work of God.' S qualifies this by referring morality to the 'Deist's God'. Later (to Godwin, 29 July 1812) he follows some contemporary opinion by ascribing the Baron d'Holbach's *System of Nature* to Hel-vetius, who had in fact heavily influenced Holbach. S would object to Helvetius's hedonistic utilitarianism and to his corresponding emphasis on the principle of self. S's criticism of the French *philosophes* throughout stems largely from his own belief in individual disinterestedness as the essential prerequisite of lasting political reform.

Condorcet. The works of Condorcet which S had in mind were probably his *Essay on the Application of Mathematics to the Theory of Decision-Making* (1785) and his *Sketch for a Historical Picture of the Progress of the Human Mind* (1795), though only the first could have had any precipitating effect on the French Revolution. In the *Speculations on Morals and Metaphysics* S reduces to absurdity an attempt to define a system of morality mathematically, as Condorcet tried to do in the first work (cf. *A Refutation of Deism*, ll. 36–8, 724–31). But elsewhere, particularly in his millennial poems, S identified his belief in man's perfectible nature with the idea of progress which Con-dorcet's sketch contributed to nineteenth-century social thought.

444–6. *Godwin... purposes.* As confirmed by his contemporary letters to Godwin, S's implication seems to be that something was lacking to make Godwin's ideas effective: for S, that something was the association Godwin deplored and S here advocates.

454–6. *a pattern... world. The Revolt of Islam* (1817) was meant to be a 'beau ideal' of the French Revolution.

465–7. *table... morsel.* S persistently and predictably attacks Malthus, though in later life he came to qualify his attacks (at least in his correspondence) with the recognition that Malthus 'is a very clever man, & the world would be a great gainer if it would seriously take his lessons into consideration' (to Peacock, 8 Oct. 1818). Malthus at times dehumanized his arguments by a rather callous rhetoric (cf. *An Essay on the Principle of Population*, London, 1798, 204: 'some human beings must suffer from want... who, in the great lottery of life, have drawn a blank') to which S here calls the attention of his audience, an audience which in S's mind certainly included the occasioner of Malthus's anti-Utopian polemic, Godwin. The following two paragraphs paraphrase and attempt to answer the major thesis of Malthus's essay since, if Malthus is right, then philanthropy is wrong.

487. *6000 years.* The period is arbitrary but probably derived in principle from Thomas Malthus, whom S clearly has in mind (cf. ll. 498–9), rather than from a biblically inferred 4004 B.C. birth date of Adam. In a letter of 8 Mar. 1812 to Godwin S implicitly takes notice of the fact that the Utopian doctrine of a perfectible human society advanced in *Political Justice* was controverted by Malthus's *Essay on the Principle of Population*, which had in effect superseded Godwin's rational optimism with an empirical scepticism concerning the social and economic future of the human race.

497. *winter must come.* Cf. S's 'Ode to the West Wind', l. 70.

542–5. *And I am induced... signification. A Proposal for Putting Reform to the Vote* contains a kindred appeal for ecumenical solidarity. Though S will later specify Catholic emancipation and repeal of the Act of Union as the purposes of this Association, he is really appealing to a condition of mind and emotion rather than to any factional expression of it. Correspondingly, he is less concerned with the ends than he is with the means (cf. ll. 523–5).

562. *meeting.* It seems clear that in early March S still did not intend any quick departure from Dublin.

564. *Lower Sackville Street.* S's Dublin address.

DECLARATION OF RIGHTS

Date: Printed Mar. 1812; distributed Aug. 1812.
Copy-text: 1812 (Huntington Library copy; shelfmark RB 23001).

Locations: PRO, Kew, Surrey (2 copies, HO 42/127 ff. 253, 427); Huntington.

Description: Broadsheet measuring 37.7 cm. × 22.8 cm. (14.8″ × 8.9″); title in large caps above an unnumbered proposition ⟨1⟩, followed by propositions 2–31 centrally numbered with arabic numerals; there is a double line above a concluding paragraph which has an italicized quotation from *Paradise Lost* centred beneath it; laid paper; wm (Huntington, PRO f. 253): posthorn in a crowned cartouche; countermark (PRO f. 427) ?C R | 1809; no author, date, or imprint. The Huntington copy is bound in a later cover which also contains *Proposals for an Association of Philanthropists*; propositions 2, 19, 28 of the Huntington copy are partially underlined in ink; PRO f. 427 is docketed 'Sam¹· Bremridge of Barnstaple | 19th August 1812'; PRO f. 253 is badly torn, with some letters and words obscured or missing. Both PRO copies have been glued to paper backings to prevent further deterioration.

Reprinted: *The Republican*, Sept. 1819; *Miscellanies of the Philobiblon Society*, xii (London, 1868–9); the *Fortnightly Review*, Jan. 1871; MacCarthy, *Early Life*; F; J. (T. J. Wise in *The Ashley Library: A Catalogue of Printed Books, Manuscripts, and Autograph Letters*, 11 vols. (for private circulation: London, 1922–36), v. 55–6, describes a limited edition of fifteen copies, apparently published in 1870.)

The *Declaration of Rights* was printed in Ireland at about the same time and perhaps by the same printer (I. Eton) responsible for one (*Proposals for an Association of Philanthropists*) and probably both of the Irish pamphlets, though, like *An Address, to the Irish People*, it contains no imprint. It appeared as a broadsheet containing thirty-one numbered declarations followed by a more personalized peroration and a defiantly Satanic coda from *Paradise Lost*. Several of its sentences and nearly all of its sentiments appear as well in the pamphlets, particularly in the *Proposals*.

The first reference to it is in a letter written by Harriet Shelley on 17 Mar. 1812 to Elizabeth Hitchener, who is advised to 'Dispense the Declarations', which were sent to her in a box apparently also containing a large number of the undistributed Irish pamphlets (see Shelley, *Letters*, i. 279–80 n.). The box was at least delayed by the Surveyor of Customs at Holyhead, England, and samples of its contents were sent to the appropriate authorities in London (see below). On ?16 Apr. 1812, unaware that his box had been intercepted, S asked Hitchener in a letter to post the *Declaration* on farmhouses, and on 7 May he warned her against letting it 'get into the hands of priests or aristocrats'. The likelihood is, then, that the box did get to Hitchener (minus the confiscated copies) and that its contents were eventually transferred to one of the 'large chests' (so heavy that it took three men to lift them) which S had with him in Lymouth,

Devonshire, in Aug. 1812 (see MacCarthy, *Early Life*, 322); S here followed his own advice to Hitchener by having the *Declaration* posted about the neighbourhood of Barnstaple through the agency of his Irish servant Daniel Healey (or Hill). Healey was promptly arrested for distributing handbills without an imprint and spent six months in prison, somewhat relieved by a weekly allowance of fifteen shillings which S had sent to him in lieu of paying a fine which S could not afford. S himself distributed his broadsheet by the relatively safe if quixotic method of placing it in sealed bottles or small boxes which he then set afloat off the Devonshire coast. Both methods of distribution doubtless contributed to its present-day rarity.

Its form and content derive most directly from comparable declarations adopted by the French National Assembly (1789) and proposed by Robespierre (1793), though countless reiterations of these seminal statements of revolutionary tenets were commonplace in broadsheets, petitions, and radical or liberal publications throughout S's lifetime. A few days before S left for Ireland the *Morning Chronicle* reported a kindred 'bill of rights' emanating from that country (23 Dec. 1811); and the radical publisher Richard Carlile (or 'Carlisle', as S spelt it) reprinted S's *Declaration* itself in the *Republican* (24 Sept. 1819) as part of an outraged public reaction to the Manchester riots (Aug. 1819), during which the rights S sets forth as axiomatic were ruthlessly violated. Historically more influential sources were Thomas Paine (who printed the French Declaration in his *Rights of Man*) and William Godwin, both of whom had provided texts for S to draw on for expansive if sometimes contradictory affirmations of the rights and duties of man which vie for priority in the piece. Also behind the piece is at least a hint of Locke's historical fiction (in the second of his *Two Treatises of Government*) of man's pristine 'state of perfect freedom' qualifying Godwin's rational insistence on man's duty to his fellows as the only right a perfectible being should wish to possess.

As their correspondence indicates, Godwin was clearly the most immediate analogue in S's mind at the time he made up his broadsheet. For Godwin duty, as 'the treatment I am bound to bestow upon others' is active, whereas right, 'the treatment I am entitled to expect from them', is passive (*PJ* i. 148). Since Godwin did not view the exercise of the unmitigated rights of man as either rational or disinterested, he felt it may become licentious and selfish. In the 1793 edition of *PJ* (which S preferred) Godwin refused to allow an unqualified right even to private judgement or to a free press because he regarded the operation of both as a utilitarian duty. Godwin would likewise question the priority and emphasis accorded to a few of the rights S asserts here, though, if he read them closely and sympathetically enough, he could have found reason to accept them as a whole because each of them suggests its complementary duty. S himself might have felt uneasy about Godwin's potential reaction, since he does not seem to have sent him a copy of the *Declaration*. In *On 'Godwin's Mandeville'* (1817) S applauds Godwin for having been the first to found his moral system on the 'negativeness of rights and the positiveness of duties'. However, it was not Godwin but Thomas Paine who provided a direct statement of the symbiotic relationships of rights and duties that S would have most readily approved and perhaps meant to illustrate in his broadsheet: 'A Declaration of Rights is, by reciprocity, a Declaration of Duties also. Whatever is my right as a man is also the right of another; and it becomes my duty to guarantee as well as to possess ⟨it⟩' (Paine, *Rights of Man*, *Writings*, ii. 355). Later, in *Speculations on Morals and Metaphysics*, S comprehended rights and duties under the classical heads of Benevolence and Justice in his unfinished attempt at deriving the elementary principles of both from the mind of man.

The provenance of the present copy-text indicates that it was among the materials seized at Holyhead, then forwarded to Francis Freeling, the postmaster òf the London post office, who in turn sent it to Lord Chicester, the Postmaster-General. He sent it back to Freeling, who kept it until he died. According to MacCarthy (*Early Life*, 309), it was advertised for sale in the 1870 catalogue of a London bookseller (apparently the same one who described his copy of the *Declarations* in *N&Q* (5 Mar. 1870, 246) and purchased by the Right Hon. Chichester Fortescue, who let MacCarthy transcribe it. (The dating here is in doubt, since the broadsheet is referred to in the *Miscellanies of the Philobiblon Society* for 1868–9 as 'purchased at the sale of Sir Francis Freeling's effects, and ... communicated by Mr. Fortescue'.) Some time before 1880 Chichester Fortescue, then Lord Carlingford, let H. B. Forman transcribe it for his edition of S's works. It was purchased by the Huntington Library from John Pearson in the early 1920s. The paper wrapper containing the Huntington copy (along with a copy of the *Proposals*) is inscribed 'Carlingford' and, towards the bottom, 'Inflammatory Irish Papers'. The fact that this latter inscription is noted by MacCarthy as appearing on the copy in the Chichester Fortescue 'collection' establishes the provenance (as far as it can be established) by identifying the Fortescue copy MacCarthy transcribed with the Carlingford copy used by Forman.

Evidence presented by MacCarthy and by William Michael Rossetti (in the *Fortnightly Review* listed below) suggests that three copies of the *Declaration* were sent to the PRO, but both writers agree that (as is presently the case) only two of them were there when they inquired about them in the early 1870s. MacCarthy states that he saw a copy of the *Declaration* at the PRO which had been sent to the Secretary of State by the Holyhead Surveyor of Customs on 30 Mar. 1812. He further states that he saw this copy with a letter from the Surveyor so dated which seems to specify a 'Declaration of rights' among its enclosures (MacCarthy, *Early Life*, 309, 314–15, 320n.). Rossetti (pp. 68–9, 77–8) likewise provides appropriately dated correspondence to confirm his inference that the two copies of the *Declaration* he had apparently seen at the PRO were both sent to Lord Sidmouth (the recently appointed Secretary of State) from Barnstaple in Aug. 1812. The correspondence Rossetti provides indicates that Sidmouth received one of these copies directly from the Town Clerk of Barnstaple, the other, less certainly, via Freeling and/or Chicester. Rossetti's assessment of the provenance of both copies seems essentially confirmed by the PRO's own records, which state that one copy was found floating in a bottle near Milford Haven, the other confiscated from Healey/Hill. The former is clearly f. 253, whose 'present tattered state' is noted in a letter of 14 Sept. 1812 (f. 250) from the Inspecting Commander of Revenue at the Port of Milford and ascribed to 'the dampness of the paper when taken out' of the 'Sealed Wine Bottle' in which it was found 'floating near the Entrance of Milford Haven on 10th Inst.' In any case, one of the PRO copies formed the basis of the inaccurate transcription Rossetti printed in his article in the *Fortnightly Review*. Besides the Huntington and PRO copies, a fourth copy, attached to a copy of *Queen Mab*, was noted in William T. Lowndes's *The Bibliographer's Manual of English Literature*, 2374. It was perhaps this copy which was used for the 1819 reprint noted above, which is accurate except for a misprint of 'we' for 'they' in l. 77. Reference is also made in the correspondence from Barnstaple printed by Rossetti, as well as in John Chanter's *Sketches of the Literary History of Barnstaple*, 56, to other copies which have since disappeared. T reproduces the copy-text, except that a redundant 'time' (l. 32) is omitted, and the 'possessions' of l. 79 is changed from the broadsheet's 'posessions', though this latter represents S's customary misspelling of the word.

Rossetti notes in his article in the *Fortnightly Review* (p. 72) the following correspondences between S's *Declaration* and the numbered declarations by the French Constituent Assembly (c) and by Robespierre (R): 2 (R16); 3 (C2, R2); 4 (C3, R15); 6 (C1, R17); 7 (C8, 9); 9 (C7); 14 (R4, 16); 15 (C5, R5, 6); 21 (C10); 27 (C6, R18); 28 (R11, 12); 29 (R3). As Rossetti says, a few of these parallels are suggestive rather than precise. Peck (*Life and Work*, i. 236–48) includes some of S's other writings, along with those of several other writers, among his sources and analogues.

Related primary and secondary materials: LETTERS (as noted above); PRO documents HO 42/127, fols. 207, 254, 424, 428–9; Paine, *Writings*, ii. 306–7, 350–6; *PJ* i. 148–69, iii. 249–60; W. M. Rossetti, 'Shelley in 1812–13: An Unpublished Poem, and Other Particulars', *Fortnightly Review*, NS 9 (Jan. 1871), 67–72; MacCarthy, *Early Life*, 307–24; Dowden, *Life*, i. 294–9; Percy Vaughan, *Early Shelley Pamphlets* (London, 1905), 24–5; MacDonald, *Radicalism*, 74–5; Peck, *Life and Work*, i. 236–48; Grabo, *Magic Plant*, 82–4; Cameron, *Young Shelley*, 195–201; *SC* vi. 948–9; Dawson, *Unacknowledged Legislator*, 64–5; Scrivener, *Radical Shelley*, 64–5.

1–2. *Government ... own*. Cf. *Proposals*, ll. 253–4 for the most obvious of several correspondences between these works. With varying emphases on rights and duties, the axiom can be found in both Paine and Godwin. A later version of the same sentiment, probably associated with *Speculations on Morals and Metaphysics*, appears in a notebook transcription by Mary Shelley of S's prose manuscripts: 'The institutions, opinions, feelings and habits by which human society is regulated, have no meaning or use, except as they tend to produce the advantage of the individuals of which it is composed' (Bod. MS Shelley adds. d. 6, p. 107).

50. *The present ... posterity*. Cf. Paine, *Rights of Man, Writings*, ii. 278: 'The vanity and presumption of governing beyond the grave is the most ridiculous and insolent of all tyrannies.'

64. *their*. That is, 'the people's'.

67. *Belief is involuntary*. This empirical (and anti-religious) axiom recurs frequently in S's early writings from *The Necessity of Atheism* through to *A Refutation of Deism*.

103. *Awake! ... fallen. Paradise Lost*, i. 330.

A LETTER TO LORD ELLENBOROUGH

Date: June–July 1812.

Copy-text: *1812* (shelfmark Bod. ⟨pr.⟩ Shelley e. 1 (1)).

Description: Undated octavo pamphlet measuring (trimmed) 18.5 cm. × 11.4 cm. (7.3″ × 4.5″), composed of three unsigned gatherings (⟨A⟩⁴ (− A1) ⟨B⟩⁸ ⟨C⟩⁴ (− C4)), which make up a title-page (verso blank), Advertisement (verso blank), drop-head title ('Letter.') and centrally numbered text (⟨1⟩–23; ⟨24⟩ blank); wove paper; WM (5/6, 15/16): 'O ?&P | 1808'; no running heads or imprint. The copy-text title-page is reproduced on page 61. The unique Shelley e. 1(1) copy is bound with *The Necessity of Atheism* (2), *An Address, to the Irish People* (3), and *Proposals for an Association of Philanthropists* (4). There are two changes in ink in the text: 'profess' to 'possess' (l. 202); 'promises' to 'premises' (l. 346).

Provenance: P. B. Shelley; Thomas Hookham; Sir Percy Shelley and Jane, Lady Shelley; Bodleian.

Reprinted: *Shelley Memorials* (portions); *F*; *J*. (An 1883 reprint called 'Shelley on Blasphemy', London, Progressive Publishing Company, uses *F*'s text and much of its headnote; Forman also lists an abridgement, New York, 1879, entitled 'Free Speech and Free Press': *The Shelley Library*, 34; T. J. Wise had a single copy printed for him by Reeves and Turner, 1887.)

On 15 May 1812 Lord Ellenborough sentenced Daniel Isaac Eaton, a radical bookseller, to eighteen months' imprisonment (including pillory time) for publishing a blasphemous libel entitled *The Age of Reason: Part the Third* and ascribed to Thomas Paine. On 11 June S wrote to William Godwin:

> What do you think of *Eaton's* trial & sentence. I mean not to insinuate that this poor bookseller has any characteristics in common with Socrates or Jesus Christ, still the spirit which pillories & imprisons him, is the same spirit which brought them to an untimely end. Still, even in this enlightened age, the moralist & reformer may expect coercion analogous to that used with the humble yet zealous imitator of their endeavours. I have thought of addressing the public on the subject, & indeed have begun an outline of the address. May I be favored with your remarks on it before I send it into the world?

On 18 June he wrote in a letter to Elizabeth Hitchener that he had 'been writing a defence of Eaton.—today I have not coolness enough to go on'. As the epigraph from the *Globe* of 2 July indicates, S had not sent the *Letter* to the printer before that date, but on 29 July he was able to send twenty-five copies of the anonymously printed work to the London publisher Thomas Hookham, whom he had apparently asked to print it before having recourse to a bookseller in Barnstaple, Devonshire, named Syle (see below). Besides the initial twenty-five copies, Hookham seems to have received another fifty (letter to Hookham, 18 Aug.), and according to Harriet Shelley's letter of 4 Aug. to the Shelleys' Irish friend Catherine Nugent copies were sent to Lord Stanhope and to Sir Francis Burdett, as well as to Nugent herself (Shelley, *Letters*, i. 320 n.). Dowden states that additional copies were sent to Lord Sidmouth and 'private friends' (*Life*, i. 291). Except for the copy-text used for this and previous printings of the work, none of the perhaps one thousand copies of the *Letter* is known to have survived, though at least one other must have remained in Harriet's possession to be used as evidence at the 1817 Chancery trial (see p. 410). A transcript in the Brewer Leigh Hunt Collection of the University of Iowa Library was evidently made from an original copy, since it correctly contains the words 'savage' in l. 82 and 'dictated' in l. 391 (printed 'some' and 'directed' in all other published versions).

S's stated reason for delaying his reaction to Eaton's sentencing is that he had hoped a 'fitter' pen would have been wielded not only in a defence of Eaton but also, as the *Letter*'s tone and content demonstrate, in an attack on the repressive governmental policies which Ellenborough's arbitrary handling of the trial had illustrated. S is pointedly defending free speech against the kind of ministerial infringements of it which Robert Southey had declared desirable in a letter written just after Eaton's sentencing: 'nothing but an immediate suspension of the liberty of debate and the liberty of the press can preserve us. Were I a minister, I would instantly suspend the Habeas Corpus, and have every Jacobin journalist confined, so that it should not be possible for them to continue their treasonable vocation' (to J. Rickman, 18 May 1812). Leigh Hunt, doubtless a 'Jacobin journalist' in Southey's sense, printed a letter in the *Examiner* of 5 Apr. which noted, as had Eaton's counsel, that the book-seller was guilty of no crime against established religion which had not already been tolerated in the writings of Hume, Voltaire, and Gibbon. When at the trial on 6 Mar. the Attorney-General argued that whereas 'one man might be injured by the works alluded to, 500 would be by this pamphlet', he implicitly acknowledged the Government's real concern, which was not so much a fear of religious dissent as of potential social unrest, to which earlier in the trial the Attorney-General had linked Eaton's publication (Howell, *State Trials*, xxxi. 955, 958, 929). In fact, portions of Paine's pamphlet quoted at the trial demonstrate that its premisses and purposes were akin to those which S held and probably implemented in the lost *Biblical Extracts* which he later wished Eaton to publish (to Hookham, 17 Dec. 1812): the Bible had no historical truth, the narrative was badly written, but 'the moral is in many parts good' (Howell, *State Trials*, xxxi. 936). S in his *Letter* consistently opposes Lockian equality (in nature and by reason) to the 'priestly and tyrannical domination' he highlights as the anachronistic institution standing in the way of a social benevolence which would eliminate religious intolerance by providing for political justice. When applied to Eaton, overt minis-terial repression such as Southey desired proved counter-productive, as Henry Crabb Robinson noted in his journal entry for 26 May: 'Walked to see D.I. Eaton in the pillory. As I expected, his punishment of shame was his glory. . . . The whole affair was an additional proof of the folly of the Ministers, who ought to have known that such an exhibition would be a triumph to the cause they meant to render infamous' (*Diary, Reminiscences, and Correspondence of Henry Crabb Robinson*, ed. Thomas Sadler, 2nd edn., London, 1869, i. 386).

While S's delayed reaction to Eaton's sentencing added little to the public discomfort of the ministers at the time, before the end of the century the *Letter* had acquired the status of a historical argument in defence of the press. It was twice reprinted during the trials of dissident publishers, in New York (1879, from *Shelley Memorials*) and in London (1883). A literal equivalent of poetic justice occurred in 1840 when *Queen Mab* and its Notes (including parts of the *Letter*) were used by the radicals as a test case to call into question the law of blasphemous libel by which Eaton was punished in 1812 (see Newman I. White, 'Literature and the Law of Libel: Shelley and the Radicals of 1840–2', *Studies in Philology*, 22 (Jan. 1925), 34–47).

The provenance of the unique Bodleian copy suggests that chance rather than intention was involved in its preservation. According to John Roberts Chanter's *Sketches of the Literary History of Barnstaple &c.*,

published in 1866 and used by Denis MacCarthy in *Early Life* (346-8), S commissioned 'Mr. Syle', a printer and bookseller in Barnstaple, to print one thousand copies of the *Letter* under the poet's supervision. When Syle discovered that S's servant Daniel Healey had been arrested for distributing the *Declaration of Rights*, he became alarmed because the pamphlet he had printed 'was quite as seditious' in its tone and contents.

He at once suppressed and destroyed the remaining sheets, and had several interviews with Shelley to endeavour to get back the ones previously delivered, but unsuccessfully, as they had been mostly distributed. One copy came into the hands of Mr. Barry, and was given by him a few years since to Leigh Hunt. (Quoted in MacCarthy, *Early Life*, 348.)

MacCarthy supposed that Hunt gave this copy to Lady Shelley, who then printed it (excluding those parts which also appear in the *Queen Mab* Notes) in her *Shelley Memorials*. Since Hunt did give other Shelleyana to Lady Shelley, the provenance suggested by Chanter and MacCarthy would seem virtually certain were it not that Forman implies that Lady Shelley told him that she used a copy 'preserved by Hookham' (F v. 402). This implication is confirmed by Hookham's endorsement on a front flyleaf of Bod. Shelley e. 1, which states that Hookham received the 'volume' from its author and presented it to Sir Percy F. Shelley in April, 1856. Hogg apparently had access to Lady Shelley's copy, since he quoted the Latin epigraph from the title-page and knew that the pamphlet contained twenty-three pages. His description of it as 'celebrated' seems gratuitous, since the only publicity it had received before he referred to it occurred in relation to the 1817 Chancery trial (*Life*, ii. 128).

There are three later references to Eaton in S's letters, the first of which (to Hookham, 3 Dec. 1812) is fragmentary but probably refers to the possibility of Eaton's publishing the lost *Biblical Extracts*, which is the subject of the other references (to Hookham, 17 Dec. 1812; 2 Jan. 1813). S later characterized Ellenborough when commenting on an address he made to the jury at the trial of John and Leigh Hunt for their famous libel of the Prince Regent: 'so barefaced a piece of timeservingness, that I'm sure his heart must have laughed at his lips as he pronounced it' (to Hogg, 27 Dec. 1812). But, as S states in the letter of 11 June to Godwin, in his published defence of Eaton he is 'addressing the public', with Ellenborough a convenient surrogate for the social and political hierarchy which the *Letter* more comprehensively condemns.

The classical development of the *Letter* helps mark it as the first sustained example of S's mature style, though portions of the *Proposals* also anticipate the rhetorical power and moral fervour which continue to increase in varying combinations through *On Christianity* and *An Address to the People on the Death of the Princess Charlotte* to culminate in the

Defence of Poetry. It often echoes S's early letters, makes direct use of the *Necessity of Atheism* (for which it is a *post factum* defence), and anticipates passages in the *Refutation of Deism* and *On the Devil, and Devils*, while certain of its philosophical inferences may be found in the *Speculations on Morals and Metaphysics*.

The following lines from the *Letter* recur in the *Queen Mab* Note on 'I will beget a Son . . .': ll. 54–7 ('It is ever . . . admission'); ll. 86–93 ('Belief . . . being'); ll. 95–8 ('before . . . life'); ll. 106–10 ('Under . . . humanity.'); ll. 130–6 ('A dispassionate . . . command.'); ll. 241–85 ('The vulgar . . . humility'); ll. 351 ('If . . . convinced'); ll. 360–3 ('Either . . . allow').

T reproduces the copy-text's variant spellings of the same word, largely because S himself used or might have used them, partly because words like 'enquiry' and 'falsehood' were also spelt, even in close contexts, 'inquiry' and 'falshood' by Regency compositors. It may however be noted that from about l. 261, where 'falshood' replaces the spelling 'falsehood' used hitherto, a different compositor was probably at work, one who typically accepted S's usual manuscript spellings.

Related primary and secondary materials: A Letter on Richard Carlisle; Howell, State Trials, xxxi. 927–58; Examiner, Mar.–May 1812, passim (on Eaton); Hogg, Life, ii. 128; Paine, Age of Reason, Writings, iv. passim; Medwin, Life, 469; Shelley Memorials, 35–46; MacCarthy, Early Life, 345–9; J. C. Jeaffreson, The Real Shelley (London, 1885), ii. 107–17; Dowden, Life, i. 288–91; Forman, The Shelley Library, 34; Percy Vaughan, Early Shelley Pamphlets (London, 1905), 26–9; Peck, Life and Work, i. 264–9; Barnard, Shelley's Religion, 32–3; White, Shelley, i. 235–6, 245–8; Hughes, Nascent Mind, 146–52; Cameron, Young Shelley, 203–10; Guinn, Political Thought, 40–1; Dawson, Unacknowledged Legislator, 25, 28; Scrivener, Radical Shelley, 65–6; Hoagwood, Scepticism, 145–7.

TITLE. Lord Ellenborough (Edward Law, 1st Baron; 1750–1818), a conservative minister and chief justice aggressively opposed to free speech, free press, and Catholic emancipation. 'The Third Part of Paine's Age of Reason', so published in 1811 by Eaton, was in fact an abridged version of a 68-page pamphlet published by Paine in New York in 1807 entitled 'An Examination of the Passages in the New Testament . . . called Prophecies concerning Jesus Christ'. The full title and a reprint of the 1807 pamphlet appear in Paine, Writings, iv. 356 ff.

EPIGRAPH. *Deorum offensa, Diis curæ.* 'An offence against the Gods is the concern of the Gods'; slightly varied from Tacitus, Annals, i. 73. The epigraph derives from Wellesley's motion to remove political disabilities from English Roman Catholics (Hansard, xxiii. 820).

25. *By what right . . . Eaton.* The 'right' by which Eaton was punished received its general sanction from Lord Ellenborough's statement that Christianity was the law of the land and had been broken by Eaton when he published a book questioning the historical truth of the Bible, the

divinity of Christ, and the authority of the Gospel writers. Particular precedents for trying Eaton were derived from the reigns of William III and George II. Ellenborough at first attempted to stop Eaton from airing his blasphemy in an oral statement to the court (a practice previously lamented by Lord Eldon) but then rather abruptly decided to let the defendant's own words convict him in the ears of the jury. When the trial was resumed on 30 Apr. Eaton's advocate, Prince Smith, admitted that his client had broken the law as defined and merely asked that the court illustrate its Christian charity by mitigating the sentence (Howell, *State Trials*, xxxi. 953). S probably derived his knowledge of the trial from the liberal press or from Eaton's own account of it, the sale of which was particularly large on 26 May, when he stood in the pillory as a living testimonial to the medieval species of governmental repression he had provoked. It was this aspect of Eaton's punishment that most outraged the liberals and aroused the sympathies of the people.

32-4. *Wherefore ... sincerity.* Cf. Howell, *State Trials*, xxxi. 955: 'The informations of the attorney-general seemed to be so denominated in derision of all knowledge, and were a complete bar to all free inquiry. An answer to this book were rather to have been wished than that it should call down the vengeance of the law.' Cf. also S's comment on the Oxford authorities' reaction to his *Necessity of Atheism* in his letter of 29 Mar. 1811 to Timothy Shelley.

38 n. *By Mr. Fox's bill ... fact.* Before Fox's bill juries were restricted to considering the facts; the judge interpreted and applied the law. S's point is that Ellenborough did not abide by the letter and implications of Fox's bill when he allowed the Attorney-General to interpret the law to the jury.

54-7. *It is ever ... admission.* Cf. *Proposals for an Association of Philanthropists*, ll. 352-8. S repeatedly uses 'coercion' and its variants to define Ellenborough's juridical practice and sanction. Prince Smith (whom S echoes elsewhere in the *Letter*) noted that it 'was quite impossible to maintain the fear of God by force; and religion ceased to be the fear of God when it became the fear of man' (Howell, *State Trials*, xxxi. 954).

59-62. *eagle-eye ... universe!* Cf. *Proposals for an Association of Philanthropists*, ll. 245-8. Other possible echoes of *Areopagitica* in the *Letter* (e.g. ll. 54-7, 141-5) suggest that here, as well as in the *Proposals*, S had in mind Milton's description in that work of the English nation 'as an Eagle mewing her mighty youth, and kindling her undazzled eyes at the full mid-day beam'.

86-93. *Belief ... being?* S first used these empirical axioms in *The Necessity of Atheism*; later in *Queen Mab* as noted above.

98. *life.* In *Queen Mab* S provided a footnote to Locke's chapter on 'Enthusiasm' in the *Essay on Human Understanding* (bk. 4, ch. 19) at this point, but the context there more obviously warrants the reference.

99–100. *If the law ... repealed.* S's use of 'has' is perhaps ironic. As Prince Smith noted, the fact that the *writ de heretico comburendo* (concerning the burning of the heretic) had been abolished demonstrated that the courts had come to distinguish between religion and morality by restricting their jurisdiction to the latter and then only in so far as the public peace was affected (Howell, *State Trials*, xxxi. 953–4).

102. *Smithfield.* A London district in which Protestants were executed during Queen Mary's reign (1553–8).

102–4. *the lash ... Vanini.* René Descartes (1596–1650), French philosopher and mathematician who spent most of his adult life in Holland, did suppress or otherwise qualify his works when they were in danger of arousing the ill will of theologians for their heretical or atheistical tendencies, but it is an exaggeration to suggest that he was driven from his country because of his beliefs or writings. Voltaire was exiled to England, later expelled from the court of Frederick the Great, and was likewise subject to the ill will of theologians, though his satirical wit was as responsible as were his beliefs for his ostracism. Galileo Galilei (1564–1642), Italian astronomer and physicist, was incarcerated by the Inquisition because of his unorthodox views concerning celestial mechanics (e.g. that the earth rotates). Lucilio Vanini (1585–1619) was an Italian freethinker strangled and burnt at the stake for atheism.

113. *lictors.* Roman functionaries who punished offenders according to the will of the magistrates whom they attended.

146–56. *Mr. Eaton... taken place.* See Howell, *State Trials*, xxxi. 928, 958. Eaton himself pointed out that he was the publisher, not the author, of the work in question. He did compose his oral statement to the court, however, which contained the same opinions. S in ll. 146–9 quotes the Attorney-General (Sir Vicary Gibbs) almost verbatim (see Howell, *State Trials*, xxxi. 928–9).

281–2. *resolution... prevailed.* Pontius Pilate found 'no crime' in Jesus but none the less allowed the Jews to crucify him (John 19: 4–16). Had he not, the messianic prophecy could not have been considered fulfilled in Jesus and Christianity in His name would not have existed.

402–6. *I have not ... virtue.* Cf. *The Age of Reason: Part the Third*, in Howell, *State Trials*, xxxi. 936: 'I am not contending with these men upon points of doctrine, for I know that sophistry has always a city of refuge.'

A VINDICATION OF NATURAL DIET

Date: 1813.

Copy-text: *1813* (Huntington Library copy; shelfmark RB 22262).

Locations: BL (2, one in Ashley); Harvard (Houghton); Huntington; Pierpont Morgan; Pf. (2); University of Texas.

Description: Duodecimo pamphlet measuring (trimmed) 15.7 cm. × 9.9 cm. (6.25″ × 3.9″) (the untrimmed Pierpont Morgan copy measures 18.5 cm. × 11.6 cm.) and made up of four gatherings (⟨A⟩² B–D⁶ E⁴), which consist of a half-title (verso blank; ⟨i–ii⟩), title-page (verso blank; ⟨iii–iv⟩), a drop-head title followed by a centrally numbered text (⟨1⟩–39; ⟨40⟩ blank), plus an Appendix (⟨41⟩–43; ⟨44⟩ blank); machine-wove paper; WM 12; no running heads; a printer's slug below 'THE END.' at the foot of p. 43 reads 'SMITH AND DAVY PRINTERS, QUEEN STREET, SEVEN DIALS.' The copy-text title-page is reproduced on page 75. The BL copy lacks the half-title and most of the title-page imprint (torn off); the University of Texas copy lacks the Appendix; the Pf. 'John A. Spoor' copy contains an inked inscription in S's hand: 'To John Grove Esqᶜ. | from the Author'; the Pierpont Morgan copy contains several critical comments on the text. The Huntington copy is followed by 24 pages of advertising for medical texts, which were issued with the *Vindication*, as is indicated by matching stab-holes. Both Pf. copies are followed by 16 pages of similar advertising; the BL (Ashley) and Pf. 'Wise–Forman' copies have WMS 1811, 1812, 1813; the Pf. 'John A. Spoor', Pierpont Morgan, and BL copies have WMS 1811, 1813; the Harvard copy has WMS 12, 1813; the University of Texas copy has only WM 1811. The Pierpont Morgan, University of Texas, and BL (Ashley) copies are in the original wrappers.

Reprinted: F; John Heywood, Vegetarian Society (1884; repr. 1886 by the Shelley Society); J. (The *BLC* lists an annotated 1922 edition by F. E. Worland and a 1947 edition with 'Extracts' from the works of William Lambe: see Wise, *Ashley Library*, v. 59; 'Shelley and Vegetarianism' (see *Related materials*) states that the work was published in *Graham's Magazine* and as an appendix to William Turnbull's *Manual of Health* in 1835.)

A Vindication of Natural Diet might have been composed as early as Nov. 1812 and was apparently published shortly before *Queen Mab*, which contains a Note that, with some variations, reprints the text of *Vindication*. The major reason for supposing that the pamphlet preceded the Note is S's concluding reference to the eight-month period during which he and his wife Harriet had been practising vegetarians (ll. 484–5). They had begun this regimen in Mar. 1812, and the Notes for *Queen Mab* were still being written in the spring of 1813, at which time Thomas Jefferson Hogg considered that S first became a strict vegetarian (*Life*, ii. 82). It was also Hogg's 'impression' that the matter contained in the Note was originally published separately (ibid. 83–4). Internal evidence likewise suggests the priority of the pamphlet: all of the changes in the Note are for the better. S's statement (ll. 277–9) that 'More than two years' had elapsed since a group of sixty persons had begun a vegetable diet which would have lasted 'more than three years' by Apr. 1814 may indicate that the *Vindication* was not composed until the spring of 1813. If S had not cribbed from one of his sources the reference to Thomas Trotter's *A View of the Nervous Temperament* referred to in ll. 391–2, the fact that he ordered this work on 24 Dec. 1812 (letter to Clio Rickman) would suggest a *terminus a quo* of early 1813 for the composition of at least part of the pamphlet. It is clear from the reference to the *Queen Mab* Note on the title-page that, however early S might have composed the *Vindication*, he held off publishing it until he had decided to include it among his Notes to the poem. As indicated, the character of the variations between the *Vindication* and the Note suggests that the pamphlet must have been in print before the Note was put into its final form. However, as the above description indicates, the pamphlet was issued in various bindings, perhaps at different times. (For further evidence that the Note followed rather than preceded the composition of the pamphlet see David Lee Clark, 'The Date and Source of Shelley's *A Vindication of Natural Diet*', *Studies in Philology* (Jan. 1939), 70–6, and Cameron, *Young Shelley*, 408–9.)

S might have been a vegetarian even at Oxford, and he remained one in theory, if not always in practice, throughout his life. The missionary zeal evident in the *Vindication* was probably inspired by his meeting with the vegetarian John Frank Newton in early Nov. 1812. The work itself derives in large part not only from S's stated source in Newton's *The Return to Nature* but also from Joseph Ritson's *An Essay on Abstinence from Animal Food, as a Moral Duty* (London: Richard Phillips, 1802; see Clark, op. cit.).

The *London Magazine and Theatrical Inquisitor* for July 1821 printed an anonymous parody of the *Vindication* (and/or the *Queen Mab* Note), with a few additions which indicate that the author—perhaps T. L. Peacock—was personally acquainted with the poet, his habits, his political and social thinking, and his sources.

Related primary and secondary materials: LETTERS, to E. Hitchener, 14 Mar. 1812, to F. Godwin, 10 Dec. 1812, to T. J. Hogg, 27 Dec. 1812, 22–3 Nov. 1813 (26 Nov. in Shelley, *Letters*), Harriet Shelley to Mrs Nugent, 21 May 1813 (Shelley, *Letters*, i. 367–8 n.), to L. and M. Hunt, 29 June 1817; anon., 'Dinner by the Amateurs of Vegetable Diet', *London Magazine and Theatrical Inquisitor* (July 1821), 31–5 (also in White, *Unextinguished Hearth*, 263–9); Medwin, *Life*, 76, 120; Hogg, *Life*, ii. 81–9; Forman, *The Shelley Library*, 58–60; anon., 'Shelley and Vegetarianism', *Book Lore*, 3/17 (Apr. 1886), 121–32; William E. Axon, *Shelley's Vegetarianism* (Manchester, 1891); Percy Vaughan, *Early Shelley Pamphlets* (London, 1905), 29–32; Grabo, *Magic Plant*, 119–22; White, *Shelley*, i. 298–303, 656–7; Hughes, *Nascent Mind*, 164–5; Cameron, *Young Shelley*, 249–58, 406–10; King-Hele, *Thought and Work*, 41–2; SC iv. 681; Crook and Guiton, *Shelley's Venomed Melody* (Cambridge, 1986), 76–83. (See also the following references in Dunbar, *Bibliography*: 17, 188, 219, 1170, 1171, 1376, 1648.)

EPIGRAPH. S found the lines from Hesiod's *Works and Days* (54–8) in Newton's *Return to Nature* (London, 1811), 12, where they are translated as follows: 'You rejoice, O crafty son of Iapetus, that you have stolen fire and deceived Jupiter; but great will thence be the evil both to yourself and to your posterity. To them this gift of fire shall be the gift of woe; in which, while they delight and pride themselves, they shall cherish their own wickedness.' (If the semicolon after ηπεροπευσασ is understood as a Greek mark of interrogation, the gist of the first sentence should be construed as follows: 'So you're happy that you stole fire and deceived me, are you?' However, it is questionable whether this is the construction intended by the author.)

10–12. *The date . . . correspondence.* Cf. *Queen Mab* Note on VI, ll. 45, 46, where S correlates the moral and intellectual improvement of mankind with the movement of the earth on its axis to a perpendicular position, whereat it will experience an eternal equinox.

19–30. *Immediately . . . rheums. Paradise Lost*, 11. 477–88. Michael (not Raphael) depicts the consequences of the 'inabstinence of Eve', related also to 'Intemperance . . . | In Meats and Drinks'. S probably took the quotation from Ritson's *Essay on Abstinence*, 39.

43–51. *Audax . . . gradum.* 'Bold to endure all things, mankind rushes even through forbidden wrong. Iapetus' daring son by impious craft brought fire to the tribes of men. After fire was stolen from its home in heaven, wasting disease and a new throng of fevers fell upon the earth, and the doom of death, that before had been slow and distant, quickened its pace' (*Odes*, 1. 3. 25–33, Loeb trans.). Newton also uses these lines.

56. *shambles.* A slaughter-house.

72–3. *sink . . . earth.* Cf. *Queen Mab*, 9. 57: 'Mild was the slow necessity of death.'

74. *primus . . . Prometheus.* 'Prometheus was the first to kill a cow'; S derived both the quotation and the source from Newton, *Return to Nature*, 9–10. S here inserts the quotation into a previous context in Newton, which he also modifies in a few minor particulars.

85–8. *But just disease . . . Man.* Alexander Pope's *Essay on Man*, Epistle III, ll. 165–8. The quotation appears in Ritson, *Essay on Abstinence*, at the top of page 56, though S's pointing indicates that he (or the printer) consulted a different text of the poem as well.

121. *Plutarch recommends.* A reference to a passage in Plutarch's essay *The Eating of Flesh*, which appears in its Greek context on p. 117 n.

133 n. 1. The reference to the article on Man in Rees ignores the fact that the entry states that no inference can be made about the vegetable diet as natural to man's inner make-up. All of the Cuvier references are evidently taken from William Lambe's *Reports on Cancer*, 27–31 (see next note).

171 n. The full title of Lambe's book is *Reports on the Effects of a Peculiar Regimen on Scirrhous Tumours and Cancerous Ulcers* (J. Mawman: London, 1809). S is perhaps concerned to distance himself from Lambe's contention in this book that it is unnatural for man to drink water at all (pp. 2–3); the distilled water he recommends is a concession to this 'unnatural habit'.

219. *Muley Ismael.* 1672-1727; Sultan of Morocco, called the Blood-thirsty because of his ruthless treatment of the peoples he conquered.

258-61. *All... youth.* Cf. *The Assassins*, ll. 198-9: 'To live, to breathe, to move was itself a sensation of immeasurable transport.'

277. *April ... statement.* This statement, if issued, has not been discovered.

289-91. *It is from that book... public.* S perhaps omitted this sentence from the Note because so much of both the *Vindication* and the Note derived from Ritson's *Essay on Abstinence*. For a full account of S's use of Ritson (whom he acknowledges in *On the Vegetable System of Diet*) see Clark, 'The Date and Source of Shelley's *A Vindication of Natural Diet*', 72-5.

341-3. *The odious ... republicanism.* The same implicit distinction between a traditional aristocracy and the *nouveaux riches* is made in *A Philosophical View of Reform*.

356-8. *Without disease ... afforded.* While S emotionally despised Malthus's panaceas for a surplus population, he recognized the demonstrated truth of the alternative and 'natural' solution.

359 n. The first part of the note could refer to either of two stays the Shelleys made in Tremodoc, North Wales, where S became involved in completing the embankment which protected the town from the sea (see the concluding portion of Appendix I). He was there both in Sept. 1812 and from mid-Nov. 1812 to late Feb. 1813. The poem by Samuel J. Pratt is entitled 'Cottage-Pictures; or, The Poor' in an 1807 edition of *Sympathy, and other Poems*. It is a decorous social satire which idealizes the relative economic well-being of the rural poor before the advent of the land monopolists and speculators, and hints that famine may drive the labouring class to violence if suggested remedies are not implemented. The specific note S refers to describes the industry of an elderly cottager who, with the help of his wife, tilled a bountiful quarter-acre in Yorkshire.

386. *pure water.* The ultimate source for this addition to the vegetable regimen is William Lambe, who (though suspicious of water-drinking in general) argued in the *Reports* S referred to that distilled water was a cure for cancer.

391-3. *Dr. Trotter... dram.* On p. 323 of an 1808 edition of Trotter's book (Wright *et al.*: Troy, NY), a specific reference is made to 'dram-drinking' and the need for total abstinence. The fully informative title is *A View of the Nervous Temperament: Being a Practical Inquiry into the Increasing Prevalence, Prevention, and Treatment of those Diseases Commonly Called Nervous, Bilious, Stomach and Liver Complaints; indigestion, low spirits, gout, &c.*

419. *lettice.* The last *OED* listing of this spelling (1713) suggests that it was at best obsolescent in S's time.

441. *find his account.* I.e. 'find his profit'.

446 n. *In . . . diseases.* S's figures suggest a specific source, perhaps in a periodical or newspaper.

The quality . . . mainland. The account of Mackenzie's travels of 1790 was published in 1811. The references to Rousseau's *Émile* which conclude the footnote derive from Ritson (*Essay on Abstinence*, 155), who himself had used a 1767 translation of *Émile* which has the references on the pages he notes. The *Émile* reference in n. 4 of the Appendix likewise appears in Ritson (pp. 72–3), though either S or his printer mistranscribed the correct page-number '48' which Ritson gave. When S earlier remarks on the preference children have for pastry and fruit (l. 152), he is again retailing Rousseau via Ritson (p. 49).

449. *foe?* The following matter in the *Vindication* is replaced in the Note by a lengthy Greek quotation from Plutarch's two essays on flesh-eating.

455+. APPENDIX. The first seven names in the longevity list, as well as their footnoted sources, derive from Ritson, *Essay on Abstinence*, 156–7, 148. However, S evidently checked the reference in Ritson to George Cheyne's *An Essay on Health and Long Life* (Edward Gillespy: New York, 1813), because not only is the reference to Old Parr on page 36 (not 62) of the New York edition but in addition Cheyne provides on p. 34 the data for the present list from St Anthony to Rombald (who appears as 'Romualdus' in Cheyne), for which S fails to provide sources. As indicated above on 446 n., the reference to Patrick O'Neale and *Émile* comes from Ritson, who notes that he had found it in Rousseau, who had himself taken it from an 'English newspaper'; 'Elkins' (l. 463) is 'Ekins' in Ritson—S probably fails to provide a source for him because Ritson provides only 'From a newspaper', though also advising, as S duly notes, that his subject had 'dy'd at Coombe in Northumberland'; the note on Aurungzebe paraphrases Ritson. James Easton, whose *Human Longevity* (1799) S used in *Vegetable System*, notes (p. xiv) a Margaret Patten, who died at the age of 137, and is doubtless the same as Ritson's 'Mary'.

While the Appendix does not appear in the Note, it recurs in substance as a footnote in *Vegetable System*, where S rather obliquely acknowledges Ritson as his source.

The titles of the footnoted sources of S's information are not italicized in *1813*.

A REFUTATION OF DEISM

Date: Late 1813–early 1814.

Copy-text: *1814* (Huntington Library copy; shelfmark RB 22752).

Locations: BL (2, one in Ashley); Bodleian; Huntington; Pf.; Pierpont Morgan; Princeton.

Description: Octavo book measuring 22.5 cm. × 13.7 cm. (8.7″ × 5.4″) and made up of eight gatherings (⟨A⟩⁴ B–G⁸ H⁴), which consist of a title-page (verso blank; ⟨i–ii⟩), Preface (⟨iii⟩–v; ⟨vi⟩ blank), errata leaf (verso blank; ⟨vii–viii⟩), a drop-head title ('EUSEBES AND THEOSOPHUS.'), and text ⟨1⟩–101 numbered to the left (verso) and right (recto) of the running heads (= the drop-head title in smaller caps); a blank ⟨102⟩ is followed by a blank leaf; wove paper; WM: W. BALSTON | 1813; a printer's slug below '*FINIS*.' at the foot of p. 101 reads 'London: Printed by Schulze & Dean, 13, Poland Street.' The copy-text title-page is reproduced on p. 93. 'Eusebes' is misprinted as 'Eusebus' in the running head of p. 101. The errata have been entered into the Huntington and BL copies in a hand other than S's, with a marginal query '?n' for '*ever*' on page 53 (l. 522) of the BL copy. This latter copy also contains the names and addresses of Thomas Hookham and Edward Dowden, along with excerpts concerning the *Refutation* from W. M. Rossetti's *Memoir* and T. J. Hogg's *Life*. Mary Shelley entered the errata into the Pf. copy. The Pierpont Morgan copy, which lacks the blank last leaf, is inscribed on the binder's blank at front: 'Given to me by Sir Percy Shelley, Bart, R. Garnett.' Vertical lines have been drawn down the margins of the Huntington copy on pp. 40-1, 81. The Ashley Library copy is described by T. J. Wise as an uncut demy-octavo (9″ × 5½″) with half-title '*A* | *Refutation,* | *&c*' (verso blank; i–ii), title-page (verso blank; iii–iv), Preface (v–vii; viii blank), text 1–101; vi, vii are misnumbered as ii, iii, and the flyleaf is inscribed from Lady Shelley to Stopford A. Brooke, 14 Nov. 1894, Boscombe, with a note indicating that the work had been written after S had been expelled from Oxford. According to Wise, this copy represents an earlier form of the work as otherwise extant. In the later form, the half-title page was omitted and the title-page and Preface put back a leaf to accommodate the errata, which were written into the unique copy by S. The signatures are the same in both issues.

Reprinted: *Theological Inquirer* (Mar., Apr. 1815); *F*; G. W. Foote (Progressive Publishing Company: London, 1890); *J*.

A Refutation of Deism was anonymously published, apparently for private circulation among the *sunetoi* ('intelligent people') of the title-page, in 1814 and probably composed in dialogue form towards the end of 1813. Much of the material is taken directly from the Notes to *Queen Mab* which S had compiled in the spring of that year, while the general subject of God and his attributes received most attention from him in his correspondence with Thomas Jefferson Hogg and Elizabeth Hitchener during 1811 and 1812. The best evidence for supposing that the dialogue was composed in the autumn of 1813 is S's references to his reading in a letter to Hogg of 26 Nov. Tacitus, Cicero, Laplace, Hume, and Plutarch on vegetarianism, all variously drawn on in the *Refutation*, are mentioned as subjects of his recent and continuing studies.

The work was reprinted in two parts in the *Theological Inquirer* for Apr. and May 1815. References to George Cannon, publisher of the *Inquirer*, in Mary Shelley's *Journals* (29 Jan. and 7 Feb. 1815) indicate that S authorized the reprint and was perhaps in some way responsible for several letters to the *Inquirer* (signed 'Mary Anne') purporting to answer the *Refutation* but finally agreeing with it. Since the reprint does not contain all of the errata corrections and does contain a few substantive differences from the 1814 text, one may infer that S's overseeing of the printing was cursory and sporadic. But the fact that he saw fit to reprint it at all—except for the *Declaration of Rights* it was apparently the only one of his prose works reprinted during his lifetime—may indicate that he eventually wished a wider audience for it than that defined in his prefatory note. Part of it (or a draft forming its basis) was converted from dialogue to straight exposition in a fair copy S transcribed into a note-book in 1817 (see headnote to and first Textual Note on *Fragment of 'A Refutation of Deism'*). In Jan. and May 1843 the *Model Republic*, a radical monthly, printed extracts from it (reprinted in 1875 by Arthur Clive as *Scintilla Shelleiana: Shelley's Attitude towards Religion*), and around 1843 George J. Holyoake, a radical atheist, made the *Refutation* a primary authority in his *Paley's Natural Theology Refuted in his Own Words*. Though noting that S did not argue his position with the 'precision and fulness' it required (p. 8), Holyoake seemed to recognize that S had previously made use of Paley's own words to refute both Paley and deism. In 1858 T. J. Hogg, in his *Life of Shelley*, printed the paragraph on vegetarianism (ll. 784–99). In providing retrospectively what may be considered the only contemporary notice the original publication received, he indicates that he somehow knew that the work was composed and printed 'in a hurry':

> The year 1814 had come upon us. In that year—and at the beginning of that year, I think—Shelley published a work entitled *A Refutation of Deism: in a Dialogue*. It is handsomely, expensively, and very incorrectly printed, in octavo. It was published in a legal sense, unquestionably; whether it was also published in a publisher's sense, and offered for sale, I know not, but I rather think that it was: the preface informs us that it was intended it should be. I never heard that anybody bought a copy; the only copy I ever saw is that which my friend kindly sent to me: it is inscribed by his own hand on the title page: 'To his friend, T. Jefferson Hogg, from P.B.S.' I never heard it mentioned any further than this, that two or three of the author's friends told me, that it had been sent as a present.... It is written in his powerful, energetic, contentious style, but it contains nothing new or important, and was composed and printed also, in a hurry. He never spoke of it to me, or in my presence. It attracted no attention; and doubtless Shelley himself soon discovered that it did not merit it. (ii. 119–20)

Both the 1815 reprint and the fragmentary fair copy of 1817 suggest that S felt the work merited more consideration than Hogg allowed it, though it is demonstrably true that its form and content were unoriginal—Hume's *Dialogues Concerning Natural Religion* and Cicero's *De natura deorum* provided major sources on both counts. As S's footnotes indicate, William Paley, the leading exponent of deism and/or natural religion during the late eighteenth century, is the other major author the poet uses (and abuses) in the *Refutation*. Thomas Paine, John Locke, other works by Hume, the Baron d'Holbach (*System of Nature*), the Marquis de Laplace, William Drummond (whose *Academical Questions* contains a dialogue on natural religion very much like S's), probably George Ensor, and contemporary periodicals provided further ammunition in the war against deism which S was ostensibly waging. Since by 1814 deism's refutation had been generally admitted—at least among the knowledgeable élite S purports to address—the dialogue might have been ulteriorly meant as a political trial balloon, sent up to ascertain whether the publishing of what in large part could have been construed as a 'blasphemous libel' would escape legal pursuit by an 'iron-souled Attorney-General', in grudging deference to its stated purpose and to its formal precedent in Hume, which had not been legally challenged. S's more specific purpose is to reiterate the grounds for a refutation of orthodox Christianity in the body of the text, while in his earlier footnotes he selects passages from the Old Testament which illustrate the immorality of the religion on which Christianity was based—an invidious use of the Bible which T. J. Hogg had employed when writing to an unnamed correspondent at about the time he and S were expelled from Oxford (cf. Bod. MS Don. e. 180, fols. 10ʳ-12ᵛ). It should be noted, however, that in keeping with the general tenor of the philosophical dialogue since Plato, S does not allow his sceptical mode to degenerate into a perfunctory dogmatism at the conclusion of the piece.

S himself wrote to the poetess Janetta Phillips in May 1811 that he had once been 'an enthusiastic Deist, but never a Christian'. His correspondence with Hogg and Hitchener indicates that in 1811 he was prepared to argue not only for a 'soul of the universe' and the 'existing power of existence' but also for a benevolent agency at work in the universe and, in some essential form, for a future state. While he would pronounce himself on occasion a devotee of reason, he would also allow (following Hume) that feeling could overturn the dictates of reason, even to the extent of inspiring a belief in an orthodox deity in those whose feelings were intense enough to so affect (or perhaps infect) their will. As late as 1819, in his *Letter on Richard Carlisle*, S seems willing to place himself (and perhaps Christ) among the deists, but his deliberately indiscriminate use of the term in this work is clearly a rhetorical gesture of defiance rather than a meaningful definition of his or anyone's religious professions.

A continuing problem during the eighteenth century was to pin down a precise definition of deism. S felt Southey's Christianity, which denied Christ's unique divinity, the inspiration of the Gospel writers, and the

Trinity, to be as clear a definition of deism as he could suppose (to Hitchener, 26 Dec. 1811). For some it was synonymous with atheism in so far as it questioned or seemed to question Christian revelation. S himself, in defining Leigh Hunt's deism, found it to be another name for atheism (to Hogg, 8 May 1811). For others it included the beliefs of those who set aside revelation and accepted only natural religion. While allowing the possibility of a revelation, Paine called the Old and New Testament accounts of it an 'imposition on the world' and deism 'the only true religion'. In *The Age of Reason* he further defines the latter as a belief in a moral God, the practice of the moral virtues, and a rationale for immortality (Paine, *Writings*, iv. 167, 315–16). For still others—such as Paley—it was implicitly identified with a natural theology which confirmed revelation. As late as 1843 Holyoake (*Paley Refuted*, 21) defined two kinds of deists: those who consider God a person and those who consider him a principle. While S suggests, before his dialogue starts, what his own theoretical definition of a deist is, Theosophus and Eusebes are not obliged to confine their arguments for and against deism within the bounds of that definition. Since philosophers as various as Hobbes, Shaftesbury, and Hume could be and were defined as deists, the only essential characteristic of a polemicist so denominated seems to have been his use of reason to pronounce on the truth or falsity of religious doctrine and the reputed facts connected with its origin and propagation.

In his prefatory note to the *Refutation* S identifies deism with the 'mode of defence adopted by Theosophistical Christians', and he supposes that this defence injures 'the cause of natural and revealed religion'. It is thus clear that, for rhetorical purposes at least, he distinguishes a presumably acceptable natural religion from deism by pejoratively associating the latter with mystical intuitions about God's relation to nature found in theosophists and quasi-theosophists from Plotinus thrugh to Jacob Boehme, Emanuel Swedenborg, and probably William Paley, who in his *Natural Theology* finds design, contrivance, adaptability, and organization in nature as evidence confirming a Christian revelation which both transcends these proofs and renders them unnecessary to the initiate. It is also clear from the work itself that through Eusebes S is opposing the 'argument from design' to prove the existence and attributes of the Christian God. In so far as he is certainly speaking through Theosophus, he is also about his customary business of refuting the Judaic-Christian revelation. While S's other writings may be adduced to support the contention that he is also advancing the cause of atheism while undermining both deism and Christianity, the dialogue itself, in keeping with its precedents in form and content, concludes with a suspension of belief and disbelief which, as noted, deliberately avoids any species of dogmatism. Here as elsewhere, the practical thrust of S's argument is at least as much moral and ethical as it is ontological and theological. The formal and substantive merit of the argument suffers (and was perhaps meant to suffer) from a failure to explore dialectically rather than merely take over from earlier philosophers the terminology of deism—'design', 'contrivance', 'order', 'power', and their standard contexts of definition and predication. The need for more stringent terminological accountability is perhaps most apparent when the theosophistic Theosophus advances an argument *from* design (ll. 586–95)—i.e. as an unarguable datum—and the empiricistic Eusebes counters with an argument *to* design (ll. 616–22)—i.e. as the contention to be proved. Given S's other relevant writings (particularly his early correspondence), his position could be either one or neither. The EC, while including and supplementing significant sources and analogues noted by previous editors and commentators, demonstrates most of all that the *Refutation* is primarily a well-articulated but not very well defined or subtly developed synthesis of much that had been thought and said several times over on the subject of deism and related topics by writers whom S made use of for his own propaganda purposes, which were not necessarily those intended by his sources. Like virtually all of the prose S published in his lifetime, the dialogue is intended to propagate derivative points of view rather than to originate a novel perspective or even to add substantively to the views so propagated.

Among the copies of the original edition of the *Refutation* yet extant, the most intriguing is the one in the Ashley Library described by T. J. Wise (in both his Ashley Library volumes and *A Shelley Library*) as a first issue containing a half-title but no errata list (errata entered by S). Dowden (*Life*, i. 399 n.) describes the more interesting of the two copies of the work he once owned (now in Pf.) as also containing errata written into the margins by S; but the hand is actually Mary Shelley's. Dowden's other copy is at the BL, and was once owned by S's publisher Thomas Hookham, apparently one of the two or three friends to whom, according to Hogg, S gave a copy of the work. The location of Hogg's copy, which he said was inscribed to him from the author, is unknown.

Related primary and secondary materials: LETTERS, to Hogg, 20 Dec. 1810, 3, 6, 11, 12, 14 Jan. 1811, to Timothy Shelley, 6 Feb. 1811, to Hogg, 24, 26, 28 Apr., 8, 17 May 1811, to E. Hitchener, 5, 11, 20, 25 June 1811, 2 Jan. 1812, to Hogg, 26 Nov. 1813; *Fragment of 'A Refutation of Deism'* (see p. 241); Bod. MS Don. c. 180, fols. 10–12, 43–5; Cicero, *De natura deorum*; John Leland, *A View of the Principal Deistical Writers that Have Appeared in England in the Last and Present Century: With Observations upon them, and Some Account of the Answers that Have Been Published against them; in Several Letters to a Friend* (2 vols., London, 1808; originally published 1754–6); Soame Jenyns, *A View of the Internal Evidence of the Christian Religion* (London, 1776); David Hume, *Dialogues Concerning Natural Religion* (1779); Paley, *Evidences*; id., *Natural Theology: Or, Evidences of the Existence and Attributes of the Deity, Collected from the Appearances of Nature* (1813; first published 1802); Paine, *The Age of Reason, Writings*, iv. *passim*; William Drummond, *Academical Questions* (1805), ch. IV; Hogg, *Life*, i. 184, ii. 119-20; Bertram Dobell, 'Shelleyana', *Athenaeum*, 2993 (7 Mar. 1885), 313 (first to note the *Theological Inquirer* reprint); J. C. Jeaffreson, *The Real Shelley* (London, 1885), ii. 208-9; Forman, *The Shelley Library*, 60-2; Grabo, *Magic Plant*, 123-9; Notopoulos, *Platonism*, 323-5; White, *Unextinguished Hearth*, 45-6, 395; Louise Boas, '"Erasmus Perkins" and Shelley', *MLN* 70 (June 1955), 408-13 (an account of S's relations with the *Theological Inquirer*); White, *Shelley*, i. 409-11, 696-7; Hughes, *Nascent Mind*, 243-4; Cameron, *Young Shelley*, 302-16, 442-8; Pulos, *Deep Truth*, 91-7; Clark, *Shelley's Prose*, 5-11; Wasserman, *Critical Reading*, 12-15; Hoagwood, *Scepticism*, 28-62; Hogle, *Shelley's Process*, 34-9.

TITLE-PAGE. ΣΥΝΕΤΟΙΣΙΝ. 'To the intelligent/wise.' If this dedication or directive is not entirely ironic, it may correlate with S's apparent concern below that the 'multitude' might be misled by the form of the argument. The *sunetoi* probably made up the 'reflecting part of the community' whose virtuous life put them beyond the need or the restraints of religion (to Hogg, 24 Apr. 1811) and 'the learned' among whom (as S wrote to Janetta Phillips, 16 May 1811) he had distributed *The Necessity of Atheism*. Notopolous traces the word to Pindar's *Olympian Odes*, 2. 85 (*Platonism*, 370).

2-3. *It is attempted ... Christianity*. The dilemma, perhaps ironically intended, is like the one with which Paley introduces his *Evidences*: 'the question lies between this religion ⟨Christianity⟩ and none' (i. 1).

8. *Theosophical*. The *OED* selects S's usage here as its first example of a disparaging variant of 'Theosophistic'. S's purpose is to associate the deist's rationalization of God's being and attributes from his observable effects in nature with the alchemico-mystical divinization of nature found in writers such as Paracelsus and Boehme.

15-16. *liable ... novelty*. While this justification is itself a species of irony meant to disarm the anticipated outrage of the orthodox Christian, it serves as well to alert the reader to S's use of a rhetorical tactic derived not only from the tradition of the inconclusive dialogue from Plato through to Dryden and Hume but, in variant form, from contemporary trials for blasphemous libel, wherein a defendant repeated the offensive libel as a necessary part of his defence, much to the irritation of the prosecution and the Lord Chancellor. S himself contrived to emulate this latter practice in *A Letter to Lord Ellenborough* and *A Letter on Richard Carlisle*. Here, in refuting deism, he is also pointing up the absurdity of the prevalent Judaic-Christian doctrine one partner in his dialogue ostensibly defends and the other seems finally willing to accept in lieu of at least one species of atheism—the kind that would deny the Christian versions of God's being and attributes.

TITLE. 'Eusebes' = 'pious' or 'religious'; 'Theosophus' = 'one who is knowledgeable or clever about the gods'. Since *A Refutation of Deism* appears only on the title-page and 'Eusebes and Theosophus' is the running head throughout the work, Forman supposes (F, vi. 35) that S might have intended this as a title either for the whole of this dialogue or for part of an originally projected longer dialogue with a number of participants. While the names by themselves would hardly have served as a sufficiently informative title, the conclusion of the dialogue does allow for a possible continuation. Analogues in S's reading and in his correspondence could have provided precedents and matter for further argumentation.

33-6. *The antient ... veracity?* The realization of Old Testament prophecy in the New Testament, the miracles which demonstrated the truth of the Christian doctrine, and the martyrs who seemingly had nothing in this world to gain by suffering *in extremis* for their beliefs were among the staples of an eighteenth-century Christian apologetics more or less subsumed under the so-called 'four ⟨later eight⟩ marks' or criteria establishing the unique truth of the Christian religion, the only religion whose attesting miracles were publicly performed for all to see and whose memorials (such as baptism and the Lord's Supper) continue to the present day (see 420-2EC). S could have found such criteria advanced in the works by William Paley (for whom the great miracle demonstrated in nature was resurrection) which he cites in footnotes *passim* below. Eusebes' historical and moral arguments throughout his introductory statement are hackneyed, as S's prospective audience among the *sunetoi* would have recognized. Many of Paley's arguments later advanced or refuted by Eusebes and Theosophus—particularly those relating to design and contrivance—had already been answered in Hume's *Dialogues*, a work which Paley therefore found it convenient to ignore. See S's *An Answer to Leslie's 'A Short and Easy Method with the Deists'* and EC.

37. *mathematical demonstration.* The *Quarterly Review* for Jan. 1818 (p. 328) quoted an unnamed source as stating that S had been expelled from Oxford for a 'mathematical demonstration of the non-existence of a God'. An unpublished letter in the Bod. MS Don. c. 180 correspondence (see the headnote to *The Necessity of Atheism*) states that T. J. Hogg (and S) wanted the truth of established religion proved 'like a problem in Euclid' (Robert Clarke to John Hogg, 13 Aug. 1811, fol. 51ʳ).

57 nn. *Suetonius.* The first (inexact) quotation is from the *Life of Claudius*, 25. 4, translated in Clark, *Shelley's Prose*, 357, as 'The Jews, who rioted at the instigation of Chrestus, were easily suppressed'; S probably found it in garbled form in one of his sources. S found the second quotation (from the *Life of Nero*, 16. 2) in Paley, *Evidences*, i. 43, where it is translated as follows: 'The Christians, a set of men of a new and mischievous (or magical) superstition, were punished.'

Pliny. S found this abridged quotation in Paley, *Evidences*, i. 46-7, where it is thus translated: 'There are many of every age and of both sexes;—nor has the contagion of this superstition seized cities only, but smaller towns also, and the open country.' The quotation is from Letter 10. 96, to the emperor Trajan.

Tacitus. From *Annals*, 15. 44: 'Therefore, to scotch the rumour, Nero substituted as culprits, and punished with the utmost refinements of cruelty, a class of men, loathed for their vices, whom the crowd styled Christians. Christus, the founder of the name, had undergone the death penalty in the reign of Tiberius, by sentence of the procurator Pontius Pilatus, and the pernicious superstition was checked for a moment, only to break out once more, not only in Judaea, the home of the disease, but in the capital itself, where all things horrible or shameful in the world collect and find a vogue. First, then, the confessed members of the sect were arrested; next, on their disclosures, vast numbers were convicted, not so much on the count of arson as for hatred of the human race. And derision accompanied their end: they were covered with wild beasts' skins and torn to death by dogs; or they were fastened on crosses, and, when daylight failed were burned to serve as lamps by night. Nero had offered his Gardens for the spectacle, and gave an exhibition in his Circus, mixing with the crowd in the habit of a charioteer, or mounted on his car. Hence, in spite of a guilt which had earned the most exemplary punishment, there arose a sentiment of pity, due to the impression that they were being sacrificed not for the welfare of the state but to the ferocity of a single man' (Loeb trans.; Paley also translates the passage, *Evidences*, i. 40–1).

57. *Lucian*. S probably cribbed this reference from a note in Paley (*Evidences*, i. 110 n.) to Lucian's *De morte Peregrini*, which is particularly concerned with emphasizing the contempt of life and suffering demonstrated by the early Christians.

71. *The morality . . . original*. S consistently denied the originality of what he regarded as the truly moral portions of the Christian religion. While Theosophus will later ridicule the patience and passivity Eusebes defines as uniquely Christian virtues, S himself elevated them to the 'sublime' in *Prometheus Unbound* and throughout most of his adult life preached against violence and revenge as a means of righting social and political wrongs. However, his early contacts with particular exponents of 'Christian mildness' led him at times to deride it (cf. letter to Hogg, 12 May 1811). At vol. ii, pp. 27–8, of *Evidences* (1811) Paley states that he could as well transcribe into his text everything that has been said on the morality of the Gospel by the author of *Internal Evidence* (see S's note) 'because it perfectly agrees with my own opinion'. Neither Paley nor S names the author, Soame Jenyns, whose book, published in 1776, went through at least ten editions before the turn of the century. Eusebes not only follows Paley's summary of the opposition *Internal Evidence* establishes between the popular virtues (friendship, patriotism, courage)

and Christian humility but uses Paley's very words when describing the heart 'quick in sensibility' (see Paley, *Evidences*, ii. 28). In *On Christianity*, as in his political writings, S recommends the passive resistance which Theosophus implicitly ridicules (ll. 348–56), though he would not accept as its corollary the 'passive submission to the will of sovereigns' which Eusebes (like Paley) advocates. S would, however, agree perfectly with the conclusion from *Internal Evidence* that if the Christian virtues were universally practised as well as preached 'the world would be a society of friends' (Paley, *Evidences*, 30).

77–81. *Friendship . . . vices.* S's point here is that Christianity (as defined by Eusebes) denies the essentially human (and classical) virtues. When one compares Eusebes' trite and superficial defence of Christianity here with his devastating (though hardly original) attack on it later, it becomes clear in retrospect that S intended him to serve as his double agent from the start.

82. *Theist.* Eusebes here uses the term comprehensively to include Christians like himself and deists like Theosophus. Later (ll. 95 ff.) he uses 'Theists' to mean monotheists who denied or did not require revelation. A deistic theist, he implies, should accept the Christian revelation as in accordance with reason. Eusebes' logic is deliberately flawed here and toward the end of the paragraph, where begged questions, circular arguments, and false dilemmas condition the fading substance of the rationale S allows him to present.

86 n. 2. S's reference is probably to the first sentence of the 'Preparatory Considerations' in Paley's *Evidences*: 'I deem it unnecessary to prove that mankind stood in need of a revelation, because I have met with no serious person who thinks that, even under the Christian revelation, we have too much light, or any degree of assurance which is superfluous' (i. 1).

93 n. 3.. *Imperfectæ . . . vocamus.* The Loeb translation of this passage from Pliny's section on God (2. 5. 27) is as follows: 'But the chief consolations for nature's imperfection in the case of man are that not even for God are all things possible—for he cannot, even if he wishes, commit suicide, the supreme boon that he has bestowed on man among all the penalties of life, nor bestow eternity on mortals or recall the deceased, nor cause a man that has lived not to have lived or one that has held high office not to have held it—and that he has no power over what is past save to forget it, and (to link our fellowship with God by means of frivolous arguments as well) that he cannot cause twice ten not to be twenty or do many things on similar lines: which facts unquestionably demonstrate the power of nature, and prove that it is this that we mean by the word "God"'.

The Lucretius quotation, from *De rerum natura*, 1. 146–50, is translated in the Loeb edition as follows: 'This terror of mind therefore and this gloom must be dispelled, not by the sun's rays or the bright shafts of day, but by the aspect and law of nature: and her first principle we will derive from this, that no thing is ever by divine power produced from nothing.'

The Euripides passage (which precedes the Lucretius excerpt in *1814*) makes up a large portion of the extant fragments of the lost tragedy *Bellerophon*. It reads as follows in a late eighteenth-century translation:

> Doth any man assert that there are Gods
> In Heaven? I answer there are none: let him
> Who contradicts me, like a fool, no longer
> Quote antient fables; but observe the fact,
> Nor to my words give credence. Kings, I say,
> Kill many, but rob more of their possessions,
> And violating every sacred oath,
> Lay waste whole cities; yet, tho' they act thus,
> Are more successful far than they who lead
> In constant piety a tranquil life.
> And I have known small cities, who revere
> The Gods, made subject to unrighteous power,
> Vanquish'd by spears more numerous. But I deem
> Should any sluggard 'mong you pray to Heaven,
> Nor earn by his own labor a subsistence,
> He soon would learn whether the Gods are able
> To shield him from calamitous events.

(*The Nineteen Tragedies and Fragments of Euripides*, trans. Michael Wodhull, four vols., Thomas Payne and Son: London, 1782, iv. 253–4.) The translator notes that 'this Atheistical language ⟨is⟩ not ill-suited to Bellerophon, who'd been badly treated by Gods' (p. 254).

102 n. *See ... Deorum*. There is nothing in this work of Cicero's concerning the magistrates' indifference to the being of God. References to the inconsistencies of the rational theism of Anaxagoras, Pythagoras, and Plato appear in i. 26–30; the superstitions of the multitude are disparaged *passim* (cf. on ll. 928–30).

113–14. *suffrage ... world*. The accepted forefather of English deism, Lord Herbert of Cherbury (1583–1648), initially proposed universality as one of the external characteristics of religious truth.

121. *vain philosophy*. Like Hume in his *Dialogues*, S reiterates this phrase (cf. l. 742, and also Coleridge's 'vain Philosophy's aye-babbling spring', 'The Aeolian Harp', l. 57; see also 223 n.EC).

123–32. *Reflect ... justice*. The appeal to self-interest, the insistence on belief as a matter of volition, the equation of God's justice with vengeance appropriately inflicted on those who do not believe, and the officiously disingenuous exhibition of Christian charity following all conspire to set up Eusebes as a rather hollow-headed straw man for Theosophus' counter-statement. As noted earlier, the simplistic establishment position Eusebes assumes here is meant to be set off retrospectively against the much stronger position he adopts as devil's advocate after Theosophus has advanced his own (derivative) case for deism while in the process of demolishing Eusebes' arguments. According to Hogg, the young S occasionally used a comparable stratagem while at Oxford (see Hogg, *Life*, i. 164–5).

156–7. *But truth ... ideas*. This empirical definition of truth, recurrent in S, separates volition and morality from epistemology and grounds Theosophus' subsequent (Godwinian) invitation to Eusebes to rescue him from his errors by rational argument rather than simply condemn them as sins. Much of Theosophus' condemnation of the Judaic-Christian testaments and practices rests on moral grounds.

178–487. *You believe ... clear?* Theosophus' biblical paraphrases and criticisms derive from Hume, Holbach, Paine, from their disciples and propagators (such as Daniel Eaton, whom S defended in *A Letter to Lord Ellenborough*), and from S's previous use of them in his Notes to *Queen Mab*. Clark, *Shelley's Prose*, 121 ff., cites several specific sources and analogues in major eighteenth-century writers, but, as the number and currency of these sources indicate, the rational absurdities and moral paradoxes Theosophus highlights had by then become part of the set of ideas already assumed to be exploded by the readership whose attention S was soliciting.

191–2. *In creating ... creatures*. Theosophus echoes Paley's premiss: 'the Deity, when he formed ⟨the universe⟩ consulted for the happiness of his sensitive creation' (*Evidences*, i. 2); however, contrary to Theosophus, Paley then advances the usual justification for the moral providence God designed for man, who had 'received faculties from his Maker, by which he is capable of rendering a moral obedience to his will, and of voluntarily pursuing any end for which he has designed him' (ibid.). As noted elsewhere, S's selective use of his sources often eliminated and sometimes reversed their major premises and conclusions.

223 n. 1. *Hobbes*. S's immediate source might well have been the comparable dialogue in Drummond's *Academical Questions*: 'If a man do an act of injustice, that is, an act contrary to the law, God, you say, is the prime cause of the law, as well as of all actions whatever, but no cause at all of the injustice, which is the inconformity of the action to the law. This is vain philosophy. You might as well say, (continues Hobbes, in whose language I am now speaking,) that one man makes a straight line and a crooked one, and that another makes their incongruity' (p. 275). The Hobbesian parable appears as well in Montesquieu's *Persian Letters*.

224–34. *Barbarous ... perfidies*. In keeping with the syncretic writers of the late eighteenth and early nineteenth centuries but contrary to their usual purpose and conclusions (to establish the priority and superiority of the Christian tradition), Theosophus implies a genetic kinship between the Judaic-Christian God and the various anthropomorphic deifications of the negative passions of primitive man. Later (in *A Defence of Poetry*) S implicitly alluded to the evidence he adduces here when he pointed out that mankind traditionally deified his vices.

231 n. 2. *Le Bon Sens*. An abridgement of Holbach's *Système de la Nature* published in Amsterdam, 1772, and subtitled 'ou Idées naturelles opposées aux idées surnaturelles'.

244 n. 1. *See Hosea*. The references here and later (sometimes supplemented with generous quotations) suggest that S had not only compiled a selection of moral excerpts from the Bible which he intended to publish as *Biblical Extracts* (see letters to Hitchener, 27 Feb. 1812, to Hookham, Nov. 1812) but also (and perhaps at the same time) a selection of immoral extracts from the same source. S evidently felt that notes were appropriate and relatively safe repositories of controversial materials (see letters to Hookham, 26 Jan. 1813, Mar. 1813).

Ezekiel. The reference here should perhaps be to ch. 15, not 16. The Latin quotation appears in Heyne's introductory 'argument' to Eclogue 4 (known as 'Pollio'): 'Horace indeed recalls the superstition of the Jews but only so that he might explode it by ridicule'; the reference is to Horace's *Satires*, 1. 5. 100–1, and their context. *1814*'s '*quidem*' is not in the 1793 edition of C. G. Heyne's Virgil (4 vols., T. Payne *et al.*: London).

248. *chief*. Moses.

249–51. *God . . . cart*. This seems to be a conflation of Exod. 25: 10 and 1 Sam. 6: 8. In William Drummond's *Oedipus Judaicus* (which S referred to in a letter to Hookham, 26 Jan. 1813), along with much else which is reductively critical of the Old Testament, the God of the Jews is described as 'a material and local god, who dwelt on a box made of Shittim wood' and was quarrelsome, vindictive, jealous, etc. (pp. vi–vii).

250. "*two . . . wide*". S reverses l. 33 of the 1798–1815 version of 'The Thorn', which reads: 'three feet long and two feet wide'.

258 n. 4. *violation*. The last line of this note reads 'three thousand', not 'twenty three thousand', in Exod. 32: 28. The following note (from Numbers) elides a few verses of 31: 7–18.

283–4. *Ferretne . . . deliquisset?* Cicero, *De natura deorum*, 3. 90: 'Would any state tolerate a law-giver who should enact that a son or grandson was to be sentenced for the transgression of a father or a grandfather?' (Loeb trans.). Cf. Ezek. 18, *passim*, where the Lord is concerned with confuting the proverb 'The fathers have eaten sour grapes and the children's teeth are set on edge' by variously asserting that the sins of the fathers would not be visited on the sons.

314–16. *what salutary . . . enlighten?* S consistently emphasized the negative practical effects of Christianity, though in less invidious contexts distinguishing from them the moral exempla offered by Christ in his parables, which, along with their summary formulations in the beatitudes, doubtless made up the substance of the lost *Biblical Extracts* and are to some degree incorporated or intimated in *On Christianity*.

320. *I come not ... sword*. Matt. 10: 34.

333–4. *worth ... fruit*. Matt. 7: 17, 12: 33.

344. *If this claim be just*. For the sake of the present argument, S allows Theosophus to grant the assumption; S himself derived the better part of Christian morality from the Greeks.

348–52. *The doctrine ... purposes*. S (as in *Prometheus Unbound*) generally regarded forgiveness, meekness, and kindred Christian virtues as most likely to effect the eventual salvation of mankind in this world. Theosophus is therefore less discriminatingly critical of Christian morality than S would be *in propria persona*.

361–2. *A total ... enjoined*. Like Blake, S was consistently critical of religious tenets which made woman's love a sin. Cf. *A Philosophical View of Reform*, where S concludes that advocacy of sexual abstinence, the real thrust of Malthus's doctrine of 'moral restraint' as a means of controlling population growth, was the sort of advice to be expected from a priest and eunuch.

373–9. *I am willing ... religion*. Theosophus' admission was presumably fundamental to S's lost *Biblical Extracts* (see letter to E. Hitchener, 27 Feb. 1812).

380. *Belief ... demerit*. Along with ll. 384–94, this empirical and amoral rationalization of belief is recurrent in S's early writings. Cf. *The Necessity of Atheism*, 17–22, *A Letter to Lord Ellenborough*, 86–93, and the Notes for 'There is no God' and 'I will beget a son' in *Queen Mab*. While rational criteria of 'intensity of belief' and 'degrees of excitement' are implied here, in *A Defence of Poetry* (also 'Hymn to Intellectual Beauty' and 'Mont Blanc') imagination and feeling replace them.

402–5. *Every case ... false*. The empirical attack on miracles here and in the following lines derives from Hume and in general outline appears in the assessment of 'testimony' in *The Necessity of Atheism*, 63–8. Perhaps because Paley (in *Evidences*, i. 6–9) had provided a plausible answer to Hume's appeal to universal experience as an argument against miracles by noting that miracles are rare and therefore not subject to such a criterion, S merely argues the relative improbability of the events and the corresponding unreliability (and implicit vested interests) of the witnesses adduced. *An Answer to Leslie's 'A Short and Easy Method with the Deists'* contains a more extensive refutation of miracles, which includes a refutation of the reciprocal support Christian miracles and Christian doctrine were supposed to provide each other.

410. *twelve old women*. S in a letter of 6 Feb. 1811 to his father compared the testimony of the twelve apostles to the testimony of twelve men who claimed they had seen a three-mile-long snake which ate nothing but elephants. Paley, in countering Hume's questioning of

Christian testimony, affirms that if 'twelve men, whose probity and good sense I had long known' should avow and then suffer for their belief in a miracle, he would accept it (*Evidences*, i. 13–14).

415 n. 1. S's reference should probably have been to the 'Preparatory Considerations' in *Evidences*, where Paley is concerned with refuting the proposition (implicitly assigned to Hume) 'That it is contrary to experience that a miracle should be true, but not contrary to experience that testimony should be false' (i. 6). Neither the 'Preparatory Considerations' nor chapter 1 (S's reference) provides S's example or his comparison.

420–2. *Every superstition . . . martyrdoms*. Christian apologists (such as Charles Leslie in *A Short and Easy Method with the Deists*, W. Onley: London, 1698) made use of the so-called 'four marks', or peculiar characteristics of its unique truth, to set off Christianity (and its miracles and prophecies) from other religions substantiated by comparable histories (see on 33–6 above). S implicitly disallows the distinction here as he later did in his *Answer* to Leslie's work. The importance of accepting the 'facts' as related in the Gospels was summed up by Francis Wrangman in his abridgement of Leslie (*Leslie's Short and Easy Method with the Deists . . . to which are Subjoined, Four Additional Marks from the Same Author . . .*, York, 1802): Christ's 'miracles, if true, establish the truth of what he delivered' (p. 2). The circular argument advanced by such apologists was that the miracles proved the truth of the doctrine and the truth (as morally stipulated) of the doctrine attested to the validity of the miracles adduced in its support.

429 n. 2. S's specific reference is not certain. M. D. Conway in *The Writings of Thomas Paine* does not index a 'Controversy of Bishop Watson and Thomas Paine', nor does Paine in his criticism of Isaiah refer to ch. 19 (which contains dire predictions concerning Egypt and an apparent prediction of Christ's birth) but to ch. 7, where he is specifically concerned with ridiculing v. 14, 'Behold a Virgin shall conceive, and bear a son.' The fragments of Paine's so-called 'Answer to the Bishop of Llandaff' (i.e. Bishop Watson) contain no reference to Isaiah. Either S is referring to a pamphlet or periodical piece dealing with the 'Controversy' or he is making a general reference to Bishop Watson's *Apology for the Bible . . . Letters to Thomas Paine* and Paine's 'Answer' to it. Richard Watson (1737–1816) had not read part two of Paine's *Age of Reason*, to which his *Apology* is an answer (see *DNB*).

448–9. *The Gospels . . . record*. S here calls into question another of the distinguishing and verifying marks of Christianity usually adduced—that the Gospels were contemporary accounts of the events they record. The anachronism which S notes in Matthew is followed in 24: 2 by Christ's prophecy of the destruction of the temple during the sack of Jerusalem, AD 70. This latter prophecy was singled out by eighteenth-century Christian apologists as certain evidence of Christ's unique gifts. Later commentators have conjectured that his actual words might have been made to conform to the historical event they preceded. The 'son of Barachias', an identification not found in the parallel context in Luke (11: 51), is likewise construed as a later addition. For the Josephus reference see *The Jewish War*, 4. 334–44.

473–4. *driving . . . pigs.* S later satirized this evidence of miraculous intervention in *On the Devil, and Devils*.

477. *historians . . . genius.* S likewise criticizes the capabilities of the Gospel writers in *On the Devil, and Devils*, also noting, as he does here (ll. 480–2), that exorcising devils was a common practice in Judaea in Christ's time.

484–5. *If the Almighty . . . convinced?* Cf. *A Letter to Lord Ellenborough*, 351. In the *Queen Mab* Note on 'There is no God' S quotes this sentence from Holbach's *Système de la Nature* in the original French. It appears in English in the Note on 'I will beget a son'.

522. *ever.* Forman (F vi. 58 and n.) thinks that the context justifies a change from 'ever' to 'even', which is plausible enough since S's holograph terminal 'n's and 'r's are often similar. But since S does use 'ever' as an adverbial modifier in comparable constructions elsewhere, it seems best to retain the *1814* reading. Whoever entered the errata into the BL copy (Edward Dowden?) likewise queried 'ever' and changed it to 'even'.

539. *monster.* S supposes that the religious would so designate an atheist in his letters to E. Hitchener of 11, 25 June 1811.

540–5. *His private . . . execute.* These are of course characteristics which S applauded.

545–7. *Iste . . . Deum.* This slightly varied quotation from Cicero's *De natura deorum* (1. 54–5) also appears, again varied, in *On the Vegetable System of Diet* (ll. 49–51): 'He does not fear a prying busybody of a god, who foresees and thinks of and notices all things, and deems that everything is his concern' (adapted from the Loeb edn.).

558–65. *I readily . . . Grace.* Theosophus does not finally keep this promise, except perhaps by ironic implication on S's part.

571. *being of a God.* While Theosophus so states his purpose, he is really concerned with defining the attributes of God. His argument throughout summarizes the standard deistic position.

575–6. *quicquid . . . natura.* Seneca, *De beneficiis*, 7. 1. 7: 'For whatever will make us better or happier, nature placed either in the open or close at hand.'

577. *From every.* The *1814* reading 'Design—every' is probably an eye-error somehow stemming from the 'Design' of l. 616. Theosophus' argument from here on is heavily dependent on the contexts from Paley and Stewart which S notes, and on other passages in Paley, Hume, Paine, and other writers which he does not note.

601–2. *tendency . . . mind.* While Hume and others called into question the theistic assumption of a natural instinct motivating the mind of man to a belief in God, S as late as the fragment *On Life* (1819) made a corresponding assumption that there is a spirit in the mind of man at war with nothingness and decay.

609 n. The reference to Dugald Stewart would be better made to the third book of *The Philosophy of the Active and of the Moral Powers of Man*, which deals with a priori and a posteriori proofs of God's existence.

610–11. *motion . . . thought.* S consistently opposed the inevitability of this logic.

616. *Design . . . inferred.* The actual 'Refutation of Deism' begins here; it is by and large a refutation of Paley's *Natural Theology*. Though S does not choose to cite him in footnotes, Hume is the major source for most of Eusebes' argument, which also makes use of Paley's own words to controvert his logic. See Clark, *Shelley's Prose*, 130 ff., for some of the specific contexts in Hume which Eusebes draws on. Whether S intended it or not, his *Refutation* could well have reminded contemporary readers that Paley had failed to answer objections to his arguments which Hume had advanced even before Paley had developed them. It should also be noted that while Eusebes is a strict Lockian empiricist in his premisses, his inferences and conclusions (particularly those on necessity) are sometimes those of the Holbachian materialist rather than of the Humean sceptic.

627–97. *Simply . . . incomprehensible.* These lines appear in *Fragment of 'A Refutation of Deism'*, ll. 35–105. For variants see the Collation for that work.

680–7. *Until . . . burthen?* A slight revision of *The Necessity of Atheism* (ll. 44–51), which is used verbatim in the *Queen Mab* Note on 'There is no God'.

688–97. *A man . . . incomprehensible.* Cf. *The Necessity of Atheism* (ll. 52–62), the *Queen Mab* Note on 'There is no God', and S's letter of 20 June 1811 to E. Hitchener. This reasoning concerning the generative power is advanced by the sceptic Philo in Hume's *Dialogues*.

698–708. *We can only . . . glaringly.* Cf. the *Queen Mab* Note on 'Necessity, thou Mother of the world'.

710–22. *These laws . . . world.* S would have found this opinion variously expressed and rationalized in philosophers from Lucretius to Dugald Stewart.

737. *Laplace.* Pierre Simon, Marquis de Laplace (1749–1827), French mathematician and astronomer. S was reading Laplace's *Système du monde* in late Nov. 1813 (to Hogg, 26 Nov.). According to a contemporary anecdote, when asked by Napoleon where in his universal system there was a place for God, Laplace replied that in his universe there was no need for a God.

739. *secular equation.* A measurable process of change which takes

place over vast periods of time. The *OED* exemplifies this meaning with 'M. De La Place ... found the secular equation of the moon to be due to the action of the sun on the moon' (*Monthly Review*, 35 (1801), 537).

741. *The necessity ... world*. The assertion appears in varied form in *Queen Mab* and stems from Holbach.

743–6. *Hypotheses ... habent*. Sir Isaac Newton, General Scholium to the *Principia*: 'I do not invent hypotheses; for whatever is not deduced out of phenomena should be called an hypothesis; and hypotheses whether of metaphysics, or of physics, or of occult qualities, or of mechanics, have no place in philosophy' (text in e.g. *Philosophiae naturalis principia mathematica*, 3rd edn. (1726), ed. A. Koyré and I. Bernard Cohen, ass. Anne Whitman, Harvard University Press: Cambridge, Mass., 1972, ii. 764). S also used the quotation in the *Queen Mab* Note on 'There is no God'.

770–2. *Light ... activity*. There is a similar passage in the fragment *On a Future State*, where, however, S seems more concerned with emphasizing differences than likenesses. Paley argues that thought, like light, gravity, magnetism, electricity, and God himself, differs from matter and motion by being caused and/or characterized by an immaterial principle (*Evidences*, 394).

784–99. *It is the necessary ... vegetables*. This paragraph echoes the anatomical arguments set forth in S's writings on vegetarianism: *A Vindication of Natural Diet*, a slight variant of this work which appeared as a Note to *Queen Mab*, and, in summary form, *On the Vegetable System of Diet*. The first two references in the footnote also appeared in the first two of these writings, and most of the last (slightly varied) in the *Queen Mab* Note. Cuvier's *Leçons d'anatomie comparée* was published in Paris 1800–5. The passages from Plutarch's *On the Eating of Flesh* are translated as follows in vol. xii of the Loeb edition of the *Moralia*: 'Are you not ashamed to mingle domestic crops with blood and gore? You call serpents and panthers and lions savage, but you yourselves, by your own foul slaughters, leave them no room to outdo you in cruelty; for their slaughter is their living, yours is a mere appetizer. (994 A–B) ... For that man is not naturally carnivorous is, in the first place, obvious from the structure of his body. A man's frame is in no way similar to those creatures who were made for flesh-eating: he has no hooked beak or sharp nails or jagged teeth, no strong stomach or warmth of vital fluids able to digest and assimilate a heavy diet of flesh. It is from this very fact, the evenness of our teeth, the smallness of our mouths, the softness of our tongues, our possession of vital fluids too inert to digest meat that Nature disavows our eating of flesh. If you declare that you are naturally designed for such a diet, then first kill for yourself what you want to eat. Do it, however, only through your own resources, unaided by cleaver or cudgel of any kind or axe. Rather, just as wolves and bears and lions themselves slay what they eat, so you are to fell an ox with your fangs or a boar with your jaws, or tear a lamb or hare in bits. Fall upon it and eat it still living, as animals do (994 F–995 B).' S, perhaps following his source, drops or misspells a few words from the Greek text as translated here, the most consequential of which is his use of σωματος and σωματι 'body' for στοματος and στοματι 'mouth, jaws'. For S's translation of a few lines of the second excerpt, see *A Vindication of Natural Diet*, ll. 119–23. For S's vegetarianism in general see the works noted and their related commentaries.

800–2. *The means ... animal*. Eusebes here and throughout this segment of his argument is suggesting a proposition the deist tended to ignore: that existences can be self-ordering and self-sustaining. S in his early prolusory letters was willing to ignore this alternative as well (cf. letter to Hogg, 6 Jan. 1811).

803. *omne ... interit*. 'Everything changes, nothing perishes.' Slightly varied from Ovid, *Metamorphoses*, 15. 165.

811. *in ... passione*. 'In which all things move, but without affecting each other.' Source untraced.

881 n. The reference to vol. i of Robert Southey's *History of Brazil* (Longman *et al.*: London, 1810), 255, apparently (and perhaps invidiously) alludes to the Brazilian natives' fear of Catholic baptism, to which they ascribed consequent physical ills and even death.

910 n. *this ... Atheism*. S provided a lengthy example of Holbach's atheistic eloquence in his *Queen Mab* Note on 'There is no God'.

928–30. *Non ... veritatis?* Cicero, *De natura deorum*, 1. 83: 'Should not the physical philosopher therefore, that is, the explorer and tracker-out of nature, be ashamed to go to minds besotted with habit for evidence of truth?' (Loeb trans.) The excerpt appears as well amidst several quotations from and references to *De natura deorum* in Bod. MS Shelley e. 4, fol. 85ᵛ. P. M. S. Dawson thinks they may be connected with the *Fragment of 'A Refutation of Deism'*, which also appears in that notebook (e. 4, p. 358).

941 n. *Chap. I, p. 1*. S's note should probably refer to ch. 1, pp. 5 ff., in Drummond.

949–51. *Intelligence ... being*. S states at the conclusion of the fragment *On Life* that it is infinitely improbable that the cause of the mind of man is like the mind of man, a distinction he anticipated in *Queen Mab* when defining Necessity or the Spirit of Nature. George Ensor, a radical political, social, and theological writer much admired by S in his early period, in his *On National Government* quoted both Malebranche and Plutarch as stating that there was no resemblance between God's mind and ours (ii, p. 393). Paley argued or assumed that God had a mind and was therefore a person (*Natural Theology*, 408–9). In Hume's *Dialogues* both Demea the Christian and Philo the sceptic deny the equation, while Cleanthes the deist (who refers to himself as a 'theist') accepts it.

956–7. *The God . . . animal.* In this context the 'rational Theosophist' might be better understood as the 'empirical Deist'. As noted above, theosophy and its variants traditionally referred to occult congruences between nature and nature's god which were permeated with mysticism and, for the uninitiated at least, were largely irrational. On any reading, S's oxymoron is ironically intended. In Hume's *Dialogues* the sceptic Philo infers that the anthropomorphic creator suggested by the 'experimental theist' Cleanthes might theoretically be, as the Stoics were found to have inferred, some 'prodigious animal'.

958–9. *You . . . sensation.* Cf. *On Life*: 'It is said that mind produces motion and it might as well have been said that motion produces mind.' S's scepticism concerning the creative powers of the mind may be traced to Hume's *Dialogues*, though S's critical emphasis is probably derived from and directed towards the traditional acceptances of Christian anthropomorphism concerning the identity, or essential kinship, of man's mind with God's originating powers.

960. *Mind . . . perceive.* S noted in a letter to Leigh Hunt of 27 Sept. 1819 that even as early as late 1811 he had 'long been persuaded' of the truth of this inference and its consequences regarding the 'imagined cause of the Universe'. In the letter S ascribes the phrasing to Charles Lloyd, a friend of the Lake poets, who had written it into a copy of Berkeley which S had borrowed from Southey when visiting Keswick. It appears as well in *On Life*, also written in late 1819.

974. *God . . . synonimous.* Cf. S to E. Hitchener, 11 June 1811: 'The word God then, in the sense which you take it analogises with the *universe* . . . In this sense I acknowledge a God, but merely as a synonime for the *existing power of existence.*'

974–79. *Omnia . . . ignoramus.* 'Everything takes place by the power of God. Nature herself is the power of God under another name, and our ignorance of the power of God is co-extensive with our ignorance of Nature. It is absolute folly, therefore, to ascribe an event to the power of God when we know not its natural cause, which is the power of God' (*The Chief Works of Benedict de Spinoza*, translated from the Latin by R. H. M. Elwes, repr. Dover Publications: New York, 1951, 25). The *1814* text is corrected (see c) from the 1670 edition of the *Tractatus*, the edition which S owned (see *SC* viii. 730–43). S has annotated this passage (on p. 14 of the edition) with his inference from it: 'God & Nature the Same' (in *SC* viii. 732). The quotation also appears in the *Queen Mab* Note on 'There is no God'.

1016. *specious.* I.e. 'attractive'; this contemporary usage is also in Hume.

THE ASSASSINS

Dates: Aug.–Sept. 1814; Apr. 1815.

Copy-text: Bod. MS Shelley adds. c. 5, fols. 38ʳ–46ᵛ.

Description: Ink manuscript consisting of seven single leaves (fols. 38ʳ–44ᵛ), measuring 35 cm. × 21.6 cm. (14″ × 8.6″), wove paper, no WM; and two single leaves (fols. 45ʳ–46ᵛ), measuring 31 cm. × 20 cm. (12.4″ × 7.9″), laid paper, WM: Britannia in a crowned oval with a 'TW&B' cipher under which is the date 1815 (fol. 46), countermark: TW&B | BOTFIELD (fol. 45); the text is continuous, except as noted in TN, from the title centred at the top of fol. 38ʳ through the top (first two lines) of fol. 44ᵛ; and from the top of fol. 45ʳ through to the bottom of fol. 46ᵛ. The eighteen pages are numbered mainly in ink (at times faded) ⟨1⟩ through 17 (there are two 14s, one in pencil; '1' and '2' are missing because the corner of the leaf has been torn off). Mary Shelley wrote fol. 38ʳ to the start of the fourteenth line of fol. 41ᵛ and fol. 45ʳ to the start of the tenth line of fol. 45ᵛ (corrections by S); S wrote the remaining pages and lines. Characteristic Shelleyan sketches of foliage, some numbers, and a good deal of smudging appear *passim*, along with jottings etc. as noted in TN.

Provenance: Mary Shelley; Sir Percy Shelley and Jane, Lady Shelley; Sir John Shelley-Rolls; Bodleian.

Printed: *1840*; F; J.

The greater part of *The Assassins* was originally composed during late Aug. and Sept. 1814. Claire Clairmont's journal entry for 25 Aug. states that 'Shelley begins his Romance in the Evening'; Mary Shelley's journal entry for the same date reads 'We . . . write part of Shelleys Romance.' Further journal entries (by either S or Mary) for 26–7 Aug. and 10, 19 Sept. record that either 'we' or S alone was busy at the 'romance'. The August entries were written in Switzerland (a probable source for some of the fragment's scenery), the entry for 10 Sept. in Holland and that for 19 Sept. in England. On 15 Sept., two days after his return to England, S read what he had then written to the publisher Thomas Hookham, which suggests that he hoped to finish it in some form acceptable for publication (Mary Shelley, *Journals*). Given the formal appearance of the manuscript title, divided and spaced as if for printer's copy, it may be that the published form would have retained the designation 'A Fragment', but the obligations of developing the plot introduced by the fourth chapter would have required even a romantic fragment to extend beyond its present limits. While the best presumption is that fols. 38ʳ–44ᵛ were composed on the Continent, the relatively finished state (substantively speaking) of the portion of the draft by Mary Shelley included in this section and the ambiguous character of the unwatermarked paper, allow the possibility of their having been both drafted by S and transcribed by Mary in England. It is true that she implies in her Preface of 1840 that the poet 'never touched' the fragment after Sept. 1814, but the English paper of 1815 used for the last two leaves (fols. 45–6) proves that he (and Mary) did return to it, probably around 8 Apr. 1815, when he copied into Mary's *Journals* a somewhat garbled note from Gibbon's *Decline and Fall of the Roman Empire*, ch. LXIV: '—all that can be known of the assassins is to be found in Memoires of the Acad⟨e⟩my of Inscriptions ⟨by M. Falconet⟩ tom. xvii p 127–170'.

There is no evidence that S consulted this work or used anything from it for his characterizations of the assassins, and the only other contemporary hint about the thematic direction the fragment might have taken is Mary's statement (in the Preface of 1840) that the mysterious stranger is 'Shelley's old favourite, the Wandering Jew'. However, Mary also states that she '⟨did⟩ not know what story he had in view'. Since S apparently did not know or did not care that the historical assassins postdated his own by several centuries, his story would probably have been a characteristic species of morally instructive myth-making. Walter E. Peck found a suggestive analogue in an 1835 translation of a history of the assassins (*Life and Work*, i. 388), while Jean Overton Fuller argues that *Le Vieux de la montagne*, a work read by Mary Shelley in Aug. 1816, contains parallels with S's fragment which identify it as his source (*Shelley: A Biography*, 159). However, other than in Gibbon, the only chronologically apropos reference to the assassins S might have come across appears in the Abbé Augustin Barruel's *Mémoires pour servir à l'histoire du Jacobinisme*, which he and Mary had been reading 23 and 25 Aug. 1814 (*Journals*); the journal entry for 25 Aug. also contains the first reference to S's 'romance'.

So far as S developed them, his assassins are construed to represent a reasonable facsimile of Godwinian Utopianism, a state of mind and of society wherein 'Every man will seek, with ineffable ardour, the good of all' (*PJ* ii. 528), and wherein an internally evolving social compact is opposed alike to the Hobbsian Leviathan and a Rousseauistic primitivism. With the intrusion of the mysterious stranger into their midst, the assassins' best-remembered activity might well have been developed with a deterministic redefinition of their historically unsympathetic character, which would then still have found its Godwinian justification: 'The assassin can not help the murder he commits, any more than the dagger' (ibid. 324). The stranger's first broken utterances suggest that a continuation of the fragment would have displayed some erosion of the assassins' benevolence and a subsequent perversion of their sense of justice, inevitable consequences of a cursing stranger, or of the god-figure he curses, or, more probably, of both. That S's millennial penchant for a happy ending would have restored the assassins' domestic and social tranquillity is a reasonable presumption.

Although Mary states in the 1840 version of a *History of a Six Weeks' Tour* that she had written *The Assassins* from S's dictation, there is some evidence that direct transcription might have replaced dictation at times: parts of the manuscript in her writing lack even minimally necessary accidentals (capitals and points at the beginnings and ends of sentences); elsewhere she uses them more responsibly. Roughly speaking, the first half of the manuscript is in Mary's hand, the second half in S's, though S's correcting hand appears *passim* and Mary returns as copyist and/or creative editor towards the end. Major and lengthy changes are much more in evidence in the latter half of the manuscript, probably because when writing in his own hand S was either creating his text from scratch or perhaps transcribing creatively from an earlier draft. That such a draft might have been the basis of Mary's transcription, whether taken directly from the draft or indirectly from dictation, can be inferred from the rough-draft continuation of fol. 44, written on the wove paper presumably used on the Continent (see 491TN), which Mary later transcribed on the Britannia paper definitely used in England (fol. 45). As a comparison of S's draft with Mary's copy indicates, either she took upon herself a good deal of editorial discretion when making her transcript in order to fill in and rectify the much-cancelled skeleton framework which S had drafted, or else S provided her with an intermediate copy (perhaps from creative dictation) for the transcript. Given the fact that S's hand resumed after the rough-draft material had been recast, the latter alternative seems more probable. Finally, the best argument for a holograph basis for Mary's transcription is its relatively correction-free appearance throughout, as compared to the variably rough to intermediate state of much of S's portion of the manuscript.

Adducible evidence of dictation appears in l. 26, where a false-start 'n' is replaced by 'Gnostics'; l. 43's 'But' originally began with a lower-case 'b' (see also l. 160c); c at ll. 145, 146, and 183 illustrates a failure to use capitals for words beginning sentences; there are as well the original use of 'there' for 'their' (l. 291c), characteristic Marian misspellings (e.g. l. 53c 'Attatched'), and un-Shelleyan spellings (e.g. ll. 61, 104 'tiger', l. 160 'sear'). Except for short-run improvements in the use of accidentals, contextual evidence for copying is relatively sparse and tends to be ambiguous: l. 63c 'accomodation' is S's spelling but Mary's hand, evidence of copying; but l. 66c 'vises' for 'vices' suggests dictation, though Mary might simply have misread S's hand. Certain deletions in context may even suggest Mary's original composition rather than S's second thoughts (e.g. l. 156c '[among the rocks]'; see also c at ll. 198, 223, 246, and 519; and TN at ll. 258 and 265, where spellings or deletions may be interpreted in support of such a thesis, as may the collaboration between them in the later drafting of *Frankenstein*: see E. B. Murray, 'Shelley's Contribution to Mary's *Frankenstein*', *K–SMB* 29 (1978), 50–68. S begins writing on 41ᵛ with a cancelled 'Is' (see c at 321) which apparently repeated an 'Is' in Mary's hand at the beginning of a previous sentence (l. 316), perhaps indicating that they were both copying from the same draft. Stylistic differences, as well as the grammatical and syntactical differences assigned to dictation or miscopying above, and the 'we' Mary sometimes used in her journal account of the composition of the romance, may be used to counter her later recollection that the creative share of the work was entirely her husband's. In some consequent deference to the possibility that her contribution was more than stenographic but largely because there is little to be gained by the attempt, her transcript has not been groomed to accord with any editorial presumption concerning her husband's practice. Her spelling 'Khaled' has been preferred to S's 'Khalib' because the former is an Arabic name and word, the latter is not. Later, as editor, Mary was also responsible for several minor substantive changes as noted in the collation and one major omission as noted at 380–93TN. See TN as well (especially at 248) for further commentary on the two hands at work in the manuscript and what division of labour this might imply in specific instances.

There are two deviations from normal editorial policy regarding manuscript accidentals: 'Assassins' has been given an initial capital throughout to accord with what seems to have been both Mary's and S's intention (cf. the change from lower-case to capital at 295C); quotation marks have also been silently supplied except for the following, which Mary provided in her portions of the text: 70–2 '"God . . . these."'; 523 '"If'; 543 'there"'; '"To'. The dashes, which may or may not be sporadically used in place of quotation marks, have been allowed to stand as well.

Related primary and secondary materials: Medwin, *Life*, 131–2; Peck, *Life and Work*, i. 386–9; White, *Shelley*, i. 357, 362–3, 682–3; Grabo, *Magic Plant*, 134–7; Hughes, *Nascent Mind*, 200, 204; Geoffrey Carnall, 'De Quincey on the Knocking at the Gate', *Review of English Literature*, 2 (Jan. 1961), 52–4; Jean Overton Fuller, *Shelley: A Biography* (London, 1968), 156–60; Dawson, *Unacknowledged Legislator*, 161; Scrivener, *Radical Shelley*, 82–3; E. B. Murray, 'The Dating and Composition of Shelley's *The Assassins*', *K–SJ* 34 (1985), 14–17.

1–12. *Jerusalem . . . city*. Most of this can be traced to Tacitus' description of the Siege of Jerusalem (*Histories*, bk. 5), which S read about the time he was drafting *The Assassins* (*Journals*, 24 Aug. 1814), though he might have supplemented Tacitus with recollections of Josephus' *The Jewish War*, which he probably read in 1813 (see *Letters*, i. 344). S's translation of the start of the relevant book of Tacitus is on paper which may be the same as that used for fols. 45–6; if so, the probability is that the translation (at least in its extant form) was made some time after the reading of Tacitus recorded in the *Journals*.

11. *strangers*. Perhaps a proleptic reference to the Assassins, but more probably 'foreigners' in general.

26. *Gnostics.* S seems specifically to have in mind the Gnostic belief that salvation was to be achieved through knowledge and understanding, a belief he would have found confirmed and applicably qualified in William Godwin's *Political Justice*, where salvation is replaced by virtue.

36. *benevolence and justice.* The *Speculations on Morals and Metaphysics* (part of which appears on the same paper used for part of *The Assassins*) is largely concerned with an account of these classical social virtues, which are mentioned again in l. 287.

70–2. *"God . . . these."* S conflates and somewhat misquotes Luke 12: 24, 27.

74–6. *The latest . . . degradation.* Most probably Lucan, who in his *Pharsalia* several times predicts 'in agony' the consequences of the civil war (whose history he recounts) instigated by Julius Caesar and fought in the main against Pompey the Great. See especially bk. 7, ll. 385–459. While S's first reference to the *Pharsalia* appears in a letter written a year after his drafting of this portion of *The Assassins*, his stated preference for Lucan over Virgil, after having only 'begun' the work, indicates that this was not his first acquaintance with at least some of it (to T. J. Hogg, end of Aug. 1815).

82–5. *Tradition . . . serene.* This may be the closest potential parallel to the Wandering Jew figure that the text provides. S might have been aware of the reported apparition of his 'old favourite' in Italy around the time that he was on the Continent (see the *Examiner*, 11 Sept. 1814).

94. *Bethzatanai.* Perhaps a coinage—'House of Satan'—which may imply the character of the change which the happy valley was to have undergone after the advent of the mysterious stranger. Newman Ivey White's belief that he is both the Wandering Jew and 'benevolent' (*Shelley*, i. 653) is based on insufficient and contradictory evidence. English equivalents of the meanings of the other Arabic names, which might have gained relevance had the fragment continued, are as follows: Albedir = the full moon, with the general suggestion of a beautiful countenance; Khaled = immortal (it is, however, a male name, most reputably attached to a sixth-century pre-Islamic poet); Abdallah = servant of God; Maimuna = fortunate, blessed. Walter E. Peck quotes an 1835 *History of the Assassins* in which 'Abdallah, the son of Maimun' is mentioned (*Life and Work*, i. 388). Peck also feels that both Albedir and Maimuna stem from Southey's *Thalaba*, although he notes that Maimuna was S's 'pet name for Mme. Boinville' (p. 387 n.).

208–12. *Alas . . . change.* Cf. 'Hymn to Intellectual Beauty', ll. 13–17.

233–4. *disinterested virtue.* Like 'sweet human love' in *Alastor* (see on 430 below), 'disinterested virtue' afflicts those who spurn its gifts. An implicit belief in man's natural benevolence seems to be the philosophical basis of both contexts. Kindred expressions or intimations of the same assumption appear in *On Christianity, Speculations on Morals and Metaphysics*, and *On Love*.

257–61. *Time . . . death.* The passage provides a helpful gloss and supplement to the affirmations of man's immortality on earth suggested or stated in *Queen Mab* and *Prometheus Unbound*.

269. *contentions of benevolence.* Here the sentimental disinterestedness ascribed to the Assassins specifically echoes the 'contests of amity' which highlight the relations of Isabella and Mathilda in Horace Walpole's *The Castle of Otranto* (Rinehart edn., p. 89) and recur in the representative Gothic romances of the 1790s.

376–8. *Having climbed . . . branch.* The impaling of the stranger has an analogue in *Zastrozzi* and an ultimate source in Matthew Lewis's *The Monk*. Jean Overton Fuller notes a parallel to the evident fall of the stranger from a higher elevation in *Le Vieux de la montagne*, which Mary Shelley read in Aug. 1816 (*Shelley: A Biography*, 159).

378. *horribly . .* The dots here and later in this context were probably provided for rhetorical effect, after the fashion of the sentimental Gothic novelists of the 1790s, who used them to heighten the suspense of a given scene of horror or of pathos. Southey's use of the two-dot point (which might have served as S's precedent) is retained in the 1909 Oxford edition of the poet's works (ed. Maurice Fitzgerald): 'All silent . . he goes in' (*Thalaba the Destroyer*, X. 8, 91); 'Them were all eyes of all the throng exploring . .' (*The Curse of Kehama*, I. 104).

414. *success . . .* The dots here and later in this context seem meant to convey the disjointed character of the wounded stranger's appropriately mangled utterance.

419–20. *'tis mine . . . destroy.* The stranger's satanic character is best illustrated in this line and the general context at this point.

430. *sweet human love.* Cf. *Alastor*, l. 203, for the most obvious of several parallels between that poem and *The Assassins* (see also ll. 111–12, 203–7 in *T*).

539. *favourite snake.* The Edenic parallel may be less relevant than canto 1 of *Laon and Cythna*, where the snake is a symbol of good. When later (ll. 586–7) Maimuna takes the snake to her bosom she anticipates a comparable happening in the poem. For the Gnostics, with whom S compares the Assassins, the snake is a symbol of human reason and opposed to evil. In another view, the appropriate analogue for this undeveloped association may be Coleridge's *Christabel*, which S might have seen in manuscript copy when visiting Southey at Keswick in 1811. The symbolic parallel would then apply to Albedir's reception of the mysterious stranger (who may or may not be the Wandering Jew). Further parallels between him and Geraldine need not be pressed to infer from his ambiguous words and actions that he might have been found out at last as a disturber of the peace in Bethzatanai, particularly if one allows

the coinage and inferences suggested above on 94. Given S's essentially poetic conception of providence, there is a good chance that (as Coleridge seems to have intended for Geraldine) the stranger would have eventually been redeemed by the good influences and offices of Albedir's family and its environment.

552. ⟨*was*⟩. The present tense (see the Collation) used in this sentence may indicate that S had a particular Alpine scene in mind (or even in view) when writing this description.

ON 'MEMOIRS OF PRINCE ALEXY HAIMATOFF'

Date: 16–17 Nov. 1814.
  Copy-text: *Critical Review*, Dec. 1814.
  Reprinted: Shelley Society Publications, Second Series, No. 2 (1886); *J*.

This review of Thomas Jefferson Hogg's novel of 1813 was printed anonymously, but the evidence that S wrote it seems conclusive. Mary Shelley's journal entry for 16 Nov. 1814 reads 'S writes his critique till ½ 3'; on 17 Nov. 'Shelley writes his critique' and then reads for the rest of the day. According to the entry for 3 Jan. 1815, the Shelleys received a parcel from the publisher of the novel, Thomas Hookham, containing a copy of the *Critical Review*, which included the critique of 'Prince Alexy Haimatoff'. Edward Dowden first identified the review as S's on the basis of the journal entries and S's letter to Hogg of 22–3 Nov. 1813, which contained diction and sentiments also to be found in the review, along with a supplementary critique:

> Your novel is now printed. I need not reassure you with what pleasure this extraordinary and animated tale is perused by me. Every one to whom I have shewn it agree with me in admitting that it bears the indisputable marks of a singular and original genius. Write more like this. Delight us again with a character so natural and energetic as Alexy—vary again the scene with an uncommon combination of the most natural and simple circumstances: but do not persevere in writing when you grow weary of your toil; "aliquando bonus dormitat Homerus" ⟨'sometimes good Homer nods': Horace, *Ars Poetica*, 359⟩ and the swans and the Eleutherarchs are proof that you were a little sleepy. (Corrected from *SC* iii. 260; dated 26 Nov. in Shelley, *Letters*.)

The correspondences suggest that S had a copy of this letter by him when a year later he took it on himself to bring his friend's book to the attention of an indifferent public.

The full title of Hogg's novel (ascribed to 'John Brown, Esq.') is *Memoirs of Prince Alexy Haimatoff: Translated from the Original Latin MSS.*

under the Immediate Inspection of The Prince. The novel relates the story of an expatriate Russian nobleman whose physical deficiencies are over-compensated for by a fine mind and an enthusiasm for learning which initially leads him to despise women as his intellectual inferiors. He soon meets the beauteous Rosalie, whose unusual intuitions and instinctive responses to nature inspire him with the realization that women may possess a more profound wisdom than mere book learning can provide. However, she soon dies and the distraught prince reacts by overcoming his physical weakness to the extent of becoming a proficient in military science and tactics, developing as well an avid and active interest in the hunt. With his tutor Bruhle, who belongs to the secret society of the Illuminati, he travels to Athens and eventually to Constantinople, where he marries a slave-girl (Aür-Ahebeh), has two children, and is on the verge of living happily ever after when his family dies of smallpox. Once more distraught, he travels, again with Bruhle, to Rome, where he learns something of the inequities of the Catholic Church. From there the two journey to Germany, where Alexy becomes a probationer in the society of the Eleutheri (who are the Illuminati). Recoiling against the most secret tenets and demands of the society, he goes to England, where he marries the daughter of a Tory aristocrat, whose principles he is willing to humour in spite of his own liberal sentiments. With the marriage and the death of Bruhle, the *Memoirs* conclude.

Edward Dowden discovered the real name of the author. Other than S's, the novel seems to have received no notice on publication. Both Mary Shelley and Claire Clairmont read it at about the time S was reviewing it, the latter with particular enthusiasm. Similarities between S and his circle and the characters of the novel have been noted by later commentators. It was reprinted in 1952, but its only (minimal) claim to posterity's attention, besides its association with S, is the word 'eleutherarch', which the *OED* gives Hogg full credit for coining.

While the over-pointing of the copy-text is not representative of S's practice, it has seemed best generally to retain it on the grounds that it would be arbitrary and futile to add to it and subtract from it in the hope of restoring S's printer's copy, which, like the great majority of his drafts, would have vacillated between formal and rhetorical punctuation. As elsewhere, some expedient changes in the accidentals have been made and are recorded in the Collation, along with substantive errors in the original printing of the review. The quotations from Hogg's novel also contain several errors, some of which impair the sense and are therefore corrected in the text. A few characteristic Shelleyan misspellings ('accomodates', 'philanthrophy') support the inference that the type was cursorily set up and indifferently proofread at most.

Related primary and secondary materials: CC 59; Edward Dowden, 'Some Early Writings of Shelley', *Contemporary Review*, 46 (Sept. 1884), 383-96; T. J. Wise,

A Shelley Library (London, 1924), 77–8; Sidney Scott, 'Introduction', in *Memoirs of Alexy Haimatoff* (London, 1952); Barnard, *Shelley's Religion*, 275–6; Cameron, *Golden Years*, 210.

28. *bibliopolism.* The trade of bookselling.
80–1. *Alfieri's . . . himself.* S read the autobiography of the Italian tragic dramatist Vittorio Alfieri (1749–1803) in 1814 (*Journals*, 86).
196. *esteem.* The pronoun 'her' is understood.
226–7. *see . . . dissimulation.* Cf. Lord Chesterfield's *Letters to his Son* (London, 1774), 22 May 1749. S may also be thinking of the distinction made by Richard Steele (1672–1729) in the *Tatler*: 'Simulation is a Pretence of what is not, and Dissimilation a Concealment of what is' (16 Aug. 1710, No. 213, p. 1). Lord Bacon also wrote an essay on the distinction. As a courtier, Philip Dormer Stanhope, 4th Earl of Chesterfield (1694–1773), gained a reputation for both simulation and dissimulation.

ON THE VEGETABLE SYSTEM OF DIET

Date: ?late 1814–?late 1815.
Copy-text: Bod. MS Shelley adds. c. 4, fols. 267ʳ–272ᵛ.
Description: Untitled ink holograph of three sheets folded to form six leaves (twelve pages), each leaf measuring 32.4 cm. × 22 cm. (12.8″ × 8″); laid paper; WM: Britannia; countermark: JOHN HALL | 1811; the text begins about 2.5 cm. (1″) from the top of fol. 267ʳ and is continuous, but fols. 271–2 (misfoliated) should precede fols. 269–70 (misfoliated); fols. 269ʳ and 271ʳ are centrally numbered '4' and '2' respectively (so confirming the misfoliation). The 1811 countermark has been traced in pen on fol. 269ᵛ. Characteristic Shelleyan trees have been sketched on fol. 268ᵛ below 'diseased organization' (ll. 95–6) and below the concluding line on fol. 270ᵛ.
Provenance: Mary Shelley; Sir Percy Shelley and Jane, Lady Shelley; Sir John Shelley-Rolls; Bodleian.
Printed: *J* (also privately printed by Roger Ingpen in 1929; an incomplete and unannotated limited edition was published in hardback by the Linden Press in 1940; a 1947 pamphlet published by the London Vegetarian Society reprints *J*).

The date of late 1815 conjectured above for the composition of the holograph is based mainly on a reference to Euripides' *Hippolytus*, a work which S requested in a letter of 27 Sept. 1815 to William Laing, an Edinburgh bookseller. Assuming that (1) he received the work shortly thereafter, (2) he had not previously read it, and (3) he had not—as he sometimes did—derived the note from another source, the date may be considered as a definitive *terminus a quo*. Other references could extend this date backward in time: S read *The Curse of Kehama* as early as 1811, though a reading on 17 Sept. 1814 reported in Mary's *Journals* seems more relevant here; a reference to Diogenes Laertius' *Lives of the Eminent*

Philosophers, appearing in the same note as the *Hippolytus* reference, bolsters this inference, since S was evidently reading this work on 4 Dec. 1814 (Mary Shelley, *Journals*). The earliest *terminus a quo* is suggested by Kenneth Neill Cameron, who feels that S's intention, expressed in a letter to T. J. Hogg of 26 Nov. 1813, to use two passages on flesh-eating he had translated from Plutarch's *Moralia* in the Preface to a work apparently completed at that date should be applied to the *Vegetable System* (Cameron, *Young Shelley*, 409–10). But the passages were used or referred to (though not translated) in the *Queen Mab* Note, *A Vindication of Natural Diet*, and *A Refutation of Deism*, all of which were written or published around the time of the reference in the letter. Still, it remains true that, while there is no Preface and S makes no direct reference to Plutarch, he does make use of examples, anatomical references, and sociological inferences which must derive either from his reading, early or late, in Plutarch or in cognate sources who made use of Plutarch (cf. ll. 173–84). The Cicero quotation (ll. 49–51) appears also in *A Refutation of Deism* (1814), and may therefore be adduced as evidence of a relatively early date for the second as well as the first vegetarian essay. The identity of subject-matter and the correspondence of diction and sources in both essays also argue for a date before 1815 for the *Vegetable System*. Most of the contemporary writers S relates to his vegetarian thesis in the holograph either definitely feature in S's research for his earlier writings on the subject or (in lieu of better evidence) may be presumed to do so. Assuming that a smeared 'Mary' doodled vertically into the right margin of fol. 268^v refers to Mary Godwin, it would most probably have been written any time after mid-1814. Taken with other evidence—the fact that the pair eloped to Europe in July of that year and did not return to England until September—late 1814 may well be the earliest period during which S would have had the time, sources, and paper to draft the holograph. Negative evidence supporting this or a still later date is the fact that none of S's original prose holographs written before his elopement with Mary are known to have survived. A possible but less probable inference which could be groomed to fit this fact is that S found time to express his renewed interest in vegetarianism by writing the draft just after his meeting with Mary in June but before their elopement in late July.

Secondary confirmation of the date in late 1815 suggested by the *Hippolytus* reference may be adduced from two letters in the Pforzheimer Collection written by S on 26 Aug. (*SC* 295, iii. 481) and 9 Nov. 1815 (*SC* 298, iv. 571), both of which are written on paper bearing the JOHN (or J) HALL watermark. The only other such watermarks in the relevant *SC* volumes so far published appear on a letter written by Godwin on 21 Sept. 1815 (*SC* 297, iv. 568) and another by S in late November 1813 (*SC* 252, iii. 259). The inductive evidence is therefore slim and slightly ambiguous, but one could speculate that in the latter part of 1815 S and his circle (barely represented by Godwin) were purchasing their paper from a stationer some of whose stock was made by John Hall. Finally, the likelihood (see *SC* iv. 496–502) that S was engaged in a revision of *Queen Mab* in late 1815 provides some grounds for supposing that he might also at that time have reassessed his thoughts on vegetarianism as set forth in a Note to that poem, which he refers to in *On the Vegetable System of Diet*.

While the chronological placing of the essay in this edition may still be regarded most of all as a concession to the necessity of placing it somewhere, it is none the less the case that a *terminus a quo* of late 1815 is the only one which can take account of all of the available evidence.

The provenance given for the holograph may be qualified somewhat by a letter of 15 Apr. 1823 from T. L. Peacock to Mary Shelley in which Peacock states that he had sent her a box containing 'a MS. on the subject of diet', though he does not specify from whom he had received it.

Related primary and secondary materials: *A Vindication of Natural Diet* and its Textual Commentary *passim*; Cameron, *Young Shelley*, 256–9, 409–12; see also this listing in the headnote to *A Vindication of Natural Diet*.

1. *The wisest*. The holograph actually begins with a series of notes apparently referring to prospective works S had in mind: 'To write the Wandering Jew. A Novel or ⟨perhaps on⟩ the Sisters—An essay on the depravations of Love'. S demonstrated his interest in the Wandering Jew in several works written during the period in which he most probably drafted *On the Vegetable System of Diet*. There is no record of a novel concerning sisters or an essay on the depravations of love, though *Alastor* comes close to treating of the latter subject (and contains a reference to the Wandering Jew).

49–51. (*esse . . . deum*). This slightly varied quotation from Cicero's *De natura deorum* (1. 54–5) appears in another variant form in *A Refutation of Deism*, 545–7. The 'torturer' is here equated, directly or indirectly, with 'a prying busybody of a god, who foresees and thinks of and notices all things, and deems that everything is his concern' (Loeb trans.). In the *Refutation* S begins the quotation with 'Iste non timet' in order to define the atheist, who does not suffer from the afflictions of the individual who believes in this kind of god; cf. Drummond, *Academical Questions*, 343.

52 n. *Curse of Kehama*. Published in London in 1810, this was a poem S was eager to purchase as soon as it was available (see Shelley, *Letters*, to the bookseller Stockdale, 18 Dec. 1810). By 11 June 1811 it had become his 'most favorite poem' (to E. Hitchener), though he felt the attributing of '*faith*' to one of his favourite characters was a 'great error' (ibid.). S read the poem to Mary and Claire Clairmont 17 Sept. 1814 (Mary Shelley, *Journals*).

82. *frantic woman*. Apparently the Virgin Mary.

120 n. The full title of James Easton's work defines its method and contents: *Human Longevity: Recording the Name, Age, Place of Residence, and Year of Decease of 1712 Persons who Attained a Century, and upwards from AD 66 to 1799*. A 'new and improved' edition was published in 1823.

149. *argali*. An Asiatic wild sheep; in *A Vindication of Natural Diet* (l. 91) S uses 'mouflon', a wild sheep of southern Europe and northern Africa, in a similar context.

164 n. 1 Here as often elsewhere S's holograph footnote-indicator should probably be understood to apply to the general context rather than to a specific word, phrase, or clause. S may be referring to either of two forms of John Abernethy's most influential work, 'Essay on the Constitutional Origin of Local Disease', one published in *Surgical Observations*, pt. II (1806), the other (more complete) version appearing in *Surgical Works*, vol. i (1811). Since the latter is closer in time to the composition of S's holograph, it is the more probable reference. The 'Essay' itself relates local diseases to disorders of the digestive system. Abernethy has mixed views on the merits of vegetable diet as a remedy for such disorders.

170 n. The text follows *J* in keying the reference to *Queen Mab* to the word which immediately precedes it in the manuscript, where, however, it appears between two parallel lines running across the page and so setting it off from the text. There is in *c. 4* no sign to indicate its place or purpose. The sentence which S refers to on p. 223 of the *Queen Mab* Note (and in *Vindication*, ll. 199–200) does in fact affirm that 'all bodily and mental derangements ⟨may be traced⟩ to our unnatural habits'. However, earlier the Note (but not the *Vindication*) does allow that 'mental and bodily derangement is attributable in part to other deviations from rectitude and nature than those which concern diet'. Here S's indicated line of argument would not only have avoided the over-simplification of but also removes a possible contradiction in the earlier works, since both of them eventually state that a vegetable diet will not cure hereditary ills. 'History of ?Re⟨?ligion⟩' is heavily written in large block letters to the right of the *Queen Mab* reference.

185–7. *The bull ... [a nature]*. This is taken nearly verbatim from the Note and the *Vindication*, in both of which, however, S completes his sentence with 'rebellious nature'.

187–9. *Sows ... [to death]*. S is recalling Plutarch's vivid description from *The Eating of Flesh* (which appears in Ritson's *Essay on Abstinence*; see on 211c (below): 'Others jump upon the udders of sows about to give birth and kick them so that, when they have blended together blood and milk and gore ... and the unborn young have at the same time been destroyed at the moment of birth, they may eat the most inflamed part of the creature' (*The Eating of Flesh*, 997 A, *Moralia*, Loeb edn. xii. 565). In *On the Devil, and Devils* S implicitly compares whipping pigs to death, boiling lobsters alive, and bleeding calves with the torments visited on the damned by the biblical coalition of God and the Devil.

193–5. *horrible . . . birth.* S's 'horrible process of torture' may be the whipping to death noted above (and in Ritson's *Essay* noted below), it may be related to the slow bleeding to death of pigs which so revolted Jude in Thomas Hardy's novel *Jude the Obscure* (Norton Critical Edition, W. W. Norton & Co.: New York, 1978, p. 54), though brawning in a general sense meant simply to fatten. The *OED* (s.v. 'brawn' *v. trans.*) quotes an eighteenth-century source as follows: 'The best way of brawning a boar is this . . . Before Christmas he will be sufficiently brawned with continual lying, and prove exceedingly fat, wholesome and sweet.' The Athenians regarded the flesh of pigs which had literally eaten themselves to death as a particular delicacy (cf. Reay Tannahill, *Food in History*, Stein and Day: New York, 1973, p. 83).

211C. [*Lambs . . . diet*]. This cancellation, along with the sentence in ll. 211–13, appears slightly varied in the Note and the *Vindication* (ll. 149–51). S first placed an '×' before and (actually) below the cancelled 'have', then implicitly replaced it with one before and above 'pidgeons' (l. 211), which originally referred to an apparent '× ?Rit' below the line concluding with 'concomitants' (l. 216), an abbreviation later spelt out and placed at the bottom of the page as '×Ritson'. An '×' after '[diet]' (see 212–13C) is the justification for keying 'Ritson' to 'aliment' (l. 213), the word which replaced '[diet]'. S does not indicate a source for this information in the earlier vegetarian writings. Joseph Ritson, whose *Essay* not only provided S with much of his material on vegetarianism but also with several of his footnotes in *A Vindication*, suffered from a nervous condition which later degenerated into brain paralysis and caused his death in 1803 (*DNB*). S's reluctance to acknowledge the full extent of his debt to Ritson's work may be related to the fate of this vegetarian, an inference which gains some justification from a letter of 29 June 1817 to Leigh Hunt in which S more or less playfully notes that advocates of a 'new system of diet' are bound to be invulnerable to disease. For further evidence of S's use of Ritson see the Editorial Commentary on *A Vindication of Natural Diet*, ll. 85–8, 289–91, 446 n., 455+.

231–2. *elations of nature.* A variation of this phrase, 'elation of spirit', is ascribed to vegetarians in the *London Magazine* parody referred to in the headnote to *A Vindication of Natural Diet* (q.v.). There is no other hint that the anonymous parodist might have seen the draft of *On the Vegetable System of Diet.* While Thomas Love Peacock, a possible author of the satire, apparently returned the holograph to Mary Shelley in 1823, there is no reason to suppose he had seen it as early as 1821.

251 n. ⟨1⟩ This list also appears in the Appendix to *A Vindication of Natural Diet.*

251 n. ⟨2⟩. There is no footnote-indicator in the text of the holograph,

although the note itself is preceded by an '×'. In the holograph this note is placed under the note here keyed to l. 256. The two Greek words in the footnote mean 'uncooked food', and come from Diogenes Laertius' 'Life of Zeno', in his *Lives of the Eminent Philosophers* (Loeb edn. ii. 138); the relevant part of ll. 952-3 of the *Hippolytus* reads 'with your lifeless food make a show of your diet, taking Orpheus as your lord'. Vegetarianism was a well-known feature of Orphic and Pythagorean asceticism. There is no reference to the *Hippolytus* as a work S might have read until he requested it from the Edinburgh bookseller William Laing (particularly known for his editing of classical Greek texts) in a letter of 27 Sept. 1815. The (lost) letter apparently indicated an edition by 'Marsh', though this might be a misreading of '(J.) Monk', who edited a *Hippolytus* in 1811 (also in 1813, though in that edition the line is numbered 957). The Eton College Library has an 1811 Greek Euripides from S's library, but there is no indication of when he got or read it.

256 n. S did not provide a footnote siglum but doubtless this note attaches to the cue after 'diet'. The full title of William Lambe's work is *A Medical and Experimental Enquiry into the Origin, Symptoms, and Cure of Constitutional Diseases, Particularly Scrofula, Consumption, Cancer, and Gout* (1805) (in the holograph 'on' precedes 'Constitutional Diseases'). For S's acquaintance with John Frank Newton's life and work, also referred to and made use of in *A Vindication of Natural Diet*, see White, *Shelley*, i. 302-4.

271. *Kanstashka*. Perhaps a contemporary English variant of 'Kamchatka', which was known as a hotbed of volcanic activity. The most active of the volcanoes there erupted in 1813, but I have not discovered any record of the event which S might have read. Another apparent variant—'Kamtskatka'—appears in S's major source for vegetarian principles and practices, Newton's *Return to Nature*, 24.

JOURNAL AT GENEVA

Date: 18 Aug.–5 Sept. 1816.

Copy-text: Bod. Dep. d. 311(2).

Description: Unnumbered ink holograph, leaves measuring 18.8 cm. × 11.9 cm. (7.4″ × 4.7″); wove paper; no WM. The text in S's hand begins just after the conclusion of Mary's journal entry for 18 Aug. 1816 and is continuous through the ghost stories; the journal entries from 29 Aug. are also continuous and, except for the entry for 29 Aug. itself, in S's hand. The notebook containing the entries is bound in original brown leather with gilt fillets and spine and measures 19.3 cm. × 12.7 cm. (7.6″ × 5″). See also Mary Shelley, *Journals*, vol. i, p. xxxii.

Printed: *1840*; *F*; *J*.

The *Journals* entry for 18 Aug. 1816 containing S's transcription of a recital by Matthew Gregory 'Monk' Lewis of four ghost stories was made immediately after S had visited Byron at Diodati, where he met Lewis and heard the stories. As Mary's note of 1840 suggests, they were probably not invented by Lewis and are presumably extant in variant forms as told by a series of story-tellers. They remain part of S's canon largely because Mary printed them as such; however, in so far as he is embellishing what he heard with his own diction, continuity, and emphasis, the tales as we have them may be considered as much his as are the majority of those assigned to compilers of folk legends and fairy-tales. Previous to its printing in 1840 as a supplement to the volume containing the *History of a Six Weeks' Tour*, the fourth story was appended by Mary to her essay 'On Ghosts' (*London Magazine*, 9 (1824), 253–6). The telling of ghost stories seems to have been a familiar part of an evening's entertainment; see *Journals*, 18 Aug. 1816, 20 Oct. 1818. The fact that S wrote out the four stories with hardly a cancel-line and no changes may suggest that he transcribed them into the journal from a copy made earlier; but he had just heard the stories, and this may account for the text's finished state, unique for an original draft. There would have been little time for any preceding rough draft.

The text follows *1840* in also printing a few later entries in the journal holograph which are (with one exception) in S's hand.

The few and generally insignificant substantive differences between Dep. d. 311(2) and *1840* indicate that Mary Shelley used the *Journals* entries as her copy-text. The text follows S's holograph accidentals except as noted in the Collation.

TITLE. *1840*'s volume ii contents-page divided the Journal into 'Journal at Geneva—Ghost Stories' and 'Journal.—Return to England'. The first page of the combined journal was introduced in the text by a drop-head title 'Journal'.

1. *Apollo's Sexton.* As Mary notes, one of Byron's genially satirical descriptions of the Gothic writer 'Monk' Lewis (1775–1818), so called from his most famous work, *The Monk* (1796); see *English Bards and Scotch Reviewers* (1809), l. 268. The answer to Lewis's question is most simply that Apollo is the god of poetry and a sexton digs graves—which would then, by some stretch of chronology and imagination, make the writer (who did compose macabre verse) a 'Graveyard Poet'. Byron's Villa Diodati (where Milton had once lived) was only a few minutes' walk from the Shelley's cottage at Lake Geneva, variously referred to as Campagne Chaupuis, Maison Chaupuis, Montalègre, and Mont Alègre (see H. W. Hausermann's 'Shelley's House in Geneva' in his *The Genevese Background*, Routledge & Kegan Paul Ltd.: London, 1952, pp. 1–7).

10. *Princess of Wales.* Caroline, wife of the Prince Regent, mother of the

Princess Charlotte, and later Queen of England. The 'Court in Germany' probably refers to her ancestral residence in Brunswick.

14. *Mina.* The use of the name by Bram Stoker for one of the heroines (Mina Murray) of his vampire classic *Dracula* may suggest a common source that justifies S's original spelling as against *1840*'s 'Minna'.

69. *Lord Lyttleton.* If a real person is intended, either George Lyttelton (1709–73; 1st baron), author of *Dialogues of the Dead*, or his son Thomas Lyttelton (1744–79), a loose liver and prodigal (known as the 'wicked Lord Lyttelton'), would have been likely subjects of a ghost story by Lewis. Thomas Lyttelton's contemporary association with ghost stories makes him the more likely candidate (cf. Samuel Taylor Coleridge, *Table Talk*, ed. Carl Woodring, Princeton University Press: Princeton, 1990, i. 17 and n.).

121+. *Thursday ⟨August⟩ 29.* Mary Shelley excluded the journal entries from 19 Aug. to 28 Aug. because they were hers; so was that for 29 Aug.

137. *Fontainbleau.* Fontainebleau was a traditional spring and autumn hunting resort for the French royal family; the palace was built by Francis I in the early sixteenth century. The palace and gardens of Versailles (l. 148) were constructed in the mid-seventeenth century by Louis XIV and served as a royal residence until the French Revolution.

172–4. *we could not . . . King.* The request was probably meant to refer to the storming of the palace on 6 Oct. 1789 by the Parisian mob, who invaded the queen's apartments. S had confused this incident with the attack on the royal family's quarters in the Tuileries, 10 Aug. 1792.

176. *Egalité.* The nickname of Louis-Philippe-Joseph, Duke of Orleans (1747–93), bestowed on him because of his egalitarian principles and practices at about the time of the French Revolution. He was for that and other reasons unpopular with the other Bourbons; his popular sympathies did not save him from the guillotine during the Reign of Terror.

177. *Mad⟨ame⟩ de Maintenon.* Françoise d'Aubigne, Marquise de Maintenon (1635–1719), first married the writer Scarron and, after his death, secretly wed Louis XIV.

191. *Auxonne.* In *SC* iv. 701–2 Gavin de Beer demonstrates that the Shelleys could not have stopped at Auxonne or Auxerre (*1840*) on 3 Sept.

197. *wind contrary.* Actually from the journal entry for 6 Sept.

THE ELYSIAN FIELDS

Date: ?Sept. 1815 or ?Nov. 1816.
Copy-text: Intermediate fair-copy holograph (no shelfmark).
Location: Berg Collection, NYPL.
Description: Unnumbered ink holograph consisting of two leaves (originally a single sheet) or four pages, each measuring 22.9 cm. × 19 cm. (9″ × 7½″); laid paper; WM: posthorn in crowned shield (with ?cipher); the continuous text starts

about 5.1 cm. (2″) from the top of fol. ⟨1ʳ⟩ and concludes about the same distance from the bottom of fol. ⟨2ʳ⟩; fol. ⟨2ᵛ⟩ contains sketches of trees by S and the start of a letter in S's hand (noted below). The manuscript is in a blue folder in a blue case with 'The Elysian Fields—Shelley—original manuscript' in gold lettering on a reddish-brown strip of paper pasted on the spine.

Provenance: ?Leigh Hunt; ?Townshend Mayer; H. B. Forman; ⟨?⟩; Dr Roderick Terry; W. R. H. Howe; Berg Collection, NYPL.

Printed: 1879; *F*; *J*.

An aborted letter in S's hand on the verso of the second page of *The Elysian Fields* holograph reads 'Sir, I am pleased with the description of your house', and so provides concrete (if ambiguous) evidence for dating the composition of the fragment either in late summer of 1815, when S was searching for a house around Bishopsgate, or towards the end of 1816, when he was in quest of his Marlow residence.

If, as is virtually certain, the speaker from Elysium is addressing his remarks to Princess Charlotte, the Regent's daughter, her much-publicized flight from the domestic tyranny of her father in the summer of 1814 would have provided S's liberal shade with all the incentive he needed to instruct the princess in a political philosophy opposed to the Regent's. Leigh Hunt's *Examiner* of 1814 echoed and emphasized Parliamentary dissension over the appropriate ways of treating and educating an heiress presumptive. The liberal concern was most of all that she should not be subject to the 'system of coercion' inspired by Lord Eldon and practised by her father, particularly concerning her political upbringing. S's sympathies with anyone oppressed by parental tyranny are well documented.

If, as suggested elsewhere (see the commentary on Appendix II), this fragment is related to a comparable one in Mary Shelley's hand and presumably addressed to the Duchesse d'Angoulême, the daughter of Louis XVI and the conservative power behind the throne recently restored to Louis XVIII, the reference there to the massacre of the Protestants at Nîmes in July 1815 would indicate a *terminus a quo* of late Aug. or early Sept. 1815 for S's holograph, since news of that event began filtering into the London newspapers at about that time. While the reference to house-hunting could then be applied to Bishopsgate and the internal evidence readily assimilated to 1815, a marginal preference may be allowed to the later date because of the continuing publicity given to the massacre at Nîmes—which received its most lurid recital in Parliament from Sir Samuel Romilly in late May 1816—and because of the marriage of Charlotte to Prince Leopold of Saxe-Coburg earlier in the same year, an event which inspired the reformist press to renewed and expanded editorial hopes for a liberal succession. Additional factors are S's detailed interest in topical political concerns as set down in his letter of 20 Nov. 1816 to Byron, and his later 1816 readings (noted in Mary's *Journals*) of Lucian and of Godwin's *Political Justice*, probable analogues in form and content (respectively) to the holograph fragment.

Harriet Shelley's suicide in December and the Chancery proceedings of Jan. 1817 would have been compelling personal reasons for S to put aside his political fiction. But there were potential public motives as well. On 28 Jan. Parliament convened in a session which S (in the letter to Byron of 20 Nov.), along with Hunt and other reformists, regarded as most crucial to England's political and social future. Shortly thereafter he was at work on *A Proposal for Putting Reform to the Vote*, a pamphlet full of a political expediency at odds with a more calculated exposition of the poet's political philosophy, such as the distancing framework of *The Elysian Fields* was meant to provide. The fragment would probably have continued the perfunctory political history of England, as read by early nineteenth-century liberals, which the speaker introduces as the piece breaks off, and then have concentrated upon the topical national concerns of the moderately radical reformists to whose immediate goals S most often accommodated his Godwinian gradualism. As modified by its quasi-fictional format, the completed work would then have anticipated the political platforms outlined in *A Proposal for Putting Reform to the Vote* and filled in with substantial additions in *A Philosophical View of Reform* (1819).

The identity of the speaker is problematical. The ideal candidate, as Forman supposed, is Charles Fox, the Whig leader who had achieved an afterlife among the generality of liberals as the cohering standard-bearer around whom a variously defined and often factional reformist movement could conceivably rally. But a speaker who in 1815–16 refers to Frederick the Great as 'having lately arrived amongst us' must have been a long time dead to regard 1786, the year of Frederick's death, as recent. While the fact that Fox died in 1806 can only emphasize the discrepancy, S's references to him in *An Address, to the Irish People* as not only 'the friend of freedom' but most pointedly the 'friend of the Prince of Wales' to whom Fox spoke '*openly* on every occasion' and so made him 'the better for his instructive conversation' may bolster the other internal evidence of the fragment and permit the rationalization (perhaps meant to feature later in the piece) that Frederick's unwillingness to believe in a personal immortality had doomed him to wander a while in limbo before gaining entry to a hereafter whose existence he continues to deny even after his arrival there. Alternatively, given S's eclectic grooming of his sources to suit his purposes, the Godwinian echoes towards the end of the fragment need not be read as presumptions invalidating John Locke as a speaker from Elysium who does not suffer from Fox's dating disqualifications. There is no evidence that S had read Locke's political tracts, but he could not have avoided a working knowledge of their essentially liberal tendency and its historical consequences.

S's concern with Charlotte's political education was probably derived from, as it was certainly reflected in, the *Morning Chronicle* and the *Examiner*. Just before S and Mary eloped to the Continent, and with special reference to the kind of education fit for a queen, Hunt wrote of the repressive measures taken by Charlotte's father after her flight from the Regent's oppression:

> The words knowledge and information, are left out . . . in the list of desirable things for the young Princess . . . and how is she to get them in that restricted condition, to which it seems to have been the intention of confining her, from first to last? There may have been as many instructors as would furnish a public school . . . but not all these . . . can impart the knowledge most requisite for a future Queen, which consists in a thorough insight into the character and society of the people she is to govern, and in the cultivation of large and liberal feelings, fostered by a free treatment and by the example of noble and generous sentiments in those about her. How is a Princess to obtain these if she is under a perpetual sense of restraint . . . is the treatment good enough . . . for a young Lady, who is . . . to take a great and public share in the national government, to deal with intelligent spirits of all kinds, and to perform under the graces of a woman the part and business of a man? (*Examiner*, 24 July 1814)

Nothing further of consequence is reported of Charlotte's treatment or activities until early in 1816, when rumours of her approaching marriage to Prince Leopold proved correct and inspired the *Examiner* to another tug of war with the Ministry and their press for the guidance of the Princess's mind and opinions. The *Examiner* for 11 Feb. announces the marriage, notes that the Prince seems a man of 'liberal opinions', and (sounding very much like S's Elysian instructor) points out that 'a Queen is a woman like other women' and that in courts 'the common feelings of our nature' predominate even over politics and should be consulted 'in the most enlarged and generous sense'. Hunt concludes that 'Private affection and manliness are the best foundations of a happy public spirit'. The *Examiner* of 12 May is even more explicit about the battle for Charlotte's political allegiance going on behind the scenes in Parliament and in the public forum provided by the press itself: 'Attempts very superfluous if they were likely to succeed, and very odious under all the circumstances, have already been made to pre-determine the political opinions of the illustrious Couple.' Hunt chooses to disavow such an attempt in the very act of repeating it when he notes that the House of Brunswick has been notable for the differences of opinion which in the 'nature of things' exist between 'the possessors and the heirs of thrones'. Like S in *The Elysian Fields*, Hunt emphasizes the relation between domestic upbringing and public governance, with a nearly overt implication that the Regent was a mixed compendium of alternating moods, from weakness to severity, which made his familial context a chaos in which a future head of state would hardly receive a disciplined education. The innuendo as advice seems comparably clear: Charlotte has seen enough indiscipline in her father to avoid his domestic character and, in consequence, his public policies. The Regent's lifestyle—he had an extended attack of gout during the late winter of 1816—provided sufficient incentive for a sanguine but necessarily repressed hope that his death would precede that of his father and so pave the way for Charlotte's early succession, a hope that perhaps gained a transferred expression in recurrent references to her as the future queen, particularly in a context which allowed for pointed allusion to the liberal expectations first aroused and then frustrated by her father when he assumed the full power of the regency in 1812: 'The people like the Princess, first, because they are always disposed to think well of Princes till they absolutely load them with disappointments,—and the Princess has yet visited them with none, and secondly and chiefly, because they think her a fine-spirited, good-hearted girl, who has warm natural affections, and promises to make a true English Queen' (*Examiner*, 9 June 1816). Since S left England on 3 May, these editorials probably escaped his notice when they first appeared, though their sentiments had (as Hunt makes clear) been the substance of public controversy for some time. In S's letter of 8 Dec. 1816 to Hunt he makes the exaggerated claim that he had read 'every' *Examiner* but that of 1 Dec.; however, his statement that he 'generally' took in the weekly allows for the possibility that he caught up on back issues when he returned from the Continent early in September.

The summer trip had broadened his political perspective and reinforced his belief that the 'spirit of the age' had achieved its tripartite expression—liberty, equality, fraternity—in the 'master theme of the epoch in which we live—the French Revolution' (to Byron, 8 Sept. 1816), a subject soon to be idealized in the poetic fiction of *Laon and Cythna*. It might more immediately have inspired the relative objectivity implied in the use of a fanciful framework for the realities of contemporary politics which *The Elysian Fields* provided. A 'radical reform of the institutions of England' (to Byron, 20 Nov.) was, he felt, necessary to condition a more moderate expression of the revolutionary theme which would preclude 'a state of anarchy' and its attendant demagoguery. In the same letter he echoed an *Examiner* (and liberal) shibboleth—'Reform or Revolution'— when he hoped that the mass of people would not be moved by the demagogues (like Henry 'Orator' Hunt and William Cobbett) who were inciting the 'popular party' to violence and inferred from their steadiness that 'reform may come without revolution'. Leigh Hunt, for all his vociferousness, resisted the extremists of the radical left and, like S, argued that a liberally constituted and instructed monarchy was, given the times, the indicated antidote to reactionary conservatism in Parliament and irresponsible republicanism among the people.

Even in its unfinished state *The Elysian Fields* demonstrates that S was willing to take what he could get at a time when reaction had reaffirmed the principle of monarchy throughout Europe. As he had earlier aimed at destroying priestcraft by ostensibly conciliating it (*An Address, to the Irish People*), he here initiates an attempt to pave the way for the destruction of the monarchical principle by predetermining its practice through a moral and political indoctrination which, if it took effect, would render the monarchy a moderating influence whose eventual purpose would be to declare itself redundant as an active agency of government. The education the princess was about to receive, historically based and liberally directed, promised to fulfil Hunt's prospects for her by requiring her to deserve the throne rather than accept it as a 'divine right', an 'exploded' doctrine which Hunt found resurgent in France and, so he designedly implied, dangerously subliminal in England.

The early provenance of the holograph text may be conjectured from Forman's statement that the review of *Rhododaphne*, published by Forman with *The Elysian Fields* and *Notes ⟨Remarks⟩ on Sculptures* in 1879, was found by Townshend Mayer among Leigh Hunt's papers. It is unlikely that the fragment would have been overlooked had it been among the Clairmont papers which included the manuscript of *Remarks*—Forman explicitly states that there was no holograph by S among the materials he received from Paola Clairmont. With the exception of *A Proposal for Putting Reform to the Vote* Forman's only direct access to prose manuscripts seems to have been through Mayer. Conceivably S asked Hunt to consider publishing a completed text, offering him the start as an indication of what the whole would be like. S would certainly have meant to publish the work when finished; the *Examiner* would have provided an ideal context for it.

Forman's expansion of the holograph title to *The Elysian Fields, A Lucianic Fragment* was based primarily on the editor's belief that S was referring to this fragment when he noted that he had 'once written a Lucianic essay to prove' that the 'popular faith' was destroyed from the bottom up, 'first the Devil, then the Holy Ghost, then God the Father' (to C. Ollier, 20 Jan. 1821). S's reference was doubtless to *On the Devil, and Devils*, but Forman rightly sensed the Lucianic overtones of the fragment, which help to date it and relate it to the comparable fragment in Mary's hand printed in Appendix II. According to Mary's journal, in 1816 S read Lucian on 29 Sept., 21, 22 Oct., and 10–14 Nov.; Mary read the author on 2, 5–7 Dec. During this period S was also reading *Don Quixote* and *Gulliver's Travels*, both works with Lucianic affiliations. Analogues to S's contemporary use of the Lucianic form for political purposes are suggested by a work of 1788, *L'Écho de l'Élisée, ou Dialogues de quelques Morts Célèbres sur les États-Généraux de la Nation et des Provinces*, and even more strongly by an earlier French listing in the *BLC*, *Entretiens des ombres aux Champs Élysées, sur divers sujets d'histoire, de politique, & de morale* (1723).

1. *dreary scene.* As the later reference to Tartarus confirms, S's Elysian Fields in this context are not the abode of the blessed but akin to Homer's Hades, particularly as this underworld is described and utilized in Lucian, whose works S and Mary were reading in late 1816.

2. *illustrate.* I.e. to render illustrious.

12. *doctrine.* Apparently Frederick's doctrine as quoted.

15–17. *Every one ... tenets.* Lucian, in the *Dialogues of the Dead*, has Pythagoras state the contrary: 'Doctrines are different among the dead.' As one commentator notes on the 'long, almost unbroken procession of writers who have made more or less use' of these *Dialogues*, many of them 'make use of the form only' (Francis G. Allison, *Lucian: Satirist and Artist*, Cooper Square Publishers, Inc.: New York, 1963, 162–3). Wittingly or not, S at times reversed the meaning of his probable sources while apparently echoing their words.

21–2. *they subsist ... dead.* E.g. the speaker in the fragment given in Appendix II.

27–9. *queen ... domestic happiness.* Evidence (1) that it is Charlotte whose accession to the throne is predicted in ll. 38–9 and (2) that the fragment was probably written after her marriage to Leopold.

42. *Pisistratus.* Forman thinks S meant to write 'the sons of Pisistratus'. In the *Cry of War to the Greeks* the 'Pisistratides' (i.e. sons of Pisistratus) are used in a kindred context, and they would better suit S's purpose here. Pisistratus, an Athenian tyrant of the sixth century BC, was once expelled from Athens but returned to resume his tyranny until his death; he was succeeded by his sons Hipparchus and Hippias. The former was murdered and the latter expelled.

53–6. *The English nation ... struggles.* S aligns himself with those reformists who recognized that England's political history through the 'Glorious Revolution' of 1688 provided at best an ambiguous context and argument for political freedom.

ON LEARNING LANGUAGES

Date: ?Autumn 1816.

Copy-text: Bod. MS. Shelley adds. c. 4, fol. 292^r.

Description: Ink holograph consisting of one leaf (folded), measuring 33.9 cm. × 21 cm. (13.25″ × 8.25″); laid paper; WM: Britannia in a crowned oval; the text starts nearly flush with the top of fol. 292^r and is continuous across the fold to the bottom of the page, where it breaks off slightly before the right edge; the verso contains the draft of *A Faustian Note*.

Provenance: Mary Shelley; Sir Percy Shelley and Jane, Lady Shelley; Sir John Shelley-Rolls; Bodleian.

Printed: *1840*. (Since reprinted in editions of S's letters.)

In the *Essays, Letters &c.* of 1840 Mary Shelley appended this fragment to a letter of 16 Nov. 1819 from S to John Gisborne, introducing it with the following note:

> I subjoin here a fragment of a letter, I know not to whom addressed; it is to a woman—which shows how, worshipping as Shelley did the spirit of the literature of ancient Greece, he considered that this could be found only in its original language, and did not consider that time wasted which a person who had pretensions, intellectual culture, and enthusiasm, spent in acquiring them. (ii. 248)

While written in the epistolary style variously associated with novels, satires, and newspaper polemics, the fragment gives no indication of belonging to S's correspondence. Mary is apparently the only editor who saw and used the holograph; later editors have followed her lead by placing the piece among the poet's letters. The Britannia water-mark and the praise of Rousseau suggest a date of composition in mid- or late 1816, though the sentiments anticipate prose writings of S's Italian period.

It is possible that it is a fragmented portion of the instruction which Princess Charlotte was to receive in *The Elysian Fields*. The internal evidence which best links this fragment with *The Elysian Fields* and its instructive purpose appears in ll. 23–5, where the author supposes that his female reader will 'require' a knowledge of those who have helped or hindered humanity in significant ways. The Princess Charlotte was in fact 'imperfectly' educated, as more or less interested observers from the King to her tutor, the Reverend Dr Nott (whom S later met in Italy), were quick to notice and deplore. She received tuition in several languages but, in spite of the aptitude for them occasionally ascribed to her, seems to have acquired a thorough familiarity only with French, and even in that language her companion, Cornelia Knight, found room for improvement as late as 1814. For accounts of her educational deficiencies and the reasons for them (usually associated with her dislike of her masters) see A. Aspinall's Introduction to his edition of the *Letters of the Princess Charlotte 1811–17* (London, 1949) and Charles E. Pearce's *The Beloved Princess* (New York, 1912), which concludes that 'as for her accomplishments, she had none, for the fact was Charlotte was very indifferently educated' (p. 106). This was precisely S's appraisal, as may be inferred from both *The Elysian Fields* and *An Address to the People on the Death of the Princess Charlotte*. The public concern over her education was politically motivated, as Parliamentary speeches and newspaper editorials around the time of her flight from Warwick House demonstrate (see e.g. the excerpt from the *Examiner* in the headnote to *The Elysian Fields*). If this fragment was in some way associated with that concern, it affords an early and practical application of S's sense of the relation between literature and legislation which later appeared in *A Philosophical View of Reform* and concluded *A Defence of Poetry*.

Forman's suggestion that Claire Clairmont might have been the object of S's recipe for acquiring languages is possible but not plausible, particularly in the context of the spring 1821 date he ascribes to the 'letter'. Claire was learning Greek in S's company as early as Sept. 1814; both she and Mary were studying Italian with the poet in Apr. 1815. In any case, there was no reason for S to write her a letter on the subject at any time. Mary's ignorance concerning the addressee fails to support a case for either Claire or Charlotte, though a lapse of nearly a quarter of a century could readily account for her failure to remember the occasion or relation of the fragment as it stands. Her association of the piece with the letter to Gisborne of 1819 was apparently made only because of the expanded reference to Theocritus which makes up the bulk of that letter.

The exaggerated Roman profiles drawn on the verso of this fragment are in a few instances very much like some of those appearing on Bod. MS Shelley adds. c. 4, fol. 195ᵛ, which makes up part of the *Speculations on Morals and Metaphysics*. An identity of watermarks in the paper used on both leaves may indicate a common stock, but there is a slight difference in measurement, probably too great to be explained by variable shrinkage.

9. *mere facts.* Here and below (ll. 13–15) S anticipates his disparagement of 'matter-of-fact history' in the Advertisement to *Epipsychidion* and of the 'detached facts' discountenanced, along with the invidious facts of a poet's life, in *A Defence of Poetry*.

16. *evanescent hues.* Cf. 'the evanescent hues of this etherial world' as a supplement to the poet's 'refined organization' and 'most delicate sensibility' in *A Defence of Poetry*. The *Speculations on Morals and Metaphysics* likewise refers to the 'peculiar hues' of the individual mind and the 'most evanescent expression of countenance' in a comparable context.

18. *What ... English?* The censure of the 'miserable and worthless inadequacy' of translation here anticipates the passage on the 'vanity of translation' in *A Defence of Poetry*.

22. *Livius or Herodotus.* Livy and Herodotus are both considered poets in *A Defence of Poetry*.

31. *Rousseau.* In a letter of 18 July 1816 to Hogg S wrote: 'Rousseau is indeed in my mind the greatest man the world has produced since Milton.' Before reading the *New Heloïse* during his trip around Lake Geneva in summer 1816, S's opinion of Rousseau was mixed or negative.

A FAUSTIAN NOTE

Date: ?Autumn 1816.

Copy-text: Bod. MS Shelley adds. c. 4, fol. 292ᵛ.

Description: See the Description of *On Learning Languages*; the text appears in the middle of the 16.9 cm. (6.7″) page formed by the folded leaf noted in that description and is written at right angles to the recto text; a bit of tree foliage appears in the space at the top; trees and a laurel-topped profile are sketched at the bottom; the rest of the leaf, which is on the other side of the fold, contains an aborted jotting in S's hand ('If the honors') and several Shelleyan sketches, including a seated ?female figure and three profiles, apparently Caesars (or perhaps Dantes), with laurels adorning their heads.

Provenance: Mary Shelley; Sir Percy Shelley and Jane, Lady Shelley; Sir John Shelley-Rolls; Bodleian.

Printed: Previously unpublished.

This *Note*—the title is editorial—may (as suggested by Sir John Shelley-Rolls on the folder containing the leaf) belong to *On Christianity*; it may form part of the many fragments which make up the *Speculations on Morals and Metaphysics*; it may form part of a fictional piece, such as *The Assassins*; it may be a self-contained reflection. While it could serve as a partial description of Christ, it seems rather a generic description of an over-reacher of the Faustian, or Frankensteinian, sort, paralleling as it does one of the moral motifs of Mary Shelley's novel—cf. 'Learn from me ... how dangerous is the acquirement of knowledge and how much happier that man is who believes his native town to be the world, than he who aspires to become greater than his nature will allow' (*Frankenstein; or, the Modern Prometheus*, Penguin Books: London, 1987, 97).

The holograph's false starts and deletions demonstrate that it was a rough draft of whatever it was meant to be or belong to. If the paper on which it appears was in use towards the end of 1816, as suggested in the headnote to *On Learning Languages*, then its composition may be tentatively assigned to the same period. A profile sketched at the bottom of the page on which this short passage appears is part of the series of profiles sketched on the other side of the fold which divides fol. 292ᵛ in two. As noted in the commentary for *On Learning Languages*, these sketches are like those appearing on MS Shelley adds. c. 4, fol. 195ᵛ, which contains part of the *Speculations on Morals and Metaphysics*. There is no way of ascertaining whether fol. 292ᵛ or fol. 292ʳ was written first. *On Learning Languages* is the more finished piece, seems to continue from a previous page, and may have continued on fol. 292ᵛ, had that side of the leaf been blank when it was written. Alternatively, the position of the *Note* on one side of the fold on fol. 292ᵛ may give priority to *On Learning Languages*, if one infers as well that the slight breaks in the ink of the strokes written across the fold of fol. 292ʳ represent flaking consequent on the folding.

DECLARATION IN CHANCERY

Date: 24 Jan.–2 Feb. 1817.

Copy-text: Bod. MS Shelley adds. c. 5, fols. 96ʳ–97ᵛ (Mary Shelley's transcript, presumably of a lost original).

Description: Untitled rough-draft ink transcript consisting of one sheet folded to two leaves (four pages), each measuring 23 cm. × 18.5 cm. (9″ × 7.2″); laid paper; wm: GOLDING | & | SNELGROVE | 1814; the text is continuous from the top of fol. 96ʳ through the bottom of fol. 97ᵛ, where it breaks off in mid-sentence; contains comments and corrections by William Godwin *passim*.

Provenance: Mary Shelley; Sir Percy Shelley and Jane, Lady Shelley; Sir John Shelley-Rolls; Bodleian.

Printed: Dowden, *Life*, ii. 86–8.

Immediately after S heard (on 15 Dec. 1816) that his wife Harriet had committed suicide, he initiated the series of unsuccessful attempts at gaining custody of their children which produced this transcribed draft of the appeal to have his paternal rights restored probably made to the Court of Chancery shortly after 2 Feb. 1817, the date on which Mary Shelley apparently made the transcription (*Journals*).

John Westbrook, Harriet's father, encouraged by her sister Eliza, had previously set up a trust fund for the two infants, Eliza Ianthe and Charles. By so doing, he put the children under the protection of Chancery, so that the case came into the hands of Lord Eldon. As early as 1815 the Westbrooks had warned S that if he attempted to gain custody of his children they would use his writings to prove his parental unfitness. In Jan. 1817 they fulfilled their threat by having their counsel, Sir Samuel Romilly, produce in court copies of *Queen Mab* and *A Letter to Lord Ellenborough* as evidence of the immorality and blasphemy which S's children would be exposed to under their father's care. As S notes at the outset of the *Declaration*, the religious accusations had been dropped. But his printed disparagement of marriage in the Notes to *Queen Mab* remained fully in evidence and was abetted by the fact that he had, until after Harriet's suicide, proved by his relation with Mary Godwin that he practised what he preached.

While S believed that this airing of his views might result in a criminal indictment, he also believed that his natural and prima-facie legal claim to his children would eventually gain him their custody. In a rather agitated and self-justifying letter to Mary (16 Dec. 1816) he wrote that his solicitor, P. W. Longdill, felt that the proposed marriage with Mary would ensure the return of his children. Timothy Shelley's attorney, William Whitton, provided the correct professional diagnosis of the case when he wrote to S's father on 17 Jan. that it was 'most certain' that Lord Eldon would not allow S's parental claim to override his moral disqualifications.

In the letter of 16 Dec. S hinted at the unfitness of the Westbrooks when he threatened to 'cover them with scorn & shame' should they bring the matter before Chancery. Nothing of the sort appears in this document or in any other associated statement made by or on behalf of S. On 17 Mar. the Chancellor handed down a judgment which, as variously implemented over an extended period of time, placed Charles and Eliza Ianthe out of the custody of and out of all communication with their father for the rest of his life. S's cousin Thomas Medwin later wrote that 'The event of this "trial" . . . acted as a continual canker on the mind of Shelley' (Life, 185), an assessment more or less directly confirmed for posterity in the poet's verse attacks on Lord Eldon, who, along with God Almighty and didactic poetry, became the major aversion of his adult life (see CC, entry for 8 Nov. 1820).

A few of the false starts and misspellings in Mary's hand may suggest that part or all of the manuscript was composed rather than transcribed by her, though a Shelleyan 'accomodate' (l. 59c) and cancelled 'alledged' (l. 73) indicate transcription (but not dictation), as may some of the pointing. Since S later refers to it—there seems to be nothing else he could be referring to—as 'my Chancery paper' (to Godwin, 11 Dec. 1817) and Godwin in his high appraisal of it as intimated in the same letter accepted it as such, one may reconcile all the evidence by assuming that Mary somewhat freely copied a rather rough draft, implementing some creative additions of her own as she copied. Both the transcript and the precedent of some other holographs by S suggest that his draft might have been rough enough to require whatever degree of editorial assistance Mary and, more substantively, Godwin had to offer. The transcription is an example of S's prose at its worst and deserves the criticism he made of its later recension in the same letter to Godwin: 'a cold, forced, unimpassioned piece . . . of cramped & cautious argument'—though it is not always as cautious as it should have been for S's purposes at the time. The final version, presumably containing at least some of Godwin's as well as S's emendations and rephrasings, doubtless improved on this transcription, but his evaluation of the end-product suggests that the improvement was negligible. Presumably this final version was presented as part of S's brief, but the fact that it was not incorporated, even in transcript, into the other documents extant at the PRO suggests the alternative possibility that S presented his argument orally from the paper. Some of the pointing—the use of the semicolon in particular—suggests that it was written and transcribed with a view to oral presentation. In its final form, however presented, it might have shared the fate of the original letters from S to Harriet, which, along with copies of Queen Mab and A Letter to Lord Ellenborough (which Eliza Westbrook stated she saw in holograph), were used in evidence, then returned to the solicitors' offices and apparently destroyed.

In order to come as close as possible to S's draft as transcribed by Mary, while still allowing for the probability that S in the presumed final version accepted at least some of Godwin's corrections, the text is printed with the holograph cancellations of S's presumed original draft in square brackets and Godwin's corrections in italic surrounded by angle brackets. The reader may therefore reconstruct both S's presumed original and a presumed later version, which could have made use of Godwin's corrections and suggestions. These latter appear to have been written at two different times, since they appear variously worked in both a thicker and a thinner nib. The possibility that the transcription is in fact Mary's composition, put together from information provided to her by S, is slight, though the tone of Godwin's comments suggest a paternal familiarity which could support such a hypothesis. However, it was also the case that by early 1817 S was himself one of the family. Dowden's statement (*Life*, ii. 86) that the manuscript is in 'Shelley's handwriting' is of course erroneous.

The transcription was apparently based on a holograph probably written just after the hearing of the case before Lord Eldon on 24 Jan. While White also wrongly assumed that S wrote the extant manuscript (*Shelley*, i. 494), his inference that Mary wrote a 'fair copy' of S's earlier draft may perhaps apply to it if one supposes that Godwin later 'corrected' it into the rougher state of the present draft, which S then presumably refashioned into an expanded and useable form some time before his next court appearance (presumably before 17 Mar., when the Lord Chancellor handed down his decision in the case). Godwin's diary during this phase of the Chancery hearings demonstrates that he was seeing a good deal of the Shelleys (who stayed at his London house on the nights of 26, 31 Jan. and 1 Feb.) and so had abundant opportunity to add his interpolations to the transcript at any time after Mary had drafted it and before S had groomed it into a final form.

Related primary and secondary materials: LETTERS, to Eliza Westbrook, 18 Dec. 1816 (PRO copy), to Mary Shelley, 11 Jan. 1817, to Byron, 17 Jan. 1817, to Claire Clairmont, 30 Jan. 1817, to Lord Eldon, 20 Sept. 1817, to Dr Thomas Hume, 17 Feb. 1821; Mary Shelley, *Letters*, to Marianne Hunt, 6 Aug. 1817; *Queen Mab* Note to 'Even love is sold'; *On Marriage* (and EC); *Examiner*, 26 Jan. 1817 (in White, *Unextinguished Hearth*, 109–10); anon., *Reply to the Anti-Matrimonial Hypothesis . . . of Percy Byssche ⟨sic⟩ Shelley . . .* (London, 1821), 6–42; 'Art. VI', *Quarterly Review*, 39 (1829), 193, 200, 210; 'Shelley v. Westbrooke', in Edward Jacob's *Reports of Cases Argued and Determined in the High Court of Chancery* (Gould, Banks & Co.: New York, 1844), 266–8; *Shelley Memorials*, 84–7; Peacock, *Memoirs*, 345–7 (in Hogg, *Life*, ii); Rossetti, *Memoir*, 72–6; Dowden, *Life*, ii. 76–95; Medwin, *Life*, 182–9, 463–86; J. C. Jeaffreson, *The Real Shelley* (London, 1885), ii. 304–14; Salt, *Principles*, 45–8; Rousseau A. Burch, 'The Case of Shelley v. Westbrooke', *Case and Comment*, 23 (1916), 181–7; Ingpen, *Shelley in England*,

490–516; Peck, *Life and Work*, i. 505–16; *Shelley's Lost Letters to Harriet*, ed. Leslie Hotson (London, 1930), *passim*; White, *Shelley*, i. 489–97, 723–7; *SC* v. 272–4, 390–1, vi. 648–52; Cameron, *Golden Years*, 48–52; Mary Shelley, *Journals*, i. 155–8 nn.; William St Clair, *The Godwins and the Shelleys: A Biography of a Family* (New York, 1989), 418–19. (Copies of S's brief petition and the Westbrook affidavits, annotated by a lawyer in the case, are in the Brewer Leigh Hunt Collection at the University of Iowa Library.)

1–3. *I understand . . . children.* See Appendix III.

36. *Selden.* John Selden (1584–1654), English jurist, legal antiquary, and oriental scholar. The reference is probably to his *Uxor Ebraica* (1646), a treatise on marriage and divorce practices among the Jews. Godwin probably replaced 'Milton' with 'Selden' for tactical reasons. Milton was controversial on every applicable ground, political, religious, and marital, while Selden was not only an ally of the Chancellor's favourite legal commentator, Sir Edward Coke, but also a sometime dissenter from the Establishment.

44–54. *If I am judged . . . heart⟨s⟩.* This is the most 'forced' and 'cramped' sentence in the fragment even as Mary originally transcribed it. Godwin's additions further encumber it but the resultant text would seem to mean and imply the following: 'If I am judged an improper guardian for my children because I express opinions which differ from orthodox positions, then the only men of an enquiring and liberal spirit who can express their opinions will be those who, unlike most men, either have no feelings to speak of or have had their feelings groomed to the satisfaction of the state. Otherwise, if they hold and express opinions kindred to mine, they must live in fear of a court of justice being used by private parties ⟨like the Westbrooks⟩ to exact private vengeance, under the guise of protecting the public good, by attacking the heartfelt beliefs of the individual whom they seek vengeance on, even though ⟨so the implication⟩ these beliefs have nothing to do with the case before the court.' Read slowly and with a due regard to the pointing the passage may, after a trial or two, allow one to infer a formal pattern which conveys the general sense rhetorically to the listening ear if not expediently to the reading eye. The use of the semicolon after 'account', like that after 'proof' in l. 71, is rhetorical rather than syntactical—it emphasizes the word it follows by requiring a pause from the speaker or reader. Still, if this pile of agglutinating clauses and convoluted negatives persisted into the final copy, Godwin's praise might have been meant to ring hollow, though he himself was responsible for the qualifying—and inflating and perhaps distorting—insertions.

51–2. *court of justice . . . vengeance.* See S's letter of 11 Jan. 1817 to Mary, where he spells out his interpretation of the Westbrooks' use of Chancery as an act of 'sheer revenge', a perspective on his situation which characteristically grew into the familiar Shelleyan context of oppression represented by 'tyranny and superstition' in a related portion of a later letter to Byron (17 Jan. 1817).

55–6. *I am aware ... country.* Godwin comments: 'This is sadly expressed. It is about as significant as if you said, I am aware the sun rises every Monday.'

63. *delicacy forbids.* S suspected Harriet of prostitution and cohabitation, though his reference here may be to his general sense of the intellectual and spiritual incompatibility which had grown up between them.

A PROPOSAL FOR PUTTING REFORM TO THE VOTE THROUGHOUT THE KINGDOM

Date: Late Feb. 1817.

Copy-texts: Holograph (Houghton Library, Harvard University, MS Lowell 36); revised proof (*P*) of the 1817 printing (Bodleian, Bod. ⟨pr.⟩ Shelley e. 3); *1817* (Huntington, shelfmark RB 22406).

Locations (of *1817*): Include BL (2, one in Ashley); Brown; Georgetown; Harvard; Huntington; Northwestern; Pf.; University of Texas; William Andrews Clark Memorial (UCLA); Yale.

Descriptions: Ink holograph written on the recto sides of eighteen leaves. The title-page measures 17.8 cm. × 15 cm. (7.1″ × 5.9″), matted (see below); wove paper; WM: 181?5; the title and author are in S's hand, the bookseller's imprint in another hand, perhaps the same that wrote 'Mr. Shelley's copy' on the verso; the pages of the text proper measure 19.3 cm. × 15.3 cm. (7.6″ × 6.1″) and are each matted into a page 24 cm. × 20 cm. (9.5″ × 7.9″); wove paper; WM: J. BUDGEN | 1814; the text is continuous; fol. 14ᵛ contains a sketch of a classical temple and a few trees which cover about two-thirds of the page, beneath which is written: 'I have no doubt that the above is a sketch by my dear friend Shelley's own hand. Leigh Hunt'; fol. 16ᵛ contains a cancelled false start ('eminence of man', scored through), rewritten on fol. 17ʳ; fol. 17ᵛ contains what may be a mailing address, written vertically, perhaps in S's hand: 'Mr. Shelley | Mr. Hunts'; correspondence between watermarked and unwatermarked leaves (fols. 1, 6–12 have watermarks), the fact that the uneven (torn) sides of fols. 13–17 are identical, and recurrent stab-holes indicate that the leaves of the text were once part of a notebook, as do the blank versos: S occasionally found it expedient to write on only one side of a notebook leaf to prevent blotting; the title-page is unnumbered, the text itself centrally numbered 1–17; the corresponding Houghton foliation is continuous from 7 (title-page) to 24, the first six leaves taken up with sale-catalogue descriptions etc.; the leaves and accompanying matter are in a maroon casing trimmed in gold foliage with a centred cartouche enclosing a motto: 'The honey for thee | the flower for me'; a folded envelope preceding the title-page has a cancelled address ('Henry Colburn, Esq.— | New Burlington Street', scored through), a docket reading 'Mr. Ollier', and the following (?)contemporary endorsement: 'Mr. P. B. Shelley's Pamphlet | "Proposal for putting Reform to the Vote", | in his own original autograph'.

The revised proof of *1817* and *1817* itself measure 22.6 cm. × 14 cm. (8.9″ × 5.5″) and are made up of a single gathering (⟨A⟩⁸), which consists of a title-page (verso blank; ⟨1–2⟩, a drop-head title ('A Proposal &c.'; written into the revised proof) followed by a centrally numbered text (⟨3⟩–15; ⟨16⟩ blank); wove paper; WM: AP | 1815; no running heads; a printer's slug below 'FINIS.' at the foot of p. 15 reads: 'C. H. Reynell, Printer, | 21, Piccadilly.' *P* varies as follows from *1817*: WM: M | 1815; pp. 3–7 (*P*) conclude with the first lines of pp. 4–8 (*1817*) respectively; pp. 13–15 vary to accommodate the insertion of ll. 162–7 ('The statement . . . reply'), written above the text on p. 13 in *P*; accidentals differ as noted in the Collation, which also records differences between *P* and the revisions appearing on it (*PC*); the great majority of the corrections are in black ink and in S's hand; corrections on the title-page and the drop-head title are in a brownish ink and in another hand; vertical lines in the margins of pp. 11–12 were probably made by Leigh Hunt, as were the two names ('Buccleuch' | 'Murray') written to the left of the vertical line on p. 12; sketches of trees by S appear in the right margin, at the bottom, and on the verso of the title-page; on the verso of the last leaf are several jottings, all, or nearly all, of which are in Leigh Hunt's hand; they are obviously notes for the Rider to the Preface he wrote for his 1832 edition of S's *Masque of Anarchy* (see Appendix IV). The unbound pages which make up *P* are contained within a thin pink wrapping attached to a brown cardboard folder. The Huntington title-page of *1817* is reproduced on page 169.

Provenances: HOLOGRAPH: Charles Ollier family; Francis Harvey; Thomas J. Wise; Sir Stuart Samuel; Amy Lowell; Houghton. PROOF: (?)Charles Ollier; Leigh Hunt; Sir Percy Shelley and Jane, Lady Shelley; Bodleian.

Reprinted: (*1817*): MacCarthy, *Early Life*; *F*; *J*. (A facsimile of the holograph was published by the Shelley Society in 1887, with an Introduction and Appendix provided by H. Buxton Forman.)

S had completed the draft of *A Proposal for Putting Reform to the Vote* before 22 Feb. 1817, since on that date he sent a messenger to its publisher, Charles Ollier, with instructions to wait for the revise. On 14 Feb. S had signed the lease for the house at Marlow from which he took his pseudonym. Previously, on 9 Feb., S had stayed up until 3 a.m. discussing 'monarchy and republicanism' with William Hazlitt (Mary Shelley, *Journals*). Earlier that day the Shelleys had visited Lord Brougham, who, like S in the *Proposal*, was an advocate of annual Parliaments and a franchise limited to those who paid direct taxes. Such evidence, concrete and circumstantial, suggests that S drafted the pamphlet some time between 10 and 21 Feb., and that the corrections and additions on the proof were probably entered soon after he had received it from Ollier. An undated letter to Ollier evidently written after that of 22 Feb. (though placed before it in *Letters*) enclosed the 'Revise' of the proof and instructed the publisher to put it 'to press when corrected, & the sooner the better'. In the *Examiner* for 2 Mar. Hunt, editor of the weekly, quoted an excerpt which he had apparently made from the revised proof of this 'little pamphlet just published' from an unidentified hand. On 14 Mar. S asked Ollier 'How does the pamphlet sell?'—a query which indicates that it had been on the market for a few days at least. S himself apparently expected the pamphlet to sell quite well. He wished 500 copies printed, about one hundred of which, in keeping with the ecumenical tenor of the *Proposal*, he directed Ollier (in the undated letter noted above) to send to reformists of all persuasions, radical, moderate, and conservative (see Appendix V). But the fact that the pamphlet is relatively scarce and was little noticed suggests that Ollier did not print 500 copies; his own notations on S's list demonstrate that he sent little more than half of the copies S had requested him to send (see *Letters*, i. 533–4). A short note to the radical bookseller William Hone, dubiously dated 20 Apr. 1817, requires 'an answer on the subject of the Pamphlet', probably S's last reference to his *Proposal*. Since S said to Ollier in the undated letter that Hone was one of those (along with Stockdale and Sherwood Neeley & Co.) likely to 'take copies on their own account', S's note to Hone probably followed up a previous attempt to 'arrange' with him (as he says he did with Hookham) to take a number of copies on his own account.

While André Koszul (K 147) supposed the holograph to be an intermediate copy, the relevant letters and the provenance (as recorded by H. B. Forman) place it in Ollier's possession from the first (which was perhaps the last) time it left S's hands. The fact that it contains on its title-page the addition, in a hand other than S's, of the publisher's name and address as they were to appear in the printed text seems to confirm Forman's inference, presumably derived not only from the provenance but also from a comparison of the holograph with *1817*, that, though heavily revised, it was the printer's copy. As indicated in the Collation, Textual Notes, and Editorial Commentary, at least a few of the errors noted in the proof evidently stemmed directly from a misreading of the extant holograph.

It can be demonstrated that, even in close context, S's proofreading was not thorough. He appropriately changes a 'their' to 'its' (l. 125) in the proof, but earlier in the sentence fails to make the same change (see l. 123C); the cancelled 'in' of l. 1 (see the Collation) was restored by the printer and was probably allowed to stand because S did not notice it; the omission in the proof of the holograph 'or' in the same line was probably allowed to stand for the same reason; the printer misread S's holograph 'alone' as 'altho' in l. 55 and S cancelled the misreading (printed as 'although') without restoring the original; in the same line he failed in the proof to restore the placing of 'then' which he clearly preferred in the holograph (see 55TN); the commas in the proof at l. 136 (see the Collation) are both unnecessary and uncharacteristic of S's practice; in two instances S changed a lower-case letter to a capital in the holograph but the change was reversed by the printer (see Collation to ll. 121 and 138).

Considering these discrepancies and given the holograph's provenance, a reasonable presumption is that the printer or Ollier himself (in spite of the possible return address noted in the Description) did not return it to S for collation when he sent him the proof, even assuming that it was customarily felt necessary or expedient to return printer's copy to the author when time was of the essence. If in fact S did have his holograph at hand, the indications are that he did not make much use of it. The discrepancies noted above, together with others listed and commented on in the Collation and Textual Notes, suggest that generally he read through the proof for sense, which he occasionally qualified and in one instance added to, paying only sporadic attention to accidentals (see the Textual Notes to ll. 22, 32). Substantive changes made by the printer were also usually allowed to stand.

The only serious editorial question is whether the words and pointing S wrote should be preferred to those which, as far as the extant evidence can demonstrate, he accepted from the corrector or printer. The appropriate editorial answer seems obvious enough from all of the above. S did not correct his proof carefully and probably did not check it against the holograph. He was clearly and for good reason concerned with getting his pamphlet into print as soon as possible, and, in his haste to get the text back to the printer, evidently overlooked discrepancies between his manuscript and the proof which he would most probably have rectified in favour of the manuscript if he had noticed them. The holograph has therefore been preferred as the basic copy-text; the revised proof has of course been used to supplement the manuscript where new material was added, and its readings are preferred for other substantives and accidentals in cases where there is evidence that S had read the proof closely. That a hand other than S's made a few of the pointing changes either before he received or after he returned the proof is possible but unprovable. The editorial presumption here is that these changes were either made or passed on by S and that, so far as the proof is concerned, they, and only they, may be accepted as his final intentions.

The *1817* printing itself, which has been previously reprinted as S's final intention, is probably the least authoritative of the three possible copy-texts, because the best inference from available evidence is that S neither made nor passed on the variants between it and the holograph and/or the revised proof. As noted above, when S sent his 'Revise'—presumably *P*—to Ollier he asked him to correct it but also made it clear that he did not himself expect to see the final clean proof before the actual printing took place. Some antecedent support for a seemingly inverted hierarchy of editorial preferences may be supplied by the printings of the Irish pamphlets, which were hastily got up and cursorily proofread at best, and would hardly have been preferred to holograph printer's copies were these extant. Questions about the authenticity of the holograph raised in R. M. Smith *et al.*, *The Shelley Legend* (New York, 1945), were convincingly answered in K. N. Cameron *et al.*, *An Examination of the Shelley Legend* (Philadelphia, 1951).

While the assumption that the corrector was responsible for the accidentals in *1817* which differ from those in *P* may be accepted on the basis of the letter to Ollier noted above, the substitution of the word 'desires' for the holograph 'wills' in l. 157 is a sole but perhaps significant item of evidence for supposing that yet another proof intervened between *P* and the published version, a supposition which might then lead one to prefer *1817* as the copy-text after all. The word 'revise', which S uses when referring to the proof in his letters to Ollier is ambiguous enough to confirm such an inference, since strictly speaking a revise means a proof corrected from an earlier corrected proof. But the fact that ll. 122–5 do not appear in the holograph indicates that the extant corrected proof could itself have been a 'revise', in this technical sense of the word, of an earlier proof made directly from the holograph. Given S's concern to get his pamphlet into print as soon as possible, the likelihood of three proofs seems negligible; indeed, the best supposition may be that S was using 'revise' loosely enough to apply it to the single proof he received (cf. W. H. Davenport in *N&Q* 177 (1939), listed below), namely *P*, and that the added lines were supplied on a separate sheet, now lost, as an addendum—or even, given their context and content, that they constitute a prudent disclaimer added by the printer and/or publisher to ward off charges of sedition which the anonymous pamphlet might have brought down on their heads. That *1817*'s 'desires' was a sole erratum sent to the printer is highly unlikely, particularly given the fact that S's emphasis throughout the *Proposal* is on the efficient and necessary place of the nation's or the people's 'will' (cf. l. 45c) in deciding the question of reform. The additional fact that 'wills' is the holograph reading unchanged in the extant proof seems sufficient grounds to accept it and suppose that the house corrector (perhaps for rhetorical reasons) or the printer (perhaps for spacing reasons) supplied the synonym. As the collations indicate, other differences between *1817* and the copy-texts as preferred here are accidental. Practically speaking, the choice of copy-text and preferred variants will probably matter very little to the common reader, since none of the substantive differences affect the general sense of the *Proposal* and very few of the accidental ones affect as much as the rhetorical disposition of the syntax.

The capitalization of certain words and phrases, such as 'Universal Suffrage', 'Annual Parliaments', and, most notably, 'Reform' itself, had to some degree become standard practice, which S might be expected to have followed once he evidenced an awareness of it. But the fact is that he did not do so in the holograph, whatever he might later have let pass as his intention in *P*, several of whose capitals were then later changed in

1817. It is also the case, as a brief survey of the relevant *Examiner*s would demonstrate, that editorial writers, correctors, and printers were not themselves consistent in capitalizing these and kindred words or phrases. Such contemporary precedents—paralleled and confirmed by the indifferent spelling of words like 'allege' ('alledge')—seem to make the decision either way a matter of *ad hoc* impressionism. S seems himself to have followed these precedents in pointing in many instances and in capitalization at all times (cf. l. 155, where 'Annual' replaces a cancelled 'annual' ⟨154c⟩). For that reason, an attempt at rectifying S's holograph in this matter is made only when traditional rather than topical usage may seem to confirm the emendation (e.g. 'Great Britain' rather than 'great Britain'). In one or two contexts a possible rhetorical distinction justifies what may seem an arbitrary inconsistency: for example, S at the start of the *Proposal* refers to the 'people' because he attaches no particular emphasis to the reference; when he enters into his formal proposal—and into the resolutions at its core—he uses 'People', a generic equivalent of 'Nation' in these latter contexts (cf. the Collation on l. 22 for an acceptance of *P*'s capital). When the printer fails to follow S's holograph capital in 'Idol' (l. 33), S is preferred, not simply out of diplomatic courtesy, but because contemporary grammars sanctioned such rhetorical emphases. The fact that *1817* apparently returns to the holograph to replace *P*'s 'universal suffrage' (passively accepted by S) merely highlights the arbitrary impressionism variably at work in both printer and author (see the Collation on l. 186).

S's concern in the *Proposal* was to unite reformists throughout the country around a principle which had been called into question as much by the heated factionalism of its supporters as by a Tory ministry and an unrepresentative, unregenerate House of Commons. With Brougham attacking Major Cartwright, and Cartwright attacking Sir Francis Burdett, and William Cobbet stigmatizing as '"Mock Reformers" some of the truest friends of freedom in the land' (*Examiner*, 2 Feb. 1817), reform as a principle on which they all agreed was subordinated to the different ways and degrees in and by which they thought it should be instituted. As Burdett noted, they were very much like the dissident Protestants who lost sight of the common cause in their divisive quibbles. 'Instead of looking at each other with captious feelings of jealousy, ⟨Burdett⟩ hoped Reformers would abstain from mutual criminations, no longer participating in that spirit of religious bigotry that illustrated its intolerance in proportion as it approximated in principle' (*Examiner*, 2 Mar. 1817). S's moderation in his stated principles of reform is therefore in large part a function of his plea for conciliation among its divided and divisive proponents. The petitions presented daily in Parliament and at reformist meetings throughout the country had demonstrated in their separate and sometimes disparate requests for Annual or Triennial Parliaments,

Universal or Limited Suffrage, that in effect the nation was uttering with a single voice an 'almost universal' demand for reform (*Morning Chronicle*, 17 Feb. 1817). S wished first the leaders and then the people in effect to place the hundreds of thousands of signatures affixed to hundreds of documents on a single document that would 'declare and publish' that demand comprehensively and unequivocally. The reason S did not in this proposal provide a section detailing the underlying and overshadowing economic motives for reform that he later wrote into both *An Address to the People on the Death of the Princess Charlotte* and *A Philosophical View of Reform* was not that in Feb. 1817 he was unfamiliar with them but rather that, in congruence with his arguments against a reformist platform full of volatile specifics, he did not care to add fuel to the fires of factionalism or otherwise alienate the economically insecure bourgeoisie by further indicating, as he must have done, his sympathies with the economic goals of a depressed and incendiary proletariat. The asserted position of the more pragmatic reformers was that parliamentary reform was a necessary prerequisite to lasting economic reform.

The immediate social and political context for S's *Proposal* was indexed by three events which illustrated the need for moderation among the reformists if they were going to attract to their cause the rather fearful and uncomfortable middle classes who were increasingly recognized as holding the balance of power between the will of the people and the restraints of the Government. On 2 Dec. 1816 a portion of a huge crowd of over 50,000 gathered at Spa-Fields to hear Henry 'Orator' Hunt preach his version of radical reform apparently caused a riot which had to be put down by force; on 28 Jan. 1817 the Regent's carriage was stoned as it carried him to the opening session of Parliament. The third event, conditioned by the first two and by a Parliamentary report alleging the serious threat of a general uprising in different parts of the country, was the suspension of Habeas Corpus, which, while not actually passed by Parliament until 4 Mar., had been anticipated for several days.

As the reformists saw it, the government were taking advantage of a few acts of violence and ultra-radical agitation to call into question the reform movement in all its variations. It was up to the reformists to demonstrate their moderation. And that is what S is doing here. It was also left up to them to demonstrate their respectability. Only by remaining the 'Hermit of Marlow' could S hope to dissociate himself from the Chancery trial of *Shelley* v. *Westbrook* (just then a subordinate feature of the press), wherein the defendant was accused of denying God and disregarding the marriage bond.

Except for Hunt's use of it, the *Proposal* seems to have fallen on indifferent ears, perhaps because it was theoretically not particularly striking (three million Englishmen speaking with one voice would merely have formulated a recognized consensus), except where it was presently infeasible. Still, if that voice could have been represented in the single document S proposed, it might have provided the irresistible force in fact which the reformists already supposed in theory. In a denigrating metaphor of the day, the tables of Parliament might well groan with unregarded reform petitions dating as far back as the 1790s, but a more significant sound might instead emanate from both chambers if *one* petition subsumed them all and avoided the contradictions and factionalism they represented. While as late as 19 Sept. 1819 the *Examiner* reminded its readers of the pamphlet when noting a slightly promising implementation of its proposal at Leeds, the only significant notice S's contribution seemed on the verge of receiving remained at best a broken purpose. Southey's anti-reform essay in the *Quarterly Review* for Jan. 1817 (actually published in Apr.), 'On the Rise and Progress of Popular Disaffection', listed the *Proposal* among those reformist tracts to be considered—and then perhaps unwittingly satirized S's work in particular by omitting any further reference to it.

Related primary and secondary materials: LETTER, to Byron, 20 Nov. 1816; *An Address to the People on the Death of the Princess Charlotte* and commentary; *A Philosophical View of Reform* and commentary; *Hansard*, xxviii. 452–79; *Examiner*, 26 Jan.–30 Mar. 1817,19 Sept., 10 Oct. 1819; H. Buxton Forman, 'The Hermit of Marlow: A Chapter in the History of Reform', *The Gentleman's Magazine*, NS 38 (May 1887), 483–97 (repr. as the Introduction to Forman's 1887 facsimile edition); Peck, *Life and Work*, i. 520–3; Grabo, *Magic Plant*, 193–5; William H. Davenport, 'Footnote for a Political Letter of Shelley', *N&Q*, 176 (Apr. 1939), 236–7; id., 'Notes on Shelley's Political Prose: Sources, Bibliography, Errors in Print', ibid. 177 (Sept. 1939), 224; White, *Shelley*, i. 515–16; Kenneth Neill Cameron, 'Shelley vs. Southey: New Light on an Old Quarrel', *PMLA* 57 (June 1942), 492–504; id., 'A Reference to Shelley in *The Examiner*', *N&Q* 184 (Jan. 1943), 42; id., 'Shelley and the Reformers', *ELH* 12 (Mar. 1945), 62–72; *SC* ii. 895 n., iii. 108 n., v. 274; Blunden, *Shelley*, 181–2; Thompson, *Working Class*, 603–49; McNeice, *Revolutionary Idea*, 81–4, 105–6; Guinn, *Political Thought*, 48–50; King-Hele, *Thought and Work*, 90–1; Cameron, *Golden Years*, 123–5, 428, 592; John Cannon, *Parliamentary Reform: 1640–1832* (Cambridge, 1973), 116–25, 158–74; Dawson, *Unacknowledged Legislator*, 53, 172–5, 184–96; Scrivener, *Radical Shelley*, 112–19; Charles E. Robinson, 'Percy Bysshe Shelley, Charles Ollier, and William Blackwood', in *Shelley Revalued*, 187, 215 n. 18; Hoagwood, *Scepticism*, 156–60; Hogle, *Shelley's Process*, 253–7.

1. The cancelled 'Sir' here and preceding l. 70 (see the Collation) indicates that S had originally intended to direct his pamphlet to a specific reformist leader, who would be responsible for convening the meeting proposed in ll. 70–1. Like the letter to Carlisle of Nov. 1819, it could then have been intended (as J notes, vi. 351) for publication in the *Examiner*. Even if, as seems probable, the addressee was the moderate Francis Burdett—often singled out or apostrophized as the particular 'Friend of the People'—S must have become convinced on reflection that

a generalized form of address was more in keeping with the political ecumenism he was soliciting. He might also have felt some uneasiness about directing his proposal to a specific reformist leader who (for reasons noted above) might be compromised should S's authorship become known.

11. *thousandth ... community.* A reformist tract dated 23 Jan. 1817 specified this disproportion by noting that an electorate of 15,000, controlled by 257, returned a majority of the members of the House of Commons while the potential adult male suffrage was three million (anon., *Common Consent, The Basis of the Constitution of England...*, T. & J. Allman: London, 48). This writer advocated public meetings and an 'irresistible expression of public opinion' to bring about a reform which he felt should be both radical and middle-class. The *Morning Chronicle* for 31 Jan. 1817 reported that at that date there were half a million signatories to various petitions for reform then before Parliament, all of them advocating universal suffrage.

12–14. *An hospital ... exhibits.* S applies to England a generalized analogy he found as follows in *PJ*: 'The supposition would be parallel, if we were to imagine ten thousand men of sound intellect, shut up in a madhouse, and superintended by a set of three or four keepers' (i. 98).

47–56. *If the majority ... people.* The *Examiner* for 2 Feb. 1817 reported George Canning's Parliamentary speech indicative of ministerial feeling concerning the questions of popular sovereignty and the people's charter which S begs in these lines: 'He trusted that when the time came, the House would repel with indignation the attempt to make them the mere creatures of the people, instead of the guardians of their rights; otherwise, from the moment they admitted the necessity of Reform, the British Constitution would be gone.' Radical reformists like Major Cartwright were explicit in their belief that members of the House of Commons were 'mere creatures of the people'. S is careful in these lines not to spell out the 'consequences of the contest that might ensue', but he makes it clear, as Hunt was then doing in the *Examiner*, that the true anarchs would not be the people but rather an unresponsive and unrepresentative Parliament, which, in refusing to admit the necessity of reform, implied the necessity of revolution.

57–67. *If the majority ... decision.* S envisages a Hobbesian majority still inert enough to prefer security to the risk of innovation. But his conclusion is Godwinian: the leaders of a reformist minority should not incite their followers to impose reform on a people whose unwillingness to accept it proves they are not ready for it. S believed, with the radical reformists, that all male adults were capable of voting knowledgeably on the general question of reform. While he later restricts that suffrage to householders paying direct taxes, and so aligns with the moderate reformists in their bid to gain middle-class support, his real reason for advocating a restricted electorate as a political expedient was also God-winian: the masses were not yet sufficiently enlightened to vote for their own best self-interests in matters more complex than the general question of reform (*PJ* i. 254–7). The radicals felt that the lower classes must be agitated first so that they might fire the middle class to reformist activity; the moderates felt that the middle class should take the lead by preparing the lower classes for a reform they were not yet ready for. S's heart, or at least part of it, was with the radicals but his head was with the moderates. In *A Philosophical View of Reform* (1819) S's advocacy of radical reform is based on his recognition of its necessity rather than of its propriety at that time. The conditions were not ideal; but they were ripe. In 1817 S still hoped for a benevolent reform perfected in modera-tion.

71. *the   of.* The final form of the *Proposal* probably omitted the date (see the Collation) because S realized he had neither the time nor the prestige to convoke a meeting of leading reformists, though it was also the case that the seventeenth of March had seditious associ-ations at least subliminally disquieting to a moderate audience. S apparently hoped that one of the reformists to whom he sent his pamph-let would implement it. Besides the excerpt in the *Examiner* (and the use of its title by Southey in the *Quarterly*), there is no evidence that anyone of consequence noticed it.

75–8. *That the most eloquent ... disunited.* Burdett's speech at the meeting in the Freemason Tavern of the 'Friends of ... Reform' on 22 Feb. 1817 echoed S: 'In obtaining Reform, he was determined ... to be all things to all men who agreed in the principle', further reminding them that 'every thing, however short of the full accomplishment, extorted from their powerful adversaries, was an advantage' (*Examiner*, 2 Mar. 1817). Both the problems and the extremes to be united were exemplified by two other men present at the meeting, Thomas Brand, MP, and Robert Waithman, both on S's mailing-list for the *Proposal*. Brand agreed that it was 'worse than idle to differ on trifling points of detail', but by noting that he did not believe in either universal suffrage or annual parliaments because they would weaken the House of Commons, he inspired Waithman to point out that the Commons had failed the people for thirty years and then query whether those present could support it as presently elected. Godwin's friend, John Philpot Curran, likewise on S's list, apparently spoke for a consensus which S adhered to in the *Proposal* when he said that 'if the words Universal Suffrage were acted upon to the extent of their meaning (which in his conscience he did not believe the people understood), he was satisfied there would be no representation at all' (ibid.). The *Morning Chronicle*, not always consistent in its essentially liberal representations, argued against both universal and householder suffrage because it feared an adverse effect on the landed interests of so extended and town-based a franchise (31 Jan. 1817). Southey, writing in the *Quarterly Review* for Oct. 1816, surveyed the reformists' dilemma from the comfortable perspective of an Establishment advocate: 'But what is meant by Parliamentary Reform? Whenever this question has been propounded among the reformists at their meetings, it has operated like the apple of discord—the confusion of Babel has been renewed,—with this difference, that the modern castle-builders are confounded in their understandings and not in their speech. One is for triennial parliaments, another for annual; and one, more simple than honest, proposes to petition for triennial only as a step towards obtaining annual. One will have a qualification for voters, another demands universal suffrage. Mr. Orator Hunt proposes voting by ballot, and one of the Penny Orators says, that if Magna Charta were made the bulwark of a General Reform the country would be speedily relieved' (pp. 252-3). S might well have had this article in mind when composing his own solution to the chaotic condition among reformists which Southey cynically but correctly described. The asociation with the rabble-rousing Henry 'Orator' Hunt was, like similarly implied kinships with the Spenceans, a calculated attempt at reducing the reformist movement to its lowest common denominator. Leigh Hunt was particularly outraged (in the *Examiner* for 24 Nov. 1816) that the Tory press had deliberately confused him with his namesake in reporting the latter's speech at Spa-Fields on 15 Nov. 1816, which, though disclaiming violence as a means, instigated a riotous aftermath, as reported in the *Examiner* for 17 Nov. Henry Hunt is conspicuously absent from the list of reformists to whom S asked Charles Ollier to send his *Proposal* (see Appendix V).

106. *"the.* S's MS quotes are retained here and in l. 118 because they represent the words which, in effect, he is assigning to the signatories of this declaration. However, one could argue that his approval of the printer's omission of the MS accidentals was more than tacit, on the grounds that he did not want to arbitrate but merely to suggest the words to be used. Two of the more or less specious reasons advanced in Parliament for rejecting reformist petitions were that they appeared in the same words as other petitions and that they were printed rather than handwritten. Godwin provided a substantive reason for questioning such petitions when he pointed out that quite often the uneducated merely parroted the dictates of their demagogic leaders (*PJ* i. 254-5).

115-16. *if we shall ... petition.* Cf. ll. 57-67. S distinguished (as Godwin did) between a minority which petitioned and a minority which agitated.

122-5. *5. . . . constitutional.* This proposition does not appear in the MS and might then have been supplied by S in a previous proof of which *P* is the 'revise'. It is possible that either Ollier or Reynell, the printer, advised S to add this common disclaimer in order to ward off *ex officio* informations (see *Address, to the Irish People*, 921EC), of which (given the anonymity of the pamphlet) they would have been the indicated targets. Alternatively, as suggested in the headnote, they could have provided the proposition themselves.

130. The words deleted here and in l. 133 (see the Collation) seem to have been meant by S to justify the 'Hermit' pen-name as well as an ulterior unwillingness to put himself forward in a cause his presence might harm. His considered decision is to keep his personal circumstances as much in the background as possible.

140–52. *I shall mention...preservation*. A vertical line appears in *P* next to this paragraph, all but the first sentence of which is used by Hunt in the *Examiner* for 2 Mar. Since Hunt preserved the proof, the best inference is that it was sent to him after the printer had incorporated S's changes and additions into his final copy. To the left of the line appear, evidently in Hunt's hand, the names 'Buccleuch' and 'Murray'. Hunt later incorporated the excerpt from l. 143 ('I have ...) into the Rider to his Preface to the 1832 edition of S's *The Masque of Anarchy* (see above and Appendix IV).

The passage's reference to 'wife and children' (S evidently had in mind his children by Harriet) establishes S's respectability, at least on paper, while the 'claims of general justice' past, present, and prospective could include Hunt himself, Peacock, Godwin, Claire and Charles Clairmont, and what Newman White refers to as 'numerous petty local charities' (*Shelley*, i. 540; cf. S's letter to Godwin of 22 Mar. 1817). After defining the phrase along these lines in a note in his Rider, Hunt adds that he 'does not dispute the phrase with him; but such were the actions of this singular "aristocrat" and most equal-sighted fellow-creature'; Hunt's concern is to deny or qualify S's supposed aristocratic leanings. His contributions to collections taken for beleaguered agitators like Peter Finnerty and William Hone were continuing signs of his material support for reformists and their kind. Neither his charity nor his sense of justice was bound to include his creditors. By October 1817 his debts exceeded £1,500 and led to his arrest (White, *Shelley*, i. 542), a fact which could then have damaged his claim to middle-class respectability and so ensured that he continued as 'The Hermit of Marlow' on the title-page of *An Address to the People on the Death of the Princess Charlotte* (Nov. 1817).

162–7. *The statement...reply*. Written at the top of p. 13 in *P*, probably because S felt the need to declare his position—typically moderate here— while maintaining his ecumenical character. The text accepts the insert's accidentals, several of which were changed in *1817*.

164. *Requisition*. I.e., the £100 of l. 147.

167–9. *It appears...measure*. By favouring annual elections and frowning on an immediate universal extension of the franchise S aligned with the moderates, or, in this respect, with those whom Godwin would call true friends of reform, because they were neither the 'friends of antiquity' nor the 'friends of innovation' (*PJ* i. 256). In stating his arguments in favour of annual parliaments, S anticipates his arguments against universal suffrage. The 'vital imperfections' present forms of government have ingrained in the 'vast multitude of men' must be gradually removed by an educative process which includes annual elections (cf. *PJ*, loc. cit.). In 'An Act for securing the Rights and Liberties of the Nation, by a Constitutional Representation of the Commons in Parliament' (1817 or earlier), the author (perhaps Major Cartwright) places S's rationale for annual parliaments in a tradition: 'It has been wisely remarked, that a free people become acquainted with their duties, by the annual exercise of their right' (p. 29). The 'general reasons' in favour of annual parliaments which S does not repeat include the historical argument (questioned not only by conservatives but even by radicals like Cartwright, who felt reason alone should determine the issue), the anti-bribery argument (annual elections would render bribery relatively unproductive and proportionally expensive), and the argument for a more responsive Commons (whose members would be subject to annual recall). The general reasons were therefore specific and mechanical reformist expedients rather than S's Godwinian argument for an organic gradualism which would eliminate bad government not only in Parliament but also in the minds of men by a kind of on-the-job training in the political process, even (so S seems to imply) if initially they do not all participate fully in it. In 1819 *A Philosophical View of Reform* provided another perspective on the same subject.

184. *Cobbett.* William Cobbett (1766–1835), English journalist whose radical sentiments at this time in his political life aligned fairly well with S's. The 'general reasonings' in favour of annual Parliaments were to be found in Cobbett's widely circulating *Weekly Political Register*, a vehicle for his reformist and sometimes demagogic views. While objecting to Cobbett's 'odious moral qualities' and his tendency to foment factionalism among the reformers, S continued to admire his 'powerful ... genius' throughout his life (to T. L. Peacock, 23–4 Jan. 1819).

186–8. *I confess ... peril.* See on 167–9 above. S's reservations about universal suffrage clearly bothered him. But they were empirically and rationally based, and deep-rooted. Political moderates like Burdett could preach a radical reform which still curtailed the suffrage because like S they realized the need to conciliate conservatives like Brougham, who spoke for the middle class whom the moderates were most concerned to conciliate, when he referred to universal suffrage as a 'delusion' which 'should be dispelled before it was too late' (*Examiner*, 16 Feb. 1817). As a political expedient, it was wise for reformists to forget about unlimited franchise if they wished to capture the constituency they needed in order to effect the people's will. Despite early disclaimers to the contrary, S, as his political writings demonstrate, was variously and even deviously expedient. In June 1818 Burdett, abetted by Jeremy Bentham, introduced a proposal into Parliament advocating the complete radical platform, including universal suffrage. As expected, it lost, and Burdett drew back, much to the apparent disgust of Major Cartwright. When S later (in *A Philosophical View of Reform*) advocated radical positions in a context which accepted triennial parliaments, he simply expanded the margins of tolerance by accommodating the ideal within the context of the expedient. He thereby continued to evince the flexibility of the moderate while still affirming the principles of Godwinian gradualism, without the latter's tacit reliance on political inertia as the preferable means to its quasi-Utopian goals. Extreme radicals (like Cartwright) felt that the Benthamite argument for universal suffrage on utilitarian principles was nearly as bad as an argument based on historical principles, since it implicitly disavowed reason as the only principle on which any sufficient and permanent reform could be based. In the final synthesis—as it appears in *A Defence of Poetry*—S recognized the essential inflexibility of a merely rational idealism by discovering a higher source of utilitarianism in the imaginative act. S's practical politics were most discriminatingly imaginative when they recognized the need for compromise as the appropriately expedient means towards the ideal ends he shared with dogmatic rationalists like Cartwright and fervent irrationalists such as Thomas Spence and the Spencean philanthropists.

191. *immediate, every*. The underscorings supplied by S in *P* and ignored by the compositor in *1817* demonstrate his desire to emphasize his strong sympathies with universal suffrage. See on 206 below.

195-201. *I allow ... man*. S again points up the mechanical and unreasonable character of untemporizing idealism, which, as S said of materialism in the fragment *On Life*, 'allows its disciples to talk and dispenses them from thinking'. Abstract rights had to be concretely deserved. Cf. *On Godwin's 'Mandeville'*, ll. 13-16. Cartwright's blinkered radicalism, however heroic, seldom deviated into the slightest compromise with expediency or even utility during the forty years he reiterated it. His attack on Burdett in an *Address to the Electors of Westminster*, 4 Feb. 1819, typifies his unanswerableness and his intransigence. See too his address of 6 Apr. to the same constituency, in which he criticizes Burdett's willingness to compromise principle by arguing for it in Benthamite terms (p. 24). Paine's republicanism, empirically derived and tested in two revolutions, was imbued with a millennial sense of immediacy akin to the fervent crisis mentality which had inspired S's Irish pamphlets but, as the Marlow pamphlets indicate, had since become less personalized and more politic. S's basic difference with Cartwright and Paine was not so much in the inutility of their principles (which he shared) as it was in the unimaginative attachment to them which made them in different ways counter-productive. Godwin defined the essential difference between theory and practice: 'He who should make these principles the regulators of his conduct, would not rashly insist upon the instant abolition of all existing abuses' (*PJ* i. 243). While this axiom had received abundant lip service from S in 1812, by 1817 it had been proved on his pulses.

201–6. *Yet... childhood*. Cf. Godwin on the unilluminated majority: 'It is an insult upon human understanding, when we speak of persons in this state of infantine ignorance, to say that the majority of the nation is on the side of political renovation' (*PJ* i. 255). In the *Examiner* for 16 Mar. 1817 Hunt echoes Godwin or perhaps S: 'The only fault... is the endeavouring to forward benevolence by violence; and the only folly, the egregious one of supposing that men are prepared for such a state of things, when as a body they have hardly yet one enlarged notion about duty, or justice, or any thing social.' Paine seems to have thought that mankind, as demonstrated by the French and American Revolutions, had in fact put off its childhood and was ready to put away its childish things, among which were aristocracy and monarchy (cf. *Rights of Man, Writings*, ii. 319–20).

206. *childhood*. The deletion following here (see the Collation)—'[Yet if the [Pub] Nation wills]'—again suggests the conflict between heart and head which assailed S each time he felt it necessary to qualify an ideal he believed in abstractly. The change from 'Pub[lic]' to 'Nation' may indicate a consciousness of Paine's distinction between the Nation, as the people, and the Government. Cf. *Rights of Man, Writings*, ii. 435: 'A constitution is the property of a nation, and not of those who exercise the government. All the constitutions of America are declared to be established on the authority of the people. In France, the word nation is used instead of the people; but in both cases, a constitution is a thing antecedent to the government, and always distinct therefrom.' Though like Paine S implicitly distinguished between a constitutional (or civil) government and a government established by conquest (as England's was perceived to be), his Godwinian gradualism, aligned with his typical belief in the perfectibility of man individually and socially, kept him from arguing, as Paine really was, for the immediate establishment of a republic in England. As indicated in the text, in the previous note, and elsewhere, he did not think the people were ready to be that kind of nation.

PREFACE TO 'FRANKENSTEIN; OR, THE MODERN PROMETHEUS'

Date: May 1817.

Copy-text: 1818 edition of Mary Shelley's *Frankenstein; or, The Modern Prometheus* (Lackington: London).

S wrote this Preface to his wife's novel as if he were she. Mary Shelley is precise about the date of its writing, noting in her journal entry for 14 May 1817 'Write Preface', which also allows her to write 'Finis' to *Frankenstein*, which her husband had on the same day corrected. In her Introduction to the 1831 edition of her novel she states that, so far as she can recollect, the Preface was written entirely by S, though there is no reason given for his having done so. While it is clear from the manuscripts of *Frankenstein* that he had a good deal to do with editing it into its 1818 form, his creative contribution to the text of the novel hardly justifies the writing of an authorial Preface on that ground alone.

Related primary and secondary materials: James Rieger's Introduction to *Frankenstein; or, The Modern Prometheus. The 1818 Text*, pp. xviii, xliv; E. B. Murray, 'Shelley's Contribution to Mary's *Frankenstein*', *K–SMB* 29 (1978), 50–68. See also the Editorial Commentary on S's *On 'Frankenstein; or, The Modern Prometheus*.

1–2. *Dr. Darwin*. Erasmus Darwin (1731–1802), a versifier of his botanical and zoological researches. As Mary Shelley notes in her 1831 Introduction, in their conversations experiments were ascribed to Darwin which he had not performed. The one which helped initiate *Frankenstein* involved a piece of scientifically animated vermicelli.

8–13. *It was recommended ... yield*. The justification is like those advanced by Horace Walpole for *The Castle of Otranto* and by Coleridge (in the *Biographia Literaria*) for his presumptive contributions to the *Lyrical Ballads*.

14–23. *I have thus ... poetry*. See the antepenultimate paragraph of S's Preface to *Prometheus Unbound* for a restatement and expansion of this aesthetic psychology, this time written under his own name.

33–8. *The opinions ... kind*. S's disclaimer, though ostensibly Mary's, probably springs from the social and legal reaction to the radical pronouncements of his earlier youth and is reiterated in a different form as late as the Notes to *Hellas*.

44–5. *German stories of ghosts*. Evidently an anonymously published collection entitled *Fantasmagoriana, ou Recueil d'Histoires d'Apparitions de Spectres, Revenans, Fantômes ...*, and purportedly translated from the German (two vols., Paris, 1812). The work, ascribed to Jean-Baptiste-Benoît Eyries, is also referred to and epitomized in the 1831 Introduction.

46. *Two other friends*. Actually Byron, John William Polidori (Byron's physician), Claire Clairmont, S, and Mary herself made up the ghost-story competition. In the last paragraph Byron and S are identified as the 'two friends'—if the trip implied refers to the journey around Lake Geneva, which began about a week after the competition was initiated (see *Letters Written in Geneva*). The particular friend of the parenthesis is Byron.

HISTORY OF A SIX WEEKS' TOUR

Date: Aug.-Sept. 1817.

Copy-text: *1817* (Huntington Library copy; shelfmark RB 23003).

Locations: Include Bodleian; BL; Huntington (2); Johns Hopkins; UCLA; University of Illinois; Princeton; University of Texas (3); Yale (2); Pf. (3).

Description: Foolscap octavo book measuring (trimmed) 15.9 cm. × 10.3 cm. (6.3″ × 4.1″), 17.5 cm. × 11 cm. (6.8″ × 4.3″) untrimmed, and made up of thirteen gatherings (⟨A⟩⁴ B–M⁸ N⁴), which consist of an unnumbered leaf with half-title (verso blank), title-page (verso imprint: 'Reynell, Printer, 45, Broad-street, Golden-square.'; ⟨i–ii⟩), centrally numbered 'PREFACE.' (⟨iii⟩–vi) and *History* text (⟨1⟩–81; ⟨82⟩ blank). A half-title leaf (⟨83–4⟩) is followed by 'LETTERS | WRITTEN ... IN ... *Geneva*' (⟨85⟩–172; see Description for that work), and, after a half-title leaf (⟨173⟩, ⟨174⟩ blank), 'MONT BLANC. | Lines Written in the Vale of Chamouni.' (⟨175⟩–183); the printer's slug is repeated at the foot of 183 (⟨184⟩ blank); machine-wove paper; no WM or running heads. The copy-text title-page is reproduced on p. 179. An 1829 issue consists of remaindered sheets of *1817*, lacks a half-title, and has a cancel title-page which contains the author's name, 'Percy Bysshe Shelley', that of the publisher, 'J. Brooks, 421 Oxford Street', and the date, '1829'. An *1817* price-label ('SIX WEEKS' TOUR. | *Price* 5s.') appears vertically on the back of the original binding, horizontally in the 1829 issue. One of the Huntington copies contains an 1817 title-page leaf with the author's name, some differences in accidentals, and the address of C. and J. Ollier printed as 'Wellbeck' street; the leaf was not part of the original binding.

Reprinted: *1829* (see above); *1840*; F; J. (Bohn's *Bibliographer's Manual of English Literature* (1864) lists an undated reprint of *1817* ascribed to 'Lumley'.)

The *History of a Six Weeks' Tour* revises, expands, and otherwise adds to entries typically made by S in the journal traditionally assigned to Mary Shelley (then Mary Godwin) but often, particularly during this Continental 'tour' (28 July–12 Sept. 1814), kept up by her future husband. Besides the Preface, written by S, the following lines of the *History* correspond, often verbatim, with the *Journals* entries in S's hand as dated: 49–52 ('The evening ... much', 28 July); 57–66 ('The wind ... Calais', 28 July); 134–6 ('On ... grass', 2 Aug.); 159–63 ('Early ... design', 8 Aug.); 192–3 ('Guignes ... war', 9 Aug.); 197–203 ('Provins ... painting', 10 Aug.); 211–14 ('Nogent ... advanced', 11 Aug.); 222–7 ('We quitted ... Cossacs', 11 Aug.); 289–92 ('We accordingly ... days', 13 Aug.); 308–25 ('As we left ... mountains', 14 Aug.); 373–80 ('Our road ... sky', 18 Aug.); 384–421 ('While ... excuses', 18 Aug.); 432–42 ('The scenery ... effect', 19 Aug.); 449–50 ('The mountains ... beautiful', 19 Aug.); 459–67 ('Two leagues ... earth', 19 Aug.); 481–7 ('A Swiss ... value', 20 Aug.); 538–49 ('The following ... month', 24 Aug.); 607–9 ('Sleeping ... Mumph', 29 Aug.); 619–22 ('We could ... down', 29 Aug.); 635–6 ('The wind ... us', 30 Aug.); 637–8 ('S*** ... Norway', 31 Aug.); 641–9 ('Suddenly ... beautiful', 30 Aug.); 653 ('The following ... canoe', 31 Aug.).

Besides these direct correspondences, many of the facts written into the journal by S were taken over and expanded by Mary. For example, the day of their departure from London, the oppressive heat which 'made ⟨Mary⟩ faint', her later seasickness, the 'two hours sail' which the seamen promised them, the 'hour after hour' which actually passed before they arrived at Calais, the rising of the sun over France were written into the journal by S in 1814 and expanded by Mary in 1817 to provide all the material in the *History* which was not taken even more directly from S's record of their first day's travel. The major difference between the two accounts is that S provides his reactions in the journal and Mary describes hers in the *History*, though, as indicated, even some of her reactions expand on those which S had noted of her in 1814.

Mary's apparent contributions to the *History* which are not expansions of her or S's entries of 1814 range from descriptions of the dress and manners of the French, ll. 72–9, to the chauvinistically reflective, ll. 79–82, to the sententious, ll. 236–7 ('but sleep is seldom denied, except to the indolent'), to the domestic, ll. 423–31 (on the relative cleanliness of the Swiss), to the implicitly satiric, ll. 442–8 (on the character of a new guide). Descriptive passages not present in 1814 are relatively few and at times appear in contexts which suggest that they might have been supplied by S (e.g. ll. 450–9). Some of the added material is mere filler (e.g. ll. 468–70), some of it seems to stem from later assessments of the trip (e.g. ll. 471–80). However, the fine description of Lake Lucerne and environs (497–537), which concludes with 'our reflections' on William Tell and the Swiss, has little or no parallel in the journal and could well have been written by S in 1817. From l. 550 to the end of the *History* the expanded account of the *Journals* entries is in all probability Mary's, except for the descriptive segments which appear in S's hand in the journal and the contexts in which they appear in the *History* (e.g. ll. 635–52). Indeed, the great majority of these entries are relatively matter-of-fact and undistinguished enough to have been written by any literate individual who had made the same trip under the same circumstances, though the recurrent emphasis on the rudeness and disgusting ways of their fellow travellers echoes Mary's sentiments as recorded in the journal (see the entry for 28 Aug.). One or two of the added descriptions (e.g. ll. 599–606) in this latter part of the *History* do not seem quite in the vein of S's earlier descriptions and may also be assigned to Mary.

The geographical facts and a few incidents are likewise the same in both works, and of course appear in both hands in the *Journals*. While in general the *History* provides more detail and description than the *Journals* do, on occasion the *Journals* helpfully supplement the *History* (see e.g. the Collation at 384–90). There are a few apparent redatings of description or event, but in the main the accounts of the tour of the couple (along with Claire Clairmont) through France, Switzerland,

Germany, and Holland are parallel. Omitted from the *History* are the personal facts of life, such as correspondence received, affectionate embracings, or detailed accounts of their miserable accommodations or of their recurrent financial concerns or the names of the individuals they met from day to day—matters which should have held little interest for the anticipated reader.

Of much more consequence is the fact that about 70 per cent of the *History* does not appear in the *Journals*, beyond a skeleton outline giving a simple recital of the places passed through and visited. Except for inferences one might hazard from stylistic parallels or scenic extensions, there is little evidence in the text itself for identifying one or other as the principal author of the bulk of the *History*. The best evidence for Mary's authorship is two leaves in her hand in the Abinger Collection (Bodleian Library) which contain a draft of ll. 357–436 ('about . . . arrived'), though this could itself have been based on a previous draft by S. The author or authors is or are contradictory about his, her, or their share in the finished work, or at least confusing in both statement and implication. Because S wrote the Preface and assigned the work to Mary, who implies at the outset that she wrote all of it, adds an 'M' to its conclusion, and does (as noted below) seem to credit herself with the authorship in her later *Journals* entries, the authorless 1817 volume could be unequivocally assigned to her—particularly since the authorial 'I' clearly refers to her— if it were the only issue of the work. But there is first of all the 1817 Huntington Library copy (see the Description) whose title-page proclaims S's authorship. While this title-page is patently suspect, it is still the case that in 1829 the remaindered sheets were published with S's name on a new title-page, and in her 1840 volumes Mary includes the *History* as one of her husband's works. It is true that the 1829 title-page might have been a publisher's inference (or promotional addition), and Mary in the very act of publishing the work as her husband's seems in her Preface to distinguish 'its author' and S, whom she designates as the motivating entrepreneur behind its publication. And she not only retained but extended (to 'M. S.') her initials at the conclusion of the *History* proper. The least equivocal assignment of authorship to respective parts of the volume is made by S in a letter of 16 Dec. 1817 to Thomas Moore:

The little volume which you have been quicksighted enough to attribute to its real authors is composed of two letters written ⟨by⟩ me signed *S*, & some ⟨two⟩ other letters & the Journal signed *M*. written by Mrs. Shelley. I ought to say that the Journal was written some years ago—the style of it is almost infantine, & it was published in the idea that the Author would never be recognized. . . . I ought to say that Mrs. Shelley, tho' sorry that her secret is discovered, is exceedingly delighted to hear that you have derived any amusement from our book.—Let me say in her defence that the Journal of the Six Weeks Tour was written before she was seventeen, & that she has another literary secret which I will in a short time ask you to *keep* in return for having *discovered* this.

While it is true that the original 'Journal' was written in 1814, it is clear from the *Journals* entries for Aug. 1817 noted below that it was being reworked—recast and expanded—much later. The rather coy attempt at both concealing and revealing the authorship of the soon-to-be published *Frankenstein* and the fact that S's 1814 journal entries were used in the *History* confirm a presumption that S's statements concerning authorship to Thomas Moore should not be accepted as definitive.

A reasonable supposition is that originally the two Shelleys had agreed implicitly to assign the 'unpresuming' and anonymously published little work to Mary—perhaps for no better or worse reason than to allow her the pride of authorship she might then have enjoyed more or less in secret, or until someone as 'quicksighted' as Moore had sufficiently discerned its authorship for S to ostensibly reveal it all. Since in 1817 S was involving himself in the more momentous matters of reformist politics and epic poetry, a by-product and left-over of his wandering youth might have seemed potentially damaging to the public image he then hoped to project.

Shelley scholars and editors have not established a firm consensus on authorship. H. B. Forman in his headnote to the *History* (in F) assumes that the 'journal kept by Mrs. Shelley was revised and to some small extent interpolated by the poet', while the editors of J suppose that Mary was 'part author' (vol. v, p. v). F. L. Jones, who, as editor of both Mary's journal and of the Shelleys' letters, might be supposed to have given the matter most consideration, feels obliged to list the *History* among S's prose works in the index to S's *Letters*, but qualifies his decision by parenthetically noting that the work was 'mainly Mary's'; Betty Bennett, in her edition of Mary's letters, indexes it as Mary's work, as do Paula R. Feldman and Diana Scott-Kilvert in their edition of Mary's *Journals*. On balance, it may finally seem that the traditional inclusion of the *History* is the best reason that can be given for continuing to print it as S's work, though it should also be noted that nearly all the substantial parts of it which can be definitively assigned to anyone (i.e. the portions which correspond with S's *Journals* entries) confirm the 1829 title-page and Mary's considered decision in 1840 to publish it as her husband's—even though when writing to Leigh Hunt as late as ?5 Oct. 1839 she is still not sure whether she should do so, because, while 'printed and corrected by Shelley', it 'was written by me'. Still later, writing to the publisher Edward Moxon, she states that 'my 6 weeks tour brought me many compliments' adding that it was written by her 'off hand' (2|6|7 Sep⟨t⟩. ⟨1843⟩). Perhaps this should be considered her final word on the matter; yet in her copy of the 1840 volume presently in the Bodleian Library (⟨pr.⟩ Shelley adds. e. 20) interleaved with notepaper containing written parallels (evidently from the 1814 text) to the facing letterpress text, Mary refers to the work as 'Shelley's journal' (opposite p. 5).

The date of the recasting and enlargement of the *Journals* entries for late July–early Sept. 1814 into the *History* is loosely established by its opening sentence as some time during the summer of 1817. More specifically, Mary states in the *Journals* entry for 9 Aug. that she (it seems) 'write⟨s⟩ the journal of our travels'; entries for 13 and 17 Aug. suggest that the writing continued through those dates. A week or so could well have been time enough for her (or S or both of them) to compose the work from the *Journals* entries, but since the 'letters from Geneva' which Mary 'wrote out' on 12 Oct. 1817 (*Journals*) were presumably the letters which appeared in the volume which contained the *History*, the concluding date for composition of the *History*, at least in its refurbishings, might be extended somewhat. On 28 Sept. 1817 Mary wrote to S asking what he had done with the 'journal of our first travels'—presumably the manuscript of the *History* rather than the original journal—which he had taken with him to London, again, one presumes, to find a publisher for that portion of the volume. If, Mary continues, S has 'any prospect' of doing anything with it, she will 'go on instantly with the letters', as she did on 12 Oct., by which time she must have heard that something had been done or was in prospect. In a letter of 14 Oct. to S Mary promises to send the 'letters' by the 16th, and apparently did send them to S via Hookham, one of the eventual publishers, on the 15th (letter of 16 Oct. to S). The 'printing' Mary mentions in the letter of 16 Oct. probably refers to some portion of the *History*, but since S was then involved in other printings (most notably of *Laon and Cythna*), the unqualified reference is ambiguous. An advertisement of Oct. 1817 bound in a copy of *Laon and Cythna* announces that, along with this poem, the *History* is 'in the Press, and will be published early in January' (*SC* v. 154–5). Advertisements appeared in the *Morning Chronicle* for 30 Oct. and *The Times* for 1 Nov. stating that the work would be on sale on 6 Nov. for 4s. 6d. Announcements for it under the heading 'This day is published' appeared in *The Times* for 12 Nov. and the *Chronicle* for 13 Nov. Forman notes that the work was not entered into the *Stationers' Register* (as published by T. Hookham) until 10 Dec., but rationalizes the discrepancy between a summer drafting of the work and a late autumn publication by inferring (1) that Mary was only beginning to 'transcribe' her journal in August (though Forman does not so specify a date) and (2) that during so busy a time for the Shelleys it might well have taken them several months to get the work to and through the press. Even if the newspaper announcements were premature, the letter to Moore of 16 Dec. indicates that it was available for distribution some time before that date. If, as Mary states in her 1840 Preface, S was the moving force behind its publication, the judgemental implications of his 1817 Preface may help account for the time it took to get it into print.

Besides S's evaluation in the Preface, justifiably modest, the only contemporary notice taken of the *History* appeared in *Blackwood's Magazine* (July 1818), where the work was found simple but amusing and the 'lady' author was commended. S indicates in a letter of 30 Apr. 1820 to Charles Ollier, who co-published the volume with Thomas Hookham, jun., that he had been disappointed in his expectation that printer's costs would be covered by the sale of the book. When the *History* was republished in the 1840 volume, the *Athenaeum*'s reviewer felt that it could have been omitted altogether, as 'telling nothing of any interest whatever, and not written by the poet,—but by the present Editor' (14 Dec. 1839).

While the text is based on *1817*, significant emendations in *1840* are preferred when they appear in S's hand in the *Journals*. Mary seems in such instances to have returned to the *Journals* for the express purpose of using portions of S's contribution which she had failed to edit into *1817*. Since Mary must be regarded as a more or less probable author as well as editor of much of the *History* (and to some extent of the Geneva letters), her *1840* emendations have unique authority in this portion of S's canon. However, in the few instances where she has added to or radically changed the *1817* text without the authority of S's holograph journal entries, her additions and changes have been placed in the Collation. Mary's later statement (quoted above) that S 'corrected' the *1817* draft means in all probability that he copy-edited it—not that (for example) he collated her creative transcript with his (or her) 1814 journal entries. *1840* corrections of place-names definitely misspelt are accepted ('Pontalier' becomes 'Pontarlier'; in the *Letters Written in Geneva* 'Mellterie' and 'Mellerie' become 'Meillerie'); the same policy applies to comparable errors in *1817*'s French (e.g. the use of 'L'Hôte' for 'l'hôtesse') when corrected by Mary Shelley in *1840* or in her subsequent editions. She apparently felt that a few other examples of schoolgirl French (as pointed out by André Koszul in the *MLR* note listed below) were either worth preserving or not worth changing; the text likewise retains them. A few place-names misspelt in *1840* are also retained in the text, but their correct spellings are noted in the Collation.

The revised portion of Claire Clairmont's journal for 14–22 Aug. 1814, printed in *SC*, vol. iii, is a particularly helpful supplement to the *History* (as it is to both her and Mary's journals) for the days it covers. See also the edition of Mary Shelley's *Journals* by Paula R. Feldman and Diana Scott-Kilvert for its italicized printing of S's portion of that text, as well as for its relevant footnotes. The collation with the *Journals* (*MWS*) is selective, providing representative rhetorical, factual, or aesthetically interesting differences between S's journal entries and the 1817 printing. Since the contexts of a few of these entries were still further recast, the collation will not always exactly fit the lemma.

Related primary and secondary materials: LETTERS, to H. Shelley, 13 Aug. 1814, to T. L. Peacock, 15 May, 12 July, 22 July 1816; Mary Shelley, *Journals*, 6–24; *CC* 21–42; *Blackwood's Magazine*, 3 (1818), 412–16; Medwin, *Life*, 128–34; Charles I. Elton, *An Account of Shelley's Visits to France, Switzerland, and Savoy . . .* (London, 1894); André Koszul, 'Notes and Corrections to Shelley's *History of a Six Weeks' Tour*', *MLR* 2 (Oct. 1906), 61–2; Claire Engel, *Byron et Shelley en Suisse et en Savoie, mai-octobre, 1816* (Chambéry, 1930); White, *Shelley*, i. 351–63; Marcel Kessel, 'An Early Review of the Shelleys' "Six Weeks' Tour"', *MLN* 58 (Dec. 1943), 623; Elizabeth Nitchie, 'Mary Shelley, Traveller', *K-SJ* 10 (Winter 1961), 29–42; *SC* iii. 342–70, vii. 42–5; Cameron, *Golden Years*, 17–19; E. B. Murray, 'A Suspect Title-page of Shelley's *History of a Six Weeks' Tour*', *PBSA* 83 (June 1989), 201–6. (See also *Letters Written in Geneva* and its Editorial Commentary.)

15. *her husband and sister.* 'Her' = Mary Shelley. Claire Clairmont, the daughter of Godwin's second wife, was no blood relation, as Mary's emendation of the word to 'friend' conceded (*1840*). In the 1814 journal of the Continental trip she is referred to as Jane, one of her real praenomens. In 1814 S was not Mary's husband.

29. *"Mont Blanc"*. S's poem was first published at the end of the *History* volume; the paragraph referring to it was dropped by Mary in editions after 1840. The 'two letters' mentioned are those to Thomas Love Peacock in the *Letters Written in Geneva*.

75. *coiffures.* Head-dresses.

79–80. *Edward . . . Calais.* Edward III (1312–77) besieged and conquered Calais in 1347. It remained under English rule until 1558.

101. *craquéed.* Cracked.

105. *femme de chambre.* Chambermaid.

115–17. *pensez-y . . . sommeil.* Think about it, it's to compensate the poor horses for their loss of sweet sleep.

137–41. *This street . . . sculpture.* In the early nineteenth century the series of boulevards surrounding Paris made up a considerably smaller circumference than those presently surrounding the city, as the figure of eight miles and the reference to the Porte St-Denis indicate. The Porte St-Denis was the traditional entry for ceremonial processions into the city. There is no evidence that the depradations Mary feared in 1817 had occurred.

144. *Impotent.* Probably = 'unrestrained'.

144–5. *destroyed . . . defeat.* A parallel is recorded in an entry for 5 Aug. 1814 which S had made in the journal concerning an officious Frenchman who 'told us he had assisted in bribing the mob to overthrow the statue of Napoleon'.

148. *a small remittance.* 'We ... received a remittance of 60£' (Mary Shelley, *Journals*, 7 Aug. 1814 ⟨S's hand⟩).

155. *We... France.* According to the journal, they had decided to walk to Uri, on Lake Lucerne (7 Aug. ⟨S's hand⟩). The 'romance' Mary associates with their planned itinerary (l. 152) would have been heightened if, as Newman White suggests (*Shelley*, i. 352), they had intended to follow the route of the title-hero in William Godwin's novel *Fleetwood; or, the New Man of Feeling* (1805).

165–6. *les Dames... enlevées.* The ladies would certainly be kidnapped.

167–8. *diligence... fiacre.* The diligence was a public stagecoach, the fiacre a privately hired cab.

181. *Napoleons.* A French coin imprinted with the effigy of Napoleon and worth about 20 francs, or a little less than a pound.

191–3. *This night... war.* The inn is identified as the Hôtel Ste-Barbe in SC iii. 362.

192. *Guignes* = Guignes-Rabutin.

193. *The little old woman.* The story she told is reported in the journal entry for 9 Aug., but the 'little old woman' herself does not seem to have come on the scene until the next day (see Mary Shelley, *Journals*, 10 Aug.). Her 'infinitely detestable beds' here become merely 'uncomfortable' (l. 207).

211. *Nogent* = Nogent-sur-Seine.

212–13. *desolated by the Cossacs.* For a brief account of the war-ravaged terrain S (or Mary) refers to here and later see SC iii. 363–4.

230–86. *The road ... at Troyes.* Derived from Mary's entries for 11–12 Aug.

257. *cabaret.* Tavern.

274. *Pavillon* = le Pavillon-Ste-Julie.

290. *voiture.* Coach.

296. *Neufchâtel* = Neuchâtel, which S used in the *Journals*.

298. *voiturier.* Coachman.

321–2. *but in the west... vapours.* Claire Clairmont, in the portion of her journal in Pf., quotes S's original reaction to this meteorological phenomenon: 'S—— said, Look there how the Sun in parting, has bequeathed a lingering look to the Heaven, he has left desolate' (SC iii. 342).

326–72. *As we ... our journey.* Derived from Mary's entries for 15–17 Aug.

327. *Chaumont* = Chaumont-en-Bassigny.

329. *Champlitte* = Champlitte-et-le Prélot.

362. *Je ne puis plus.* I can't go any further.

374–80. *From... sky.* Cf. *Prometheus Unbound*, II. iii. 19–27.

395. *auberge.* Inn.

458–9. *in time of war . . . across it.* The iron chain is not noted in Mary's journal, but Claire records it (*SC* iii. 348).

459. *we saw the Alps.* Claire describes S's reaction to the Alps more vividly: 'How great is my rapture he said, I a fiery man with my heart full of Youth, and with my Beloved at my side, I behold those lordly immesurable Alps—they look like a second world gleaming on one, they look like dreams more than realities, they are so pure and heavenly white' (*SC* iii. 349).

474. *£38.* Claire recorded £50 (*SC* iii. 350).

silver upon discount. The fact that earlier S had pawned his watch (Mary Shelley, *Journals*, 4 Aug.) makes it difficult to infer that he had bills of exchange to discount at this stage of his travels. His usual willingness to sign post-obits at exorbitant rates of interest suggests that the 38 pounds in silver be brought back to the 'astonishment and consolation' of Mary and Claire Clairmont were the result of a similar transaction (see Mary Shelley, *Journals*, 20 Aug. 1814, and *SC* iii. 350).

481–3. *A Swiss . . . Lucerne.* Claire wrote that Mary felt such 'perfect strangers' took so helpful an interest in the trio because they were 'captivated by Shelley's countenance and manner' (*SC* iii. 350).

493. *Altorf* = Altdorf, most famous as the place where William Tell (see l. 524 and commentary) shot an apple from his son's head.

524. *chapel of Tell.* The fifteenth-century story of the Swiss hero William Tell's personal rebellion against the tyrannical Austrian bailiff Gessler was still popularly accepted in the early nineteenth century as a historical account of the origin of the Swiss Confederacy, which was in fact founded at Brunnen in the early fourteenth century. Friedrich von Schiller's drama *Wilhelm Tell* (1804) more than counterbalanced the doubts which had been cast on the legend by seventeenth-century sceptics such as Voltaire. The William Tell chapel here referred to (there were at least three associated with him) was probably that on Tell's Platt, a shelf of rock projecting into Uri (the southern bay of Lake Lucerne), which, according to one version, was the site of the hero's slaying of the tyrannical bailiff.

546. *Siege . . . Tacitus.* In *Histories*, 5. 1–13.

578–9. *S*** . . . upon.* After S had written (Mary Shelley, *Journals*, 20 Aug. 1814) of his returning from the Neuchâtel banker 'staggering under the weight of a large canvas bag full of silver' (cf. on 474 above), he added 'S alone looks grave on the occasion, for he alone clearly apprehends that francs & ecus & louis d'or are like the white & flying cloud of noon . . .'. While in ll. 561–8 a quasi-dramatic account of a mutual discussion of their finances is put into the 1817 *History*, there is very little in the 1814 *Journals* to qualify S's assessment of his solitary awareness of the seriousness of their plight. As late as 27 Aug. Claire Clairmont understood so little of their financial straits that she commented on their leaving Brunnen for England 'All because the stove did not burn brightly & there were too many Cottages' (*CC*). However, the fact that immediately before they decided to return to England they were still proposing to push on across St Gothard to Italy suggests that even S was still hoping to test his dictum that desire will somehow create capacity (Mary Shelley, *Journals*, 26 Aug. 1814).

586–7. *diligence par-eau*. Water-coach.

587. *Loffenburgh* = Laufenburg.

588–90. *Our companions . . . disgusting*. Mary Shelley later recalled the contrast between their fellow passengers and the beautiful scenery they were passing through in *Rambles in Germany and Italy* (1844), i. 170 (quoted in *Journals*, 20 n.).

604. *Rhône*. Probably an error for 'Rhine', though a recent reading of Byron's *Childe Harold*, canto III (1816), might have put the writer in mind of the 'blue rushing of the arrowy Rhône' (st. 71); cf. l. 704. The canto was written at about the time S and Byron made the excursion around Lake Geneva described in Letter III of *Letters Written in Geneva* (see S's letter to T. J. Hogg, 18 July 1816 ·.

619. *Mumph* = Mumpf.

632. *Mayence* = Mainz.

637–8. *Letters from Norway*. *Letters Written during a Short Residence in Sweden, Norway, and Denmark* (1796) contained the descriptive but less personal portions of the letters written by Mary Wollstonecraft to Gilbert Imlay, the father of her first daughter Fanny.

685–7. *C'est . . . noyés*. It's only a boat, that was only overturned, and all the people are only drowned.

692. *bombardment*. In 1792 Mainz accepted French rule, but for the next few years it was the scene of several military engagements.

705–6. *third . . . Harold*. Probably a reference to the lyric addressed to his half-sister Augusta which Byron placed after stanza 55. If so, the portion of the Rhine described from here is in the vicinity of Bonn. The remembrance following ('We read these verses with delight') is in any case anachronistic: Canto III of *Childe Harold* was not written until 1816.

724. *borderers*. I.e. those who lived along the Rhine.

766–8. *At Nimeguen . . . Montague*. The reference is to Mrs Montagu's letter to Sarah Chiswell, 13 Aug. 1716: 'I must not forget to take notice of the Bridge ⟨at Nimeguen = Nijmegen⟩, which appear'd very Surprizing to me. Tis large enough to hold hundreds of Men with Horses and Carriages. They give the value of an English two pence to get upon it and away they go, bridge and all to the other side of the river, with so slow a motion, one is hardly sensible of any at all' (*The Complete Letters of Lady Mary Wortley Montagu*, ed. Robert Halsband, 3 vols., Clarendon Press: Oxford, 1967, i. 252).

LETTERS WRITTEN IN GENEVA

Date: Late 1817.

Copy-text: *1817* (Huntington Library copy of *History of a Six Weeks' Tour*, shelf-mark RB 23003).

Description: See the Description of *History of a Six Weeks' Tour*. The text of the Letters section proper is introduced by 'LETTERS.' (⟨83⟩; ⟨84⟩ blank) and drop-head title (here partially normalized): 'LETTERS | written | DURING A RESIDENCE OF THREE MONTHS IN | THE ENVIRONS OF GENEVA, | *In the Summer of the Year 1816*.' (⟨85⟩).

Location: See Locations for *History of a Six Weeks' Tour*.

Reprinted: *1829*; *1840*; F; J.

The first two *Letters Written in Geneva* were assigned to and probably written for the most part by Mary Shelley; the second two by her husband. While the letters were originally written in the summer of 1816, their published versions were evidently not transcribed and re-created until late 1817. The literary character and intention of these letters are formally established by their presence in the 1817 volume including the *History of a Six Weeks' Tour*. The descriptions of landscapes in the letters by S are generally superior to those recorded either in the *History* or in the portions of Mary Shelley's *Journals* on which the *History* is based. Betty Bennett (Mary Shelley, *Letters*, i. 19) argues that Mary's original letters were probably written to her half-sister Fanny Imlay; S's were written to T. L. Peacock. While there are no extant manuscripts of Mary's letters, there seems little reason to suppose that she created them from scratch in 1817 for inclusion in the *History* volume. However, as noted below, part of Letter I was derived from a letter of 15 May 1816 to Peacock, first printed by Charles Middleton in *Shelley and his Writings* (London, 1858), i. 321–5.

Further confirmation of the literary purpose of these letters is established by SC 571 (vii. 25–35), a transcription of the original letter of 17 July to Peacock, the latter portion of which contains an 'abstract' of the 'voyage' around Lake Geneva. Forman had pointed out (F vi. 185 n.) that the start of Letter IV (22 July) implied a gap which in his opinion was filled in by a letter published by Middleton that was itself (Forman rightly inferred) in some way continuous with Letter III (12 July), as published in the *History*. What Middleton had printed (op. cit. ii. 38–44) was the letter of 17 July as published in Jones's edition of S's letters. As the SC transcription demonstrates, the letters of 12 and 17 July were originally one and the same letter. Evidently a copy of the portion which Middleton used had been left with Robert Maddocks, a Marlow carpenter and land agent who had rendered some services to S for which he had not been paid, along with other Shelleyana which Maddocks retained in his possession long after S's death (see *SC* iv. 490–1). Since the complete letter of 17 July to Peacock was lost to sight until 1975, and the implications of Forman's note overlooked, editors of S's letters have reprinted as separate letters the Middleton portion and the *History* portion.

The letter as printed by Middleton may be supposed to have derived from a safe-keeping copy of the first and business part of the letter of 17 July: it is most of all concerned with a request to Peacock that he locate and rent an appropriate house for the Shelleys in the vicinity of Windsor Forest. A probable reason for Middleton's not having the larger descriptive portion of that letter is that the Shelleys had made no copy of it, since, as noted below, it not only appeared in a more finished original form in the notebook which S had with him when he and Byron sailed round Lake Geneva but also might well have been recopied in a yet more finished form in the lost *Journals* notebook which quite possibly formed the basis of the published letter. Because of the nature of its contents, it is highly unlikely that the copy of the earlier and business part of the letter was (as suggested in *SC* vii. 40) intended for publication in the *History* volume, though the use of part of the letter of 15 May indicates that the descriptive portions of that letter *were* originally meant for publication. The Middleton portion of the letter of 17 July, having no literary purpose, is merely a copy, except in so far as the original copyist or Middleton decided to omit, abbreviate, or otherwise garble what he or she was transcribing. In any case, Mary's entry in the *Journals* for 12 Oct. 1817 seems to establish the precise date on which the printer's copy of the letters as published in the *History* was made up: 'write out letters from Geneva'.

As indicated, the two letters signed 'M' have been included not merely because of editorial precedent but also because the first one is in part (ll. 10–20, 41–7, 77–9, 82–4) cribbed, either directly or in paraphrase, from S's letter of 15 May 1816 to Peacock. It is worth noting that where relevant substantive differences exist between the printing of this letter in Middleton's book (i. 321–5) and in F. L. Jones's edition of the letters, the printing of Letter I in the *History* volume is marginally closer to the Middleton version, which, however, lacks ll. 10–20.. It is also the case that there is no manuscript evidence to prove definitely who wrote the rest of Letter I and all of Letter II. They of course remain, even more than the *History* itself, a dubious part of S's canon.

The following pre-*1817* forms of Letters III and IV appear, or once appeared, in Bod. MS Shelley adds. e. 16, where they were written in pencil from the back to the front of the notebook: Letter III, ll. 77–80 (now in Bod. MS Shelley adds. c. 4, fol. 65ʳ); ll. 102–9 (now in Bod. MS Shelley adds. c. 4, fol. 65ᵛ); ll. 213–16 (p. 56 rev.); ll. 246–53 (p. 55–54 rev.); ll. 274–5, 278–81 (pp. 53–52 rev.); ll. 296–310 (pp. 51–49 rev.); ll. 315–29 (pp. 49–48 rev.); Letter IV, ll. 14–28 (p. 45); ll. 68, 76–80 (p. 66).

Except for p. 66 (drafted by Mary), the portions of the two letters in MS Shelley adds. e. 16 are in S's hand. While the drafts are quite different from the original letters to Peacock, they are quite like the corresponding segments of these letters as published in the *History* volume. However, a comparison between corresponding portions of the manuscript and the entry in the *Journals* for 21 July (see *Journals*, i. 112–13) makes it clear that the *History* version of that portion of Letter IV was derived from the journal entry, itself based on MS Shelley adds. e. 16. The corresponding portion of the actual letter to Peacock (the Pierpont Morgan holograph as printed in *Letters*) could be a condensation of either MS Shelley adds. e. 16 or the journal entry. Since in the Bodleian manuscript the leaves following the aforementioned portion are missing, it is impossible to be sure whether S continued to keep this continuation of his Geneva diary in that notebook or whether he allowed a copy of the actual letter to Peacock from 22 July to serve as the sole record of his excursions to and around Mont Blanc. But the fact that the *Journals* entries corresponding to the post-21 July entries are in Mary's hand combines with the fact that from that point there is relatively little difference between the letter to Peacock as sent and the letter as printed in the *History* volume to support the inference that Mary used a copy of the original letter when writing it out for publication. Mary's use of the few lines she had drafted on p. 66 of MS Shelley adds. e. 16 in her continuation of the *Journals* entries from 22 July does seem to indicate that S's Geneva diary became to some extent a Chamonix diary, used by both Mary and S as a quarry for their respective contributions to the journal's account of the later excursion.

While the scantiness of the extant materials in MS Shelley adds. e. 16 makes the induction risky, the fact that S creatively redrafted some lines from this manuscript into the *Journals* entry from 21 July which almost certainly served as the basis for the start of Letter IV supports an analogous inference that at least some of the description of the trip round Lake Geneva in MS Shelley adds. e. 16 was also drafted into the lost *Journals* notebook, which would have contained entries through 20 July and could then have served as the basis for the *History* printing of Letter III. Except for the first paragraph, very little of Letter III could have come directly from S's letter to Peacock containing the account of the trip round Lake Geneva. (The letter as printed in Shelley, *Letters*, is merely a reprint of the text in *History*, since Jones did not have access to the holograph of the letter actually sent to Peacock as reproduced in *SC* vii.) A probable chronology of the variant forms of Letter III may therefore be outlined as follows: (1) MS Shelley adds. e. 16 draft of the Geneva trip as it was taking place; (2) original letter to Peacock abstracted from the foregoing; (3) *Journals* entries (no longer extant); (4) *History* copy-text and printing. However, neither the substance nor the implications of this chronology should be accepted uncritically: the few changes between the extant draft in MS Shelley adds. e. 16 and the corresponding portions of Letter III hardly argue the necessity of a journal source, though, again, the correspondences noted above in Letter IV indicate that S could well be continuing a creative reprocessing of the Bodleian draft which began with the Geneva diary. Most of the Bodleian draft has been printed in *VP* 83–7 and *Journals*, 110–12; see also Robert Brinkley's *K–SJ* article listed below.

Regardless of the various relations suggested above for both letters, it seems to be the case that the copy-text for the actual printing of the *History* version of all of the letters was provided by Mary (see *Journals*, 12 Oct. 1817), who might well have supplied her own variants into whatever copy she was using, though the disparities between the *SC* transcription of the letter to Peacock and Letter III argue for some other intermediate copy (e.g. MS Shelley adds. e. 16 or its creative transcription into the lost *Journals* notebook) in S's hand which she may or may not have further embellished. The collation of the *SC* transcript of the letter to Peacock with the 1817 printing of Letter III, like the collation of the *History* with Mary Shelleys *Journals* (*MWS*), does not always exactly fit the *1817* lemmata, nor is it exhaustive.

Related primary and secondary materials: 'Mont Blanc'; LETTERS, to Hogg, 18 July 1816, to Byron, 22 July 1816; Mary Shelley, *Letters*, i. 19, 21–2; F vi. 160, vii. 349 n.; Mary Shelley, *Journals*, 109–21; Medwin, *Life*, 153–4; Peacock, *Memoirs*, 338, 344, 366–88; Charles S. Middleton, *Shelley and his Writings* (London, 1858), i. 321–5, ii. 38–44; Rossetti, *Memoir*, 63 n.; Gavin de Beer, 'The Atheist: An Incident at Chamonix', in *On Shelley* (London, 1938), 35–54; E. B. Murray, 'Mont Blanc's Unfurled Veil', *K–SJ* 18 (1969), 43–4; *SC* iv. 690–701, vii. 37–45; Robert Brinkley, 'Documenting Revision: Shelley's Lake Geneva Diary and the Dialogue with Byron in *History of a Six Weeks' Tour*', *K–SJ* 39 (1990), 66–82. (See also this listing in *History of a Six Weeks' Tour* and the Editorial Commentary for that work.)

Letter I

4. *Lavalette*. Antoine-Marie Chamans, Comte de La Valette (1769–1830), an office-holder under Napoleon, imprisoned and condemned to death at the Bourbon restoration, but escaped to England in Dec. 1815.

11. *last invasion*. The invasion and later occupation of France by the English and continental armies during and after Napoleon's 'Hundred Days' return to power, which ended at the Battle of Waterloo (18 June 1815). The 'detested' Bourbon dynasty was again restored in the person of Louis XVIII.

24. *Neufchâtel* = Neuchâtel.

Letter II

ADDRESS. C⟨haupuis⟩. The name of the Shelleys' cottage.
4. *aiguilles*. Literally, 'needles'.

Letter III

ADDRESS. *T. P.* = Thomas ⟨Love⟩ Peacock.
VEVAI = Vevey.
4. *Julie*. The reference is to Jean-Jacques Rousseau's *Julie, ou La Nouvelle Héloïse* (1761). The trip which S and his 'companion' Byron took around Lake Geneva roughly followed the itinerary Rousseau had described in his diary; see *SC* iv. 690 and n.
5–6. *enchantment...arises*. That is, the scene (or natural setting) which he had just visited lent an 'enchantment' to the 'delineations' of that scene in Rousseau's novel; reciprocally, the 'most touching charm' of the scene arises from the (memory of the) description of it in the novel. S's proclivity for synergistic effects appears not only in the dialectics of his metaphysical writings (e.g. in his *Speculations on Morals and Metaphysics*) but also in his poetry (e.g. the mutual reinforcements of Asia and Prometheus, Love and Imagination, in *Prometheus Unbound*), in his politics (e.g. the coalescing reforms of institutions and the individual argued for in his letters and political writings), and in his aesthetics (e.g. the relation between poetry and imagination as defined in *A Defence of Poetry*).
9. *23d of June*. For a reassessment of the actual dates of the Geneva excursion see *SC* iv. 691 ff.
24. *Nerni* = Nernier.
28. *"beached margin."* *A Midsummer Night's Dream*, II. i. 85.
74. *besolets*. An unmodified 'besolet', or 'bezolet', is Swiss-French for a whiskered tern (*chlidonias hybridus*; 'Guifette Moustac' in French). However, S's description of the birds as having 'purple on their backs' best fits the *bezolet noire*, or black tern, a summer migrant to Lake Geneva, whose coloration may seem to vary from black to purple in bright sunlight.
88–9. *"Diespiter, per pura tonantes egit equos"*. From Horace, *Odes*, I. 34. 5–8: 'Jupiter through the pure skies drove his thundering horses'. Horace claims to have been converted from Epicureanism to a belief in the traditional gods by the thunder he describes. Lucretius had argued that if thunder and lightning were caused by the gods (and were not natural phenomena), they would occur in a clear ('purum') sky. (*De rerum natura*, 6. 400).
92. *Evian*. Evian, on Lake Geneva in Savoy, was then ruled by the king of Sardinia. Mary wrote in *Journals* (end of the entry for 22 July): 'At the in at servreaux ⟨Servoz⟩ among other laws of the same nature there was an edict of the king of Sardinia's prohibiting his subjects from holding

private assemblies on pain of a fine of 12 francs & in default of payment imprisonement.'

97. *eaux savonneuses.* Foamy waters.

111. *Empress Maria Louisa.* Consort of Napoleon I.

114-29. *How beautiful... production.* Largely omitted from *SC* because the political moralizing would have been needlessly sententious in a letter to Peacock. As a public expression, it was not only in line with S's sentiments but also appropriate to a contemporary travel journal, as was the aside on honey which follows and appeared later in *SC.* Ll. 111-14, on Maria Louisa and St Preux, also appeared later in the original letter.

128-9. *Probably ... production.* 'Miel' = 'honey', though the form 'Mellerie' in *1817* would not have conveyed the derivation so exactly.

148. *My companion... coat.* Byron also refers to the incident (letter to John Murray, 27 June 1816). Thomas Moore later wrote that S refused Byron's offer to save him by 'seating himself quietly upon a locker, and grasping the rings at each end firmly in his hands' and declaring his resolution to go down in that position (*Life of Byron*, 1844, 320).

153. *St. Gingoux* = St Gingolph.

212. *See... 4.* In this letter St Preux points out to Julie the mouths of the Rhone, 'dont l'impétueux cours s'arrête tout à coup au bout d'un quart de lieue, et semble craindre de souiller de ses eux bourbeuses le cristal azuré du lac'. The same letter refers to the 'besolets' on Lake Geneva, which S describes in ll. 74-5.

212-18c. *immaterialism.* The inclination to immaterialism noted in *SC* is a significant gloss on the soon-to-be written 'Mont Blanc', whose scepticism is restricted to the senses and/or rational inferences from them and is subordinated to the concluding, if rhetorically queried, idealism of the poem it conditions. The reference to the 'prejudices' of *La Nouvelle Héloïse*, along with the praise of Rousseau, appears as well in a letter of 18 July 1816 to T. J. Hogg, where S concludes that Rousseau was the 'greatest man the world has produced since Milton'.

221. *We passed ... dungeons.* It was during this visit that Byron heard the story which inspired *The Prisoner of Chillon*, written during the poets' stay at Ouchy.

241. *"pernicies humani generis".* 'Destruction of the human race'. I have not found this precise quotation in Tacitus' works. It is possible that S misremembered the 'odio humani generis' ('hatred of the human race') which Tacitus assigned the Christians in his well-known description of the sect (*Annals*, 15. 44).

268-70. *the spot... lake.* The two incidents also appear in part IV, letter 17, of *Julie.*

275-7. *We gathered... absent.* These lines do not appear in *SC* but the terrace might be represented or suggested by the 'tessallated pavement near which L.B. agreed with me in aspiring to visit'.

307–14. *We were shewn ... solitary.* On completing *The History of the Decline and Fall of the Roman Empire*, Edward Gibbon (1737–94) felt a 'sober melancholy', as if he had taken 'leave of an old and agreeable companion' (*Miscellaneous Works*, London, 1814, i. 255).

315. *My companion ... leaves.* A sprig of the acacia gathered by Byron was sent to John Murray in the letter of 27 June noted above.

329. *fire.* The descriptive portion of SC concludes here. S allows only a few words to each of the three remaining days of the journey home and then returns to the affair of the house, with which the earlier (and separated) portion of the letter had dealt.

Letter IV

1–2. *Whilst ... it.* In the letter of 17 July as it now appears in Shelley, *Letters*, S had commissioned Peacock to find a house for him, 'with as good a garden as may be, near Windsor Forest, and take a lease of it for fourteen or twenty-one years'. (See the headnote for the relation between this letter and that of 12 July to Peacock.) Since S returned to England in September and did not move to his Marlow residence until the following March, Peacock's commission presumably came to nothing, at least in the short run. However, at the time of the letter of 17 July S did not intend to return to England until spring.

51–2. *Egyptian statue.* The 'statue' (along with its accompanying veil) seems to have been later generalized into the 'unsculptured image' of 'Mont Blanc', ll. 26–7. The waterfall itself has been identified as the Nant d'Arpénas (*Journals*, 113 n.).

64. *St. Martin ... Sallanches.* Two nearly facing villages on opposite sides of the Arve, apparently identified on the maps because of their proximity.

78. *cascade.* Identified as the Cascade de Chède in MS Shelley adds. e. 16.

96–7. *natural ... Bethgelert.* Here and in l. 308 S seems to be referring to contemporary collections of natural curiosities of a kind that Peacock would have been familiar with. As S also seems to be suggesting, they had no particular distinction, except for the horns he notes. A contemporary travel guide describes 'a cabinet of natural history' offered for sale in both Chamouni and St Martin, which contained 'minerals of Mont Blanc and S. Gothard; seals, necklaces, &c. made of the crystal of Mont Blanc, together with insects and plants indigenous to the higher Alps' (Mariana Starke, *Travels on the Continent: Written for the Use and Particular Information of Travellers*, John Murray: London, 1820, p. 63).

99–100. *bouquetin ... stag.* S's association of this not particularly rare animal with the goat family in the original letter was more appropriate; the *OED* identifies it with the ibex.

114–30. *Mont Blanc... divinest.* An important supplement and gloss to the climactic experience described in 'Mont Blanc'. Cf. also S's letter of 22 July 1816 to Byron.

209. *Saussure.* Horace Bénédict de Saussure (1740–99), Swiss geologist and alpinist, who felt that the Alps provided the key to the true theory of the earth's formation. Some of the speculations in sections III and IV of 'Mont Blanc' may derive from S's knowledge of Saussure's *Voyages dans les Alpes* (1779–96); Saussure was among the first to make a recorded ascent of Mont Blanc.

221. *Buffon's.* Georges-Louis Leclerc, Comte de Buffon (1707–88), French naturalist, whose *Histoire naturelle*, vol. i (1749), contained the theory of the earth S is referring to.

225. *Ahriman.* The 'Destructive Spirit' of evil in the dualistic and essentially Manichaean Zoroastrian doctrine. For an excellent account of Peacock's unfinished poem on the subject and its relation to S and his works see *SC* iii. 226–44.

248. *Mauvais pas.* Bad step.

277. *like the god... animal.* The same description of the Stoics' god is assigned to the Theosophist in *A Refutation of Deism* (ll. 956–7).

298–9. *fell... valley.* See *Journals*, 119 n., for a contemporary account of this catastrophe.

309. *Clifton.* The reference allows the biographical inference that while S and Mary were in Clifton (a suburb of Bristol) in early August 1815 he visited its repository of natural curiosities. A similar visit in Matlock is also implied both here and in l. 43. S could have passed through Matlock (in Derbyshire) on earlier trips north to York and Keswick, though I have discovered no reference to his stopping there.

319. *Celandine.* The repetition (with 'classic') suggests a mildly ironic reference to Wordsworth's poems on the flower.

322–3. *Did... mountains?* On a copy of the *History* in the Pforzheimer Collection appears the pencilled reaction of William Beckford (1759–1844, author of *Vathek*) to this sentence: 'No you did not ⟨tell me that there are troops of wolves among these mountains⟩ but had you told me there were troops of wild *Bores* & yourself their Captain, as raving *mad* about Mountains as Hares in March about Love, I should have believed you ...'. Beckford continues with a criticism of S's 'pompously picturesque' prose and an assessment of 'Mont Blanc', the concluding piece in the 1817 volume, as 'an avalanche of nonsense' (quoted in *SC* vii. 44). His earlier reactions to the volume as a whole were generally neutral.

328. *Adieu.* The original letter concludes with a paragraph of personal matters, mainly having to do with bills and their disposition.

AN ADDRESS TO THE PEOPLE ON THE DEATH OF THE PRINCESS CHARLOTTE

Date: 11–12 Nov. 1817.

Copy-text: ?*1843* (Huntington Library copy; shelfmark RB 439067).

Locations: Include BL (2, one in Ashley); Bodleian (3); Boston Public; Columbia, Cornell; University of Delaware; Harvard; Huntington; University of Illinois; Newberry (Chicago); Indiana University; Lehigh; Peabody Institute (Baltimore); Pf. (23); Princeton; University of Texas (5); Yale.

Description: Undated octavo pamphlet measuring 21.2 cm. × 13.4 cm. (8.3″ × 5.25″) and made up of two gatherings (⟨A⟩–B⁴), which consist of a title-page ('*Reprinted for Thomas Rodd, 2, Great Newport Street.*' at the foot of the verso; ⟨1–2⟩), drop-head title ('An Address, &c.') and centrally numbered text (⟨3⟩–16); the paragraphs are numbered I–XI; machine-wove paper; original stitching through three stab-holes; no wm or running heads; a printer's slug below '*FINIS*' at the foot of p. 16 reads: '*Compton & Ritchie, Printers, Middle Street, Cloth Fair, London.*' The copy-text title-page is reproduced on page 229.

Printed: 1817; ?1828–30; ?1843; MacCarthy, *Early Life*; F; J. (For an 1883 Aungervyle Society reprint, see below.)

The Princess Charlotte, daughter of the Regent and heiress presumptive to the English throne, died in childbirth on 6 Nov. 1817; the next day three working men were hanged for treasonable utterances and actions which they had been entrapped into making and performing by a Government *agent provocateur* going by the name of William Oliver. The liberal press seized on the coincidence, as S does here, to point out that there was at least as much cause for grieving over the deaths of these three working men and the suppressing of liberty their cases exemplified as there was for the death of the princess. For S, as for the liberal press, there was the additional connection between the princess and the working men implicit in reformist anticipations that she would have provided the nation with a reform-minded succession.

Mary Shelley's journal entry for 11 Nov. reads 'S. begins a pamphlet'; for 12 Nov. 'Shelley finishes his pamphlet'. On the morning of 12 Nov. S posted what he had 'written of a pamphlet on the subject of our conversation the other evening' to Charles Ollier, who had previously published *A Proposal for Putting Reform to the Vote*, with the request that it 'be sent to press without an hours delay' and the promise that he would send the rest of the printer's copy that evening, after he had received the first part from the printer. On 15 Nov. Mary records that, after a walk to both 'Olliers & Hookhams' (another publisher), they (presumably) 'read Shelley's pamphlet'.

The pamphlet referred to was undoubtedly *An Address to the People on the Death of the Princess Charlotte*, but there is no extant holograph or 1817 printing of the work. The bookseller Thomas Rodd, who issued the pamphlet in 1843, listed the work in his catalogue for that year as a 'fac-simile reprint' of an original edition which he said was limited to twenty copies. The provenance of Rodd's copy-text and the source of his infor-mation are not given, but it is possible to assign a *terminus a quo* of 1828 to his undated reprint, since Compton and Ritchie, its printers, formed their partnership in that year (see Philip A. H. Brown, *London Publishers and Printers c. 1800-1870*, London, 1982, 44). S's authorship of the pamphlet is demonstrated not only by the pseudonym 'Hermit of Marlow', used as well for *A Proposal for Putting Reform to the Vote*, but also by Thomas Medwin's reference to it in *The Shelley Papers* (1833): 'The title was only a masque for politics. Under the lament of the Princess he typified Liberty, and rung her knell' (p. 18). If an inscription in a Pf. copy —'Given to me by Mr. T. Rodd, July 31, 1830'—is authentically dated, the reprint's publication can be confined to 1828–30, which would then make it possible for Medwin to have seen the reprint rather than an 1817 printing. Medwin's reference tends to confirm the dating of the in-scription, though it does not, *per se*, altogether counter Thomas Wise's sceptical suggestion in *A Shelley Library*—that there had been no 1817 printing and that Rodd had in fact received from some source a holograph of the work left behind at Marlow and printed it himself for the first time (p. 46). Wise was obviously unaware of the *Journals* entries which make it clear that in some form the *Address* had reached the stage of printer's copy and had even, in view of the implications of the entry for 15 Nov., been printed.[1]

It is not clear why or how the original pamphlet (or holograph) came into Rodd's possession, nor why, once he had 'reprinted' it, he delayed publishing it. The apparent contradiction between S's insistence that the pamphlet be printed as soon as possible and Rodd's statement that only twenty copies were printed may provide some answers. Ollier or his printer (probably Buchanan McMillan, who was at about this time objecting to *Laon and Cythna* because of its anti-Establishment represen-tations) might have recognized some danger to themselves (if not to 'The Hermit of Marlow') in printing and distributing a pamphlet which could well have irritated the people at large, and the Ministry in particular, by its use of the princess's death as an occasion for explicit anti-Government propaganda and implicit exculpation and glorification of a set of convicted traitors. The fact that Rodd is precise about the number of pamphlets printed in 1817 indicates that he was at least informed of that

[1] Writing to Richard Garnett, 9 Nov. 1898, Wise was much more willing to trust Rodd's assertion: 'As to "We pity the Plumage" I have heard of the discovery of no copy as yet of the original edition. Rodd was a very different sort of fellow to Stockdale, and I have confid-ence in his imprint asserting that his issue was reprinted from a—now missing—original' (in W. R. Thurman's 1972 unpublished University of Texas dissertation, 'Letters about Shelley from the Richard Garnett Papers', p. 377).

fact and, since no copy of this printing has been recovered, there is a probability that the entire lot was given or sold to him, perhaps by Ollier or by the printer.[1] His claim of 'fac-simile' reproduction probably means only that he used one of the originals as a copy-text for his printing. Having printed it, Rodd might himself have decided to limit circulation of the pamphlet until the private opposition to publishing such works by S was laid to rest with the death of Timothy Shelley, which, however, did not take place until 1844. Any more public opposition would have lost much of its legal sanction when in 1841 a judge set free a convicted publisher of *Queen Mab*, whose trial for blasphemous libel had been forced by contemporary radicals to precipitate just such a result and provide the kind of precedent which Rodd might have felt he had to have, even so long after the specific events retailed in the pamphlet had passed out of the public mind. More cynically, one might care to suppose that Rodd advised Timothy Shelley of his reprint and accepted an appropriate recompense from S's father when he agreed not to distribute it at large. Sir Timothy had enforced a comparable arrangement with Mary Shelley when he advised her in 1824 that he would provide her with funds only if she promised 'not to bring dear S's name before the public' while his father lived (Mary Shelley, *Letters*, to Leigh Hunt, 22 Aug. 1824). When he rescinded his ban in 1838, her publication of S's prose in 1840 would then have served as a precedent for Rodd's assumption that previous agreements in restraint of such publication were no longer in force or enforced.

Given the suspect printing history of the pamphlet, it is tempting to infer from S's covering letter to Ollier, of 12 Nov. 1817, in which he writes that he does not think 'the whole will make a pamp⟨h⟩let so large as my last', that the later reprint might have represented an expansion of the 1817 printing (or drafting). The *Address to the People* is in fact over half as long again as S's 'last' pamphlet, *A Proposal for Putting Reform to the Vote*. Since S intended to finish the pamphlet before the evening of the same day on which he sent Ollier the first part of it, one may suppose that he knew what he wanted to put into it and about how much longer it would be. The inference is only worth making because a sizeable portion of the pamphlet, paragraphs VIII and IX, have the appearance of economic and historic digressions which in the first instance are very much like a portion of *A Philosophical View of Reform* and in the second parallel the

---

[1] An Aungervyle Society reprint of 1883 (published in *Aungervyle Society Reprints*, second series, privately printed, Edinburgh, 1884) was printed from a copy in the possession of the editor Edmund Goldsmid, who implies that his copy was an original. However, house style and corrector changes or lapses were most likely responsible for the many differences in accidentals and the few negligible differences in substantives between this reprint and Rodd's, which probably based Goldsmid's. Forman notes (*The Shelley Library*, p. 68) that 'fraudulent book-sellers' occasionally removed the Rodd imprint and sold his copies as originals.

form and content of the *Fragment on Reform* (*I*). Paragraph viii has no formal connection at all with its context, while paragraph ix's allusions to the Derby hangings and their context seem written from the point of view of a historian at some distance from the event—a perspective, however, which S might purposely have taken at the time (cf. letter to Hogg, end of Aug. 1815). Paragraph viii's references to and inferences concerning the 'double aristocracy' appear again in *A Philosophical View*, which also repeats or parallels the figures concerning the different amounts of time the labourer worked and those relating to the national debt. But this may simply mean that S, in Italy in 1819, made use of the *Address to the People* (in some form) when drafting the later work, which itself contains examples of the kind of digression which this paragraph seems to be. All in all, it appears more reasonable to assume that the work as issued by Rodd was the work as S originally drafted it than to speculate that at some later time, in some mysterious way, the paragraphs made their way into it.

Poems and pamphlets recounting and lamenting the princess's death, along with its effect on her loved ones and the nation, began appearing even before her funeral took place and continued well into the following year. By devoting most of their pages for several days to detailed accounts of the event and its aftermath, the Tory press likewise helped obscure the executions at Derby, mentioning them only to justify them and to absolve the Government of the charge of using *agents provocateurs* uttered by the convicted men and repeated by the liberal press. Leigh Hunt's *Examiner*, while pointedly avoiding a political reaction to the princess's death in its lead editorial for 9 Nov., attacked the Tory press the following Sunday for using the occasion as an excuse for avoiding full treatment of the Derby hangings and their political ramifications. From 9 to 12 Nov. S visited Hunt daily (cf. *Journals*). The fact that both Hunt's editorial of 16 Nov. and S's pamphlet have corresponding political motives for relating Charlotte's death to the executions suggests a shared intention, which was partly to compensate for the Tory press's relative failure to report the hangings but mainly to point up the Government's role as the instigators of the abortive Midlands uprising for which the three men were hanged.

With the inevitable exception of the succession itself, which eventually put Victoria where Charlotte would have been, the hangings at Derby, largely because of the governmental machinations they exposed, were of more lasting political consequence than the death at Windsor. One can only conjecture as to what reformist tendencies Charlotte might later have had the will and power to implement. The extent to which the princess had by 1817 become a stalking-horse for liberal hopes rather than their embodiment is suggested by S's patronizing definition of her attributes and potential, which echoes the assessments of the liberal press. After the pamphlets and poems of mourning had gone their ephemeral way and the commemorative medals were relegated to trunks and attics, the memory of the working men continued to work as a yeast in the ferment of radical change. Abetted by the liberal press and the political motives he shared with them, S's historical perspective on the relative significance of the topical events he parallels and contrasts tends to illustrate the objective view of passing events he occasionally claimed for himself and later summed up as a proclivity to look behind the visible for the truth it veiled (letter to T. L. Peacock, 6 Nov. 1818).

Related primary and secondary materials: *The Trials of Jeremy Brandreth ... and Others for High Treason, under a Special Commission at Derby* (London, 1817); *SP* 18; Forman, *The Shelley Library*, 68-9; Charles E. Pearce, *The Beloved Princess* . . . (New York, 1912), 105-6, 206, 218, 231, 279, 281, 301; J. L. and Barbara Hammond, *The Skilled Labourer, 1760-1832* (London, 1920), 341-76; Newman I. White, 'Shelley and the Active Radicals of the Early Nineteenth Century', *SAQ* 39 (July 1930), 248-61; Grabo, *Magic Plant*, 195-200; Kenneth Neill Cameron, 'Shelley, Cobbett, and the National Debt', *JEGP* 42 (Apr. 1943), 197-209; William Davenport, 'Notes on Shelley's Political Prose: Sources, Bibliography, Errors in Print', *N&Q* 177 (23 Sept. 1939), 223-5; Notopoulos, *Platonism*, 486; R. J. White, *Waterloo to Peterloo* (London, 1957), pp. ix, 152-75 (and *passim*); *SC* v. 125 n.; Thompson, *Working Class*, 648-69; Cameron, *Golden Years*, 125-7, 593, 595-6; Scrivener, *Radical Shelley*, 108-12, 133-9; Robinson, *Shelley and Byron*, 260 n.; Webb, *Voice not Understood*, 107; Dawson, *Unacknowledged Legislator*, 49-50, 176-8; Hoagwood, *Scepticism*, 160-1.

TITLE-PAGE. *Epigraph.* "WE ... BIRD." This sentiment, from Thomas Paine's *Rights of Man* (*Writings*, ii. 288), is sometimes listed as the title of the pamphlet. It refers most directly to Edmund Burke's 'pity' in his *Reflections on the French Revolution* for Marie Antoinette and the French aristocracy (the 'plumage'), and his relative indifference to the condition of the French people in general (the 'dying bird'). S's application might have seemed invidious enough to forestall the dissemination of a printing of the pamphlet in 1817.

The Hermit of Marlow. Though S actually wrote the pamphlet in London, his permanent residence was then in Marlow. If there was an ulterior motive for the use of the pseudonym, it was S's fear that the mild notoriety he had already achieved, partly because of the Chancery trial (see *Declaration in Chancery* and commentary), might compromise the reformist cause. S's life at Marlow, as later reported by Hunt, was ascetic and reclusive.

15. *too deep for words.* Cf. Wordsworth's 'Ode: Intimations of Immortality', l. 204.

33-5. *And have ... blood?* Cf. *The Merchant of Venice*, III. i. 60-8. The general context is obviously concerned with democratizing Charlotte's death in preparation for the analogy soon to be set up with the Derby hangings, though the reader might have appropriately recalled that 'revenge' was the end of Shylock's ruminations: 'The villainy you teach me, I will execute.' The actor Edmund Kean's landmark portrayal of Shylock from 1814 on would have contributed to the force of the allusion in the public mind; it was also used in the *Examiner*'s account of the hangings on 16 Nov.

39–41. *The Athenians . . . genius.* Cf. S's translation of Plato's *Menexenus* (a dialogue largely concerned with funeral panegyric). In a compendious entry in her journal, 23 Feb.–6 Apr. 1817, Mary Shelley notes that S had read 'several works of Plato' during that period. Notopoulos (*Platonism*, 486) traces this sentence to *Menexenus* or, less probably, to Thucydides' *History of the Peloponnesian War*, 2. 35–47.

41. *illustrated.* I.e. 'made illustrious'.

41–5. *Men . . . voyage.* W. H. Davenport (*N&Q* 177 (23 Sept. 1939), 225) traces these lines to William Godwin's *Essay on Sepulchres* (1809), which S apparently had in mind when he wrote the review of *Mandeville* that appeared in the *Examiner* for 28 Dec. 1817.

45. *"that . . . returns."* A variant of *Hamlet*, III. i. 79–80.

65–6. *Horne Tooke and Hardy.* John Horne Tooke (1736–1812) and Thomas Hardy (1752–1832), English radical reformers, both tried for and acquitted of high treason in 1794.

79. *Brandreth . . . Turner.* Relevant biographical data for Jeremiah Brandreth, the apparent leader of the militant labourers, Isaac Ludlam, and William Turner may be found in the extended account of the 'insurrection', its causes and aftermath, in Thompson, *Working Class*, 656–69.

84–7. *But there were . . . grief.* The levelling of Princess Charlotte accords with the Godwinian estimate of public utility as the proper gauge for public concern.

92–6. *She had accomplished . . . rule.* While S's criticism of Princess Charlotte's political acumen and knowledge was probably not altogether fair (cf. *Letters of the Princess Charlotte 1811–17*, ed. A. Aspinall, London, 1949, xvi, 9, 18, 60, 95, 236, and *passim*), it justifies S's earlier attempt (through his persona) to instruct her in such matters, something about to take place when *The Elysian Fields* breaks off. She preferred the *Morning Chronicle* and the *Examiner* to the Tory press, and her liberal uncle Sussex to her other politically motivated relations, received special tuition in political history and in the laws of England (cf. *The Auto-biography of Miss Knight* ⟨Charlotte's governess⟩, ed. Roger Fulford, London, 1960, 115, 162), maintained an allegiance to Charles Fox, whom her father had abandoned, and, as the reformers were pleased to observe, gave early promise of being an actively progressive monarch quite in accord with the 'spirit of the age' as they defined it. When it suited his purposes, as it does in *The Elysian Fields*, S accepted this conception of her political character. His purpose here is rhetorical and relatively invidious.

99–101. *Princes... regret.* Cf. George Ensor, in his *Defects of the English Laws and Tribunals* (J. Johnson: London, 1812): 'princes in infancy ... are ... prevented from thinking, seduced from truth' (p. 254). As noted elsewhere, Ensor, a radical writer whom S much admired and highly recommended (cf. letter to E. Hitchener, 5 June 1811), might well have provided immediate sources and certainly provides analogues for sentiments recurrent in S's prose from the *Address, to the Irish People* through to *A Defence of Poetry*. See White, *Shelley*, i. 624–6. Ensor was among those to whom S asked Ollier to send copies of *A Proposal for Putting Reform to the Vote*.

113. *Her husband.* Prince Leopold of Saxe-Coburg, whom Charlotte married in May 1816.

113–14. *father... brethren.* While S is here concerned with emphasizing the intrinsic unnaturalness of the royal condition, Princess Charlotte's adversary relationship with her father and her enforced estrangement from her mother are specifically alluded to.

119. *hurdle.* The *Examiner* for 9 Nov. described it as a 'very simple machine, formed of a few boards nailed upon two long beams'. Until 1870 those convicted of high treason were conveyed through the streets on this sledge-like contrivance to the place of execution.

127. *What is death?* Cf. *On the Punishment of Death, On a Future State,* and several of the Esdaile poems, particularly 'Reality'.

128 n. *Cymbeline.* Not italicized in the pamphlet.

147. *depending on.* I.e. flowing or resulting from.

158–9. *circumstances ... consequence.* I.e. governmental oppression, political and economic, through the means indicated in paragraph VIII.

165. *check.* S probably refers to the institution of the Sinking Fund in 1786, which seemed to provide a mechanism for retiring the national debt but in fact provided an excuse for raising it. Much of Cobbett's *Paper against Gold* (1815) was concerned with exaggerating the duplicity of Pitt's Government in formulating what Cobbett saw as an additional tax on the people. S seems here to have the following passage from Cobbett in mind: '⟨The Sinking Fund⟩ took from the Ministers that check to the making of wars and the paying of foreign armies, for the want of which check the Expenses and Taxes and Debt of the country have been so fearfully augmented, to say nothing, at present, about the dreadful changes which those wars have made in our affairs both at home and abroad' (p. 37). Reformers such as Burdett and Grenville related the increased power of the Crown and the consequent oppression of the people to the proliferation of tax-collectors and a standing army, themselves creatures of the burgeoning national debt. One may surmise that S meant to (or perhaps did) write 'until *after* the American War'.

170. *fundamental defect.* In *A Philosophical View of Reform* S more explicitly defines this defect as 'an original imperfection in the equal distribution of suffrage'.

173-5. *improved ... created.* In 1694, in order to subsidize the wars undertaken during King William III's reign, the Bank of England was founded with a series of loans which were to be paid for by increased taxes. In his *Paper against Gold* Cobbett traces the consequent increase of the debt from £16.3m. in 1701 to £811.12m. in 1809. With the abandonment of the gold standard in 1797, the debt tended to inflate geometrically.

179. *placemen.* Individuals appointed to public office regardless of their qualifications.

181-2. *double aristocracy.* Kenneth Neill Cameron ('Shelley, Cobbett, and the National Debt', *JEGP* 42, Apr. 1943, 201-2) traces the concept of a fund-holder aristocracy supplementing the traditional aristocracy of landholders to David Hume's 'Essay on Public Credit', which S apparently read as early as 1812. But Cobbett was probably S's immediate source. The context through much of this paragraph anticipates *A Philosophical View of Reform*.

189. *old aristocracy.* Cf. *A Philosophical View of Reform*. S recognized that certain acquired and transmitted characteristics of the traditional aristocracy represented a diluted form of the human perfectibility he envisaged in his millennial poetry. More practically, he recognized the need to conciliate the traditional aristocracy by setting them off from the fund-holding breed. S initially derived his own cultural values from the economic and social status of the landholding aristocracy. While suspicious of oligarchy, S might have seen a benevolent overseership by the landed class—a conscionable squirarchy—as a tolerable interim expedient in a collective reform movement which would accelerate as the masses' capacity to reform themselves was activated and enlarged. In an early letter to T. J. Hogg S criticized the 'bigotry of commonplace republicanism', insisted that he was himself a 'very resolved republican', but none the less allowed that the 'noblest feelings might conduct some few reflecting minds ⟨like David Hume's⟩ to aristocracy' (3 Dec. 1812).

sans ... tache. 'Without fear and without stain'. The French military hero Pierre Bayard (?1474-1524) was referred to as 'le chevalier sans peur et sans reproche ⟨or tache⟩'.

191. *funds.* The *OED* provides the following 1809 definition: 'a general term for money lent to government, and which constitutes the national debt'; a 'fund-holder' is then one who invests ('lends' or 'gambles') this money.

193. *"Corinthian ... society".* Cf. Edmund Burke, *Reflections on the French Revolution* (J. M. Dent & Sons Ltd.: London, 1953, 135). S's source for this quotation is probably the *Rights of Man*, where the metaphor is

singled out for particular censure during the course of Paine's recurrent criticism of Burke's anti-revolutionary and pro-aristocratic biases: 'Mr. Burke, in his first essay, called aristocracy *"the Corinthian capital of polished society"'* (*Rights of Man, Writings*, ii. 471). There is no evidence that S ever read the *Reflections*, though he would have been familiar with its arguments and their counter-arguments in both Paine and Godwin (see ibid. 357–68 and *passim*; *PJ* ii. 86–103). The phrase had become an ironic commonplace in reformist speeches and tracts.

196. *sixteen . . . eight.* Cf. *A Philosophical View of Reform.*

201. *forty-four millions.* The *Examiner* for 9 Mar. 1817 listed the 'unfunded debt' at £44.6m. S uses this figure and a higher one in *Philosophical View*, written two and a half years later (see on ll. 173–5 above). Adam Smith defined the 'unfunded debt' as a national debt contracted by 'borrow⟨ing⟩ on what may be called personal credit, without assigning or mortgaging any particular fund for the payment of the debt' and prophesied in 1776 that in the long run it would probably lead to the ruin of all the great nations of Europe. (*An Inquiry into the Nature and Causes of the Wealth of Nations*, two vols., ed. W. B. Todd, Liberty *Classics* repr.; Oxford University Press, Oxford, 1979, ii. 911). As S indicates, these unfunded appropriations were used to pay for 'extraordinary services' (Smith, ibid.), such as a standing army, and were to be reimbursed at the expense of the nation at large. In his Preface to *The Masque of Anarchy* Hunt builds an anecdote around S's interest in the amount of the national debt which probably relates to mid- or late 1817 (p. xiii).

203–4. *necessity . . . submit.* In line with his concern to allay the fears and gain the support of an anticipated middle- and upper-class audience, S here makes an anti-radical accommodation to an established system of injustice with which that audience generally identified its prerogatives. S's poetic qualification of Godwinian gradualism and 'hard necessity' is love, or the outgoing of the spirit, which will eventually replace the principle of self here exemplified by the regressive fund-holding aristocracy, the real 'enemy of freedom' (ll. 210–11) because they are the prospective cause of anarchy.

212. *two chasms.* Apparently anarchy and misrule.

222–3. *The government . . . play.* As S construes it, the Government's purpose was to discredit reform by tempting the lower classes into acts of violence which would intimidate and alienate the middle class and quell the 'nobler spirit' of liberty (essentially the extension of the franchise) abroad in the land.

226–7. *causes before mentioned.* The creation of the national debt, which in turn (so S, following Cobbett) created the fund-holding aristocracy.

227. *manufacturers.* I.e. factory hands.

236–8. *It is impossible . . . agents.* Hunt specifically involves Castlereagh in the 'guilt' of the *agents provocateurs* (*Examiner*, 16 Nov. 1817), as did Brandreth on the scaffold. Lord Sidmouth was Oliver's immediate superior among the ministerial hierarchy.

259–60. *eighteen dragoons.* The number reported in the *Examiner* for 9 Nov.

262–4. *The cruel instigators . . . villainy.* The statement seems to imply a later knowledge of Oliver's recompense for his part in the conspiracy, as does the plural subject. At the time of the trial Oliver was kept in the wings as a possible witness for the prosecution, though the Government's hope was that it would not be necessary to call on him and so risk publicly bringing into question their own part in the affair.

264. *public voice.* The significant public voice which S meant to appeal to and strengthen was probably that of the middle class, who were becoming increasingly prominent in the reform movement, though remaining fearful of the anarchy of the mob. (See John Cannon, *Parliamentary Reform: 1640–1832*, Cambridge, 1973, 115, 165–6, 183, concerning British public feeling as identified with the middle classes.)

267. *extraordinary powers.* Probably a reference to the suspension of Habeas Corpus and to the Seditious Meetings Act, both of which were passed by Parliament in Mar. 1817.

275. OLIVER. As S notes, he derived his information about the hangings from the *Examiner* for 9 Nov.; some of the material not in quotation marks is in fact also from that source. However, the *Examiner* for 16 Nov. uses phrases and allusions which are also found in *An Address to the People*, presumably already printed (e.g. the reference to the dying man's words and the allusion to Shylock noted above on ll. 33–5), though they could have been part of the common conversational stock which the two friends shared when they spoke of the event earlier in the week.

282–3. *while the executioner . . . neck.* The italicized words are taken verbatim from the *Examiner*.

285–6. *chaplain . . . observations.* This was construed by the liberal press as the denial of a traditional right of last words by the condemned, which in this instance might have proved embarrassing to the Government.

289 n. *Examiner.* Not italicized in the pamphlet. S could as well have taken the expressions from the *Morning Chronicle* of 10 Nov. (and probably other newspapers), where they appear in precisely the same form.

301. *delusion.* The definitive source and reference of 'delusion' in such a context is doubtless Paine's *Decline and Fall of the English System of Finance* as quoted in Cobbett's *Paper against Gold*: 'When people find . . . reservedness among each other in giving gold and silver for bank-notes . . . they will go for payment to the Bank . . . and the truth, or delusion of the funding system, will then be proved' (p. 119). Earlier Cobbett himself refers to the system as 'the fatal delusion'. In a letter of 6 Nov. 1819 to the

Gisbornes S notes that the 'peculiar circumstances of the delusion are such that none but a very few persons will ever be brought to see its instability but by the experience of loss'. The 'delusion' was variously compounded of paper money, the sinking fund, and the public debt itself, any or all of which might be meant by a given writer in a given context.

327–33. *Let us follow ... Queen.* The positive elements of the traditional elegiac conclusion appear as Hope creating from its own wreck the thing it contemplates, through what seems to be a violent overthrow of the established hierarchy. The revolutionary coda—not really veiled by the allegory—might have contributed to a printer's or publisher's reluctance to attach his name to the work in 1817. The positive emphasis, however, as in *Laon and Cythna*, is the eternal resurgence of liberty, whatever temporal defeat it may incur.

FRAGMENT ON REFORM (I)

Date: ?1817.

Copy-text: Bod. MS Shelley adds. c. 4, fols. 282^r, 283^r.

Description: Untitled ink holograph appearing on the rectos formed by a single lined sheet folded into two leaves or four pages, each measuring 19.7 cm. × 15.8 cm. (7.7″ × 6.3″); laid paper; WM: J CRIPPS 1811; the text is continuous from below a few sprigs of characteristic Shelleyan drawings of foliage 4.5 cm. (1.7″) from the top right of fol. 282^r and concludes about half-way down fol. 283^r; the numeral '2' is centred at the top of fol. 283^r. Both versos are blank. Sir John Shelley-Rolls's folder containing the fragment entitles it 'Essay on English Constitution'.

Provenance: Mary Shelley; Sir Percy Shelley and Jane, Lady Shelley; Sir John Shelley-Rolls; Bodleian.

Printed: J.

While the watermark suggests that this fragment could have been drafted in England at any time from 1811, the fact that none of S's original prose manuscripts are extant before he began living with Mary Godwin makes it probable that it was not written until after the summer of 1814. Since S's interest in reform was mainly evidenced in print during 1817, the conjectured date provided above seems plausible.

The Julian editors printed the holograph along with a fragment of comparable length, originally printed in Richard Garnett's *Relics of Shelley* (London, 1862), as two 'Fragments on Reform', but there is no real connection between the two. While the other fragment, written after the Shelleys had left England, may have some relation to *A Philosophical View of Reform*, this one seems less an expository work than a fictionalized account of the post-Napoleonic period in England seen from the perspective of someone living after a revolutionary crisis such as English radical reformers had been anticipating since the early 1790s. The major reason for placing the fragment after *An Address to the People on the Death of the Princess Charlotte* derives from the comparable historical perspective developed towards the conclusion of that work (see pp. 236–7). The title provided by the Julian editors is preferable to that written on the Bodleian folder (see the Description above), if only because it is more generalized.

4C. *year   was.* The space after 'year' suggests that S wished to specify a time for the 'crisis' he was describing; this may support the inference that the fragment was intended as a fictional account of a potential crisis and aftermath which S anticipated from current conditions in England.

FRAGMENT OF 'A REFUTATION OF DEISM'

Date: ?Late 1817.

Copy-text: Bod. MS Shelley e. 4, fols. 1ʳ–5ʳ.

Description: Untitled fair-copy holograph, in ink except as noted in the Collation, measuring 22.9 cm. × 18.2 cm. (9″ × 7.2″); wove paper (lined); WM: the leaves of the gathering which contains the fragment do not have the watermark W TURNER & SON appearing elsewhere in this manuscript; a variable but consistently wide right margin was left on each page; a first division of the text seems originally to have been continuous from fol. 1ʳ through the top of fol. 3ᵛ, but since the outer half of fol. 1 has been torn away and fol. 1ʳ concludes a paragraph c.3.6 cm. (1.5″) from the bottom of the page, the continuity is not certain; a second division of the extant text begins at the top of fol. 4ʳ and concludes about two-thirds of the way down fol. 5ʳ. Characteristic Shelleyan foliage and doodles appear in the spaces left above and below the text on fol. 1ʳ, in the wide right margin of fol. 1ᵛ rev., and below the text concluding at the top of fol. 3ᵛ rev.; additional foliage and two or three towered structures appear under the text on fol. 5ʳ. See also Dawson, *e. 4*, p. xii.

Provenance: Mary Shelley; Sir Percy Shelley and Jane, Lady Shelley; Bodleian.

Printed: Koszul, *Shelley's Prose*; J; Dawson, *e. 4*.

Since the *Fragment of 'A Refutation of Deism'* appears at the beginning of a notebook containing material which either must have been or was most probably written no earlier than late 1817 (drafts for 'Ozymandias', 'Prince Athanase', and two 'Constantia' poems), and since, along with the drafts of *On Christianity* and *On Marriage*, it almost certainly preceded the poetry drafts, Sept.–Nov. 1817 seems reasonable as a date of composition for this fair-copy holograph. However, not only must a *terminus a quo* remain uncertain but the chronological relationship of the fragment to *A Refutation of Deism* is ambiguous. While 1817 is the earliest plausible date one can assign to this draft, the fact that it is a fair copy indicates that it could have been based on a rougher draft rather than on the 1814 *Refutation*, which it might otherwise seem partially to transcribe in expository rather than in dialogue form. Either because or in spite of the fact that internal evidence is often dubious and its interpretation tendentious, it is arguable that the *Refutation* is a more finished version of the argument as presented here, which not only conflates antithetical portions of the reasonings offered by the *Refutation*'s controversialists but is also rhetorically less sophisticated than the dialogue (see the Collation and related commentary *passim*; see also James Notopoulos, 'The Dating of Shelley's Prose', *PMLA* 58 (1943), 484). While it is unclear why in 1817 S would have cared to transcribe a draft written before the 1814 printing, it is likewise unclear why he would have cared at that date to rewrite an argument which had already been printed twice. And other hypotheses are no doubt possible. In any case, when taken with the relatively fair-copy hand at work in *On Christianity* and *On Marriage*, the very careful, printer's-copy hand used for this piece (as well as its position) suggests that it was the first entry into a notebook which was perhaps originally intended to serve as a repository of final transcriptions and recensions of works previously drafted or even printed elsewhere, with the intention diminishing along with the less careful hand used for the other two prose drafts. The stubs of two leaves between fol. 1 and the front pastedown of the notebook could have contained an earlier portion of the fragment.

Like the 1814 *Refutation*, the fragment is heavily indebted to Hume and probably to Holbach as well. For further comment see K 123–5 and the relevant commentary on *A Refutation of Deism*.

105+ HEADING. *Of . . . existence.* 'Universality' was a 'mark' of the truth of a particular belief among some eighteenth-century Deists.

151–7. *The only knowledge . . . occurrence.* Cf. *1814*, ll. 931–6, where S notes his source in Hume.

ON CHRISTIANITY

Date: ?Mid- to ?late 1817.

Copy-texts: Bod. MS Shelley e. 4, fols. 7ʳ–33ᵛ; Bod. MS Shelley adds. c. 4, fols. 276ʳ–279ᵛ. (A transcription of the *e. 4* fragment among the Abinger materials at the Bodleian Library, Dep. d. 393, was evidently made for the 1859 printing and has no independent authority.)

Description: *Bod. MS Shelley e. 4*—untitled and occasionally numbered ink holograph measuring 22.9 cm. × 18.2 cm. (9″ × 7.2″); wove paper (lined); WM: W. TURNER & SON; there are several breaks in the text as noted in the Textual

Notes. *Bod. MS Shelley adds. c. 4*—untitled ink holograph consisting of two sheets folded to make four folio leaves and eight pages each measuring 19.7 cm. × 16 cm. (7.8″ × 6.3″); laid paper; wm: Britannia; the text is continuous from the top of fol. 276ʳ to the bottom of fol. 279ᵛ except as noted in the Textual Notes.

Provenance: *e. 4*—Mary Shelley; Sir Percy Shelley and Jane, Lady Shelley; Bodleian; *adds. c. 4*—Mary Shelley; Sir Percy Shelley and Jane, Lady Shelley; Sir John Shelley-Rolls; Bodleian.

Printed: *e. 4*—*Shelley Memorials*; *F*; *K*; *J*; *TT*; *c. 4* (fols. 277ʳ—278ᵛ) *J*; (fols. 276ʳ–279ᵛ) *TT*. A facsimile edition of the *e. 4* notebook, ed. P. M. S. Dawson, has been printed by Garland Publishing Inc. in the Bodleian Shelley Manuscripts series; it is referred to in the apparatus as *e. 4(D)*.

A date of late 1817 for the *e. 4* holograph of *On Christianity* may be conjectured from its placing in a notebook whose most datable contents are the drafts of poems written no later than early Jan. 1818—'Ozymandias', published 11 Jan. 1818, 'To Constantia', and 'To Constantia, Singing'—one of which Claire Clairmont partially copied on 19 Jan. 1818 (see *CC*). Along with a carefully drafted recension of part of *A Refutation of Deism* and the draft of the fragment *On Marriage*, *On Christianity* preceded the other contents of the notebook, which seems originally to have been meant exclusively for prose drafts. Though not so carefully drafted as these other prose fragments, *On Christianity* is *passim* a relatively fair copy which might have been creatively transcribed from a rougher draft. But the fact that its parts are themselves fragmented, at times repetitious, and obviously in need of an authorial reordering and integration indicates that at best such a draft, if it existed, must have been a large part no more than a series of notes.

The portion of the text in *adds. c. 4* may be a segment of that earlier draft, though the only evidence for its having been written before at least some of *e. 4* is its relatively rough state. The Julian editor established a reasonable precedent for placing the *c. 4* leaves where they are placed in this edition. The material is not redundant and it does seem to follow from the first paragraph of *e. 4*, which breaks off mid-sentence—thus confirming, as its appearance also indicates, that the early leaves of the holograph were intermediate copy. The nearly two blank pages which follow this break clearly indicate that S intended to continue the draft, perhaps from the rougher *c. 4* leaves. The generalized and introductory nature of the content in *c. 4* likewise seems to confirm its placing early in the context of *e. 4* (once the decision has been taken to include it at all). The only concrete internal evidence for incorporating and locating *c. 4* in this way is the reference late in the text of *e. 4* (ll. 591–3) to a refusal to consider the Gospel miracles which is made in *c. 4* (ll. 24–6). The probability is that the *c. 4* draft preceded the *e. 4* draft, and that it was written no earlier than mid-1817. The piece as a whole, however, has been placed in accordance with the ordering indicated in the *e. 4* notebook, which has the bulk of *On Christianity* after the *Fragment of 'A Refutation of Deism'*. As the Textual Notes demonstrate, the *1859* text of *e. 4*, followed by *F*, was incomplete and inaccurate; *K* provided the first complete and generally accurate printing of this manuscript.

The subject-matter of the fragment divides into three sometimes overlapping parts—Christ on revenge, Christ on God, Christ on equality—and a fourth part concerned with justifying Christ's rhetorical methods and criticizing the integrity of the Gospel writers' reportage. S himself assumes the rhetorical posture of both an exegete and higher critic of the New Testament texts he chooses to quote, paraphrase, and comment on. The predictable result is that Christ is found, like S, to preach non-violence, social and political equality, and belief in a pantheistic (perhaps panentheistic) god who animates the moral and material world. While S may not be so sanguine as his Christ in believing that this God's benevolence extends to a species of personal immortality in the spirit, he is at one with him in believing that such a God would not condone, much less practise, retributive justice. Like S in *Queen Mab* and in the fragment *On Life*, Christ refuses to identify the mind of man with the mind of God. The section on equality, which derives much of its substance from S's imaginative enlargement of what Diogenes Laertius implied on the subject rather than from Christ's words, suggests that S would finally have directed his selective exegetal concerns towards a contemporary political application within a larger philosophical context such as that he was soon to initiate (or had already initiated) in his *Speculations on Morals and Metaphysics*. The discursive subject of justice and benevolence which makes up much of this latter work is not only echoed or anticipated in *On Christianity* but implicitly demonstrated by the exemplary benevolence ascribed to Christ and the exemplary justice which in S's judgement had been meted out to Julius Caesar. In so far as Christ's critical methodology is associated with major pagan philosophers from Socrates to the later Academics, he is found, like them, to demonstrate an independent mind, a sceptical attitude, and a moral empiricism particularly concerned with reassessing traditional dogmas according to humanistic standards. The resultant spiritualizing of the biblical moral codes is correspondingly found to have its appropriate antecedents and condition in the larger context of a civilization evolving from national ideals rooted in the primitive virtues of courage and patriotism towards receptivity to a subjective moral idealism rooted in love and expressed through social and political utilitarianism. Largely de-anthropomorphized and altogether non-sectarian, Christ's God is none the less a direct reflection of the moral imagination and thereby retains an essential benevolence (and a more questionable will) so as to serve ideally as a positive sanction for the equality among mankind which, S concludes, Christ effectively if prematurely preached. S's criticism of the egalitarianism he supposed in force in the early Christian communities stemmed from a grounding belief, emphatically inculcated in *An Address, to the Irish People*, that individual moral improvement collectively demonstrated was a necessary prerequisite for lasting institutional reforms. In the gospel according to S, Christ himself is historically re-imagined as a poet rather than as a prophet, a prototype of a legislator of the world, still unacknowledged because still misunderstood and mis-applied.

S's interest in Christ and Christianity was lifelong, though at its most intense in his early letters, where, in a continuing context of often vitriolic censure levelled at the Christian system, he first outlined and eventually proposed to himself the critical task of providing an appropri-ately bowdlerized recension of the Bible which might serve a socially constructive purpose. Writing to his friend Hogg on 26 Apr. 1811, he allows that Christianity, with its 'disgusting excrescencies' lopped off, its 'selfish dogmas' qualified, and only its 'virtuous precepts' retained, would do no harm and might even be 'highly requisite for the vulgar'. Later, in writing to Elizabeth Hitchener, he suggests the motive for his lost *Biblical Extracts*, a compendium apparently much like what *On Christianity* was at least partially intended to be: 'I have often thought that the moral sayings of Jesus Christ might be very useful if selected from the mystery and immorality which surrounds them; it is a little work I have in con-templation' (27 Feb. 1812). The gist of several letters S wrote to his London publisher, Thomas Hookham, from Nov. 1812 to 2 Jan. 1813 indicates that he had finished the little work, had sent it to Hookham for publication either by him or by the radical bookseller Daniel Eaton (subject of *A Letter to Lord Ellenborough*), and had failed to persuade either of them to print it or at any rate to publish it.

The likely date of *On Christianity* makes it probable that it was not, as has been argued, an early draft of the *Biblical Extracts*, though it could represent a draft made up from some early notes for that work or from a recollection of some of its contents. The 'mystery' and perhaps the immorality which S meant to exclude from the lost *Extracts* may be linked to his refusal here to take up the question of the divinity and miracles ascribed to Christ and his particular concern with denying that eternal (or even temporal) damnation was part of Christ's authentic teaching. But S seemed inspired by any given reading of the Bible for some sort of commentary on it (as his annotations to Luke in Bod. MS Shelley adds. e. 9 illustrate), and it would not have required any impetus other than a recurrent concern with Christianity, non-violence, justice and benevolence, and political equality to have inspired the fragment. The comparatively finished state of much of the holograph's phrasing may itself indicate that old associations were being reiterated and regrouped around the epicentres provided by the relatively few Gospel excerpts S chose to deal with here, for a comprehensive purpose which this fragment may only begin to define.

Besides the primary materials noted above and below, *An Address, to the Irish People*, *A Letter to Lord Ellenborough*, 'Hymn to Intellectual Beauty', 'Mont Blanc', *Alastor, Adonais, Prometheus Unbound, A Philosophical View of Reform*, and *A Defence of Poetry* all contain more or less obvious echoes or anticipations of parts of the fragment. Parallels to the several definitions of God and to many of the political inferences in the fragment appear in works by Spinoza, Paine, and Godwin which S had been familiar with since at least 1812. Diogenes Laertius and Tacitus certainly, Plutarch and Gibbon very probably, were also drawn on for philosophical parallels and historical data. The format of the fragment could have been influenced by William Paley's *Evidences*, which consists in large part of paraphrases of and inferences concerning the Gospels.

Related primary and secondary materials: LETTERS, to E. Hitchener, 11, 25 June, 24 Nov. 1811, 2 Jan. 1812; *A Refutation of Deism* (and related primary materials); *The Assassins*; *On the Punishment of Death*; *An Answer to Leslie's 'A Short and Easy Method with the Deists'*; *On a Future State*; *On Life*; MS Shelley adds. e. 9, pp. 1–8 (nn. on Luke 1–20); Paine, *Age of Reason, Writings*, iv. 26–8; *K*, 7–12 and nn.; J. M. Robertson, *A History of Freethought in the Nineteenth Century* (London, 1929), 94–5; Bennett Weaver, 'Shelley's Biblical Extracts: A Lost Book', *Papers of the Michigan Academy of Science, Arts and Letters*, 20 (1935), 523–38; Grabo, *Magic Plant*, 154–60, 255–6; Barnard, *Shelley's Religion*, 67–73; A. M. D. Hughes, 'Warton Lecture on English Poetry: The Theology of Shelley', *Proceedings of the British Academy*, 24 (1939), 191–203; Notopoulos, *Platonism*, 326–7, 329–30; David Lee Clark, 'Shelley's Biblical Extracts', *MLN* 66 (Nov. 1951), 435–41; Pulos, *Deep Truth*, ch. VI; Roy R. Male, jun., and James A. Notopoulos, 'Shelley's Copy of Diogenes Laertius', *MLR* 54 (Jan. 1959), 10–21; Cameron, *Golden Years*, 163–9, 510; Robinson, *Shelley and Byron*, 118–19; Webb, *Voice not Understood*, ch. VI; Dawson, *Unacknowledged Legislator*, 84–5, 181–2; Scrivener, *Radical Shelley*, 87–107; Hoagwood, *Scepticism*, 131–4; Hogle, *Shelley's Process*, 261–2.

TITLE. None in MS. The editorial title indicates the subject of the fragments without further defining the specific form, content, and purpose S might have intended, except to suggest that Christ's recorded pronouncements, their meanings and applications, were his primary concern. Whether the fragments would have evolved into a self-sufficient essay, formed part of a larger work, or continued as 'Biblical Extracts' therefore remains an open question.

48. *God or man*. In a preliminary note on fol. 6ᵛ S rather dubiously interprets a verse from Scripture to accord with his own understanding of Christ's divinity: 'Acts C. 18. V. 25. That [God]Xt was not thought to be god'.

49. *doctrines*. In discounting the miracles and advancing the doctrines, S implicitly discountenances Christian apologists (such as William Paley)

who argued that the miracles were a necessary demonstration of the truth of the doctrines. Elsewhere S will point out that even the doctrines had their historical antecedents among the Greek and Roman philosophers.

52c. *Esseneians.* That is, Essenes. I have not been able to locate S's pencilled reference. It is possible that he wished to associate Christ with this exacting order of historical Judaism. See on l. 766 below.

62-85. *The most abject... venom.* This passage anticipates the relation between the calculating principle and the decline of poetry variously defined and implied in *A Defence of Poetry*.

93. *Rome... Greek.* See the Collation. The insertion suggests that S wanted to associate the Greek loss of religion with the Roman, in cause as well as in effect, and, since it was written later, is preferred to the uncancelled reading ('the Roman republic') which it replaced.

97-103. *Without... it.* These conclusions could have been drawn from Cicero's *De natura deorum.* Entries from this academical dialogue in Bod. MS Shelley e. 4, fol. 85ᵛ indicate that S was reading it while drafting *On Christianity*, with one of them (here translated from S's Latin) paralleling the thought of these lines in c. 4: '... and in all probability the disappearance of piety towards the gods will entail the disappearance of loyalty and social union among men as well, and of justice itself, the queen of all the virtues' (1. 4, Loeb trans.). References below to the Stoics, Epicureans, and Sceptics may likewise stem from Cicero's work, which is a discussion among representatives of these three schools of thought.

105. *Scævola... Regulus.* S could be referring to any one of several members of the Scaevola family but most probably either Gaius Mucius Scaevola, the legendary founder of the name (Scaevola = 'left-handed'), who when threatened with death or torture by a king he had been sent to assassinate illustrated his contempt for pain by holding his right hand in an altar fire until it was burnt away, or Quintus Mucius Scaevola (*fl.* 106-82 BC), Pontifex Maximus, who at the end of an illustrious and honourable life of public service was slain while attempting to make peace between the opposing parties of Marius and Sulla. S's probable reading of Cicero's *De natura deorum* (see on ll. 97-103), wherein Quintus Scaevola is relevantly mentioned (3. 80), suggests that he could well have been in S's mind at about the time *On Christianity* was being drafted (his feeling that men of intellect had no need for traditional religion, which was for the unreasoning multitude, would have appealed to S); Publius Decius Mus, the name of two consuls, father and son (*c.* 340-295 BC), who died heroically and selflessly fighting for their country; Regulus (*fl.* 267-250 BC), consul and general, who when captured by the Carthaginians was brought to Rome to win his freedom by persuading the Senate to make peace. He instead told them to continue the war and, in fulfilment of his promise to his captors, returned to Carthage, where he was put to death.

115-16. *internal sanctity*. S specifically ascribes this Stoic tenet to Christ's teaching in l. 174. His general distinction is between the external virtues of the Roman national religion and the internal virtues eventually ascribed to Christ's teachings but derived from the pagan philosophers. Much of S's argument throughout is grounded in Godwinian perfectibility and a congruent necessity spiritualizing not only religious beliefs and ethical codes but also the political ideals they implied.

124. *Dualist*. It is clear from the cancellation (see the Collation) that S was thinking most of all of the Manichaean concept of an eternal opposition between warring principles of good and evil. He probably used the less specific designation because it was more appropriate to his context and more comprehensive in its application.

146. *made audible*. Under these words, at the end of the line, and in the space left after 'heart' (l. 147), S has written 'Mr. Malthus book', which (if it has application here) may suggest S's association of the 'still, sad music of humanity' with the Malthusian population theory, according to which misery and poverty are the necessary consequences of unchecked population growth.

148-50. *The still ... subdue*. Slightly misquoted from Wordsworth's 'Lines Composed a Few Miles above Tintern Abbey' (ll. 91-3).

151-3. *He had contemplated ... crimes*. The word 'vacancy' is written (perhaps in another hand) in the left margin with a line under it extending through this sentence. Again the application is uncertain. In *Prometheus Unbound* Christ, through Christianity, becomes the 'prophanation' he is here supposed to have contemplated: 'Thy name ... hath become a curse' (i. 603-4).

160. *Proteus*. S is thinking of Proteus not as the prophetic old man of the sea but, in the Orphic mystical sense, as the source of the elemental material world, a symbolic application of his character derived from his ability to change into whatever shape he pleased until caught in one of them, on which occasion he was obliged to answer truthfully any query put to him. On the front pastedown of e. 4 S had drafted a fragmentary poem which refers to Proteus and indicates that it might have dealt specifically with his elemental powers.

160-4. *the word ... things*. This and comparable definitions of God later are anticipated in S's early letters (e.g. to T. J. Hogg, 3 Jan. 1811; to E. Hitchener, 11 June 1811), *Queen Mab*, and *A Refutation of Deism*.

173. *Blessed ... God*. Matt. 5: 8.

218-21. *There is a power ... will*. The sentence, like the paragraph as a whole, is a close anticipation of *A Defence of Poetry*, where S defines the imaginative principle and the power motivating it in similar terms and metaphor.

238-42. καὶ ... ειρηται. The entire passage from Thucydides which S refers to (and largely quotes) is translated as follows: 'As to the speeches that were made by different men, either when they were about to begin the war or when they were already engaged therein, it has been difficult to recall with strict accuracy the words actually spoken, both for me as regards that which I myself heard, and for those who from various other sources have brought me reports. Therefore the speeches are given in the language in which, as it seemed to me, the several speakers would express on the subjects under consideration, the sentiments most befitting the occasion, though at the same time I have adhered as closely as possible to the general sense of what was actually said' (*History of the Peloponnesian War*, 1. 22, Loeb edn. 39). The 'number of instances' S refers to may be the speeches with which Thucydides provides his historical characters. While he does not quite apply it, S clearly intends the Thucydides reference to bolster his argument for a loose interpretation of the Gospels. S also knew that the Roman historians Tacitus, Suetonius, and Lucan provided speeches for their historical figures (cf. on 682 below).

243–5. *Tacitus . . . temples.*" The quotation is from *Histories*, 5. 5, which S had probably read in Aug. 1814 (see Mary Shelley, *Journals*, 24 Aug.). The corresponding portion of S's fragmentary translation of Tacitus on the Jews is very much like the one he provides here.

250–1. *quodcunque . . . virtus.* S's recension of Lucan's *Civil War* (*Pharsalia*), 9. 579–80 (reversed and shortened), means: 'whatever you see, whatever motion you make, that is the divine, that is excellence.' S has left sufficient space above, before, and after his garbled quotation to correct it from a text, which might well have been his intention.

261–4. *"Love . . . unjust."* A conflation of Matt. 5: 44–5 and Luke 6: 28, partly repeated in ll. 285–8. A final draft would doubtless have eliminated the redundancy.

276–8. *He is said . . . bone.* Perhaps a heightened expansion of Matt. 25: 41.

285–8. *Love . . . God.* Luke 6: 27–8. S apparently intended to provide more Gospel evidence of Christ's view of a non-retributive God, as *K* infers from the manuscript spacing (here filled in with Luke and Matt. 5: 44). Forman had earlier noted that 'it seems likely that it was a part of the scheme of this Essay to examine and illustrate the Beatitudes *seriatim*' (F vi. 344). On fol. 6ᵛ S wrote what seems to have been a preliminary reference to Matt. 5: 'From v. 38 to 45. Against revenge'. The fact that S does a good deal of eddying about in Matthew further indicates that *e. 4* may derive from a series of notes still in need of further integration.

297. *purest quality.* Christ's utilitarianism, like S's, is not merely quantitative. The *summum bonum* is to see God, which is to be ideally virtuous.

301–8. *Such . . . deeds.* Probably a recollection of Suetonius' *Life of Caesar*, 1. 75; S was reading Suetonius in late 1814 and in 1815.

301–28. *Such . . . sacrifice.* The characters of Julius Caesar and his assassins seem appropriately detailed and heightened to fit S's purpose. Suetonius, Plutarch, and probably Shakespeare were among his sources.

308. *enormous.* I.e. 'very wicked'.

316. *venerable and dear.* These words may be underlined for reconsideration rather than for emphasis; or they could have been underlined by mistake for *father and their friend*, l. 319, the error remaining uncorrected. However, S's disenchantment with the perversion of shibboleths like 'country' and 'liberty', along with certain customary expressions of 'virtue', helps confirm an editorial decision to retain the MS reading in italic.

319. *father and their friend.* The emphasis here needs no special justification (contrast the preceding n.); however, it may suggest that S meant the pair of emphases to be considered together, perhaps with some sense of the interplay of ironies that characterize the emotional paradox he is here developing as a conflict of loyalties. Perhaps the (apparently unwritten) note (see the Collation) was meant either to explain the paradox according to S's (or Godwin's) understanding of the relation between human affection and civic duty or to provide the reader with the source for his example.

341. *models.* The uncancelled original rather than the inserted 'clothes' (see the Collation) seems preferable here. Cf. the use of 'plastic' in a kindred context in *Adonais*, l. 381, where S develops an essentially Neoplatonic conception of God/Power like that ascribed to Christ here.

351–3. *The supposition ... pain.* The anthropomorphic extension of Shaftesburian natural benevolence to God's will may be implicitly 'according to Christ' but has Shelleyan roots as well in the eclectic associations of poems such as *Queen Mab* and 'Mont Blanc'.

355. *some ... world.* The diluted Manichaeism which S ascribes to Christ recurs in *Prometheus Unbound*, II. iv, and in *On the Devil, and Devils*. At the temporal level, S believed that the principle of self was the dominant evil spirit in the world, a belief which, for practical purposes, he seems to ascribe to Christ as well.

355–7. *But ... power.* S personifies or metaphorically realizes such a power in poems like 'Hymn to Intellectual Beauty', *Prometheus Unbound*, and *The Witch of Atlas*.

357–70. *Men ... be.* S uses similar phrasing in *On a Future State*, though there is some indication there that, as in the fragment *On Life*, he would also have suggested a happier hereafter such as that which he imagines Christ asserting from l. 371 to l. 402, a passage which has metaphorical and conceptual correspondences with several other writings by S.

365–6. *"there ... ⟨wisdom"⟩.* Eccles. 9: 10. S used this passage as a motto for his early poem 'The pale, the cold, and the moony smile' ('Reality'), which anticipates l. 362: 'Though the fine-wrought eye and the wondrous ear | No longer will live to hear or to see' (ll. 21–2). The fragment from

'They' to 'is' (ll. 364–5) is an insertion, in a cramped uncharacteristic hand, lacking S's usual slant.

431–6. *An Athenian soldier . . . Athens.* From Herodotus, *The Persian Wars*, 5. 101, 105; the retributive action against Athens is described later in the same source (8. 53).

443–6. *The desire . . . completion.* Quintus Curtius, *History of Alexander the Great* and Plutarch's *Life of Alexander*, both read by S in Nov. 1816 (see *Journals*), could have served as his sources.

458–9. *Mardonius and Zerxes.* Mardonius was a Persian general who served under Xerxes, the Persian king (485–465 BC). After several military successes, culminating in the conquering of Athens, Xerxes retreated to Persia when his fleet was defeated at Salamis (480 BC) and Mardonius was slain in battle when his army was defeated at Plataea (479 BC).

459–60. *extinction . . . Macedon.* As S notes above (ll. 445–6), Alexander the Great initially defined his Persian war as a war of reprisal on behalf of the Greeks, but it soon became clear that his real motive was to destroy the Persian empire to gratify his own ambition for world domination. S read Plutarch's *Life of Alexander* 28 Nov. 1816 (Mary Shelley, *Journals*).

463c. *"Men of Athens.* S apparently realized that an attempt at emulating Thucydides (and the Gospel writers) by composing a speech for Jesus Christ in the guise of a Persian ambassador would have verged on the egregious and disproportionate, though it is clear that the ambassador's message would have been conciliatory had S continued it (as it was in a possible source in Herodotus, *The Persians Wars*, 8. 140). A 9 cm. (3.5″) gap concluding the line most probably indicates that S had realized that his fanciful associations were about to run away with his argument and broke them off before they did so. Later (from l. 682) S more successfully integrates a quasi-speech by a Diogenes/Christ figure into his argument.

464–79. *The emptiness . . . law.* Cf. *On the Punishment of Death*, where S argues against capital punishment from a comparably utilitarian view of justice. See also ll. 510–12 below. The blank third of a page following from here indicates that S meant to write more on the subject, which a possible colon after 'law' (see Collation to l. 479) would have then introduced, perhaps (as Dawson suggests, *e.* 4 352) with an appropriate quotation from Godwin's *Political Justice*.

482–4. *have not failed . . . own.* Cf. *A Defence of Poetry*: 'Every epoch, under names more or less specious, has deified its peculiar errors'.

494. *and from the actions and opinions.* Previous editors omit this, apparently because they regard it as an inadvertent repetition of the preceding phrase. But S seems in fact to be distinguishing private from public acts and opinions. Again the grammatical discrepancies between 'its' and 'theirs' reflect the fact that S is trying to talk about a nation and individuals at the same time.

496–7. *instructed . . . is perfect.* Matt. 5: 48.

502. *itself.* S's depersonalizing of God (disallowed by *1859*) is not altogether consistent with this context, but it accurately reflects his earliest and continuing views of a divine essence free of human limitations.

505. *perfection.* Previous editors apparently supposed that S meant to underline 'actual', and so print '*actual* perfection', which may then seem to contrast more neatly with '*abstract*' above. But S may instead be contrasting the attributive nature of human perfection with the substantive nature of the divine. It is also possible that S underlined this word and the '*perfectness*' of l. 486 because he wanted to replace one of them.

515–18. *The peculiar ... crime.* See *On the Devil, and Devils* and the Preface to *Prometheus Unbound* for other references to the Christian doctrine of retributive justice as eternal damnation.

546–8. *But ... truth.* S's lost *Biblical Extracts* was apparently based on this assumption.

560–2. *return ... head.* The source of this doctrine is actually in a Pauline text (Rom. 12: 20), itself derived from Prov. 25: 21–2. The context in Romans indicates that Paul includes the retributory forgiveness of the Old Testament among the beatitudes and kindred utterances of Christ.

592. *I.* In the manuscript this is followed by the references to Francis Bacon's discussions of the 'Idols of the Cave', below which is a broken line running across the page. Under this line, on the left, is an 'x' followed by what may be 'as in—', probably keyed to the 'x' over the cancelled 'persecution' (see Collation to l. 578). The lower quarter of the page is blank, indicating that S meant to provide a note which could then have dilated on the distinction between the essential and attributed (or non-essential) character of Christ that he is discussing by e.g. noting and perhaps 'vindicating' Christ's 'righteous indignation' in driving the money-lenders from the temple (Matt. 21: 12) or his insisting that he has come to 'cast fire upon the earth' and breed division within families (Luke 12: 49, 53).

597. *familiar Spirit.* Plato's *Apology* contains the best known of several references Socrates supposedly made to this 'form of augury', as S characterized it in a manuscript note (see Notopoulos, *Platonism*, 505–7).

601–2. *the established religion ... write.* A further if unneeded confirmation that the manuscript was drafted in England. The consequent allusion to the final hours and fate of Socrates (as recounted in the *Phaedo*) suggests as well the trial and condemnation of Daniel Eaton (who also approved of the moral teachings of Christ but queried the Gospel history), which S reacted to in *A Letter to Lord Ellenborough*. As P. M. S. Dawson points out (*e. 4* 353), S is very probably recalling Blackstone's *Commentaries*, according to which 'christianity is part of the laws of England' (Blackstone, iv. 59).

606. *sacrifize ... Esculapius.* Aesculapius, the Greek god of medicine, was appropriately propitiated by the sacrifice of a cock. The reference is to the *Phaedo*, where Socrates, just before dying of the hemlock he had been forced to drink, asks a friend to make this sacrifice, which he felt he owed the god. S's irony is perhaps derived from his understanding of Socrates'.

612–13. *He accommodated ... addressed.* Christ is therefore supposed to have done what S attempted to do in his Irish pamphlets. In *The Missionary* by Sydney Owenson (Lady Morgan) (London, 1811), a novel which very much impressed the young S (see letters to Hogg, 19 June, 28 July 1811), the protagonist participates in certain pagan rituals 'In submission to those prejudices, which he could only hope to vanquish by previously respecting' (i. 82). S's point is that Christ's rhetorical misrepresentations are themselves misunderstood when taken as authentic parts of his doctrine.

621–4. *"Think not ... fulfilled."* A version of Matt. 5: 17–18.

627. *own.* While S's asterisk actually appears before 'Thus' (l. 624), his reference to Cicero's *De oratore* not only includes the sentence ending here but seems also to have application to other parts of the rhetorical discussion following. S would have been familiar with Cicero's work from his Eton days and does himself (as in the Irish pamphlets) practise the venial and requisite rhetorical hypocrisy he here ascribes to Christ. The footnote actually reads: 'See Cicero de Oratore', and appears in the body of the text (see Collation to l. 624). S's specific reference is probably to *De oratore*, 2. 42–4.

652 n 2. S refers to the following verses from Matt. 5: 'Ye have heard that it was said to them of old time, Thou shalt not kill; and whosoever shall kill shall be in danger of the judgment' (21); 'Ye have heard that it was said, Thou shalt not commit adultery' (27); 'It was said also, Whosoever shall put away his wife, let him give her a writing of divorcement' (31); 'Again, ye have heard that it was said to them of old time, Thou shalt not forswear thyself, but shalt perform unto the Lord thine oaths' (33). S was doubtless more interested in Christ's readings of and additions to these laws, which make up their context in Matthew and conclude, as S notes (l. 654), by renouncing retribution as an act of God or of those who would 'be perfect, as your heavenly Father is perfect' (48).

653 n. The verse reads 'Ye have heard that it was said, An eye for an eye, and a tooth for a tooth', and is followed by Christ's counter-admonition: turn the other cheek.

666–7. (*Luke ... 18.*) Ll. 662–6 are nearly an exact quotation (originally from Isa. 61: 1) of Luke. S quite possibly meant to insert here (as elsewhere) further scriptural evidence of the 'equality of mankind', since the evidence he does offer seems too sparse and tangential for the 'enunciation of all that Plato and Diogenes have speculated' on the subject which he maintains he has presented. In an early letter to Elizabeth Hitchener (25 July 1811) S defines and justifies his understanding of the perfectible nature of equality.

677–9. *Plato . . . power.* Cf. Plato's *Republic*, bk. 4.

682. *He said.* The following account of Diogenes' thoughts on equality, property, etc. seems largely S's invention, perhaps conflated with his understanding of Christ's thoughts on the same subjects. As the Greek quotation in ll. 763–5 indicates, S derived his knowledge of Diogenes the Cynic (fourth century BC) from Diogenes Laertius (third century AD), who implies in a little what S infers at large (see *Lives of the Eminent Philosophers*, 6. 72). His concurrent readings in Thucydides and Josephus perhaps prompted S to follow their practice of imagining appropriate speeches for their historical figures, a practice which he might have thought that the Gospel writers were themselves occasionally following.

700. *oppression.* See the Collation: neither this word nor the original 'subserviency' is deleted. *1859* supplies an 'and', retaining both words, which does align with S's occasional lumping together of the oppressors and the oppressed on the grounds that they were victims as well as occasions of oppression. The 'subservient' of l. 708 probably led to S's change.

714–15. *Among . . . common.* Cf. Diogenes Laertius, *Life of Diogenes*, 6. 72: '. . . friends share all property in common' (Loeb trans., ii. 73).

763–5. ευγενειας . . . κοσμω. The full quotation from Diogenes Laertius' *Life of Diogenes* (6. 72) is so translated: 'He would ridicule good birth and fame and all such distinctions, calling them showy ornaments of vice. The only true commonwealth was, he said, that which is as wide as the universe' (Loeb trans., ii. 75). S has somewhat modified the quotation to suit his syntax and emphasis. An asterisk over κοσμω (see the Collation) was apparently meant to key the source, which was not given.

766c. [*The wise man . . . marriage*]. K notes of this deletion: 'This is the only quotation which suggests how S could assimilate, as he says in an unpublished note on the same *MS.*, the views of Christ and those of the Cynics' (p. 45). The note K refers to appears on fol. 6ʳ and reads: 'The similitude of doctrine between Jesus Christ and the Cynics on the subject of marriage and love.' Christ (Matt. 22: 30; Mark 12: 25; Luke 20: 34–5) states that after the resurrection there will be no marriage or giving in marriage. Diogenes Laertius, immediately after the sentence quoted in ll. 762–4, notes that Diogenes the Cynic advocated a community of wives, a scheme of social planning paralleled in Plato's *Republic.* K also states that S did not interpret the deleted clause 'as a plea for celibacy, but as a deprecation of ritual' (p. 56). But, given the note on the Essenes (see on 52 above), it may be that S actually associated Christ's (apparently not his own) thoughts on the subject with the first order of Essenes as described by Josephus in *The Jewish War* (2. 120–1): 'Marriage they disdain, but they adopt other men's children, while yet pliable and docile, and regard them as their kin and mould them in accordance with their own principles. They do not, indeed, on principle, condemn wedlock and the propagation thereby of the race, but they wish to protect themselves against women's wantonness, being persuaded that none of the sex keeps her plighted troth to one man' (Loeb trans., ii. 369).

777–84. *Rousseau ... Rousseau.* A probable reference to Jean-Jacques Rousseau's *Discours sur l'origine de l'inégalité parmi les hommes* (1754).

790. *literal and strict.* S's reiterated criticisms of literal interpretation were commonplace among biblical rationalizers from Spinoza to Paine and appear with reference to Christ in his own works as early as *An Address, to the Irish People.*

798–806. *Rousseau ... society.* Rousseau's early discourses on art and inequality were highly critical of the artificial present-day society which had necessarily evolved from a happy state of nature once man had introduced the concept of property. However, in *On the Social Contract* (1762) he allowed that the 'original state ⟨of nature⟩ cannot subsist any longer, and the human race would perish if it did not alter its mode of existence' (trans. and ed. Donald A. Cress, Hackett Publishing Company: Indianapolis, 1983, 23), though this mode of existence was best defined by social and political conventions which allowed the individual as much natural freedom as was compatible with reason.

809–49. *He simply exposes ... field.* The basic text for S's expansion of Christ's reported utterances is Matt. 6: 19–34, though other verses such as Matt. 18: 2–3 and 19: 23–4 are also hinted at.

831. *its nature.* Apparently refers to 'frame of thought'.

852–3. *Government ... depravity.* Paraphrased from Thomas Paine's *Common Sense, Writings,* i. 69.

875–80. *The wisest ... state.* Hesiod (*Works and Days,* ll. 109–20) is the *locus classicus* for this poetic conception, which appears as well in Virgil (*Aeneid* viii. 319–25) and Ovid (*Metamorphoses* i. 89–112).

886–7. *the   period.* 1859's 'Saturnian' (see the Collation) is a plausible conjecture here, though the space in MS is too small to accommodate this word.

900. *more, or more universal, knowledge.* Only *TT* among previous editions retains 'more, or'; *K* notes that 'it is a pity that S should have forgotten a word after the first "more," as it would no doubt have corrected the purely intellectualistic and Godwinian nature of the statement' (p. 51). But this reads an unnecessary lapse into S's prose by stipulating a Godwinian meaning for 'universal' which S probably did not intend. Universally, the knowledge S seems to have in mind would include that great secret of morals, the love which he notes as a product of the 'knowledge of truth' below.

903. *abolition... distinctions.* S finds Christ refuting by anticipation not only medieval Christian apologists of the social and political hierarchy but also contemporary writers such as Paley and Malthus, who likewise found religious sanctions for the continuance of material inequalities.

907–12. *A young man... ⟨sorrowing⟩.* Cf. Matt. 9: 17–22.

919. *&⟨c⟩.* S's quotation concludes with verse 46, though he perhaps meant to imply a continuation to comparable passages in Acts (e.g. 4: 32–7).

931. *demagogues... sect.* Presumably beginning with Paul and extending through to the early church fathers, though Christ had himself given ample warrant for subordinating this world to the next. S's point seems to be that the temporal benefits of Christ's moral teachings were subverted by an increasing emphasis on his divinity and the salvation promised his followers.

942–5. *The system... kind.* Cf. *An Address, to the Irish People* for S's earliest public statements on self-reform as a prerequisite to lasting social and political reform. The Godwinian tenor of the paragraph becomes increasingly obvious in ll. 953–5 and in the implicit promise of a perfectible humanity gradually accommodating itself to the visions of unacknowledged legislators such as Christ had been and continued to be. Then, as in S's time, 'arbitrary institutions' stood in the way of the inevitable self-reform that would eventually lead to their overthrow and to the equality Christ's followers had attempted to practice before the collective mind of man had become sufficiently imbued with his true doctrine to replace the principle of self with love, a conversion S again predicted and demonstrated in *Prometheus Unbound.*

963–9. *Still ... them.* S here generalizes from the expansiveness of man's minds and hearts briefly achieved through Christ's agency to kindred historical moments of social 'crisis' such as that which he had himself tried to take advantage of in 1812. See *An Address, to the Irish People*, 479–84; *Proposals for an Association of Philanthropists*, 26–49.

969–71. *They... justice.* In *Laon and Cythna* S provided his own version of such a 'trophy', the French Revolution, recreated in terms of its promise rather than its accomplishment.

ON THE DOCTRINES OF CHRIST

Date: ?late 1817.

Copy-text: Pierpont Morgan Library holograph (shelfmark MA 1069).

Description: Untitled single-leaf ink holograph measuring 32.7 cm. × 20.5 cm. (13″ × 8.1″); laid paper; WM: W | 1813 *or* 1815; the text is continuous from the unnumbered top recto through nearly one half of the verso; the upper left corner (recto), with space for two or three letters on both recto and verso, is missing, as is a triangular segment of about the same size at the centre (left margin recto) of the leaf, where a heavily creased fold had been made (a paper backing has been supplied to prevent further attrition of the leaf); the manuscript is contained in a blue morocco half-leather casing docketed 'P. B. Shelley—Portion of Manuscript of "Essay on Christianity".' The Editorial Commentary and Textual Notes contain supplementary descriptive information about the holograph.

Provenance: Leigh Hunt; Townshend Mayer; H. B. Forman; Jerome Kern; Pierpont Morgan.

Printed: *St. James Magazine* (Mar. 1876), 665–6; *F*; *J*.

This fragment was first printed in the *St. James Magazine* by Townshend Mayer, who had found it among the Leigh Hunt papers in his possession. H. B. Forman reprinted it in his 1880 edition of S's works at the end of *On Christianity* because he thought it 'part of a recapitulation and conclusion' to that fragment. It appears as a separate prose fragment entitled *On the Doctrines of Christ* in the Julian edition. Variations among these three printings indicate that each editor had used the holograph itself as copy-text. Tatsuo Tokoo (who presumed that the manuscript was lost) reprints the Julian text, though including it as part of his edited version of *On Christianity* (TT).

In a note to S's translation of part of Moschus' 'Elegy on the Death of Bion', Forman states that the translation was 'written upon the same paper with the concluding portion' of *On Christianity*. In a note to *SC* 394 (v. 192), which catalogues the holograph of the Moschus elegy (as 'Lament for Bion'), the editor quotes the 1920 sales catalogue for the Forman collection as describing what purports to be, but cannot be, this same portion of the supposed conclusion as appearing at the 'top of the page' of the manuscript which also contained what became *SC* 394. Since the 1920 catalogue described a folio sheet and the 1934 catalogue for the Roderick Terry sale a single quarto page containing only the Moschus, the two leaves of the original sheet must have been separated during the interval. *SC* 394 actually contained the cancelled jottings quoted below from F vi. 344. Forman in a note on the same page had clarified in advance the confusion between the cancellation and the 'conclusion' perpetrated by the 1920 catalogue:

> The passage now printed as the conclusion of the Essay ⟨*On Christianity*⟩ occupies a page and a half of a sheet of foolscap paper: on the other leaf of the sheet, and not continuously with the rest, are written and cancelled the following passages:—

> "I, the Redeemer of mankind;
> I who dare to . . . . .
> Lament no more ye meek and gentle beings: bear on against the oppressions of the hard and unfeeling world—with resolute and

tranquil mind; for in the calmness of your own spirit shall be your reward, and the . . . .

Blessed are the poor in Spirit for theirs is the Kingdom of Heaven. —Neither . . . . .

Know in what manner to estimate the bearing of . . . . ."

These notes are followed, in the same page, by the beautiful fragment of a translation of Moschus's Elegy on the Death of Bion, given in Vol. IV, p. 235, of the Poetical Works.

It is therefore the above cancellation (which contains words not in an earlier printing in *St. James Magazine*), not the stipulated conclusion, which in 1920 must have appeared at 'the top of the page' containing the translation. Such an inference must in any case have been made, given the length of the holograph fragment and its appearance on a complete leaf. Since *SC* 394 measures 22 cm. × 20.5 cm. (8.7″ × 8.1″) and its once conjugate Pierpont Morgan (MA 1069) leaf 33 cm. × 20.5 cm. (13″ × 8.1″), its detached upper portion must have measured about 11 cm. (4.3″). *SC* 394 (190 n.) describes a fragment of a 'conjugate sheet at lower-left-hand corner of manuscript' which 'has several letters written *reverso* on both sides'. As noted in the Description above, a small portion of the upper left-hand corner of its leaf (recto) is missing. A collation of a photocopy of the Pierpont Morgan holograph with the *SC* 394 holograph does in fact prove that they were once portions of the same leaf, since the word 'The' and the letters 'Gr' appear in the fragment noted and, when attrition is given its due, provide the beginnings of the first two lines of the recto of MA 1069 while traces compatible with the word 'Let' appear on the verso and so provide the needed word at the end of the first line on the verso of the holograph. 'The' and 'Gr' are reversed relative to the Moschus translation, as was probably the cancellation. A fold in MA 1069 (see the Description) does not appear in *SC* 394, thus indicating that it was made after the leaves had been separated. Both holographs have a triangular segment missing at what was once their conjugate centre, or near centre, probably the result of the same tear.

The purpose and placing of *On the Doctrines of Christ* in the canon cannot be definitively inferred, but the internal evidence strongly corroborates Forman's conclusion that it relates in some way to *On Christianity*. The note in the *St. James Magazine*, perhaps informed if not written by Forman, suggests that it might have been meant as 'memoranda' for the conclusion of *On Christianity*. The heading 'Chap 2' is a certain indication that it represented a continuation of, or notes for, a much larger draft. If the passage is in fact the beginning of a chapter, rather than an insert into one, then it could hardly be construed as a conclusion, particularly since S stopped writing the draft in mid-sentence. There is no physical connection between this leaf and the portion of *On Christianity* in Bod. MS c. 4 adds. (as printed here), which is on different paper.

Internal correspondences are the best if not very firm arguments for supposing that *On the Doctrines of Christ* was written at about the same time as *On Christianity*. An additional argument for a date in late 1817, or at least much later than the paper's 1813 (or 1815) watermark, is plausibly suggested by Forman and expanded in the commentary on *SC* 394—namely, that the Moschus fragment was written in competition with Leigh Hunt, whose translation of the same piece appeared in his *Foliage* of 1818. Since the Pforzheimer leaf seems to have preceded the Pierpont Morgan leaf, one may further infer that the Moschus was probably in place when the matter relating to Christ and Christianity above and following it was drafted.

On the Doctrines of Christ has been associated with a comparable fragment, *On The Moral Teaching of Jesus Christ*, with which it exhibits some internal correspondences. But both fragments also exhibit kindred correspondences with other prose works by S, and the holograph of the *Moral Teaching* fragment appears on Italian paper which S was using around 1821-2. While it is clear that *On the Doctrines of Christ* belonged to (or was meant to belong to) a larger context, this edition leaves it to the reader to conjecture from internal evidence and correspondences where else, if anywhere, it may be better placed among S's extant writings. The Julian title has been accepted here, mainly to prevent confusion in further references to the fragment.

The manuscript presents a few problems in arrangement and syntax which may be most conveniently dealt with here. The heading 'Chapter 2' appears as 'Chap 2' at the beginning of the fragment, where it was inserted below the first of two parallel lines which set off ll. 23-6 ('The most eminent . . . Man') from the material following it, which in this edition begins the fragment ('No mistake . . .'). An 'X' to the right of these lines corresponds with two 'X's at either end of a space enclosed by another pair of parallel lines between 'announced' (l. 22) and 'The universality . . .' (l. 26). It is therefore clear that S wished the lines at the top of the page to be placed where they appear in the text. (An 'X' before 'Nor', l. 19, was probably misplaced and may be deleted.) The fact that 'Chap 2' is a later insertion between the upper parallel line and the first line of the enclosed text indicates that S wished the chapter-heading to appear before ll. 23-6, not before l. 1.

Below the manuscript line which concludes with 'minds' (l. 9) S left a space partially filled in with a separation-line which extends nearly to 'Thus mankind is', which are the only three words in the space containing the separation line, and which conclude at the right margin. It seems clear that S meant to continue the fragmentary sentence ending with 'minds', perhaps with text from another leaf. There is also a space below the manuscript line which concludes with 'impostor' (l. 12). This space contains the four words 'Such has been, most' towards the right margin. Again, it seems clear that S meant to continue the fragmentary sentence ending with 'impostor' in this space. A single underlined word— '?indeed'—is written in pencil horizontally up the page towards the left of this space (which at this point measures 1.8 cm., 0.7″) and was perhaps meant to key in whatever S might have intended to place here.

Related primary and secondary materials: Notopoulos, *Platonism*, 331. (See also this listing in *On Christianity*.)

18–19. *The doctrines . . . law*. Cf. *On Christianity*, l. 650, where S says that Christ proceeds to 'qualify' and 'abrogate' the Jewish law.

27–8. *internal purity*. Cf. 'internal sanctity of soul' at *On Christianity*, l. 174. The philosophical correspondences implied in this context are like those which S notes and enlarges on in the 'Equality of Mankind' section of *On Christianity*, where he is more specifically concerned with interpreting in their generic relations what he also sums up as 'the doctrines of Jesus Christ' (l. 767).

28. *Pythagoras*. Greek philosopher of the sixth century BC who felt that internal purity was achieved through silence, temperance, vegetarianism, and knowing oneself.

Diogenes. Diogenes the Cynic, Greek philosopher of the fourth century BC who scorned wealth, rank, and sensual pleasures, arguing that spiritual freedom and inner peace came through self-control and self-denial.

Zeno. Zeno of Citium, Greek philosopher of the fourth century BC, the founder of Stoicism, who felt that if men would do their duty by living their lives rationally and virtuously each individual would be at peace with himself, and the world through the collective efforts of such individuals would develop into a harmonious and well-ordered society.

34. *its*. Probably refers to 'doctrines'.

45. *priests*. The manuscript breaks off in mid-page as well as in mid-sentence. The abrupt conclusion, along with the repeated phrase noted in the Collation to l. 37, may suggest that S was copying from a previous draft.

ON MARRIAGE

Date: ?late 1817.

Copy-text: Bod. MS Shelley e. 4, fols. 39^r–40^v.

Description: Untitled ink holograph measuring 22.9 cm. × 18.2 cm. (9″ × 7.2″); wove paper (lined); WM: W TURNER & SON; the text is continuous from the top of fol. 39^r to the top of fol. 40^v.

Provenance: Mary Shelley; Sir Percy Shelley and Jane, Lady Shelley; Bodleian.
Printed: *K*; *J*; Dawson, *e. 4*.

While *On Marriage* could stand by itself as a complete note tracing the background of the marriage contract as an example of the self-interested process by which national laws and social institutions evolve, it was probably meant to form part of a larger work. The holograph notebook in which it appears contains two jottings which may relate it to *On Christianity*, the major prose writing in the notebook. On fol. 6^r S wrote 'The [compa] similitude of doctrine between Jesus Christ & the Cynics ⟨*the word looks like* Cyneis⟩ on the subject of marriage & love'; at the top of fol. 35^r he wrote 'Jesus Christs idea of marriage. See Milton on Divorce'. *On Christianity* does contain a cancelled reference to the subject, '[The wise man neither marries nor is given in marriage]' (fol. 27^v), and, given occasional examples of such practice elsewhere in S's prose (*On Life* apparently grew out of a cancelled segment of *A Philosophical View of Reform*), it may be that *On Marriage* was a spin-off from the longer draft, whose larger purposes would have been diverted by a treatment of the historical social issue S chose to advance in the present fragment, where there is no reference to Christ or to Christianity. It is also possible that it was intended as part of a *magnum opus* on morals and metaphysics whose nucleus would have been the *Speculations on Morals and Metaphysics*.

The probable date for the holograph is late 1817, though the fact that it is, as Koszul noted, 'remarkably free from corrections' (K 56) suggests that much of it might have been transcribed from an earlier and rougher draft or notes, as *On Christianity* might also have been; a *Fragment of 'A Refutation of Deism'* is either a partial recension of the 1814 text of *A Refutation of Deism* or a partial redaction of a draft which formed the basis of that text. These three items were almost certainly the first to be entered in the notebook, which therefore seems originally to have been intended exclusively for prose drafts or redrafts. The fact that fols. 34^r–38^v contain drafts of other works would tell against this supposition were it not that the pagination occasionally apparent in *On Christianity* is consistently extended on the rectos of these leaves from '52' (fol. 34^r) through to '60' (fol. 38^r) to indicate that S had reserved these pages for a possible continuation of *On Christianity* when he began his excursus (as it might have been) on marriage. When that continuation did not occur, the leaves were filled in with other works, two of which (translations of Euripides' *Cyclops* and Virgil's fourth *Georgic*) also appear after *On Marriage*, presumably because the latter fragment was in place when they were written. The earliest datable contents in the notebook (drafts of 'To Constantia, Singing' and 'Ozymandias') help to support a *terminus ante quem* of late 1817, while its position indicates that it was the last of the three prose drafts to be written here. The *terminus a quo* of all these works is a matter of conjecture, even as they appear here; it is reasonable to infer the existence of earlier drafts not only from the appearance of the holographs but also from corresponding content in S's earlier writings.

With the possible exception of laws relating to capital punishment, S felt that civil and religious sanctions regarding marriage were most in need of reconsideration. Specimen attitudes towards the institution appear more colourfully and vehemently in his early Gothic novels (*Zastrozzi* (1810) and *St. Irvyne* (1811)), achieve subjective expression in letters to T. J. Hogg—in which he recommends anti-matrimonialism as a philanthropic step in the right direction for those who are virtuous enough to take it (9 May 1811) and describes marriage as the 'most horrible of all the means' by which the world 'binds the noble to itself' (20 June 1811)—and a limited but, for S, unfortunately effective public currency in *Queen Mab* (cf. the Note on 'Even love is sold', where the abolition of marriage is advocated). While S allowed himself to be convinced by Hogg, Harriet, and his recurrent pragmatism that not only the idea but also the implementation of marriage had to be endured even by the virtuous, the rationale for not practising what he continued to preach remained essentially disinterested: extra-marital cohabitation is socially injurious to the woman and may be politically disabling for the man who, like S, wished to work selflessly for the good of the state and the reform of the world.

In 1817 the decision against him in Chancery was largely based on his anti-matrimonial pronouncements in *Queen Mab* and corresponding practice (while Harriet was still alive), as exemplified by his relationship with Mary. A good if not real reason for S printing his political pamphlets of 1817 under the pseudonym 'The Hermit of Marlow' was that he did not want to embarrass the reformist cause by the publicity he had received from the Chancery proceedings and their reminders and revelations about his thoughts on marriage. Even his early antagonism towards marriage was qualified by the Godwinian recognition that a 'previous reformation in morals' (to Hitchener, 26 Nov. 1811) was requisite before the 'evil' could be remedied. S continued (in letters to Mary, 16 Dec. 1816, and to Byron, 23 Apr. 1817) to regard the ceremony as a politic expedient, while emphasizing his opposition to it. The relative objectivity of *On Marriage* suggests that it is, and was supposed to be, a calculated distillation of his later reflections on the subject, which, while avoiding the recurrent selfishness implicit in his earlier pronouncements, none the less continue to represent marriage as S found it represented in Godwin's *Political Justice*, where it is described as the worst of properties and the worst of laws (1st edn., 1793, p. 850; cf. *PJ* iii. 219-20).

Dissatisfaction with the marriage laws was not new when Godwin wrote against them in 1793 and was a complaint on the fringe of the radical reformists' agenda in 1817, when S is supposed to have written a letter (signed 'Delta') to the *Examiner* protesting against the hypocrisy which dissenters were forced into when legally obliged to bind them-selves in marriage by a ceremony they did not believe in (see *Letters*, i. 558–9). The style and details of this letter indicate, as does S's presence in Italy when other 'Delta' letters appeared in the *Examiner*, that he did not write it. But as one of several letters on the subject to appear in this and other more or less radical publications around that time, it indicates the historical and topical concern which S would eventually have dealt with in this draft, which has all the appearances of an introductory overview preparatory to an application and thesis characteristic of contemporary pamphlets and polemical reviews. These letters were uniform in protesting against the religious sanctions of the ceremony, but almost from its inception in 1753 the Marriage Act had been subject to criticism in and out of Parliament by liberals denouncing it on popular grounds as a 'rich man's' law (those who had to abide by it were assumed to have a certain amount of time and money at their disposal) and on sentimental grounds because of the impediments it put in the way of true love. Godwin, and later S, went beyond agitation for repeal of a particular law or dispensation from the religious ceremony by arguing on essen-tially moral grounds for the abolition of the institution in any form. An early letter to Sir James Lawrence, whose *Empire of the Nairs* illustrated a species of free love, indicates S's awareness of contemporary and his-torical precedent for his own reservations about institutionalized cohabi-tation and comes to a conclusion much like that which William Blake suggested in the *Visions of the Daughters of Albion*: 'Your "Empire of the Nairs", which I read this Spring, succeeded in making me a perfect convert to its doctrines. I then retained no doubts of the evils of mar-riage,—Mrs. Wollstonecraft reasons too well for that; but I had been dull enough not to perceive the greatest argument against it, until developed in the "Nairs", viz., prostitution both *legal* and *illegal*' (17 Aug. 1812). S's criticism of Hogg's treatment of free love in his review of his friend's *Memoirs of Prince Alexy Haimatoff* as 'pernicious and disgusting', taken at face value, illustrates the distinction S always meant to imply between sexual freedom and sensual licence.

Related primary and secondary materials: LETTERS, to Hogg, 8, 9 May, 4, 20 June, 3, 15 Aug., 17–18 Nov. 1811 (and commentary on these letters in *SC* ii, iii; see also SC 169, ii. 840–2), to E. Hitchener, 8 Oct. 1811, to W. Godwin, ⟨?26 Jan. 1812⟩, to L. Hunt (*Examiner*), 26 Sept. 1817 (though probably not by S); *Queen Mab* Note on 'Even love is sold'; *Alastor* Preface; *On Love*; *Epipsychidion*, ll. 149–73; Mary Wollstonecraft, *A Vindication of the Rights of Woman*, ed. Ulrich H. Hardt (Troy, NY, 1982), 157–9; *PJ* ii. 506–11, iii. 110, 219–20; Rosa Matilda ⟨Charlotte Dacre⟩, *Confessions of the Nun of St. Omer*, 3 vols. (London, 1805), i. 114–15, 126–33, 150–1, ii. 58–63; anon., *Reply to the Anti-Matrimonial Hypothesis and Supposed Atheism of*

Percy Bysshe ⟨sic⟩ *Shelley as Laid Down in Queen Mab* (London, 1821); John Todhunter, *Shelley and the Marriage Question* (London, 1889); Salt, *Principles*, 45-8; K 56-7; MacDonald, *Radicalism*, 36-65; Walter E. Peck, 'Shelley's Indebtedness to Sir Thomas ⟨for James⟩ Lawrence', *MLN* 40 (Apr. 1925), 246-9; Walter Graham, 'Shelley and the *Empire of the Nairs*', *PMLA* 40 (Dec. 1925), 881-91; Barnard, *Shelley's Religion*, 275-96; Hughes, *Nascent Mind*, 211-20; Cameron, *Young Shelley*, 293-8; id., *Golden Years*, 177-81; Nathaniel Brown, *Sexuality and Feminism in Shelley* (Cambridge Mass., 1979), 95-116.

23-5. *a contrivance...preoccupying.* Cf. *PJ* ii. 508: 'So long as I seek, by despotic and artificial means, to maintain my possession of a woman...I am guilty of the most odious selfishness.' S's later inclination to 'think the Godwinian plan is best' (to Hogg, 16 Nov. 1811) probably refers to this social and moral criticism and to its corollary, that a woman should be free at all times to choose the man whose various virtues best qualify him to share her company and favours. The Godwinian objection to man's exclusive proprietary rights over the woman of his choice was likewise related to his selectively utilitarian hedonism. In dutiful consequence, S avowed that, Harriet willing, he would not 'be so sottish a slave to opinion as to endeavour to monopolize what if participated would give my friend pleasure without diminishing my own' (to Hogg, 16 Nov. 1811; in the 1793 edition of *PJ* marriage was the 'most odious of all monopolies', p. 850; *PJ* iii. 220). S in 1811 objected to Hogg's attempt at seducing Harriet because he felt that Hogg was being both sensual and selfish and because Harriet indicated that she objected. Later, S demonstrated not only in theory but also in practice a readiness to set up a *de facto* ménage when Mary Godwin seemed an amenable object of Hogg's attentions (to Hogg, 26 Apr. 1815).

44-5. *A superficial...universal.* Cf. S's letter to Hogg, 9 May 1811: 'a crime in England ... becomes praiseworthy at Algiers'. In James Lawrence's *Empire of the Nairs*, which S read and admired, the narrator points out that the free love which is honourable in Malabar is a sin in England. Like S in his letters, Lawrence in his Introduction asks whether society should favour an institution which 'debases the female into a slave' and 'cramps the genius and vigor' of the male (p. xli).

ON 'GODWIN'S MANDEVILLE'

Date: 9-11 Dec. 1817.

Copy-text: *Examiner* (28 Dec. 1817), 826-7.

Description: About three and a half columns under the heading of 'Literary Notices. | No. 37. | Godwin's Mandeville.'

Reprinted: *Athenaeum* (27 Oct. 1832; several variants); *F*; *J*.

The date of the composition of this review can be restricted to a three-day period. S wrote in a letter to William Godwin on 11 Dec. 1817 that he had been inspired to write it because Godwin had caused to be printed in the London *Morning Chronicle* for 9 Dec. an extract from S's letter to him of 7 Dec. in praise of *Mandeville* (1817). The extract provides a generous supplement to the review and reads as follows in S's letter, which the *Chronicle* printed as 'Extract of a Letter from Oxfordshire' (substantive differences in the *Chronicle* printing appear in angle brackets):

> I have read Mandeville, but I must read it again soon. For the interest is of that irresistible & overwhelming kind, that the mind in it's influence is like a cloud borne on by an impetuous wind, like one breathlessly ⟨breathfully⟩ carried forward who has no time to pause, or observe the causes of his career. I think the *power* of *Mandeville* is inferior to nothing that you have ⟨the author has⟩ done, & were it not for the character of Falkland, no instance in which you have ⟨he has⟩ exerted that power of *creation* which you possess ⟨he possesses⟩ beyond all contemporary writers might compare with it. Falkland is still alone: power is in Falkland not as in Mandeville Tumult hurried onward by the tempest, but Tranquillity standing unshaken amid its fiercest rage! But Caleb Williams never shakes the deepest ⟨om.⟩ soul like Mandeville. It must be said that in the latter you rule ⟨the author rules⟩ with a rod of iron. The picture is never bright, & we wonder whence you ⟨he⟩ drew the darkness with which its shades are deepened until ⟨om.⟩ the epithet of tenfold night almost ceases to be metaphor. The NOUN *smorfia* touches some chord within us with such a cold & jarring power, that I started, & for some time could scarce believe but that I was Mandeville, & that this hideous grin was stamped upon my own face.
>
> In style & strength of expression Mandeville is wonderfully great, & the energy & the sweetness of the sentiments [are] scarcely to be equalled. Cliffords character as mere beauty is a divine & soothing contrast, & I do not think, if perhaps I except (& I know not if I ought to do so) the speech of Agathon in the Symposium of Plato that there ever was produced a moral discourse more characteristic of all that is admirable & lovely in human Nature ⟨and⟩ more lovely & admirable in itself than that of Henrietta to Mandeville as he is recovering from madness—Shall I say that when I discovered that she was pleading all this time secretly for her lover, & when at last she abandoned—weakly abandoned poor Mandeville I felt an involuntary & perhaps an unreasonable pang?

In the letter of 11 Dec. S indicated his surprise and pleasure at Godwin's having sent the above to the *Chronicle*, and wrote that he had already sent his review to Leigh Hunt for inclusion in the *Examiner*.

Mandeville: A Tale of the Seventeenth Century in England (3 vols.; London, 1817) is a psychological study of a man whose unnatural upbringing inevitably leads him to become a morbid misanthrope who none the less cherishes beauty, benevolent sensibility, and Godwinian principles as they appear in his sister Henrietta, who had been raised apart from him, and more characteristically comes to hate them as they appear in his classmate Clifford, who remains the object of his hatred and becomes his foil through his later life. After the historical context intrudes into the novel's plot long enough for Mandeville, a royalist among royalists, to be thought a Commonwealth spy, his mental balance is further disturbed when he discovers that Henrietta is to be married to Clifford. Unable to prevent the marriage by abducting his sister and feeling with some justice that his motives have been misconstrued by the world in general, he retreats into a seclusion whose only solace is the writing of the dismal memoirs which make up the novel.

S's enthusiastic response to this rather gloomy novel was not generally shared—the *Quarterly Review* found it 'a very dull novel and a very clever book' (18 (1817), 176)—though readily traceable to the extremes of characterization which it developed. Henrietta comes close to his own idealizations of women both fictional and real—the 'Angel' Luxima of Sydney Owenson's *The Missionary*, Sophocles' Antigone, Elizabeth Hitchener (the sister of his soul who became the 'Brown Demon'), and the Emilia Viviani of *Epipsychidion* (1821)—though like the latter Henrietta tended in his estimate to diminish from a Juno to a cloud at last (cf. letter to John Gisborne, 18 June 1822). The creative paranoia of Charles Mandeville—who conjured up visions of Clifford and Henrietta 'trampling on ⟨his⟩ lifeless limbs with looks of scorn' (iii. 322)—was bound to find a sympathetic audience in one who had imagined the self-tormenting idealist of *Alastor* (1816) and would later create a barely vicarious self-portrayal in the madman of *Julian and Maddalo* (1819), who was 'a nerve o'er which do creep | The else unfelt oppressions of this earth' (ll. 449–50). Indeed, contemporary writers felt that S was a proto-type of Mandeville, though the morally flawless Clifford might have been a character he would have preferred to be identified with (see George Woodcock, *William Godwin*, London, 1946, p. 192).

The later printing of the review by Thomas Medwin in the *Athenaeum*, entitled 'Remarks on "Mandeville" and Mr. Godwin', might have derived from a copy of the text as sent to the *Examiner*, which S's letter to Godwin of 11 Dec. indicates that he made, or it could have come from an original draft, which may account for the variants that are not obviously Medwin's transcribal errors. Medwin reprinted his version in *The Shelley Papers* (1833). Forman, who was not aware of the *Examiner* printing, used Medwin's text in the 1880 edition of S's works.

Related primary and secondary materials: Adeline E. Glasheen, 'Shelley's First
Published Review of Mandeville', *MLN* 59 (Mar. 1944), 172–3.

13–15. *Political justice . . . duties.* The general arguments concerning the
relations between rights and duties appear towards the end of book ii, ch.
iv, and continue through the following two chapters in F. E. L. Priestley's
edition of *Political Justice.* Godwin's social utilitarianism led him to
conclude that the only right an individual had was a right to his private
judgement, which itself was necessarily abrogated when it interfered with
his duties to his fellow men.

17. *Caleb Williams. Things As They Are; Or, the Adventures of Caleb
Williams*, the first and best of Godwin's novels, was published a year after
the first edition of *Political Justice* (1793) and illustrated several of its
doctrines in describing the persecution of the title-hero by his employer,
Falkland, a gentleman, who feels he can preserve his honour only by
preserving the secret of a murder he has committed which only Caleb is
aware of. The plot is generally concerned with the various adversities
Caleb is afflicted with as a result of Falkland's nefarious efforts to
maintain his reputation by continuing to pursue his servant even after the
latter has left his employment. In a climactic scene Caleb, whose own
moral character has been changed for the worse by his trials, confronts
his former master, pleads his case, and brings Falkland to admit his crime,
praise his accuser, and so die to that extent redeemed in the eyes of the
reader. Not only the vanity and pretensions of aristocracy but also
positive institutions—the legal system most obviously—are called into
question by the novel as it proceeds in different ways to illustrate Godwinian attitudes towards coercion, punishment, the power of opinion,
and moral necessity.

21. *St. Leon. St. Leon: A Tale of the Sixteenth Century* (1799) is a Gothic
allegory of the philosopher's stone and the elixir of life providing
boundless wealth and the gift of eternal youth to its hero, who predictably does not live happily ever after—at least partly because Godwin was
explicitly concerned with emphasizing the emotions as the true source of
human happiness and so repair a sin of omission which *Political Justice*
had incurred by its rational disparagement of marriage and the affections
which ideally ground it. In writing to Mary Shelley, 22 Sept. 1818, S
encourages his wife in her proposed translation of Alfieri's *Myrrha* by
reminding her that the 'second volume of St. Leon begins with this proud
& true sentiment, "There is nothing which the human mind can conceive,
which it may not execute"'.

Fleetwood: Or, The New Man of Feeling (1805) is the tale first of a youth
and then of a man of sensibility whose sentimental education in nature is
sufficiently qualified by the corruptions of England and the Continent
for him to become mildly dissolute, recurrently misanthropic, and

irrationally jealous before he is redeemed at last by the domestic affections. Newman Ivey White has pointed out several parallels between
Fleetwood and S's life and work, including the itinerary of the *History of a
Six Weeks' Tour* (*Shelley*, i. 229, 320, 349, 352, 635, 700–1; see also *SC* iii.
364, 373).

23. *Essay on Sepulchres*. The *Essay on Sepulchres: or, A Proposal for erecting
some Memorial of the Illustrious Dead in All Ages on the Spot where their
Remains have been interred* (1809) argued that such memorials would
inspire emulation in the hearts and minds of the descendants of the noble
dead. Except for a suggestion to his publisher Thomas Hookham that the
'type & size' of Godwin's *Essay* would be 'a good model for The Biblical
Extracts' (2 Jan. 1813), the only other significant indication that S was
himself affected by the work may be his incomplete translation of Plato's
Menexenus, which treats of inspirational funeral oratory.

33. *Mr. Malthus or Dr. Paley*. In his Preface to *Prometheus Unbound* S
again yokes these two in a more emphatic opposition: 'For my part I
would rather be damned with Plato and Lord Bacon, than go to Heaven
with Paley and Malthus.' Both William Paley (1743–1805) and Thomas
Malthus (1766–1834) were apologists for the political and social status
quo that both S and Godwin questioned. Malthus is particularly apt in
this context because the Utopian premiss of Godwin's *Political Justice*
(1793) inspired an *Essay on the Principle of Population* (1798), wherein
Malthus argued that the perfectibility of all mankind was quite literally a
physical impossibility, given the limited amount of tillable soil and the
ever-increasing number of people who had to gain their sustenance from
it. War and famine, he initially contended, were the only ways to decrease
the surplus population, an increasing number of which were bound to
live out their lives in poverty and misery. In 1820 Godwin published *Of
Population: An Answer to Mr. Malthus's Essay*, a work which S had eagerly
anticipated but which proved a less successful rebuttal than he had hoped
for (see *Shelley, Letters*, ii, Nos. 471, 582, 605, 634, 668).

36. *Wordsworth is in poetry*. A probable reference to Wordsworth's
'Preface' to his 1800 edition of the *Lyrical Ballads*, in which he justified
the common language and commonplace subject-matter of those poems
in contradistinction to the 'poetic diction' and (by implication) the
exalted subject-matter of his immediate predecessors. As the following
sentence demonstrates, S is also accusing Wordsworth of compromising
his reformist principles in poetry by the conservative tendency of his
later politics. S is more explicit in a later letter: 'What a beastly and pitiful
wretch that Wordsworth! That such a man should be a poet! I can
compare him with no one but Simonides, that flatterer of the Sicilian
tyrants, and at the same time the most natural and tender of lyric poets'
(to T. L. Peacock, 25 July 1818).

47–50. *the writings ... country*. William Godwin's publication of the

Memoirs of the Author of the Vindication of the Rights of Woman in 1798 contained a straightforward account of Mary Wollstonecraft's illicit sexual connections which was probably a primary cause for the 'stifling' of her writings S refers to, though a general reaction against liberal thinking which had set in during the 1790s and continued through the early part of the century doubtless contributed to it, as S further suggests. He perhaps exaggerates the currency of Wollstonecraft's continental writings in translation, which are only minimally represented in major library catalogues (British Library, Bibliothèque Nationale, National Union). The admittedly incomplete index to continental interest in her work contained in Janet M. Todd's *Mary Wollstonecraft: An Annotated Bibliography* (Garland Publishing Inc.: New York, 1976) has very few and generally mixed French reactions to her work during the early nineteenth century and there are no others.

53–6. *Falkland . . . abhorrence.* Except for his murder of the boorish and brutal Tyrrel and his consequent but largely secret persecution of Caleb Williams, Falkland was uniformly just and benevolent in his dealings with his fellow men. S's own grudging admiration for the traditional aristocracy (cf. *An Address to the People on the Death of the Princess Charlotte*, ll. 188–9) was a concession to their superiority to the *nouveaux riches*, typically qualified by his recognition, expressed in *A Philosophical View of Reform*, that 'at the bottom it is all trick'.

87–9. *How . . . lute. Comus*, ll. 475–7.

104. *"fades . . . day."* William Wordsworth's *Ode: Intimations of Immortality*, l. 77.

117. *"all . . . vanity".* Cf. Eccles. 1: 2.

117–18. *"the house . . . feasting".* Eccles. 7: 2.

131. *these. 1832*'s 'objections' (see the Collation) is an appropriate supplement.

144. *Smorfia.* Usually translated 'grimace', though S translates it as 'grin'. Two pages before the conclusion of the novel Mandeville first describes his physical disfigurement, 'The sight of my left eye is gone; the cheek beneath is severed, with a deep trench between', and then decides it is best described by the 'noun, *smorfia*', which he finds defined by the Renaissance lexicographer John Florio 'to signify "a blurting or mumping, a mocking or push with one's mouth"' (iii. 365).

149. *E. K.* = 'Elfin Knight'. S seems to have been the first to ascribe the name to himself but it probably derived from Mary's reading on 6 May 1815 of Spenser's *Faerie Queene*, Canto I, in which the Red Cross Knight is so denominated (see *Journals*, 77, 80 and n.). Keats ascribed the review to Leigh Hunt's sister-in-law, Elizabeth Kent (letter to George and Tom Keats, 5 Jan. 1818). A note preceding the *Examiner*'s publication on 19 Jan. 1817 of the 'Hymn to Intellectual Beauty' by Percy B. Shelley

states that the poem was 'originally announced under the signature of the *Elfin Knight*'.

ON THE GAME LAWS

Date: Mar. 1816–Feb. 1818.

Copy-text: Library of Congress notebook (shelfmark MSS. 13, 290).

Description: Three-and-a-half page ink holograph on leaves measuring 19 cm. × 15.7 cm. (7.5″ × 6.2″); wove paper; no WM; the text is continuous on alternate leaves of the notebook (pp. 11, 13, 15, 17); a smear towards the lower right of p. 11 obscures a few words, as noted in the Collation. The notebook itself is bound in worn grey marbled boards with a brown leather binding, measures 19.8 cm. × 16.5 cm. (7.7″ × 6.5″), contains 68 pages (only the first 33 are numbered), and is entitled 'Manuscript Pieces of Percy Bysshe Shelley and his wife Mary—1814–1822'. On what is now the inside back cover appears, in her hand, 'Mary Wollstonecraft Godwin | May 16th 1814'. The contents are as follows: 1–10 Latin exercises (Mary); 11, 13, 15, 17 *On the Game Laws*; 12, 14 16 *On 'Frankenstein; or, The Modern Prometheus'* (conclusion); 18–31 Italian transcription (Claire Clairmont); 32–3 Latin exercises (Claire Clairmont); ⟨34⟩ blank; ⟨35⟩–⟨65⟩ Apuleius translation (Mary); ⟨66⟩–⟨68⟩ *On 'Frankenstein; or, The Modern Prometheus'* (beginning). The first four pages of S's *An Answer to Leslie's 'A Short and Easy Method with the Deists'* have been inserted into the front of the notebook.

Provenance: Mary Shelley; Sir Percy Shelley and Jane, Lady Shelley; Richard Garnett; V. E. Neale; John A. Spoor; Mrs Matthew John Whittall; Library of Congress.

Printed: Frederick L. Jones, 'Unpublished Fragments by Shelley and Mary', sect. II, *Studies in Philology*, 45 (July 1948), 475–6.

A certain *terminus a quo* for this fragment is set by the reference to the discontinuance of the income tax (l. 12), which occurred in Mar. 1816; but that date may be modified depending on how one interprets the spatial and chronological relationships among the three hands at work in the notebook containing *On the Game Laws*. A conservative *terminus ante quem* may be fairly well established by the fact that the fragment is interdigitated with the concluding three pages of *On 'Frankenstein; or, the Modern Prometheus'*. S would seem to have left the three pages blank so that he could provide notes or insertions for *On the Game Laws*. He failed to continue the work and, when he ran out of space for the review at the end of the notebook, made use of the blank pages to finish it. If *On the Game Laws* had not been in place when he wrote the review, he would perhaps not have written the latter on alternate pages, though his practice elsewhere of skipping versos to avoid blotting makes that an uncertain inference. It is conversely possible that the pages on which *On the Game Laws* appears had been left blank for insertions or notes for the review, but the existence of the review in two places in the notebook makes that the less probable hypothesis, particularly since *On the Game Laws* follows immediately after Mary Shelley's Latin exercises, evidently the first entry put into the notebook.

There are two ways of assessing the chronological relationships among the contents of the notebook in order to arrive at a more precise date of composition than that conservatively indicated by the dating 'Mar. 1816–Feb. 1818' provided above. If one supposes that S was the first to use the notebook after Mary had written her Latin exercises into it, then an earlier date of composition may be inferred. This inference further implies that after he had written *On the Game Laws* Claire Clairmont took over the notebook at some uncertain period (she was at work on Italian as early as 1815 and may be presumed to have resumed her studies when in late 1817 the Shelley ménage was making plans to go to Italy), then gave it over to Mary, who in her journal does provide an exact period for her translation of the Cupid and Psyche episode from Apuleius' *The Golden Ass*—early to mid-Nov. 1817—and that she in turn passed it back to S, who wrote his review of *Frankenstein* in it. On this view, the *terminus ante quem* for the fragment may be moved back to Sept.–Oct. 1817. However, since it is quite possible that six pages of the notebook were left blank between Mary's Latin exercises and Claire's Italian composition, another assessment of the same evidence could be that S did not in fact receive the notebook until both Mary and Claire had finished with it. If that was the case, then the *terminus ante quem* of Feb. 1818 must be restored as an outside possibility. While also possible, a *terminus a quo* as early as the spring of 1816 is highly unlikely. The best presumption is that the fragment was composed late in 1817, not long before the composition of the *Frankenstein* review.

The fact that agitation for the repeal or amendment of some aspect of the game laws was recurrent during S's lifetime does not greatly help to pinpoint his concern with it here. The apologists for the law in some form argued that it kept the lower classes from falling into idle and depraved ways, noting as a general corollary that to allow them the privilege of hunting would render them unfit for the station in life they were meant to fill. In his *Observations on the Game Laws with Proposed Alterations for the Protection and Increase of Game, and the Decrease of Crimes* (London, 1813; repr. in the *Pamphleteer*, 1816–17), Joseph Chitty anticipated one of S's concessions (but not his consequent qualificattion) by arguing that a change in the game laws would do away with the country gentleman (p. 183). Chitty quotes one advocate for repeal or modification of the laws who, like S, felt that disputes about game divided the nation and encouraged what 'remains among us of savageness and brutality, ⟨which is⟩ chiefly preserved by the mean and greedy selfishness of those who possess a thousand peculiar advantages, and who yet meanly contend for an exclusive right to destroy the game' (p. 186). A particularly severe set of penalties enacted during the summer of 1816 had by Feb. 1817 inspired liberals such as Sir Samuel Romilly to argue in Parliament against both the specific Act and the game laws in general, though their intermediate object was merely to legalize the sale of game and so discourage poaching. S's polemical interest in reform had reached a high point at about this time, as demonstrated by *A Proposal for Putting Reform to the Vote*, drafted in Feb. 1817. It is clear from the introductory paragraph that his overall concern is with the reform of a House of Commons whose empty claim to 'virtually' represent the people is used to introduce a particular example of whose interests the Commons actually represented. Depending on the weight one cares to allow such correspondences, one may consider early 1817 as the most probable period during which *On the Game Laws* was composed.

Abetted by a few echoes from S's earlier writings on vegetarianism, the direction of the argument seems to take a moral and aesthetic turn about half-way through its course, which may suggest that S was on the point of extending the boundaries of his projected essay beyond its indicated subject-matter and into the realm of the metaphysical speculations which he was also engaged in drafting during the period 1816–17.

While F. L. Jones (in *Studies in Philology*) and D. L. Clark (*Shelley's Prose*) have printed independent transcriptions of the fragment, nearly all of the substantive differences between their texts and that of this edition are in the cancellations and have therefore not been recorded in the Collation; a few differences have been noted in the Textual Notes. The first notice of *On the Game Laws* appeared in Ruth Granniss's *A Descriptive Catalogue of the First Editions . . . of the Writings of Percy Bysshe Shelley* (Grolier Club: New York, 1923).

Related primary and secondary materials: Hansard, xxxv. 338–47.

ON 'FRANKENSTEIN; OR, THE MODERN PROMETHEUS'

Date: ?Early Jan.–early Mar. 1818.

Copy-texts: Library of Congress (incomplete) holograph (shelfmark MSS. 13, 290); *Athenaeum* (10 Nov. 1832), 730.

Description: Six-page untitled ink holograph on leaves measuring 19 cm. × 16 cm. (7.5″ × 6.2″); wove paper; no WM; the text is continuous from p. ⟨66⟩ to p. ⟨68⟩, resuming after a gap at p. 12, thence to p. 14, and concluding at the bottom of p. 16; p. ⟨67⟩ has some scribbling and drawings of foliage by S on its bottom half; p. 12 is slightly smeared towards the top; p. 14 has the block letters 'HOW H HO' written between the lines of text about two-thirds of the way down the page (see also Description of *On the Game Laws*); ll. 38–51 ('Human . . . which') are from the *Athenaeum*, second column.

Provenance: Mary Shelley; Sir Percy Shelley and Jane, Lady Shelley; Richard

Garnett; V. E. Neale; John A. Spoor; Mrs Matthew John Whittall; Library of Congress.
    Printed: *Athenaeum* (10 Nov. 1832; see below for reprintings); *F*; *J*.

Since *Frankenstein* was evidently in print (though not bound) by 23 Dec. 1817 (letter to Lackington *et al.*) and copies for private circulation were being distributed by 2 Jan. 1818 (letter to Sir Walter Scott), a probable inference is that S wrote his review between early Jan. and early Mar. 1818, when the Shelleys were preparing to depart for Italy. So late a *terminus a quo* is left open to question on the grounds of S's familiarity with the novel from its inception, which would have made the writing of a brief critique a task of a few hours at any time after it had, with his help, achieved its finished state in May 1817. The fact that S did not, as was customary among periodical reviewers, quote from the work he was reviewing may even suggest that the novel had not yet reached the state of printer's copy, though the same fact could also suggest that, like his review of Godwin's *Mandeville*, the review of *Frankenstein* was intended for Leigh Hunt's *Examiner* (see W. E. Peck's note in *MLN*, listed below), where space was relatively limited. On another view, the holograph is evidently a first draft which would almost certainly have been expanded and could well have been supplemented with quotations in the printer's copy. The first three pages of the review are at the end of the notebook, beginning on what was originally the verso of Mary's translation of the Cupid and Psyche episode from Apuleius' *The Golden Ass*; while its concluding three pages appear on what were originally the blank versos of the *Game Laws* draft towards the front of the notebook, assuming that this draft preceded the review. A reasonable conclusion, therefore, is that the review was the last item written into the notebook. See the Description and Editorial Commentary for *On the Game Laws* for further information about the notebook and the relative dating of its contents.

While Thomas Medwin, in his biography of Shelley, states that he gives only the 'greater part' of the review there, he does in fact (with variant and corrupted readings) provide all of the extant part of it, plus a portion no longer extant in holograph (Medwin, *Life*, 157–9), as he had when he first printed it in the *Athenaeum* (repr. in Medwin, *The Shelley Papers*). The implication that he was aware of more than he provides should probably be taken simply to mean that the whole, as he copied it from the notebook, impressed him as a rough and incomplete draft that S must have expanded in a fairer copy. The lines for which Medwin is the sole authority would have taken up about a page of the holograph, which is, in spite of lapses in transcription and editing, clearly the basis of his text, which subsequent editors have relied on as the basis of theirs. The missing last leaf of the notebook, which presumably contained the lines now extant only in Medwin's printings, must then have been removed after late 1820, when Medwin was transcribing from S's notebooks. In the appendix to his 1913 edition of Medwin's *Life* Forman was able to confirm a few readings on the basis of the holograph, which he had seen when it was in the possession of Richard Garnett (p. 456).

The review itself is in general rather poorly written even by the contemporary journalistic standards it emulates and would doubtless have received further grooming before reaching the stage of printer's copy. S's appraisal of the novel received some implicit qualification, apparently induced by what he conceived of as its negative public reception, a few years later when he asked Charles Ollier not to publish Mary's second novel, *Valperga*, as the work of the author of *Frankenstein* (letter, 27 July 1821).

Related primary and secondary materials: Medwin, *Life*, 456 n.; W. E. Peck, 'Shelley's Reviews Written for the *Examiner*', *MLN* 39 (Feb. 1924), 118–19. See also the *Preface to 'Frankenstein; or, The Modern Prometheus'* and commentary.

44. *obligations*. The word makes a sufficient and even subtle sense, when considered in the light of S's necessarianism, but the fact that it is seldom used without a positive moral or legal connotation suggests that Medwin might have mistranscribed.

51. *social*. Forman notes (Medwin, *Life*, 456 n.) that the word is 'rather unconvincing' in this context and led one commentator to suggest 'soured', which is the least that can be said to describe the modification of the Being's nature in consequence of the negative reactions he inspired in those whom he wished to befriend. While the necessarian trend of S's thought would again justify 'social', there is a possibility that its introductory context—which is provided only by Medwin—was garbled in the transcription. Taken as it stands, the sentence as a whole seems to mean that the treatment the Being necessarily received from men (given his appearance) led to consequences necessarily springing from his (also) being a social nature, or someone capable of reacting for better or for worse in a social context (cf. ll. 43–44).

63–5. *The encounter ... Falkland*. In the 'sea of glass' (that is, 'Mer de Glace', a glacier on the northern slope of Mont Blanc) encounter between Frankenstein and his creation the latter rationally and sympathetically pleads his case while the former proudly and disdainfully rejects him. There are several more or less comparable scenes between Falkland and Caleb Williams, though S probably had in mind the one in which Falkland demands that Caleb sign a paper declaring Falkland guiltless of the murder he had committed and Caleb rationalizes his case for refusing to do so (see the Rinehart edition, New York, 1960, 326–30).

67. *admirable writer*. William Godwin, Mary's father. (S's use of the masculine pronoun accords with the anonymity of the work and the grammatical presumptions of the period.)

69–71. *imitation ... Ireland.* Like Caleb Williams, Frankenstein is unjustly accused of a crime he did not commit. Godwin's implicit criticism of the social inequities of the legal system in *Caleb Williams* seems combined with his criticisms (in *Political Justice*) of the unenlightened masses in the consequent trial in *Frankenstein.*

ON 'RHODODAPHNE OR THE THESSALIAN SPELL'

Date: 20–3 Feb. 1818.

Copy-text: Mary Shelley transcript.

Location: The Brewer Leigh Hunt Collection, University of Iowa Libraries, Iowa City (shelfmark 733.S54n).

Description: A six-page ink transcript by Mary Shelley, with corrections by S and Leigh Hunt; the first three pages measure 18.3 cm. × 11.5 cm. (7.2″ × 4.5″); wove paper; no WM (pages ⟨1⟩–2 appear on the first leaf; page 3 on one side of the second; page 4 on one side of the third); the last two pages measure 18.3 cm. × 11.2 cm. (7.2″ × 4.3″); laid paper; WM: ?HOMIAS | ?1816 (page 9 appears on one side of the fourth leaf; page 10 on one side of the fifth); pages ⟨1⟩–4 are continuous, as are pages 9–10; the numbers are in Mary Shelley's hand. (See also the Textual Note on the title.) The transcript is contained in a diagonal corner-pocket attached to the back of a copy of Buxton Forman's 1879 *Notes on Sculptures ...* (privately printed: London).

Provenance: Mary Shelley; Leigh Hunt; Townshend Mayer; H. Buxton Forman; The Brewer Leigh Hunt Collection, University of Iowa Libraries.

Printed: H. Buxton Forman (1879); *F*; *J*.

This incomplete fair-copy transcript of a review of Thomas Love Peacock's *Rhododaphne* was made from S's draft very soon after the poem was published early in 1818, and seems to have been intended as printer's copy. In her journal Mary Shelley writes that she was copying 'S's critique on Rhododaphne' on 20–1 Feb. and that she finished copying it on 23 Feb. Since the transcript was found by Townshend Mayer among Leigh Hunt's papers, the best presumption may be that it was meant for publication in the *Examiner* (see W. E. Peck's note in *MLN*, listed below), though it does not seem to have been printed until Buxton Forman, who received it from Mayer, published it in 1879, along with *Notes ⟨Remarks⟩ on Sculptures* and *The Elysian Fields*. The pages numbered 5 through 8 are missing, which suggests that a complete bifolium has been lost from the middle of the review, while the fact that the extant transcript ends in the course of a quotation from the last canto suggests that a concluding paragraph at least is missing.

S could have written the original draft at any time from early Dec. 1817, when Mary was transcribing what was probably the printer's copy of Peacock's poem (Mary Shelley, *Journals*, 4–10 Dec.), though the probability is that he wrote it immediately after he had received a copy of the printed text from either Peacock or the bookseller. S's only other comment on *Rhododaphne* is descriptive rather than judgemental. Writing to Hogg immediately after Peacock had finished the poem and read some of it to him, S defines it as 'a story of classical mystery and magic,—the transfused essence of Lucian, Petronius & Apuleius' (28 Nov. 1817).

Because S's correcting hand often lacks the characteristic slant and flow of his representative drafting hand, it is not always clear whether he, Leigh Hunt, or Mary Shelley made some of the corrections in the transcript. Luther Brewer, most knowledgeable in Leigh Hunt's hand, assigns 'a few minor corrections' to him (*My Leigh Hunt Library: Huntiana and Association Books*, Iowa City, 1938, 65); Buxton Forman and Roger Ingpen (in the Julian edition) assign them all to S, though Ingpen may be merely accepting Forman's judgement. The insertion noted in the Collation to ll. 26–7 is probably Hunt's, the inserted 'statues' at l. 23 (see the Collation) may be his or (less likely) Mary's, but none of the other corrections are distinctive enough to conjecture a hand other than S's, and the greater portion of them are definitely in his hand. Except for a very few accidental variants and one substantive difference ('may' for 'can' in l. 119), the quotations exactly reproduce the 1818 printing of *Rhododaphne*.

Related primary and secondary materials: W. E. Peck, 'Shelley's Reviews Written for the *Examiner*', *MLN* 39 (Feb. 1924), 118–19; Notopoulos, *Platonism*, 51–4; Marilyn Butler, 'Myth and Mythmaking in the Shelley Circle', in *Shelley Revalued*, 10–17.

5. *religio loci* = 'religious feeling of the place' (cf. Virgil's *Aeneid*, 8. 349).

6–8. *author . . . stood*. The 'Pythian cavern' alludes to the cave on the side of Mt Parnassus, the lair of the Python, a large serpent killed by Apollo. However, S is specifically referring to the temple of Apollo at Delphi, originally a town built on the side of Mt Parnassus, which contained an opening in the ground from which intoxicating vapours issued. A priestess sitting on a tripod over this opening was inspired to oracular utterances which were written down by the attendant priests. Cf. *Prometheus Unbound*, II. iii. 4–10, for a parallel use of the myth.

8–9. *Peneus . . . Tempe*. The Peneus is a river flowing through the vale of Tempe in Thessaly, where Apollo purified himself after having slain the Python.

10. *Ilissus . . . Plane tree*. The setting of Plato's *Phaedrus* is under a plane-tree, on the banks of the Ilissus, a river flowing through the east side of Athens.

11. *sallows* = willows.

12. *nightingale . . . pine*. The Chorus in Sophocles' *Oedipus at Colonus*, 671–5, sings of the 'clear-voiced nightingale' who 'trilleth her ceaseless song' among the 'wine-dark ivy', where, however, the sun never comes (Loeb trans.).

19. *"the . . . stream"*. Slightly varied from Canto III of *Rhododaphne*: 'The life, the intellectual soul | Of vale, and grove, and stream . . .'.

25–6. *Syria . . . Apuleius*. Peacock in the 'Preface' to his poem refers to the contributions which the 'treatise on the Syrian goddess' of Lucian (*fl.* second century AD) and the *Metamorphoses* or *The Golden Ass* of Apuleius (*fl.* second century AD) made to it. Of the first he simply notes its 'wild and wonderful imagery', which he implies has been drawn on and paralleled in his poem. S's ll. 20–4 are themselves drawn from and parallel Peacock's comment on and quotation from Apuleius with which his 'Preface' begins:

> The ancient celebrity of Thessalian magic is familiar, even from Horace, to every classical reader. The *Metamorphoses* of Apuleius turn entirely upon it, and the following passage in that work might serve as the text of a long commentary on the subject. 'Considering that I was now in the middle of Thessaly, celebrated by the accordant voice of the world as the birthplace of the magic art, I examined all things with intense curiosity. Nor did I believe any thing which I saw in that city ⟨Hypata⟩ to be what it appeared; but I imagined that every object around me had been changed by incantation from its natural shape; that the stones of the streets, and the waters of the fountains, were indurated and liquified human bodies; and that the trees which surrounded the city, and the birds which were singing in their boughs, were equally human beings, in the disguise of leaves and feathers. I expected the statues and images to walk, the walls to speak; I anticipated prophetic voices from the cattle, and oracles from the morning sky.' (*The Works of Thomas Love Peacock*, 10 vols., ed. H. F. B. Brett-Smith and C. E. Jones, London, 1931, vii. 3)

78. *laurel-rose* = 'Rhododaphne'.

83. *he has*. Since S elsewhere gives little more than a summary of the poem interspersed with excerpts from it, Forman assumes that the missing pages contained a comparable résumé of cantos 3 and 4, which he provides as follows:

> As soon as Anthemion has thrown the flower into the water he hears a sudden cry, Calliroë's voice:

> > He turned to plunge into the tide,
> > But all again was still:

The sun upon the surface bright
Poured his last line of crimson light,
Half-sunk behind the hill;
But through the solemn plane-trees past
The pinions of a mightier blast,
And in its many-sounding sweep,
Among the foliage broad and deep,
Aërial voices seemed to sigh,
As if the spirits of the grove
Mourned in prophetic sympathy
With some disastrous love.—

Canto II, pp. 43–4.

Canto III shews Anthemion, on his way back to Thespia, repelled by sounds of revelry, and seeking solitude by 'Aganippe's fountain-wave.' Musing on Calliroë, he hears music, prelusive to the appearance of the 'radiant maid' whom he had met in the Thespian temple: he learns that her name is Rhododaphne, and receives her declarations of love. She utters the words

These lips are mine; the spells have won them,
Which round and round thy soul I twine;
And be the kiss I print upon them
Poison to all lips but mine!—

Canto III, pp. 66–7.

Stung by the thought of Calliroë, he escapes this time from the encircling arms of Rhododaphne. The fourth Canto sets forth that 'magic and mystery' have been chased away by Reason; but the poet adds

Yet deem not so. The Power of Spells
Still lingers on the earth, but dwells
In deeper folds of close disguise,
That battle Reason's searching eyes:
Nor shall that mystic Power resign
To Truth's cold sway his webs of guile,
Till woman's eyes have ceased to shine,
And woman's lips have ceased to smile,
And woman's voice has ceased to be
The earthly soul of melody.—

Canto IV, pp. 72–3.

This is introductory to the working of the spell. Seeking Calliroë, he finds her recovered, rejoices with her one evening, kisses her, and sees her fade and at once become as one dead. Fleeing along the shore, he is seized by pirates (Canto V), on board whose ship he is set beside a maiden similarly snatched away, who turns out to be Rhododaphne. By her incantations she raises a storm; the boat is wrecked, and Anthemion is borne to shore by the magic of Rhododaphne. Such is the portion of the poem that the missing leaves of the MS. doubtless epitomize. Shelley would scarcely have failed to quote the following description of Rhododaphne preparing for the storm:

> She rose, and loosed her radiant hair,
> And raised her golden lyre in air.
> The lyre, beneath the breeze's wings,
> As if a spirit swept the strings,
> Breathed airy music, sweet and strange,
> In many a wild phantastic change.
> Most like a daughter of the Sun
> She stood: her eyes all radiant shone
> With beams unutterably bright;
> And her long tresses, loose and light,
> As on the playful breeze they rolled,
> Flamed with rays of burning gold.—
>
> Canto V, p. 105.

The extract with which the next leaf of the MS. opens is the conclusion of Canto V; and the paragraph beginning with *They now find themselves* epitomizes Canto VI. (*Works*, vii. 20–1)

99. *Uranian Love*. Peacock in a note states that Uranian Love 'in the mythological philosophy of Plato, is the deity or genius of pure mental passion for the good and the beautiful; and Pandemian Love, of ordinary sexual attachment' (p. 91). Like the spirit of sweet human love in S's *Alastor*, Peacock's Uranian Love is vengeful when its powers have been abused (see on ll. 132–4).

99–100. *Love . . . beauty*. In commenting on the source of this paradox in the *Symposium*, S had earlier written that he would reply to it by saying that Eros 'neither loved nor was loved but is the *cause of* love in others—a subtlety to beat Plato' (Bod. MS Shelley adds. e. 16, p. 37).

106. *Armida . . . Bliss*. The gardens of Armida and Alcina are described, respectively, in Tasso's *Gerusalemme Liberata* and Ariosto's *Orlando Furioso*, while the Bower of Bliss appears in the second canto of Spenser's *Faerie Queene*.

112. *thyrsus*. An ivy-wreathed staff or spear carried by Dionysus (Bacchus) and his followers.

114. *nebris*. A spotted fawn-skin worn by Dionysus and his followers.

115. *thiasus*. A company of Bacchic dancers; perhaps here the dance itself is meant.

125. *Corybantic*. Pertaining to the wild and noisy dances performed by

the Corybantes, priests of the earth-goddess, Cybele, whose rites were closely associated with those of Dionysus.

132–4. ⟨*Ever* ... *148–50.*⟩ Again, Forman's inferences about the content of the presumably missing leaves are worth including here:

> There must have been another leaf or two of the MS. The last leaf I have ends without completing the extract: and I have added the final couplet. Doubtless Shelley followed his friend's narrative to the catastrophe,—the slaying of Rhododaphne by Uranian Love, who, as he sends his shaft into her breast, exclaims
>
> > With impious spells hast thou profaned
> > My altars; and all-ruling Jove,
> > Though late, yet certain, has unchained
> > The vengeance of Uranian Love!—
> >
> > > Canto VII, p. 159.
>
> How Anthemion finds himself with the dead Rhododaphne near Calliroë's door, how Calliroë comes out, the spell of her trance being broken, to greet her lover, Shelley doubtless told in few words, and perhaps concluded with verses that must have commended themselves to him—
>
> > But when the maid Anthemion led
> > To where her beauteous rival slept
> > The long last sleep, on earth dispread,
> > And told her tale, Calliroë wept
> > Sweet tears for Rhododaphne's doom;
> > For in her heart a voice was heard:
> > —''Twas for Anthemion's love she erred!'—
> >
> > > Canto VII, pp. 165–6.
> > > (*Works*, vii. 23)

Collations

When a letter or word is written through or cancels another letter or word, the cancelled letter or word appears in square brackets with the letter or word replacing it appearing immediately to the right of the closed bracket. For example, 'th[o]ese' means that 'o' has been cancelled by an 'e' written through it; '[scorn]contempt' means that 'scorn' has been cancelled by 'contempt' written through it. A dropped letter is indicated by an en-space. In a few instances it has been expedient to place certain (usually lengthy) collations in the Textual Notes. The MS folio- or page-number appears immediately after the first word (occasionally words) on the leaf or page.

THE NECESSITY OF ATHEISM

Collated: *1811*; *Queen Mab* Note on *Queen Mab*, 7. 13, 'There is no God' (*QM*).

Parts of the *Queen Mab* Note on 'There is no God' collated below clearly derive more directly from *A Letter to Lord Ellenborough*, which was the first later work to make an extended use of *Necessity*, than they do from the original; the Note itself was the direct source of passages in *A Refutation of Deism* which ultimately derive from *Necessity*. Differences in accidentals between *1811* and *QM* are not recorded unless they appear in the lemmata.

ADVERTISEMENT. possession] posession *1811*

1 A close] *see* EC   2 proposition . . . way] ~, is the only secure ~ *QM*   3 upon] on *QM*   11 belief;] ~, *1811*   12 immediate;] ~, *1811*   15 perception] ~ of the relation which the component ideas of the proposition bear to each *QM*   20 so] incapable *QM*   21–2 The strength . . . excitement.] Belief, then, is a passion, the strength of which, like every other passion, is in precise proportion to the degrees of excitement. *QM*   29 degree.] ~. (*par.*) (A graduated scale, on which should be marked the capabilities of propositions to approach to the test of the senses, would be a just barometer of the belief which ought to be attached to them.) *QM*   31 reason;] ~, *1811*   32–3 we . . . consider] it is to be considered *QM*   34 them to] them, which should *QM*   39 existence.] ~. But the God of Theologians is incapable of local visibility. *QM*   40 claims the 2nd. place] *om. QM*   place—] ~, *1811*   41 or] ~ have *QM*   42 eternity;] ~, *1811*   43 Where this] When this reasoning *QM*   existence of] *om. QM*   44 created;] ~, *1811*   46 eternity.—In] eternity. We must prove design before we can infer a designer. The only idea which we can form of causation is derivable from the constant conjunction of objects, and the consequent inference of one from the other. In *QM*   47 less] least *QM*   incomprehensible;] ~, *1811*   49 being] ~ beyond its limits *QM*   it. If] it, if *1811*   53 only] ~ that *QM*   there was . . . exist] once he was not *QM*   exist;] ~, *1811*   54–5 But . . . prove? We] But our idea of causation is alone derivable from the constant conjunction of objects and the consequent inference of one from the other; and reasoning experimentally, we *QM*   55 We] we *1811*   57 particular] certain *QM*   61 Almighty] omnipotent *QM*   62 ⟨same⟩] same *QM*   63 The 3rd. . . . Testimony] 3d. Testimony *QM*   it] testimony *QM*   73 passive. From] passive, from *1811*: ~, or involuntarily active. ~ *QM*   74 not] no *QM*   75 God;] ~, *1811*   we have] It has been *QM*

76 they] They alone, then, *QM*   77 they only] *om. QM*   78 From this] Hence
QM   any] either *QM*   79 a] ~ creative *QM*   80 God. It] God, it *1811*
81 can be attached] is attachable *QM*   disbelief;] ~, *1811:* ~; and that *QM*
82 willingly] *om. QM*   83 the subject.] any subject of discussion. *QM*   84–6 It
... mankind.—] *om. QM*   88 Q.E.D.] *om. QM*

AN ADDRESS, TO THE IRISH PEOPLE

Collated: 1812; Letter to Elizabeth Hitchener, 16 Jan. 1812 (*H*, for ll. 161–77); *F; J*;
Pforzheimer Collection corrected copy (*Pf*).

4 Englishman;] ~, *1812*   56 brother.] ~, *1812*   58 as] *Pf*: than *1812*   that,] *Pf*:
~$_\wedge$ *1812*   feel,] *Pf*: ~$_\wedge$ *1812*   68 prefer to] profer[s] [for] to *Pf*: profers for *1812*:
profess for *F, J*   others,] *Pf*: ~$_\wedge$ *1812*   73 must,] *Pf*: ~$_\wedge$ *1812*   74 you;] *Pf*: ~,
1812   76 impudent] ~[ly] *Pf*:~ *F, J*: ~ly *1812*   say,] *Pf*: ~$_\wedge$ *1812*   81 high,] *Pf*:
~$_\wedge$ *1812*   95 churches,] *Pf*:~$_\wedge$ *1812*   96 wasted,] *Pf*: ~$_\wedge$ *1812*   100 found,]
Pf: ~$_\wedge$ *1812*   131 given] can give *J*   135 virtuous;] *Pf*: ~, *1812*   136 them;]
Pf: ~, *1812*   166 soul] souls *H*   167 the will of] *om. H*   168 God.] ~? *H*
No, certainly,] No, if God makes any distinction *H*   170 values] loves *H*   a poor] ~
a ~ *1812*   Priest,] priest. Jesus Christ has said as much *H*   173–4 ceremonies ...
wonders] ceremonies confessions masses burials processions wonders *H*   174 away.]
~$_\wedge$ by these things. *H*   175 to charity] ~ love and ~ with all men *H*
196 Servetus;] ~, *1812*   209 *toleration?*] ~ ? *1812*   210 tolerates;] ~, *1812*
215 sat] *?for* sit   229 cannot;] ~, *1812*   devilish] develish *1812*   235 you;] ~,
1812   236 used:] ~, *1812*   245 yet we] [we] ~ ~ *Pf*: we ~ ~ *1812*
248 were] [have] ~ *Pf*: have *1812*   249 is,] *Pf*: ~$_\wedge$ *1812*   better;] ~, *1812*
255 said,] *Pf*: ~$_\wedge$ *1812*   263 vain.] ~ *1812*   273 said,] *Pf*: ~, *1812*
283 intolerant;] ~, *1812*   302 and] aud *1812*   304 damned—] ~, *1812*
327 subjects;] ~, *1812*   354 or good.] ~ ~, *1812*   390 blush.] ~$_\wedge$ *1812*
violence] violenee *1812*   392 people,] ~; *1812*   employed;] ~, *1812*
419 coolly] cooly *1812*   436 days.] ~, *1812*   477 right] right[s] *Pf*: rights *1812*
498 this;] ~, *1812*   504 others'] ~$_\wedge$ *1812*   505 devilish] develish *1812*
544 as you] ss you *1812*   552 spread,] ~[?], *Pf*: ~? *1812*   556 do] [so] ~ *Pf*: so
1812   They] they *1812*   562 multiply] mu tiply *1812*   627 happiness]
happinees *1812*   696 to be] /~/ ~ *Pf*: be *1812*   literally.] ~, *1812*   698 heart;]
~, *1812*   730 wish] ~, *1812*   convince] convice *1812*   764 should] shall *J*
768 ⟨to⟩] *J's emendation*   774 unaccustomed] nnaccustomed, *1812*   783 hope,]
~$_\wedge$ *1812*   791 ⟨is⟩] is *J*: in *1812, F*   795 us,] ~; *1812*   807 is] as *1812, F, J*
(*see 806-8* EC)   818 principles,] ~$_\wedge$ *1812*   824 will] who ~ *1812*
829 Europe,] ~$_\wedge$ *1812*   842 on] [a] ~ *Pf*: a *1812*   851 glory in] ~ /~/ *Pf*: glory
1812   853 men;] ~, *1812*   854 cheek] check *1812*   turn] ~ [in] *Pf*: ~ in *1812*
883 House] house *1812*   899 beings,] ~$_\wedge$ *1812*   901 there] their *1812*
902 there] their *1812*   912 "The] $_\wedge$~ *1812*   953 confinement.] ~$_\wedge$ *1812*
965 are,] ~$_\wedge$ *1812*   967 religion,] *Pf*: ~$_\wedge$ *1812*   976 own;] ~, *1812*
997 terrible,] ~$_\wedge$ *1812*   1017 you] yuu *1812*   1032 vibrate] [vitiate] ~ *Pf*: vitiate
1812   1043 incompetent] imcompetent *1812*   1044 the abuses] theabuses *1812*
1049 introduction] inroduction *1812*   millennium] millenium *1812*   1053 are] [or]
/~/ *Pf*: or *1812*   1054 upon] npon *1812*   1065 his] this *J*
1068 philanthropy] philanthrophy *1812* (*so spelt in ll. 1071, 1122*)   1069 one] onc *1812*
1088 love] ~, *1812*   1108 select] seleet *1812*   1124 *revolution*] revo ution *1812*
1143 to bring] ~ to ~ *1812*   1159 discussion";] ~$_\wedge$; *1812*   1165 it."] ~.~$_\wedge$ *1812*

PROPOSALS FOR AN ASSOCIATION OF PHILANTHROPISTS

Collated: 1812.

7 Philanthropy] Philanthrophy *1812* (*see* TN)   18 ⟨which⟩] what *1812*: which *J*
66 basilisk.—] ~‿— *1812*   75 universe?] ~; *1812*   86 Catholic] Cathol c *1812*
111 England,] ~‿ *1812*   130 alive] a li e *1812*   love for] lovefor *1812*
133 ⟨e⟩ffect] effect *F, J*: affect *1812*   149 benefiting] benefi ing *1812*
151 association] assoc ation *1812*   166 grandmother's] grandmothers *1812*
171 united] unit d *1812*   173 principles] princ ples *1812*   174 honour] hononr
1812   194 rejoice] rejo ce *1812*   197 them,] ~; *1812*   198 shoulders;] ~,
1812   199 necessity] necessi y *1812*   212 these are] these a e *1812*
unquestioned] unquest oned *1812*   221 disseminating] disseminati g *1812*   may,]
~‿ *1812*   234 concealment] conccalment *1812*   244 lets] ~, *1812*
260 government is] goverument is *1812*   271 secret,] ~‿ *1812*   280 constituted]
constitu ed *1812*   impossible] im- | ~ *1812*   291 tightening] tightning *1812*
319 controvert] contravert *1812*   362 believe,] ~‿ *1812*   366 philanthropists.]
~, *1812*   387 poetic] p etic *1812*   387 n. *Mémoires du Jacobinisme*] Memoires de
Jacobinisme *1812*   Barruel] Baruel *1812*   390 these,] ~‿ *1812*   391 appear]
~, *1812*   403 Thus] ~, *1812*   certain,] ~‿ *1812*   441 revivification]
revivification *1812*   467 n. on ... *Population.*] on Population. *1812*
487 millennium] millenium *1812*   490 foliage] foilage *1812*   501 ⟨analogies⟩]
analysis *1812* (*see* TN)

A LETTER TO LORD ELLENBOROUGH

Collated: 1812; Note on *Queen Mab*, 7. 135, 'I will beget a Son' (*QM*); *Shelley Memorials* (*1859*).

54 It] But it *QM*   56 power and] *om. QM*   57 admission.—] ~—*1812*   and
persuasion] *om. QM*   65 is] has *1859*   73 which] *om. 1859*
82 savage] some *1859*   84–98 You consider ... life.] *om. 1859*   86 and disbelief]
om. QM   87 volition. They] volition; it is *QM*   88 which] that *QM*   Belief is]
~ ~ a passion, or *QM*   91–5 How then ... punishment;] *see* TN   96 which]
whether *QM*   105–10 And where? ... humanity.] *om. 1859*   106 Under]
Even under *QM*   108 in ... country] *om. QM*   130–6 A dispassionate ...
command.] *om. 1859*   133 unwillingness] ~ or incapacity *QM*   134 activity,]
energies *QM*   147–9 and imposture ... Christ] *om. 1859*
168 circumstances] cirumstances *1812*   202 possess] profess *1812* (*see* TN)
205–9 A bear ... elephant!] *om. 1859*   212 analogous] analagous *1812*
234–82 Jesus ... existed.] *om. 1859*   245 ages,] ~, met with the reveries of Plato and
the reasonings of Aristotle, and *QM*   248 disprove] impugn *QM*   must] ~ be
contented to *QM*   255 murder] assassination *QM*   257 is.] *see* TN   belief]
faith *QM*   259 Does not analogy] Analogy seems to *QM*   260 it has]
Christianity has *QM*   261 violence and falshood] violence, darkness, and deceit *QM*
265 obsolete] *see* TN   then] *om. QM*   270–1 by ... fitness,] *om. QM*
275 facts, physical and moral, which] facts, whose evidence *QM*   277 acknowledged]
~ as satisfactory *QM*   280 barbarous and] *om. QM*   283–5 Man! ... humility;]
see TN   299 give⟨s⟩] giving *1812*   326–30 When ... age.] *om. 1859*
346 premises] promises *1812* (*see* TN)   351–74 *If God* ... belief.] *om. 1859*
361 not] false *QM*   391 dictated] directed *1859*   395 approaching—] ~, *1812*
396 arrival—] ~, *1812*

A VINDICATION OF NATURAL DIET

Collated: 1813; Note on *Queen Mab*, 8. 211–12, '. . . No longer now | He slays the lamb that looks him in the face' (*QM*).

31 thousand] thousands *QM*   44 vetitum] vetetum *1813*   48 macies et] macieset *1813*   50 Semotique] Semotiq *1813*   68 which the] which this *QM* 74 *primus* . . . *Prometheus*] primus . . . Prometheus *1813*   74 n. *Nat⟨uralis⟩ Hist⟨oria⟩*] Nat. Hist. *1813*   76–7 the inventions] these inventions *QM*   83 grave"] *see* TN 89 Man,] ~: *1813*   107 question.] *see* TN   128 except] unless *QM*   133 in . . . exists] , which live on different food, *QM*   133 n. *Leçons d'Anat⟨omie⟩ Comp⟨arée⟩* . . . 169, 373, 448, 465,] Lecons d'Anat. Comp. . . . 169. 373. 448. 465. *1813*   Cyclopædia] Cyclopœdia *1813*   140 cæcum] cœcum *1813*, *QM* (*see* TN)   151 accustomed] natural *QM*   160 possess] possesses *QM*   171 n. apparent.] ~∧ *1813*   Reports on Cancer] Reports on Cancer *1813*   185 lay] lie *QM*   205–6 at . . . stream] with pure water *QM*   210–11 drank . . . and] *om. QM*   212 that] *om. QM* 226 impossible,] *QM*: ~∧ that *1813*   228 had] ~, *1813*   237 insidious] insiduous *1813*   238 n. *Reports on Cancer*] Reports on Cancer *1813*   240–1 apparently . . . passions] by which He has there excited and justified the most ferocious propensities *QM* 277 In April] Hopes are entertained that, in April *QM*   289 essay.] ~∧ *1813* 289 n. *Return . . . Regimen*] Return . . . Regimen *1813*   289–91 It . . . public.] *om. QM* (*see* EC)   391 n. ⟨,A . . . Temperament⟩ on the Nervous Temperament *1813* 400 the same] such *QM*   408 more] ~ to be *QM*   409 that] which *QM* 419 lettice] lettuces *QM* (*see* EC)   446 n. ⟨Travels . . . Iceland⟩ Hist. of Iceland *1813* *Emile*, i, . . . 54,] Emile, i. . . . 54. *1813*   449 foe?] *see* EC   477 n. 2 *Return to Nature*] Return to Nature *1813*

A REFUTATION OF DEISM

Collated: 1814; *The Theological Inquirer* (*TI*); '(*cor.*)' following '*TI*' refers to marginal corrections in the Harvard copy of the periodical, though it is doubtful whether any of them have the autograph status the cataloguer has assigned to them (no record is given of words underlined in this copy because they are corrected in the errata); see also the Collation to *A Fragment of 'A Refutation of Deism'*.

TITLE. A . . . Dialogue.] ~ . . . ~∧ between a Deist and a Christian. *TI* Preface.] *om. TI* 6 The . . . shew] It is endeavoured to be shewn *TI*   8–9 he . . . himself] the task proposed will be accomplished *TI*   11–16 The . . . novelty.] *om. TI*   57 n. 1 ⟨Claudio⟩] *Tib 1814*   62 his holy] holy *1814* (*corrected in Errata*) 77 n. 1 *Evidences*] Evidences *1814*   86 n. 2 *Evidences*] Evidences *1814* 93 n. 3 Plin⟨y⟩] *Plin. 1814*   Discuti⟨a⟩nt] Discutient *1814*   Ορκους τε] Ορκουστε *1814* Πολεις τε] Πολειστε *1814*   Euripides] *Euripides 1814*   102 n. de Natura Deorum] de Natura Deorum *1814*   209 wondering] wandering *TI*   215 world.] ~∧ *1814* 219 had foreseen] and ~ *TI*   231 n. 2 *Le Bon Sens*] Le Bon Sens *1814* 244 n. 1 *Hosea . . . Ezekiel*] Hosea . . . Ezekiel *1814*   Heyn⟨e,⟩] Heyn. *1814* 250 n. 2 Sam⟨uel,⟩ . . . V,] Sam. . . . V. *1814*   n. 3 *Lyrical Ballads*] Lyrical Ballads *1814* 256 unarmed] unharmed *TI* (*cor.*)   258 n. 4 Who is of] *TI* (*cor. changed* of *to* on) Chap. . . . 26] *Chap. . . . 26 1814*   ⟨wroth⟩] *om. 1814*, *TI* (*cor.*)   Chap. XXXI] *Chap. XXXI 1814*   Chap. III, v. 6] *Chap. III, v. 6 1814*   Chap. X] *Chap. X 1814*   II . . . Chap. XII, v⟨v⟩. 29] *II . . . Chap. XII, v. 29 1814*   288 other] *om. TI* (*cor.*)   295 Deity] Diety

TI (cor.)   erase] erace *TI (cor.)*   322 it] them *1814, TI (corrected in Errata and in TI)*
349 loving] loveing *1814 (corrected in Errata)*   361 sexual] social *1814 (corrected in Errata)*   362 n. 1 I . . . Chap. VII] 1 . . . *Chap. VII 1814*   363 n. 2 *Decline and Fall*]
Decline and Fall *1814*   367 n. 3 *Decline and Fall*] Decline and Fall *1814*
405 immutable] inimitable *1814 (corrected in Errata)*   415 n. 1 *Evidences,* Vol. I,]
Evidences, Vol I. *1814*   429 n. 2 *Isaiah*] Isaiah *1814*   438 n. 3 Chap. XXIV] *Chap.
XXIV 1814*   455 n. 1 *Matthew*] Matthew *1814*   519 Atheism.] ~_∧ *1814*
522 ever] *TI (cor. changed* ever *to* even)   528 futurity] fraternity *1814 (corrected in
Errata)*   536 sympathise] sympathize *TI (cor.)*   553 designer] designers *1814
(corrected in Errata)*   577 From every] Design—every *1814 (corrected in Errata)*
583 necessitated] ncessitated *1814*   593 animals;] ~_∧ *1814*   relation,] ~; *1814, TI
(cor. deletes the punctuation)*   598 new display] open display *1814, TI (corrected in
Errata and in TI)*   609 n. Outlines . . . *Philosophy*] outlines . . . Philosophy *1814
Natural Theology*] Natural Theology *1814*   621 infering] inferring *TI*
650 insect's] insects *1814*   696 leaves] not only leaves *TI*   719 hypotheses]
hypothesis *1814 (corrected in Errata)*   720 its] his *TI*   722 of] in *TI (cor.)*
736 corrected] connected *1814 (corrected in Errata)*   744 *quicquid . . . deducitur*] no
spaces between words *1814*   755 would] could *1814 (corrected in Errata)*   769 it,]
~_∧ *1814*   770 active] light *TI*   797 conf(o)rmation] conformation *TI*:
confirmation *1814*   798 anatomy,] ~_∧ *1814*   799 n. Leçons d'Anat⟨omie⟩
Comp⟨arée⟩] Leçons d'Anat. Comp. *1814   Rees's Cyclopædia*] Ree's Cyclopædia *1814*
'Οτι] Ότι *1814*   ⟨επι⟩] απο *1814*   σ⟨το⟩ματος] σωματος *1814*   κοπιδι,] ~. *1814*
σ⟨το⟩ματι] σωματι *1814*   εκεινα.] ~·*1814*   ⟨α⟩] β *1814*   824 testimony to] ~
of *TI (cor.)*   836 n. *Political Justice*] Political Justice *1814*   I,] I. *1814*
837 antelope] antilope *TI*   837–8 a defenceless] or ~ ~ *TI (cor.)*   847 Populous]
Popular *TI*   881 n. *History of Brazil*] History of Brazil *1814*   898–9 of
properties] by ~ *1814 (corrected in Errata)*   910 n. *Le . . . Nature*] Le . . . Nature *1814*
929 ex] *et 1814 (corrected in Errata)*   932 ⟨derivable⟩] deniable *1814, TI (corrected to*
derivable *in the BL copy, in F, and in TI)*   941 n. *Academical Questions,* Chap. I, p. 1.]
Academical Questions, chap. I. *p. 1, 1814*   946 is] is ~ *1814*   976 *certum*] artem
1814, TI   eatenus] catemus *1814, TI*   977 eandem] eandam *1814, TI*   978 hoc]
sive *1814, TI*   979 n. Spinosa, *Tract⟨atus⟩ Theologico-Pol⟨iticus,⟩* Chap.] Spinosa.
Tract. Theologico-Pol. chap. *1814*   985 lurks] works *1814 (corrected in Errata)*
991 urged] used *1814 (corrected in Errata*   1002 Epicurus] Epiphanes *1814 (corrected
in Errata)*

THE ASSASSINS

Collated: MS, 1840

TITLE. The Assassins ⟨&c.)] *fol. 38ʳ*   4 hope] [hohe] ~ *MS*   9 city,] ~_∧ *MS*
preparations,] preparations_∧ *MS*   10 of] ~ [the] *MS*   13 East] east *MS*
14 Christians. They] Christians they *MS*   15 importance. They] importance they *MS*
16–17 poets. Acknowledging] poets acknowledging *MS*   19 on] [and] ~ *MS*   And]
and *MS*   23 slavery] slave[s]/ery/ *MS (S's change)*   26 Gnostics] [n] ~ *MS*
29 than] tha[t]an *MS*   strenuous] streneous *MS*   37 persuaded] [/particular/] ~ *MS*
39 another,] ~_∧ *MS*   40 master,] ~_∧ *MS*   should] *perhaps* would *MS*   41 The]
fol. 38ᵛ   42 regarded] [had] ~ *MS*   43 persecution] pers/ec/ution *MS*   But]
[b]~ *MS*   44 degree] dgree *MS*   45 rich] [great] ~ *MS*   46–7 destiny. Had]
destiny [and] had *MS*   49 views] ~ [& sect] *MS*   53 Attached] Attatched *MS*
despising] d[i]espising *MS*   54 the ⟨de⟩generate] /the/ regenerate *MS (see* TN)
mankind,] ~_∧ *MS*   57–8 attractions. It] ~/./ [i]~ *MS*   63 accommodation]

accomodation *MS*   64 a] /~/ *MS*   66 vices,] vises_∧ *MS*   67 philanthropy]
?philantrophy *MS*   69 that] [?that] ~ *MS*   Others] others *MS*   73 her] /~/
MS   76 mind,] ~_∧ *MS*   77 temples,] ~_∧ *MS*   81 depth] debth *MS*
82 awe,] ~_∧ *MS*   solitary] *fol. 39ʳ*   84 being,] ~_∧ *MS*   man,] ~_∧ *MS*   85 a
visage horribly serene] [the ghastly paleness of a] /a visage/ horribl[e]y seren[ity]e *MS*
86 multitude] [~ *MS* (*see* TN)   91 throne] [thone] ~ *MS*   93 After] after *MS*
98 some] /~/ *MS*   99 than] tha[t]n *MS*   101 the] /~/ *MS*   odoriferous]
odorifruous *MS*   103 their] [its] /~/ *MS* (*S's change*)   106 sound,] ~_∧ *MS*
108 assisted,] ~_∧ *MS*   113 accomplish] ' /ork] /~/ *MS* (*S's change*)   116 But]
[but] ~ *MS*   117 consummate] [coms] ~ *MS*   120 perfect,] ~_∧ *MS*
121 history,] ~_∧ *MS*   122 obscure] [dark] /~/ *MS*   129 valley;] ~_∧ *MS*
130 sky,] ~_∧ *MS*   grotesque] gro[tesque *fol. 39ʳ⁻ᵛ*   134 vale,] ~_∧ *MS*   then] [and]
/~/ *MS* (*S's change*)   136 those] these *1840*   137 sun,] ~_∧ *MS*   139 their]
the/ir/ *MS*   140 mirrors,] ~_∧ *MS*   144 become] [beg] ~ *MS*   145 She] she
MS   146 The] the *MS*   147 the] /~/ *MS*   148 chrystalline] chrytaline *MS*
149 mingled] migled *MS*   pine] [pne] ~ *MS*   150 boughs] bows *MS*   among] [on]
/~/ *MS*   152 effulgent] efulgent *MS*   153 around] [along] /~/ *MS*
156 Through] Th/r/ough *MS*   east,] ~_∧ *MS*   [among the rocks] *MS*   the] /~/ *MS*
157 unnumbered] unumbered *MS*   158 world,] ~_∧ *MS*   broad] [broard] ~ *MS*
moon,] ~_∧ *MS*   160 The] [t]~ *MS*   163 shone] [was] ~ *MS* (*pencil change*)
164 winter,] ~_∧ *MS*   clear,] ~_∧ *MS*   165 before the] ~ /~/ *MS*   166 sulphur]
sulpher *MS*   arrested] arested *MS*   167 the] ~[ir] *MS*   168 whirlwind]
wirlwind *MS*   169 through] though *MS*   171 Such] ~ [These] *MS* (These *written
first*)   172 to] ~ [the de] *MS*   173 tranquillity.] tran[quillity. (*fols. 39ᵛ-40ʳ*) [No
storm deconded to desolate Bethzatanai] *MS*   175 solitudes] [sublimities] /~/ *MS*
176 mystery.] ~. [The] *MS*   178 is seldom] [cannot often be] /~ ~/ *MS*   of] ~
[history] *MS*   180 breath of] ~ ~ [on] *MS*   181 through] [thou] ~ *MS*   skirts,]
~_∧ *MS*   183 heath,] ~_∧ *MS*   And] and *MS*   184 Arabians] arabians *MS*   of]
/~/ *MS*   Bethzatanai,] ~_∧ *MS*   185 nature, to] nature. To *MS*   187 Thus]
[Now] /~/ *MS*   world,] ~_∧ *MS*   190 with] /~/ *MS*   194 beneficence]
benificence *MS*   195 descended] deconded *MS*   196 epidemic] epedemic *MS*
communicated] [comun] ~ *MS*   198 To live] [existence] ~ ~ *MS*   201 delight,]
~_∧ *MS*   203 contain] ~[ed] *MS*   204 love,] ~_∧ *MS*   206 inexhaustible]
inexaustible *MS* (*see* TN)   213 dissolved] disolved *MS*   218 occupation] occuppa⌈tion
MS (*irrelevant notation*)   219 which] [whitch] ~ *MS*
human] *fol. 40ᵛ*   bear,] ~_∧ *MS*   220 smothered,] ~_∧ *MS*   extinguished,] ~_∧ *MS*
221 communicated] ~ [towards] *MS*   222 all;] ~_∧ *MS*   223 influence.] ~. |
[During three centuries] *MS*   HEADING. Second] second *MS*   224 polluted]
poluted *MS*   227 Constantine,] ~_∧ *MS*   229 successors,] suc/c/essors_∧ *MS*
232 sepulchre] sepuchre *MS*   233 disinterested] ~[ness] *MS*   236 of] [and] /~/
MS (*S's change*)   241 operation] opperation *MS*   246 corresponding]
coresponding *MS*   moral being] [natures] ~ ~ *MS*   247-8 by . . . intelligences]
[which] /~ . . . ~/ *MS* (*S's change*)   248 been] /~/ *MS*   redeemed] ~
[their   intelligences] *MS*   256 but] ~ [it] *MS*   ⟨in the⟩] in the
1840   258 between] [with] /~/ *MS* (?*S's change*)   and] /&/ *MS*   nation] ~ [of the
happy nation] *MS*   259 Assassins] [a]~ *MS*   or] nor *1840*   262 condition]
conditi|on *fols. 40ᵛ-41ʳ*   265 formed,] [became] /~_∧/ *MS*   were,] ~_∧ *MS*
266 divided . . . by] [in which there was] /~ . . . ~/ *MS*   267 Every] [In which] every *MS*
268 Each   devoted] [e]Each   devot[ing]ed *MS*   273 calamities] calamaties *MS*
274 possession] possessions *1840*   unimagined] ~ [by them] *MS*   275 embarrassed]
embarassed *MS*   279 in every case] /~ ~ ~/ *MS*   280 preference] ~ [will] *MS*
obviously] oviously *MS*   282 causing] [producing] /~/ *MS*   284 germinate in]
[be the cause of] /~ ~/ *MS* (*S's change*)   286 over whom] [in which] /~ ~/ *MS* (*S's

change)   288 prevail| pre|side|/vail/ *MS* (*S's change*)   291 whereby their| ~
|there| ~ *MS*   293 is| ~ |so| *MS*   consonant| con|n|sonant *MS*
294 invincible| invincinible *MS*   295 predilections| predelictions *MS*   Assassin|
|a|~ *MS*   296 accidentally| accidentaly *MS*   299 should| |w|/sh/ould *MS*
300 magnificence| magnificience *MS*   301 conceptions,| conception∧ *MS*
Heaven,| ~∧ *MSe*   305 presumption| presum|t|ion *MS*   307 passion| ~ /human/
MS (*irrelevant notation*)   illustrious| *fol. 41ᵛ*   308 remuneration| renumeration *MS*
311 but| except *1840*   314 viper's| vipers *MS*   the excess| /~/ ~ *MS*
devastation,| ~∧ *MS*   316 indefeasible| indefeasable *MS*   317 prerogative|
perogative *MS*   319 oppressed| opressed *MS*   or| ~ |of| *MS* (*S's change*)
320 tyrannize| tyranize *MS*   321 The| |Is| the *MS* (*S's hand from here*)
322 superstition| |religion| /~/ *MS*   323 endures| ~ |the| *MS*   329 priviledged
condition| |surpassing nature| /~ ~/ *MS*   330 |Nature| | |~| |The customs| |Those who
?remained| *MS* (Nature *inadvertently deleted*)   The … vicious—| /~ … ~~/ *MS*
332 of the| ~ ~ |destroyer| *MS*   333 this beautiful| th|e|is |lovely| /beautiful/ *MS*
334 on| |in|~ *MS*   335 in| /in/ *MS*   337 thro'| thro *MS*
338 marked| |mar| |known| ~ *MS*   oppressor| oppressor|s| *MS*   340 and venerable|
/& ~/ *MS*   341 holy| |sacred| /~/ *MS*   guise,| ~∧ *MS*   342 charnel,| ~∧ *MS*
343 green and| /green &/ *MS*   slimy| /~/ *MS*   344 of| ~ |successful & atrocious| *MS*
344–5 rooted … detested| /~ … ~/ *MS*   345 detested| *apparently added in MWS's hand*
345–59 |The … felicity.| | *see TN*   345 respectable| |honorable| /~/ *MS*   smooth,| ~∧
|secret| *MS*   smiling,| ~∧ *MSe*   346 honours,| ~∧ *MS*   349 eyeless … the| /~
… ~/ *MS*   351 Yet … imbued| |How gentle & benignant |are| were| /~ … ~/ *MS*
pure| here *1840*   352 with … benignity| /~ … ~/ *MS*   355 ⟨id⟩ly| *see TN*
356 evening| |sunset| /~/ *MS*   357 faith| |religion| /~/ *MS*   358 |to| | |~ n| |/&/|
|they had not| *MS* (to *inadvertently deleted*)   Nor … they| /~ … ~/ *MS*   had| *fol. 42ʳ*
361 graves| ~ |with| *MS*   364 of| /~/ *MS*   365 mothers'| mothers *MS*   Men|
men *MS*   366 many … luxuriant| the |flowering| |wild flowering| /many … luxiant/
MS (the *inadvertently retained*)   weed| weed|s| *MS*   367 had| /~/ *MS*   round|
around *1840*   370 rainbow| |quiet hues| ~ *MS*   HEADING. Third| 3d *MS*
371 Where| |An incident at length occurred … slight indeed; & such as the historian of a
|more| less inglorious race would omit recording| |Four centuries had passed away, & in the|
~ |no| *MS*   is| /~/ *MS*   calm| ~ |& uninterrupted| *MS*   circumstance| |incident| /~/
MS   372 remembered.| ~. |A stranger at length visited Bethzatanai| |An incident at
length occurred: the arrival of a str| *MS*   sixth| |fifth| /~/ *MS*   one| /|a singular| /~//
(*see TN*)   372–3 incident … strange| /~ … ~/ *MS*   named Albedir| /~ ~/ *MS*
(*darker ink*)   374 woods,| ~, |found a mangled & bloody corpse| |beheld the| |found a
human |spiked| body |on a broken branch| impaled on the a /sharp/ point of a broken
cedar |of a |high| /branch/| /lofty cedar/| |a naked human body, maimed & mangled every
limb bent & bruised| *MS* (*see TN*)   375 saw| |beheld| ~ *MS*   376 |of a lofty
cedar|| of a cedar *1840* (*see TN*)   376–8 Having … branch.| *see TN; Having fol. 42ᵛ*
376–7 he beheld| |he surveyed in horror & astonishment| /~ ~/ *MS*   378 a| |the| /~/
MS   379 into| ~ |the most| *MS*   380 most| /~/ *MS*   A| |On the gushing
marrow of one broken leg| a *MS*   381 that| *om. 1840*   381–3 fed … jaws…| *om.
1840*   382 worms| s *blotted in MS*   disputed| ~ ||the|at his| *MS*   383 Above|
and above *1840*   hungry| |famished| /~/ *MS*   383–93 who … ground.| *om. 1840*
384 not| ~ |even| *MS*   tho' mad| /tho mad/ |in| *MS*   with| /~/ *MS*   eyes| ~ |so
sparkling full of| *MS*   385 endowed … with| /~ … ~/ *MS*   empire| |power| /~/ *MS*
386 victim,| ~∧ *MS*   gluttonous| /~/ *MS*   387 sated| |glutted| /~/ *MS*
390 ribs, whilst the| ribs. /whilst/ The *MS*   391 tortured| /~/ *MS*   was| /slow/|
MS   slowly| |slowly| /~/ *MS*   392 hung,| ~∧ *MSe*   393 From| |His eyes| ~
MS   amid| amidst *1840*   396 power| |spirit| /~/ *MS*   397 of| ~ |a deathless| a
|mighty spirit| *MS* (a *inadvertently retained*)   a … mind| /~ … ~/ *MS*   They| he *1840*

398 measure| ~ |the scene| *MS*   399 the| ~ |mangle| *MS*   400 scorn| ~|ed| *MS*
lips.| ~, |but in his eyes the [serenity] cal tranquil[liti] greatness of a mighty mind [shone] /as
throned/ like the /very/ monarch of ruin, tempering with majesty the torture of
dissapointment & the fury of disdain.| *MS*: lip *1840*   402 reluctantly| relunctantly *MS*
403 dank| ~ |cave| *MS*: dark *1840*   404 vulture,| ~_∧ *MS*   meal,| |prey| /~_∧/ *MS*
404–5 pecked ... mountains| fled to the mountain *1840*   405 to| ~ |his| *MS*
406 reechoed with| reechoched |to| /with/ *MS*   of triumph| *om. 1840*   triumph.| ~. |All
was deadly silent| *MS*   409 It| |It| It *MS*   411 strange and| strange *1840*
soliloquy.| ~. |& seemed to pursue| |"The Almighty Tyrant has done well in creating
to himself an immortal foe. The torturers curse has armed its victim with| *MS*
412 apparent| /~/ *MS*   wide| |the| /~/ *MS*   414 Joy!| ~_∧ *MS*   415 under|
|beneath| /~/ *MS*   416 Ha!| ~! |the| *MS*   his| /~/ *MS*   this| the *1840*
418 beneath| |in| /~/ *MS*   black| |gre| ~ *MS*   419 There| Here *1840*   'tis| tis *MS*
420 design ...| |Build| ~.: *MS*: *om. 1840*   execute ...| ~:. *MS*: *om. 1840*   was| ~ |your|
MS   421 Thousands| ~ |knee| *MS*   422 golden| ~ |?the| *MS*   head,| ~_∧ *MS*
422–4 the golden crown whose ... brain."| *om. 1840*   423 gnawing| |poisonous| /~/
/whos/ *MS*   mingled| *fol. 43ʳ*   mingled with| |eaten into| /~ ~/ *MS*
424 ?cankered| |corrupted| /?~/ *MS*   He| ~ |was s| *MS*   silence| |stillness| /~/ *MS*
425 Albedir| |The youth| /~/ *MS*   tree;| ~_∧ *MSe*   428 voice,| ~_∧ |so soft & musical
that it seemed the response| *MS*   Albedir: ... God| /~! ... ~/ *MS*   429 approach.|
~. |Thou needest not| *MS*   430 of| ~ |all hum| *MS*   delight| delight[s| *MS*
431 pity's| pitys *MS*   approach,| ~_∧ *MS*   432 tones were mild| |voice| /tones/
w[as]ere |soft| /mild|ness|/ *MS*   433 of| ~ |old| *MS*   ⟨They⟩| It *MS*   floated|
float|ing|ed *MS*   435 to his| into his *1840*   was| ~ |a brother| |it was a friend| *MS*
as ... a| /~ ... ~/ *MS*   436 of ⟨his⟩ childhood| ~ his – *1840*: a|s|f this childhood *MS* (*S*
neglected to change a *to* o *and to delete* t)   438 resisted| restisted *MS*
440 deposited| deposit|ing|ed *MS*   441 on| |up|on *MS*   ground.| ~_∧ |gave / |sate|/
vent to the emotions of an uncontrollable sympathy. He wept in ungovernable sorrow. He
could not repress his deep & mingled feelings until exhausted he sate down beside his
charge, sobbing |with| almost to suffocation. Awe and cold| *MS*   443 succeeding|
succe|ed|ing *MS*   to| /~/ *MS*   444 silver| ~ |tones of| *MS*   the same| th[is|at|]e
/same/ *MS*   447 a friend| and ~ ~ *1840*   you,| ~_∧ *MS*   450 brother.| ~, |your
beautiful little ones must learn to regard me| *MS*   I must| *perhaps* I must *MS*   of| *fol. 43ᵛ*
451 children;| ~, *MS*   all| *om. 1840*   father's| fathers *MS*   453 indeed,| ~_∧ *MSe*
453 less| ~ |strange| *MS*   455 Albedir",| ~_∧∧ ... *MS*   he continued—| /~ ~_∧/ *MS*
456 solemnity—"in| solemnity ... |th|at|ou darest not trifle with my high|—|Th| In *MS*
456–7 "in ... submission."| *see* TN   457–9 Albedir ... deference| /~ ... ~/ *MS*
458 Not| |The| ~ |the| *om. 1840*   459 He| |Albedir| /~/ *MS*   towards the|
to/wards the/ |his| *MS*   460 Khaled| Khalib *MS* (*see* 518 TN)   461 |the| stranger|
|the| |/the/| |stranger| *MS* (*underlined for retention*)   462 habitation. He| ~: |an| ~ *MS*
464 following| |third| /~/ *MS*   465 Khaled| Khalib *MS*   466 unaccustomed| /~/
MS   467 blighting,| ~_∧ *MS*   curse.| ~. |Khalib, the mother of his children, the
partner of his inmost thoughts, the idol of his early love knew not what entranced| *MS*
468 stranger's| stranger *MS*   469 imagination| |expectation| /~/ *MS*
470 denomination| |?shape or ?relation| /~/ *MS*   471 modelled| |all| *MS*
473 troubled| |dark &| troubl|ing|ed *MS*   473–4 thought ... waves| ~ /over ... ~/
|which inexorable fate| *MS*   474 preside,| ~_∧ *MSe*   475 unforeseen| /~/ *MS*
476 cottage,| ~_∧ *MS*   revolving| ~ |⟨   ⟩| |⟨   ⟩| *MS*   477 the incident|
th[is]e incident *MS*   478 intense| intense[st| *MS*   478–9 In ... controlled.| /~ ...
~./ *MS*   479 Astonishment,| ~_∧ *MS*   480 a| /~/ *MS*   481 all| ~ |powers of
callm judgment| *MS*   activity of judgement| /~ ~ ~/ *MS*   overwhelmed| and ~ *1840*
482 stunning| |rapid| /~/ *MS*   deliberation| delinberation |inquisition into the nature of
his state &| *MS*   483 His| ~ |reflexions| *MS*   return| *fol. 44ʳ*   Khaled| Khalib *MS*

484 that scene of] ~ [sanctuary of their] /~ ~/ MS   repose,] ~_∧ MS   485–6 [the . . .
world]] [~ . . . ~] [as enter [thier] this place of rest] [⟨   ⟩] MS: that change might as soon
overwhelm the eternal world, *1840*   487 Without . . . he] [He] /~ ... ~/ MS
488 Khaled's] Khalibs MS   489 breathless] [fervent] /~/ MS   490 staggering]
[stunning] ~ MS   491 confused] [ton] ~ MS   countenance.] ~. [But habits of]
[But habits of uniformity soon overflowed the universal excitement, and] MS (*for folio-
division see* TN)   Chapter Fourth] Chapter (*fol. 45ʳ*) 4th MS (*Mary's hand resumes*)
495 singularly] singurlarly MS   499 from] [by] ~ MS   502 find?] ~_∧ MS
awhile;] ~_∧ MS   505 silent,] ~_∧ MS   507 he;] ~, MS   508 ground,] ~_∧ MS
509 too,] ~_∧ MS   515 employment] em[p]loyment *fol. 45ʳ⁻ᵛ*   these,] ~_∧ MS
517 spoke.] ~. [But [benevo] the benevolence and sincerity of his feelings w[h]ere so
profound] MS   518 the] [they] ~ MS   519 him,] ~[.], [His gaiety seemed to be
revived by her presence] MS and taking] *S's hand resumes*   520 attentively] ~ [& long]
MS   countenance.] ~. [Sister he said] MS   521 sleep.] ~_∧ [and if the]
MSe   523 Albedir's [said]] Albedirs [said—She cannot be more tenderly beloved] MS
524 love] ~ [?resound] MS   525 sleep, sister,] ~_∧ ~_∧ MSe   526 than] ~ [the
cloud of ?noon] MS   528 you . . . of] ~, [among] /in . . . ~/ MS   529 Khaled,] ~_∧
[replied] MS   531 stranger's] strangers MS   manner,] ~_∧ MSe   534 arrival,]
~_∧ MS   536 of] *fol. 46ʳ*   544 children,] ~_∧ MS   Albedir's] Albedirs MS
545 thro'] thro MS   546 with [odoriferous shrubs]] ~ [~ ~] [whose] MS (*see* TN)
whose] *om. 1840*   547 blooms] [?flowers] /~/ MS   gleamed] which ~~ *1840*
thro'] thro MS   548 chasms,] ~_∧ MSe   550 after] [threading a] MS   wound]
~ [among the rocks to the] MS   thro'] thro MS   551 wilderness,] ~_∧ MS
552 ⟨was⟩] is MS (*see* EC)   554 gazed] *perhaps* gased MS   555 countenance]
contenance MS   but] ~ [conte] MS   556 contemplatively] contemplatingly *1840*
she] he *1840* (*see* TN)   gazed] *perhaps* gased MS   557 voice,] ~. [Look] MS
560 her soul] ~ [bos] ~ MS   inaudibly.—] ~_∧— MS   561 hair] ~ [fallen] MS
562–3 by . . . utterance] ~ /such/ love /as/ exceed[ing]s ~ [& expression] MS   564 in]
fol. 46ᵛ   below;] ~, MS   eyes,] ~_∧ MS   566 apparently] ~ [twelve years] MS
eight] ~ [years & the girl] MS   two] 2 MS   younger.] younger— MS   The] Th[ier]e
[beauty was] MS   567 form] ~ [of] MS   568 overwhelmed] [bewildered] /~/ MS
570 thro'] thro MS   570–1 form appeared.] ~ [sho] ~. [like] MS   573 sails of] ~
~ [feathers] MS   577 language.] ~. [It unwreathed its] MS   578–9 no . . . it
entered] [it entered] /~ . . . had/ ~ ~ MS   583 last] ~ [the] MS   586 The] [Then]
the MS   587–8 answered . . . song] [called it] /~ . . . ~/ MS   588 glided] [crept]
/~/ MS   from] ~ [beneath] MS: ~ beneath *1840*   hands,] ~, [toward] MS
589 While] [As] /~/ MS   employed,] ~_∧ MS   seeing] s[aw]eeing MS
591 Abdallah,] ~_∧ MS   leaving his snake,] /~ ~ ~_∧/ MS

ON 'MEMOIRS OF PRINCE ALEXY HAIMATOFF'

Collated: *Critical Review* (CR); Shelley Society Publications, Second Series, No. 2
(SS); '(D)' after 'SS' indicates that the latter's 1886 correction had been anticipated
by the unbracketed (and unquestioned) correction silently supplied by Edward
Dowden in the 1884 *Contemporary Review* (see *Related Materials*). Obvious
typographical errors are corrected unbracketed in the text but collated below.

4 The] the CR   12 infamy] ⟨infamy?⟩ SS (D): infancy CR   15 If] if CR
25 refrains] ⟨re⟨f⟩rains⟩ SS (D): rerains CR   41 accommodates] SS (D): accomodates
CR   49 eve⟨r⟩] ⟨ever?⟩ SS (D): even CR   51 character] ~, CR   67 the]
thə CR   75 novelist—] ~, CR   76 poet—] ~, CR   78 merit⟨s⟩] SS (D):
merit CR   80 counterpart] SS (D): counter part CR   Alfieri's] SS (D): Alfien's CR

85 philanthropy] *SS* (*D*): philanthrophy *CR*   103 the] *SS*: thy *CR*   106 sex] *SS*
(*D*): six *CR*   108 Debesh-Sheptuti,] ~∧ *CR*   112 incidents;] ~, *CR*
113 which] and ~ *CR*   115 therefore,] ~∧ *CR*   118 delineation:] ~, *CR*
Her] her *CR*   139 fineness] *SS*: finenoss *CR*   143 Aür-Ahebeh] *SS*:
Aür-Ahebch *CR*   149 Rosalie] *SS*: Rosalic *CR*   153 stalk⟨s⟩] *SS*: stalk *CR*
161 on] *SS*: or *CR*   163 circum⟨am⟩bient] *SS*: circumbient *CR*   165 autumnal
beech] autumual ~ *CR*   171 sepulchral;] ~∧ *CR*   187 a⟨r⟩id] amid *SS*, *CR*
212 Fulke] *SS* (*D*): Eulke *CR*   tory;] ~, *CR*   214 party;] ~, *CR*   226-7 (see
... dissimulation,)] *S's interpolation*   236 knew.'] ~." *CR*   244 *Homerus*] *SS* (*D*):
Homenus CR   254 East] east *CR*   265 worship] *SS*: worships *CR*
269 embodies] embody *SS*   passions] *SS*: of ~ *CR*

ON THE VEGETABLE SYSTEM OF DIET

Collated: MS; Julian (*J*).

TITLE. *None in MS*   1 The] *fol. 267ʳ* (*see* EC)   7 themselves,] ~ *MSe*
11 cherished] [cherished] *MS* (*underlined for retention*)   12 rendered] [cons] ~ *MS*
12-13 and ... custom] [& ... custom] *MS* (*underlined for retention*)   14 their] ~ [erro]
MS   error.] ~; [which] [/The origin/] *MS*   15 This therefore] /~ ~/ *MS*
scientific disquisition.] /~/~ [& must] *MS*   16 consequence,] ~∧ *Mse*   21-2 of
human beings] /~ ~ ~/ *MS*   23 will] ~ [freeze] *MS*   25 science;] ~∧ *MS*   that]
~ [the mind] [mind] [the energy of thought is so connected with our body as] to *MS* (to
inadvertently retained)   25-6 the faculties ... they] /~ ~ ... ~/ *MS*   26 body]
[organs of the] ~ *MS*: organs of the ~ *J*   that] [ ]~[to] *MS*   27 perfection,] ~∧ *MSe*
Does] ~ [not] *MS*   28 of] *fol. 267ᵛ*   in some degree] /~ ~ ~/ *MS*   29 some
slighter] /~ ~/ *MS*   perversities] pervers[e]ities [desires] *MS*   29-30 of passion] /~
~/ *MS*   30 Is] [Is that which generates] /~/ *MS*   31 the] *perhaps changed to a* *MS*
33 whilst ... of] /~ ... ~/ *MS*   those] Those *MS*   34 have] ~ [been] *MS*
35 the subject ⟨of⟩] [subjected] /the subject/ to *MS*   philosophical] philoso[ph]icial *MS*
(ph *inadvertently deleted*)   investigation.] ~. [It has been thought] *MS*
36 instruction] inspiration *J*   38 science,] ~, [are perhaps] *MS*: sciences *J*   when
perceived,] /~ ~∧/ *MS*   39 conduct:] ~,: [wherever they are perceived]: *MS*
41 by] ~ [securing] [for] *MS*   an] ~ [un[diseased] /vitiated/] *MS*   understanding,] ~, [& a
physical] [the advantage of a natural state of body] *MS*   41-2 unvitiated ... disease.]
/~ ... ~./ *MS*   42 With] [what] with *MS*   43 terrifying] terryfiing *MS*
44 refuting] [inflicting] [bearing] /~/ *MS*   with the indisputable] ~ [them] /~ ~/ [the] *MS*
45 sense,] ~, [& refuting] *MS*   reason] [philosophy] /~/ *MS*   45-6 whilst portentous
dreams ... [that]] /~ [monstrous] /~/ ~ ... ~/ *MS*   45 portentous] politicians' *J*
48 torturer] torture *J*   49 vitals] vitals *MS* (*perhaps underlined for reconsideration*)
49-51 (*esse ... deum*)] (/[esse da] esse/ ... deum) *MS*   50 animadvertentem]
animadvertem *MS*   51 forces him] [goads him] ~ ~ [/like Ladurlad/] *MS* (*see* TN)
every] [a] /~/ *MS*   51-2 sight and sound] [countenance] /~ & ~/ *MS*
53 inspire] ~ [with] *MS*   that ... with] /~ ... ~/ *MS*   54-5 and ... life] /& ... /life//
MS   55 is] ~ [changed] *MS*   56 constituted] [into] /~/ *MS*   sensibilities?] ~?
⟨ ⟩ [The impetuousness of the animal appetites, which arises from unnatural excitability, &
that [exhau] languor which] *MS*   The] ~ (*fol.* 268ʳ) [absurdity would be more palpable] *MS*
57 attempt ... common] /~ ... ~/ *MS*   is scarcely less] /~/ ~ /~/ *MS*   58 lunatic]
[madman] [/man/] /~/ *MS*   from] [that] [/from/] [the] /~/ *MS*   man] ~ [should [cont]
exert] *MS*   the exertion of] /~ ~ ~/ *MS*   59 for] [from] /~/ *MS*   which] ~ [in]
[during] [his] *MS*   59-60 when in health] ~ /~/ h[e]alth *MS*   60 conspicuous.]
~∧ *MS*   61 of ardent] ~ [of] /~/ *MS*   61-2 the ... degree] *see* TN

63 inebriety] [gluttony] ~ MS   subversive] laborious J   65 ?the ?slave . . . Passions]
/?~ ?~ . . . ~/ MS   66 ?Mixed] morbid J   70 remoter] remote J
71 mistakes] ~ [had] MS   73 society,] ~, [as producing] [wars, revolutions] [hatred] MS
trace] ~ [murder tyranny] MS   73–4 to the . . . life] /~ ~ . . . ~/ MS   74 and] &
[violence] MS   76 A] [It may be] [objections] [It is] a MS   fails] fol. 268ᵛ
78 so] ~ [?has] MS   79 spark] ~ [of fire] MS   well kindled] /~ ~/ [will involve] MS
80 palace.] ~: MS   81 Monarch's] Monarchs MS   may] [will] /~/ MS
82 lighted] ~ [all the ⟨   ⟩] MS   84 complicated] [several] /~/ MS   87 The
vital principle] [Volition] [/The/] [Mind] [/of ?memories/] /~ ~ ~/ MS   88 influences]
[acts upo] ~ MS   90 suspended] [deranged] /~/ MS   lethargy,] ~, [& the] MS
91 therefore] therefore [/?that/] MS (see TN)   92–4 and . . . philosophy,] /~ which /is/
neither [the] . . . ~ₐ/ MS   93 subtile] simple J   94 profound] profane J   ⟨is⟩]
is J   100 mere] /~/ MS   dietetics.] ~. If [disease] [the misery produced by
disease[d]s [is not limited to the [/suffering/] individual] pervades /& corrupts/ every fibre of
the social system how [novel] [important must] worthy of [in] [cons] our consideration
is—the cause of this universal desolation.] MS (If inadvertently retained)   Much] [If] much
MS   that] fol. 271ʳ (see TN)   101 and] [then] & MS   the] [their]~ MS
102 constitutions. It] ~[;]. [i]~ MS   104 investigate] ~ & [to oppose] (& inadvertently
retained)   and] & [to oppose] MS   107 Disease] [/organic/] [Disease] MS (underlined
for retention)   a] blotted MS   109 preserve] [produce] perserve MS
109–10 organic derangement] [disease] /~ ~/ MS   110 It] [That the[re] there are
certain habits] [is] ~ MS   112 malady] [unnatural] ~ MS   The] [In this] ~ MS
113 life] possibly ~; MS   114 objection.] ~. [Almost] MS   To . . . excepting] /~/
every /species of/ animal, [but] /~/ MS   115 his] [the] ~ MS   116 dominion,]
~ₐ ⟨MSe⟩ [attains to an equal age.] [Their youths; their] [The period ?of ?their] [Few fail to
[arrive at the es] to attain or to exceed the] [established] [/average/] [period of thier
existence.] MS   is] [an]~ MS   117 which few exceed] Which [which] few
[suc]exceed MS   and] [but]& MS: but J   117–18 But . . . man] /~/ No hour of
[human] /the/ life /of ~/ MS   118 malady.] ~. [One half of [the]every generation
perishes] MS (retained by J)   120 natural term of] [indefinite extent] /~ ~/ ~ /is/ MS (is
inadvertently retained)   ordinarily] [in] ordinar[y]ily [life], MS   121 upon] ~ the
[infant] & MS (inadvertent retentions)   childhood] [infancy] /~/ MS   121–2 Not the
innocence of infancy,] /Not/ The /innocence of [infancy] ch infancy/ MS   122 the
bloom] ~ [By the nature of man, I understand] [I state of the human] ~ MS
124 destroyer.] ~ₐ MSe   125 Human] [Hum] ~ MS (fol. 271ᵛ)   possesst] /posesst/
MS   126 their] the/ir/ MS   127 Beings] [Men] /~/ MS   anxiously] [the]
anxious/ly/ [regard] [for] MS   to their] /to/ thier MS   128 whom] [to] ~ MS
129 concord,] [peace] /~ₐ/ MS   130 exertions,] ~ₐ MSe   swept] [taken] ~ MS
132 children.] ~. [This is the consequence of a diseased organization, which results from
unnatural habits of life.] MS   135 us—] ~ₐ MS   these] th[is]ese MS
137 innumerable ages] [ages] /~ ~/ MS   138 By an] [I am] [The use of the] [The word]
[unnatural] [nature in this enquiry] [is to be justified] ~ /~/ MS   habit . . . understood] ~ [I
mean] /is to be ~/ MS   as] ~ [is analogous] [pernicious] [/bears no analogy/] [to the
/structure of/ human frame; and its] [perni] [pernicious] [& I esteem it] [such an habit] as MS
(as inadvertently retained)   139 conformation] [anatomical economy of] ~ MS   and]
& [I esteem] MS   141 It is probable that no] [It /is to be/ presumed /that/ no one will
deny] /~ ~ ~ ~/ No MS   anatomist] anatomist[s] MS   142 deny] [dispute] [/assert/]
/~/ MS   grass] [fruits] ~ MS   flesh] ~ [the health] MS   145 boar] bear J
147 rendered] reduced J   147–9 has rendered . . . filthy,] [&] has /[ren]dered . . .
miserable [weak] /languid/ & filthy,/ MS   148 omnivorous] fol. 272ʳ   consequence]
?consequences MS   149 him] ~ [a variety of that] MS   150 of] ~ [won] MS
151 and] /&/ MS   152 would be] [is] /~ ~/ MS   innumerable] /~/ MS
153 butcher's] butchers MS   ⟨did⟩] does MS   154 end.] ~. [it were] [an endless] MS

157 object| |su| ~ MS   158–9 It . . . the substances| [That] The /It is confessed/ ~ MS:
The ~ J   161 stomach;| body, MS (see 160–1 TN)   groundless| [the ⟨   ⟩|
|vertigo| |hypocondriasis,| /~/ |vain| MS   166 strongly and| /strongly &/ MS
167 therefore,| ~∧ MS   disorders| [diseases| /~/ MS   168 discovered,| ~, [the|
|principal source| MS   168–9 successfully . . . source| /~/ assailed /in its ~/ MS
169 system| |natural| ~ MS   173 The| |⟨   ⟩ and| ~ MS   175 destruction,|
~∧ MSe   with| /~/ MS   176 carnivorous| fol. 272ᵛ   178 artifices . . . from|
|artificial| ~ |of a state which| /which result/ |may be| |considerable| /~/ MS   184 he
. . . by| /~ . . . ~/ MS   185 construction| construction[s] MS: constitutions J
186 wether| ~ |that| MS   188 indeed| /~/ MS   stamped| ~ |to death| MS, J   upon
. . . die| /~ . . . ~/ MS: om. J   190 inarticulate| |imperfect| inarculate MS
194 repasts| respasts MS   196 torments?| ~? [They destroy & devour it immediately
with as little scruple| MS   197–8 The . . . flesh| Th[is]e /single/ |consideration|
|/argument/| /consideration/ |alone| /that . . . flesh [without the most]/ MS   199 did|
|was| ~ MS   carcases| |flesh| /~/ MS   200 Custom . . . to| [Habit (fol. 269ʳ) will| /~
. . . ~/ MS   reconcile| reconcile MS (see TN)   202 ceased| |failed| /~/ MS
204 Every| [It is the| ~ MS   206 situation;| ~; |it does not fail however to| [?it|
nevertheless| /~/ MS   exhausts| exhauts |however| MS   207 energy. A| ~[,|. |and a|
~ |tree| |oak will grow upon the barren rocks, but it |will at| is capable of| |attaining to
greater age & perfection| a MS (a inadvertently repeats and lower-cases A)   to| ~ |greater
perfection| MS   its perfection| /~ ~/ MS   209 ⟨in⟩| J   tree:| tree, : [&| /~/
209–10 indeed . . . will| /~ . . . ~/ MS   210 diseased| |stunted| ~ MS   211 shrub.|
~. |Lambs ˣhave eaten flesh, until they have refused their natural diet| MS (see EC)
sheep,| ~∧ MS   212 their| ~ |accustomed aliment| MS   212–13 natural aliment|
/~ |dietˣ| ~/ MS   215–16 observed . . . unfailing| ~ to /among/ |be its| /~/ MS (its
deleted for to)   216 concomitants.| ~∧ MSe   217 Here| [It| ~ MS (see TN)   lies|
|is| /~/ MS   218 man.| ~. |It is clear| |that| MS   If . . . force| /~ . . . ~/ MS
these| then J   reasoni⟨n⟩g⟨s⟩| reasoning J   219 habit,| ~, [& that| [/therefore/|
MS   219–20 consequences of which| ~ |of this habit| /~ ~/ MS   221 himself,|
|those w| ~∧ MSe   to posterity,| /~∧/ MS   223 health and| /health &/ MS   for
any . . . their| ~ |their support| /~ . . . ~/ MS   224 happiness, resolutely| ~, |& to
posterity| /~/ MS   unnatural| |?this| ~ |& destructive| MS   224–5 thus . . .
calamity.| /~ . . . ~∧/ |resolutely & at once|. |It is| MS   225 measureless| om. J   are|
~ |convinced by these reasonings| MS   227 bound| fol. 269ᵛ   of morality| /& ~ ~/ MS: ~
228 adopt| ~ |the| MS   231 content| control J   and more constant| /& ~ ~/ MS: ~
~ consistent J   232 of nature| |of nature| |which| |the practise of virtue &| [/to the
breast/| /~ ~/ MS   invariably| invarialy MS   virtuous| |benevolent| ~ MS
234 Before [?the]| [If the| /~/ [/?all/| [/?~/| MS   shall be| |is| /~ ~/ MS   considerable|
|further| /~ ~/ MS   235 happiness| ~ |which| MS   236 must| ~ |previou| MS
237 unsparingly| /~/ MS   239 custom| |habit| /~/ MS   hereditary. The| hereditary.
[&| the MS: hereditary |and| the J   240 a| |the| ~ MS   241 With what rapidity|
|In| /~/ ~ |degree| /~/ MS   242 might| ~ |?arrive ?at| MS   diminish| |⟨   ⟩|
~ MS   246 may| /~/ MS   247 may| /~/ MS   251 n.⁽¹⁾ Hungary| hungary
MS   113| /113/ MS   103| /103/ MS   instances| ~ |of longevity| MS   Easton's|
Eastons MS   from another source| /~ ~ ~/ MS   251 n.⁽²⁾ τρ⟨ο⟩φη| τρωφη MS
252 hermits| |fathers of the| ~ MS   Christianity,| ~, |the| /to/ |/the one from a sense of
duty & the/| /others/ MS (to and others inadvertently retained)   system of| ~ ~
|abstinence from w| MS   253 the| |all|~ MS   excluded;| ~, MS   254 they|
|⟨   ⟩| /~/ MS   examples| |instances| ~ MS   longevity.—| ~.—|Among the
Moderns| MS   255 yielded| yeilded MS   256 n. Return to Nature . . . ⟨cure of⟩
Constitutional Diseases.| Return to Nature . . . on Constitutional Diseases∧ MS   fairly| /~/
MS   257 here| fol. 270ʳ   260 invincible| |unaccountable| /~/ MS
261 frequently,| ~ |over| MS   invaded . . .| ~ . . . |His temper| MS   263 So far as| [If

ever] /~ ~ ~/ *MS*　　264 shall] ~ [be found to] *MS*　　266 in] ~ its [genuine] *MS* (its *inadvertently retained*)　　268 any] ~ [animal] *MS*　　being,] ~, [unattended [by] by the] *MS*　　270 animated beings] [the human species] /~ ~/ *MS*　　276 With what] /with/ What *MS*　　of ... and] /of evil/ [does] /is/ [Revenge] /anger, vengeance &/ *MS*　　277 malignity] ?Malignity *MS*　　series] [chain] ~ *MS*　　278–9 produced] *perhaps* produed *MS*　　279 It] [Who] ~ *MS*　　281 beings,] ~_∧ *MS*　　and] *fol. 270ᵛ* 282 of the] ~ ~ [duties of social life] *MS*　　282–3 offices ... society.] /~ ... ~./ *MS* 283 brutal,] ~_∧ *MS*　　coarse,] ~_∧ *MS*　　284 Their habits form] [They are eminently qualified by their] ~ [train of] [/bloody/] ~ [is] [are] /~ [no less]/ *MS*　　even a more] /~ ~ ~/ *MS* (*the inserted words underlined twice*): om. *J* (*see* TN)　　285 more] /~/ *MS*　　wide] om. *J*　　wickedness] [desolation] /~/ *MS*　　hired] [paid] ~ *MS*　　286 beings by] ~, [that tyrants & courtiers ⟨countries *J*⟩ may profit by] the [confusion] ~ *MS* (*the inadvertently retained; J prints* [that ... profit] *unbracketed*)　　287 preserve] [be indued with] /~/ *MS* 288 with carnage,] [to]~ [blood], [/murder/] /~/ *MS*　　290 axe] [butchers] ~ *MS* 291 harmless] [innocent] ~ *MS*　　292 in] [with] /~/ *MS*　　292–3 is ... altho'] /is ... altho/ *MS*　　293 massacre] [death & agonies] ~ *MS*　　294 the use ... consequence] ~ [use of] [destruction of animals] [/con/] /~ ... ~/ is *MS* (is *inadvertently retained*) subversive to] ~ [/⟨　　⟩/] [of]~ (*perhaps* [to]of) *MS*　　295 unwarrantable] unwarrantabl[y]e *MS*　　296 exercised ... victims.] exersised ... victims_∧ *MS* (*see* TN) 297 human] /~/ *MS*　　artifice,] artific[ial]e [?resources of propagation], [only] *MS* 297–9 that ... disease] (*see* TN)　　297 that] /~/ *MS*　　may be] [are] /~ ~/ *MS* 298 then] /~/ *MS*: om. *J*　　outraged] [are] ~ *MS*　　they may] they may [lead a life] *MS* 299 disease.] ~_∧[d] [diet] *MS*

JOURNAL AT GENEVA

Collated: Bod. Dep. d. 311(2) (*MS*); *1840*.

2 or] nor *1840*　　4 also] om. *1840*　　6 or,] ~_∧ *MS*　　7 loneliness] [th] ~ *MS* 12 The] the *MS*　　14 This] no par. *MS*　　Mina] Minna *1840* (*so in ll.* 22, 31, 34) 15 and] ~ [had] *MS*　　16 and] to *1840*　　18 husband's] husbands *MS* 19 habiliments,] ~_∧ *MS*　　22 ear,] ~_∧ *MS*　　23 had] ~ [died] *MS*　　24 that] om. *1840*　　26 had] om. *1840*　　29 witty,] ~_∧ *MS*　　30 her,] ~_∧ *MS* 31 thro'] thro *MS*　　Mina,] ~_∧ *MS*　　32 attentions,] ~_∧ *MS*　　33 peal,] ~_∧ *MSe* deep,] ~_∧ *MS*　　34 ghost's] ghosts *MS*　　38 He] Lewis *1840*　　four] [three]~ *MS* 39 man] ~ [had] *MS*　　41 Germany.—] Germany—— *MS*　　42 o'clock] o clock *MS* 43 already] om. *1840*　　46 expressive] om. *1840*　　48 man,] ~_∧ *MSe*　　troubled,] ~_∧ *MS*　　49 or as] or *1840*　　51 which] wh[ere]ich *MS*　　preparing] employed in ~ *1840*　　52 portrait,] ~_∧ *MSe*　　54 portrait] ~[s] *MS*　　minister] ~ [who] *MS* 56 He] no par. *MS*　　60 with] /~/ *MS*　　HEADING. 2] 2 *MS*　　70 stranger.—] ~_∧— *MS*　　72 gentlemen,] ~_∧ *MS*　　73 concluded,] ~_∧ *MS*　　74 astonished,] ~_∧ *MS*　　76 on,] ~_∧ *MS*　　78 his] the stranger's *1840*　　83 stranger's] strangers *MS*　　84 locked.] ~[,]. [& when they] moment's] moments *MS* 85 ground—] ~—[cover] *MS*　　87 himself,] ~_∧ *MS*　　90 more.] ~_∧ *MS* 91 night] ~ [in his] *MS*　　92 when] ~ [he was sur] *MS*　　97 Lord] L. *MS* servant] ~ [denied his knowledge of] *MS*　　106 that] ~ [the li] *MS*　　107 at the gate] om. *1840*　　108 thro'] thro *MS*　　109–10 at that moment] om. *1840* 110 gentleman,] ~_∧ *MS*　　112 retreat] retreats *1840*　　113 friend's] friends *MS* 114 hour, who] ~[. His friend had] /~/ *MS*: hour, who had *1840*　　waiting] om. *1840* 117 friend] friends *1840*　　119 friend's] friends *MS*　　122 morning.—] ~_∧— *MS* 123 mount;] ~_∧ *MS*　　124 The] the *MS*　　beaut⟨iful⟩] beauty *MS* 125 views.—We] ~_∧—we *MS*　　*La Vattaz*] La Vattay *MS*: om. *1840*　　126 were] was

deep in *1840*   HEADING. 30] 30ᵗʰ *MS*   127 Morrez] [Mor]ez *MS*   128 day.]
~_∧ *MS*   HEADING. 31] ~. *MS*   129 thro'] thro *MS*   130 to] than *1840*
131 two] 2 *MS*   134 streams,] ~_∧ *MS*   bottom.] ~_∧ *MS*   136 arrive] arrive [in
the] *MS*   o'clock] o clock *MS*   137 we] we [left] *MS*   139 granite,] ~_∧ *MSe*
thro'] thro *MS*   140 wild,] ~_∧ *MS*   141 shaded] [covered] ~ *MS*   142 and
... palace] *om. 1840*   Fontainbleau.] Fontainbleau_∧ *MSe*   145 passed] proceed
1840   148 those of] *om. 1840*   149 of the ... workmanship] *om. 1840*
150 colonnades.—] ~_∧— *MS*   154 Grand] grand *MS*   155 palace,] ~_∧ *MS*
magnificent.—] ~_∧— *MS*   161 We] *no par. MS*   Palace.—] ~_∧— *MS*
163 Fontainbleau] Fontanbleau *MS*   164 colours,] ~_∧ *MSe*   ceiling] cielig *MSe*
165 exquisite] *om. 1840*   166 precious] *om. 1840*   has] ha[ve]s *MS*   in it] ~
[them]~ *MS*: in them *1840*   true,] ~_∧ *MSe*   168 Versailles] versailles *MS*
171 us] ~ through *1840*   174 Opéra,] Opera_∧ *MSe*   176 Egalité] Egalitè *MS*
178 girl,] ~_∧ *MS*   The] [We saw] ~ *MS*   180 held] [known] ~ *MS*
191 Auxonne] Auxerre *1840*   192 thro'] thro *MS*   194 disappoints] dissapoints
MS   burial] ~ [of] *MS*   195 fine] [   ]~ *MS*   196 Yvetot] Yvetor *MS*

THE ELYSIAN FIELDS

Collated: MS; F.

TITLE. The (*fol.* ⟨*1ʳ*⟩) Elysian fields *MS*: The Elysian Fields: A Lucianic Fragment *F*
3 altho'] altho *MS*   5 in] ~ [th] *MS*   7 even] ~ [when the grave] *MS*
16 accommodates] accomodates *MS*   18 I] [I have] ~ *MS*   19 airy] *fol.* ⟨*1ᵛ*⟩
31 doubt,] ~_∧ *MS*   35 pieces] peices *MS*   38 you,] ~—[you recollect yourself, &
if] the [prejudices of the age have not deprived you of all] [That] [/that/] [learning] *MS* (the
inadvertently retained)   41 depraving] *fol.* ⟨*2ʳ*⟩   42 Tarquin] ~ [But if these
motives] *MS*   If] if *MS*   43 actions,] ~; *MS*   44 but] ~ [if] *MS*: ~ if *F*
discipline] [lessons] ~ *MS*   narrow] ~ [& s] *MS*   may have] [is to] [prevent⟨   ⟩] [has] /~
~/ *MS*   45 thirst] [the] ~ *MS*   50 evident] ~ [to you] *MS*   52 counsellors]
consellors *MS*   53 imagined,] ~_∧ *MSe*   55 institution] /~/ *MS*   it in] [them]
/~/ ~ *MS*   56 which] [& this has been] ~ *MS*   acquirement] [conquest] /~/ *MS*

ON LEARNING LANGUAGES

Collated: MS; 1840.

TITLE. *None in MS*   1 it] *fol. 292ʳ*: It *1840* (*see* TN)   they] you *1840*
2 language.] ~. & [&] *MS*   6 the] th[ose]e [eloquent] *MS*   thei⟨r⟩] the *1840*
7 institutors] ~ [of liberty] *MS*   11 actors—] ~_∧ *MS*   12 or principles] /~ ~/ *MS*
13 conduct.] ~. [Those hues] *MS*   poetry,] ~_∧ *MS*   history,] ~_∧ *MS*   14 men,] ~_∧
MSe   panegyric] panygeric *MS*   15 divisions,] ~_∧ *MSe*   16 delicate] [subtle]
/~/ *MS*   18 English?] ~_∧ ⟨*MSe*⟩ [good for] [look at Paradise lost in French & a person]
MS   19 Lost] lost *MS*   20 obtain an analogical] [posess] ~ [some] /~ ~/ *MS*
22 Herodotus] [Hero]dotus *MS*   24 benefit,] ~_∧ *MS*   enlighten,] ~_∧ *MS*
25 injure] ~ [the] *MS*   28 and which] & [which] wh[o]ich *MS*   28–9 Ariosto,
Tasso,] ~_∧ ~_∧ *MS*   29 Goethe, Schiller,] ~_∧ ~_∧ *MS*   30 female] woman *1840*
31 it] it[s] *MS*   32 well] ~ that *1840*   33 it.] ~_∧ *MS*

A FAUSTIAN NOTE

Collated: MS.

TITLE. *None in MS*   1 It| |Some| *fol. 292ᵛ* |The bound| ~ *MS*   1–2 the knowledge| ~ |age in which they live, &| ~ *MS*   2 live.—| ~.—|These were in remote antiquity| & to |posess powers which have never yet been equalled.| |powers| |& it often| happens |that circumstances| |/these ?primarily arise from/| |foreign from| |/unconnected/| |the| |with any superior wisdom in the individual whom they invest|. *MS* (*inadvertent retentions*)   Circumstances| ~ |from thier own| *MS*   3 from| ~ |any| *MS* conspire| |in| ~ *MS*   4 Let| |Let none suppose| ~ *MS*   5 possessor!| posessor! |He is| *MS*   If| ~ |the| *MS*   8 misfortune.| *Centred under the bottom line but with no clear relation to the text S wrote:* may be, is & must /may/ be *MS*

DECLARATION IN CHANCERY

Collated: MS; Dowden (D). (Godwin's insertions appearing in T are not noted as such—i.e. with surrounding slashes—here unless the context in which they appear is collated for other reasons. MWS = Mary Wollstonecraft Shelley.)

TITLE. *see* TN   1 I| *fol. 96ʳ*   6 |differed|| |differd| *MS*   12–17 I understand . . . reasoning.| *bracketed in MS*   12 I understand that| |I understand that| /~ ~ ~/ *MS* that it is argued| *om. D*   14 because| ~ |of| *MS* (*MWS's deletion*)   17 reasoning.| ~. |All this| *MS* (*MWS's deletion*)   17–20 If . . . me| *original portion bracketed in MS: om. D*   17 of| *fol. 96ᵛ*   19 rights,| ~. *MS*   21 |This| ⟨*The*⟩| |X| Th|is|e *MS* 22 mind,| ~ₐ *MS*   24 heterodoxy,| ~, /not even/ *MS* (*see* TN)   31 dissolved| ~ |in s| *MS* (*MWS's deletion*)   causes| cause *D*   32 destructive| distructive *MS* 33 institution. Adultery| institution—adultery *D*   36 choice| *fol. 97ʳ* 40 institution| instition *MS*   44 founded.| ~. |am| *MS* (*MWS's deletion*) 50 |must not|| |~ |I| ~| *MS* (|I| *is MWS's deletion*)   54 ⟨their⟩ heart⟨s⟩| his heart *MS* 56 |exists|| |exist|ing|/s/| *MS* (*MWS's correction*)   exist| ~|ing| *MS* (*MWS's correction*) 57 my| |me| ~ *MS* (*MWS's correction*)   58 peculiar| |pecliar| ~ *MS* (*MWS's correction*) 59 accommodate| accomodate *MS*   myself| *fol. 97ᵛ*   as| *om. D* 61–2 commencement| |time| ~ *MS* (*MWS's correction*)   65 that| |~| /This/ *MS* (*Godwin's insertion; see* TN)   marriage|| |~| ⟨|/contracted at 18 years of age/|⟩ *MS* (*Godwin's insertion and deletion; see* TN)   69 "wife"| ₐ~ₐ *MS*   73 consequence| |~| |I /protest against my previous connexion with her being interpreted into a consequence/| *MS* (*Godwin's insertion and deletion*)

A PROPOSAL FOR PUTTING REFORM TO THE VOTE THROUGHOUT THE KINGDOM

Collated: MS; proof of *1817* (*P*); revisions appearing on *P* (*PC*); *1817*. (In order to prevent confusion about the authority behind preferred variants, all variants and their sources are reported below. Since *1817*'s accidentals are assumed to be least authoritative, their occasional unique agreement with editorial preference should be regarded as coincidental.)

TITLE-PAGE. A Proposal | |for a National Meeting| |of the| | for putting Reform to the Vote | throughout the Kingdom | by the Hermit of Marlow | London | Printed for C & J Ollier | Welbeck St Cavendish Sqr. | 1817 *MS* (London . . . 1817 *in a hand other than S's*)

TITLE. A Proposal &c.] [An (*fol. 1ʳ*) Address | to the Reformers] *MS*: A Proposal &c. *PC*
(*added in ink in another hand*), *1817* (*heads p.* ⟨*3*⟩)   1 A] [Sir] | ~ *MS* (*see* EC)
agitating] ~ [in] *MS*: ~ in *P, 1817*   nation,] ~, [which waits] *MS*   or] *MS: om. P, 1817*
2 decide;] ~; [or to foresee] [& which] [& the manner of the decision of which] [No] [no one is
able to predict.] *MS*   indeed] /~/ *MS*   2–3 there ... result.] /~ ... ~./ *MS*
3 Yet on its] [On [its] /the/] /~ ~ ~/ *MS*   4 we] we *MS* (*the underline is probably a
mistake*)   5 reform] *MS*: Reform *P, 1817*   7–8 remains,] *MS*: ~ₐ *P, 1817*
8 is] *MS*: ~, *P, 1817*   to] ~ [be represented or not] *MS*   legislate] legis]]late *PC*
9 laws] ~ [assented] [which] *MS*   10 of] ~ [somewhat less] *MS*   11 not] /~/ *MS*
12 lunatics] *p. 4 1817*   13 mournful] mornful *MS*   14 exhibits:] ~: [as that] *MS*
15 possessed] posessd *MS*   16 trampling and spitting] trample & spit *MS* (*fol. 2ʳ*)
tho'] tho *MS*: though *P, 1817*   20 abhorrence.—] *MS*: ~.ₐ *P, 1817*
21 Parliament] ~ [have been exercised in contempt] *MS*   a] *PC:* ~ a *P*   is] [has been]
/~/ *MS*   22 people,] *MS*: People *P*: People, *PC, 1817*   in] ~ [obedience] [obedien]
[consist] *MS*   strict] /~/ *MS*   23 nature,] *MS*: ~ₐ *P, 1817*   24 people's]
peoples *MS*: People's *P, 1817*   despise,] *MS, PC, 1817:* ~ₐ *P*   men] *MS, PC, 1817:* nem
P   25 instinctively] *MS, PC, 1817:* ~, *P*   wretched,] *PC, 1817:* ~ₐ *MS, P*
26 secure.] *PC, 1817:* ~. [It is the object of] *MS*: secured. *P*   26–7 people to] ~ ~ [thier
rights, or rather to excite them to posess themselves of those rights] [/sovereignty which has
been usurped/] *MS*: People ~ *P, 1817*   27 a ... contempt.] /~ ... ~./ *MS*
29 the] *p. 5 1817*   people] *MS*: People *P, 1817*   30 enslaved,] *MS*: ~; *P, 1817*
31 famished. Perhaps] ~ₐ [/perhaps/ the fanaticism of custom has [so securely] wooed them
to its enchantments so securely that they would rather (*fol. 3ʳ*) [part with thier wives & thier
children] see thier wives & children starve by inches [than dare] [to] rather hear /& see/
without indignation all the contumelies [of the proud & the powerful, rather work sixteen
hours a day]] ~ *MS*: famished; perhaps *P, 1817*   Custom] *MS*: custom *P, 1817*
32 worshippers] *PC, 1817:* ~, [& they] *MS*: ~, *P*   waste] [pine] /~/ *MS*   33 Idol.
Perhaps] *MS*: idol; perhaps *P, 1817*   they will] ~ [shall] /~/ [live in squalidness & want,
that they will not] *MS*   34 not to] ~ /~/ *MS*: not *P, 1817*   of] ~ [th[is]at] *MS*
35 the] th[is]e *MS*   condition] ~ [of paying the] *MS*   36 exist.] ~. [Is such] [If such
be] *MS*   37 champions] *MS, PC, 1817:* Champions *P*   rights,] ~, [of] *MS:* ~ₐ *P,
1817*   38 retire] *perhaps* return *MS*   39 until] ~ [suffering] *MS*
40 reason:—] *MS*: ~.ₐ *PC, 1817*   41 issue,] *MS*: ~ₐ *P, 1817*   is] *MS*: ~ₐ *P, 1817*
42 Great] great *MS*   Ireland,] ~, [a complete] *MS:* ~ₐ *P, 1817*   43–4 Assembly.—]
Assembl[ies]y.— *MS* (*fol. 4ʳ*): Assemblies. *P*: ~.ₐ *PC, 1817*   45 I have] [If that question
is answered in the affirmative] ~ ~ *MS*   will] [desire] /~/ *MS*   and] & [that this] [such is]
MS   is the] [opinion] /~ ~/ [private] *MS*   46 public] *MS*: the ~ *P, 1817*
47 But] *p. 6 1817:* ~ [it ought] *MS*   proceed.] ~. [If the Reformers are really in the] *MS*
48 population] [shall] *MS*   49 that] ~ [they should be adequately represented] *MS*
50 House] *P, 1817:* house *MS*   Parliament] ~[,] [if] *MS*: ~, *P, 1817*   51 of] *MS*: to
P, 1817   52 petitioned] *MS*: ~, *P, 1817*   52–3 for ... effect; and] *P, 1817:* [for
the purpose] /~ ... ~ₐ/ ~ *MS*   53 refuse—] *MS*: ~, *P, 1817*   54 might] [would]
/~/ *MS*   ensue,] *MS:* ~ₐ *P, 1817*   its] [thier] /~/ *MS*   55 alone] /~/ *MS:* , although
P: [, although]. *PC: om. 1817*   then] *om. P, 1817*   56 people.] ~, then.— *MS*: People:
then— *P*: People then. *PC, 1817*   57 shall] *fol. 5ʳ*   58 opinion], ~, [th] *MS*
determine] *PC, 1817:* ~, *MS, P*   59 by reform in] [in] /~ ~ ~/ *MS:* ~ ~ ~ *P:* ~ Reform
~ *1817*   60 the] ~ [abuse of pow] *MS*   misgovernment] *PC, 1817:* ~ [which springs
from its being made the instrument of private] [which we all] [this] *MS:* ~, *P*   61 which
Parliament has] ~ [it] /~ ~/ *MS*   sanction ...] *MS:* ~, *P, 1817*   62 silent.—] *MS*: ~;ₐ
P, 1817   guilty] ~ [as] *MS*   63 which] [of] ~ [we] *MS*   Commons *p. 7 1817*   if]
MS, PC, 1817: ~, *P*   64 unequivocal] [an] ~ [expression] *MS*   evidence] /~/ *MS*
that ... national] of [the general] /~ ... ~/ *MS* (*of inadvertently retained*)   will to
acquiesce] *PC, 1817:* ~, [that] ?~ [they] /it/ ~/d/ *MS*: will acquiesced *P*   65 system]

PC, *1817*: ~, MS, P   65-6 the multitude] PC, *1817*: ~ [people, or] ~ MS: the multitudes P   66 acts,] PC, *1817*: ~ₐ MS, P   disturb] [overawe] ~ MS, *1817*: distrust P: [distrust] / [that]~/ PC   this] [their] [/its/] /~/ MS   67 decision.] P, *1817*: ~.—[Let the national will be sacredly] [The] [Let the nation be free if it wills to be] MS 68 The] [Let this [then] point is] [t]~ MS   reform] MS, P: Reform *1817*   point.] P, *1817*: ~ₐ MSe   For] [It] (*fol. 6ʳ*) [I conc] | ~ MS   which] PC, *1817*: [this]~ MS: this P 69 effectual:—] P, *1817*: ~.ₐ MS   70 That] [To call a meeting] [That you, Sir, should call a meeting to be held] ~ MS   meeting] MS: Meeting P, *1817*   71 on the of   ] PC, *1817*: ~ ~ seventeenth ~ March MS, P (see EC) 71-2 to … consideration] [& that all the friends of reform be [all] invited to attend that meeting.] [for the purpose of] /to take into/ consider[ing]ation MS   73 is] [was] /~/ MS   74 Nation.—] MS: ~.ₐ P, *1817*   75 That] [That the friends of reform [be inv] residing in any part of the country should be earnestly entreated to be present at this meeting.] | ~ [all the friends] MS   eloquent] MS: ~, P, *1817*   virtuous] MS: ~, P, *1817* 76 the Friends of Liberty] PC: ~ ~ ~ ~, *1817*: you MS, P   their] *1817*: thier PC: all your MS, P   77 all] *fol. 7ʳ*   77-8 animosity and even] PC, *1817*: ~, ~ ~ ~ P: /animosity, & even/ MS   78 discussion] MS, PC, *1817*: ~, P   79 love] ~ [which] MS: ~ which P, *1817*   country] MS, PC, *1817*: ~, P   conjure] [entreat] /~/ MS 80 rest.—] MS: ~ₐ— P, *1817*   81 whether] *p. 8 1817*: [Does] /~/ MS   desires] desire/s/ MS   reform] MS: Reform, P, *1817*   82 country,] ~, [be conjured] MS 83 intreated] MS: entreated P, *1817*   last] ~ [effort which] MS   and] & [the] MS: ~ the *1817*   84 rest.—] MS: ~;ₐ P, *1817*   can,] MS: ~ₐ P, *1817*   go] P, *1817*: come MS 85 cannot] ~ [should address a letter to the chairman of the meeting] MS: ~, P, *1817* 86 beneficial] MS: ~, P, *1817*   86-7 chairman … meeting] MS: ~ … ~, P: Chairman … Meeting, *1817*   87 sentiments—] MS: ~: P, *1817*   88 day.] ~. | [Let (*fol. 8ʳ*) the following Resolutions be proposed.] [?or ?1ˢᵗ something which should resemble or ?som] MS   Resolutions] MS: ~, P, *1817*   90 That those] P, *1817*: [That the Reformers deny the imputation w] [That] [t]Those MS   that it] P, *1817*: that MS 91 Nation] MS: nation P, *1817*   exact] ~ [a full representation] MS   reform] MS: Reform P, *1817*   Parliament] MS: ~, P, *1817*   92 a] ~ [full a] MS   93 duty,] ~, [are now] [have] MS   assemble here] ~[d] /~/ MS   95 duty] MS: ~, P, *1817* to] /~/ MS   96 right.] P, *1817*: ~.—[for they deny] [For that purpose they divide the] [If [the] [a] [/the opinion/] majority of the nation [determine] [/determ/] shall be found on examination [to be] to determine to continue to be governed as they are now governed, the] | [This meeting shall [be] continue to be held day after] | [For (*fol. 9ʳ*) that purpose they divide the United Kingdom of great Britain & Ireland into 40 districts equal in each of which] MS 97 2.] *p. 9 1817*   That] [For this purpose they divide] /~/ MS   be divided] /~ ~/ MS 98 three hundred] [4]300 MS   99 of inhabitants] [of persons. .] /~ ~/ MS   and … be] [& they] /& 300 persons be/ MS   commissioned] ~, P, *1817*: commission/ed/ [300 friends of reform [/persons, if possible disinterested, if not, ?men/] or persons who might be hired for the purpose, to visit] MS   100 each] /~/ MS   101 inquire] MS: enquire P, *1817* 102 sign the] ~ [declaration No 2.] ~ [second resolution, with] MS   declaration … third] /[The] ~ … [second] /~// MS   resolution,] P: ~ₐ MSe: Resolution, *1817* 103 explanation] ~ [he might think fit] MS   104 sentiments] MS: ~, P, *1817*   on] in MS   105 declaration] MS, P: Declaration *1817*   proposed for signature.] P: /~ ~ ~ₐ/ MS: ~ ~ ~:— *1817*   106 3. That] [2]3 [~] ?2 [That] MS: 3 ~ P, *1817*   ⁱthe] MS: ₐ~ P, *1817* (see EC)   Commons] ~ [is not] MS   106-7 will of the] /~ ~ ~/ MS 107 Nation;] ~; [& that] [& it is the duty of the (*fol. 10ʳ*) People to require that House to originate such measures, as shall remedy this enormous corruption as are requi] MS   we the undersigned therefore] We [therefore resolve &] /the undersigned therefore/ MS 108 declare and publish,] PC: ~, ~ ~ ~, *1817*: /publish &/ declare, MS: declare, and our signatures annexed shall be published, P   109 conviction] MS, PC, *1817*: ~, P liberty,] P, *1817*: ~ₐ MS   happiness,] P, *1817*: ~ₐ MS   110 nation] MS, PC, *1817*: ~,

P belong,] ~, [are endangered] [are ill-secured] [by] *MS*   111 have ... thro'] /have ... thro/ *MS:* have ... through *P, 1817*   decay] *PC, 1817:* ~, *MS, P*   112 which] ~ [the members of that Assembly which [assumes] falsely assumes to itself the title] [which falsely [call] [styles] style themselves the representatives of the nation, are] *MS*   members] *MS:* Members *P, 1817*   chosen] *p. 10 1817*   113 Commons'] *MS:* ~‸ *P, 1817* Parliament.—] *MS:* ~;‸ *P, 1817*   We] *MS:* we *P, 1817*   express,] ~, [in the] *MS* 114 Country,] ~, [calling] *MS:* country, *P, 1817*   a] [our] /~/ *MS*   115 duty] *MS:* ~, *P, 1817*   we ... found] ~ [are found] /shall be ~/ *MS*   in this] [o]~ ~ *MS*   question] *MS:* ~, *P, 1817*   116 incessantly] /~/ *MS*   petition;] *P, 1817:* ~, *MS*   majority] *MS:* ~, *P, 1817*   and exact] /& exact/ *MS*   118 members] *MS (fol. 11ʳ):* Members *P, 1817*   representatives] *MS:* Representatives *P, 1817*   nation."] *MS:* Nation. *P, 1817 (see 106*EC*)*   119 meeting] *MS:* Meeting *P, 1817*   until it determines] until [its object be] it [shall have] [/has/] determine[d]s *MS*   120 whole ... the plan] [manner in which] /~ ... the/ ~ ~ *MS (inadvertent redundancy)*   121 Nation] [n]~ *MS:* nation *P, 1817* reform] *MS:* Reform *P, 1817*   Parliament] ~ [shall be put in execution] *MS* 122–5 5. ... constitutional] *om. MS (see* EC*)*   122 meeting] Meeting *P, 1817* 123 ⟨its⟩] their *P, 1817*   124 schemes,] *P:* ~‸ *1817*   125 its] *1817:* ~' *PC:* their *P* 126 6.] 5 *MS:* ~. *P, 1817 (see 122-5* EC*)*   127 plan] *MS, P:* Plan *1817* 128 Resolutions] *MS:* ~, *P, 1817*   be] *p. 11 1817*   130 detail. If] *P, 1817:* ~; [it being the principal feature in my design to excite others to a task of which I am no less incapable thro habits of seclusion & delicacy of health, than] [feel], [i]~ *MS (see* EC*)*   degree] ~ [beneficial] [practicable or beneficial] *MS*   131 men] ~ [of established popularity] *MS:* ~, *P, 1817*   132 sacrifices] *MS:* sacrifices *P, 1817*   eminence] *PC, 1817:* ~, *(fol. 12ʳ)* [which] *MS:* ~, *P*   133 rival,] ~, [it belongs to them] *MS*   pursue] ~ [the suggestions afforded by the] *MS*   develope] ~ [the cause which they] [suggestions which in the retirement of my closet have involuntarily presented ⟨prevented *J*⟩] [a cause] *MS (see 130*EC*)* 134 suggestions relating to] ~ [which] ~ ~ [/a/ cause] *MS*   the ... Liberty] /~ ... ~/ *MS:* the ... liberty *P, 1817*   135 nurtured] [/alone/] ~ *MS*   their] *1817:* thier *MS, PC:* that *P*   136 sweat] *MS:* ~, *P, 1817*   blood] *MS:* ~, *P, 1817*   Some] *MS:* some *P, 1817*   tended] [cherished] /~/ *MS*   137 famine,] *P, 1817:* ~‸ *MSe* 138–9 Power.—So] [p]~‸—— *MS:* power:—so *P, 1817*   139 begun.—] *MS:* ~.‸ *P, 1817* 140–52 I ... preservation] *see* EC   140 therefore] /~/ *MS*   one] ~ [technical] *MS* 141 proposal] *MS, P:* Proposal *1817*   Considerable expenses] *P, 1817:* /considerable/ Expenses *MS*   142 necessarily] [necess] ~ *MS*   incurred:] *1817:* ~, *P:* ~[,] *PC:* ~. [This must be met by] *MS*   funds] *P, 1817:* Funds *MS*   143 these demands] this/e/ [expense] demands *MS*   144 year] *MS:* ~, *P, 1817*   on] [from] /~/ *MS*   wife] *fol. 13ʳ, p. 12 1817*   145 comfort] *MS:* ~, *P, 1817*   from which] [from w] ~ ~ *MS* 146 justice.—] *MS:* ~.‸ *P, 1817*   any] [my] ~ *MS*   proposed,] *MS:* ~‸ *P, 1817* 147 you,] *P, 1817:* ~‸ *MSe*   £100,] *P, 1817:* ~‸ *MS*   148 income,] *P, 1817:* ~‸ *MS* object. And] ~. ~ [when I confidently] *MS:* object; and *P, 1817*   149 myself] *MSe:* ~, *P, 1817*   alone] ~ [confident when ⟨or where⟩ devotion to the public good] *MS*   in this respect] /~ ~ ~/ *MS:* ~ ~ ~, *P, 1817*   any] ~ [temperate &] *MS*   150 benefit] [good] /~/ *MS*   151 those] th[e]ose *MS*   men,] *MS:* ~‸ *P, 1817*   153 A] [The leading feature in my plan is] | [The only] [An indis] | ~ *MS*   friends] *MS, P:* Friends *1817* Reform] *MS:* ~, *P, 1817*   154 proposal.] ~. [The advocates of annual Parliaments & Universal Suffrage] [It requires some sacrifice of the selfish the [envious]] *MS* 155 Universal ... limited Suffrage] Universal ... limited suffrage *MS:* universal ... limited suffrage *P:* Universal ... Limited Suffrage *1817*   156 Parliaments,] *P, 1817:* ~‸ *MS* on] [of] ~ *MS (fol. 14ʳ)*   157 is] ~ [certain that] *MS*   the Nation wills] the nation wills *P:* [th[is]e] Nation wills [any Re] *MS:* the nation desires *1817*   160 no.—] *MS:* ~.‸ *P, 1817*   161 nothing ... but] [it will be asked w] /~ ... ~/ [I am bound] *MS*   state] *p. 13 1817*   162 subject] *PC, 1817:* question *MS, P*   Reform.—] ~.—[I am] [Annual Parliaments appear] *MS:* ~.‸ *P, 1817*   162–7 The ... reply.] *PC, 1817: om. MS, P (see*

EC)   164 it,| *PC*: ~ₐ *1817*   Requisition| *PC*: requisition *1817*   165 ask| *PC*:
~, *1817*   166 scheme| *PC*: ~, *1817*   170 nation. It| ~[,]. |by enabling men to
cultivate energies which have n| ~ *MS*: nation; it *P, 1817*   172 state| *MS*, *PC*, *1817*: ~,
P   173 depends. It| *MS*: ~; it *P, 1817*   familiarise| *MS*: familiarize *P, 1817*
174 liberty| *PC*, *1817*: ~, *MS, P*   175 forms.] ~. [It would render innovations| *MS*
is| ~ [ind] *MS*   susceptible| *fol. 15ʳ*   176 consider| ~ [as] *MS* (*underlined for retention
or reconsideration*)   possible so long as| *PC*: ~, ~ ~ ~ *1817*: possible in *MS*: possible, in *P*
177 the vital| *p. 14 1817*   178 system| ~ [has] *MS*   179 men shall subsist| *PC*, *1817*:
men.— *MS*: men.   *P* 179–80 beneficial innovations| /~ ~/ *MS* (*see* TN): ~ ~, *P, 1817*
180 caution,| *MS*: ~; *P, 1817*   181 freedom| *MS*, *PC*, *1817*: ~, *P*   friends of reform|
~ ~ ~ [comp] *MS*: friends of Reform *P*: Friends of Reform *1817*   182 despotism|
despositism *MS*   183 intire assent.—| *MS*: entire assent.ₐ *P, 1817*   184 favour
which| ~ [which Mʳ. Cobbett has placed already beyond the reach| ~, *MS*: ~, ~ *P, 1817*
185 mind.—| *MS*: ~.ₐ *P, 1817*   186 Universal Suffrage| *MS*, *1817*: universal suffrage *P*
I confess| ~ [cannot but] ~ *MS*   187 adoption| *MS*: ~, *P, 1817*   188 those who|
~ [~ pay a] *MS* (who *inadvertently deleted*)   190 present,| ~, [to poss] *MS*   members|
MS: Members *P, 1817*   Parliament| *fol. 16ʳ*   191 *immediate*| *PC*: immediate *MS, P,
1817* (*see* EC)   every| *PC*: every *MS*, *P*, *1817* (*see* 191 EC)   192 adult| *MS*: ~, *P, 1817*
place| ~ [the happiness| *MS*   193 It| *p. 15 1817*   195 endow| [qua] /~/ *MS*
196 unanswerable;| ~; [it is the right] *MS*   197 have| [be] ~ *MS*
198 unanswerable;| ~; [& who is bold enough to say that he would abolish the Lords & pull
down the King, careless of all the ruin & bloodshed that must ensue. I am intimately
persuaded that theoretically a pure republic is the| *MS*   199 irresistible,| *P, 1817*: ~ₐ
MS   200 and| [or] ~ *MS*   201 eminence| *fol. 17ʳ*   Yet, nothing| *PC*, *1817*:
[—]/Yet/ /Nothing/ *MS*: Nothing *P*   202 issue| *MS*: ~, *P, 1817*
203 aristocratical| ~ [powers be] *MS*   204 thro'| *MS*: through *P, 1817*
205 improvement,| *PC*, *1817*: improvent, *MS*: ~ₐ *P*   206 childhood.| ~. [Yet if the
[Pub] Nation wills| *MS* (*see* EC)

HISTORY OF A SIX WEEKS' TOUR

Collated: *1817*; Mary Shelley, *Journals* (*MWS*), selectively collated; *1840* (*K* = the
Koszul corrections noted in *Related Materials*).

15 sister| friend *1840* (*see* EC)   20 Meillerie| *1840*: Mellerie *1817*   36 It|
JOURNAL. | ~ *1840*   49 beautiful; there| beautiful; the sand slowly receded. There
MWS   52 produced a sea| became *MWS*   66 the gale| a wind that came in
violent ⟨g⟩usts *MWS*   93 A cabriolet is| Our ~ was *1840* (*subsequent tenses also
changed*)   99 harnesses were| harness was *1840*   131 ante-chamber| *1840*:
anti-chamber *1817*   135 and uninteresting| *MWS*, *1840*: om. *1817*   136 any|
MWS, *1840*: om. *1817*   156 my sister| as C*** *1840*   160 market| merchant
MWS   162 l'hôtesse| *1840*: L'Hôte *MWS, 1817*   192–3 Guignes, in . . . war.|
Guignes. There we heard that the Emperor Napoleon & some of his generals slept in the
same Inn. *MWS*   213–14 Cossacs. Nothing . . . advanced;| The houses were redu⟨c⟩ed
to heaps of white ruins, & the bridge was destroyed. *MWS*   224–6 St. Aubin . . .
dilapidated| St. Aubin a beautiful village situated among trees. This village was also
completely destroyed *MWS*   294 writing| ~ letters *1840*   360 Mort| Morre *K*
362 *plus*| *1840*: pas *1817*   382 Noé| Nodz *or* Nouaille *K*   384–90 While . . .
forest| at Noè, whilst our postillion waited, we walked into the forest of pines. It was a scene
of enchantment where every sound & sight contributed to charm. One mossy seat in the
deepest recesses of the wood was enclosed from the world by an impenetrable veil. *MWS*
397–409 At . . . The| ~ Maison Neuve he had left a message importing that he should

proceed to Pontalier 6 leagues distant, & that unless he found us there should return.—We dispatched a boy on horseback for him—he promised to wait for us at the next village. We walked two leagues in the expectation of finding him there. ~ *MWS*   398 Pontarlier| *1840*: Pontalier *1817* (T *so corrects subsequent spellings in 1817*)   410 and . . . fatigue| *om.* *MWS*   413 vallies| ~ which *MWS*, *1840*   enclosed| included *MWS* 417–18 journey, but . . . We| journey. We found, according to our expectation, that M. le voiturier had pursued his journey with the utmost speed. We *1840*   419 cart, and in| cart, S*** being unable to walk. The moon became yellow, and hung low close to the woody horizon. Every now and then sleep overcame me, but our vehicle was too rude and rough to permit its indulgence. I looked on the stars—and the constellations seemed to weave a wild dance, as the visions of slumber invaded the domains of reality. In *1840* (Shelley being . . . horizon. *MWS*)   420 conductor| driver *1840*   433 spots| scenes *MWS* 441 to us| *1840*: *om.* *1817*   450–9 We . . . across it.| *om. MWS*   459–60 range after range| Pile after pile *MWS*   460 extending one before| extending its craggy outline before *MWS*   462–3 but . . . heavens| *om. MWS*   467 they . . . earth| they are indeed mountains *MWS*   484–7 This . . . value.| *MWS*, *1840*: *om.* *1817* 487 value.| ~. On the 21st August, we left Neufchâtel, our Swiss friend accompanied us a little way out of the town. *1840* (*slightly recast from Mary Shelley's* MWS *entry*)   Lucerne| *1840*: this place *1817*   516 avalanche| *1840*: avelanche *1817*   560 supplied.| ~. Our amusement meanwhile was writing. S*** commenced a Romance on the subject of the Assassins, and I wrote to his dictation. *1840*   561 These| Our *1840* 562 situation. The| situation. At one time we proposed crossing Mount St. Gothard into Italy; but the *1840*   577 for| on *1840*   600 feet.| ~. Most of the passengers landed at this point, to re-embark when the boat had descended into smooth water—the boatmen advised us to remain on board. *1840*   623 who| they *1840* 682 *batelier*| *1840*: batalier *1817*   701 talked,| ~, and got tipsy *1840*   752 we for| *1840*: and for *1817*   767 Mary| ~ Wortley *1840*   768 T⟨h⟩iel| Triel *1817* (*present-day* Tiel)   785 rolled| backed *1840*   802 September| *1840*: August *1817* 804 Marsluys| Maasluis *K*   810 hills.| ~. During our stay at Marsluys, S*** continued his Romance. *1840*

LETTERS WRITTEN IN GENEVA

Collated: *1817*, *1840*, *Journals* (*MWS*).

Letter I: Letter to Peacock, 15 May 1816 (*L*); Middleton, *Shelley and his Writings*, i. 324 (*M*).

Letter III: Letter to Peacock, 17 July 1816, in *SC* 571, vii. 25–35.

Letter IV: Letter to Peacock, 22 July 1816 (*L*).

The Collation at times provides or refers to parallel rather than to identical passages from otherwise equivalent contexts and is not exhaustive.

Letter I

11–12 the last . . . Allies| *om. L*   35 mountain| *om. 1840*   43 Sometimes . . . descending| ~ ~ they *L, M*   44 the distorted trees| clothing the precipitous rocks & *L, M* 45 road| *M*: route *L*   46 regions| *M*: region *L*   then the| there these *L*   scattered| *M*: scantier *L*   46–7 and . . . trees| *om. L, M*   47 snow| the ~ *L, M*   55 dark| *om. 1840*   78 and stand| *M*: but ~ *L*   79 over| *M*: in *L*   81 or| nor *1840* 92 Gentlemen's| *1840*: Gentlemens' *1817*

Letter II

ADDRESS. C⟨haupuis,⟩| C****** *1817*: *Chapius 1840*   61–2 one to another| *1840*: to

one another *1817*   82 several⟨; and⟩ ... we] several, when you shall again hear of us;
and we *1817 (see* TN)

Letter III

HEADING. MEILLERIE—CLARENS—CHILLON]   MELLTERIE—CLAREN—
SCHILLON *1817*   5 enchantment] charm *SC*   9 We] 1st day. We *SC*
Montalègre] Montalegre with Lord B. his servant, & two bateliers *SC*   9–10 at ... arrived]
om. SC   10–23 at ... find.] *expands and recasts* At Hermance we saw a ruined tower,
one of four which the Genevese had demolished for their fortifications in 1560. The marks of
the chisels of Caesar's liberticide legions yet remain on the wall. I wondered at the massy
structure, cursed its builder & departed. *SC* 24–58 Leaving ... return.] *expands and recasts*
This night we slept at Nerni, and sat on the wall in the twilight watching the children at
play; most of the children (this is Savoy, the King of Sardinia's dominion) were exceedingly
deformed and ugly and very unlike those of Switzerland. One child however was far more
beautiful than I had ever seen. He was a boy of ten years old a model of grace both for mein
& motions, & with a countenance overflowing with such expression as made it more
beautiful than any mere combination of lineaments however exquisite.—Lord Byron, a new
convert to Wordsworth, reminded me of the Highland girl. *SC* 59–91 The ... Horace.]
expands and recasts 2d day. We passed the promontory of Ivoire, which bounds the western
side of the bay of Thonon, this bay is sheltered by an amphiatre of mountains (for the plain
ends here) luxiantly covered with interminable forests of chestnut & walnut & pine ... the
forests of pines become darker & more immense until the ice & snow mingle with the points
of naked rock that pierce the blue air. We pass the mouth of the river drance which descends
from between a chasm in the mountains & makes a plain near the lake intersected by its
divided streams. Thousands of besolets, beautiful water birds take their station where its
waters mingle with the lake Besolets are birds like seagulls but smaller & with purple on
their backs. As we approached Evian the mountains came nearer to the lake & masses of
wood & mountain overhung its shining spire. The day was changeable & wild. Gusts of
wind—sudden showers—then a warm south wind with summer clouds hanging thier white
volumes below the mountain tops with intervals of sky dazzlingly blue. When we arrived at
Evian flashes of lightning & thunderpeals suddenly came on, & continued after a black
cloud which brought them had dispersed. "Diespiter per pura tonantes egit equos." a
phenomenon I never witnessed before. *SC* 92–102 The ... Rhine.] *om. SC*   103 We] 3d
day. I must tell you now that our boat is English, very like, but somewhat larger [that of]
that with which we ascended the Thames. It is rigged with four sails & is exceedingly
manageable & convenient.—When we *SC*   106 Meillerie] Mellerie *1817*
114–29 How ... production.] *om. SC*   130 exile; but] ~. I had not yet read enough of
Julie to enjoy the scene as I do by retrospect. ~ *SC*   131–5 Groves ... thyme.] *recast
and shortened from* Groves of chestnuts overshadow it, magnificent & extensive forests to
which England affords no parallel. The grandeur & beauty of this scene augments with the
turn of every promontory. Loftier points of elevation descend still closer to the lake & on
high the aerial mountains cherish vast depths of snow in their ravines & the paths of their
winter torents. The rocks & forest open in parts & leave interstices of lawney expanse
covered with moss & odorous with thyme. thousands of delightful flowers unknown in
England cover these lawns. It makes a distinct picture in my memory from all other
mountain scenes which I have ever visited until now. *SC*   136–63 The ... shore.] *recast
and expanded from* We went from Mellerie to St Gingoux, & were overtaken by a
tremendous storm which made the waves at least 15 feet high. We all prepared for a swamp
as it was impossible to keep the smallest sail & the water began to break over the head. *SC*
164–72 St. ... visited.] *om. SC*   173–212 As ... unwillingly.] *recast and expanded from*
In the evening we went to see the Rhône enter the lake among its pines & willows—strange
mixture! We went thither through chestnut woods beneath mighty mountains & turning to

the right proceeded as far as the Tour de Beaverie, separating La Suisse & Savoie. We saw the snowy mountains of La Valais, & the gigantic couch of the Rhône thro the portcullised gateway & returned. (*par.*) Day 4th We left St Gingoux & crossed the lake leaving Villeneuve an old wretched town to the right & landed at the Château de Chillon. The waters of the Rhône mixed with the blue lake turbidly. *SC*   212–18 I . . . were] *recast from* I read Julie all day. I forgot its prejudices—it is an overflowing of sublimest genius & more than mortal sensibility.—It ought to be read amongst its own scenes which it has so wonderfully peopled. Mellerie, Chillon Clarens the mountains of La Valais & Savoy are monuments of the being of Rousseau. like the valley path of a mighty river—whose waters are indeed exhausted but which has made a chasm among the mountains that will endure forever. The feelings excited by this Romance have suited my creed, which strongly inclines to immaterialism—The beings who inhabit this romance, were *SC* (*see* EC)   221–45 We . . . escape!] *recast and expanded from* We saw the Castle of Chillon; it is an old castle built on a rock by the Lake which close to the very walls is 800 feet perpendicular deep.—The dungeons of this castle are excavated below the lake & have outlets which connect with it by the means of which it could be let in upon the prisoners by the sudden opening of the sluice. The large dungeon is supported on seven carved columns whose outbranching capitals support the roof. A narrow cell is near it, & beyond one large & far more lofty & quite dark supported by three unornamented arches Across one of these arches was a beam now black & rotten on which prisoners were hung in secret.—a terrible monument was this castle altogether of the tyranny of that loathsome superstition which the great Tacitus so prophetically announced as the pernicies humani generis. There at the reformation thousands pined to death for religious disbelief. The exterior of the Castle is not at all remarkable, & only constructed for strength. *SC*   256 trees;] ∼.—All breathed the spirit of Rousseau—*SC*   259–66 who . . . them?] *om. SC*   275–7 We . . . absent.] *om. SC* (*see* EC)   278–90 We . . . sublime.] *om. SC*   301 afar.] ∼. As we approached Ouchy the spires of Lausanne shone behind. *SC*   301–5 In . . . up.] *om. SC* 309–14 from . . . solitary] *om. SC*   315–23 My . . . Gibbon.] *om. SC*   329 fire.] ∼. The waves broke over the pier. *SC* (*see* EC)

Letter IV

15 eight in the morning.] 8. having taken horses beforehand *MWS*   64–7 Martin . . . recesses.] Martin. Clouds had overspread the evening & hid the summit of Mont Blanc—Its base was visible from the Balcony of the Inn. *MWS*   64 (called . . . Sallanches)] *see* TN 74–5 more profound . . . mountains] profounder as it approached the regions of snow *L* 94 thawing] *om. L*   96 of natural curiosities] *om. L*   100 stag kind] goat kind but considerably larger *L*   101 twenty-seven] 25 *L*   122 vast . . . space] great number of miles *L*   126 above] ∼—was close to our very footsteps *L*   144 saw . . . themselves] saw the torrent also spread itself *L*   145 couch.] ∼.—We arrived at Chamounix at 6 o'Clock *L*   146 intended] designed *L*   *des Bossons*] de Boissons *1817, 1840* (T *corrects subsequent spellings*)   147 descends] comes *L*   148 least] leisure *L*   150 pyramidical] pyramidal *L*   172 rush] fall *L* 180–1 pinnacles, which . . . silver] pinnacles. *L*   186 descended] been *L* 195 irresistible] ∼ progress of the *L*   204–5 to . . . base] *om. L*   217 existence] subsistence *L*   222 globe] earth *L*   223–4 by . . . earth] *om. L* 227 adamantine] unsparing *L*   232 most] all *L*   235 disdain to regard.] disdain. It presents views, a development of which I reserve for conversation. *L*   237 slanting] flat *L*   237–8 of Montanvert . . . Ice] *om. L*   249 mountain.] ∼.—The guide continually held that which Mary rode. *L*   250 stones] ∼ detached from the rock above *L*   253 descent] fall *L*   259–61 upon them. . . . they] there. They *L* 273 bursts] rises *L*   274–6 The . . . moment.] *recasts* From the precipices which surround it the echo of rocks which fall from their aerial summits, or of the ice & snow

scarcely ceases for one moment. *L*   277 like ... animal] was a living being *L*
280 clear.] ~. We met I lament to say some English people here. I will not detail to you the
melancholy exhibitions of tourism which altho they emanate from the profusion &
exigences of these vulgar great corrupt the manners of the people, & make this place another
Keswick. But the inhabitants of Cumberland are not for a moment to be compared with
these people, on whose stupidity, avarice & imposture engenders a mixture of vices truly
horrible & disgusting. *L*   280–3 We ... o'clock.] In the evening we returned to
Chamo[u]nix. *L*   286 sunset] ⟨?sunrays⟩ *L* (*Jones's conjecture*)   287 shone] *om. L*
288–90 the ... heads] *om. L*   303 vales.] ~∧ and destroying many persons. *L*
313 the sick] ~ blood of the ~ *L*   314 all] *om. L*   328 Adieu.] *om. L* (*see* EC)

FRAGMENT ON REFORM (*I*)

Collated: MS, J.

TITLE. *None in MS*   1 The] *fol. 282ʳ*   bound ... the] [at issue together with] the /~
... ~/ *MS* (the *inadvertently retained*)   3 abolish the] [cast down those] /~ ~/ *MS*
3–4 those impostures] /th[at]ose/ imposture/s/ *MS*   4 sanctity.] ~. [In the great
question] [They claimed to be governed] [The year   was the crisis when [the crisis] it]
MS (*see* EC)   7 benefit] ~ [the institutions] *MS*   it was declared,] [it was desirable
that a system of so] /~ ~ ~∧/ *MSe*: ~ ~ ~∧ or declaimed that *J*   8 subsist.] ~. [Most] [It]
MS   9 of] *fol. 283ʳ*   as to] [what should be] /~ ~/ *MS*   of] ~ [the institutions] *MS*
12 thousands] ~ [famished] [of naked & famished wretches] *MS*   13 thro'] thro *MS*
famished,] ~∧ *MSe*   14 houseless] homeless *J*   cottages] [the] ~ *MS*   tenantless]
tenanted *J*   whilst] ~ [new] *MS*

FRAGMENT OF 'A REFUTATION OF DEISM'

Collated: MS; *A Refutation of Deism* (1814); K.

TITLE. *None in MS*   1 The] *fol. 1ʳ*   2 be] he *K*   4 of] [to] /~/ *MS*: *om. K*
7 its] ~ A *K*   15 proofs] prroofs *MS*   then] [then] *MS* (*deleted, then underlined in
pencil for retention*)   18 in] *fol. 1ᵛ*   in ... Deity.] *in pencil in MS*   20–34 ine ...
ntrivance] *see* TN   20 structure] s̆tructure *MS*   25 shall be] [has] /~/ ~[en] *MS*
27 philosophical] ?*par. MS*   30 thence infer] infer *K*   a] the *1814*   33 popular]
?*par. MS*   34 ntrivance?] ntrivance? [This | tion of the mind] *MS*   35 Simply] *fol.
2ʳ*   37–8 if having no] [had we no] /~ ~ ~/ *MS*   38 knowledge] previous
knowledge *1814, K*   contrivance of art] artificial contrivance *1814* (*see* TN)   we had]
[and] /~/ ~ [we] *MS*   accidentally] /~/ *MS*   39 have been] /have/ be/en/ *MS*
41–2 the attempt] any attempt *1814*   44 some philosophers have attempted] you
attempt *1814*   49–50 But our entire ignorance] But [we are] /our/ entire[ly]
ignoran[t]ce *MS*: Our entire ignorance, therefore, *1814*   51 defective] [imperfect] /~/
MS   52 What] [Why]~ *MS*   then remains] remains *1814*   55 that] [w] /t/hat
MS   whose] wh[ich]/ose/ *MS*   56 invariable] changeless *1814*   systems] *fol. 2ᵛ*
57 thro'] thro *MS*   veins] viens *MS*   58 insect's] insects *MS*   lymph] [?blood]~
MS   61 for] [to]~ *MS*   63 we ... proposition] have we arrived at the substance
of your assertion *1814*   66 could] would *1814*   67 eternity,] ~∧ *MSe*
derives] must have derived *1814*   69 respects] respect *1814*   does ... from] do
these arguments apply to *1814*   Universe?] ~, and not apply to God? *1814*
70 admirable] *om. 1814*   70–3 end the Deist ... conspicuous] end you infer the
necessity of an intelligent Creator. But if the fitness of the Universe, to produce certain
effects, be thus conspicuous *1814*   70 infers] ~ [a God] *MS*   70–1 that ...

created.] /~ ... ~./ MS   71–3 How ... evident,] *om.* K   73 more] ~ exquisite
1814   75 from ... arrangement] /~ ... ~/ MS   77 feel] perceive *1814*: percieve
K   78 whose] *fol. 3ʳ*   79 The] *par. 1814, K*   81 their] his *1814*   than ...
foregoing] /~ ... ~/ MS   82 these premises] the premises which you have stated *1814*
85 The] *no par. 1814, K*   88 proved] clearly proved *1814, K*   94 increase]
encrease *1814*   95 burden] burthen *1814*   99 effects; but there] ~; But ~MS:
effects. There *1814, K*   100 inherent] *fol. 3ᵛ*   104 Eternal, Omniscient and
Omnipotent Being,] eternal Omnipotent and Omniscient Being, *1814*   HEADING. Of]
fol. 4ʳ   Of ... existence] *om. 1814*   106–7 God ... Universe.] *om. 1814*
106 God may be defined] [The word] ~ ~ ~ [thus] ~ MS   an] [the]~ MS
107–8 believe in this Being] really believe in God *1814*   108 the thousands] ~
[multitudes] /~/ MS   prevented] prevent[ing]ed MS   109 one thought] a serious
thought *1814*   to the] and the *1814*   110 butterflies,] ~ₐ *MSe*   monkeys,] ~ₐ MS
111 abstractions,] ~ₐ MS   113–15 Certainly ... mind.] *om. 1814*   113 reasoning]
[propositions] /~/ MS   117 mankind,] ~. MS   118 a snake, an ape] ~ ~ₐ ~ ~
MS: an ape, a snake *1814*   calabash,] ~ₐ MS   119–23 The ... Cause] *om. 1814*
124 But ... mind.] There is a tendency to devotion, a thirst for reliance on supernatural aid
inherent in the human mind. *1814*   125 any] *fol. 4ᵛ*   128–30 they ... conceive.]
they firmly confide in the holiness and power of these symbols, and thus own their
connexion with what they can neither see nor perceive. *1814*   132 strictly consistent]
in strict consistency *1814*   134 those] the[e]ose MS: the *1814*   136 sacrifizes
and prayers] prayers and sacrifices *1814*   138 beneficence] benevolence *1814*
malevolence] malignity *1814*   139–40 by supplications] ~ [abjectness &] ~ MS
141 fury] anger *1814*   144 and] *fol. 5ʳ*   146 source then of] source of *1814*
147 winds,] ~ₐ MS   149 in his own mind] within himself *1814*   150 is
instigated] ~ [impelled by] ~ MS   151–7 The ... occurrence.] *parallels 1814, ll. 931–6*
151 arriving,] ~, /Mankind/ MS (*irrelevant marginal notation*)

ON CHRISTIANITY

Collated: e. 4; c. 4; Shelley Memorials (1859); K; J; TT. (Readings from the Garland
'Bodleian Shelley Manuscripts' series facsimile edition of the Bod. e. 4 notebook
are collated here and in TN as *e. 4(D)*.)

TITLE. *None in e. 4*   1 The] *e. 4, fol. 7ʳ*   2 Christ.] ~. [Two hundred
millions of the race of man call upon his name as their Redeemer & their God.] *e. 4*
3 devotional] [religious] /~/ *e. 4*   5 authority] ~, [& are imbued in some slight degree
by the Spirit of his doctrines] *e. 4*   5–6 from ... are] /~ ... ~/ *e. 4*   6–7 and to a
certain extent are [imbued by ⟨their⟩ spirit.]] & to a certain extent are [imbued by the spirit
of his doctrines] *K, TT: om. 1859*   7 He is the God] he is the hero, the God, *1859*
8–9 doctrines, his] ~, [the]~ *e. 4*   12 man] ~ [have] *e. 4*   17 walked] *fol. 7ᵛ* (J.C.
actually heads the leaf)   thro'] thro *e. 4*   19 to] to *e. 4* (*see* TN)   22 I] *c. 4 begins
here (fol. 276ʳ), no par.*   controversy] [dispute] /~/ *c. 4*   indeed] ~ [there is] *c. 4*
24 was] [be] /~/ *c. 4*   whatever] ~ [divine] [of] *c. 4*   27 The remarkable] [J.C. was
born in a humble station & in a country remote from the metropolis of the civilised world.]
~ ~, *c. 4*   28 historians] ~ [among his immediate followers who] *c. 4*
30 genius,] ~ₐ *c. 4*   virtues,] ~ₐ *c. 4*   these] the[y]se *c. 4*   32 tale.] ~. [They relate
a series of events to which] [/They relate no/] [/It is a/] *c. 4*   32–3 It ... truth.] /~ ...
~ₐ/ *c. 4*   33 Every] every *c. 4*   34–5 with ... particulars] /~ /~ regard to [in] some
of [the] /its/ ... ~/ *c. 4*   35 events.] ~ₐ *c. 4 MSe*   A man] *fol. 276ᵛ*
36 perishes] perish[ing]es *c. 4*   stern] ?sten *c. 4*   37 tyranny,] ~ₐ *c. 4 MSe*
superstition.] ~. [What alone may be considered as unparrallelled is the wisdom & the

gentleness [of] of the] *c. 4*   He refuses,] he refuses∧ *c. 4*   38 the torturing] th[is]e ~
c. 4   40 on] o[f]n *c. 4*   42–3 is ... make] /~ ... can/ can ~ *c. 4* (can *repeated*)
44 heart,] ~, [is] *c. 4*   the] [a]~ *c. 4*   46 unparalleled] unparrallelled *c. 4*   the ...
mankind] [human annals] /~ ... ~/ *c. 4*   46–7 the human race] [mankind] /~ ~ ~/ *c. 4*
48 be] *fol. 277ʳ*   a God] a *is obscured by* G *in c. 4*   48–9 the profound wisdom] ~
[wisdom] ~ ~ [of the] [obscurely visible,] *c. 4*   51 for] [to produce] /~/ *c. 4*
52 men.—] ~.— | The Esseneians 195.111 *c. 4* (*see* EC)   53 The birth] [The period of] the
birth *c. 4*   55 race.] ~. [The m] [Liberty & heroism] *c. 4*   splendour] [magnificence]
/~/ *c. 4*   Roman] roman *c. 4*   56 vanished.] ~. [Sentiments of liberty & heroism
[survived] no] [no longer inspired] *c. 4*   57 and power] & [/they put/] [honour]
/power/ *c. 4*   57–8 no longer] /~ ~/ *c. 4*   59 lived] *fol. 277ᵛ*   61 they
were] [it]~ [was]~ *c. 4*   64 on] ~ [the] *c. 4*   65 The] [The] ~ *c. 4*
65–6 they accurately corresponded] [their]~ [were pernicious] /~ ~/ *c. 4*   67 letters] ~
[unnaturally] *c. 4*   natural] national *J*   71 care.] ~. [Men] *c. 4*   72 slave,] ~,
(*fol. 278ʳ*) [or] [all sti] *c. 4*   73 prerogative] prerogation *J*   74 a system] ~
[calculated] ~ *c. 4*   75 ascertained that] [estimated] /~/ ~ [the precise] *c. 4*
inclined] upturned *J*   76 minutest] smallest *J*   76–7 as intellectual objects
betray] ~ [mind may with greater facility be] /~ ~/ ~[ed] *c. 4*   77 their ... readily] /~
... ~/ *c. 4*   pursuer] presence *J*   78 pleasures] ~ [challenged] *c. 4*   hence] Hence
c. 4   82 affections] ~ [having] *c. 4*   84 men,] ~∧ *c. 4 MSe*   serpent's] serpents
c. 4   85 venom.] ~. | The [national religion of the Roman world] *c. 4* (The *inadvertently
retained*)   86 Meanwhile] *no par. c. 4* (*fol. 278ᵛ*): The meanwhile *J* (*see* 86TN)
88 few ... affairs] [no consequences] /~ ... ~/ *c. 4*   89 of] o[n]f *c. 4*   90 state.] ~.
[Any action or series of actions is to be pronounced beneficial or the contrary when [the
result] after a comparison of the good & evil [they] it contains the result which remains shall
be ascertained & estimated. This process is eminently difficult.] *c. 4*   which] [of] /~/ *c. 4*
91 essentially] ~ [unjust] *c. 4*   93 Rome ... republics] the /Rome & of the Greek/
Roman republic/s/ *c. 4* (*see* EC)   Rome] [it] /~/ *c. 4*   94 was] ~ [inseparably] *c. 4*
96 by] *fol. 279ʳ*   97 Polytheism] [religion of] ~ *c. 4*   98 belief] [faith] /~/ *c. 4*
tranquillize] [repress] /~/ *c. 4*   99 from] ~ [& from] *c. 4*   100 mind.] ~.
[Connected with the religion of Rome was its moral system: the thirst for glory] [/An
important moral system, which carried with it/] *c. 4*   faith] ~ [gradually recieved its]
c. 4   101 [and] lost] [& gradually lost] lost *c. 4* (& *inadvertently deleted*)
104 splendid devotions] [ostentatious & splendid virtues] /~ ~/ *c. 4*   105 such] [the]
[/to/] /~/ *c. 4*   Scævola,] ~∧ *c. 4*   107 allotted] [due] /~/ *c. 4*   108 accurate]
fol. 279ᵛ   maxims] [feelings] [/knowledge/] /~/ *c. 4*   duty] [duties] /~/ *c. 4*
109 replace the ... of] ~ [an unrefined & barbarous impetuosity] [the springs of which] /~
... ~/ *c. 4*   which derived no] [deriving no] /~ ~ ~/ *c. 4*   110 from] ~ [custom &]
c. 4: ~ custom and *TT*   immemorial] immemmoral *c. 4*   and which] /&/ ~ *c. 4*
112 science,] ~, [had] [matured the] [silently] *c. 4*   to] ~ [the] *c. 4*   120 assent] ~
[indispensable to all] *c. 4*   121 was] *c. 4 ends here*   HEADING. God.] *e. 4* (*fol. 8ᵛ, 8ʳ*
blank): *om. 1859*   122 The ... which] [God, the most venerable of names]
[The meaning of] /~ ... ~/ *e. 4*   God,] ~, [is] [varies] [suggests various] *e. 4*
123–5 The ... differ] ~ Stoic, the Platonist, & the Epicurean, the Polytheist, the Dualist,
and the Trinitarian, ~ *1859*   124 Dualist] [Manic] ~ *e. 4*   127 names,] ~∧
e. 4 MSe   a] [th] ~ *e. 4*   devised] [calculated] /~/ *e. 4*   132 influencings]
influences *1859*   133 opinions] opinion *1859*, K, J, TT   134 interes⟨ting)]
J: interes *e. 4 MSe*: ⟨interesting) *1859*   135 term.] ~∧ *e. 4 MSe*   136 We]
[He probably] ~ *e. 4*   138 his] *fol. 9ʳ*   139 his] [the]~ *e. 4*   141 years,]
~∧ *e. 4*   142 meditations.] ~∧ *e. 4*   143 *Job*,] Job, *e. 4*   had] ~ [probably]
e. 4   145 *Ecclesiastes*] Ecclesiastes *e. 4*   147 heart] ~
     Mr. Malthus book *e. 4* (*see* 146EC)   148 sad] [?mild] /~/ *e. 4*
152 sanctioning] sanction[it]ing *e. 4*   154 both from] from *1859*   155 from the]

the *1859*   156 Jupiter] [Jehovah of the Jews,] ~ *e. 4*   157 thro'] thro *e. 4*
things] *blotted in e. 4*   158 the terrestrial] /~/ ~ [fire] *e. 4*   element] *fol. 9ᵛ*
161 Jesus Christ] J.C. *e. 4*   162 interfused] ⟨interpoint⟩ *1859*   163 Spirit] ~ [of
all] [the Power] [the ?term] *e. 4*   energy] [Power] ~ *e. 4*   164 It is important] [It is
important] *e. 4 (underlined for retention)*   165 Christian] Xtian *e. 4*   173 they]
[thier]~ *e. 4*   blessed] ~ [ind] *e. 4*   174 soul,] ~, ?& *e. 4*   175 conscious] *fol.*
10ʳ   deceit,] [sin] ~ₐ *e. 4*   176 no thought,] ~[thing] ~ₐ *e. 4*   of thought,] ~ ~ₐ
e. 4 MSe   179 What!] ~[ ] *e. 4 (illegible point)*   180 Heaven, shall] Heaven? Shall
1859   181 gaze] *perhaps* gase *e. 4*   183 These are] [Away with] /~ ~/ *e. 4*
184 visionary] ~ [vulgar] *e. 4*   186 dwarfish ... conceptions] [designs] /~ ... ~/ *e. 4*
and] or *1859, K, J, TT*   Jesus] *par. 1859*   has] *om. TT*   187 than] tha[t]n *e. 4*
expressed—that] ~. ~ *e. 4*   189 genius,] ~ₐ [& the] *e. 4*   190 poet,] ~. *e. 4*
not] *om. K (see 190 TN)*   true,] ~ₐ ⟨because⟩ *1859 (see 190 TN)*   192 God, it has]
[What] ~ₐ ~ is ~ *e. 4 (is inadvertently retained)*   contemplated] [considered] /~/ *e. 4*
every] *fol. 10ᵛ*   193 contemplated] ~ [him] *e. 4*   194–5 express the] ~ ~
[collective] *e. 4*   196 world.] ~. [The human] *e. 4*   therefore ... simple] ~ [the
simple & the sincere shall] /no more than that/ a a ~ *e. 4 (redundant a inadvertently retained)*
197 an] [that requisite] [the most es] ~ *e. 4*: the *1859*   knowledge] science /~/ *e. 4*: science
1859, K, J, TT (see TN)   198 happiness.] ~. [[If God is infinite, every atom /& every
thought/ of the ?moral & material world must be pervaded by his spirit]] *e. 4 (see TN)*
200 the] ~ [surrounding] *e. 4*   201 surrounded.] ~ₐ *e. 4 MSe*   Whosoever] *par. 1859*
204 and the] & *1859*   autumn,] Autumnₐ *1859, K, J, TT*   205 solitary] /~/ *e. 4*:
softened *1859*   206 or destroyer] /~ ~/ *e. 4*   flatterer,] ~ₐ *e. 4*   206–7 may
walk] /~/ ~[s] *e. 4*   209 God.] ~ₐ *e. 4 (fol. 11ʳ)*   210 confidence,] confidene, *e. 4*
214 God.] ~ₐ *e. 4 MSe*   215 We] [For the] ~ *e. 4*   216 arbiters] rulers /~/ *e. 4*
217 own] /~/ *e. 4*   masters] ~ /arbiters/ *e. 4 (see TN)*   220 breath] breath *e. 4*
221 imperial] imperial *e. 4*   stupendous] stupendous *e. 4*   qualities,] ~, [are] *e. 4*
222 and] & the *1859, K, J, TT*   223 to the inferiour] ~ [its] ~ [its] ~ *e. 4*   indeed]
/~/ *e. 4*: *om. 1859*   225 omnipresent] omnipotent *1859*   Power] [p]~ *e. 4*
226 periods] [moments] /~/ *e. 4*   227 been] ~ [moulded by] *e. 4*   will,] ~ₐ *TT*
so] [that] /~/ *e. 4*   a] /~/ *e. 4*: [~] *1859, K, J, TT*   228 of] ~ [po] *e. 4*   powers,]
power *1859*   of] *fol. 11ᵛ*   230 That] [The] ~ *e. 4*   231 assertions] ~. [The
truth] [Both of] *e. 4*   231–2 The former of] /~ ~ ~/ *e. 4*   232 is] [may be
considered as] /~/ *e. 4*   234 institutor] nature *1859*   235 They ... it] *om. 1859*
it] ~ [seems that whosoever] *e. 4 (see TN)*   236 Thucydides] Thucydydes *e. 4*
instances] ~ /from/ *e. 4*   237–42 establish ... ειρηται] *om. 1859*   237 establish
this opinion:] establish th[e]is [difficulty of relating speeches] /opinion/ *e. 4*
242 ειρηται.] ~ₐ *e. 4*   243 Tacitus] *fol. 12ʳ: par. 1859, K, J, TT*   244 supreme,]
~ₐ *e. 4 MSe*   245 temples."] ~ₐ" *e. 4*   The] [It may be] [God] the *e. 4*
246 which deny] [by] /~/ [?been] ~[ing] *e. 4*   247 existences.] ~. [So soon as] *e. 4*
253 of] ~ [God] *e. 4*   254 ordinar⟨il⟩y] ordinarily *1859, K, J, TT*
255 virtuous,] ~ₐ *e. 4*   258 disapprobation.] dissaprobation. [That most pernicious
propensity in human nature to [inflict] derive satisfaction] *e. 4*   261 man:] ~ₐ *e. 4*
enemies, bless] ~ₐ ~ ⟨fol. 12ᵛ⟩ *e. 4*   262 the] *om. TT*   Father] ~ [tha] *e. 4*
267 compassion!] *perhaps* ~? *e. 4*   267–8 They ... him] ~ [have] /have ... ~/ *e. 4*
268 asserting] assert[ed]ing *e. 4*   269 this] the *1859, K, J, TT*   earth] ~ [all] *e. 4*
270 influencings] influences *1859*   271 of] /~/ *e. 4*   272 to] [the]~ *e. 4*
creatures of] ~ [all]~ *e. 4*   274 scheme] ~ [whereby when the body moulders] *e. 4*
277 then] /~/ *e. 4*   278 And] *par. e. 4*   279 supposition] suppo[si]tion *fol. 13ʳ*
280 moral] /~/ *e. 4*   281 improved] emproved *K, TT*   tortures] tortures—it *1859*
284 Jesus Christ] J.C. *e. 4*   288 God;] ~; [that is, if ye would [be a] cultivate true virtue]
e. 4   289 example] ~ [& ?model] *e. 4*   is] ~ [benignant] *e. 4*   291 large]
perhaps huge *e. 4*   292 protracted] protraicted *e. 4*   294 to] ~ [the f] *e. 4*

295 other] ~ [?shall] *e. 4*   297 the purest] purest *1859, K, J, TT*   action is] ~; ⟨this⟩
~ *1859*   298 justice.] ~. [Whatsoever] [The words mercy (*fol. 13ᵛ*) & justice which
have been] To [confound the words of justice & mercy [is the] has ever been the
of slavery & imposture] *e. 4* (To *inadvertently retained*)   299 Inslaved] Inslavd *e. 4: om.*
1859   to] by *K*   300 their] these *K, TT*   mankind] [cannot distinguish between]
e. 4   receives] recieeves *e. 4*   301 and] or *1859, K, J, TT*   302 atchieved]
achieved *1859, TT*: atcheeved *K* (*see* TN)   303 country] ~ [/has/] [acquires] *e. 4*
304 possessing] posessing *e. 4*   304–5 slay and torture] [slay & torture] (*underlined for*
retention) [/thousands of ?good/] he [contented himself] *e. 4*: slay *1859* (he *inadvertently*
retained)   306 and arrogat⟨ed⟩] /&/ arrogating *e. 4*: arrogating *1859, K, J, TT*
himself] ~ [that] *e. 4*   merit] ~[, which] *e. 4*   307 only] /~/ *e. 4*
308 enormous deeds] deeds *1859*: ⟨~⟩ ~ *K, TT*   311 murdered] ~ [from] *e. 4*   him.]
~. [If to be merciful is to be benevolent & just these men are the benefactors of mankind] *e. 4*
313 said,] ~ₐ *e. 4* MSe   was] *fol. 14ʳ*   314 friend. Most] friend, most *K, TT*
316 *venerable and dear*] venerable and dear *1859, K, J, TT* (*see* EC)   317 country,] ~ₐ
e. 4   319 *father and their friend.*] father and their friend. *1859, K, J, TT:* ~ ~ ~ ~.
x/Note/ *e. 4* (*see* EC)   320 have] ~, *e. 4*   322 sacrifice] sacrifices *1859*   They]
~ [desired that] *e. 4*   323 bloodshed] blood shed *e. 4*   324 thought,] ~ₐ *e. 4 MSe*
participate] participitate *e. 4*   327 they] [their]~ *e. 4*   328 Jesus Christ] J.C. *e. 4*
330 and upon the] and *1859*   unjust.] ~. [If whatever ha] *e. 4*   332 incompatible] *fol.*
14ᵛ   to] ~ [render impossible] *e. 4*   inaccessible even to] ~ /~/ ~ *e. 4:* inaccessible to
1859   333 influencings] influences *1859*   334 propensities] ~ [Such does Jesus
Christ represent the character of God] *e. 4*   336 consistently] consistenly *e. 4*
338 good.] God. *1859*   339 enjoying.] ~. [because God is the model & example] *e. 4*
340 Jesus Christ] J.C. *e. 4*   [Power]] [~] ? *e. 4:* ₐ~ₐ *1859, K*   or] and *1859*   thro'] thro
e. 4   341 models] ~ /clothes/ *e. 4* (*see* EC)   343 nature] [virtue]~ *e. 4*
343–4 Jesus Christ] J.C. *e. 4*   346 Jesus Christ] J.C. *e. 4*   347 Thus] This *1859*
348 certain,] ~ₐ *e. 4*   Jesus Christ] J.C. *e. 4*   represents] *underlined or deleted in e. 4*
350 motive] *fol. 15ʳ*   351 cause] ~ [acts] *e. 4*   352 it] ~ [can] it *e. 4*
353 benevolent] bene[ficent]/volent/ *e. 4:* beneficent *1859*   slightest] ~ [unnec] *e. 4*
355 case,] ~, . *e. 4*   358 ground,] ~, [worms shall eat] *e. 4*   thro'] thro *e. 4*
362 neither hear nor see,] *om. 1859*   364 surrounded.—] ~ₐ *e. 4*   364–5 They
... is] /~ ... ~/ *e. 4*   ⟨to⟩ the grave] *J:* to graves; *1859*   365 "there is] *e. 4:* then?
1859 (*see* EC)   365–6 ⟨no ... wisdom".⟩] *TT* (*first suggested by K*)   366 we] ~ [are]
e. 4   dust, a] ~; to ~ *1859*   368 fallacious,] ~, [& that instead of [becoming] *e. 4:* ~,
and *1859, K, J, TT*   369 conception] ~, [of] *e. 4*   371 Another] *fol. 15ᵛ*
373 misery,] ~ₐ *e. 4*   pain,] ~ₐ *e. 4*   374 the evil Spirit] evil spirits *1859*   extends]
Extends *e. 4*   375 irradiations] ?Irradiations *e. 4*   376 that] ~ [has] *e. 4*
379 varies] [vary]~ *e. 4:* varyes *K:* var⟨i⟩es *TT*   when] *perhaps* where *e. 4*   cease] *e. 4 has*
an x *over the* 'a'   380 untram⟨mel⟩led] *perhaps* untainted *e. 4:* untrammelled *1859:*
unt⟨rammel⟩led *K, J, TT:* untamled *e. 4(D)*   385 affections] ~ [whic] *e. 4:* feelings
1859   thro'] thro *e. 4*   389 fulfilment] *fol. 16ʳ*   [and]] [& most] *e. 4:* ₐ~ₐ *1859, K,*
J, TT   391 Jesus Christ] J.C. *e. 4*   languor] langour *e. 4*   392 All] all *e. 4*
394 with] /~/ *e. 4* (*pencil*): ⟨~⟩ *K* (*see* TN)   the nature of our being;] *om. 1859, K, J* (*see* TN)
396–7 and illustrious] *om. 1859*   397 is] [a]~ *e. 4*   400 is impatient,] /~ ~ₐ/ [is]
e. 4: ~ ~ₐ and *1859, K, J, TT*   401 which] ~ [his own perishable] *e. 4*
402 portion] potion *1859*   405 the picture] th[is]e picture [was] *e. 4:* this picture *1859,*
K, J, TT   it] is *1859*   heartmoving] heart-moving *1859, K, J, TT*   406 lovely;] ~,
e. 4   hope,] ~ₐ *e. 4 MSe*   407 mortal] morbid *1859*   fear and] /fear &/ *e. 4*
anguish,] ~ₐ *e. 4*   consist] [be the torturing of] /~/ *e. 4*   millions] *fol. 16ᵛ*   408 of
torture] /~ ~/ [of] *e. 4*   omniscient] omni[potent]/scient/ *e. 4*   411 enslaved] *or*
inslaved *e. 4*   for] of *TT*   412 Nations] *par. e. 4*   414 ten] [two]~ *e. 4*
416 with] [th]~ *e. 4*   417 desolation.] ~. [It is human to ?envy] [It is human to desire

that what others posess should be our own] *e. 4*   417–18 The ... revenge] /~ ... ~/
e. 4 (pencil)   417 spirit] ⟨~⟩ *TT*   418 been] /~/ *e. 4*   in] [on]~ *e. 4*
419 Retaliation] ~ [of injuries] *e. 4*   remedy] ~ [of] *e. 4*   421 repetition.] ~. [Thus,
the serpent is avoided because its bite is mortal, & it lives securely in the recesses of the
wilderness.] [Thus] *e. 4*   422 measure [of]] /~/ [portion of] *e. 4*   received.] recieved.
[Then] *e. 4*   423 from] of *1859*   424 no ... from] /~ ... ~/ *e. 4*   the] ~
[robber] *(fol. 17ʳ) e. 4*   destroys ... or] /~ ... ~/ *e. 4*   427 remembrance,] ~, [or
from] *e. 4*   that] ~ [men may know the] *e. 4*   428 clearly] /~/ *e. 4*   and feel] /&
feel/ *e. 4*   peace] [rig] ~ *e. 4*   of] ~ [the comm] *e. 4*   429 society.] ~. [?Pursuing]
e. 4   Such] such [principles] *e. 4*   arising] [ari]sing *e. 4 (inadvertent deletion)*
431 An Athenian soldier in] /~ ~/ [A] ~ [of] /~/ *e. 4*   433 being] [was] /~/ *e. 4*
434 Persians] Persian/s/ [King] [invaded Greece] [to] [to retaliate] [considered] *e. 4*
437 ruin] ~ [A] *e. 4*   438 Græcian] ~ [nations] *e. 4*   was] ~ [laid wa] [utterly
destroyed,] *e. 4*   burned ... ground,] /~ ... ~ₐ/ *e. 4 MSe*   439 contain⟨ed⟩.]
containing *e. 4*: contained ⟨destroyed⟩. *1859*: ⟨was⟩ containing. *K*   439–40 The ...
?tracery] /~ ... ?~/ *e. 4*: om. *1859*: The ... & the *given as a footnote in K*   440 markets,]
~ₐ e. 4   columns,] ~ₐ *e. 4*   442 impotent] im[potent *fol. 17ᵛ*   447 this]
the[e]/is/ [career of this leader] *e. 4*   consummation ... ruin] /~ ... ~/ *e. 4*   448 If]
[If] ~ *e. 4*   449 engines] [instruments] /~/ *e. 4*   450 aggression] [attack] ~ *e. 4*
451 falshood] falsehood *1859, K, J, TT*   which] ~ [these] *e. 4*   452 deluded and
goaded] [hastening] /deluded & goaded/ *e. 4 (pencil insertion)*   deluded ... ruin] om. *1859*
ruin] ~, *e. 4*   454 and extend] /~ ~/ *e. 4*   real] ~ /destin/ *e. 4*   man,] ~ₐ *e. 4*
455 society.] ~! *1859, K, J, TT*   456 on] in *1859*   science from] ~ [on] /~/ *e. 4*:
science, upon *1859*: science, on *K, TT*   457 happiness and the power] power and
happiness *1859, K, J, TT*   458 of the] ~ ~ [extin] *e. 4*   459 Zerxes] Xerxes *1859,
K, J, TT*   460 outrage?] ~? [& in ?its] *e. 4*   461 of spoliation] *fol. 18ʳ*
former?] ~? [The serpent is avoided & des ?ly] [All things] [/All men/ make war upon the
serpent because its bite is mortal, because it inflicts death upon the heel that tramples it.
?But] *e. 4*   462 in this instance] /~ ~ ~/ *e. 4*   463 mass] [sum *or* scale] /~/ *e. 4*
world?] ~? | [If Jesus Christ had been the King of Persia /after the burning of Sardis/ he
would have sent [an herald to] an [herald] /ambassador/ to the Athenian nation with
instructions very different from those which the herald   bore. He
would have said "Men of Athens] *e. 4*   464 The] [If] ~ *e. 4*   is] are *1859*
466 have] [has]~ *e. 4*   467 is,] ~ₐ [attempt to provide] *e. 4*   472 without]
with/out/ *e. 4*   accommodation] accomodation *e. 4*   propensities] *fol. 18ᵛ*
473 destroy] ~ [Still is it] *e. 4*   recognize] [destr] [/a/] [to] ~ *e. 4*: recognizes *1859*
476 unjust, of] ~, [so long] /~/ *e. 4*   long as] that *1859*   478–9 Such ... law.] om.
1859   478 only justifiable] /~ ~/ *e. 4 (pencil)*   principles] ~ [of law] *e. 4*   true]
/~/ *e. 4*: [~] *K, J*: om. *TT*   of] *may have* for *written through it in e. 4*
479 law.] ~?: *e. 4 (see 464-79*EC)   480 this] [the] /~/ *e. 4* (this *in pencil*)
481 horrible] om. *1859*   accumulated] ~ [retaliations] *e. 4*   484 image] ~,
[therefore], *e. 4*   this] ~ [great] *e. 4*   invisible,] *fol. 19ʳ*: invisible *e. 4*: om. *TT*
mysterious] /~/ *e. 4*   485 its] [the] /~/ *e. 4*   and object] om. *1859*
486 *perfectness*] perfection *1859*: perfectness *K, TT*   487 the nation] th[at]e nation *e. 4*:
that *1859*   488 moral] [mental] /~/ *e. 4*   that God] ~ [only true] ~ [whose nature]
e. 4   488–9 the ... real] /~ ... ~/ *e. 4*   489 attributes] ~ [are to be] [is to] *e. 4*
⟨has⟩] *K*: /have/ *e. 4*: is *1859*   been] [be]~ *e. 4*   490 religion.] ~. [Thus] [And] *e. 4*
?nature of the] /~ ~ ~/ *e. 4*: reason of the *1859, K, J, TT*   491 also] /~/ *e. 4*
492 or indiv⟨id⟩uals] /or indivuals/ *e. 4*: or individual *1859, J, TT*: indiv⟨id⟩ual *K*
493 entertain] entertains *e. 4, 1859, K, TT*   be] [in]~ *e. 4*   494 and ... opinions]
om. *1859, K, J, TT (see* EC)   496 Christ,] Xt, *e. 4*   498 perfection] [consisted] *e. 4*
e. 4   required] requires *1859, K, J, TT*   or] and *1859*   499 shapes.] ~. [Between]
[the] [ch] *e. 4*   The ... human] /~ ... the/ ~ *e. 4*   500 is] are *e. 4*   same:] ~: [The

theology] *e. 4* 502 within] ~ [his nature] *e. 4* itself] himself *1859* (*see* EC) 503 Thus] ~ the (*fol. 19*ᵛ) [one] *e. 4* (the *inadvertently retained*) God] /god/ *e. 4* thro'] [by] /thro/ *e. 4* man] [the other] /~/ *e. 4* 504 measured] estimated /~/ *e. 4*: estimated *1859, K, J, TT* abstract] abstract *TT* 505 actual *perfection*] actual perfection *1859, K, J*: *actual perfection TT* ⟨be⟩] *K*: be *1859* 506 views as] ~ ~ [those] of *e. 4* (of *inadvertently retained*) 510 or] and *1859* 512 the] /~/ *e. 4* 514 shewn. But] shewn; but *K* consign] [watch] consign[s] *e. 4* beings] [living] ~ *e. 4* 516 God] [hi] ~ *e. 4* 520 happiness] *fol. 20*ʳ 521 doctrine] doctrines *1859* 523 these] their *1859, K, J, TT* 523–4 world, and] world, [as in the spirit of atheistical] [bigotry] [superstition] & [could] *e. 4* 525 to it] [him with] /~ ~/ *e. 4* 526 love] [beneficence] /~/ *e. 4* to] ~ [a princ] *e. 4* 527 of] ~ [mischief &] *e. 4* calamity.—] ~ₐ— *e. 4* 528 that] th[e]at *e. 4* 530 confound.] ~. [He asserts that God is good, perfectly good] *e. 4* doctrine] doctrines, *1859, K, J, TT* 531 have been] /have/ be/en/ *e. 4* enquire,] ~ₐ *e. 4 MSe* 532 incentive] ~ [to hope] *e. 4* the] [all] [that is great & good] /~/ *e. 4* 533 whilst] [which]~ *e. 4* holds out] [affords] /~ ~/ *e. 4* 535 It] To belong to some other part. Introduction] ~ *e. 4* (*see* TN) precisely ascertained] [discovered] /~ ~/ *e. 4* to] in *1859*: [in] *K, TT* 536 accommodated] accomodated *e. 4* opinions] [persuasions] /~/ *e. 4* or] *fol. 20*ᵛ 537 said.] ~ₐ [In the picture which ⟨is⟩ here attempted to be delineated of his system & his character the most liberal construction is carefully put on those circumstances which have been considered most equivocal.] *e. 4* 538 written] /~/ *e. 4* himself,] ~, [but a variety] *e. 4* 539 information] [histories] /~/ *e. 4* 541 guides,] ~, [abound with contradictory] *e. 4* 542 other.—] other[s]ₐ— *e. 4* 543 represent him as narrow, superstitious,] [impute sentiments of] /represent him as/ narrowₐ supertitio[n]us ₐ *e. 4* or] ~ [deliberately &] *e. 4*: and *1859* exquisitely vindictive] ~ [cruel[ty]] [revengeful] /~/ *e. 4* 544 malicious.—] ~.!? *e. 4*: ~!ₐ *TT* 545 exhortation,] ~ₐ *e. 4 MSe* 548 truth,] ~ₐ *e. 4* 549 of the object] *om. 1859* left] *fol. 21*ʳ 550 genuine] [real] /~/ *e. 4* Christ] ~. [We learn from them [words] [/expressions/] which they would never have dreamed of forging th] [have been incapable of inventing] *e. 4* 553 falsehood] falsehood *TT* 554 is] [his]~ *e. 4* 555 vindicated.] ~. [That he is this, the meekness & the majesty of his demeanour, as well as the [connections] /unbroken ?series/ of his doctrines contribute to establish.] *e. 4* 557 thoughts] thought *1859, K, J, TT* 558 unmoved and] [?both] /unmoved &/ *e. 4*: unmoved, *1859* serene] severe *1859* 559 that] ~ [you ought to return good for evil, that by such trivial sacrifize of revenge] *e. 4* hated] hate *1859* 561 such] ~ a *1859* 562 upon] on *1859* 563 general] *fol. 21*ᵛ of] ~ [his] *e. 4* 564 which] ~ [his] his[torians betray] *e. 4* is] ~ [unanimously] *e. 4* possess.—] ~ₐ— *e. 4* 565 The] [The opposite] [This rule of c] It is [incumbent on every enquirer to adopt] th[at] /e/ *e. 4* (It is *inadvertently retained*) criticism] critisism *e. 4* life,] ~ₐ *e. 4 MSe* 567 narrow.] ~. [It is said that we should decide from facts or from the relation of faˣcts.] *e. 4* We] ~ /Bacon/ *e. 4* (*see* TN) 568 image] [view] /~/ *e. 4* 569 whole] ~ [the several] *e. 4* of action . . . speech] /~ ~ . . . ~/ *e. 4* action] actions *1859, K, J, TT* of] *om. 1859* 571 have] ~ taken *1859* Jesus Christ] J.C. *e. 4* 573 scheme of] ~ ~ [moral feeling &] *e. 4* 575 no] [some] /~/ *e. 4* 576 disapprobation] dissapprobation *e. 4* 577 folly.] ~. [But that the essential basis of char] *e. 4* Those] Th[at]ose [only] *e. 4* deviations] ~ [which are] [from the [documents] histor[y]ical documents] [alo] *e. 4* life] *fol. 22*ʳ 578 which] ~ [assert] *e. 4* 579 itself.] ~. . , [which represent the mildest of men [as a] breathing malice revenge & peˣrsecution] *e. 4* (*see* 592 EC) Lord] *om. 1859* 580 *idola specus,*] idola specus, *e. 4* the] ~ [?inl] *e. 4* 581 essential] [peculiar] /~/ *e. 4* 582 word] ~ [is to] *e. 4* bears] have *1859* 583 depicturing] depicting *1859* 584 genuineness] [genuiness] ~ *e. 4* those] these *1859* 585 determined] *see* TN 585 n. *Novum . . . Scien⟨tiarum⟩*] Novum . . . Scien *e. 4* 587 geniuses] geniusses *e. 4* most] /~/ *e. 4* 588 His story] History *1859*

589 thus] /~/ e. 4   be] ~ made 1859, K, J, TT   590 his deceit] deceit 1859
591 have] fol. 22ᵛ   593 falsehood] falsehood TT   596 determine] ~ [whether he
had indued some div] e. 4   597 it] [he] /~/ e. 4: [it] 1859   597–8 that . . . to] [to
have asserted] /~ . . . ~/ e. 4   598 attend] ~[ed] e. 4: ~ on 1859   [the]] ∧~∧ 1859, K,
J, TT   601 country] ~ [wit] e. 4   603 introducing] introducting TT
abolishing] [denying] /~/ e. 4   605 tho'] tho e. 4   607 for the] [as his] /~ ~/ e. 4
609 inferences] ~ [contradictory] e. 4   610 deduced] adduced 1859   from] fol. 23ʳ
613 prepossessions] preposessions e. 4   615 you,] ~∧ e. 4   616 fact,] ~∧ e. 4
of the] ~ th[ose]e e. 4: ~ those 1859, K, J, TT   617 original] /~/ e. 4   law and] law
& [your] e. 4   618 constitution] constitutions 1859   of] ~ [these] e. 4
619 altered,] ~, [thro] e. 4   621 and] [or]& e. 4   622 not come] come not 1859
Till] till e. 4   623 pass] ~ away 1859   624 law] Law K, TT   fulfilled."—]
~."—[whosoever therefore shall break the least commandments /one of these/] /See Cicero
de Oratore/ e. 4 (see 627EC)   Thus] ˣ~ e. 4 (see 627EC   625 induces]
[seduces] /~/ e. 4   by] ~ [a representation of his] e. 4   627 own] see EC
627 n. 1 de Oratore] de Oratore e. 4   628 the success] fol. 23ᵛ   629 cause]
~, 1859   the judges] [those] /~ ~/ e. 4   to] ~ [judge] e. 4   630 those . . . religious]
[the] /~ [individual] . . . [or]& ~/ e. 4   636 admission.] ~. [Th[e]is represen] e. 4
have been] [are] /~ ~/ e. 4   642 expression.] ~. [But the scheme of human things is
imperfect] e. 4   of] ~ [abstract truth] [would avail but little, if] e. 4   642–3 entire
sincerity] /~ ~/ e. 4: utter ~ 1859   646 required] requird e. 4   an] fol. 24ʳ
647 in which] on ~ 1859   650 proceeds] pro[d]ceeds e. 4   652 absolutely]
[finally] /~/ e. 4   654 is] [in]~ e. 4   655 most daring] [the boldest] /~ ~/ e. 4: the
~ ~ 1859   impassioned] [enthusiastic] /~/ e. 4   657 singularity] ~ [& extravagance]
e. 4   659 mankind.] ~. [He loses sight of the] e. 4   chains] claims 1859
661 and become] /& become/ e. 4: and receive 1859   imitators] imitator 1859   and] &
[the] e. 4   662 ministers] minister 1859   God.] ~. [Government &] e. 4
HEADING. Equality] [Relat] (fol. 25ʳ, 24ᵛ blank) Equality e. 4   665 recovery]
recover[ing]y e. 4   666 Luke,] Luke. e. 4   667 iv,] iv. e. 4   669 upon of]
upon 1859   saw] ~ [the human species] e. 4   671 imbecility,] ~∧ e. 4   672 to]
/~/ e. 4   678 laws] law 1859, K, J, TT   679 external] /~/ e. 4   unequal
power:] [inequality,] /~ ~;/ e. 4   680 Diogenes] ~ /&/ e. 4 (see TN)   681–2 the
. . . tyrant] [injustice] /~ . . . ~/ e. 4   682 said, it] said I [do not consent to esteem]
(fol. 25ᵛ) [benefits] /posessions/ [whose unequal distribution you lament to be [benefits]
beneficial.] It e. 4 (inadvertent retentions)   684 he really occupies] he occupies 1859
689 possesses] posesses e. 4   691 yield . . . to] ~ in meek reverence ~ 1859
693 apparel] apparrell e. 4   694 O] TT: o e. 4: om. 1859   695 social] [poli] ~ e. 4
696 possessors] posessors e. 4: possessions 1859: posessons K (see TN)   Circumscribe]
[Decrease] /~/ e. 4, TT: Decrease 1859, K, J   697 concerned,] ~∧ e. 4   698 air;]
~. e. 4   699 of your] fol. 26ʳ   700 oppression] subserviency /~/ e. 4:
subserviency and ~ 1859 (see EC)   With] [But if ye are wise] ~ e. 4   701 entire] ~[ly]
e. 4   702 possessions] posessions e. 4   love] live 1859   702–3 one another]
onnother e. 4: [wisely] 1859: on[e a]nother K, TT   703 the . . . of] /~ . . . ~/ e. 4
706–7 of philosophy] ~ [mankind] /~ e. 4   707 and [mankind]] ~ ∧~∧ TT: and e. 4:
philosophy; and, if 1859: and—if J   among men,] [between ye] /~/ ~∧ e. 4
710 thro'] thro e. 4   711 should] [to] /~/ e. 4   712 peace] power, 1859
713 In] [And] in e. 4   716 as] om. 1859   718 of] fol. 26ᵛ   718–9 nations . . .
religions] nations, societies, families, and religions, 1859   720 with] [in]~ e. 4
their] ther e. 4   721 men.] ~. [I love my wife,] e. 4   721–2 born, my . . . care,] ~/,
~ . . . ~∧/ e. 4   722 city,] ~∧ e. 4   724 to an] [that] ~ ~ e. 4   725 indirect]
/~/ e. 4: evident 1859   duty] Unity 1859   727 comp⟨re⟩hended] comprehended
1859, K, J, TT   728 it.] ~? 1859, TT: ~⟨?⟩ K   729–30 the . . . circle] your [wife
less & children] [/relatives/] /~ . . . yr. domestic ~/ e. 4 (your inadvertently retained)

730 less,] ~. e. 4   love] ~ [mankind more] .. e. 4   exist] ~[s] e. 4   731 and affection] ~ of ~ 1859   736 dawn] da[y]wn e. 4   shall] ~ [the absence] e. 4 progress of] ~ ~ [general] e. 4   737 disperse in] ex[t]~ ~ [in] e. 4   737–8 and slavery,] ~ ~ₐ e. 4 MSe: and 〈curb the〉 1859 (omitting slavery) ministers] fol. 27ʳ 739 Your] [Your] e. 4 (underlined for retention)   741 complication.] ~ₐ e. 4 MSe former men] ~ ye /~/ e. 4 (men over ye, neither deleted): former, you 1859: ~, ~ K, TT 742 themselves] yourselves /them/ e. 4 (them over your, neither deleted): yourselves 1859 cultivated] ~ [the power of indulgence of] e. 4   743 meaner] /~/ e. 4   nothing] ~ so 1859   744 but] [as] 1859   Hence] ~ [they seek, as the instruments of their [desires] [/attainment/] fame wealth & power, &] e. 4   745 end which] end 1859 747 idolatry.] [superstition] /~ₐ/ e. 4 MSe   748 is] are 1859   749 its] the 1859 750 properties] [original] ~ e. 4   752 the discord] discord 1859   torpor and] ~ ~ indifference, 1859   755 admired] admitted 1859   fragile.] ~ₐ e. 4 MSe 756 Before] [They (fol. 27ᵛ) bind us to] ~ e. 4   equal] ~, [such as a wise man would wis] e. 4 759 are:] ~: [&] e. 4   760 the meanness] th[at]e meanness e. 4   761 leisure] reason 1859   764 προ〈σ〉κοσμ〈η〉ματα] προζκοσμεμata e. 4   765 κοσμω] κοσμω* e. 4   766 Such, with] [The wise man neither marries nor is given in marriage. It is one of the most] [such are, to] ~, [with some] [seem to have been the doctrines of Jesus Christ] ~ e. 4 (see EC)   766–7 the state] state 1859   772 was] ~ [ill under] e. 4 imperfectly] fol. 28ʳ   772–3 but thro' a] [practic] but [practic] /thro/ a[n] e. 4 773 considerably] considerabbly e. 4   on] om. 1859   774 or] and 1859, K, J, TT 775 founded] found TT   776 instances,] ~ₐ e. 4   778 philosopher] [man am] ~ e. 4   781 those passionate words] th[is]ose [enthusiastic burst of] [ind] [indignation] /passionate words/ e. 4   782 strongly] stronly e. 4   784 Jesus Christ] J.C. e. 4 785 Take] (fol. 28ᵛ) no par. 1859, K, J, TT (see 784-7TN)   therefore] therfore e. 4 the morrow,] ~ ~, [what ye shall eat] e. 4: to-morrow 1859   789 〈it〉 employ〈s〉] K: they employ e. 4   790 and strict] /& strict/ e. 4   of] [as]~ e. 4   791 Christ] C. e. 4   here] om. 1859, K, J, TT   than it] ~ 〈to imagine that〉 ~ 1859: than 〈that〉 TT 795 among men] [of mankind] /~ ~/ e. 4   796 savages] [a] savage/s/ e. 4   and beasts] & [a] beast/s/ e. 4   Philosophy] [Jesus] ~ e. 4   797 mysteries] fol. 29ʳ 800 life,] ~ₐ [&] e. 4   805 aspect] ~ [of civilized s] e. 4   overshadowed] overgrown /~/ e. 4: overgrown 1859, K, J, TT (see TN)   with] ~ [luxur] e. 4   807 Jesus Christ] J.C. e. 4   808 frame] [provide] /~/ e. 4   809 He] [Such interpreters would do well to beware] [It is]~ e. 4   816 society] fol. 29ᵛ   honour,] ~ₐ e. 4: power, 1859 or empire] [emp] /~/ ~ e. 4   818 that] ~ [those] e. 4   819 suppose,] ~ₐ e. 4 820 subserviency] ~ /as they ?personate a/ e. 4   821 it ... of] /~ ... ~/ e. 4   being] ~ [has a right] e. 4   possess] posess e. 4   822 degree.] ~., [for those who arrogate to themselves a superfluous portion] (period replaced comma after deletion) e. 4   825 your] ~ [mi] ~ words,] ~ₐ e. 4   826 degree of] ~ ~ [requisitions] e. 4   827 you] ~[r] e. 4   829 that] /~/ e. 4   832 are willing] [desire] /~ ~/ e. 4 833 possess] [attain] /posess/ e. 4 (see TN)   objects] fol. 30ʳ   subsistence.] ~. [This system is inconsistent with] e. 4   834 invocated] 〈impelled〉 1859 835 participation in] /~ ~/ e. 4: participate in 1859   nature's gifts.] natures gifts. [Obtain each what suffices to t]he e. 4   835–46 Ye ... contain.] see TN   836 mechanisms] mechanism 1859, K, J, TT   837 pride.] ~ₐ e. 4   838 nature!] ~ₐ e. 4   bodily] /~/ e. 4   841 this] the 1859, K, J, TT   844 are] ~ [the] ~ to the] ~ be ~ 1859, K, J: ~ 〈be〉 ~ TT   nutriment] ~ & [consummation] e. 4 (& inadvertently retained) 846 that] om. 1859   your] pure 1859   847 swift ... coloured] /~ ... ~/ e. 4 848 as the] ~ ?? ~ e. 4 (see TN)   852 they] fol. 30ᵛ   Government] Goverm[nm]ent & e. 4 (& inadvertently retained)   the] ~ [happiness & majesty of] e. 4   854 without] ~ [the strong] e. 4   860 depends on] [sanctions] /~ ~/ e. 4   862 men] [men & equals] /~/ e. 4   863 men,] ~ₐ e. 4   frail] [perverse] /~/ e. 4   864 possess] posess e. 4   866 to pervert,] [of] /to/ ~[ing]ₐ e. 4: to prevent, 1859   together ...

own] (~ . . . ~) *1859*   own,] ~∧ *e. 4*   869 exhibiting . . . proper] [rendering vile] /~ . . . ~/ *e. 4*   worthlessness] & worthless/ness/ *e. 4* (& *inadvertently retained*) 871 wherever] *fol. 31ʳ* whereever *e. 4*   873 is] [in]~ *e. 4*   by] by this [disease] ~ *e. 4* (by this *inadvertently retained*)   the] an *1859*   874 is blind] ~ [stup] ~ *e. 4* 877 conceptions] conception *1859, K, J, TT*   879 which] [whi]ch *e. 4* 880 state] *perhaps* estate *e. 4, as in e. 4* (D)   881 have] *om. TT*   885 without mixture] *om. 1859*   886 referred indeed] referred, in truth, *1859*   886–7 the period,] ~ Saturnian ~; *1859*   889 the parents] parents *1859, K, J* mysterious] /~/ *e. 4:* man's *1859*   890 moralist,] ~∧ *e. 4*   metaphysician,] /~∧/ (*fol. 31ᵛ*) *e. 4*   ⟨a⟩ poet] ∧~∧ ~ *1859*   891 have referred] ~ [institu] /~/ *e. 4* 892 themselves] ~; *1859, K, J, TT*   ⟨the⟩ progress] ∧~∧ ~ *1859:* [thier] progress *e. 4:* this progress *K, TT*   894 these] [they]~ *e. 4:* the *1859*   Poets] /~/ *e. 4* 895 imagined.] ~. [He compared as is probable, the] [He firmly believed that if men [are now] might transcend the limits of their ignorance & their] *e. 4*   896 The] [That Jesus Christ] ~ *e. 4: no par. 1859, K, J, TT*   897 Jesus Christ] J. C. *e. 4*   899 justice among mankind,] ~. /~ ~∧/ [Domestic slavery & pr] is [abolished in the] [The immense distinction of] *e. 4* (is *inadvertently retained*): justice, *1859*   900 more, or more universal,] ~, ~ ~ ~∧ *e. 4:* more *1859, K, J* (*see* EC)   knowledge.] ~. X———X Slaves *e. 4* (*see* TN)   To] *par. 1859, K, J, TT*   901–2 Jesus Christ] J C [directed] *e. 4* 902 extended,] /~/[;], [ ] [that] [& so clearly did he forsee] [th[ier]e /a/ progress] [/caus/] [in conjun] [on] *e. 4:* ~; *1859, K, J, TT*   903 artificial] [personal] /~/ *e. 4* 906 produced,] ~∧ *e. 4*   907 A] —— *e. 4*   Jesus Christ] J.C. *e. 4*   908 and simplicity] & *fol. 32ʳ* ~ *e. 4*   909 uttered.] ~∧ *e. 4 MSe*   be] ~ [admitted on] *e. 4* 911 philosopher,] ~∧ *e. 4*   give . . . poor] /~ . . . ~/ *e. 4*   912 possessions] posessions *e. 4*   he ⟨went away sorrowing.⟩] *see* TN   913 Christ's death,] C's ~∧ *e. 4* 914 things] ~ in *1859*   918 heart"] ~∧ *e. 4*   918–19 *Acts,* Chap. 2, v. 44 &⟨c⟩.] *Acts Chap. 2 v 44 & e. 4*   920 of] *fol. 32ᵛ*   921–2 have been expected.] [be] /~ ~/ ~. [No] *e. 4*   924 Men to . . . possessions] Men [again] /to . . . posessions/ *e. 4*   these] ample *1859*   926 those] th[e]ose *e. 4*   928 withheld] witheld *e. 4* 929 their] *om. 1859*   930 another's] anothers *e. 4*   to] /~/ *e. 4*   majesty] dignity *1859*   931 Christian] Xtian *e. 4*   932 thro'] thro *e. 4*   933 its] [the]~ *e. 4:* their *1859, K, J, TT*   934 all.] ~. [When] *e. 4*   935 voice] [mor] ~ *e. 4* 938 of] ~ [Heaven] *e. 4*   939 those] [   ] /~/ *e. 4*   which] *fol. 33ʳ*   940 or] and *1859, K, J, TT*   ⟨to⟩] *TT*   946 Jesus Christ] J.C. *e. 4*   948 would] could *1859, K, J, TT*   949 treasurers] ~ [or stewards] *e. 4*   950 considerable] [immense] /~/ *e. 4*   to his] ~ [the degree of] /~/ [wisdom] & *e. 4*   952 steward and] steward /[of]/ & *e. 4*   953 possess] posess *e. 4*   wisdom,] ~∧ *e. 4 MSe* 955 discretion.] ~∧ [Such is] *e. 4 MSe*   955–6 the annihilation] ~ [origin of equality] ~ *e. 4:* ~ ⟨~⟩ *1859*   957 subs⟨is⟩ting] existing *1859, K, J, TT*   world, and so] world∧ & so *e. 4:* world, so *K*   958 accommodated] accomodated *e. 4*   to] *fol. 33ᵛ* 961 basis] *or* ?bases *e. 4*   962 have] ~ [fail] *e. 4*   963 foundation,] formation *1859* 965 men] m[a] /e/n[kind] *e. 4*   consented to] [would] /~ ~/ *e. 4*   966 luxury,] ~∧ *e. 4* 967 possession] posession *e. 4*   968 which] /with/ ~ *e. 4* (*see* TN)   authority] [weight] /~/ *e. 4*   968–9 made . . . them.] [swelled their imaginations]. /~ . . . ~∧/ *e. 4* (*K reads* [riveted] *for* [swelled])   970 enemies'] ~∧ *e. 4:* enemy's *1859:* enem⟨y's⟩ *TT* 971 justice.] ~∧ *e. 4*   972 Christ] C. *e. 4*   the] *om. K* (*e. 4 fragment ends here; see* TN)

ON THE DOCTRINES OF CHRIST

Collated: MS; *St. James Magazine* (*SJ*); *F*; *J*.

TITLE. *None in MS*   1 No] [The doctrines of Jesus Christ] ~ *MS*   2 derive] ~ [its] *MS*   3 either] /~/ *MS*   circumstance] ~ [either] *MS*   4 not] ~ [bec] [for] *MS*

7 ⟨abstract⟩] F: ⟨   ⟩ MS   ⟨u⟩seful] useful SJ   8 of] for J   accommodate]
accomodate MS   11–12 deluded . . . impostor] om. J   11 deluded] [&] ~ MS: and
~ SJ, F   14 doc⟨trin⟩es] doctrines SJ   16 a superstition] ~ [system] /~/ MS:
superstitions SJ, F, J   17 them] [these doctrines] /~/ MS   18 The] [Let us
proceed to vindicate] ~ MS   19 Nor] [The philosophers of Greece, & their imitators
the Romans, bear] ~ MS   21 to] ~ [the] MS   22+ Chap⟨ter⟩ 2] Chap (fol. ⟨1ʳ⟩) 2
MS (see 1 TN): om. SJ, F, J   23 The] [doctrines were speculations of] the MS   long]
/~/ MS   24 ⟨o⟩n] on SJ   24–5 on . . . world] /~ the /visible/ ~ & on/ MS
25 the intellectual] intellectual SJ, F, J   28 asserted] [direc] ~ MS   Pythagoras,
Plato,] [the Platonists] /~‸/ ~[nists & Stoics]‸ MS   Diogenes,] ~‸ MS   31 Christ's]
Christs MS   32 practicability.] ~. It [promises] [would persuade man not to be tyrant
of man,] MS (It inadvertently retained)   33 mysteries,] ~‸ MSe   we] fol. ⟨1ᵛ⟩
34 its] ~' MS   liberty and truth] [our fellow men] /~ ~ ~/ MS   37 may not be] ~ be
[incited] not be ~ ~ ~ MS (inadvertent repetition)   everlastingly] everlasting/ly/ MS
38–9 their fellow beings] [our] ~ ~ [men] /~/ MS: fellow men SJ   39 turns] returns J
41 with] [&]with MS   of] to J   42 is] ~ [a cold & [palsying] tame thought] MS
43 to] ~ [share the fate] MS   45 priests] see EC

ON MARRIAGE

Collated: MS; K.

TITLE. None in MS   1 Before] [In] (fol. 39ʳ) /~/ MS   society,] ~, [it is probable that]
MS   4 practise.] ~‸ MSe   9 possession] posession [of] MS   12 possessor]
posessor MS   13 possession] posession MS   13–14 are the . . . thro'] ~
[subjugated by] /the . . . thro/ MS   14 and] ~ [nations by the] MS   men] never K
17 are] [ar]e MS (inadvertently deleted)   18 to] fol. 39ᵛ   21 possession] posession
MS   21–2 those laws or opinions] ~ [laws which] [institutions] /~ ~ ~/ MS
23 institution] ~[s] MS   a] ~[n] [institution which] [device whereby] MS   24 that] ~
[posession] MS   26 undergone] u[d]ndergone MS   27 circumstances] ~
[connec] MS   27–8 as I describe] ⟨undubitably⟩ K   28 marriage] [its]
[monogamy]. ~ MS   29 If any] [With] [Together with the law ?spring up the ideas of
duty & of crime] /If/ Any MS   agree to] [may] /~ ~/ MS   30–1 commission]
comission MS   32–3 the denomination] ~ [term w] ~ MS   33 practise] function
K   36 consider] fol. 40ʳ   40 equivocal] [incorrect] ~ MS   42 standard
peculiar] ~ [more or less deceptive] ~ MS   44 A] [Those] ~ MS   considers] [calls]
/~/ MS   45 in] &[~] MS   manner] ~ [as mathemeticians call all that at] MS
46 to] /~/ MS   48 The] [With] the MS   altho'] altho [it was only the consequence
of] MS   51 another.—Every . . . the] ~‸[Every ?law supposed the] /~ . . . ~/ MS
53 consideration] [mistake] /~/ MS   54 right,] ~‸ MS   55 the [greatest] fol. 40ᵛ
56 Such] [This] /~/ MS   cause] ~ [of justice & virtue having been confounded] MS
57 doctrinal] ~ [perversities] [of] MS   have] ~ [confounded all those] MS

ON 'GODWIN'S MANDEVILLE'

Collated: Examiner (1817); Athenaeum (1832).

TITLE. see TN   1 SIR,—] om. 1832   2 in] of 1832   6 comprehension] om.
1832   13 Political] no par. 1817   17 other] om. 1832   25 interests]
interest 1832   and] om. 1832   34 still] om. 1832   40 foundation] foundations
1832   morals] minds 1832   42 Wordsworth's] his 1832   47 reverence] ~
and admiration 1832   48 Wollstonecraft] Wolstonecroft 1817   51–2 The . . .

of] In interest it is perhaps inferior to *1832*   53 Yet] *om. 1832*   59 of a] *om. 1832*
sprang] spring *1832*   60 a] *om. 1832*   61 in virtue] virtue *1832*   62 arose]
sprang *1832*   63 the majesty of] *om. 1832*   66 undefiled] unassailed *1832*
68 if] *om. 1832*   70–1 useful occasions for] powerful sources of *1832*   71 in
favour of] for *1832*   73 fiction,] ~; as such *1832*   75 The language] *no par. 1817*
81 and] ~ of *1832*   84 perspicuous] perspicacious *1832*   view] river *1832*
85 scarcely] not *1832*   88 as . . . suppose,] *om. 1832*   89 lute.] ~, *1817*
97 has] have *1832*   104 withdrawn] undrawn *1832*   105 with] to *1832*
106 purity] sincerity *1832*   107 and is] *om. 1832*   110 for] to *1832*   accidents]
accident *1832*   112 have] yet ~ *1832*   unshrinkingly] unshrinking *1832*
115 overturned] overthrown *1832*   would] might *1832*   127 executing] execrating
1832   to] in *1832*   131 these] ~ objections *1832*   core] close *1832*
132–43 The . . . of mind] *appears after* Author., *l* 74, *in 1832*   132 on] *om. 1832*
133 and growing] growing *1832*   134 there is no shock] no shock *1832*
136 Author] author *1817*   137 profound] fearful *1832*   138 complete] so ~
1832   139 gossamere] the gossamer *1832*   142 *Mandeville*] Mandeville *1817*
which] that *1832*   147 the] that *1832*   149 E. K.] *om. 1832* (*see* EC)

ON THE GAME LAWS

Collated: MS.

TITLE. On] *p. 11*   1 tho'] tho *MS*   2 people.—] ~.—[It is said, that tho' not
?chron] [If even] *MS*   3–4 actually . . . shadow;] /~ represent /that which is/ a
distortion & a ~ₐ/ *MS*   8 Assembly] [Assem] ~ *MS*   10 Game . . . its] ~ [to
contemplate] [which will expose] /to [contemplate]/ /set/ in [the] /~/ *MS* (to *inadvertently
retained*)   10–11 view, . . . exercised] view, [a] /the/ despotism /which is/ exersised *MS*
11 us.] ~[,]. [which fully to unveil were to overthrow].— *MS*   13 the incomes] th[ier]e
incomes *MS*   of its] of *badly smeared in MS*   own] /~/ *MS*   14 it ?loads] [the
necess] ~ [taxes] /?~/ *MS*   the] *badly smeared in MS*   necessaries] ~ [of the] *MS*
15 with] *blotted in MS*   16–17 spared— . . . wealth—] ~ₐ[; namely a vast accum]
/namely, . . . ~ₐ/ *MS*   17 possession] posession *MS*   19 question.—But]
question—but *MS*   the] *p. 13*   21 bring] ~[s] *MS*   assembly,] ~ₐ [which assumes
to speak the will of the nation], [/country/] *MS*   21–2 taste and morals,] /taste &/
morals_ₐ *MSe*   22 lives,] ~, [outraging the] *MS*   23 of this same country] /~ ~ ~
~/ *MS*   that] ~ [without] *MS*   24 even] /~/ *MS*   25 good,] ~, [for] *MS*
26 from] /~/ *MS*   27 shrinks in] [contemplates with] /~ ~/ *MS*   29 There]
[First, to consider it as a violation of property, the] | ~ *MS*   the inequality] [there are
degrees] /~ ~/ *MS*   30 us; so] [us] ~; [so that] ~ *MS*   36 literature,] ~ₐ *MS*
and the] & [the] the *MS*   37 by the] by th[is]e *MS*   38 is] *p. 15*   39 possess]
posess *MS*   40 courage,] ~ₐ *MS*   42 system of the] /~ ~ ~/ *MS*   laws,]~ₐ *MS*
so far as it ?proceeds,] /~ ~ ~ ~ ?~ₐ/ *MSe*   44 was] [h]~ [been] *MS*   the] th[em]e *MS*
46 right] [d]~ *MS*   so] [how] /~/ *MS*   50 they persecute] [?test] ~ ~ *MS*
neighbours;] ~, *MS*   54–5 their flesh] the[y]ir /flesh/ *MS*   56 unforseen—] ~ₐ
MSe   of the] [for] of th[is]e *MS*   man] *p. 17*   57 indispensible.—] ~.—[Some of the
most ?refined thinkers have even disputed this necessity. But in theory no one has ever said
that to destroy & mangle] But [But to the destruction of game no] *MS* (But *inadvertently
retained*)   justifiableness] [innocence] /~/ *MS*   58 authors] [framers] /~/ *MS*
59 on] [t]~ *MS*   60 man] [criminal] ~ *MS*   ⟨they are⟩] he is *MS*   61 beasts.—]
~ₐ— *MS*   62–3 for . . . rights of] [to] /~ the/ preserv[e]/ation/ but [to] /for the/ insult
/& outrage of the ~ ~/ *MS*   64 as] /~/ *MS*   64–5 the mode of death of] [an] /~ ~
~ ~ ~/ *MS* 65 that] /~/ *MS* as] ~ [The former is the necessity for] *MS*

ON 'FRANKENSTEIN; OR,
THE MODERN PROMETHEUS'

Collated: MS; Athenaeum (1832).

TITLE. *None in MS*   1 The] *p.* ⟨66⟩   2 undoubtedly,] undoubed[t]dly, [one] *MS*
complete] [striking] /~/ *MS*   3 age] [pres]ent [day] ~ *MS*: day *1832*   We] ~ [wonder,
when we read it w] *MS*   wonder] [astonishment] /~ [& a] / *MS*   4 been] /~/ *MS*
6 conducted] ~, *MS*: conduced *1832*   author's] authors *MS*   6–7 of . . . incidents]
[of the relations of human motives & actions,] /~ motives [of] & ~/ *MS*   8 perhaps] ~
[po] *MS*   9 it is] /~ ~/ *MS*   But] ~ [this] *MS*   10 discrimination,] [&]
discriminati[ng]on *MS*   11 is] ~ [the] *MS*   12 advances] ~ [as the] *MS*
13 conclusion] con[clusion *p.* ⟨67⟩   14 held] led *1832*   15 incident,. . . passion.]
~, /& . . . ~./ *MS*   16 cry] [think that] ~ *MS*   hold, hold,] ~∧ ~∧ *MSe*
17 something to come] [more] /~ ~ ~/ *MS*   20 seen, blank,] ~[.], [The] /~/∧ *MSe*
21 giddy,] ~∧ *MS*   22 Novel] ~ [cannot] *MS*   thus] /~/ *MS*: om. *1832*   on] [to] ~
MS   23 emotion.] [excitement] /~∧/ (*perhaps a colon after* emotion *in MS*)   The
elementary feelings] [Thus are] ~ ~ [passions of] ~ *MS*   24 who] ~ [think] *MS*
25 their] thier [tendencies &] *MS*   can] [will] /~/ *MS*   26 the full] th[is]e (*p.* ⟨68⟩)
full *MS*   in . . . of] [with] /~ . . . ~/ *MS*   27 But,] ~∧ *MS*   are,] ~∧ *MS*
28 will] ~ [feel] *MS*   29 his] [the] ~ *MS*   31 strange] /~/ *MS*   are] ~ [so] *MS*
32 such] /~/ *MS*   mind.—] ~∧— *MS*   33 every where] /~ ~/ *MS*: om. *1832*
33–4 The . . . deep.] /~ . . . ~./ *MS*   33 pathos] father's *1832*   34 Nor are the]
[The] /~ ~/ /~/ *MS*   34–5 the single Being,] [him on whom] one, /~ ~ ~∧/ *MS* (one,
inadvertently retained)   35 tho'] [are] /tho/ *MS*   tremendous,] ~, [but they] *MS*
36 evil] [crime] /~/ *MS*   inevitably] ~ [from the nece] *MS*: irresistibly *1832*
37 causes] ~ [whi] *MS*   38 were,] ~∧ *MS*   Human] *see* TN   51 led]
[counteracted] (*p. 12*) [have rescu] ~ *MS*   his] ~ [to] *MS*   52 was] ~ [as it were] *MS*
tho'] tho *MS*   53 formed] framed *1832*   it,] ~∧ [amiable considerate &] *MSe*
54 were] are *1832*   55 that] ~ [all who look] *MS*   56 gradually] /~/ *MS*
57 the fuel of] om. *1832*   an] [his] /~/ *MS*   misanthropy and revenge] [hatred]
/misanthropy/ & [rage] revenge *MS*   58 blind] ~ [old m] *MS*   de] De *1832*
60 recollect] [read] ~ *MS*   60–1 this dialogue— . . . feeling] [of] /~ ~∧ . . . character∧/
without [the heart] ~ *MS*   61 other situations] others *1832*   62–3 and . . .
cheeks!] "~ . . . ~." *1832*   64 Frankenstein] *p. 14*   ice] ~ [reminds us of] *MS*
65 Falkland] [his persona] ~ *MS*   67 writer] [Author,] ~ [of which indeed this Author
ap] *MS*   and] & [of] *MS*   work,] ~, [& of] *MS*   68 studied.] ~. [Not t] *MS*
69 imitation,] ~∧ *MSe*   70 is, . . . Frankenstein's] is, /[the inci] / [in] /the conduct of the
incident of/ Frankensteins *MS*   70–1 and trial] om. *1832*   71 Ireland.—]
~.—[But we know not] [After the death of Elisabeth, the story] *MS*   74 magnificent]
p. 16   75 as] om. *1832*   tempest.] ~. [The journey of Frankenstein is at once the
terrible animation of a] [The catastrophe] [His] [quitting Geneva] *MS*   78 Ocean,] ~∧
MS   resembles at once] [is] [like] /~ ~ ~/ *MS*: resemble at once *1832*   79 The] [The
catastrophe] the *MS*   81 Being's] Beings *MS*   82–3 we . . . acknowledge] [in ficti]
/~ . . . ~/ *MS*   83 surpassed.] ~∧ *MS*

ON 'RHODODAPHNE OR THE THESSALIAN SPELL'
Collated: MS.

TITLE. *Rhododaphne* ⟨&c.⟩] *p.* ⟨1⟩ *MS*   3 under] [under] ~ *MS*   8 stood. We] ~[;].
[w]~ *MS*   Peneus,] *perhaps* ~[,] *MS*   11 there] the[m] /re/ *MS*   13 so] /~/ *MS*

15 in] *p. 2*   16 their] [there] /th[ie]eir/ *MS*   18 sacrifize] sacrifi[s]ze *MS*
19 stream,"] ~_∧_" *MS*   21 speak] [open] ~ *MS*   22 their] the[e]/ier/ *MS*
23 statues] [forms] /~/ *MS*   25 fancy,] ~_∧_ *MS*   26 have] ~ [crom] *MS*
26–7 this . . . poem] ~ [poem] /portion of the/ ~ *MS*   30 we] [he] ~ *MS*   its] [the] /~/
MS   31 so] /~/ *MS*   32 charmed—] ~/—/ *MS*   feeble] *p. 3*   33 that]
th[e]at *MS*   it] /~/ *MS*   be] /~/ *MS*   34 it] /~/ *MS*   40 Love] [Uranian] ~
MS   55 offer] ~ [to offer] *MS*   56 mistress] [mis] ~ *MS*   57 flowers]
flow[ers *p. 4*   60 wreath,] ~_∧_ *MS*   he] /~/ *MS*   69 vacant] [a] ~ *MS*
77 He] [h]~ *MS*   78 which grows] [th] /~ ~/ *MS*   84 away] /~/ *MS*
90 safety] [saft] ~ *MS*   94 They] [The scene in which they now find themselves is then
described] ~ *MS*   97 where,] [which is] /~,/ *MS*   99 Love] [l]~ *MS*
101 bids] [bi[s]d] ~ *MS*   102 After] ~ [a] *MS*   the] [their] /~/ *MS*   103 of the
lovers] /~ ~ ~/ *MS*   105 we . . . to] /~ . . . ~/ *MS*   106 Bliss;] ~_∧_ [should have left
nothing unsaid]: *MS*   107 description] ~[s] *MS*   many,] ~_∧_ *MS*   107–8 is . . .
fertile . . . imagination:] [is worthy remark]: /~ . . . [a] ~ . . . ~_∧_/ *MS*   111 oak] oack *MS*
113 vest] ~[al] *MS*   125 timbrel] [ty] ~ *MS*

End-line hyphens

The following words are hyphenated or separated at the end of a line in the copy-text: 'Irish-men' (p. 12, l. 139); 'your-selves' (p. 23, l. 567); 'man-kind' (p. 42, l. 31; p. 45, l. 149; 'child-hood' (p. 71, l. 338); 'fore-runner' (p. 86, l. 344); 'pre-disposition' (p. 87, l. 383); 'fore⟨⟩told'* (p. 126, l. 75); 'over-hanging' (p. 129, l. 213); 'over⟨⟩powering' (p. 130, l. 243); 'pre-rogative' (p. 140, l. 20); *Mid-summer*' (p. 177, l. 17); 'sea-sick' (p. 185, l. 53); 'pig-tail' (p. 186, l. 101); 'mid-night' (p. 192, l. 321); 'over-looked' (p. 193, l. 369); 'over-hanging' (p. 195, l. 455); 'wax-work' (p. 197, l. 506); 'over-taken' (p. 200, l. 623); 'well-informed' (p. 202, l. 703); 'boat-men' (p. 202, l. 720); 'brick-work' (p. 204, l. 795); 'pass-port' (p. 208, l. 67); 'over-come' (p. 216, l. 157); 'over-looks' (p. 218, l. 273); 'over-flow' (p. 220, l. 9); 'over-hanging' (p. 221, l. 50); 'over-thrown' (p. 225, l. 204); 'up-rooted', 'over-whelmed' (p. 225, l. 207); 'land-holders' (p. 236, l. 203); 'farm⟨?⟩houses' (p. 240, l. 14) (*perhaps hyphenated in MS*); 'extra-ordinary' (p. 276, l. 19).

All hyphens between compound words and after prefixes appearing in this volume reproduce the copy-text, except for the following, which are editorial: 'your-selves' (p. 35, l. 1035); 'wher-ever' (p. 83, l. 248); 'be-gotten' (p. 95, l. 21); 'ever-lastingly' (p. 127, l. 126); 'pre-eminence' (p. 131, l. 300); 'for-gotten' (p. 133, l. 358); 'through-out' (p. 150, l. 129); 'under-stand' (p. 233, l. 94); 'blood-shed' (p. 235, l. 163); 'man-kind' (p. 247, l. 62).

The following words, hyphenated at the end of a line in the copy-text, might have been meant to be unhyphenated: 'co-operation' (p. 54, l. 526); 'ever-present' (p. 100, l. 178); 'brick-kiln' (p. 103 n.); 'blood-thirsty' (p. 106, l. 370); 'custom-house' (p. 186, l. 85); 'post-office' (p. 196, l. 481); 'death-rattle' (p. 231, l. 19). The word 'touchstone' (p. 110, l. 533) is actually endline 'touch-stone' in copy-text. The word appears both with and without the hyphen in S's copy-texts.

End-line hyphens supplied between syllables in the copy-text which clearly

---

* ⟨ ⟩ indicates that the word was separated but not hyphenated in MS: S did not consistently hyphenate words he presumably meant to hyphenate or join. The above list includes only those words which precedent or relevant contemporary authority suggests S might have hyphenated as indicated had they appeared mid-line.

would have appeared unhyphenated were they not at the end of a line (e.g. 'im-partially', 'na-ture', 'excite-ment') are not listed, nor are words with prefixes and suffixes which S did not set off by hyphens, except when they appeared at a line break.

Textual Notes

AN ADDRESS, TO THE IRISH PEOPLE

68 profer to] S's correction in *Pf* must be preferred to the received 'profess for', which might otherwise seem the more probable reconstruction from *1812*'s 'profers for'. Given his prospective Catholic audience, S might have felt 'profer' rhetorically more positive.

79 a . . . slower] In the *Pf* copy S has underlined each word in this phrase but, like the 'X's used later, the underscorings were probably meant only to call his father's attention to the qualification. The 'X's appear before 'very worst way' (101), 'cease' (158), 'smooth-faced impostors' (164), and 'see' (185).

104 and Bishops] This addition to 'Kings' seems incongruous; the printer perhaps dropped a qualifying phrase or clause (or misplaced these words).

136 them;] It is possible that the stroke over *1812*'s comma is a deletion, though I read it as a hyper-extended dot meant to form a semicolon.

161–77 think . . . ambition] This portion of the *Address* appears with some variation in S's letter to Elizabeth Hitchener of 16 Jan. 1812.

213–14 not a . . . intolerant] Underlined in *Pf*.

324 burden] A preceding 'the' might have been dropped by the printer.

351 the cultivation] A preceding 'in' might have been dropped by the printer.

372–3 All . . . bad] Underlined in *Pf*.

380 may] Again, a preceding 'and' might have been dropped by the printer; but in this instance the parataxis is rhetorically appropriate enough in an 'Address'.

392 people, . . . employed;] The reversed order of the comma and semicolon in *1812* (see the Collation) suggests a printer's transposition.

490 prosecute] Forman (F v. 334 n.) feels this is probably a misprint for 'persecute'. But S could very well have intended 'prosecute' in a legal sense. If not, the *OED* indicates the synonymity of the two words in contexts with which S could well have been familiar.

768 ⟨to⟩] S did not correct this in *Pf*, but the 'to' supplied by *J* seems necessary for the modern reader's ready comprehension. However, the fact that Forman did not question the original reading indicates that he read it as a contemporary locution rather than as a printer's error.

791 ⟨is⟩] Forman suggested that *1812*'s 'in' was probably a misprint for 'is' but retained 'in'; *J* accepted 'is'.

812 even] As previous editors have noted, 'ever' might well have been the word S wrote; however, the *OED* documents uses of 'even' that could apply here.

816 ⟨to⟩] Alternatively, a semicolon may be placed after 'feel' (l. 819). But 'to' provides a less strained and more Shelleyan construction.

839 on⟨e⟩] Forman annotated 'on' with 'sic'; *J* suggested 'one' but retained 'on'. The colloquial style S affects in the pamphlet justifies a rather loose construction to the sense which 'one' provides, while the printer's lapses elsewhere justify a supposition that he might have dropped an 'e' (or perhaps misread S's hand).

851 glory in] Forman's rationale for correctly inferring the readings here and in l. 854 (confirmed in *Pf*; see Collation) is worth noting: 'Probably ⟨"in"⟩ was inserted as a correction in the margin of a proof, and was put in by the printer in the wrong place' (F v. 348 n.). But the large number of errors in the text make it improbable that S ever saw a proof; clearly the printer was quite capable of displacing words without the distraction of a marginal correction.

853 men;] While the semicolon replacing *1812*'s comma is regarded as editorial (see the Collation), it is possible that an ambiguous stroke at this point in *Pf* was meant to convert the comma to a semicolon.

991 ⟨not⟩] Forman first suggested that 'not' was probably omitted; *J* accepted the reading (in brackets).

1053c [or]] The underline in *Pf* is meant to call attention to the word to be replaced by 'are' (i.e. it does not indicate reinstatement).

1065 his] The reference must be to 'any one', in so far as the grammar can be justified in spite of the intervening 'they' of l. 1063, which assumes the plural implications of 'any one' which 'his' immediately elides. While one may infer a dropped 't'—as *J* appears to have done—the resulting 'this' still makes for a rather indistinct reference.

PROPOSALS FOR AN ASSOCIATION OF PHILANTHROPISTS

7 Philanthropy] As in the *Address, to the Irish People*, this word and its variants are spelt with 'oph' here and in the following lines: 19, 29, 39, 71, 137, 160, 183, 194, 205, 214, 240, 380, 443, 457, 462, 482, 523, and 543. Elsewhere the word is spelt correctly.

18 ⟨which⟩] *1812*'s 'what', which Forman retained, might have had a nineteenth-century colloquial acceptance as a plural pronominal referent that the *OED* does not record. *J* silently introduced a 'which' that, appropriately bracketed, seems preferable, particularly when it is also possible that the printer erred.

43 misfortune] Possibly, as Clark suggests (*Shelley's Prose*, 61), a compositorial misreading of 'importance'.

63 root not out] Possibly a printer's transposition, but S might have intended a rhetorical emphasis which the inversion supplies.

75 universe? Are] In *1812* 'universe' is followed by a semicolon; however, the 'Are' following it suggests that the printer read S's '?' as a semicolon. Alternatively, the semicolon may be correct and the 'A' a misread 'a'.

84–101 I . . . wicked] The general sense of this paragraph is clear enough but its organization and some of its syntax (e.g. ll. 93–6) suggest that the printer might have missed or miscopied some of S's text.

143 discussing] Perhaps, as Clark suggests (*Shelley's Prose*, 63), a compositorial error for 'diffusing'; cf. 'discussing' at l. 146.

197–8 them . . . shoulders] Both the original pointing (see the Collation) and the sense suggest that the printer might have dropped some words from S's text.

302 devilish] In the *Address, to the Irish People* the word is spelt 'develish', which suggests a different compositor, if not printer, for each work.

387 executive] Either S is using the word in a plural sense or the compositor dropped an 's'. S's reference is in any case either uncertain or deliberately generalized, though the context suggests that the French aristocracy are at least included in the prediction.

441c revivivication] The OED lists an erroneous usage, 'revification', which S or the printer might have compounded here by transposing 'v' and 'f'.

501 ⟨analogies⟩] Forman's emendation of 'analysis' (F v. 386 n.) seems sufficiently confirmed by the construction to warrant its acceptance into the text.

558 institution] The compositor might have dropped a defining phrase here (e.g. 'of such an Association').

DECLARATION OF RIGHTS

38 discussion,] The use of the comma to represent a strong pause more formally represented by a semicolon or colon is characteristic of both the broadsheet and the Irish pamphlets.

89 philanthropy] The spelling 'philanthrophy' of the Irish pamplets may suggest a different printer or merely a different compositor for this broadsheet.

A LETTER TO LORD ELLENBOROUGH

13 intolerance] There is a four en gap after this word in the copy-text.

57–62 Falsehood ... universe!] This sentence was first reprinted (somewhat varied) in 1866 in J. R. Chanter's Sketches of the Literary History of Barnstaple ... (pp. 55–6). S used substantially the same metaphor (along with the Macbeth quotation) in Proposals for an Association of Philanthropists (ll. 243–8).

91–5 How ... punishment] S recast this as follows in the Queen Mab Note on 'I will beget a Son': 'But the Christian religion attaches the highest possible degrees of merit and demerit to that which is worthy of neither, and which is totally unconnected with the peculiar faculty of the mind, whose presence is essential to their being.'

96 which] The 'whether' which replaces 'which' in the Queen Mab Note on 'I will beget a Son' (see the Collation) makes only a strained and contradictory sense. The probability is that eye error caused the compositor of QM to place 'whether' both here and where it belonged (l. 97 in the Letter).

146–59 Mr. Eaton ... opinions] A vertical pencilled line appears here in the margin of 1812. Similar lines appear adjacent to ll. 174–7 ('An ... natures'), 259–68 ('Does ... spirits'), and 338–48 ('The system ... superstructure').

202 possess] The copy-text originally read 'profess' but has been corrected in ink to 'possess', presumably by S.

257 is] QM inserts the following here in the Note on 'I will beget a Son': 'The blood shed by the votaries of the God of mercy and peace, since the establishment of His religion, would probably suffice to drown all other sectaries now on the habitable globe.'

261 falshood] From this point on the compositor adheres to S's characteristic spelling of this word, which was (like 'alledge') a contemporary variant spelling. Other differences in spelling may be traced to similar acceptance by the

compositor of S's variant (and variable) spelling; e.g. l. 302 'inquiry' (elsewhere 'enquiry'). For S's uncertain spelling of 'certain words', see F iv. 554–5.

265 obsolete] *QM* inserts the following here in the Note on 'I will beget a Son': 'that Milton's poem alone will give permanency to the remembrance of its absurdities.'

283 opinions] The 'p' is barely discernible in *1812*.

283–5 Man!. . . humility] Considerably recast in the *Queen Mab* Note on 'I will beget a Son': 'on so feeble a thread hangs the most cherished opinion of a sixth of the human race! When will the vulgar learn humility? When will the pride of ignorance blush at having believed before it could comprehend?

294 convulsionists] This occurrence predates by over forty years the first usage of this word recorded in the *OED*. However, in its earlier form ('convulsionary') the word refers specifically to a sect of eighteenth-century French Jansenists whose induced convulsions at the tomb of one of their deceased predecessors were supposedly accompanied by miraculous cures.

296 demand] S tended to use 'demand' in the relatively neutral sense 'ask' rather than with the peremptory overtones usually associated with the English word; see F. S. Ellis's *A Lexical Concordance to the Poetical Works of Percy Bysshe Shelley* (London, 1892).

310 festinating] 'hastening'. The *OED* lists S as the last of a small group of writers to use this Latin borrowing.

322 your] There is a three-en gap before this word in the copy-text.

346 premises] The copy-text originally read 'promises' but was corrected to 'premises', presumably by S.

351 If. . . spoken] S uses this verbatim in the *Queen Mab* Note on 'I will beget a Son'; in the Note on 'There is no God' he gives it in French and in large capitals as the concluding portion of a long passage from the Baron d'Holbach's *Système de la Nature*.

391 opinion] A very small comma may be penned in after this word in *1812*.

A VINDICATION OF NATURAL DIET

83 grave"] S provided a footnote in the *Queen Mab* Note: '*Return to Nature*, Cadell, 1811.'

107 question] S inserted the following paragraph at this point in the Note: 'It is true that mental and bodily derangement is attributable in part to other deviations from rectitude and nature than those which concern diet. The mistakes cherished by society respecting the connection of the sexes, whence the misery and diseases of unsatisfied celibacy, unenjoying prostitution, and the premature arrival of puberty necessarily spring; the putrid atmosphere of crowded cities; the exhalations of chemical processes; the muffling of our bodies in superfluous apparel; the absurd treatment of infants:—all these, and innumerable other causes, contribute their mite to the mass of human evil.' S apparently intended to insert these sentences (which qualify the over-simplification of the *Vindication*) into the draft of *On the Vegetable System of Diet* as well (see *Vegetable System*, l. 170EC).

140C cœcum] S perhaps took over the spelling from Newton (*Return to Nature*, 18 n.). There seems to be no authority for it, and Newton's probable source in

William Lambe read 'cæcum' (p. 31). Alternatively, the fact that '*Cyclopædia*' in the same footnote actually reads 'Cyclopœdia' may suggest a printer's error (or expedient) for both spellings.

226 impossible, had] In *QM* S (or the house corrector) removed the redundant 'that' (226c) and added the comma (226). The *QM* reading is preferred here.

THE ASSASSINS

TITLE. The title is formally centred, as if for printer's copy, and suggests—as do the first several pages of the draft—that Mary Shelley was transcribing (or S was dictating) from an earlier draft. To the right and slightly above the title appears the following cancelled verse fragment in S's hand and in a darker ink than that of the draft: 'Like a worm in the bud | Was the ?knife in the blood | As I pierced ?near the heart.'

CHAPTER-HEADING. A pencilled word, '? Hibberil', appears to the left and slightly above this heading.

22 them] A word which looks like 'Ilighton' or perhaps 'Highton' has been heavily printed above and to the right of 'them' and keyed into place immediately after it by a square bracket. It seems to be a later insertion, written over a pencilled word with a broader nib than the text around it, and in a stylized hand which may not be either S's or Mary's.

54 ⟨de⟩generate] Mary's emendation of 'regenerate' to 'degenerate' in post-*1840* editions indicates that she felt she must have misheard (less probably miscopied) S's word, though the *OED* does note an Elizabethan usage of 'regenerate' which could justify the reading in *MS*.

67 philanthropy] *MS* is badly smudged and the word seems strangely elongated, even if one reads '?philanthrophy'; but Mary's reading (*1840*) of her own writing is probably definitive (and the smudging may have occurred after she had made up her printer's copy).

68 industry] Obscured by the smudge noted in the previous note, but probable.

73 of . . . self] The few letters which have not worn away confirm the reading of *1840*.

86 multitude] The pencilled bracket preceding this word (see the Collation) might have been meant to key an insert or suggest a possible deletion. The sentence it interrupts seems a *non sequitur*, as does the rest of the paragraph.

111 ancient] S's preferred spelling was 'antient' (cf. l. 545).

180 crowding] If Mary was transcribing from S's draft, a following space may indicate her inability to read S's hand.

187 securely] A sharper nib begins with the cancelled 'Now' before 'securely' but quickly degenerates and is resharpened at l. 208 ('Alas!').

216 It is true] Mary's paragraph indentations, as here, are generally 2.5 cms. to 4 cms. (1″ to 1.5″) wider than S's, which normally allow space for no more than three or four letters.

218c occuppa |tion| The pencilled bracket which encloses 'tion' on three sides may have something to do with an encircled '193 ?r' (perhaps 'B') above and at the end of the word.

223c influence. [During three centuries]] The false start probably represents

S's change of mind rather than Mary's original composition. It appears indented below the last line of 'Chapter First'. S decided at this point that he wished to begin a new chapter, hence the cancellation.

235 Monstrous] A bracketed '[X' follows here, perhaps to key an unwritten footnote; a short vertical dash through the bracket might have been meant as a cancel.

246C [natures] moral being] The cancel may represent Mary's error in transcription (see l. 245) or, less likely, S's recognition in dictating (perhaps from his own rough draft) that he was repeating words in close proximity.

247–8C [which] /by ... intelligences/] The short diagonal strokes deleting 'which' are those often used by Mary, but S seems to have inserted 'by ... intelligences', which in effect replaced '[their   intelligences]' of l. 248C. The space before '[intelligences]' was probably left by Mary because she could not read S's hand. If this probability is allowed, it also means that around this point in the process of transcription Mary was working directly from a draft by S, an inference that may gain some backing from the fact that the punctuation increases and improves somewhat through the next two pages. It may then be the case that the 'limited' which S supplied before his inserted 'intelligences' was the word which Mary could not read and left a space for before the cancelled '[intelligences]'. Since the other changes, before and after this one, are in Mary's hand, S's scribal intrusion into the correcting process may be explained by the illegible word, which Mary had asked him to clarify. He not only did that first hand but changed the construction as well, apparently omitting the 'been' following, which appears to be in Mary's hand.

258C nation [of the happy nation]] The cancelled repetition may be read as further evidence that Mary was copying directly from the transcript.

265C [became] /formed/] This change, as well as those in 266C and 282C, appears to be in Mary's hand. These alterations could represent her own creative editing or they could be changes made from S's dictation or at his direction.

268C [e]Each devot[ing]ed] Originally part of the preceding sentence; the period was added when the words were mended.

279C /in every case/] The insertion in Mary's hand may indicate that she was editing, creating, or checking the work against the draft she was copying from— or that S decided on the insertion after having dictated its surrounding context.

307C /human/] MS's 'human' written under 'passion' seems irrelevant and may have some connection with an irrelevant '/ ?life/' noted in 218C, since both words are at the very bottom of their respective leaves and taken together repeat the 'human life' of l. 218.

310 Who] Sharper nib from here.

venemous] An alternative spelling at best obsolescent in the early nineteenth century.

321C [Is] the] The 'Is the' of a previous sentence in Mary's hand (l. 316) suggests that S was here transcribing from the same draft that she had been using.

340 crimes] A superscript 'x' above the 's' of 'crimes' keys in 'How ... cunning', which follows a corresponding 'x' about two-thirds of the way down fol. 42^r, between the words 'mad' and 'with' (l. 384). S apparently wrote the insertion on the blank fol. 42^r, then later wrote around it. See the following note. Because of S's practice of writing or interpolating on different leaves material

meant to appear consecutively in the same context, the MS pagination keyed to the first word of a given leaf as noted in the Collation will from this point sometimes be followed by line-references which actually appear on other MS pages. A close reading of the relevant notes below should allow the reader to reconstruct the manuscript ordering relative to that of the text as printed here.

345–59 [The . . . felicity.]] This passage immediately follows 'crimes' (l. 340) in *MS* but has been deleted with a large 'X'. If the 'X' is S's, Mary's decision to restore it is probably without authorial warrant, though—with the qualification provided by the brackets—seems worth abiding by, on the grounds that the passage is an important adjunct to S's characterization of the Assassins. See on ll. 358–9 below.

355 ⟨id⟩ly] Inserted with a caret just above the 'g' of 'hang'. The reconstruction of the word is based both on the sense and on the fact that the blot which obscures the first part probably covers no more than two letters.

358–9 Nor . . . felicity.] This sentence appears twice in *MS*. S originally wrote it at the top of fol. 42ʳ; Mary copied it above the last line on fol. 41ᵛ, with a caret before it. S's original is not deleted, though Mary's copy shares in the deletion covered by the large 'X' noted above on ll. 345–59.

372C [a singular] /one/] The insert 'one' is actually written above '[occurred]' in the preceding line in *MS* but is clearly meant to replace '[a singular]'.

374C woods [found . . . bruised]] The syntactical order of the insertions and deletions is not clear, nor does *MS* contain the received 'a cedar'. See the following note.

376 *and* C [of a lofty cedar]] *1840* accepts the need for some nominal reference to the cedar, though all references to it by name have been cancelled. The choice is between '[broken cedar]' and '[lofty cedar]'; the latter is preferred because it replaced the former and because S uses 'broken' to qualify 'branch' in the same context (l. 378).

376–8 Having . . . branch] These sentences appear at the top of fol. 42ᵛ, where they are set off from the text following them (ll. 393 ff.) by a line running across the page. They are keyed into their location here by a separating line above 'It was maimed' etc. towards the middle of fol. 42ʳ after the lengthy cancel of l. 374C.

380–93 A monstrous . . . . ground] *1840* and subsequent editions bowdlerize these lines as follows: 'A monstrous snake had scented its prey from among the mountains—and above hovered a hungry vulture.' Mary probably felt an aesthetic qualm about retaining the general mass of gory detail which S himself seems to have sporadically relished throughout his life and in any case felt appropriate here.

383 jaws . .] The two dots are followed by a six-letter space in *MS*.

384 mad] This word is separated from the 'with' which follows it by the insert for the previous page which appears at ll. 340–5 (see on l. 340 above). A half-bracket before and over 'with' separates it from the insert and indicates the continuation from 'mad'.

393 ground] There is a line across the bottom of the page at this point, below which is written what looks like 'ares are'. The line emphasizes the separation between this context and the two sentences which follow at the top of fol. 42ᵛ (see on ll. 376–8 above).

397–9 They . . . life] These two sentences appear on fol. 43ʳ in a lined-off space below 'creeping horror' (l. 427). Mary changed 'They' to 'he' when she placed both this and the following sentence after 'lips'. *MS* is ambiguous about the correct placing. Mary perhaps supposed that a small ?'x' above a cancelled 'throned' (see 400c) keyed in the sentence after her reading 'lip'. But, so construed, S's 'they' would have had to apply to 'lip', which makes no grammatical or literal sense. To change the pronoun avoids rather than attempts to decide the question of authorial intention. In fact, S seems to have intended 'They' to refer to the 'eyes' of l. 394. The lined-off space contained room for another two or three lines of text under 'mass of life'.

404–5c fled to the mountain *1840*] Mary might have changed these lines for aesthetic reasons (see above on ll. 380–93). Alternatively, she might have felt that the vulture's pecking out the reptile's eyes and then fleeing with it ('writhing prey' could not refer to the eyes alone) to the mountains contradicted ll. 383–7, where the vulture may appear afraid of the snake; however, the real cause of its fear is the wounded but still living man. The 'ignobler victim' of those lines is probably the soon-to-be-sated snake. At Albedir's approach the vulture's frustration leads it to attack and make off with the retreating serpent even though the latter remains unsated.

422–4 the golden crown . . . brain."] Mary probably omitted this (see the Collation) because of the near illegibility of some of the words. S originally wrote 'unholy head whose poisonous rust' etc.; he later inserted 'the golden crown', though misplacing it (and its caret) by putting it after rather than before 'whose'.

433 *and* c ⟨They⟩] S failed to change 'It' when he replaced 'voice' with 'tones'.

456–7 "in . . . submission."] The clause appears as a complete sentence near the top of fol. 44ʳ. It is keyed into its context here by the introductory word 'In' which appears after the deletion '[. . . high]' (l. 456c) on fol. 43ᵛ. That is, 'In' appears twice. The several cancellations, false starts, and insertions probably account for the upper-case 'In', which is changed to 'in' so that the clause can follow the introductory 'Albedir /he continued/' above.

A sketch of what seems to be a full body profile of a statue of a man on a three-tiered pedestal appears in the space containing the insertion on fol. 44ʳ, which is large enough to have contained a line both above and below this clause.

475 hand] A longer gap than usual after this word may indicate a break.

491c countenance. [But . . . universal excitement, and]] There is a space both in the *MS* and apparently in time of composition between this last deletion on fol. 44ʳ and the following text, which is S's rough draft of the beginning of 'Chapter Fourth' (later transcribed by Mary on fol. 45ʳ):

[Albedir's family consisted of a son and a daughter] [When] On the following morning Albedir arose at sunrise & visited the stranger. He had already risen, & was employed in adorning his lattice with flowers from the garden There was something in his attitude [in an ex] and occupation which expressed in an extraordinary degree [his familiarity & which impressed his host with an invincible feeling of the naturalness & that he was] /his/ entire[ly] familiar/ity/ with the scene—that Albedir's habitation was his accustomed home.—[that Albedir] He [welcomed] /addressed/ his host with a mein of gay & affectionate welcome, that communicated itself by sympathy [to Albedir's] [A] The balm of the dew of our vale my friend said he is sweet, as this garden [It] is the favoured spot where the winds conspire to scatter the best [⟨   ⟩] odours that they

find:—|we know that the sun has arisen &| Come |said he, motioning to walk
forth| |lend me your arm |⟨   ⟩| |?while| awhile, I feel very weak. He
|Observing a spade standing against the house he said| motioned to walk forth,
but feeling himself unable to proceed rested on the seat before the door.—
|There| You have only one spade my brother—|/⟨   ⟩/| |I am| not |well
enough today| We must |make another, but| but procure another quickly—I
cannot (*to fol. 44ᵛ*) |to| earn my supper of tonight, but henceforward I do not
mean |to abuse your affection towards me| to be a burthen on you—
(The rest of fol. 44ᵛ is blank.)

515c em|ployment| A cancelled '2' in the upper right-hand corner may indicate
that the two watermarked leaves (fols. 45-6) were numbered separately from the
others; a number '15' replaced the cancel.

517c spoke. |But ... profound|| There is a 5-cm. (2ʺ) vertical gap across the
page and under the deletion noted in the Collation. A line in the left margin
indicates that 'As' is meant to follow 'spoke'. Either S advised Mary to leave the
space (he might have intended to repeat and expand the deleted material) or she
could not read his writing.

518 Khaled| At this point Mary changed the name S had been using hitherto
('Khalib'), and when S resumed composition (or transcription) in the next line he
continued to use the form Mary supplied here. In *1840* Mary used 'Khaled'
throughout her text. Either Mary or S must have discovered that 'Khalib' was not
an Arabic name. S's later use of 'Khaled' implies a correction of his previous uses
of 'Khalib', which are therefore changed in the text.

522 placing| That is, the stranger placed one of Khaled's hands in Albedir's.

526-7 I ... of| S seems to have picked up a duller nib at this point; several
words here and further down the page (ll. 531-3) are much lighter than others in
the immediate vicinity.

546 with |odoriferous shrubs|| S probably meant to replace '|odoriferous
shrubs|' (deleted because of the 'odoriferous shrubs' of l. 549) with something
comparable. Mary's solution was to omit the deleted words, along with the
'whose' before 'many', and add a 'which' before 'gleamed'. S's intention seems
better indicated by allowing the deletion a place in the text.

556 she| While it is possible that S meant to write 'he' (see the Collation), it is
clear from what follows that Khaled, like the stranger, is gazing below. S is then
contrasting the emotions inspired by the scene both are 'gazing' at. The stranger
is relatively cold; Khaled is ardent, eager, and loving.

564c in| In keeping with the pagination supplied by Mary (see the Descrip-
tion), this page was finally numbered '17'; however, a pencilled '18' in the upper
left-hand corner of the page suggests that the original pagination had included fol.
44ᵛ, which, along with fol. 45ʳ, is numbered '14'. The repagination would then
seem to have followed the recasting in Mary's hand of the material S had roughly
drafted on fol. 44ʳ⁻ᵛ.

591 joyfully.| Below the text there is a sketch of foliage and the following three
faded ink jottings, reversed, in the lower right-hand corner of the page: '?Quiretes
| Pliny's letters | Tacitus Annals'. They seem to be in Mary's hand. ('Quiretes' =
the Roman citizenry.)

ON THE VEGETABLE SYSTEM OF DIET

TITLE. The text uses the title supplied by the Julian editors. There is an illegible word cross-written in large letters in the right margin of fol. 267ʳ and over the first five lines of text.

12–13c [& . . . custom]] Probably underlined for retention, but the line at the bottom of the phrase could have been meant as an additional strikeover.

46 testify [that]] The cancel is retained in the text as a further indication that S intended to add to this clause.

47 How] A bracket before 'How' in MS is taken to indicate a paragraph; but it is possible that S intended to place something else here or to place the matter following the bracket elsewhere.

50 putantem] There is an illegible word above and slightly to the right of 'putantem' which may belong to this quotation.

51c [/like Ladurlad/]] The cancelled 'Ladurlad' is followed by a kind of siglum—a vertical bar with two short horizontals across it at either end—which may indicate the context to which S wished to attach the quotation from The Curse of Kehama, which appears on the following page.

52 anguish?] A space after 'anguish?' may also indicate that S intended to key the Southey quotation to this sentence rather than to include it in the body of the text after 'revolutions' (l. 75), as J does. A line across fol. 268ʳ separates the quotation and its introductory clause from the rest of the text to indicate that they make up a footnote, which was probably written before the text above it. In the quotation S wrote 'And' for Southey's 'But' (l. 2) and omitted the essential point after 'care' (l. 4), supplied here in the text; J reads 'hear' for 'bear' (l. 5). The colon after 'pencil' to introduce the quotation replaces a full point in MS.

56 constituted] J places 'constituted' after 'is' (l. 55), but in MS it is over '[into]', which was cancelled along with '[changed]' (see the Collation), though J retains it before 'the canting'.

56c [The . . . which]] The illegible word before [The] may be a cancelled ampersand or a siglum of some sort (it looks like an open scissors). Following and below '[which]', at the bottom of the page, is a short line under which S has written what looks like 'Feinars Ghosts', perhaps a footnote related to the Southey reference.

61–2 the . . . degree] S actually wrote 'in a greater or less degree the mental faculties', then placed a '1' over 'the mental faculties' and a '2' over 'in . . . degree'. He emphasized the transposition by underlining the entire phrase.

64–6 (The . . . ?Mixed)] The relation of this parenthetical list to the context is unclear. If, as is probable, the suggested categories derived from his reading, S might have placed them here as a reminder to use and better integrate them into the body of his text later.

87–91 The . . . fever] These sentences appear in MS after a 2.5 cm. (1ʺ) gap following and below the line concluding with 'organization' (ll. 95–6). They are set off from what precedes and follows them by two lines running across the text, S's usual method of indicating that he wants a piece of text to be moved. Placing this passage after 'other' (which may have a siglum following it) allows the overall context to cohere somewhat better than allowing it to stand (as in J) after 'organization'; for example, the 'conclusion' (l. 91) to which S arrives seems best followed by the reference to 'this axiom' which begins the next paragraph.

91–6 The . . . organization] The confused relationships in this sentence may be illustrated if not clarified by reproducing their appearance in the holograph:

> The
>
>   is
> and which neither [the] contradicted by the experience of daily life,
>   ?that
> conclusion therefore to which we have arrived . . (that much
>   nor the more subtle speculations of profound philosophy
> of the violent & unreasonable conduct of human beings
>
> is to be ascribed to diseased organization)

The major question is how to treat the parenthetical element, which is also the major statement of the sentence, or potential sentence, which S was constructing here. He quite possibly meant to recast his 'conclusion', and put it into a parenthesis to indicate that he was not satisfied with its present phrasing and/or placing. The text printed above essentially accepts *J*'s syntax as closest to S's original intention. The parentheses are therefore ignored as authorial sigla, as are the two dots after 'arrived', though S did occasionally use a pair of points to indicate some sort of constructive syntactical relationship. Here they seem merely to reinforce the syntactical break introduced by the parenthesis.

91 therefore] *J* reads the cancelled '[/?that/]' (see the Collation) as an uncancelled 'then' and ignores the 'therefore' (partially underlined for reconsideration).

100c that] The leaves are misnumbered in the Bodleian foliation; S's '2' at the top of fol. 271ʳ validates a sequence which is in any case obviously correct.

116 there] Sharper nib and lighter ink from here; also apparent in the insertion noted in the Collation to 114.

120 life] The 'x' keying in S's footnote 'Easton' (given in this abbreviated form and also preceded by an 'x' in *MS*) actually appears over the preceding 'of'. A caret after 'life' may confirm its editorial placing but more probably is meant to place the superfluous 'is' (see the Collation); S perhaps meant to insert a 'what' before 'the natural term'.

120c [life],] The comma was probably meant for the cancelled portion of the context and is therefore omitted from the text.

122c [By . . . human]] The deletions do not seem to form part of the continuous text. They are in a darker ink than their context, which they probably preceded in time of composition, perhaps as the start of a cancelled footnote.

132c [This . . . life.]] This sentence was set off by parallel lines running across the page; it was perhaps originally a note to himself which S deleted when he used its content in the following text.

145 boar] S might originally have written 'bear' (*J*'s reading) but mended it to 'boar'—probably at once, since it is doubtful whether he ever meant 'bear', an animal which is omnivorous and seldom domesticated.

148c ?consequences] S might have written an unidiomatic 'consequences', though he might instead have curled the tail of the 'e' back and over the letter itself.

153 ⟨did⟩] S failed to change 'does' to 'did' when he changed 'is' to 'would be' above (see the Collation).

155 disease . . . life] What may be an inverted comma before 'disease' and what looks like two inverted commas after 'life' could be intended to indicate a quotation from an unidentified source.

158–9 It . . . the substances] S originally began the sentence with 'That', replaced it with 'The', and then inserted 'It is confessed' after both words without restoring 'that' or lower-casing 'The' (see the Collation).

160–1 The . . . stomach] S wrote:

$$\underset{}{\text{The}} \; \underset{2}{\text{stomach}} \; \underset{}{\text{sympathise[s]}} \; \underset{}{\text{[with]}} \; \underset{}{\text{the}} \; \underset{}{\text{remotest}} \; \underset{}{\text{parts}} \; \underset{}{\text{of}} \; \underset{}{\text{the}} \; \underset{1}{\text{body,}}$$

It is possible that S meant to underline rather than delete 'with', which is needed to complete the English idiom. The Collation for l. 161 therefore has 'stomach;' before and 'body,' after the bracket because the editorial semicolon in the text is after 'stomach' while the comma in the MS is after 'body', whose syntactical position 'stomach' takes in the text.

166 regularly] Followed by a six-letter space for a word in the holograph. On the assumption that the 'strongly and' inserted before 'regularly' provided what the space was left for, it has not been recorded in the text or Collation.

187 to [a nature]] The space after the cancel indicates that S intended to provide some sort of object for the uncancelled 'to'; the cancel is retained in the text to confirm that fact and perhaps to give a clue to the kind of insertion S may have intended (see EC on 185–7).

199 animals] A space intermittently filled with numerals and sums appears in MS below the line concluding with 'animals' and apparently inspired the mis-foliation reported in the next note.

200C [Habit]] The Bodleian foliation is contradicted by the numeral '4' at the top of the page, indicating that it follows the sequence established by the '2' at the top of fol. 271ʳ.

reconcile] The holograph appearance of the underline (see the Collation) indicates that it was drawn in error.

202 [produce]] S might have meant to replace this word, in view of 'produce' below, but here the repetition is rhetorically effective.

215 [its]] S probably meant to cancel 'to', not 'its', when he added 'among' and 'unfailing' and cancelled 'be' (see the Collation).

217 Here] The paragraph beginning here is separated from the preceding text by a line across the page. Below the line, above and to the right of 'Here', S has written 'X: X: X:', sigla he uses elsewhere to key in inserts from other contexts. Material from the *Queen Mab* Note and the *Vindication* (from l. 151) could perhaps have been inserted to help make up the 'reasonings' which S refers to in l. 218. Given the earlier reference to a specific context of the *Queen Mab* Note, one might suppose that S was in fact marking a copy of that work with sigla matching those he uses here.

218 these] *J* reads 'then', which is possible. However, below (see the Collation to l. 225) S cancelled 'these reasonings' when, parallels suggest, he decided to insert 'If these reasonings have any force' at the beginning of this sentence. The argument for 'then' is that S did not make 'reasoning' plural, but since he actually wrote 'reasonig' one may suppose he was writing hurriedly enough to omit more

than one letter in the word. The 'then' in the preceding line provides a strong stylistic argument against S's repeating the word here.

228 He] Following on 'Those' (l. 225), 'He' illustrates S's recurrent indifference to consistency in such matters.

234 Before] Two slightly convergent horizontal strokes before this insertion indicate S's indention in *MS*.

245 particular] An '18' in block figures appears about two inches to the right of this word in *MS*. It is apparently a free-hand attempt at reproducing the '1811' tracing of the countermark above (over 'food might', l. 242); fol. 270ʳ has the '11' so traced in the space left by the paragraph conclusion at 'outrage' (l. 267).

251 food] The keying in of the footnote, which actually appears at the bottom of fol. 270ʳ, is a guess, but a probable one. *J* combines the note with the one here keyed to 'diet' (l. 256); *J* omits the Zeno note. In the footnote itself a period has been used throughout to separate the personages listed, though in *MS* S sometimes uses a comma. *MS* has a cancelled '[of longevity]' after 'instances' (perhaps cancelled because the phrase is used twice in the text where S most probably wished to key the note); '113' and 'from another source' are insertions (with no point after 'source'). *J* reads 'Eldems' for 'Elkins', 'Rombold' for 'Rombald', and 'produced' for 'procured'. When the names in the holograph are difficult to read they have been assumed to correspond with the list in the printed 'Appendix' to *A Vindication of Natural Diet*. The 'other source' S refers to is probably Ritson, though in the 'Appendix' S makes a show of indicating separate sources for the first seven of the names on the list. Several of the names also came from George Cheyne's *Essay on Health and Long Life* (see *Vindication*, commentary on APPENDIX). The list makes up the bulk of the 'Appendix' to the *Vindication*, from which S apparently transcribed it, though not always in the same order. It does not appear in the *Queen Mab* Note.

276 expedient? With what] S seems to have changed a period after 'expedient' to a comma and then inserted above it a malformed question-mark when he inserted 'with' before 'What' (see the Collation).

284 even a more] S placed this insert below its line because a cancelled 'no less' occupied the corresponding space above the line. The double line below the phrase (see the Collation) may be meant to emphasize the relation of the insert to its appropriate context.

286 beings] The comma (see the Collation) was probably meant to introduce the cancelled 'that' clause and so is omitted from the text.

296 exercised . . . victims] It is not clear whether the phrase was meant to be cancelled—a faint line through parts of the words may be a cancel—and restored by an underline, underlined for reconsideration, or simply cancelled (see the Collation). The text assumes reconsideration or restoration.

297-9 that . . . disease] The clauses appear as follows in *MS*:

that they may [lead a life]

2

drag out a short & miserable existence of slavery & disease[d]

that   may be then   1

[diet], their bodies [are] mutilated, thier social feelings [are] outraged

S was apparently trying (with little success) to rectify an awkward syntax without recasting it. S typically used underscorings (represented in *J* by italic) to call further attention to numbered transpositions.

301 misery.⁽ⁱ⁾] There is no indication where S wished to key the note, which appears at the bottom of the page after a space (occupied by the sketch of a tree) of about 6.5 cm. (2.5″). After 'confutation' *MS* continues with the following cancel: '[The man who ?shd. act upon this supposition ⟨   ⟩ ⟨   ⟩ would ?be the greatest brute of them]'; for 'monstrous . . . machines' *J* reads 'monstrous sophism that beasts are pure unfeeling machines'; 'very', 'monstrous', and 'unfeeling' are insertions.

ON LEARNING LANGUAGES

1 they] Mary changed 'they' to 'you' and so obscured the fact, likewise indicated by the initial lower-case 'it' which she capitalized, that the holograph continued from another page which would have contained the pronoun's referent.

13–14 poetry . . . panegyric] As usual, S provides no commas in this series. It is therefore possible that 'in satire or in panegyric' is meant to modify 'in the lives of men' but more likely that S used the latter phrase generally to include both biography and autobiography.

16 ⟨with⟩ which] Because of their similarity S might have omitted 'with' before 'which' in rapid drafting; alternatively the need for two 'in's in l. 17 may have been overlooked.

18 expresses] S perhaps unwittingly omitted 'them' after 'expresses' at the conclusion of the sentence, but his penchant for comparable locutions elsewhere (e.g. 'together with their own' at the conclusion of the *Alastor* Preface) suggests otherwise.

33 it] There is space for a word or two after 'it' in the holograph, which perhaps indicates that the word concluded a paragraph; there is no room for another line on this page.

DECLARATION IN CHANCERY

TITLE. There is no title in *MS*, but Mary refers to it as 'Shelley's Declaration' in her *Journal* entry for 2 Feb. 1817. There are in the PRO a 'Brief Petition' and an 'Answer' which are assigned to S but were evidently written by his lawyers (see Medwin, *Life*, 470–3, for a transcript of the 'Answer').

12–17c I understand . . . reasoning.] Bracketed and variously lined for omission in red ink by Godwin, who (rightly) felt that the entire paragraph was unnecessary ('this is all tautology', he wrote in red ink) and ineffectively phrased. 'I understand that' as written by Mary was deleted only to be replaced with the same phrase by Godwin, written in from the left margin apparently to indicate a paragraph indentation.

17c [All this]] This false start is one of the best indications that Mary was composing or partially recreating the text; see also the Collation to ll. 61–2.

17–20c If . . . me] Bracketed in red ink by Godwin. Dowden omitted this sentence while retaining the previous one, also bracketed by Godwin, probably because he read it as ungrammatical. S may be using 'if' to mean 'whether' and inverting the clauses for rhetorical effect.

19c rights.] The period following 'rights' is clear enough but must be an error. Given the awkward inversion noted in the previous note, it is possible that S in his draft had used a '2' and a '1' over the respective clauses of the sentence to indicate that he wished them transcribed in reverse order (his customary procedure). On this view Mary would have transcribed his period but failed to reverse the clauses.

21c |X| Th[is]e] The enclosed 'X' (in black ink) may key in or suggest the need for an insertion. 'Th[is]e' represents Godwin's 'e', written through S's 'is'.

24c heterodoxy, /not even/] Godwin apparently began to enter a third negative 'whether' clause.

40 [have]] What looks like '71' deleted by two lines is written through 'have'.

54c his heart] Godwin and Mary forgot they were dealing with a plural subject by the time they reached the end of this sentence; in this instance, it seems preferable to maintain consistency.

65c [marriage] ⟨/contracted...age/⟩] When Godwin cancelled 'and...that' he initially retained the following 'marriage' and inserted 'This' (see the Collation to l. 65). At that time he also inserted ⟨contracted...age⟩ and then deleted it. His reading would then have first been 'This marriage, contracted at 18 years of age' and was left incomplete when (except for 'This') it was deleted. A period was first placed after 'dissentions' then deleted. He likewise deleted his own insertion as represented in the Collation to l. 73. While Mary's spelling 'dissentions' is probably idiosyncratic, the last use of the spelling listed in the *OED* is 1807.

77 respect] Since 'respect' is written at the very bottom of the page and to the extreme right margin, it is clear that the draft continued on a lost leaf.

A PROPOSAL FOR PUTTING REFORM TO THE VOTE THROUGHOUT THE KINGDOM

1 A great question] See l. 81.

agitating] The text accepts the reading of *MS*, which deletes an 'in' apparently retrieved by the printer because he felt S should have preferred a contemporary idiom in this context which S himself does use elsewhere (e.g. in *A Letter on Richard Carlisle*). But the *MS* deletion is emphatic, and this should weigh more heavily than the fact that the printer's preferred construction was allowed through to the published version, particularly since S does not appear to have checked the proof against *MS*. See also the notes below on ll. 34, 46, 50, 55.

3 Yet on its] S first wrote 'On its' and replaced 'its' with 'the' before writing the received reading below the line.

11 intire] Like 'allege/alledge', 'entire/intire' were used interchangeably by Regency printers. S used both spellings.

22 people,] S here returns to the pointing of *MS*, which had been changed by the printer. See also the Collation to ll. 24, 25, 26, 60, 63, 78, 79, 109, 110, 172, 181, 205. S typically lets the printer's capitalizations stand.

32 worshippers] S here changes the pointing in *P*, even though the printer followed *MS*. See also the Collation to ll. 58, 65, 66, 77–8, 111, 132, 174.

34 not to] The printer omitted the 'to', which S had inserted over a caret in *MS*, and S did not restore it in the proof. However, the reading of *MS* seems confirmed by the emphatic '*their* will' of l. 36 as S's considered intention.

36 *their*] The MS actually reads '*theer*', with a dot indicating that one of the 'e's was originally an 'i'. Given S's spelling, it should have been the first one. Cf. *On Christianity*, l. 302c and TN.

46 public] The previously received 'the' before 'public' was introduced by the printer (see the Collation).

50 Parliament] S emphatically deleted the comma in *MS* which the printer restored and S let stand in *P*. S's conscious decision seems preferable to his passive acquiescence.

55 alone] The printer apparently read the *MS* 'alone' as 'altho', since *P* read 'although' until S deleted it without replacing it—evidence that he did not have the *MS* at hand when he corrected the proof. The *MS* again represents a more authoritative because a more considered reading, particularly so because it calls attention to the exclusive blame which S assigns in advance to a Parliament whose inaction would have fomented rebellion.

then] 'then' appears in *MS* after 'people'; S circled it and ran a trailing arrow to the position after 'would' reflected in the text. S either did not note or did not concern himself with the fact that the printer ignored his direction.

64 evidence] The *MS* insertion may be in another hand.

will to acquiesce] Originally 'acquiesced' in *P*, with 'to' inserted by a caret and 'd' deleted. The *MS* comma after 'will' was meant to introduce the aborted 'that' clause and was therefore not retained in the revision. The *MS* changes are unclear enough to account for the printer's misreadings.

66 disturb] *P*'s 'distrust' is again a justifiable misreading of S's ambiguous script. The deleted and partially overwritten 'that' in *P* suggests that S himself might at first have misconstrued his own intention here, though the greenish ink may indicate another hand.

67c decision.—] The purpose of the dash in *MS* was probably to introduce the cancellation following.

68 which] *P*'s 'this' (see the Collation) probably resulted from the compositor's inability to read the *MS* 'which', which is not only smeared but written in a very light reddish ink partially over and somewhat beyond the word it replaced. S probably changed it to 'which' because of the 'this' two words back. *PC* may indicate that S did collate the holograph at this point, though his dislike of words repeated in close context would have been sufficient impetus for him to change the word without reference to his earlier emendation.

71 on the] The spaces following represent the number of letters taken up by 'seventeenth' and 'March', S's date both in holograph and proof. *1817* left a space of about 4 ems on either side of 'of'.

79c love [which]] The probability is that S failed to note that *P* restored the 'which' that S had deleted in *MS* (see the Collation). The deletion represents S's considered intention, in keeping with his dislike of repetition (another 'which' appears earlier in l. 78), and is thus preferred in the text.

83 and] A deleted 'the' after 'and' in *MS* was restored by *P* (see the Collation); the text follows *MS* as representing S's active intention.

84 go] The *MS* 'come' (see the Collation) might well have been S's intention:

his reference to the *Crown and Anchor* suggests a London perspective. It would then seem that the corrector noted the incongruity of the verb from the standpoint of a hermit ostensibly located in Marlow and thus substituted 'go', which S would have had reason to accept.

90 That] Since the parellelism of the numbered series beginning here requires 'That', its deletion in *MS* may be supposed inadvertent and its restoration in *P* a necessary inference; see on l. 97 below.

that it] The 'it' is probably a corrector's insertion (see the Collation), but is none the less retained in the text because it more readily conveys S's sense and syntax.

97 That] 'That' was written over the deleted 'For this' (see the Collation) in *MS* in a large bold hand, apparently when the adjacent '2' was inserted. The emendation suggests that S finally decided on the 'That' construction as the rubric of the propositional series. On that assumption, the text restores 'That' at ll. 90 and 106, which, along with the occurrence in l. 97, appear in both *P* and *1817*, thus indicating an inference on the part of the printer or corrector which S was content to follow.

102 third] The *MS* insert (see the Collation) may be in Mary Shelley's hand.

106 That] See above on l. 97.

108 declare and publish] See the Collation. The printer was confused by S's placing of 'publish &' in *MS*, inserted as part of a legalistic formula which S reinstated when correcting *P*. *P* gives 'declare, and our signatures annexed shall be published, and be evidence', and the corrections were made thus: 'declare[,] /and publish,/ and our signatures annexed shall [be published,] [and be] evidence'. S apparently deleted one of the 'be's inadvertently, though he might conceivably have intended 'shall evidence our' (if so, he failed to delete 'of').

123 ⟨its⟩] The text changes *P* to accord with *PC*'s emendation of 'their' to 'its' in l. 125 (see the Collation).

141c /considerable/ Expenses] 'Expenses' was originally given an initial capital as the start of a sentence; 'considerable' should have been given one when inserted.

142c Funds] Originally capitalized because it began a sentence.

147 you] S perhaps forgot to change this 'you' to 'Friends of Reform' etc., as he changes the others.

153 A certain] A sharpened nib and lighter ink at this point in *MS* may indicate that S had left off writing at the conclusion of the preceding paragraph. Some scribbled sketches of foliage appear over or under the *MS* deletion in l. 154 (see the Collation).

157c [th[is]e]] A single line seems to cancel the whole in *MS*, but S apparently then wrote an 'e' over the end of the line, expecting the printer to infer (as he did) that the first two letters of the word were in fact to be restored.

Nation] The only capital 'N' so written in this *MS* may suggest S's intention for at least some of those written with a more or less enlarged lower-case 'n', his characteristic cap.

wills] *1817*'s 'desires' seems to have been a corrector's emendation or a compositor's mental slip or expedient. It appears neither in *MS* nor in *P*. If the presumption that *P* was the final proof corrected by S is incorrect, then the reading of *1817* could well have been validated by a still later 'revise' no longer extant. The arguments against such a proof are outlined in the introductory commentary; the chance of a last-minute authorial erratum sent to the printer for a single word is negligble, particularly since the 'national will' seems to have been a concept S was concerned to emphasize throughout the pamphlet. See the Collation to l. 45, which shows 'will' replacing 'desire' in a kindred context.

162 subject] S probably changed the *MS* 'question', correctly printed in *P*, to avoid a clash with the occurrence of 'question' in the sentence which he added at this point on the proof.

179–80 beneficial innovations] The words are crammed into and extend beyond a space left in *MS* for an insertion; S used the same words in a kindred context in *Proposals for an Association of Philanthropists* (l. 104).

HISTORY OF A SIX WEEKS' TOUR

TITLE.] The heading preceding the text is transferred from a half-title page in *1817*.

417–18c We . . . speed.] *1840* retrieves a sentence in *MWS* which is in S's hand. But since it seems to obscure rather than enhance the sense of its context *1817* has been preferred.

433 rocks] Changed to 'cliffs' in Mary Shelley's post-*1840* editions, probably because of 'rocks' at l. 435.

484–7 This . . . value.] This sentence from *1840* appears in S's hand in *MWS* and is therefore adopted here. However, the sentence which follows it in *1840* (see the Collation) is in Mary's hand in *MWS* and is therefore omitted. *1840*'s 'Lucerne' (l. 487) is required for clarity, though in Mary's hand.

516c avelanche] The *1817* spelling has no authority according to the *OED*, and should probably be considered a mistake, though one that the Shelleys often preferred.

560c Our . . . dictation.] The *1840* insertion recasts and expands *MWS* (25 Aug.; in Mary's hand), clarifying Mary's role in the composition of *The Assassins*. See the Editorial Commentary on that work.

562c proposed . . . Gothard] While the substance of *1840*'s insertion is found in S's hand in *MWS*, an earlier reference to this broken purpose renders its repetition here unnecessary. *1817* is therefore preferred.

810c During . . . Romance.] The substance of the *1840* insert comes from *MWS* (10 Sept.).

LETTERS WRITTEN IN GENEVA

Letter I

77–9 never . . . wilderness] These clauses are reversed in *Letters* and in Middleton's printing, appearing directly after what is here printed as l. 47 ('loaded with snow').

Letter II

82 several⟨; and⟩ . . . we] As the Collation shows, *1817* reads 'several, when you shall again hear of us; and we'. While *1840* and subsequent editors accept this

reading, it seems preferable to suppose that Mary did not notice that the printer had misread copy, and to provide a reading that retains *1817*'s words and pointing but places them in an order which makes sense and most probably restores what Mary had actually written.

Letter III

   106 Meillerie] Consistently spelt 'Mellerie' in *1817*; silently corrected in the text.

   156 know] Post-*1840* editions read 'knew'.

Letter IV

   ADDRESS–13 Hôtel ... Geneva] This passage was transcribed nearly ver-batim from the letter of 22 July to Peacock as printed in *Letters*. The reference to the 'home' connects this separately printed letter with that of 17 July as printed in *J* and in *Letters*.

   13 20th] F. L. Jones notes that this is an error for the 21st (Shelley, *Letters*, i. 495).

   14–64 We ... Martin. This passage appears with slight variations in S's hand in the *Journals* entry for 21 July 1816, where it has been set off by brackets, probably to indicate an intention to use it in the *History* volume.

   64 (called ... Sallanches)] Except for the material noted in the next note, from this point on Letter IV follows the original letter to Peacock. The changes as noted in the Collation seem sometimes motivated by a desire for greater accuracy, but in general either omit material unrelated to the descriptions or improve the diction and syntax. The collation is not exhaustive.

   76–88 On ... progress.] This is the only segment of the *History* version of the letter which does not derive nearly verbatim from either the *Journals* or the *Letters* version. It appears to be a conflation and recasting of Bod. MS Shelley adds. e. 16 and the *Journals* entry for 22 July, both of which are in Mary's hand. The original letter to Peacock states only that they had 'visited a waterfall which was very fine'.

   138 earthly] Does not appear in Mary Shelley's post-*1840* editions.

   146 *Bossons*] Mary Shelley first printed the correct spelling of the glacier in her 1845 edition of *Essays, Letters from Abroad*.

   148 least] *L*'s 'leisure' may seem sufficiently preferable to permit the inference that 'least' is a mistranscription.

   180–1 which ... silver] This clause may replace *L*'s 'It is more steep, more broken & more,' a fragment which F. L. Jones says 'seems to have been cancelled by smearing the ink with the finger' (Shelley, *Letters*, i. 498).

FRAGMENT OF 'A REFUTATION OF DEISM'

1–157 In *1814* the fragment was assigned to the members of the dialogue as follows: ll. 1–19 not in *1814*; ll. 20–6/7 Theosophus, *1814*, ll. 577–84; ll. 28–33, 34–84, 88–105 Eusebes, *1814*, ll. 616–22, 626–79, 680–97; ll. 105+ ('Of the argument ... existence') not in *1814*; ll. 107–19 ('How ... Unity') Eusebes, *1814*, ll. 917–26; ll. 119–23 ('The ... Cause') not in *1814*; ll. 124–30 Theosophus, *1814*, ll. 601–8;

ll. 131–51 ('That ... revenge') Eusebes, *1814*, ll. 878–97; ll. 151–7 ('The ... occurrence') Eusebes, *1814*, ll. 931–6 (much changed; the argument is recurrent in S). Lines 88–105 also appear in *The Necessity of Atheism* (ll. 43–62) and in the *QM* Note on 'There is no God'. For a plausible reconstruction of the missing portions of ll. 1–18 see Dawson, *e. 4*, 5–6.

5 legitim⟨ate⟩] While the missing ends of this and other such foreshortened words through to l. 17 are inferable, they cannot be completed by collation with *1814* (as stated in *K* 126 n.) because the passage does not appear there. The bracketed ends here and through l. 16 were first supplied by *K*, except for l. 4's 'sen⟨ses⟩' (*K* read 'ser').

7 its] *K* sees part of S's sketch of foliage following 'its' as an 'A'.

16 usua⟨lly⟩] The top of an 'l' after 'a' is visible at the tear in *MS*, as is part of a tail characteristic of S's 'y'.

18 in ... Deity.] Written in pencil, perhaps as a working title for the material below it (ll. 20–34).

19 a Deity.] The positioning of these words suggests that they concluded a paragraph with a sentence such as that which begins Theosophus' argument in *1814* ('I will readily state the grounds of my belief in the being of a God'). It is also possible that the pencilled line 18 provides some of the words which preceded these two words in the missing part of the *MS* leaf.

20–34 ine ... ntrivance?] *1814* (ll. 577–81, 583–5) completes and reproduces this segment as follows (brackets distinguish *1814* from *e. 4*): '[If we exam]ine the structure of a [watch, we shall readily confess the existence of a watch-m]aker. No work of man ⟨*sic 1814*⟩ [could possibly have existed from all eternity. From] the contemplation of [any product of human art, we conclude that there] was an artificer [who arranged its several parts. . . . If the parts of the Universe have been de]signed, [contrived and] adapted[, the existence of a God is manifest.]' The word 'philosophical' does not appear in this or any associated context in *1814*, but the material after it does appear in another context as part of Eusebes' answer to the argument from design: '[Design must be proved before a designer can be] inferred. The [matter in controversy is the existence of design in the Univ]erse, and it [is not permitted to assume the contested premises and] thence infer the ⟨*sic 1814*⟩ [matter in dispute. Insidiously to employ the words contrivanc]e, design and [adaptation before these circumstances are made ap]parent in the [Universe, thence justly infering a contriver, is] a popular [sophism against which it behoves us to be watchful ⟨ll. 616–22⟩. . . . Why do we admit design in any machine of human co]ntrivance? Simply' (ll. 626–7) etc.

20 structure] There is no corresponding siglum to indicate an insertion or note for the 'x' over 'st' (see the Collation).

27 philosophical] The spacing below this word indicates that the missing line following it concluded a paragraph.

33 a popular] A period preceded by a fragmentary letter below this line indicates that a paragraph concluded at that point.

36 art] This word appears at the end of a line in *MS* and is followed by a space and the word 'They' in a bolder, larger, perhaps different hand.

38 knowledge] *K*'s 'previous knowledge' (see the Collation) is the *1814* reading but 'previous' does not appear in the fragment. As the Collation indicates, several substantive misrepresentations of the fragment in *K* were apparently

derived by the editor from *1814*. There are likewise a good many misrepresentations of the fragment's accidentals (not recorded in the Collation), altered to the form in which they appear in *1814*. Koszul evidently used *1814* rather than *e. 4* for some parts of his transcription.

contrivance of art] *1814*'s 'artificial contrivance' is one of many stylistic changes (here made to eliminate repetition) which indicate that *MS* might have preceded *1814*. See also l. 50, where 'entire ignorance' (mended from 'entirely ignorant' in *MS*) is the *1814* reading; l. 52, 'What' written over 'Why'; l. 56, where 'invariable' became 'changeless' in *1814* (again to avoid repetition); l. 81 where 'their' became 'his' in *1814*, a grammatical change for the better.

71-3 How . . . evident] Omitted in *K*, who then capitalizes the following 'how' and prints it after 'created'. The omission apparently stemmed from an eye-error in *K* (which subsequent editors have reproduced).

72 itself] An instance of S's apparent failure to provide, even in fair copy, the exclamation or question mark which the sentence seems to require. Printing style in his time, as in ours, would probably prefer either point to the period S used here and on rhetorically comparable occasions elsewhere. In at least some of these instances S seems to have considered the given clause declarative. But cf. 'universe.' (l. 74), which is 'Universe?' in *1814*.

85 The assumption] In *1814* this sentence is placed within the previous paragraph before the sentence which it follows here. The *1814* ordering is clearly preferable, suggesting that this isolated sentence is not so much a separate paragraph as it is an afterthought meant to be integrated into the preceding paragraph where most appropriate.

HEADING. Of . . . existence] Appears as a single line in *MS*. Both the form of this phrase and a short separation mark under 'of a' suggest that it is a heading for the material following here. Cf. l. 18.

134 those] Since 'those' is 'the' in *1814*, it may be that the ambiguous relation between deletion and revision (see the Collation) should be reversed, contrary to the received and present reading.

ON CHRISTIANITY

6-7 and . . . Spirit] The text's conflation of part of the deleted matter (see the Collation) with the fragmentary conclusion of this sentence is meant to preserve S's overall intent as inferable from *MS*: 'The institutions of the most civilised portion of the globe derive their authority, [& are imbued in some slight degree by the Spirit of his doctrines] /from the sanction of his doctrines & to a certain extent are/ '. The insertion was clearly meant to replace the deleted material. The fact that it was neither completed nor deleted suggests that S meant to retain the sense it introduced once he had decided on a phrasing that would avoid the repetition of the word 'doctrines'.

19c to] *K* plausibly suggests that 'the underlining of "to" was probably meant as a criticism of S on his own sentence; as an unwary reader might connect it with the verb "attribute," and not—as it should be—with the noun "application"' (*K* 14).

21 who] The nearly two-page gap from this point on fol. 7ᵛ to fol. 8ᵛ ('God', l. 121+) indicates that S meant to add (or transcribe) a good deal more than a

conclusion to this incomplete sentence. *K* suggests that the segment labelled 'Introduction' on fol. 20ʳ (ll. 535–662; see the Collation to l. 535) might be placed here, but he did not have the material in *c. 4*, which contains the reservation about miracles (ll. 24–6) very likely referred to in ll. 591–3. (For further discussion of the placing of ll. 535–662, see below on 535c.) *J* placed fols. 277ʳ–278ᵛ (ll. 48–96, 'be . . . lost the') here, interpolating '⟨may⟩' to join 'who' with 'be'. The text follows this order with the addition of the fols. 276ʳ⁻ᵛ (ll. 22–48, 'I . . . he') and 279ʳ⁻ᵛ (ll. 96–121, 'by . . . was') which *J* did not use. Dawson, *e. 4*, feels that the sporadic pagination S began to supply later in the draft indicates that he did not intend the matter before this break as part of the continuous essay (p. xiii).

27c [J.C. . . . world.]] Perhaps underlined for reconsideration rather than deleted. The text from 'The remarkable' in *MS* is written in a sharper nib with a lighter ink.

33 truth. Every] Since S wrote 'every', it is possible that he meant to reinstate the deleted '[to which]' (see the Collation to l. 32) and join the clauses as follows: '. . . full of heart moving truth to which every religion . . .'.

35 genius] The numeral '2' was added in a darker ink over the word 'genius' in the first line of fol. 276ᵛ but in a hand which may not be S's. This intermittent attempt at paginating these leaves was continued at fols. 278ᵛ ('5'), 279ʳ ('6'), and 279ᵛ ('7'). However, the paginator did not count fol. 278ʳ, which should have been '5', and so fell one short of the number '8' he ought to have placed on fol. 279ᵛ.

86 Meanwhile] The 'The' which *J* places before this word actually appears as an uncancelled introduction to the cancellation at the bottom of fol. 278ʳ (see the Collation). Immediately following the numeral '5' (see the previous note) at the top of fol. 278ᵛ, S has written 'Milton Areopagitica', an apparent allusion to something which he had incorporated, or meant to incorporate (from a previous draft or note), into his text at this point.

90–2 The . . . despotism.] Footnoted by previous editors, these sentences are set off by horizontal lines and preceded by 'xx' but with no indication of where S might have wished to place them.

96 the   by] S left a space for two or three words at the top of fol. 279ʳ, before 'by'.

121 virtue] *TT* places *On the Moral Teaching of Jesus Christ* (written in Italy) here, and follows it with *On the Doctrines of Christ*.

was] The portion of the text in *c. 4* ends mid-sentence at the bottom of fol. 279ᵛ, which indicates that it originally continued on a following leaf, now lost.

TITLE. God] *TT* places this segment through to l. 534 after l. 662.

122–5 The . . . Trinitarian] The comma in *MS* divides the philosophical from the religious triad in this syntax; to introduce commas further dividing the series would obscure a contrast S apparently intended.

133 opinions] The 's' may instead be an accidental stroke; previous editions print 'opinion'.

172 capable] A 5 cm. (2.3″) space follows 'capable'. Below this line there is a 2.4 cm. (1″) vertical gap, with a caret and the word 'Insert' written diagonally up the right margin. *K* feels that ll. 243–51 belong here (p. 20).

188 an] S only half-formed the 'n'; or mistakenly wrote 'as'.

190 but . . . true] The clause does not require the bracketed 'because' supplied by *1859*, and its meaning is reversed by *K*'s deletion of 'not' (see the Collation). S

is saying that poetic conceptions *are* repugnant to the multitude, or to their 'mistaken conceptions'. *K*'s reference to the attack in ll. 233–5 on literal interpretation does not really support his reading because S is using 'literally' metaphorically or rhetorically in l. 190. *K* notes that it 'seems very like S to have written one negative form ("the less") to correct the other ("not") and to have forgotten to cancel the former' (p. 17). *MS* does not back *K*'s supposition, though S's meaning would have been clearer if he had placed 'clearly . . . multitude' after 'poet'. S's occasional tendency to convolute and invert clauses and phrases (perhaps encouraged by his familiarity with inflected languages) is most notoriously represented by ll. 72–3 of *The Sensitive Plant. F* accepts *1859*'s reading, *J* accepts *K*'s. For a different explanation of these lines see *TT* 27.

197 knowledge] The text prefers S's insertion to the uncancelled original, though the previously received reading is 'science' (see the Collation), not only because it was written later but also because it expresses S's meaning more clearly to a modern, as perhaps it would have to a contemporary, reader.

198c [[If . . . spirit]]] The sentence was first bracketed by S, then apparently cancelled by him, though the cancel-line is not that typically used by him, while the sentiment is one which he elsewhere professes. It is possible that he initially meant to move the sentence elsewhere—so the brackets—perhaps before the sentence it now follows. He might then have recognized that the gist of the sentence was contained in the sentence beginning at l. 194 and consequently decided to cancel rather than transpose.

205 solitary] 'The word is doubtful, being an insertion in a very small hand-writing, but certainly looks more like *solitary* than the (unbracketed) *softened* of *1859*' (*K*18).

217 masters] The text follows previous editors in receiving the insertion 'arbiters' in l. 216 and retaining the original 'masters' here, though 'arbiters' would be equally appropriate in either place. Except for rhetorical effect, S tried to avoid repetition of the same word in close context; the supposition here is that in revision he would have avoided it in this place.

220–1c breath, imperial, stupendous] These words are probably underlined in *MS* for reconsideration rather than for emphasis.

235 it] The incomplete sentence ending here is followed below by a note or jotting which may indicate what S intended to conclude it with: 'antient evil state of man'. The words are written in the middle of a one-line space which had probably been left for a continuation of the incomplete sentence. A rather free-floating 'from' (see 236c) inserted in a smaller hand was perhaps meant to further specify either this reference or the Thucydides reference following.

237c th[e]is [difficulty of relating speeches]] Perhaps underlined rather than cancelled. It may be S's note to himself epitomizing the passage from Thucydides he wished to use, or it may be replaced by 'this opinion'.

242 ειρηται.] There is a 4 cm. (1.5″) gap from here to the bottom of the folio.

243–51 Tacitus . . . virtus.] *K* feels that there is 'little doubt' that these lines should be placed after l. 172, since from l. 252 'quite a different question is henceforward discussed, that of Future Retribution'. Given the disjointed state of many of these notes, there does not seem to be enough evidence to warrant the change of context. The fact that 'quodcunque . . . virtus' appears in a 3 cm. (1.3″) vertical gap below and after 'expressed' suggests that S might have left a space for a much larger quotation, an inference which seems abetted by the disposition of the quotation as reproduced in the text.

254 ordinar⟨il⟩y] The *OED* lists an adverbial usage of 'ordinary' dated 1798 which may justify S's spelling, but the text follows previous editors in supposing that he omitted two letters. If S was transcribing from a previous draft, 'ordinary' might have slipped in two words before its time: 'ordinary operations of the Universe' would have appropriately defined S's meaning, which is in any case clear.

256–7 seems ... shapes] *MS* reads 'in all its shapes seems to have been contemplated', a self-editing form S often used to indicate transpositions. The *1859* editor apparently overlooked the numbers and half the underlining to read *in all its shapes* as an emphatic phrase.

285–7 curse you ... such he] A 3.9 cm. (1.5″) gap after 'curse you' concludes the holograph line, while a 15 cm. (6″) gap precedes 'such he', which appears towards the end of the next line. The inference is that S intended to insert more of the text he was essentially quoting.

292, 294 protracted .., good ..] *MS* points are retained because a more orthodox alternative might arbitrate without necessarily conveying S's syntactical purpose. Previous editors have used several different points to variously formalize the syntax, a disparity that tends to justify a decision to let the reader infer authorial intention according to his understanding of what S meant by two dots. (Cf. the Editorial Commentary for *The Assassins*, on ll. 378 and 414.)

295 This ... justice.] S perhaps meant to eliminate this sentence, repeated in l. 298.

299–300 tyrants ... usurpation] *1859* reads 'tyrants ⟨   ⟩ to the usurpation of their rulers ...'; *F* deleted what appeared to be an incoherent fragment to read 'tyrants. Mankind ...'. *K* recovered 'Enslaved by' to complete the sense.

302 achieved] As *K*'s 'atcheeved' suggests, the *MS* letter looks more like 'e' than 'i', but S at times made his 'i's like 'e's (e.g. the first 'i' of 'dominion', l. 310, and probably the 'i' of 'basis', l. 961).

306 and arrogat⟨ed⟩] The ampersand (see the Collation) was a later insert; S apparently neglected to mend the participle accordingly.

340c [Power] ?] The question mark in *MS* may be S's reminder to himself to reconsider the cancellation.

366–7 dust, a few] *1859*'s 'to a' (see the Collation) clarifies the appositive construction.

379 cease] The 'x' over 'cease' (see the Collation) was perhaps meant to key in the Gospel text S is here paraphrasing.

394 with] *K* thinks that this word (in pencil) was added, 'probably by another hand' (p. 27).

the nature of our being] Though typically omitted by previous editors, the uncancelled phrase seems rhetorically apt as an introduction to the appositive clause which specifies and emphasizes its meaning.

405 heartmoving] S sometimes wrote this as one word, sometimes as two.

417–18 The ... revenge] *K* places this pencilled insertion in a footnote. But it is meant to replace the first deletion noted in the Collation to l. 417.

424c [robber]] There are two columns of numbers at the top of fol. 17ʳ.

439–40 The ... ?tracery] K (29) reads the part of this fragment he places in a footnote (see the Collation) as an inserted appendage, 'with a very dry pen', to the preceding sentence; *e. 4(D)* reads ' ?tracery' as 'treasures'. While the gap in the text following ' ?tracery' approximates the gap between the end of the insert and a justified right margin, it is most of all an editorial means of separating the fragment from the sentence following it.

459 Zerxes] Previous editors have supposed that S must have intended an 'X', but the holograph 'Z' here is identical with that which S uses several times for 'Zonoras' in the *e. 4* draft of *Prince Athanase*. The *OED* notes that during the seventeenth and eighteenth centuries 'Z' was on occasion used in place of initial 'X'.

484 mysterious] The word 'mysterious' was inserted above 'invisible' and might have been meant to replace it; it is possible that S did provide a very small ampersand before 'mysterious', though an initial squiggle is more probably part of the 'm'.

486 *perfectness*] Perhaps underlined for reconsideration rather than for emphasis.

489 ⟨has⟩] Another example of an interruptive qualifying phrase containing a plural noun ('attributes') governing S's verb ('have'; see the Collation), which it would be misleading to retain.

490 ?nature] The text tentatively accepts the reading in *e. 4(D)*; 'doctrine' may also be possible.

492 indiv⟨id⟩uals entertain] The *MS* 'entertains' (see the Collation) agrees with the original subject 'nation'. When S inserted 'or indivuals' he neglected to change the verb.

503c Thus the [one]] That 'the' was accidentally retained seems confirmed by the deletion later of 'the other', with which it was originally in parallel.

535c To belong to some other part. Introduction] While the text maintains the order of *MS*, it is clear that in a final version the segment beginning 'It cannot be' would have been placed elsewhere. *K* summarizes the content of the section by stating that it 'dwells on what might be called the principles of his investigation', and then infers that it 'would no doubt have found a place, in a final transcript, before the chapter on "God," which precedes it in the *MS*' (pp. 8–9). Or it may perhaps introduce 'some other part' not yet written. *TT* places it after the fragment *On the Doctrines of Christ*, which the editor considers to be part of *On Christianity*.

535 to] *K*, who follows *1859* in printing 'in' here, notes that 'to' is cancelled. But in fact 'to' was blotted (along with the second 'a' of 'imaginable' on fol. 19ᵛ, l. 518) when the leaf was turned.

537c [In ... equivocal.]] *K* notes this deletion as 'a very clear and outspoken statement of S's method' (p. 34). It has been set off by parallel lines, as if for possible use elsewhere; it is also possible that another hand made the deletion.

544c malicious.!?] The assortment of points in *MS* probably indicates S's negative to uncertain reactions concerning the series of epithets he had just written and partly cancelled, though it is possible that the exclamation mark was offered as a (questionable) replacement for the period. There seems to be a semi-bracket (perhaps keying in a potential insertion) separating all of the punctuation marks from the sentence they follow.

554 neither] The clause may be more readily understood if 'neither' is read before 'bloodshed'.

567c Bacon] The name and 'x' above cancelled 'facts' were probably meant to remind S of the reference to Bacon which he placed on the next page.

576 disapprobation] A 'his' before 'disapprobation' (and possibly 'of' in place of the following 'against') would dispel some syntactical confusion here.

585 determined] The (unkeyed) footnote actually reads: 'Bacon Novum Organum / [Sec] / /Aph/ 53.—De aug. Scien. [B]Lib. V. C. 4.'

598 [the]] Previous editors have accepted 'the' uncancelled; it may not be required for the generic sense S intends.

618–19 constitution . . . have] Another example of a singular subject supplied with a plural verb because a plural attributive phrase intervened.

652–3 nn. See . . . 38.] The notes appear below a blank space of 1.5 cm. (0.7″) under the last line of MS. The text has rearranged and normalized the notes, which are on the same line as follows in the holograph:

¹ See /verse/ 21. ,27. 31. 33   ² 38   Matt. Chap. V.

654 speech] There is a 7 cm. (2.8″) space after this word in e. 4.

680 and   .] The period suggests that S meant to add only one or two words here.

680c Diogenes /&/] S apparently meant to add a name here.

696 possessors] K reads 'posessons' in MS, which likewise does away with the 'i' received by previous editors in their texts. Ordinarily S provided a clear downstroke after an 'i' when writing 'io' combinations. There is none here. Given the missing 'i', 'r' rather than 'n' seems a better choice for the admittedly ambiguous loop which precedes the final 's'.

702–3c onnother] 'one another' seems to be S's intention. Possibly the 'an' of 'another' is partially written through 'one'.

706–7 philosophy and [mankind]:—] S gives no certain indication of what he might have added here, though both the ampersand and 'common' make some sort of addition obligatory. TT supposes that the cancelled '[mankind]' might have been meant to be reinstated after '&'. Since S occasionally dropped his 'c's in '&c' formulae (see 918–19TN), it is possible that he was referring to material from another source which he wished to add here later. The dash concludes the line on which it appears in MS, but S did not begin the following line with an indentation. None the less, the present text accepts TT's suggestion, though supplies square brackets to indicate that, in so far as the word may be S's choice, it was one which not only came earlier in the holograph line but was also cancelled. The fact that S had already used 'mankind' twice in this paragraph might have led him to reject the word here, though not the correlation, which makes excellent sense in this context and might well have been reasserted with an appropriate synonym in a later draft.

721 born,] A caret (for an inserted 'parents') partially obscures the comma after 'born'.

730c love [mankind more]] Sharper nib from here.

748–9 is . . . its] A representative example of S's recurrent use of the singular verb and/or pronoun with a compound subject.

772 thro'] e. 4(D)'s 'thro' seems preferable to a possible 'this'; previous editors omit the word.

784–7 "No ... thereof."] The large space left after 'masters' (see the next note) may, as *K* notes, be meant for the full quotation from Matt. 6: 24–34, whose beginning and end S quotes; however, ll. 813–49 provide a close paraphrase and expansion of the verses omitted here.

785 Take] The top third of fol. 28ᵛ (7 cm.; 2.7″) is blank, as is the bottom third of fol. 28ʳ (6 cm.; 2.5″) following 'masters'. It is clear that S intended to extract and perhaps comment on more Gospel texts.

789 ⟨it⟩ employ⟨s⟩] Again the *MS* reading ('they employ'; see the Collation) indicates that S is thinking in the plural after beginning his sentence in the singular.

805c overgrown/overshadowed/] Neither word is deleted in *e. 4*; S might have meant to retain both.

820c subserviency ... a] S perhaps meant to replace 'to their subserviency to' with 'as they ?personate a' but the replacement is unclear and apparently incomplete.

833c [attain]] Perhaps underlined for reconsideration rather than cancelled.

835–46 Ye ... contain.] These lines appear as follows in *MS*: 'ˣ(The man ... contain.(ˣ(Ye ... nature)'. The parentheses and the 'x's, and another 'x' at the top of fol. 30ʳ, indicate the transposition adopted in the text.

848 as the] Question marks after 'as' (see the Collation) suggest that S questioned his simile. A caret after 'the' was probably meant to be placed below the inserted 'swift ... coloured' of the previous *MS* line.

861 [system]] The fact that 'of' is retained after '[system]' suggests that S meant to underline rather than delete the word, which is retained by previous editors as necessary to the sense; alternatively, S might have meant to delete 'of'.

894c [they]these] The word 'these' was written through 'they' when 'Poets' was inserted.

894–5 Jesus Christ ... imagined.] Previous editors print this sentence as a footnote, but S gives no indication that he intended to place this important distinction outside the body of the text.

900c X———X Slaves] Apparently meant to key an insertion.

912 and he ⟨went away sorrowing⟩] The text accepts *1859*'s conclusion to this incipient quotation (from Mark 10: 22). S probably intended to fill the rest of the vertical gap of 7.5 cm. (3″) with examples of Christ's disavowal of material values, such as that following in Mark (10: 23–31).

918–19 *Acts*, Chap. 2. v. 44 &⟨c⟩.] The ampersand is retained here because S apparently meant it to stand for 'et cetera'. See EC.

927 court] Possibly 'couch', as in *e. 4(D)*.

932 its] Previous editors replace 'its' with 'their' because they suppose S is referring proleptically to 'institutions'; but he could instead be referring back to 'republic' or 'sect'. The 'its' is not clear but probable.

936 engaging them] The text accepts the received 'them', though in *MS* the word looks more like 'thin'; *e. 4(D)*'s 'their' supposes that S meant to write a word such as 'hearers' after it.

961 basis] A clearly formed but nevertheless dotted 'e' makes 'bases' a possible reading in this context. However, as elsewhere noted, S at times wrote his 'i's like 'e's.

968c /with/ which] As *K* notes, S's failure to delete 'with' when he changed his construction led to 1859's rather contrived reading of the sentence's conclusion: 'with which the accumulated authority of ages had made them dear and venerable'.

972 to the] A five- or six-line space (5 cm.; 2.1″) from here to the bottom of the page indicates that S broke off this part of *On Christianity* with an incomplete sentence. The pagination which S continued to supply on the rectos through to fol. 38ʳ indicates that he intended to continue his essay to at least that point in the notebook. Fol. 85ʳ contains a pencilled jotting that may belong to this fragment (perhaps after 'them' in l. 133): 'It was not about these names & these opinions that they disputed but about the possession of power of which these names & these opinions were the symbols'.

ON THE DOCTRINES OF CHRIST

TITLE.] Supplied by *J*; none in *MS*.

1 No. The holograph is headed 'Chap 2' and actually starts with '[doctrines . . .] Man' (see the Collation to l. 23), which is enclosed by two lines and keyed in (with corresponding 'X's) to the position after 'announced' (l. 22) where it appears in the text. As noted in the commentary, the word 'The' preceded '[doctrines]' but was torn off when the leaf containing the 'Lament for Bion' now in the Pforzheimer Collection was separated from the Pierpont Morgan holograph.

14 doc⟨trin⟩es] Unlike 'The' (see above on l. 1), 'Gr' (l. 23 and TN below), and 'Let' (l. 34 and TN below), 'trin' does not appear at all in SC 394, which, like MA 1069, is missing a triangular segment at this point.

23 The] The sentence which begins at this point appears at the start of the holograph. See above on l. 1.

Greece] The 'G' (and a portion of the 'r') appears in SC 394 (see the commentary). The 'ece' of the conjugate MA 1069 leaf justifies an unbracketed printing of the word.

34 its] Probably refers to 'doctrines'.

Let] As noted in the commentary, 'Let' is sufficiently clear in SC 394 to adopt it here as a certain reading. It appears unbracketed in *J* and *F*, presumably because the missing corner of the leaf containing it was in place in 1876 and perhaps in 1926 (though *J* might simply have accepted *F*).

ON MARRIAGE

14 men] The word in *MS* looks like 'nun'; it could not be 'never' (*K*'s reading); 'men' is the only plausible alternative.

28 describe] When the page was turned a heavily inked deletion of 'calls' on fol. 40ʳ blotted 'cribe' on fol. 39ᵛ. That the ink was wet enough to blot half way up the page indicates that S was writing rapidly and adds support to the hypothesis that he might have been creatively transcribing from a rougher draft.

marriage] This word was perhaps supplied later than the other *MS* changes.

ON 'GODWIN'S MANDEVILLE'

TITLE. 'Godwin's Mandeville.' in *1817*, followed by 'To the Editor of the Examiner' (in small capitals); 'Remarks on "Mandeville" and Mr. Godwin' in the *Athenaeum*

75 The language] *1832* places ll. 132-43 ('The events ... of mind.') before this paragraph.

79 has] Another example of S's use of a singular verb with a plural subject which he construed as singular. Since both *1817* and *1832* use 'has', one may care to infer that the press correctors of the day did not consider the usage a solecism. But see the Collation and note below on l. 97.

84 view] *1832*'s 'river' (see the Collation), if not a printer's error, is a probable misreading of S's rough drafting hand, indicating that Medwin might well have been copying from a lost holograph rather than the one sent to the *Examiner*.

97 has] Here the correcting hand (or perhaps Medwin's transcribing hand) has preferred 'have' in *1832* (see the Collation and above on l. 79).

106 purity] *1832*'s 'sincerity' may seem preferable here.

ON THE GAME LAWS

3 distortion] Clark (*Shelley's Prose*, 342) and P. M. S. Dawson (*Unacknowledged Legislator*, 46) read 'deception', a plausible alternative, though S does seem to have made an 's', not a 'c', and there is no discernible descender to make up the 'p'. F. L. Jones could decipher only 'actually represent' in the clause in which the word appears, while Clark read it, with some variation, as cancelled, except for 'actually', which he placed (with a conjectural 'and') before 'virtually' in the next clause. Neither transcription includes 'that which'. Both supply an unbracketed 'They' after a supplied period and before 'virtually'.

18-19 tho' ... question] That is, the question whether they should be allowed the possible justification which 'ignorance or ill-faith' might provide.

24 even] Omitted by Jones and Clark.

ON 'FRANKENSTEIN; OR, THE MODERN PROMETHEUS'

22c /thus/] The word and its caret are each placed a line below the point in *MS* where the text supposes that they belong. If inserted according to the *MS* placing the reading would be '... a source of thus powerful', a strained and unlikely alternative to the assumption that S simply inserted his correction at the wrong point.

38 Human] The part of the text for which *1832* is the sole authority begins here and ends at l. 51 'which'.

83 surpassed] Both the content of the last paragraph, which concerns the conclusion of *Frankenstein*, and the space after this word suggest that S had completed his review, though the notebook gave him little room to continue here even if he had had more to write. There is in fact only one page blank in the entire notebook and that is far removed from this reviewing context.

ON 'RHODODAPHNE OR THE THESSALIAN SPELL'

TITLE. In the transcript 'Pub.—1818' is written above the title; to the right, 'Mary Shelley's writing' is enclosed between parallel lines; below this, 'see Dowden's Shelley, vol. II, 182.' The publication date probably refers to the poem, though it is possible that the writer thought that the review was published then. All these entries are in pencil. To the right of the last line of the title ('a Poem') there is a dash followed by 'Hookhams', the name of the publisher of the poem, in Mary's hand. Except for the editorial 'On' the title is reproduced as it appears in the transcript (italic type and quotation marks are also editorial).

58 up] The word has been crammed in, a later addition.

63–7 Some . . . me] In *MS* this quotation has quotation marks before each line and after the concluding 'me'. The text normalizes the passage to accord with other displayed quotations.

79 wea⟨r⟩] A segment of *MS* is torn out at the ends of four lines; 'wea' concludes the third of these and seems to be the only part of the text affected. Since *F* reads 'wear' the word was apparently complete when Forman transcribed it.

131 hair,] *MS* breaks off here, at the bottom of p. 10.

Bibliography

A selective list of works cited or consulted.

ALLISON, FRANCIS G., *Lucian: Satirist and Artist* (Cooper Square Publishers, Inc.: New York, 1963).

[Anon.], *Reply to the Anti-Matrimonial Hypothesis and Supposed Atheism of Percy Byssche* ⟨sic⟩ *Shelley, as Laid down in Queen Mab* (W. Clarke: London, 1821).

[Anon.], 'Dinner by the Amateurs of Vegetable Diet', *The London Magazine and Theatrical Inquisitor*, 4 (July 1821), 31–5 (also in White, *The Unextinguished Hearth*).

ASPINALL, A[RTHUR], *Politics and the Press, c. 1780-1850* (Home and Van Thal: London, 1949).

AXON, WILLIAM E., *Shelley's Vegetarianism* (The Vegetarian Society: Manchester, 1891).

BAKER, CARLOS, *Shelley's Major Poetry: The Fabric of a Vision* (Princeton University Press: Princeton, 1948).

BARNARD, ELLSWORTH, *Shelley's Religion* (Russel & Russell Inc.: New York, 1964; repr. of the 1937 edn.).

BARRUEL, ABBÉ AUGUSTIN, *Mémoires pour servir à l'histoire du Jacobinisme* (D. Le Boussonier & Co.: London, 1797); trans. as *Memoirs, Illustrating the History of Jacobinism*, 4 vols., trans. Robert Clifford (Privately printed: London, 1797–8).

Blackwood's Edinburgh Magazine, 8 (July 1818), 412–16.

BLUNDEN, EDMUND, *Shelley: A Life Story* (The Viking Press: New York, 1947).

—— 'Shelley is Expelled', in *On Shelley* (Humphrey Milford, London, 1938).

BOAS, LOUISE, '"Erasmus Perkins" and Shelley', *MLN* 70 (June 1955), 408–13.

BRADLAUGH, CHARLES, 'Percy Bysshe Shelley', *Half-hours with the Freethinkers*, 1/4 (15 Nov. 1856), 25–32.

BREWER, LUTHER, *My Leigh Hunt Library: Huntiana and Association Books* (University of Iowa Press: Iowa City, 1938).

BRINKLEY, ROBERT, 'Documenting Revision: Shelley's Lake Geneva Diary and the Dialogue with Byron in *History of a Six Weeks' Tour*', *K-SJ* 39 (1990), 66–82.

BROWN, NATHANIEL, *Sexuality and Feminism in Shelley* (Harvard University Press: Cambridge, Mass., 1979).

BROWN, PHILIP A. H., *London Publishers and Printers c. 1800-1870* (The British Library: London, 1982).

BURCH, ROUSSEAU A., 'The Case of Shelley v. Westbrooke', *Case and Comment*, 23 (June 1916–May 1917), 181–7.

BUTLER, MARILYN, 'Myth and Mythmaking in the Shelley Circle', in Kelvin Everest (ed.), *Shelley Revalued: Essays from the Gregynog Conference* (Leicester University Press: Leicester, 1983).

BYRON, Lord, *The Works of Lord Byron, with his Letters and Journals and Life by Thomas Moore, Esq.*, ed. Thomas Moore, 17 vols. (John Murray: London, 1832–3).

CAMERON, KENNETH NEILL, *The Young Shelley: Genesis of a Radical* (Collier Books: New York, 1962; first published 1950).

—— *Shelley: The Golden Years* (Harvard University Press: Cambridge, Mass., 1974).

—— 'Shelley vs. Southey: New Light on an Old Quarrel', *PMLA* 57 (June 1942), 492–504.

—— 'A Reference to Shelley in the *Examiner*', *N&Q* 184 (16 Jan. 1943), 42.

—— 'Shelley, Cobbett, and the National Debt', *JEGP* 42 (Apr. 1943), 197–209.

—— 'Shelley and the Reformers', *ELH* 12 (Mar. 1945), 62–85.

CANNON, JOHN, *Parliamentary Reform: 1640-1832* (University of Cambridge Press: Cambridge, 1973).

CARNALL, GEOFFREY, 'DeQuincey on the Knocking at the Gate', *Review of English Literature*, 2 (Jan. 1961), 49–57.

CHANTER, JOHN ROBERTS, *Sketches of the Literary History of Barnstaple* . . . (E. J. Arnold: Barnstaple, 1866).

CHARLOTTE, Princess, *Letters of the Princess Charlotte 1811-17*, ed. A[rthur] Aspinall (Home and Van Thal: London, 1949).

CHIAPPELLI, BICE, *Il pensiero religioso di Shelley con particolare riferimento alla 'Necessity of Atheism'* . . . (Edizioni di Storia e Litteratura: Rome, 1956).

CHITTY, JOSEPH, *Observations on the Game Laws with Proposed Alterations for the Protection and Increase of Game, and the Decrease of Crime* (London, 1812; repr. in the *Pamphleteer*, 1816–17).

CICERO, *De Natura Deorum; Academica*, Eng. trans. by H. Rackham (Loeb Classical Library; William Heinemann Ltd.: London, 1967).

CLAIRMONT, CLAIRE, *The Journals of Claire Clairmont*, ed. Marion Kingston Stocking (Harvard University Press: Cambridge, Mass., 1968).

CLARK, DAVID LEE, 'Shelley and *Pieces of Irish History*', *MLN* 53 (Nov. 1938), 522–5.

—— 'The Date and Source of Shelley's *A Vindication of Natural Diet*', *Studies in Philology* 36 (Jan. 1939), 70–6.

—— 'Shelley and *Biblical Extracts*', *MLN* 66 (Nov. 1951), 435–41.

CLARK, GEORGE, *Further Evidences of the Existence of the Deity... Intended as an Humble Supplement to Archdeacon Paley's Natural Theology* (Printed for the Author: London, 1806).

CLIVE, ARTHUR, *Scintilla Shelleiana: Shelley's Attitude towards Religion* (William McGee: Dublin, 1875).

COBBETT, WILLIAM, *Paper against Gold and Glory against Prosperity: Or, An Account of the Rise, Progress, Extent, and Present State of the Funds and of the Paper-money of Great Britain; and also of the Situation of that Country as to its Debt and Other Expenses, its Navigation, etc.*, 2 vols. (J. McCreery: London, 1815).

CROOK, NORA, and GUITON, DEREK, *Shelley's Venomed Melody* (Cambridge University Press: Cambridge, 1986).

CURRAN, JOHN PHILPOT, *Speeches of the Right Honourable John Philpot Curran* (J. Stockdale: Dublin, 1811).

DACRE, CHARLOTTE: *see* MATILDA.

DARVALL, FRANK ONGLEY, *Popular Disturbances and Public Order in Regency England* (Oxford University Press: London, 1934).

DAVENPORT, WILLIAM H., 'Footnote for a Political Letter of Shelley', *N&Q* 176 (8 Apr. 1939), 236–7.

—— 'Notes on Shelley's Political Prose: Sources, Bibliography, Errors in Print', *N&Q* 177 (23 Sept. 1939), 223–5.

DAWSON, P. M. S., *The Unacknowledged Legislator: Shelley and Politics* (Clarendon Press: Oxford, 1980).

—— 'Shelley and the Irish Catholics in 1812', *K-SMB* 29 (1978), 18–31.

DE BEER, GAVIN, 'The Atheist: An Incident at Chamonix', in *On Shelley* (Humphrey Milford: London, 1938).

—— 'An Atheist in the Alps', *K-SMB* 9 (1958), 1–15.

DILLON, JOHN JOSEPH, *Considerations on the Necessity of Catholic Emancipation or the Propriety of Repealing the Act of Union with Ireland* (J. Ridgway: London, 1811).

DIOGENES LAERTIUS, *Lives of Eminent Philosophers*, Eng. trans. by R. D. Hicks, 2 vols. (Loeb Classical Library; Harvard University Press: Cambridge, Mass., 1965).

DOBELL, BERTRAM, 'Shelleyana', *Athenaeum*, 2993 (7 Mar. 1885), 313.

DOWDEN, EDWARD, *The Life of Percy Bysshe Shelley*, 2 vols. (Kegan Paul, Trench & Co.: London, 1886).

—— 'Some Early Writings of Shelley', *Contemporary Review*, 46 (Sept. 1884), 383–96.

DRUMMOND, WILLIAM, *Academical Questions* (Cadell and Davies: London, 1805).

—— *Oedipus Judaicus* (A. J. Volpy: London, 1811).

DUNBAR, CLEMENT, *A Bibliography of Shelley Studies: 1823-1950* (Garland Publishing, Inc.: New York and London, 1976).

ELTON, CHARLES I., *An Account of Shelley's Visits to France, Switzerland, and*

Savoy in the Year 1814 and 1816: With Extracts from 'The History of a Six Weeks' Tour' and 'Letters Descriptive of a Sail round the Lake of Geneva and of the Glaciers of Chamouni', First Published in the Year 1817 . . . (Bliss, Sands & Foster: London, 1894).

ENGEL, CLAIRE, *Byron et Shelley en Suisse et en Savoie, mai-octobre, 1816* (Chambery, 1930).

ENSOR, GEORGE, *On National Government*, 2 vols. (J. Johnson: London, 1810).

—— *On National Education* (Longman *et al.*: London, 1811).

—— *Defects of the English Laws and Tribunals* (J. Johnson: London, 1812).

ERSKINE, THOMAS, *The Speeches of the Hon. Thomas Erskine . . . on Subjects Connected with the Liberty of the Press*, collected by James Ridgway (London, 1810).

EVEREST, KELVIN, ed. *Shelley Revalued: Essays from the Gregynog Conference* (Leicester University Press: Leicester, 1983).

FORMAN, H. BUXTON, *The Shelley Library: An Essay in Bibliography. Shelley's own Books, Pamphlets & Broadsides, Posthumous Separate Issues and Post-humous Books Wholly or Mainly by Him* (The Shelley Society Publications; London: Reeves and Turner, 1886).

—— 'The Hermit of Marlow: A Chapter in the History of Reform', *The Gentleman's Magazine*, NS 38 (May 1887), 483–97.

FROTHINGHAM, WASHINGTON, *Atheos: Or, The Tragedies of Unbelief* (Shelden & Co.: New York, 1862).

FULLER, JEAN OVERTON, *Shelley: A Biography* (Jonathan Cape Limited: London, 1968).

GIBBON, EDWARD, *The Miscellaneous Works of Edward Gibbon with Memoirs of his Life and Writings*, 5 vols. (John Murray: London, 1814).

GINGERICH, SOLOMON, 'Shelley's Doctrine of Necessity versus Christianity', *PMLA* 33 (Sept. 1918), 444–73.

GLASHEEN, ADELINE E., 'Shelley's First Published Review of Mandeville', *MLN* 59 (Mar. 1944), 172–3.

GODWIN, WILLIAM, *An Enquiry Concerning Political Justice and its Influence on General Virtue and Happiness*, 2 vols. in 1 (G. G. J. and J. Robinson: London, 1793); 3rd edn. (1798) repr. as *Enquiry Concerning Political Justice and its Influence on Morals and Happiness*, 3 vols., ed. F. E. L. Priestly (University of Toronto Press: Toronto, 1946).

GRABO, CARL, *The Magic Plant: The Growth of Shelley's Thought* (The University of North Carolina Press: Chapel Hill, 1936).

GRAHAM, WALTER, 'Shelley and the *Empire of the Nairs*', *PMLA* 40 (Dec. 1925), 881–91.

GRANNISS, RUTH, *A Descriptive Catalogue of the First Editions . . . of the Writings of Percy Bysshe Shelley* (Grolier Club: New York, 1923).

GUINN, JOHN POLLARD, *Shelley's Political Thought* (Mouton: The Hague, 1969).

GURNEY, WILLIAM BRODIE, *The Trials of Jeremiah Brandreth, William Turner, Isaac Ludlam, George Weightman, and Others for High Treason, under a Special Commission at Derby . . . with the Antecedent Proceedings . . . Taken in Short Hand by William Brodie Gurney*, 2 vols. (Butterworth & Son: London, 1817).

HALÉVY, ÉLIE, *England in 1815*, trans. E. I. Watkin and D. A. Barker (Ernest Benn Limited: London, 1949).

—— *The Liberal Awakening*, trans. E. I. Watkin (Ernest Benn Limited: London, 1949).

HAMMOND, J. L. and BARBARA, *The Skilled Labourer, 1760-1832* (Longmans & Co.: London, 1920).

HANSARD, T. C., ed. *Parliamentary History of England from the Earliest Period to the Year 1803* (London, 1803); continued as *Parliamentary Debates*.

HARVEY, A. D., *Britain in the Early Nineteenth Century* (St Martin's Press: New York, 1978).

HERODOTUS, *The Persian Wars*, Eng. trans. by A. D. Godley, 4 vols. (Loeb Classical Library; William Heinemann Ltd.: London, 1922).

HOAGWOOD, TERENCE ALLAN, *Scepticism & Ideology: Shelley's Political Prose and its Philosophical Context from Bacon to Marx* (University of Iowa Press: Iowa City, 1988).

HOGG, THOMAS JEFFERSON, *The Life of Percy Bysshe Shelley, As Comprised in The Life of Shelley By T. J. Hogg, The Recollections of Shelley & Byron by Edward J. Trelawny, Memoirs of Shelley by Thomas Love Peacock*, with an Introduction by Humbert Wolfe, 2 vols. (J. M. Dent & Sons: London, 1933).

HOGLE, JERROLD E., *Shelley's Process: Radical Transference and the Development of his Major Works* (Oxford University Press: New York and Oxford, 1988).

HOLBACH, PAUL HENRI THIRY, Baron d', *Système de la Nature* (first published under the name of Mirabaud; London, 1770).

HOLYOAKE, GEORGE J., *Paley's Natural Theology Refuted in his Own Words* (1843; J. Watson: London, 1851).

HORACE, *The Odes and Epodes*, Eng. trans. by C. E. Bennett (Loeb Classical Library; William Heinemann Ltd.: London, 1960).

—— *Satires, Epistles, and Ars Poetica*, Eng. trans. by H. Rushton Fairclough (Loeb Classical Library; William Heinemann Ltd.: London, 1955).

HOWELL, T. B. and THOMAS JONES, *A Complete Collection of State Trials and Proceedings for High Treason and Other Crimes and Misdemeanors from the Earliest Period to the Year 1783, with Notes and Other Illustrations: Compiled by T. B. Howell, Esq. F.R.S. F.S.A. and Continued from the Year 1783 to the Present Time by Thomas Jones Howell, Esq.*, 31 vols. (Longman et al.: London, 1816).

572 BIBLIOGRAPHY

HUGHES, A. M. D., *The Nascent Mind of Shelley* (Clarendon Press: Oxford, 1947).

—— 'Warton Lecture on English Poetry: The Theology of Shelley', *Proceedings of the British Academy*, 24 (1939), 191–203.

INGPEN, ROGER, *Shelley in England: New Facts and Letters from the Shelley-Whitton Papers* (Kegan Paul, Trench, Truber & Co.: London, 1917).

JEAFFRESON, JOHN CORDY, *The Real Shelley: New Views of the Poet's Life*, 2 vols. (Hurst and Blackett: London, 1885).

JONES, FREDERICK L., 'Hogg and The Necessity of Atheism', *PMLA* 52 (June 1937), 423–6.

—— 'Unpublished Fragments by Shelley and Mary', sect. II, *Studies in Philology*, 45 (July 1948), 472–6.

JOSEPHUS, *The Jewish War*, Eng. trans. by H. St J. Thackeray, 9 vols. (Loeb Classical Library; Harvard University Press: Cambridge, Mass., 1928).

KESSEL, MARCEL, 'An Early Review of the Shelleys' "Six Weeks' Tour"', *MLN* 58 (Dec. 1943), 623.

KING-HELE, DESMOND, *Shelley: His Thought and Work* (Associated University Presses, Inc.: Cranbury, NJ, 1971).

KNIGHT, ELLIS CORNELIA, *The Autobiography of Miss Knight*, ed. Roger Fulford (William Kimber: London, 1960).

KOSZUL, A. H., 'Notes and Corrections to Shelley's *History of a Six Weeks' Tour*', *MLR* 2 (Oct. 1906), 61–2.

LANG, A., 'Shelley's Oxford Martyrdom', *The Fortnightly Review*, NS 81 (Feb. 1907), 230–40.

LAWRENCE, Sir JAMES HENRY, *The Empire of the Nairs, or the Rights of Women: An Utopian Romance*, 4 vols. (London, 1811).

LELAND, JOHN, *A View of the Principal Deistical Writers that Have Appeared in England in the Last and Present Century: With Observations upon them, and Some Account of the Answers that Have Been Published against them; in Several Letters to a Friend*, 2 vols. (1754–6; Crosby & Co.: London, 1808).

LOWNDES, WILLIAM T., *The Bibliographer's Manual of English Literature*, 6 vols., rev. Henry G. Bohn, 1857–64 (Henry G. Bohn: London, 1864).

LUCAN, *Pharsalia*, Eng. trans. by J. D. Duff (Loeb Classical Library; William Heinemann Ltd.: London, 1962).

MAC-CARTHY, DENIS FLORENCE, *Shelley's Early Life from Original Sources: With Curious Incidents, Letters, and Writings, Now First Published or Collected* (John Camden Hotten: London, 1872).

MACDONALD, D. F., *The Age of Transition: Britain in the Nineteenth and Twentieth Centuries* (Macmillan: London, 1967).

MACDONALD, DANIEL J., *The Radicalism of Shelley and its Sources* (Phaeton Press: New York, 1969; privately printed 1912).

MACNEVEN, WILLIAM JAMES, and EMMET, THOMAS ADDIS, *Pieces of Irish History, Illustrative of the Condition of the Catholics of Ireland, of the Origin and Progress of the Political System of the United Irishmen; and of *their Transactions with the Anglo-Irish Government* (Bernard Dornin: New York, 1807).

McNIECE, GERALD, *Shelley and the Revolutionary Idea* (Harvard University Press: Cambridge, Mass., 1969).

MALE, ROY R., jun., and NOTOPOULOS, JAMES A., 'Shelley's Copy of Diogenes Laertius', *MLR* 54 (Jan. 1959), 10–21.

MALTHUS, THOMAS R., *An Essay on the Principle of Population* (1798; 5th edn., 3 vols., J. Murray: London, 1817).

MANSEL, PHILIP, *Louis XVIII* (Blond and Briggs: London, 1981).

'MATILDA, ROSA' (pseud. for Charlotte Dacre), *Confessions of the Nun of St. Omer*, 3 vols. (London, 1805).

MEDWIN, THOMAS, *The Life of Percy Bysshe Shelley*, ed. H. B. Forman (Humphrey Milford: London, 1913).

—— *The Shelley Papers: Memoir of Percy Bysshe Shelley* (Whittaker, Treacher, & Co.: London, 1833).

MIDDLETON, CHARLES S., *Shelley and his Writings*, 2 vols. (T. C. Newby: London, 1858).

MONTGOMERY, ROBERT, *Oxford: A Poem*, 3rd edn. (Clarendon Press: Oxford, 1833).

MORGAN, Lady [SYDNEY OWENSON], *The Missionary*, 3 vols. (J. J. Stockdale: London, 1811).

MURRAY, E. B., '"Elective Affinity" in *The Revolt of Islam*', *JEGP* 67 (Oct. 1968), 570–85.

—— 'Mont Blanc's Unfurled Veil', *K-SJ* 18 (1969), 39–48.

—— 'Shelley's Contribution to Mary's *Frankenstein*', *K-SMB* 29 (1978), 50–68.

—— 'The Trial of Mr. Perry, Lord Eldon, and Shelley's *Address to the Irish*', *SiR* 17 (Winter 1978), 35–49.

—— 'Shelley's *Notes on Sculptures*: The Provenance and Authority of the Text', *K-SJ* 32 (1983), 150–71.

—— 'The Dating and Composition of Shelley's *The Assassins*', *K-SJ* 34 (1985), 14–17.

—— 'A Suspect Title-page of Shelley's *History of a Six Weeks' Tour*', *PBSA* 83 (June 1989), 201–6.

NEWTON, JOHN FRANK, *The Return to Nature, or, A Defence of the Vegetable Regimen; with Some Account of an Experiment Made during the Last Three or Four Years in the Author's Family* (T. Cadell and W. Davies: London, 1811).

NITCHIE, ELIZABETH, 'Mary Shelley, Traveller', *K-SJ* 10 (Winter 1961), 29–42.

NOTOPOULOS, JAMES A., *The Platonism of Shelley: A Study of Platonism and the Poetic Mind* (Duke University Press: Durham, NC, 1949).

—— 'The Dating of Shelley's Prose', *PMLA* 58 (June 1943), 477–98.

OWENSON, SYDNEY: see Lady Morgan.

PAINE, THOMAS, *The Writings of Thomas Paine*, ed. Moncure Daniel Conway, 4 vols. (1894–6; AMS Press, Inc.: New York, 1967).

PALEY, WILLIAM, *A View of the Evidences of Christianity in Three Parts* (1794; 2 vols., Vernor, Hood & Sharpe: London, 1813).

—— *Natural Theology: Or, Evidences of the Existence and Attributes of the Deity, Collected from the Appearances of Nature* (1802; Longman and Co. et al.: London, 1813).

PEACOCK, THOMAS LOVE, *Essays, Memoirs, Letters & Unfinished Novels*, ed. H. F. B. Brett-Jones and C. E. Jones (The Halliford Edition of the Works of Thomas Love Peacock [10 vols., 1924–34], 8; AMS Press, Inc.: New York, 1967).

—— *Memoirs of Shelley*: see HOGG.

PEARCE, CHARLES E., *The Beloved Princess: Princess Charlotte of Wales, the Lonely Daughter of a Lonely Queen* (Stanley Paul & Co.: London, 1911).

PECK, WALTER E., *Shelley: His Life and Work*, 2 vols. (Ernest Benn: London, 1927).

—— 'Shelley and the Abbé Barruel', *PMLA* 36 (Sept. 1921), 347–53.

—— 'Shelley's Reviews Written for the *Examiner*', *MLN* 39 (Feb. 1924), 118–19.

—— 'Shelley's Indebtedness to Sir Thomas ⟨for James⟩ Lawrence', *MLN* 40 (Apr. 1925), 246–9.

PLUTARCH, *Moralia*, Eng. trans. by H. Cherniss and W. C. Helmbold (Loeb Classical Library; William Heinemann Ltd.: London, 1957).

PULOS, C. E., *The Deep Truth: A Study of Shelley's Scepticism* (University of Nebraska Press: Lincoln, 1954).

RATCHFORD, F. E., 'Shelley Meets the Texas Legislature', *Southwest Review*, 30 (Winter 1945), 161–6.

ROBERTSON, J. M., *A History of Freethought in the Nineteenth Century* (Watts & Co.: London, 1929).

ROBINSON, CHARLES E., *Shelley and Byron: The Serpent and Eagle Wreathed in Flight* (Johns Hopkins University Press: Baltimore, 1976).

—— 'Percy Bysshe Shelley, Charles Ollier, and William Blackwood', in Kelvin Everest (ed.), *Shelley Revalued: Essays from the Gregynog Conference* (Leicester University Press: Leicester, 1983).

ROBINSON, HENRY CRABB, *Diary, Reminiscences and Correspondence of Henry Crabb Robinson*, ed. Thomas Sadler, 3 vols. (Macmillan and Co.: London, 1869).

ROSSETTI, WILLIAM M., *Memoir of Percy Bysshe Shelley* (Edward Moxon, Son & Co.: London, 1870).

—— 'Shelley in 1812–13: An Unpublished Poem, and Other Particulars', *Fortnightly Review*, NS 9 (Jan. 1871), 67–85.

ST CLAIR, WILLIAM, *The Godwins and the Shelleys: The Biography of a Family* (W. W. Norton & Company: New York, 1989).

SALT, HENRY S., *Shelley's Principles: Has Time Refuted or Confirmed them?* (William Reeves: London, 1892).

SCOTT, SIDNEY, 'Introduction', in *Memoirs of Alexy Haimatoff* (Folio Society: London, 1952).

SCRIVENER, MICHAEL HENRY, *Radical Shelley* (Princeton University Press: Princeton, 1982).

SHARPE, CHARLES KIRKPATRICK, *Letters from and to Charles Kirkpatrick Sharpe, Esq.*, ed. Alexander Allardyce, 2 vols. (William Blackwood and Sons: Edinburgh, 1888).

SHELLEY, MARY WOLLSTONECRAFT, *Frankenstein: Or, The Modern Prometheus. The 1818 Text*, ed. James Rieger (The University of Chicago Press: Chicago, 1982).

—— *Mary Shelley's Journal*, ed. F. L. Jones (University of Oklahoma Press: Norman, 1947).

—— *The Letters of Mary Wollstonecraft Shelley*, ed. Betty T. Bennett, 3 vols. (The Johns Hopkins University Press: Baltimore, 1980–7).

—— *The Journals of Mary Shelley 1814-1844*, ed. Paula Feldman and Diana Scott-Kilvert, 2 vols. (Clarendon Press: Oxford, 1987).

—— *Rambles in Germany and Italy, in 1840, 1842, and 1843*, 2 vols. (Edward Moxon: London, 1844).

[SHELLEY, PERCY BYSSHE], 'A Refutation of Deism, in a Dialogue between a Deist and a Christian', *The Theological Inquirer, or Polemical Magazine* (London), 1 (Mar. 1815), 6–24; ibid. (Apr. 1815), 121–31 [anonymous].

—— *Essays, Letters from Abroad, Translations and Fragments, by Percy Bysshe Shelley*, ed. Mary Shelley (Edward Moxon: London, 1840 ⟨actually 1839⟩).

—— *Shelley Memorials: From Authentic Sources. To Which is Added an Essay on Christianity*, ed. [Jane,] Lady Shelley (Smith, Elder and Co.: London, 1859).

—— *Relics of Shelley*, ed. Richard Garnett (Edward Moxon & Co.: London, 1862).

—— *Notes on Sculptures in Rome and Florence, together with a Lucianic Fragment ⟨The Elysian Fields⟩ and a Criticism of Peacock's Poem "Rhododaphne" by Percy Bysshe Shelley*, ed. Harry Buxton Forman (privately printed: London, 1879).

—— *The Works of Percy Bysshe Shelley in Verse and Prose*, ed. Harry Buxton Forman, 8 vols. (Reeves and Turner: London, 1880).

—— *Review of Hogg's Memoirs of Prince Alexy Haimatoff by Percy Bysshe Shelley: Together with an Extract from Some Early Writings of Shelley by Prof. E. Dowden*, ed. T. J. Wise (Shelley Society Publications, Second Series, No. 2; Reeves and Turner: London, 1886).

—— *Essays and Letters by Percy Bysshe Shelley*, ed. Ernest Rhys (Walter Scott: London, 1886).

—— *A Proposal for Putting Reform to the Vote ...*, Facsimile of the

Holograph Manuscript with an Introduction by H. Buxton Forman
(Reeves and Turner: London, 1887).

[SHELLEY, PERCY BYSSHE], *The Prose Works of Percy Bysshe Shelley*, ed.
Richard Herne Shepherd, 2 vols. (Chatto & Windus: London, 1888).

—— *An Address, to the Irish People*, ed. T. J. Wise (Reeves and Turner:
London, 1890).

—— *Shelley's Literary and Philosophical Criticism*, ed. John Shawcross
(Henry Frowde: London, 1909).

—— *Shelley's Prose in the Bodleian Manuscripts*, ed. A. H. Koszul (Henry
Frowde: London, 1910).

—— *The Complete Works of Percy Bysshe Shelley*, ed. Roger Ingpen and
Walter E. Peck, 10 vols. (1926–30; Gordian Press: New York, 1965).

—— *Shelley's Lost Letters to Harriet*, ed. Leslie Hotson (London: Faber &
Faber Limited, 1930).

—— *Verse and Prose from the Manuscripts of Percy Bysshe Shelley*, ed. John
C. E. Shelley-Rolls and Roger R. Ingpen (Curwin Press: London, 1934).

—— *Selected Poetry, Prose and Letters*, ed. A. S. B. Glover (Nonesuch Press:
London, 1951).

—— *Shelley's Prose: Or, The Trumpet of a Prophecy*, ed. David Lee Clark
(University of New Mexico Press: Albuquerque, N. Mex., 1954).

—— *Shelley and his Circle 1773-1822*, ed. K. N. Cameron (vols. i–iv) and
Donald H. Reiman (vols. v–viii) (Harvard University Press: Cambridge, Mass., 1961–86).

—— *The Letters of Percy Bysshe Shelley*, ed. Frederick L. Jones, 2 vols.
(Clarendon Press: Oxford, 1964).

—— *The Complete Poetical Works of Percy Bysshe Shelley*, ed. Neville
Rogers, 2 vols. (Clarendon Press: Oxford, 1972–5).

—— 'Bodleian Shelley MSS. Re-examined: A Re-edited Text of Some of
Shelley's Prose Works in the Bodleian MSS. (II)' (*On Christianity*), ed.
Tatsuo Tokoo, *Humanities: Bulletin of the Faculty of Letters, Kyoto Pre-
fectural University*, 35 (Nov. 1983).

—— *Bodleian MS. Shelley e. 4*, ed. P. M. S. Dawson (The Bodleian Shelley
Manuscripts, 3; Garland Publishing, Inc.: New York, 1987).

SOUTHEY, ROBERT, *The Life and Correspondence of Robert Southey*, ed.
Charles Cuthbert, 6 vols. (Longman *et al.*: London, 1849–50).

STOCKDALE, JOHN JAMES, *Stockdale's Budget* (London, 1827).

TACITUS, *The Annals*, Eng. trans. by John Jackson (Loeb Classical Library;
Harvard University Press: Cambridge, Mass., 1962).

—— *The Histories*, Eng. trans. by Clifford H. Moore (Loeb Classical
Library; Harvard University Press: Cambridge, Mass., 1962).

THOMPSON, E. P., *The Making of the English Working Class* (Victor
Gollancz: London, 1963).

THUCYDIDES, *History of the Peloponnesian Wars*, Eng. trans. by Charles

Foster Smith, 4 vols. (Loeb Classical Library: William Heinemann Ltd.: London, 1928–35).

THURMAN, WILLIAM RICHARD (ed.), 'Letters about Shelley from the Richard Garnett Papers' (unpubl. doctoral diss., University of Texas at Austin, 1972).

TODHUNTER, JOHN, *Shelley and the Marriage Question* (Privately printed: London, 1889).

VAUGHAN, PERCY, 'Early Shelley Pamphlets, IV: The Irish Pamphlets', *The Literary Guide and Rationalist Review*, ns 101 (1 Nov. 1904), 169–70; repr. in *Early Shelley Pamphlets* (Watts & Co.: London, 1905).

WASSERMAN, EARL R., *Shelley: A Critical Reading* (The Johns Hopkins Press: Baltimore, 1971).

WEAVER, BENNETT, 'Shelley's Biblical Extracts: A Lost Book', *Papers of the Michigan Academy of Science, Arts and Letters*, 20 (1935), 523–38.

—— 'Pre-Promethean Thought in the Prose of Shelley', *Philological Quarterly*, 27 (July 1948), 193–208.

WEBB, TIMOTHY, *Shelley: A Voice not Understood* (Manchester University Press: Manchester, 1977).

—— 'The Avalanche of Ages: Shelley's Defence of Atheism and *Prometheus Unbound*', *K-SMB* 35 (1984), 1–38.

WERKMEISTER, LUCYLE, *A Newspaper History of England 1792-3* (University of Nebraska Press: Lincoln, 1967).

WHITE, NEWMAN IVEY, *Shelley*, 2 vols. (Alfred A. Knopf: New York, 1940).

—— *The Unextinguished Hearth: Shelley and his Contemporary Critics* (Duke University Press: Durham, NC, 1938).

—— 'Literature and the Law of Libel: Shelley and the Radicals of 1840–2', *Studies in Philology*, 22 (Jan. 1925), 34–47.

—— 'Shelley and the Active Radicals of the Early Nineteenth Century', *SAQ* 39 (July 1930), 248–61.

WHITE, R. J., *From Waterloo to Peterloo* (William Heinemann: London, 1957).

WISE, THOMAS JAMES, *A Shelley Library: A Catalogue of Printed Books, Manuscripts and Autograph Letters by Percy Bysshe Shelley, Harriet Shelley and Mary Wollstonecraft Shelley* (Privately printed: London, 1924).

WOLLSTONECRAFT, MARY, *A Critical Edition of Mary Wollstonecraft's 'A Vindication of the Rights of Woman: With Strictures on Political and Moral Subjects'*, ed. Ulrich H. Hardt (The Whitston Publishing Company: Troy, NY, 1982).

WOOD, ANTHONY, *Nineteenth Century Britain 1815-1914* (David McKay Company, Inc.: New York, 1960).

WOODCOCK, GEORGE, *William Godwin: A Biographical Study* (Porcupine Press Ltd.: London, 1946).

WOOLLEN, WILFRED H., 'Shelley and Catholic Emancipation', *Downside Review*, 44 (Oct. 1926), 271–84.

YOUNG, ART, *Shelley and Nonviolence* (Mouton: The Hague, 1975).

Index

Names and titles listed in the Chronology and under 'Printed' (or 'Reprinted')
and *Related materials* in the Editorial Commentary are not indexed; elsewhere
names of letter recipients, book titles, place names, and quotations are selectively
indexed. Certain of S's ideas, for example those related to 'morality', permeate
nearly all of his writings and cannot be fully represented in an index. Numbers in
parentheses refer to the number of references on a particular page.

Abdallah: 137, 139, 388(2)

Abernethy, John: 151 n., 395(2)

Academics: 323, 461

Act of Union: xlii, xliii, xlix, 8, 17, 37(2), 41, 43, 44, 55, 292, 293, 294(3), 295, 299, 328, 332, 348

Ahriman: 226, 446

Albedir: 133, 134, 135 *passim*, 136(4), 137(3), 388(2), 390, 544 *passim*

Alembert, Jean le Rond d': 51, 345, 346

Alexander the Great: 97, 257, 258, 468

Alfieri, Vittorio: 142, 392, 484

Allison, Francis G.: 405

Anaxagoras: 98, 374

Andrew, Miles: 158(4)

Angoulême, Marie-Thérèse Charlotte, duchesse d': 303, 304, 305(3), 306(2), 307(3), 308(2), 400

Apollonius Tyanaeus: 299

Apuleius, Lucius: 285, 487, 488, 490, 493, 494(2)

Ariosto, Ludovico: 164, 314(3), 496

Aristotle: 501

Aspinal, A(rthur): 406, 452

Athenaeum: xxxii, xxxiii, 434, 483, 489, 490, 565

Bacon, Francis: 1 (quoted), 118, 123, 261 and n., 326, 346, 392, 469, 485, 527, 562(2)

Barachias: 108(2), 379

Barrabbas: 69

Barruel, Abbé Augustin: 51, 339, 345; *Mémoires pour servir à l'histoire du jacobinisme*, 51 n., 339, 345(2), 385

Barry, Mr.: 356

Bayard, Pierre: 454

Bayle, Pierre: 346

Beaumaris (S's speech at): 301

Beckford, William: 446

Behrendt, Stephen: xxiii n.

Bennet, Mr.: 316

Bennett, Betty: 432, 439

Bentham, Jeremy: 426(3)

Berkeley, George (Bishop): 383

Bethzatanai: 126, 127, 128, 388, 389, 504, 505

Bible: xxiii n., xli, 66–7, 77 (Adam and Eve), 83, 95–109 *passim*, 322, 348, 355, 357, 367, 368, 371, 375, 376(2), 389 (Eden), 461(2), 462(2), 478 (quoted); OLD TESTAMENT: *Deuteronomy*, 102 n.; *Ecclesiastes*, 249, 254 (paraphrased), 279 (quoted), 486; *Exodus*, 102 n., 376(2); *Ezekiel*, 102 n., 376(2); *Genesis*, 77 (allusion), 154 (allusion); *Hosea*, 102 n., 376; *Isaiah*, 107, 378, 470 n.; *Job*, 249; *Joshua*, 102 n., 103 n.; *Numbers*, 102 n., 376; *Proverbs*, 469; *Psalms*, 334; *Samuel*, 102 n., 103 n., 376; NEW TESTAMENT: *Acts*, 269 (quoted), 463, 473; *Corinthians*, 105 n.; *John*, 359; *Luke*, 110 (paraphrased), 263 (quoted), 379,

Bible (*cont.*)
462, 466(3), 469, 470, 471; *Mark*, 471, 563(2); *Matthew*, xli, 26 (quoted), 43 (paraphrased), 104 (paraphrased), 104–5 (paraphrased), 107 n. (quoted), 108 and n., 125–6 (paraphrased), 250 (quoted), 253 (2; paraphrased), 259 (paraphrased), 262 (quoted), 263 and n., 264–5 (allusions), 266 (2; quoted), 267–8 (allusions), 269 (paraphrased), 335, 377(2), 378–9, 465, 466(4), 468, 469, 470(3), 471, 472(2), 473, 475 (quoted), 478 (paraphrased), 563; *Romans*, 260 (paraphrased), 469; *see also* Christ (Jesus)

Birmingham Hampden Club, The: 316
Blackstone, William: 32, 336, 469
Blackwood's Magazine: 434
Blake, William: xliv, 377, 480
Boas, Louise: 320
'Bodleian Shelley Manuscripts, The': xxx
Boehme, Jacob: 368, 370
Boinville, Mrs (Jean Baptiste Chastel de): 388
Bonaparte, Napoléon: 30, 83(2), 187, 189, 191, 215, 305, 308, 380, 435, 436, 442(2), 444, 517
Boulanger, Nicolas-Antoine: 51, 345, 346
Bourbons, the: 83, 161, 215, 305, 306(3), 307, 442(2)
Brand, Thomas: 316, 422(2)
Brandreth, Jeremiah: xliv, 233(2), 234(2), 237, 238(2), 452
Brew, Claude: xxx
Brewer, Luther: 493
Brighton Magazine: 320
Brinkley, Robert: 442
Brooke, Stopford A.: 365
Brougham, Henry Peter (Lord): 316, 414, 418, 425
Brown, Philip A. H.: 448
Bruce, Mr.: 317
Buccleuch, Walter Francis Scott, 5th Duke of: 314(2), 424
Buffon, Georges-Louis Leclerc, comte de: 226, 446

Bulkeley, Lord: 302
Burdett, Jones: 317
Burdett, Sir Francis: 311, 316, 354, 418(2), 420, 422, 425, 426(4), 453
Burgoyne, Montague: 316
Burke, Edmund: 295, 451, 454, 455(2)
Byron (George Gordon Noel, 6th Baron), Lord: xliii, xliv n., 156 and n., 180, 202, 213(2; 'my companion'), 214, 215, 216, 217, 218, 220, 398(3), 428, 438, 440, 443, 444(3), 445, 519; *Childe Harold*, 202, 438(2); *English Bards and Scotch Reviewers*, 156 n., 398; *The Prisoner of Chillon*, 444

Cæsar, Julius: 212, 254, 461, 466, 519
Calvin, John: 14, 333
Cameron, Kenneth Neill: 417; *Young Shelley*, 292(2), 326, 337, 361, 393, 454
Canning, George: 421
Cannon, George ('Erasmus Perkins'): 365
Cannon, John: 456
Carlile, Richard, *see* Carlisle, Richard
Carlingford, Lord: 351 *passim*
Carlisle, Richard: *Republican*, 350, 352
Caroline of Brunswick, Princess of Wales (Princess Charlotte's mother): 156, 398, 453
Cartwright, John (Major): 176, 316, 418(2), 421, 425(2), 426 *passim*
Castlereagh (Robert Stewart, 2nd Viscount), Lord: xliii, 337, 455
Catholic emancipation: xliii, 8, 14, 17, 23(2), 25, 29, 37, 41, 42–3, 55, 291, 292, 294(2), 295, 299, 327, 328(2), 330, 332, 341, 343(2), 348, 357
Cervantes, Miguel de: *Don Quixote*, 189, 404
Chanter, John: *Sketches of the Literary History of Barnstaple*, 352, 355–6, 539
Charles IX: 303, 308
Charlotte, Princess: xxxi(2), xliv, 156, 305(2), 306(4), 307(2), 333, 398; *see also An Address to the People on the Death of the Princess Charlotte* and Editorial Commentaries for that

work, for *The Elysian Fields*, and for *On Learning Languages passim*

Chesterfield, Philip Dormer Stanhope, Lord: 392; *Letters to his Son*, 145, 392

Cheyne, George: 90 n., 364(3), 549

Chicester, Lord: 351, 352

Chitty, Joseph: 488(2)

Christ (Jesus; also referred to as Redeemer and Son of God): xlix, 15, 26 (quoted), 33, 46, 66, 67, 69(3), 71(2), 95(3), 96 and nn., 97, 98, 100, 101, 103, 104(2; quoted), 107, 108(4; quoted), 125(2), 125–6 (quoted), 152, 272–3, 295 (allusion), 321, 354, 357, 358, 359, 367(2), 371, 372, 376, 378, 379, 408, 461, 474, 477, 478(2), 526; *see also* s.v. Bible and *On Christianity* and Editorial Commentary *passim*

Cicero, Marcus Tullius: 98 n., 103 (quoted), 110 (quoted), 121 (quoted), 148 (quoted), 262 n., 365, 367, 374, 376, 379, 382, 393, 394, 464(2), 470, 528

Clairmont, Charles: 424

Clairmont, Claire (Clara Mary Jane): xxxiii, 188(3), 191(2), 227, 391, 394, 404, 407(3), 435, 460, 487(2), 488(3); her journal, 384, 410, 424, 428, 430, 434, 436, 437 *passim*, 438, 460

Clairmont, Paola: 404

Clark, David Lee: 361(2), 363; *Shelley's Prose*, xxix(2), xxxi and n., 371, 375, 380, 489, 538(2), 565(3)

Clark, George: 324

Clarke, Robert: 320, 371

Clive, Arthur: *Scintilla Shelleiana*, 366

Cobbett, William: xliv, 175, 316, 403, 418, 425, 453(3), 454(3), 455, 456(2); *Weekly Political Register*, 425

Cochrane, Lord: 316

Coke, Sir Edward: 412

Coleridge, Samuel Taylor: 374, 399; *Christabel*, 389, 390, 428

Compton and Ritchie (printers): 448

Comyns, John (Lord Chief Baron): 32, 336

Condorcet, Jean-Antoine-Nicolas Caritat, marquis de: 51, 52, 345, 346, 347

Constantine (the Great): 105–6, 129

Conway, Moncure D.: 378

Corn Law (1815): as an index to political and social relations during the Regency, xlv–xlvi

Creevy, Mr.: 317

Critical Review: xxvi, 390

Crown and Anchor Tavern: 172, 553

Curran, John Philpot: 316, 328, 422

Curtius, Quintus: 468

Cuvier, Georges: 80 n., 117 n., 362, 381

D'Alembert, Jean le Rond, *see* Alembert, Jean le Rond d'

Darvall, Frank Ongley: xliii n., li n.

Darwin, Erasmus: 177, 428

dating of Shelley's prose: xxxi–xxxiv; *see also Editorial Commentaries for individual works*

Davenport, W. H.: 316, 452

Dawson, P. M. S.: xxx, xxxi and n., 344–5, 382, 468, 469, 556, 558, 561, 562, 563(2), 565

Davy, Humphry: *Elements of Agricultural Chemistry*, xxiii n.

de Beer, Gavin: 399

Decii, the: 248, 464

de Lille, Abbé (Jacques): 306

Delisle, Fanny: *Study of Shelley's 'A Defence of Poetry': A Textual and Critical Evaluation*, xxx

Democritus: 97

Descartes, René: 65, 359

Diderot, Denis: 299, 346(2)

Diogenes Laertius: 392, 397, 461, 463, 470, 471(4)

Diogenes (the Cynic): 263(2), 273, 468, 471 *passim*, 477

Dowden, Edward: xxix, 365, 379, 390, 391, 507, 550; *The Life of Percy Bysshe Shelley*, 292, 326, 354, 369, 411, 566; *Transcripts and Studies*, xxix

Drummond, William: *Academical Questions*, 121 n., 324, 367, 375, 382, 394; *Oedipus Judaicus*, 376

Dryden, John: 370

Dublin Evening Post, The: 294, 328
Dublin Freeman's Journal, The: 293, 338
Dublin Journal, The: 295, 298
Dublin Weekly Messenger, The: 291(2), 298, 301, 339(2), 341(2), 342
Ducrée (guide): 225
Duncan, Andrew: 316

Easton, James: 150 n., 153 n., 364, 395
Eaton, Daniel Isaac: 62–73 *passim*, 353–9 *passim*, 375, 462, 469
Edward III: 186, 435
Eldon (John Scott, 1st Earl) (Lord Chancellor): xliv(2) and n., 166, 310, 311(3), 312, 333, 358, 400, 409(2), 410(2), 411(2), 412; as Attorney-General, 31–2, 335, 336(2)
Elizabeth, Queen: 233
Ellenborough, Lord: 336; see also *A Letter to Lord Ellenborough* and Editorial Commentary *passim*
Ellis, F. S.: *Concordance*, 540
Emmet, T. A.: 329
Encyclopédie: 346 *passim*
Encyclopedists: 51, 345, 345–6
Ensor, George: 317, 334 (2; quoted), 336 (2; quoted), 337, 367, 382, 453(2)
Epicurus: 97, 123
Epiphanes: 503
Erskine, Thomas: 335(2), 336(2), 345
Esculapius: 261, 470
Essenes: 464, 471–2, 523
Essex, Lord: 316
Eton, I (printer): 338, 349
Euclid: 371
Euripides: 97; *Bellerophon*, 97–8 n. (quoted), 374; *Cyclops*, 478; *Hippolytus* 153 n., 392, 393, 397(3)
Examiner, The: xxvi, xlii, l, 238 n., 292, 304, 305(2), 306(2), 308, 310(3), 311(2), 312, 314(2), 316, 334, 337, 355, 388, 400, 402(4), 403(3), 404, 414, 418(3), 420(2), 421(2), 422(2), 423(2), 424, 425, 427, 450, 452(2), 453, 455, 456 *passim*, 480(2), 482, 483(2), 486, 490, 492, 565
Eyries, Jean-Baptiste-Benoît: *Fantasmagoriana*, 178 (alluded to), 428

Faber, George S.: 320, 321 *passim* (quoted), 327
Feldman, Paula: 432, 434
Ferguson, Sir R.: 317
Fingal, Lord: 340
Finnerty, Peter: 33, 298(2), 299, 336, 337, 342, 424
Florio, John: 486
Fontescue, Chicester, *see* Carlingford, Lord
Forman, H(arry) B(uxton): xxiii n., xxix, xxxi, 401, 404(4), 405, 415, 433, 449 n., 474, 491(2), 492, 493, 566; his ed. of *The Prose Works of Percy Bysshe Shelley* (F), xxiii n., xxviii, xxix(2), xxxi n., 351, 356, 371, 379, 407, 432, 439, 440, 461, 466, 474(4), 475(2), 476, 483, 494–7 *passim*, 537(4), 538(3), 539, 540, 559, 560, 564, 566
Fortnightly Review: xxix, 351, 352(2)
Fouché, Joseph: 304
Fox, Charles: xliii, 20(2), 333–4; his Libel Act, 64 n., 307, 335, 358, 401(4), 452
Framebreaking Act of 1812: xliii
Francis I: 399
Frank, Frederick S: xxiii n.
Frederick (the Great): 162, 346, 359, 401(3), 405
Freeling, Francis: 351(3), 352
French Revolution: xlviii, 1, 19, 36, 50–2, 161, 295, 303, 309, 346, 347, 348, 399(2), 403, 473
Fuller, Jean Overton: 385, 389

Galileo (Galilei): 65, 359
Game Laws: 1, 280–1, 488–9
Garnett, Richard: 365, 448 n., 491; *Relics of Shelley*, xxviii and n., 457
Gentleman's Magazine: 90 n.
George II: 358
George III: xlii, xliv, 20, 21, 334
Gibbon, Edward: 105 n.(2), 219, 220(2), 355, 385(2), 445, 463
Gibbs, Sir Vicary (Attorney-General): 64, 66 and n., 67, 334, 355(2), 359
Gisborne, John: 406, 407, 483
Globe (London): 61, 326, 354

Glover, A. S. B.: *Selected Poetry, Prose and Letters of Percy Bysshe Shelley*, xxx n.

Gnostics: 124, 386, 388, 389

Godwin, Mary Jane (Mrs William): 435

Godwin, William: li, 52, 166 n., 276, 277(4), 283, 293, 328 *passim*, 329, 330(4), 337(2), 338, 339(4), 340(3), 341, 343(2), 345, 347, 348(2), 393, 394, 409, 410(3), 411 *passim*, 412(3), 413, 421, 424, 426, 427, 455(2), 463, 465, 472, 473, 479(2), 480, 481(2), 482(2), 483, 484, 485(4), 491, 492, 513, 550(4), 551(4); *Caleb Williams*, 276, 277, 278, 279(2), 283, 482, 484, 486, 491, 492; *Essay on Sepulchres*, 276, 452, 485(2); *Fleetwood*, 276, 436, 484, 485; *Mandeville*, 276–9, 452, 482–3, 486, 490; *Memoirs of the Author of the Vindication of the Rights of Woman*, 486; *Of Population: An Answer to Mr. Malthus's Essay*, 485; *Political Justice (PJ)*, 118 n., 276, 278(2), 337, 339(2), 340, 345, 348, 350–1 *passim*, 353, 354, 385(2), 388, 401, 421, 422, 423(2), 424–5, 425, 427(2), 455, 468, 479, 481(2), 484(3), 485, 492; *St. Leon*, 276, 484(2)

Goethe, Johann Wolfgang von: 164

Goldsmid, Edmund: 449 n.

Goodbehere, Alderman: 317

Gordon, Lord George (riots): xlix

Graham, Edward: 320, 326

Granniss, Ruth: 489

Grenville, William Wyndham: 453

Grey, Lady Jane: 233

Grey, Lord: 316

Grosvenor, Lord: 316

Grove, Harriet (Shelley's cousin): 324

Hall, John: 394

Hallet, Mr.: 317

Hampden Clubs: xlvii, 316, 317, 330

Hansard, Parliamentary Debates: 357

Hardy, Thomas (novelist): 396

Hardy, Thomas (reformer): 232, 452

Hausermann, H. W.: 398

Hazlitt, William: 414

Healey, Daniel: 350, 352, 356

Helvétius, Claude-Adrien: 52, 347(3)

Hennuyer, Jean le (Bishop), *see* le Hennuyer, Jean

Herbert, Lord (of Cherbury): 374

Herodotus: 164, 407, 468(2)

Heron, Sir R.: 316

Herostratus: 298

Hesiod: 78, 361, 472

Heyne, Christian Gottlob: 102 n., 376

Hill, Daniel, *see* Healey, Daniel

Hipparchus: 405

Hippias: 405

Hitchener, Elizabeth: 293, 325, 341(2), 345, 349(3), 350, 354, 365, 483, 500

Hobbes, Thomas: 101 n., 368, 375, 385, 421

Hogg, John: 320, 321, 322

Hogg, Thomas Jefferson: xxxii, 320–1 *passim*, 322(3), 323, 325, 326, 341, 356, 365, 366, 367(2), 369(2), 371, 479, 481(2); *Memoirs of Prince Alexy Haimatoff*, 141–6, 390–2, 480; *The Life of Percy Bysshe Shelley*, 291(2), 322, 323, 356, 360(2), 365, 366 (quoted), 375

Holbach, Baron Paul-Henri d': 72 (quoted), 101 n., 326, 346, 347, 367, 375, 376, 379, 380, 381, 382, 459, 540

Holland, Lord: 316

Holyoake, George: 366(2), 368

Homer: 164, 286, 405; *Iliad*, 177

Hone, William: xlvi, 415(3), 424

Hookham, Thomas (bookseller): 329, 330, 339, 340, 354(2), 356 *passim*, 365, 369, 384, 390, 415, 433(2), 434, 447, 462, 485, 566

Horace, 78 (quoted), 146 (quoted), 214, 362, 376, 390, 443, 494

House of Commons: xlii, 21, 31, 171, 172(2), 173(3), 174, 280, 515

Howell (T. B. and T. J.): *State Trials*, 355(2), 358(3), 359(4)

Hume, David: 123, 324, 346, 355, 365, 367(3), 368, 370, 371, 374, 375, 377(2), 378 (quoted), 379(2), 380(4), 382, 383(3), 454(2), 459(2)

Hunt, Henry ('Orator'): xlvi, xlvii, 403, 419, 423(3)

Hunt, John: 356, 383
Hunt, Leigh: xlii, 305, 306(3), 308(2), 313–15 *passim*, 355, 356(3), 368, 400, 401, 402(4), 403, 404(3), 413, 414(3), 419, 421, 423, 424 *passim*, 427, 432, 450(2), 451, 455(2), 474, 476, 482, 486, 490, 492(2), 493(3)
Hutchinson, Thomas: xxxix n.

Illuminati: 339, 344–5
Imlay, Fanny: 438, 439
Imlay, Gilbert: 438
Independent Whig: 317
Ingpen, Roger: xxix, 442, 493
Irish pamphlets: xxv, xxxii, xlii, xlviii, li, 329, 340, 341, 349, 416, 470, 539; see Shelley: Prose Works, *An Address to the Irish People* and *Proposals for an Association of Philanthropists*
Ismael, Muley: 82, 363

Jeffreys (Judge): xliii
Jenyns, Soame: *View of the Internal Evidence of the Christian Religion*, 97 n., 327(2), 372
Jones, Frederick L.: 432, 440, 441, 489, 555(2), 565(2)
Josephine (consort of Napoleon): 189
Josephus, Flavius: *The Jewish War*, 108 n., 379, 387, 471, 472 (quoted)
Julian edition of Shelley's works (J): xxiii n., xxvii n., xxix(4)., xxxi n., 432, 457, 458, 460, 474(2), 476, 493, 537(3), 538(3), 546(4), 547(3), 548, 549(3), 550(2), 558(3), 559, 564(2)

Kean, Edmund: 452
Keats, John: 486
Keats–Shelley Journal: xxxvi n.
Keats–Shelley Memorial Bulletin: xxx(2)
Keepsake, The: xxvii n.
Kent, Elizabeth: 486
Kenyon, Lord: 336(2)
Khaled: 135(2), 136(2), 137 *passim*, 138, 387, 388, 506, 545 *passim*
Khalib, *see* Khaled
Kinnaird, Lord: 316
Knight, Ellis Cornelia: 406, 452

Koszul, A(ndré) H(enri): *Shelley's Prose in the Bodleian Manuscripts (K)*, xxix(2) and n., 313, 314, 415, 434, 459, 461, 466, 471(3), 472, 478, 556(6), 557(3), 558(3), 559(6), 560(4), 561(4), 562, 563(2), 564

Lafayette, marquis de: 38, 51, 338, 345
Laing, William (bookseller): 392, 397
Lambe, William: 81 n., 84, 154 n., 362(2), 363, 397, 541
Lancaster, Joseph: 337
Laplace, Pierre Simon, marquis de: 115, 365, 367, 380, 381
La Valette, comte de: 206, 442
Le Vallière, Louise Françoise: 160, 161
Lawless, John: 292, 293, 341(2)
Lawrence, Sir James: *Empire of the Nairs*, 480(3), 481
le Hennuyer, Jean (Bishop): 12, 332
Leigh, Augusta: 438
Leland, John: 324
Leopold, Prince (husband of Princess Charlotte): 400, 402(2), 405, 453
Leslie, Charles: 378
Lewis, Matthew Gregory ('Monk'): 156 *passim* and n., 398(5), 399; *The Monk*, 389, 398
Limerick Evening Post, The: 38, 338
Livy (Titus Livius): 164, 407
Lloyd, Charles: 383
Locke, John: 72, 82, 121, 123, 324, 346, 350, 355, 358, 367, 380, 401(2)
London Hampden Club: 317
London Magazine and Theatrical Inquisitor: 361, 396
London *World*: 335
Longdill, P. W.: 409
Louis-Philippe-Joseph, Duke of Orléans ('Egalité'): 161, 300, 399
Louis XIV: 160, 161, 399(2)
Louis XV: li
Louis XVI: 161, 305, 307, 308, 400
Louis XVIII: 303, 304, 305 *passim*, 306(2), 307(2), 308, 400, 442
Lowndes, William T.: *The Bibliographer's Manual of English Literature*, 352

Lucan, Marcus Annaeus: 252, 388(2), 466(2)

Lucian: 96, 285, 372, 401, 404(3), 405(2), 493, 494

Lucretius (Titus Lucretius Carus): 97, 269, 373, 374, 380, 443

Luddites: xliii(2)

Ludlam, Isaac: xliv, 233(2), 234(2), 237, 238, 452

Lyttelton, George: 399

Lyttelton, Thomas: 399

Lyttleton, Lord: 158 *passim*, 399

MacCarthy, Denis Florence: *Shelley's Early Life*, xxviii, 292, 293, 301, 337, 350, 351 *passim*, 356(4)

Machiavelli, Niccolò: 164

Mackenzie, Sir George: 88 n., 364

McMillan, Buchanan: 448

MacNeven, W. J.: 329

Maddocks, Robert: 439

Madocks, Mr.: 317

Madocks, William Alexander: 301(2)

Maimuna: 137, 139, 388(3)

Maintenon, Françoise d'Aubigné, marquise de: 161, 399

Malebranche, Nicolas de: 382

Malthus, Thomas R.: 53(2) and n., 277, 337, 348 *passim*, 363, 377, 465, 473, 485 *passim*, 523

Mandeville, Bernard: 337

Manichaeism: 465, 467

Mansel, Philip: 307

'Manuscripts of the Younger Romantics': xxx

Marat, Jean Paul: 300, 303, 309

Mardonius: 258, 468

Marie-Antoinette: 161, 308, 451

Marie Louise: 189, 214, 215, 444(2)

Martini, F. M.: *Le prose di Percy Bysshe Shelley*, xxx n.

Mary I (Mary Tudor): 304, 305

Mayer, Townshend: 404(2), 474, 492(2)

Medici, Catherine de: 303, 308, 332

Medwin, Thomas: xxvi, xxvii and n., 323, 448(2), 483(4), 490(3), 491(3), 565(2); *Angler in Wales*, xxvii and n.; *Life of Percy Bysshe Shelley*, xxvii, 323,

410, 490, 491(2), 550; *New Anti-Jacobin*, xxvii; *Shelley Papers*, xxvii, 448, 483, 490

Medwin, Thomas Charles: 341, 342

Melitus: 69

Messiah, *see* Christ (Jesus)

'Meyton, Charles' (Shelley pseudonym): 321

Middleton, Charles: 439(4), 440 *passim*, 554

Milnes, Richard Monckton: 332

Milton, John: 167, 232, 398, 407, 412, 444, 478; *Areopagitica*, 358, 558; *Comus* 278 (quoted), 486; *Paradise Lost*, 60 (quoted), 77 (quoted), 164, 177, 349, 353, 362, 540

Mina: 156, 157, 399

Model Republic: 366

Montagu, Basil: 311, 312

Montagu, Mary Wortley: 203, 438

Montesquieu, Charles Louis de Secondat, baron de: 346, 375

Montgomery, Mr.: 317

Monthly Review: 381

Moore, Thomas: 431, 432(2), 433, 444

Morning Chronicle (London): 310, 311, 317, 333(3), 334, 335, 337, 350, 402, 419, 421, 422, 433(2), 452, 456, 482(4)

Morning Post (London): 90 n.

Moschus: 'Elegy on the Death of Bion', 474(2), 475(3), 476(2)

Moses: 69, 102 and n. *passim*, 103, 376

Moxon, Edward: 432

Munday and Slatter (Oxford booksellers): 320

Murray, E. B.: xxxvi n., xlviii n., l n., 386

Murray, John: 445

Murray, William: 314(2), 424

Nero: 372(2)

Newton, Isaac: 64, 72, 116 (quoted), 118, 123, 327, 381

Newton, John Frank: 78–9, 84 and n., 88 n., 90, 154 n., 361(3), 362(2), 397(2), 540(2)

Nicholson, William: *Encyclopedia*, 323

North Wales Gazette: 301

Notopoulos, James: xxxi n., 370, 452, 459, 469
Nott, George Frederick: 406
Nugent, Catherine: 354

O'Connell, Daniel: 295, 332 *passim*
Oliver, William: 238(3), 447, 456(4)
Ollier, Charles: 314(2), 316(2), 413, 414(3), 415(5), 416(2), 417(2), 423(2), 434, 447(2), 448, 449(3), 453, 491
Ovid (Publius Ovidius Naso): 472; *Metamorphoses* 117 (quoted), 382
Owen, R(obert): 317
Owenson, Sidney (Lady Morgan): *The Missionary*, 470, 483
Oxford University and City Herald: 320, 333

Paine, Thomas: 51, 107 n., 344(4), 346, 350, 351, 353, 355, 357, 367, 375, 378(2), 379, 426(2), 427(2), 456, 463; *Age of Reason*, 353, 355, 357, 368, 378; *Common Sense*, 334(3), 472; *Rights of Man*, 338, 343(2), 344, 346(2), 350, 351, 353, 427(2), 451, 454, 455(2)
Paley, William: 277, 324, 327, 337, 366(2), 367, 368, 371(3), 372(2), 373, 379, 380(2), 463, 473, 485(2); *A View of the Evidences of Christianity*, 97 n.(2), 107 n., 370, 371(2), 372, 373(4), 375(2), 377(2), 378(2), 379, 463; *Natural Theology*, 112, 368, 380, 381, 382
Paracelsus: 370
Parr, Thomas ('Old'): 90(3), 91, 364
Paul, St: 469, 473
Peacock, Thomas Love: xxxii(2), 361, 394, 396, 424, 435, 439, 440, 442, 445(3), 446; *Rhododaphne*, 285–8, 492–7
Pearce, Charles E.: 406
Pearson, John: 351
Peck, Walter E.: xxix, 345, 352, 385, 388, 490, 492
Peele, Robert: 332
Perry, James: 32, 334, 335 *passim*, 336(2)
Peters, Mr.: 316
Petrarch (Francesco Petrarca): 164

Petronius, Caius: 493
Pforzheimer, Carl H.: xxix
Philip II (of Spain): 162
Philips, Mr.: 316
Phillips, C. and W. (printers): 320
Phillips, Janetta: 367, 370
Pickering, Mr (clergyman): 234
Pieces of Irish History: 329
Piggott, Sir A.: 311
Pilate, Pontius: 70, 359, 372
Pindar: 370
Pisistratus: 163, 405
Pitt, William: xliii, 453
Place, Mr.: 316
Plato: 98, 263(2), 273, 278, 285, 286, 287, 367, 370, 374, 470, 485(2), 496(2), 501; *Apology*, 469; *Menexenus*, 452(2), 485; *Phaedo*, 469, 470; *Phaedrus*, 493; *Republic*, 471(2); *Symposium*, 287 (allusion), 482, 496
Pliny (the Elder): 79 and n., 97, 373
Pliny (the Younger): 96 and n., 371, 545
Plotinus: 368
Plutarch: 80, 117 n., 362, 364, 365, 381, 382, 393(4), 395, 463, 467, 468(2)
Polidori, John William: 428
Political Register: 320
Pope, Alexander: 79 (quoted), 362
Pope Gregory XIII: 332
Pratt, Samuel J.: 86 n., 363
Priestley, F. E. L.: 484
Prince Regent (Prince of Wales, later George IV): xlii(2), xliii(3), xlvii, li, 20–1 *passim*, 54, 55, 292, 306, 310, 311, 328, 329, 333 *passim*, 341, 356, 400, 401, 402, 403(3), 419, 447, 453
Prince of Wales, *see* Prince Regent
Prometheus: 78, 79, 361, 362(2)
Proteus: 250, 465(2)
Pythagoras: 98, 273, 374, 405, 477

Quakers: 17
Quarterly Review: 371, 420, 422, 423, 483
Quesnay, François: 346

Rees, (Abraham): *Cyclopædia*, 80, 362
Regulus: 248, 464

Reiman, Donald H.: xxix, 313 n.
Reynell, C. H.: 314(2), 423
Rhys, Ernest: *Essays and Letters by Percy Bysshe Shelley*, xxx n.
Ridley, C. J.: 326
Ritson, Joseph: 152 n., 153 n., 361, 362(2), 363(2), 364 *passim*, 395, 396 *passim*
Robespierre, Maximilien de: 82, 303, 308, 309, 350, 352
Robinson, Henry Crabb: 355
Rodd, Thomas: 447, 448–9 *passim*, 449 n., 450
Rogers, Neville: xxiv n.
Rolleston, T. W.: xxix, 330
Romilly, Sir Samuel: 310(2), 311(2), 312, 400, 409, 489
Rossetti, William Michael: 351(2), 352 *passim*, 365
Rousseau, Jean-Jacques: xlviii, 52, 164, 210, 212, 215(2), 220, 232, 266(3), 299, 343, 345, 346, 347 *passim*, 364(2), 385, 406, 407, 443, 444(2), 472(2); *Confessions*, 347; *Émile*, 88 n., 364(4); *New Heloise* (*Julie, ou La Nouvelle Héloïse*), 212, 215(2), 216, 217, 218(4), 219(3), 220, 407, 443(2), 444(2); *On the Social Contract*, 472

St Bartholomew's Day Massacre: xlix, 11–12, 303, 308–9, 332(2)
St. James Magazine: 474, 475(2)
Saunder's News-Letter: 295
Saussure, Horace Bénédict de: 225, 446
Savine, A.: *Percy Bysshe Shelley Œuvres en prose*, xxx n.
Scævola (Mucius): 248, 464
Scarron, Paul: 399
Schiller, Friedrich von: 164; *Wilhelm Tell*, 437
Scot's Magazine: 90 n.
Scott, Sir Walter: 314
Scott-Kilvert, Diana: 432, 434
Scourge: 333
Scriptures, the, *see* Bible
Selden, John: 167, 412
Seneca (the Younger): 111 (quoted), 379

Servetus, Michael: 14, 333
Shaftesbury (George Anthony Cooper), third earl of: 337, 368, 467
Shakespeare, William: 344; *Cymbeline*, 234 n. (quoted); *Hamlet*, 452; *Julius Caesar*, 467; *King Lear*, 164; *Macbeth*, 47 (quoted), 64; *Merchant of Venice*, 451–2; *Midsummer Night's Dream*, 177, 443; *Tempest*, 177
Sharpe, Charles Kirkpatrick: 320
Shawcross, John: *Shelley's Literary and Philosophical Criticism*, xxx n.
Shelley and his Circle (*SC*): xi, xxix, xxx(2), 383(2), 390, 393(5), 394, 399, 433, 434, 436(3), 437(4), 439(2), 440(2), 441, 442, 443(2), 444(4), 445, 446(2), 474(3), 475(4), 476, 485, 564(2)
Shelley, Sir Bysshe (Shelley's grandfather): 323
Shelley, Charles: 409, 410
Shelley, Eliza Ianthe: 409, 410
Shelley, Harriet: 91, 168, 292, 330, 339, 342(2), 349, 354(2), 360, 401, 409(3), 410, 413, 424, 479, 481(3)
Shelley, Jane, Lady: xxix, 315(2), 356(3); *Shelley Memorials* (1859), xxviii, 355, 356, 461, 559(2), 560(3), 561, 563, 564
Shelley, Mary Wollstonecraft (Godwin): v, xxvi(3), xxvii, xxviii n., xxxi, xxxii(2), xxxiii(3), 166 n., 167, 168, 227, 304(2), 305, 306(2), 307, 308(2), 310, 315, 365, 369, 384–7 *passim*, 391, 393(3), 396, 398(5), 406(2), 407(2), 409(3), 410(3), 411(4), 412, 428 *passim*, 430–4 *passim*, 435(4), 436, 437(2), 439(3), 441(5), 449, 481, 484, 487(4), 488(5), 490, 491, 492, 493(2), 541–2 *passim*, 543(4), 544(5), 545 *passim*, 550(2), 551(3), 553, 554(4), 555(5), 566(2); *Frankenstein*, 282–4, 408, 428(3), 489–92, 565; her 1840 edn. of Shelley's prose, *Essays, Letters from Abroad, Translations and Fragments*, xxv, xxvii–xxviii, 406, 555; *Journals*, xxxii(3), xxxiii(2), 365, 384(2), 385(2), 387, 390, 392, 393, 394, 397(2), 398(3), 399, 401, 404, 406, 407(2), 409, 414, 428, 429–30 *passim*,

Shelley, Mary Wollstonecraft (*cont.*)
431(2), 432(3), 433(5), 434(4), 435,
436(5), 437(5), 438(2), 439, 440(2),
441(5), 442(4), 443, 446, 447(3), 448,
452, 466, 468, 486, 492, 493, 550, 555;
projects 1823 edn. of Shelley's prose,
xxvii and n.; 'On Ghosts', 398;
Rambles in Germany and Italy, 438;
Valperga, 491

SHELLEY, PERCY BYSSHE: on associations, 8, 18, 30, 31, 36, 37, 41–55 *passim*, 67, 329, 338–42 *passim*; on
atheism, 94, 98, 110–11, 114–23 *passim*, 241–3, 368(2), 379, 394, see also
The Necessity of Atheism and Editorial Commentary; on belief, 3–5,
14–16, 58, 65, 67, 72, 99, 106, 119–21
passim, 243–5 *passim*, 258, 319, 321,
327, 353, 374, 377, see also *A Refutation of Deism passim*; on capital punishment, 234, 258, 468, 479; on
causation, 4, 43, 50, 51, 53, 71, 77, 78,
82, 86, 101, 104, 111–16 *passim*, 118,
121–2, 147, 149, 151, 243, 245, 248,
346; on Christianity, 69–73, 319, 324,
see also *On Christianity, A Refutation of Deism*, and their commentaries *passim*, and s.v. Christ (Jesus);
on the constitution, 22, 25, 29, 35
and n., 47–8, 64, 166, 172, 344; on disinterestedness, 21, 41–2, 44, 46, 50,
95–6, 125, 130–1, 142, 301, 330, 341,
343, 345, 347, 388–9; on the 'double
aristocracy', xliv, 235, 236, 363, 450,
454, 486; on equality, xlviii, xlix, 12,
13, 16, 23, 24, 26, 46, 56, 58, 86, 125,
263–71, 273, 280–1, 295, 461(3), 470–
1, 471, 477; on a future state, 98, 123,
255–6, 367, 467; on God, 3–5, 10,
11(3), 12, 13(2), 16(2), 17, 19, 34(2),
43(2), 48, 50, 65, 66, 67, 68 *passim*,
72(4), 77, 83(2), 87, 88, 124, 125(2),
127, 130, 132, 134, 135(2), 156, 165,
171, 234(2), 239, 241–4 *passim*, 246,
249–55 *passim*, 258(2), 259 *passim*,
263, 267(3), 270, 273(2), 299, 319(2),
321(2), 323(4), 324(3), 325(2), 326,
347, 367, 368(4), 370(2), 373, 374(2),

375, 376, 379, 380, 382, 383(3), 404,
410, 461 *passim*, 463(2), 465, 466(2),
467(2), 469, see also *A Refutation of
Deism* and *Fragment of 'A Refutation
of Deism' passim*; on government, 20,
21 *passim*, 24–5, 29, 30, 32, 37, 45–50,
56–9 *passim*, 65, 67, 162–3, 235, 236,
237, 247–8, 268, 341, 455; his use of
science, 64, 79–80, 116–18 *passim*,
362, 380–1; on liberty of the press,
31–3, 38, 62–73 *passim*, 354, 367; on
mind, 3–5, 19, 22, 52, 53, 72, 82, 112,
113, 114, 116, 118, 120, 121–2, 124,
141, 147–8, 217, 244, 248, 249, 250,
255, 261, 262, 264, 265, 282, 324–5,
383, 407, 461, 484; on miracles, 4, 64,
66–7, 69, 95, 96, 100, 106–7, 108, 246,
261, 377, 378(4), 379, 460, 462, 463–4;
on morality, xlix, 3, 5, 47, 49, 54, 57–
8, 63, 67, 68, 77, 82–3, 96–7, 99–106,
118–19, 124–5, 130–1, 142, 147, 148,
153, 247, 248–9, 272–3, 274–5, 276–9,
283, 347, 367, 372–3, 377, 388, 461,
462(3), 465, 472, 473, 479, 480, 481,
482, *see also* the Irish pamphlets, *A
Letter to Lord Ellenborough*, and *On
Christianity passim*; on necessity, 4,
5, 15, 114, 115, 116, 117, 236, 277, 283,
323, 324, 465, 491; on the oppression
of the poor, xliv, xlvii, 17, 30–1, 43,
44, 48, 51, 53, 161, 235–8 *passim*, 240,
280–1, 340, 453; on perfectibility, 21,
24, 29–30, 34–5, 43, 52, 60, 69, 83, 297,
330, 347, 348, 427, 465, 473; as
reformer, xlvi, xlvii, li, 10, 16–19, 21–
9, 31, 34–6, 37, 45, 53–5, 56–60, 86,
240, 280–1, 313, 338, 340, 341, 401,
403–4, 405, 479–80, 489; see also *A
Proposal for Putting Reform to the
Vote* and Editorial Commentary;
relates religious and political
oppression, xlix–l, 34, 45–6, 49–50,
62–73 *passim*, 119, 132; on religious
persecution, 10–15, 62–73 *passim*,
101, 102, 103, 105, 291; on religious
toleration, 14–17, 33–4, 58, 59, 73,
291, 297; on revenge (retribution),
98–9, 103, 104, 123, 234, 252, 253,

256–9, 262–3, 372, 374, 461, 462, 466, 469(2), 470; on revolution (rebellion), xlvii–xlviii, l, 19–20, 27, 37, 328, 341; on self-reform, 17–19, 22–9 *passim*, 34, 86, 270, 330, 337, 462, 473; on suffrage, 140, 175–6, 421–2, 425, 454; POETICAL WORKS AND TRANSLATIONS: *Adonais*, 463, 467; *Alastor*, 388, 389, 394, 463, 483, 496; *A Poetical Essay on the Existing State of Things* (lost), 298 (alluded to), 337; 'Constantia' poems, 458, 460, 478; 'Elegy on the Death of (*or* Lament for) Bion', 474(3), 475, 476(2), 564; *Epipsychidion*, 407, 483; *Hellas* (and Notes), xxiii(2), 428; 'Hymn to Intellectual Beauty', 377, 388, 463, 467, 486; *Julian and Maddalo*, 483; 'Lament for Bion', 564; *Laon and Cythna* (*The Revolt of Islam*), xlviii, l, 348, 389, 403, 433(2), 448, 457, 473; 'Mont Blanc', 180, 377, 435, 444, 445, 446(3), 463, 467; 'Ode to the West Wind', 347, 348; 'Ozymandias', 458, 460, 478; 'Prince Athanase', 458, 561; *Prometheus Unbound*, 330, 372, 377, 389, 428, 436, 443, 463, 465, 467(2), 473, 493; *Queen Mab* (and Notes), xxiii(2), xxiv, xlvi, 151 n., 293, 311, 322, 323, 324(2), 325, 326, 327, 330, 334, 345, 346, 352, 357, 358(2), 360(2), 361 *passim*, 362(2), 363, 365, 375, 377, 379(2), 380(3), 381(4), 382(2), 383, 389, 393, 394, 395, 409(2), 410, 449, 461, 465, 467, 479(2), 499, 539(4), 540(4), 541, 548(2), 549, 556; 'Reality', 453, 467; *The Mask of Anarchy*, xliv, 313 and n., 414, 424, 455; *The Sensitive Plant*, 559; *The Triumph of Life*, 346, 347; *The Witch of Atlas*, 467; PROSE WORKS AND TRANSLATIONS: novels, xxiii; *A Defence of Poetry*, xxviii, xxix(2), xxxvi, xlii, 293, 330, 344, 346, 357, 376, 377, 407(4), 426, 443, 453, 463, 464, 465, 468; *A Definition of Atheism*, xxiii, 323 and n.; *A Discourse on the Manners of the Antient Greeks*, xxvii n., xxx; *A Faustian Note*, xxiii, xxvi, xxxi; *A Letter to Lord Ellenborough*, xxiii–xxiv, xxv, xxviii, xxxii, xxxvii, xl n., 325, 344(2), 370, 375, 377, 379, 409, 410, 462, 463, 469, 499; *A Philosophical View of Reform*, xxviii(2), xxix(2), xxx, xliv, xlviii, li, 293, 345, 363, 377, 401, 407, 419, 422, 425, 426, 449, 450, 454(3), 455(2), 457, 463, 478, 486; *A Proposal for Putting Reform to the Vote throughout the Kingdom*, xxv, xxvi, xxvii, xxxii, xxxv, xxxvi(2), xl n., xli n., xlii(2), xlvii, xlviii, 311, 313, 314, 348, 401(2), 404, 447, 448, 449, 451, 453, 489; *A Refutation of Deism*, xxiv, xxv(3), xxxii, xxxiii, xxxv, 322, 325, 327, 347, 353, 357, 393(2), 394, 446, 458, 459(5), 465, 478, 499; *A System of Government by Juries*, xxiv; *A Vindication of Natural Diet*, xxiii, xxv, xxxiii, 381, 382, 393, 395(4), 396(5), 397, 548, 549(3); *Alastor* Preface, xxxiv, 550; *An Address, to the Irish People*, xxv, xxvii, xxxv, xxxvi, xlii, xliv, 291, 338 *passim*, 339(2), 342(3), 345, 349, 353, 401, 404, 423, 453, 462, 463, 472, 473(2), *see also* Irish pamphlets; *An Address to the People on the Death of the Princess Charlotte*, xxiv, xxvi, xxviii, xxxii(2), xlii, xliv(2), xlv, 346, 356, 406, 419, 424, 458, 486; *An Answer to Leslie's 'A Short and Easy Method with the Deists'*, xxiii, xxx, 371, 377, 378, 487; *Arch of Titus*, xxvii; 'Bacchus and Ampelus', xxvii; *Biblical Extracts* (lost work), xxxiii, 292, 355, 356, 376, 377(2), 462(3), 469, 485; *Cry of War to the Greeks*, xxiii, 304, 405; *Declaration in Chancery*, xxiii, xxvi, xxvii, xxxii, 310, 311, 451; *Declaration of Rights*, xxv(2), xlii, li, 320, 325, 329(2), 331, 335, 338, 339, 340, 344, 345, 356, 366; *Fragment of 'A Refutation of Deism'*, xxvi, xxix n., 380, 382, 460, 461, 478; *Fragment on Reform* (*I*), xxvi, xxxii, 450; *Fragment on Reform* (*II*), xxviii; *History of a Six*

SHELLEY, PERCY BYSSHE (*cont.*)

Weeks' Tour, xxiii, xxiv, xxv, xxvi, xxxii(2), xxxv, 385, 398, 439(4), 440(5), 441(6), 442(2), 485; *Hubert Cauvin* (lost novel), l; *Journal at Geneva*, xxvi, xxxii; 'Laocoon', xxvii; *Letter on Richard Carlisle*, xxiii, 367, 370, 420, 551; *Letters Written in Geneva*, xxiii, xxvi, xxxii, 347, 428, 435, 438; *Menexenus*, 485; *Note on Love in Plato's 'Symposium'*, xxviii; *On Beauty*, xxviii and n.; *On Christianity*, xxvi, xxviii, xxix, xxx, xxxiii(2), xlix, l, 292, 356, 373, 377, 389, 408, 458, 459, 474(3), 475(2), 476(2), 477(3), 478(5), 553, 561; *On Contraception*, xxiii; *On the Devil, and Devils*, xxviii, xxx, xxxviii, 357, 379(2), 395, 404, 467, 469; *On the Doctrines of Christ*, xxvi, 558, 561; *On 'Frankenstein; or, The Modern Prometheus'*, xxvi, xxvii, xxxiii(2), 487(3), 488(2); *On a Future State*, xxvii, xxxiv, 381, 453, 467; *On the Game Laws*, xxvi, xxxiii(3), xli n., l, 489, 490(2); *On Godwin's 'Mandeville'*, xxv, xxvi, 345, 351, 426, 452; *On the Improvvissatore Sgricci*, xxiii, xxx; *On Learning Languages*, xxiii, xxvi, xxxi(2), xxxix n., 346, 347, 408(4); *On Life*, xxvii, xxx, xxxiv, 325, 380, 382, 383(2), 426, 461, 467, 478; *On Love*, xxvii n., xxx(2), xxxiv(2), 389; *On Marriage*, xxvi, xxix n., xxxiii, l and n., 312, 458, 459, 460; *On 'Memoirs of Prince Alexy Haimatoff'*, xxv, xxvi, xli n.; *On the Moral Teaching of Jesus Christ*, 476(2), 558; *On Polytheism*, xxviii n.; *On the Punishment of Death*, 453, 468; *On the Revival of Literature*, xxiv, xxvii; *On 'Rhododaphne or The Thessalian Spell'*, xxvi, 404; *On Shakespeare's Sonnet 111*, xxviii; *On the Vegetable System of Diet*, xxvi, xxviii(2), xxix, xxxii–xxxiii, xl n., 363, 364(2), 379, 381, 540; *On Zionism*, xxiii, xxx; *Preface to 'Frankenstein'*, xxvi, xxxiii; *Preface to 'Prometheus Unbound'*, 428, 469; *Proposals for an Association of Philanthropists*, xxv, xlii, xlvi, l, 298, 329(2), 330(2), 331(2), 349(2), 353(2), 356, 358(2), 473, 539, 554, see also Irish pamphlets; *Remarks ⟨Notes⟩ on Sculptures in the Florentine Gallery*, xxiv, xxvii(2), xxxvi n., xlii, 404(2), 492(2); *St. Irvyne: Or, the Rosicrucian, A Romance*, xxiii n., 325, 479; *Speculations on Morals and Metaphysics*, xxiv(2), xxix, xxx, xxxiv, 347, 351, 353, 357, 388, 389, 407(2), 408(2), 443, 461, 478; *The Assassins*, xxvi, xxxii, xl n., xli n., 363, 408, 560; *The Coliseum*, xxvii; *The Elysian Fields*, xxvi, xxvii, xxxi(2), 304, 305, 306(3), 307, 308(2), 406(3), 407, 452(2), 492; *The Elysian Fields: An Addition?* (Appendix II), 400, 405; *The Necessity of Atheism*, xxiii, xxv, xxxii, xxxv, xlii, 353, 357, 358(2), 370, 371, 377(2), 380(2), 556; *Una Favola*, xxviii; 'View from the Boboli Gardens', xxvii; *Zastrozzi, A Romance*, xxiii n., 325, 389, 479

Shelley, Percy Florence (Shelley's son): 315, 356, 365

Shelley, Timothy (Shelley's father): xxvii n., 292, 297, 319, 321, 323, 331, 409, 449(3)

Shelley-Rolls, Sir John: 408, 442, 457

Shepherd, Richard Herne: *The Prose Works of Percy Bysshe Shelley*, xxviii–xxix

Sicilian Vespers, the: xlix

Sidmouth, Lord: 352, 354, 456

Simonides: 485

Smith, Adam: 455(2)

Smith, Prince (D. I. Eaton's consul): 355, 358(2), 359

Smith, R. M.: 417

Socrates: 64, 69(2), 71(3), 261, 354, 461, 469, 470(2)

Solomon: 88, 126

Sophocles: 285, 286, 483, 494

Southey, Robert: xlvii, 119 n., 328, 329, 354-5, 355(2), 367, 382, 383, 388, 389(2), 420, 422, 423(2); *Thalaba the*

Destroyer, 388, 389; *The Curse of Kehama*, 148 n., 389, 392, 393, 546(4)
Spence, Thomas: 426
Spenser, Edmund: 486, 496
Spinosa, Benedict: 122 (quoted) and n., 383, 463
Stanhope, Lord: 354
Starke, Mariana: 445
Statesman: 317
Stationer's Register: 433
Steele, Richard: *Tatler*, 392
Stewart, Dugald: 112 n., 379, 380(2)
Stoker, Bram: 399
Studies in Philology: 489
Sturch, Mr.: 317
Suetonius, Gaius: 96, 371, 466(3), 467
Sussex, Duke of: 317, 452
Sussex Weekly Advertiser: 342
Swedenborg, Emanuel: 368
Swift, Jonathan: *Gulliver's Travels*, 404
Syle, Mr. (bookseller): 354, 356(3)

Tacitus, Cornelius: 96, 164, 198, 218, 252, 357, 365, 372, 387, 437, 444, 463, 466(2), 545
Tannahill, Reay: 396
Tarquin: 163
Tasso, Torquato: 164, 496
Taylor (Sen. and Jun.): 316
Tell, William: 197, 430, 437(2)
Terry, Roderick: 474
Theocritus: 314(3), 407
Theological Inquirer, xxv, 365, 366, 502
Thomas, J.: 316
Thompson, E. P.: 452
Thucydides: 252, 452, 465–6, 468, 471, 559(2)
Thurman, W. R.: 448 n.
Times (London): 433
Todd, Janet M.: 486
Tokoo, Tatsuo (*TT*): xxx, 472, 474, 558(2), 559, 561, 562(2)
Tooke, John Horne: 232, 452
Tremadoc (embankment at): 301–2, 363
Trotter, Thomas: 87 n., 360, 363
Turner, Edward: 234

Turner, William: xliv, 233(2), 234(2), 237, 238(2), 452
Twiss, Horace: xliv n.

Vanini, Lucilio: 65, 359
Victoria, Queen: 450
Virgil (Publius Vergilius Maro): 269, 388, 472, 478, 493
Viviani, Emilia: 483
Volney, Constantin François, comte de: xlviii n.
Voltaire, François-Marie Arouet de: 52, 65, 232, 303, 310, 346 *passim*, 347, 355, 359, 437

Waithman, Robert: 316, 422(2)
Walker, Mr.: 316
Walpole, Horace: *Castle of Otranto*, 389, 428
Wandering Jew: 126 (allusion?), 385, 388(2), 389, 394(3)
Watson, Richard (Bishop of Llandaff): 107 n., 378
Weishaupt, Adam: 345
Wellesley, Marquis: 61, 357
Werkmeister, Lucyle: *A Newspaper History of England*, 335
Westbrook, Eliza: 409(2), 410(2), 412(2)
Westbrook, John: 312, 409(2), 410, 412(2)
White, Newman Ivey: xliii n., 293, 301, 332, 334, 342, 355, 388, 397, 411, 424(2), 436, 453, 485
Whitton, William: 409
Wieland, Christoph Martin: 164
William I (the Conqueror): 48, 344
William III: 235, 358, 454
Williams, John: 301(2)
Williams, Sir Robert: 302(2)
Wise, Thomas J.: 330, 365(2), 369, 448 and n.
Wodhull, Michael: 374
Wollstonecraft, Mary: 277, 480, 486(2); *Letters from Norway*, 200, 438
Woodcock, George: 483
Woodring, Carl: 399
Wordsworth, William: 102 (quoted) and n., 277(2), 376 ('The Thorn'), 446,

Wordsworth, William (*cont.*)
451, 465, 485(3), 486, 519; 'Intimations' Ode (quoted), 278
Woulfe, Chief Baron: 293
Wrangman, Francis: 378
Wyse, Thomas: 291(3), 292

Xerxes (Zerxes): 258, 468

Zacharias ('son of Barachias'): 108(2), 379
Zeno: 153 n., 273, 477, 549